LIGHTWAVE 3D® 8 REVEALED

Kelly L. Murdock

THOMSON
COURSE TECHNOLOGY
Professional ■ Trade ■ Reference

Publisher and General Manager of Course PTR:
Stacy L. Hiquet
Associate Director of Marketing:
Sarah O'Donnell
Marketing Manager:
Heather Hurley
Manager of Editorial Services:
Heather Talbot
Senior Acquisitions Editor:
Kevin Harreld
Senior Editor:
Mark Garvey
Marketing Coordinator:
Jordan Casey
Project Editor:
Karen A. Gill
Copy Editor:
Carla Spoon
Technical Reviewer:
Angela Murdock
PTR Editorial Services Coordinator:
Elizabeth Furbish
Interior Layout Tech:
Susan Honeywell
Cover Designer:
Steve Deschene
Indexer:
Katherine Stimson
Proofreader:
Kezia Endsley

THOMSON™

COURSE TECHNOLOGY

Professional ■ Trade ■ Reference

Thomson Course Technology PTR, a division of Thomson Course Technology

25 Thomson Place
Boston, MA 02210
http://www.courseptr.com

ISBN: 1-59200-582-9

Library of Congress Catalog Card Number: 2004114415

Printed in Canada

05 06 07 08 09 WC 10 9 8 7 6 5 4 3 2 1

A true friend doesn't care if you're rich or poor,
Only that you are happy.
A true friend doesn't require fame or glory,
Only that you're pleased with your success.
A true friend isn't demanding,
But is always supportive.
A true friend never laughs at your embarrassments
Until much later with you in private.
A true friend knows how you'll act in certain situations
And still likes you just the same.
A true friend knows all the buttons to set you off
But chooses not to use them.
A true friend is someone you trust
And someone who trusts you.
A true friend is there to comfort you
When the world has turned against you.
A true friend will give you the shoes off his feet
And gladly receive the shoes off your feet.
A true friend has a true friend.

To Christian, Todd, and Todd, 2005.

Acknowledgments

I would like to acknowledge several individuals who were great to work with on this project. First of all, thanks to Kevin Harreld, who has been my main point of contact with Thomson. He has made me feel like I could do no wrong.

I'd also like to thank Karen Gill, who worked as project editor. In addition, I'd like to thank all the people at Thomson who work behind the scenes to create such great titles.

Juan Gonzalez Diaz, thank you for creating and allowing us to use the stunning cover image. I contacted Juan at the last moment, and he was extremely helpful in his support.
His work is representative of the types of images that are possible with LightWave and is an example to us all.
You can view more of Juan's work at his Web site,
http://www.genesisvisual.com.

Thanks to Chuck Baker and all the great people at NewTek for software support. And thanks to the super development team for creating such a great software package.

As always, I'd like to thank my family, without whose support I'd never get to the end of a book. To Angela, for often driving me harder than I drive myself; to Eric, for helping me with my other business so I could work on this book, and to Thomas, for occasional breaks that helped me keep my sanity.

About the Author

KELLY L. MURDOCK has a background in engineering, specializing in computer graphics. This experience has led him to many interesting experiences, including using high-end CAD workstations for product design and analysis, working on several large-scale visualization projects, creating 3D models for several blockbuster movies, working as a freelance 3D artist and designer, doing 3D programming, and writing several high-profile computer graphics books.

Kelly's book credits include five editions of the *3ds max Bible*, *Maya 6 Revealed*, two editions of the *Illustrator Bible*, *Adobe Creative Suite Bible*, *Adobe Atmosphere Bible*, *gmax Bible*, *3D Graphics and VRML 2.0*, *Master Visually HTML and XHTML*, and *JavaScript Visual Blueprints*.

In his spare time, Kelly enjoys rock climbing, mountain biking, skiing, and running. He works with his brother at his co-founded design company, Logical Paradox Design.

CONTENTS AT A GLANCE

CONTENTS

Chapter 2
Creating and Selecting Objects 35

CONTENTS

Chapter 3 Transforming Objects 69

Chapter 4 Extending, Duplicating, and Dividing Objects 101

CONTENTS

Chapter 5 Constructing and Detailing Objects 137

Chapter 6 Surfacing Objects and Mapping Textures 173

Chapter 8 Modify Layout Objects 247

CONTENTS

Chapter 9
Animating Objects 281

Chapter 10
Working with the Graph Editor 307

CONTENTS

Chapter 12 Rendering the Scene 355

Chapter 13 Using LScript 379

Revealed Series Vision

A book with the word "Revealed" in the title suggests that the topic that is being covered contains many hidden secrets that need to be brought to light. For LightWave, this suggestion makes sense. LightWave is a powerful piece of software, and finding out exactly how to accomplish some task can be time-consuming without some help. Well, you're in luck, because the help you need is in your hands.

As you dive into the *Revealed* series, you'll find a book with a split personality. The main text of each lesson includes a detailed discussion of a specific topic, but alongside the topic discussions are step-by-step objectives that help you master the same topic that is being discussed. This unique "read it and do it" approach leads directly to "understand it and master it."

—The *Revealed* Series

Author Vision

Writing computer books is always a journey. As an experienced 3ds max author, I was anxious to spread my wings to try out other 3D packages. I've always heard amazing things about LightWave and its fiercely loyal users. So, what was all the noise about? LightWave is just another run-of-the-mill 3D package, isn't it? Boy, was I in for a shock!

After many months of intense use, all I can say is, Wow! LightWave is awesome, and its approach to modeling, animating, and working with materials is easy to grasp, powerful to use, and actually fun to work in. It feels like the developers didn't over-engineer the software, but also took the straightest path to get it to do what they wanted.

A good example of LightWave's simplicity is how NewTek has broken the interface into two parts: one for modeling and the other for building scenes and animating. This is a simple idea, but by separating the two, each interface becomes much simpler, and it can actually load quicker than the time it takes to microwave two frozen burritos. Even Photoshop takes longer to load than both LightWave interfaces. Another good example of LightWave's elegance is how the menu buttons are dynamically selected with tabs across the top of the interface. Only the features that you currently need are visible, and all other junk is hidden so that the interface is clean. This means that you need to hunt for certain features when you begin, but after you learn their location or hotkeys, you can really fly.

Okay, now that you know that I'm a fan of LightWave, you need to understand my approach. This book is intended for the beginner, although we start to get into more advanced topics later in the book. A couple of months ago, I, too, was a beginner to LightWave, and with this perspective, I've described the software as I've uncovered it.

The first chapter explains the two LightWave interfaces and how to work with them. By taking a quick tour of the interface elements, you'll learn where the major interface elements are located. The next six chapters go through the Modeler interface, explaining how to model and add surfaces to objects. The final six chapters discuss the Layout interface, explaining all the details of creating, animating, and rendering a scene.

Along with every discussed task are several step-by-step objectives that show you a simplified example of the discussed topic. Each of these examples was created to be extremely simple to keep the number of steps to a minimum. I've tried to add some variety here and there, but none of these examples should be overwhelming (or will win a prize at the county fair). The real creative work is up to you, but these simplified examples will be enough to show you the way. Each objective example begins from the default setting that appears when the program is first loaded, but you don't need to close and reopen the software to begin each example; just select the File, New menu command, and you'll be ready to go. For some of the more complex examples, the steps instruct you to open an example file. You can download these files from the Course Technology Web site, or you can use your own files as a beginning point. You can also go to the Course Technology Web site to download the copy of each example file that is saved for comparison.

As a final note, LightWave is an extremely powerful piece of software with a boatload of features. Given that this book doesn't have enough pages to cover every aspect, I've taken the liberty to cover a select set of features. If I didn't cover a particular feature to your satisfaction, I apologize, and I'll try to include it in the next version if I can find some extra pages. I've had a lot of fun using this software, and I hope you will, too.

—Kelly L. Murdock

LIGHTWAVE 3D 8 REVEALED

CHAPTER 1

LEARNING THE LIGHTWAVE INTERFACES

1. Launch the Layout and Modeler.
2. Use the pop-up menus.
3. Work with files.
4. Set interface options.
5. Explore the viewports.
6. Get help.

CHAPTER 1
LEARNING THE LIGHTWAVE INTERFACES

LightWave consists of two main interfaces: the **Layout**, where you position, light, animate, and render objects; and the **Modeler**, where you build objects. You can move objects seamlessly between these two interfaces.

The Layout and the Modeler also share several interface elements. Both interfaces have a toolbar of menu buttons located on the left side of the screen, and **menu tabs** along the top edge. At the top of the toolbar are four menu buttons that are always available including File, Edit, Window, and Help.

When you click a menu button in the toolbar, its associated menu opens:

- The File menu includes commands to reset the scene, load and save files, import and export files, and exit the program.
- The Edit menu includes commands to undo and redo actions, customize the interface, and set interface options and preferences.
- The Window menu includes commands to access different utility panels such as the Layers panel in the Modeler and the Backdrop Options panel in the Layout.
- The Help menu lets you access, as you'd expect, the online help.

Another common element is the viewports. Located in the center of the interface, the viewports provide a view into the objects in the scene. They also work the same way in both programs. **Viewports** include menu buttons along their top edges, which you can use to change the view and display options, in addition to panning, rotating, and zooming within the viewport.

This lesson introduces the two LightWave interfaces and explains many of the different interface elements that will be used throughout this book. Coverage of using files to load and save your work is included, along with several tips on configuring the interface to your liking.

Tools You'll Use

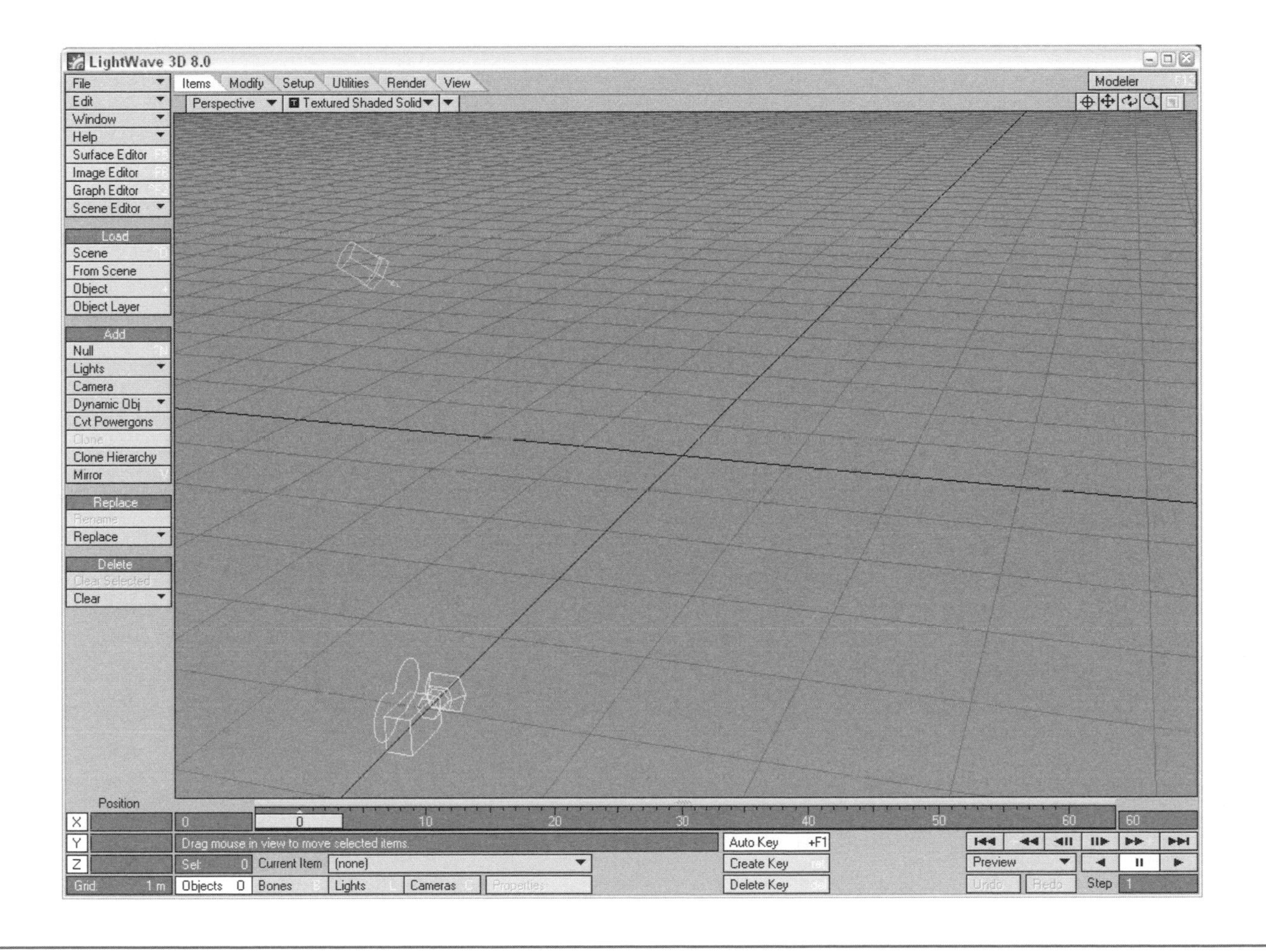

Tools You'll Use

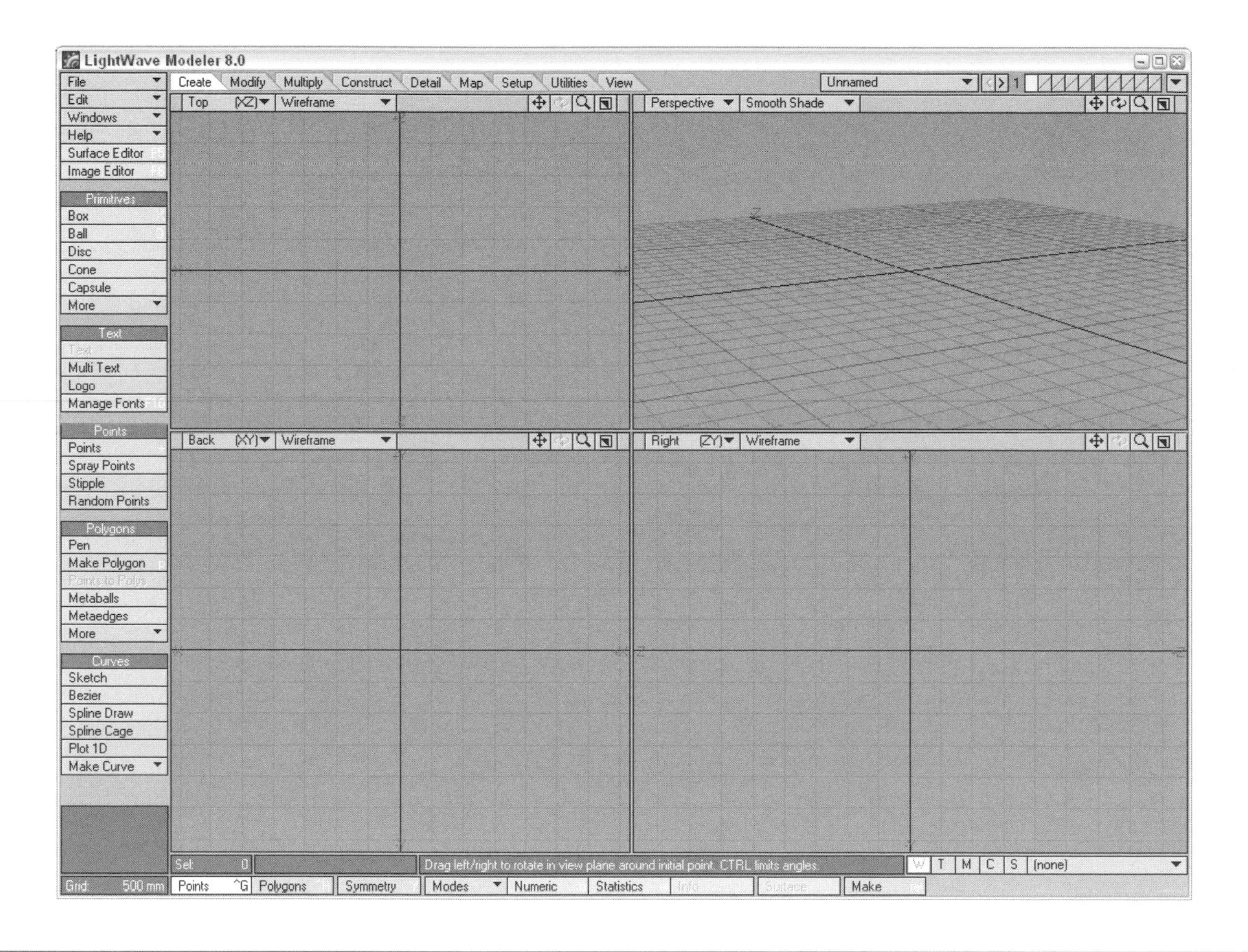

Tools You'll Use

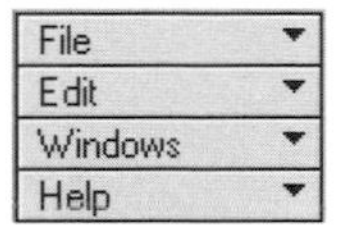

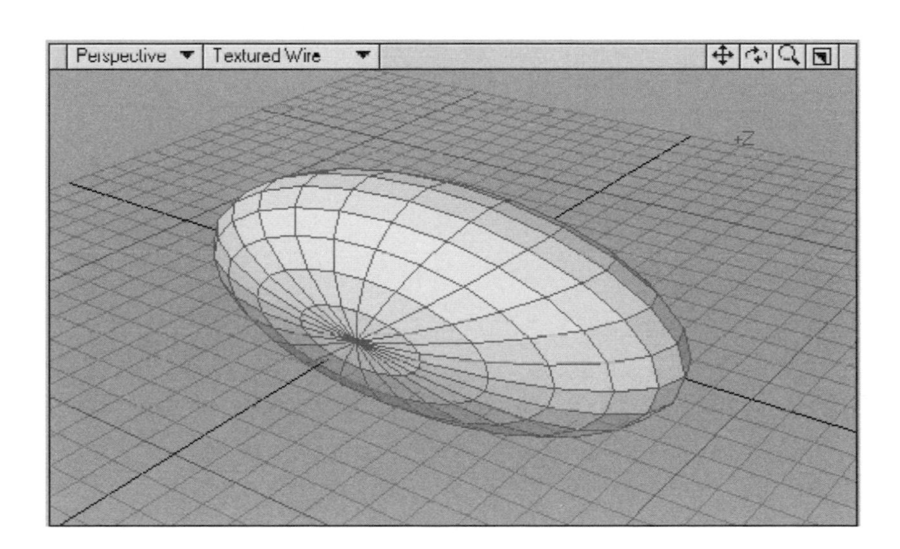

LESSON 1

LAUNCH THE LAYOUT AND MODELER

What You'll Do

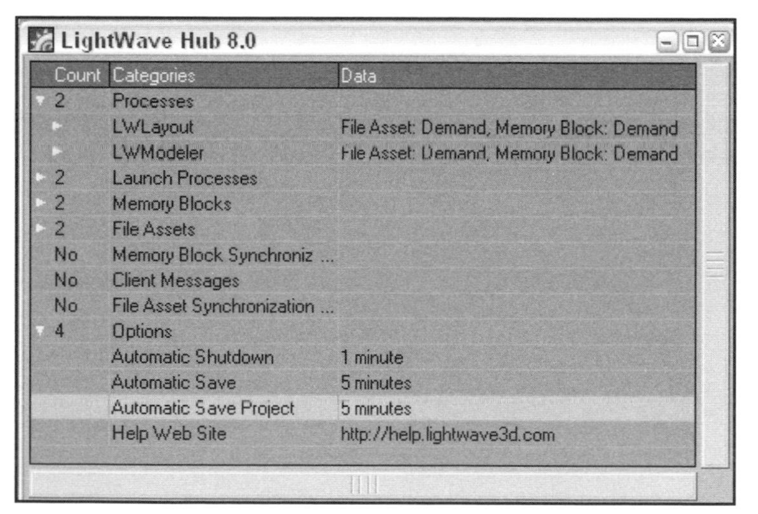

In this lesson, you'll learn how to launch the Layout and Modeler interfaces.

3D modeling, animation, and rendering software is complex. Because a wide variety of features are packed into each new release, it can be difficult to find exactly what you need. Newtek's elegant solution is to divide the software into two separate interfaces: one to handle the task of modeling (the Modeler), and the other to handle animation and rendering (the Layout, which is accessed with the LightWave icon). Each interface has its own startup icon, as shown in Figure 1.1.

FIGURE 1.1

Modeler and Layout interfaces are separate programs

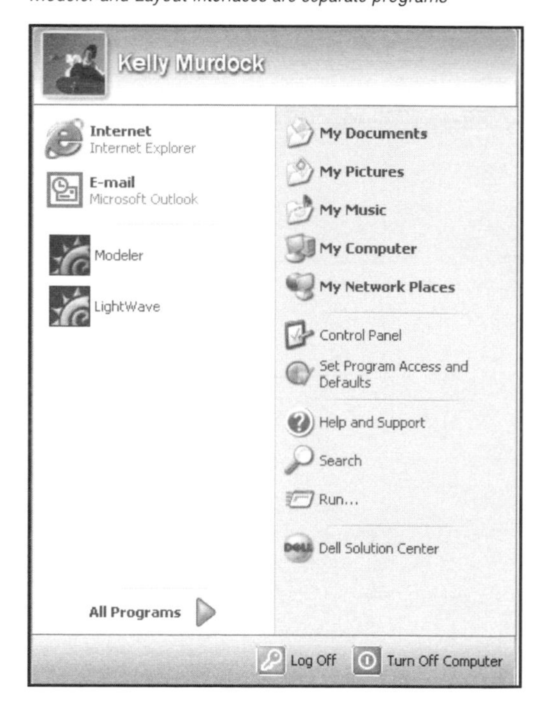

Launching the Modeler and Layout Interfaces

Because the Modeler and the Layout interfaces are separate programs, you can launch each one separately. You can also launch each application using the available interface. For example, you can launch the Modeler from the Layout interface and vice versa.

To launch the Modeler from Windows, click the Start button, click All Programs, click NewTek LightWave 3D, and then click the Modeler icon. To launch the Layout interface from Windows, click All Programs, NewTek LightWave 3D, and then click the LightWave icon.

On a Macintosh computer, you can launch the programs using the Modeler and LightWave icons in the Applications, LightWave folder.

Learning the Common Interface Elements

The Layout and Modeler interfaces have common elements, including a toolbar, menu tabs, and workspace, position, and grid displays. Figure 1.2 depicts how these common elements appear in the Modeler.

FIGURE 1.2
Common interface elements

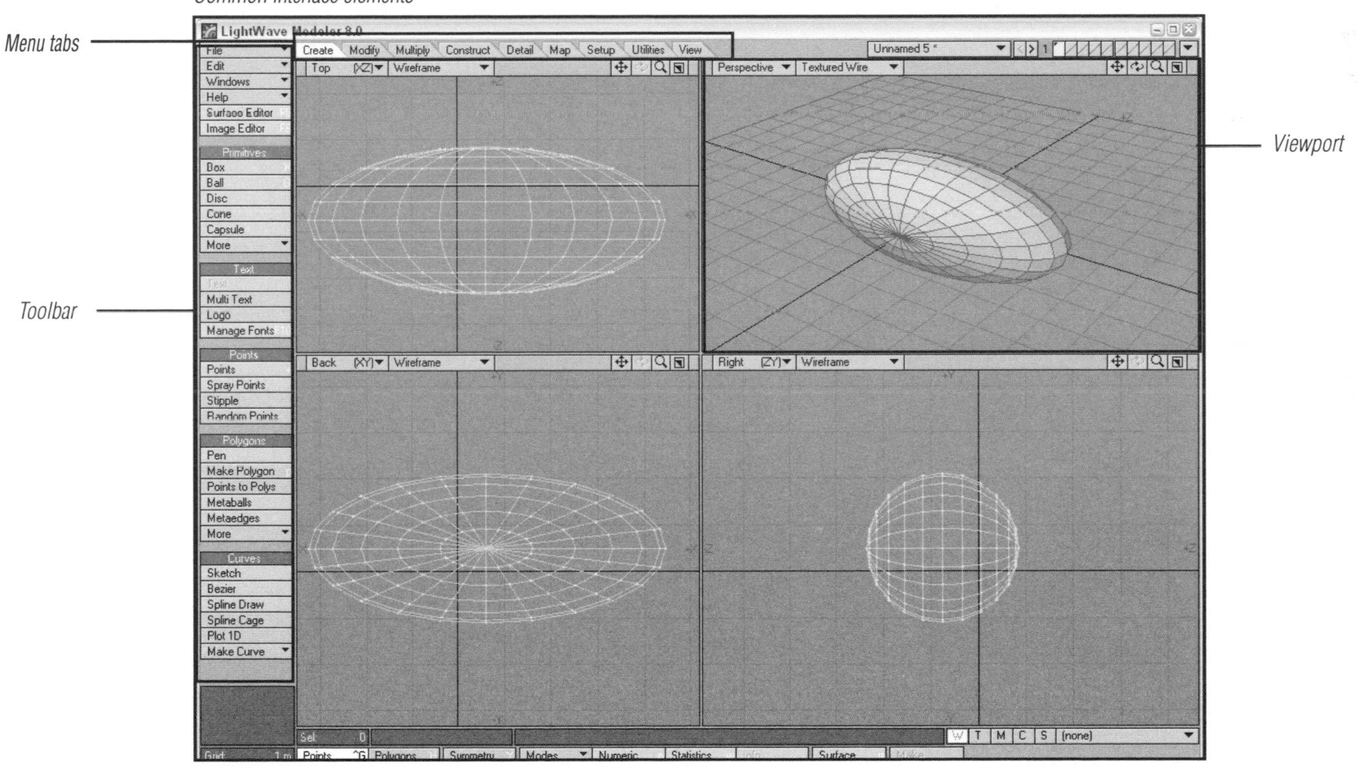

The toolbar is located along the left side of the interface and includes buttons you can use to access menus and dialog boxes. Menu tabs are located along the top edge of the interface. By clicking on the various menu tabs, a specific set of menu buttons appear in the lower half of the toolbar. The buttons on the lower half of the toolbar change for every menu tab.

The workspace is the central view of the scene. It can be divided into several different viewports. Along the top edge of each viewport are several drop-down menus and viewport control buttons that you can use to change what is displayed within the viewports.

Other common interface elements are the object position and grid value fields located in the lower-left corner.

Using the LightWave Hub

The **LightWave Hub** is a background program that automatically runs when either LightWave interface is open. It keeps track of the different processes and the amount of memory in use. The Hub icon appears in the system tray in Windows, or as a separate running program icon on Macintosh computers.

You can use the Options section of the Hub, shown in Figure 1.3, to configure LightWave to automatically save a file after a given amount of time. The Automatic Shutdown option defines how long the Hub waits until it shuts down after you exit LightWave.

FIGURE 1.3
LightWave Hub

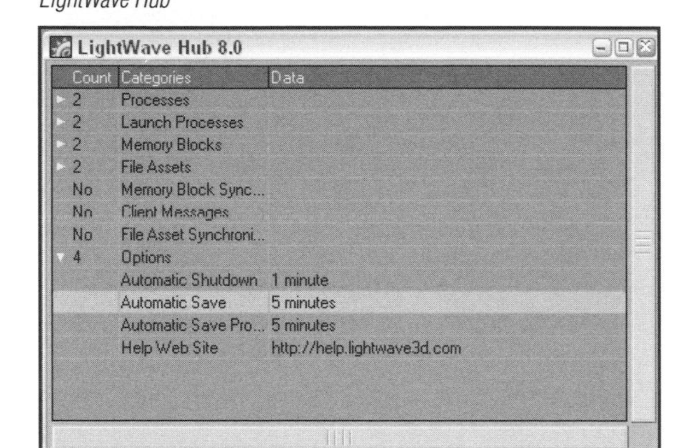

Enabling Automatic Saving

If you expand the Options menu in the Hub and click the Automatic Save option, you can specify how often the current object or project is saved. The options include Never, 1, 5, 15, 30, or 60 minutes.

Switching Between Interfaces

From within either interface, you can access or launch the other interface. To do this in the Modeler, click the down arrow icon in the upper-right corner to open a menu from which you can select the Switch to Layout menu command. If the Layout interface isn't available, it will be launched and selected.

Within the Layout interface, a button in the upper-right corner labeled Modeler is available for launching or accessing the Modeler interface.

> **TIP**
>
> Press F12 from either interface to switch to the other interface.

Launch LightWave

1. To launch the Layout interface in Windows, click the Start button, click All Programs, click NewTek LightWave 3D, and click LightWave. For Macintosh systems, open the Applications folder, open the NewTek LightWave folder, click the LightWave icon, and press Enter.
2. To launch the Modeler interface in Windows, click the Start button, click All Programs, click NewTek LightWave 3D, and click Modeler. For Macintosh systems, open the Applications folder, open the NewTek LightWave folder, click the Modeler button, and press Enter.

   When either interface opens, the Hub automatically starts up.

Use the LightWave Hub and enable Automatic Save

1. Double-click the LightWave Hub icon in the system tray in Windows. On a Macintosh computer, click the LightWave Hub icon.
2. In the Hub window, expand the Options menu to find the Data column for the Automatic Save row, click the row, and then click the 5 minutes option from the drop-down menu that appears.

   The current file will be saved to a temporary directory every five minutes.
3. Repeat step 2 for the Automatic Save Project option.

   The LightWave Hub window should now look like Figure 1.4.

Switch between interfaces

1. With the Modeler selected, click the down arrow button in the upper-right corner of the interface, and then click Switch to Layout.

   The Layout interface is active.
2. Click the Modeler button in the upper-right corner of the Layout.

   TIP You can also press F12.

   The Modeler becomes active.

FIGURE 1.4
LightWave Hub with Automatic Save enabled

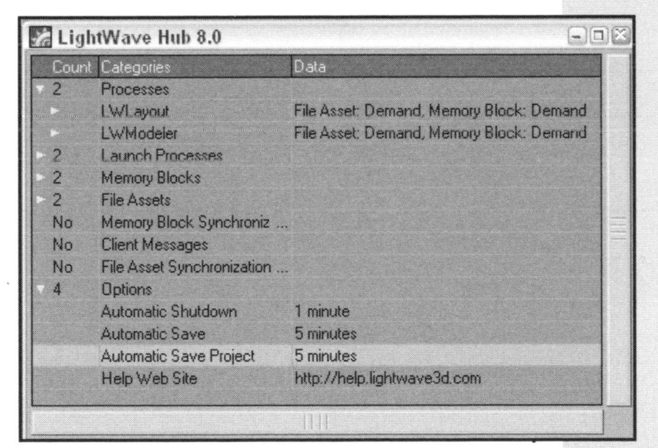

LESSON 2

USE THE POP-UP MENUS

What You'll Do

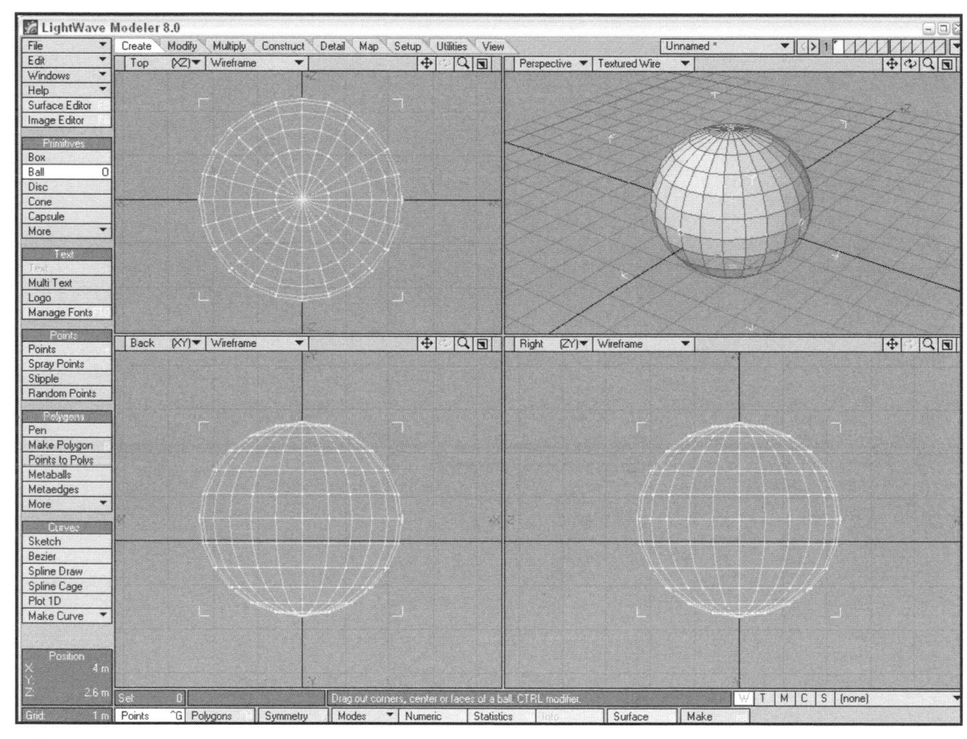

In this lesson, you'll learn how to use the pop-up menus.

Both the Layout and Modeler interfaces have four buttons (File, Edit, Windows, and Help) in their upper-left corners, as shown in Figure 1.5. These buttons are part of the top toolbar. When you click one of these buttons, a command menu opens. To execute one of these commands, click it. If a black arrow appears to the right of the menu command, clicking that command opens a submenu.

FIGURE 1.5
Four default menus are in the top toolbar

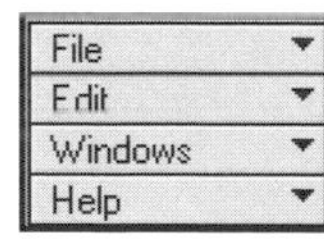

Using Keyboard Shortcuts

If a **keyboard shortcut** for a command (also known as a hotkey) exists, it is listed to the right of the command on the menu. Pressing the hotkey has the same effect as using the menu to execute that command.

For example, in the File menu, there is a capital N next to the New menu command. Pressing the Shift+N keyboard shortcut combination executes the same command as selecting the File, New menu command.

> CAUTION
>
> When using the keyboard shortcuts, be aware that the case of the letter is important. The keyboard shortcuts for a, A, Ctrl+A, and Alt+A are all different, and each has a different effect.

Editing Keyboard Shortcuts

You use the Edit, Edit Keyboard Shortcuts menu command to open the Configure Keys dialog box, shown in Figure 1.6 This dialog box displays a list of all the current keyboard shortcuts for the selected interface. Here you can assign hotkeys to commands and save the keyboard shortcuts you defined as a file you can use whenever you work with LightWave.

> TIP
>
> The Configure Keys dialog box displays a list of all the current keyboard shortcuts for the selected interface, which is helpful if you want a complete list of all keyboard shortcuts.

Switching Menus with the Menu Tabs

The menu tabs are located along the top edge of the interface, as shown for the

FIGURE 1.6
Configure Keys dialog box

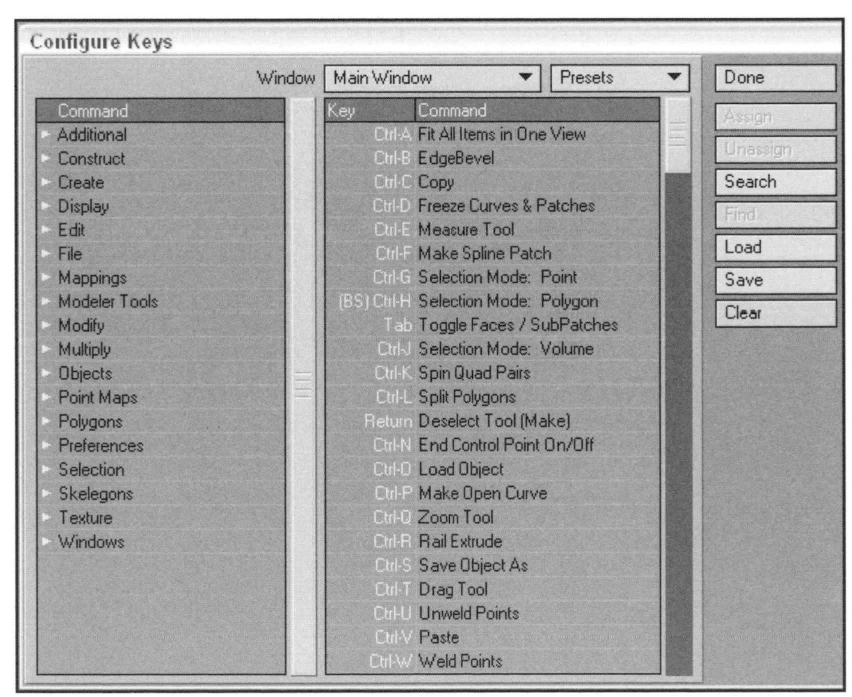

FIGURE 1.7
Menu tabs

Modeler in Figure 1.7. Clicking a menu tab changes the lower portion of the toolbar. The selected menu tab is displayed in white. For example, clicking on the Create menu tab in the Modeler interface makes several sets of buttons appear. These button sets include the Primitives, Text, Points, Polygons, and Curves button sets. Selecting another menu tab would replace all these button sets with several different ones.

Understanding Menu Button Colors

The buttons in the toolbar are color coded to define their functions. Gray buttons open submenus of commands when clicked, and grayish-yellow buttons represent modal commands. Clicking a grayish-yellow button turns the button white and lets you use this command multiple times until you click the button again. The light blue buttons perform a single action, and the light green buttons open dialog boxes. If you pay attention to these colors, you can better understand what to expect from the various command buttons.

Editing Menu Layouts

If you prefer to work with menus in a different way than the default layout offers, you can change their layout using the Edit, Edit Menu Layout command. This command opens the Configure Menus dialog box, shown in Figure 1.8, where you can add, delete, and rename commands. The Configure Menus dialog box includes menus found in the toolbar, along the bottom edge of the interface, and the menus you can access using the left, right, and middle mouse buttons.

FIGURE 1.8
Configure Menus dialog box

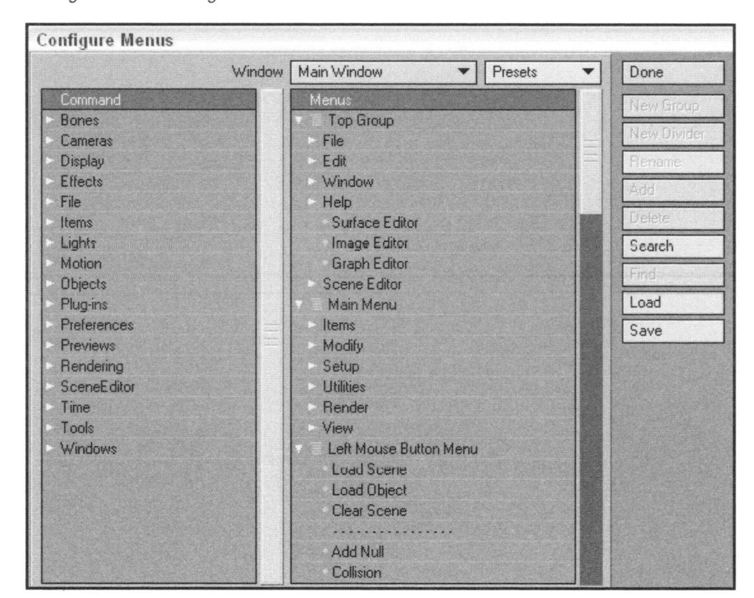

FIGURE 1.9

Ball menu creates a ball object

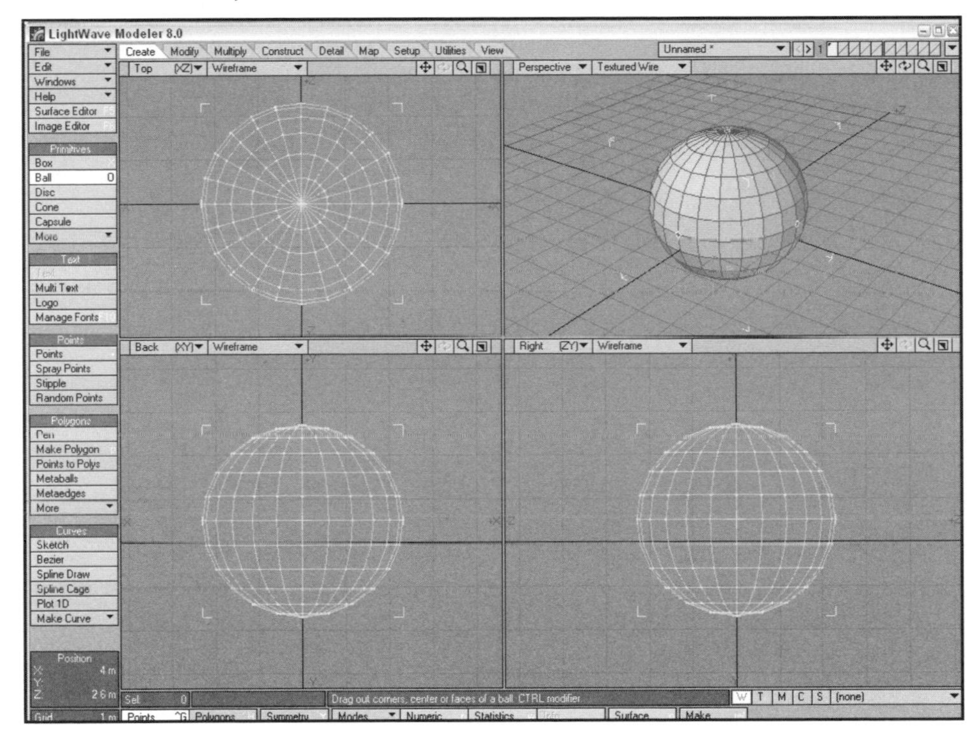

Use a menu command

1. Open the Modeler interface.
2. Click the Create tab, and then click the Ball button in the toolbar.

   The Ball button turns white to indicate that it is the active button.
3. Drag your mouse in the Top viewport to create an elliptical shape, and then drag in the Back viewport to define the ball's height.

   The ball object appears in all four viewports, as shown in Figure 1.9.
4. Press the Ball button to exit ball creation mode, or press the Enter key to accept the created object.

Create a keyboard shortcut

1. Select the Edit, Edit Keyboard Shortcuts menu command.

   The Configure Keys dialog box opens.
2. Click the arrow to the left of the File command to expand the list of commands available on the File menu.

   In the Command list, all commands that already have an assigned keyboard shortcut are dimmed.
3. Under the File command in the Command list, click Close All Objects.

4. In the Command list, click Shift+F10, and then click Assign. Click the Done button to exit the Configure Keys dialog box.

   The Close All Objects command is now assigned to the Shift+F10 keyboard shortcut, as shown in Figure 1.10.

Change the menu layout

1. Select the Edit, Edit Menu Layout menu command.

   The Configure Menus dialog box opens. All commands are listed on the left, and all menus are listed on the right.

2. Click the arrow to the left of Create to expand the list of Create commands.

   In the Command list, all commands that are already part of a menu are dimmed.

3. Under the File command in the Command list, click Switch to Layout.

4. In the Menus list, click Top Menu Group, click File, click Quit, and then click Add. Then click the Done button to exit the Configure Menus dialog box.

   The Layout command is added to the bottom of the File menu, as shown in Figure 1.11.

FIGURE 1.10

Configure Keys dialog box lets you assign keyboard shortcuts

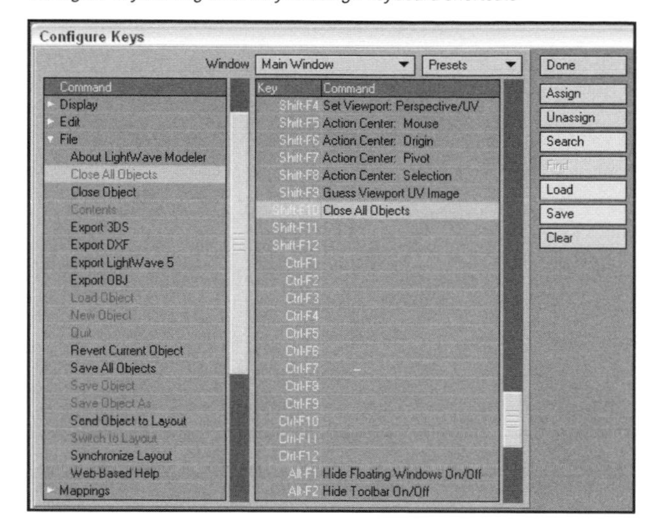

FIGURE 1.11

Menus can be altered

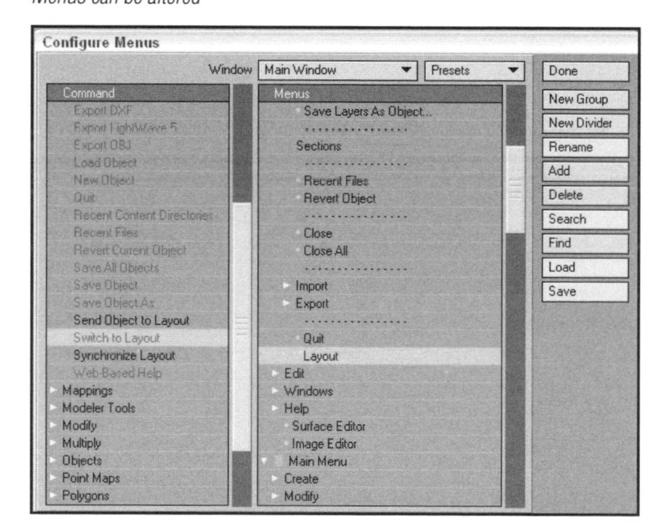

LESSON 3

WORK WITH FILES

What You'll Do

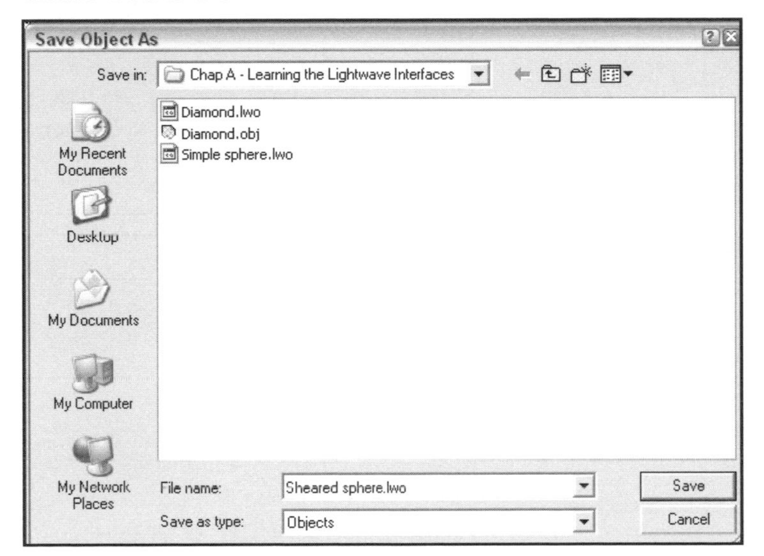

In this lesson, you'll learn how to use the File commands to open, save, and close files.

The File menu includes commands to load and save files. Objects saved from the Modeler interface have an LWO file extension, and scenes saved from the Layout interface have an LWS file extension. LightWave also uses several other data formats for data, such as motion and envelope files.

You can also import and export files from and to several different file formats, including OBJ, DXF, 3DS, VRML97, and Shockwave.

Learning the Native File Types

LightWave deals with several different file types. In fact, a single scene file can reference hundreds of external files. Of the many supported file formats, several are unique to LightWave, including these:

- **LightWave Object (LWO).** 3D data saved as an object you can open in the Modeler.
- **LightWave Scene (LWS).** Lights, cameras, and data added using the Layout interface.
- **Motion data (MOT).** Animated sequences you can save and reuse.
- **Envelope data (ENV).** Used to mark a region where a feature, such as weight, has an effect.
- **Surface attribute file (SRF).** Data that defines the material and texture of an object's surface.
- **Plug-in (P).** Files that add new functionality to the program.

Loading a File

To load LightWave files into the various interfaces, click the File menu and the appropriate menu command. The Modeler includes a Load Object command for loading files with the LWO extension. The Layout interface includes the File, Load, Load Scene and File, Load, Load Object menu commands, allowing you to load both LWO and LWS files into the Layout interface. Both commands open a file dialog box, like the one shown in Figure 1.12.

> TIP
>
> To reload a file that was recently opened, select the File, Recent Files menu command in the Modeler or the File, Load, Recent Scenes in the Layout interface.

FIGURE 1.12
Load Scene dialog box

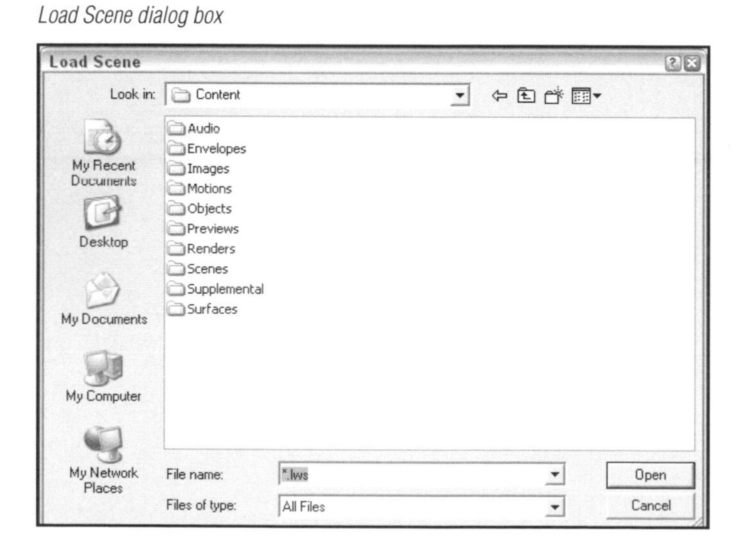

Saving Files

You can save files using commands on the File menu. Using the File, Save menu command in the Modeler saves the object file using the named file without opening a dialog box. However, the File, Save As menu command opens a dialog box where you can save the file with a different file name. The File, Save Incremental menu command saves the current object as a new file without overwriting the last saved file.

The same menu commands are available for the Layout interface in the File, Save menu, except that the Layout interface can save the current scene file or the selected object.

> TIP
>
> Modified objects have an asterisk (*) displayed next to their names at the top of the Modeler interface until you save them.

Importing and Exporting Files

You can import objects into LightWave from other 3D packages using the OBJ, DXF, 3DS, and FACT file formats. You can also export objects using the LW5 (LightWave 5.x), OBJ, DXF, and 3DS formats. You can export scene files to VRML97 and Shockwave 3D formats for viewing on the Web. Commands for importing and exporting objects are on the File menu.

Learning the Supported File Types

You can use image and video files in LightWave in many different capacities, including materials, backgrounds, projections, and others. LightWave supports many different image file formats, including PSD, Alias, BMP, Cineon FP, Flexible Image Format, IFF, JPEG, PCS, PICT, PNG, Radiance, PLA, RPF, SFI, Sun, TIFF, Targa, VBP, and YUV. Supported video file formats include QuickTime, RTV, Flexible Image Format, Storyboard, and Film Expand.

FIGURE 1.13
Open file in Modeler

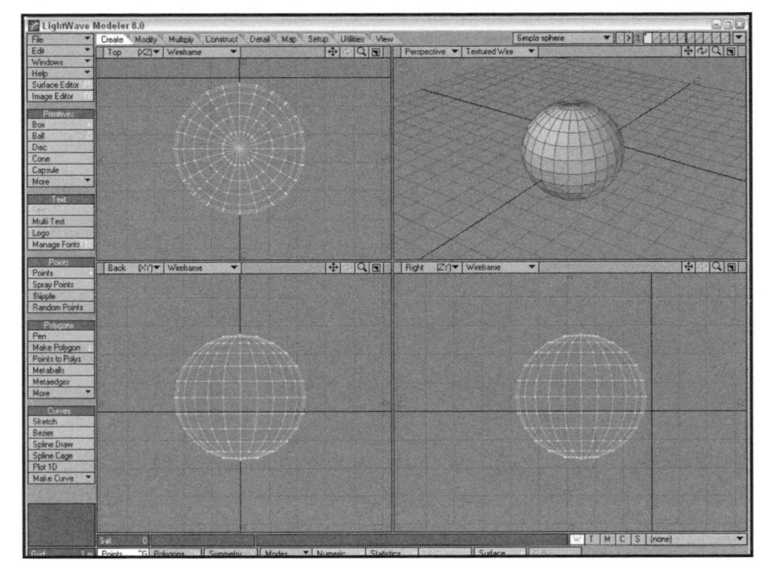

FIGURE 1.14
Saved file

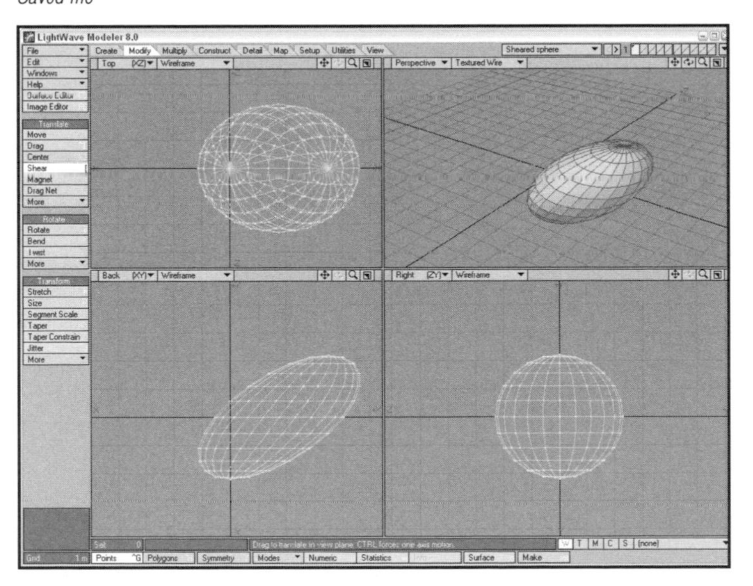

Load a file

1. Switch to the Modeler, if necessary.
2. Click File, and then click Load Object.

   The Load Object dialog box opens.
3. Select the Simple sphere.lwo file, and then click Open.

   The file opens. It consists of a simple sphere object, as shown in Figure 1.13.

   > NOTE You can download all example files for this book from the Course Technology Web site, at http://www.course.com.

Save a file

1. With the Simple sphere.lwo file open, click the Modify menu tab. Then click the Shear button in the Translate section of the toolbar.
2. Drag the sphere in the Top viewport to shear the ball object.
3. Click the File, Save As menu command.

   The Save As dialog box opens.
4. Enter the file name, Sheared sphere, and click Save.

   The directory where the file is to be saved is shown in Figure 1.14.

Export a file

1. Switch to the Modeler, if necessary.
2. Click File, and then click Load Object.

   The Load Object dialog box opens
3. Select the Diamond.lwo file and click Open.

   The file opens. It consists of a diamond-shaped object.
4. Click File, click Export, and then click Export OBJ.
5. Enter the file name, **Diamond.obj**, and click Save.

SET INTERFACE OPTIONS

What You'll Do

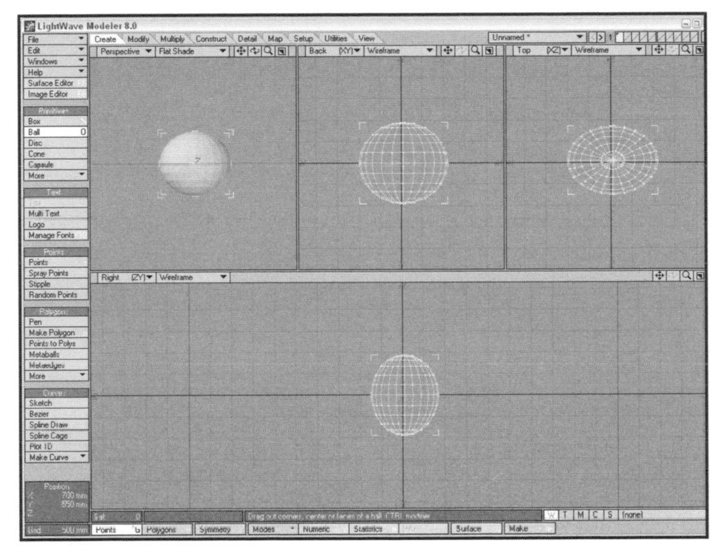

In this lesson, you'll learn how to undo mistakes, change options, and set layout preferences.

The Edit menu in both interfaces includes menu commands to open the General and Display Options dialog boxes. These dialog boxes are different in the Modeler and the Layout interfaces, but they share many of the same settings. Both the General Options and Display Options are displayed as panels in the Preferences dialog box in the Layout interface, as shown in Figure 1.15. They are displayed as tabbed panels in the Modeler interface (see Figure 1.16).

FIGURE 1.15

Layout interface's Preferences dialog box

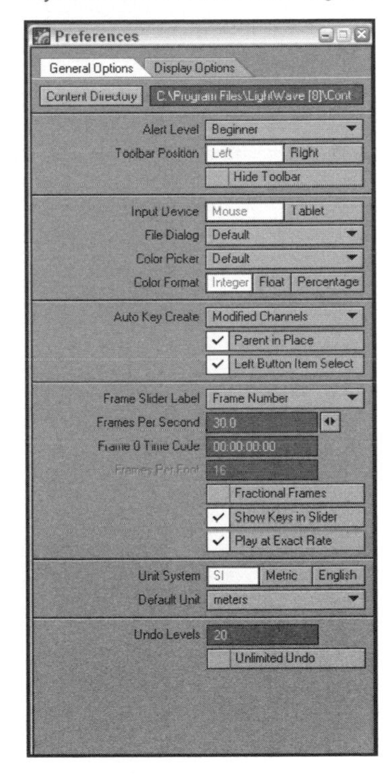

FIGURE 1.16
Modeler interface's Display Options

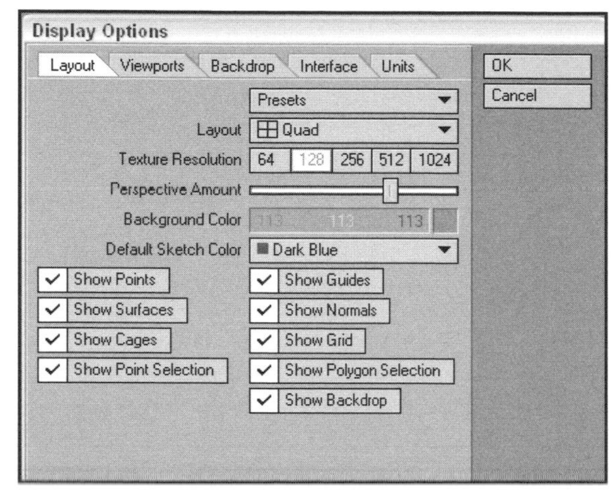

Setting the Content Directory

A text field that defines the **Content Directory** is located at the top of the General Options dialog box for both interfaces. The Content Directory is the directory that you access when you open a file dialog box. Clicking the Content Directory button lets you browse to this directory from a file dialog box.

TIP

If you know where all of your project's files will be saved, setting the Content Directory will save you a lot of time looking for the correct directory.

Using the Undo Feature

If you make a mistake, you can use the Edit, Undo feature to remove the effect of the last command. You can specify the number of actions kept in the Undo buffer in the General Options dialog box. If you undo an action, you can perform the action again using the Edit, Redo command.

Setting the Number of Viewports

The Viewport Layout list appears in the Display Options dialog box, shown in Figure 1.17. Use this list to select the number and position of the viewports. For the Modeler, you can also set the view, rendering style, upright rotation, and background color for each viewport.

FIGURE 1.17
You can divide the workspace into viewports of different sizes

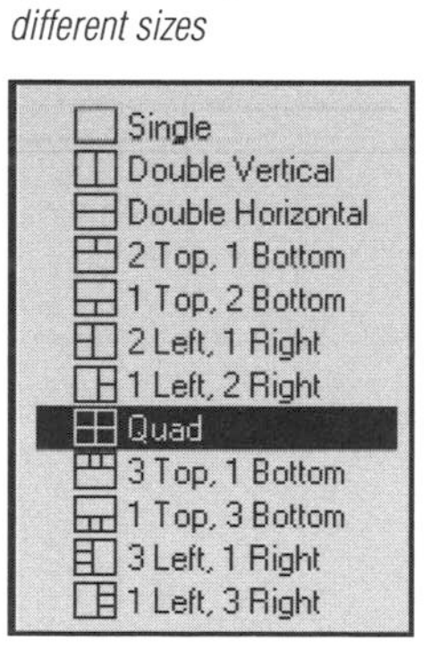

Positioning and Hiding the Toolbar

You can use the Options dialog boxes to position the toolbar to the left or right, or to hide the toolbar. Use the General Options dialog box in the Layout interface and the Display Options dialog box in the Modeler, shown in Figure 1.18. If the toolbar is hidden, you can press Alt+F2 to redisplay it.

FIGURE 1.18
Display Options dialog box

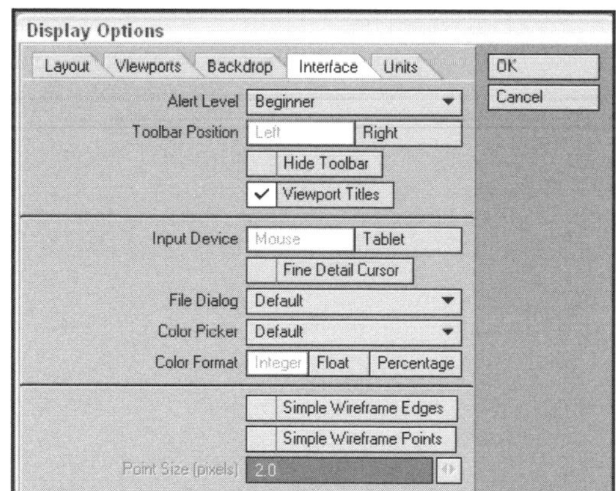

Setting the Default Units

You can set the units used by the system in the Options dialog boxes. The options include SI, Metric, and English. For each option, you can choose the default unit to be millimeters, meters, or kilometers. The unit system setting is located in the General Options dialog box in the Layout interface and within the Units panel of the Display Options dialog box in the Modeler.

FIGURE 1.19
Changing the Content Directory

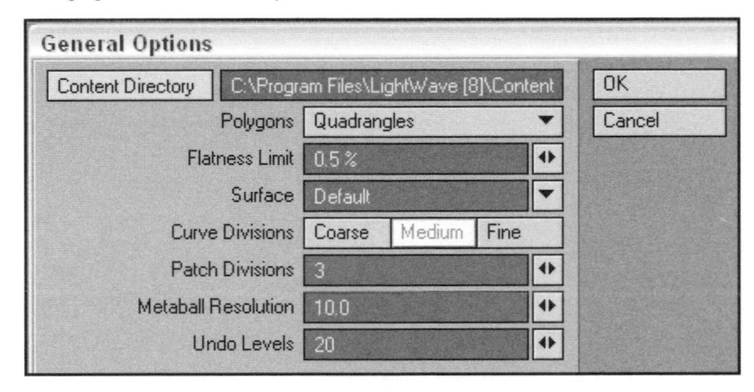

FIGURE 1.20
Drawing a sphere in the rearranged viewport layout

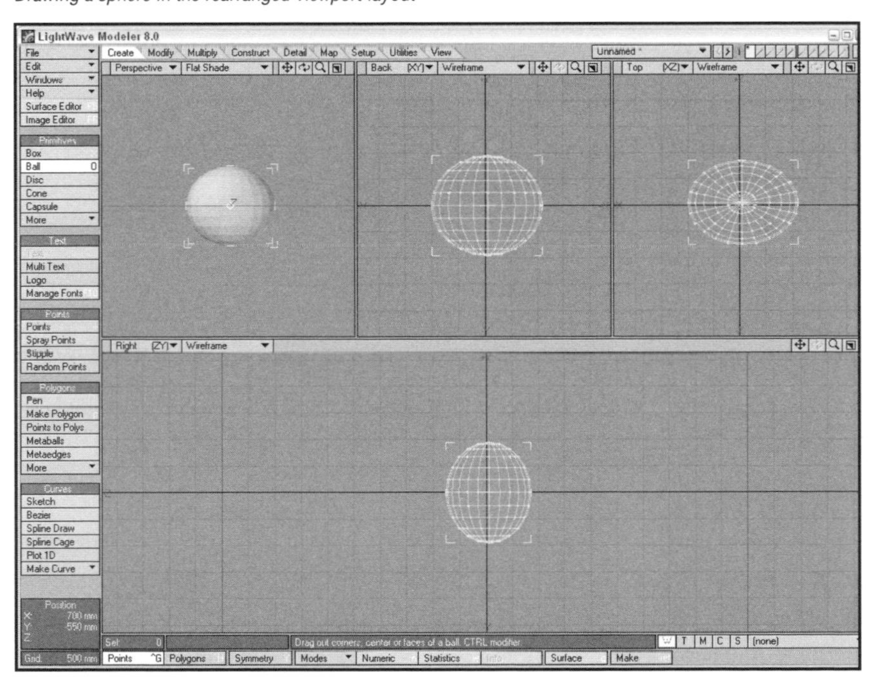

Set the default Content Directory

1. Switch to the Modeler interface, if necessary.
2. Select the Edit, General Options menu command.

   The General Options dialog box opens.
3. Click the Content Directory button at the top of the dialog box.

   The Browse for Folder dialog box opens.
4. Browse to the directory that you want to use as the default Content Directory, such as the My Documents directory, and then click the OK button.

   The path to the Content Directory is added to the General Options dialog box, as shown in Figure 1.19.

Change the viewport layout

1. Switch to the Modeler, if necessary.
2. Select the Edit, Display Options menu command.

   The Display Options dialog box opens.
3. In the Layout drop-down list, click the 3 Top, 1 Bottom option, and then click OK to close the Display Options dialog box.

   The viewports are rearranged.
4. Click the Ball button on the toolbar and drag into the viewports to create a sphere object.

   The sphere is displayed in the rearranged viewports, shown in Figure 1.20.

Change the system units to kilometers

1. Switch to the Modeler, if necessary.
2. Select the Edit, Display Options menu command.

   The Display Options dialog box opens.
3. Click the Units tab, click the Metric button, and then, in the Default Unit list, click Kilometers.

   The Display Options dialog box looks like Figure 1.21. After you click OK, LightWave updates the system units for all viewports.

FIGURE 1.21
Changing the system units

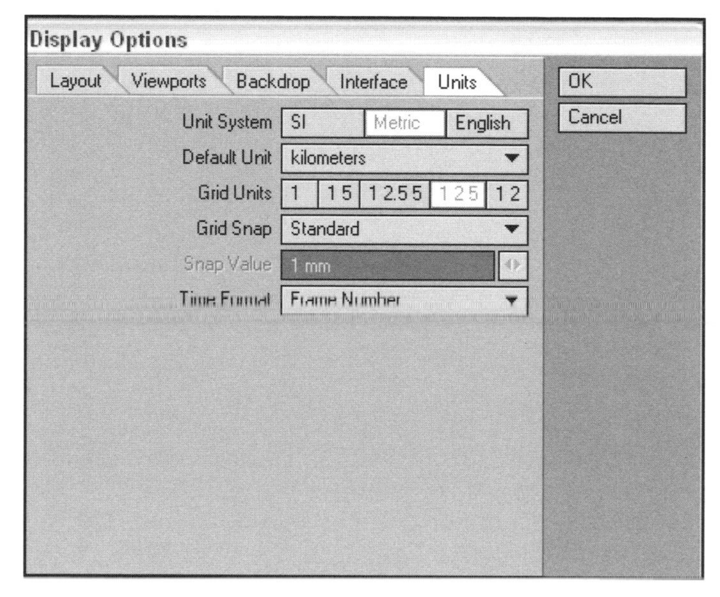

EXPLORE THE VIEWPORTS

What You'll Do

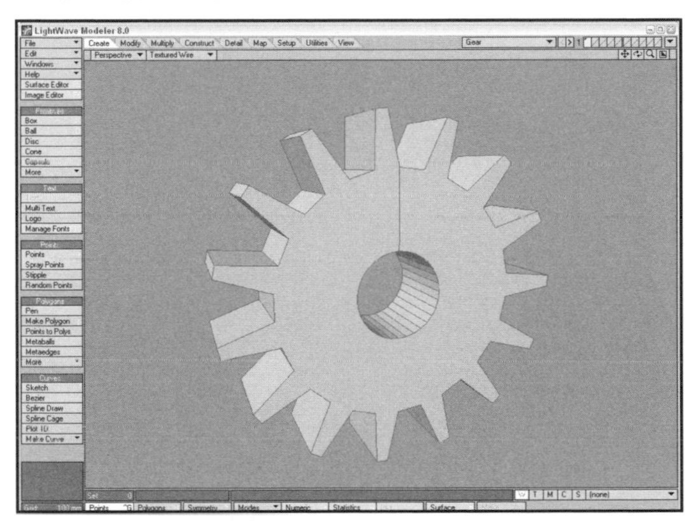

In this lesson, you'll learn how to use the viewports to see objects in different ways.

The viewports fill the central workspace and provide a way to see the objects within the scene. The viewport title, its rendering method, and four viewport control buttons are located along the top edge of each viewport, as shown in Figure 1.22. Using these controls, you can alter what to show in the viewports.

Moving, Rotating, and Zooming Viewports

You can use the buttons in the upper-right corner of the viewport to change the viewport's point of view. Clicking and dragging the Move button pans (moves) the viewport in the direction that the mouse is dragged. Clicking and dragging the Rotate button causes the view to be rotated about its center point, and doing the same with the Zoom button zooms in and out of the view.

FIGURE 1.22
Viewport controls

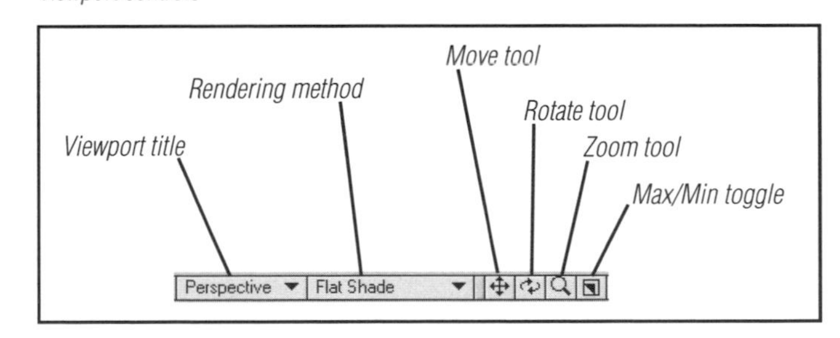

Maximizing the Viewport

To the right of the Zoom button is the Maximize/Minimize button. Clicking this button causes the selected viewport to enlarge to fill the space allotted to the viewports. Figure 1.23 shows a maximized viewport.

Manually Changing the Viewport's Size

If several viewports are visible in the workspace, you can manually resize any of them by dragging the borders between adjacent viewports. Using this method, you can increase the size of a single viewport while decreasing the size of a less important one.

Changing the Viewport's View

The button located in the upper left of the viewport shows the name of the view that is

FIGURE 1.23
Maximized viewport

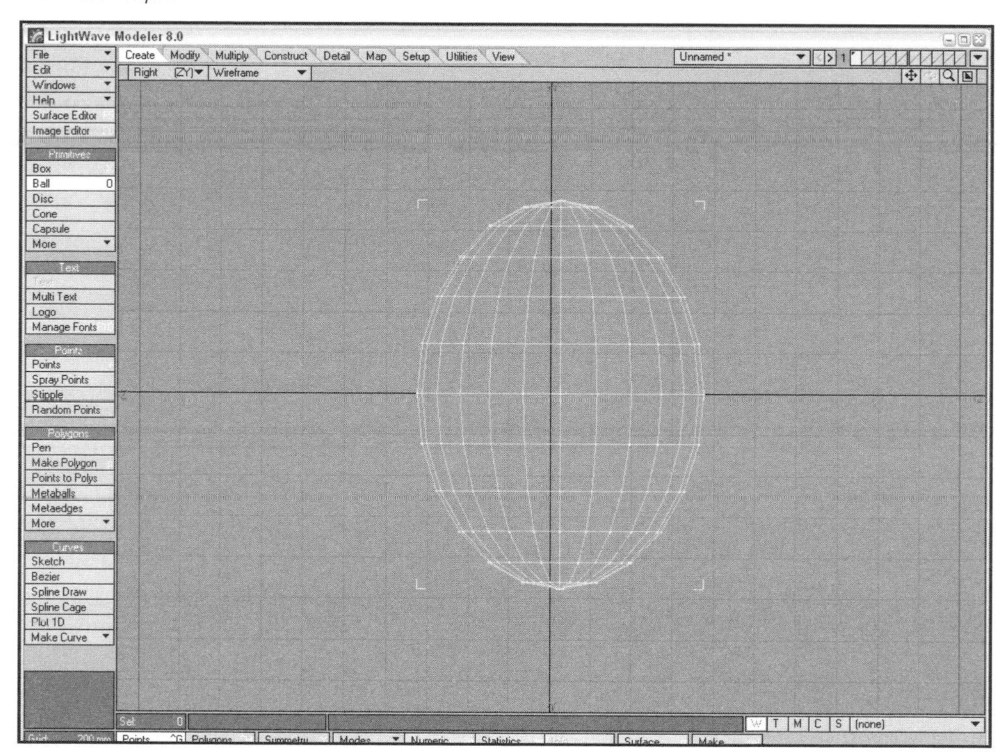

active. If you click this button, you can select a new viewport view from the drop-down list. The options include Top, Bottom, Back, Front, Right, Left, and Perspective. These views are available in both the Modeler and Layout interfaces.

Changing the Viewport's Display Mode

The button to the right of the view lets you change the display mode you use to draw the scene objects. The available options in the Modeler (listed from fastest to slowest) include Wireframe, Color Wireframe, Hidden Line, Sketch, Wireframe Shade, Flat Shade, Smooth Shade, Weight Shade, Texture, and Textured Wire. The latter options look much more realistic, but they require more time to be redrawn, and this extra time is significant when you're working with complex objects. The Layout display modes are Bounding Box, Vertices, Wireframe, Front Face Wireframe, Shaded Solid, Textured Shaded Solid, and Textured Shaded Solid Wireframe. Figure 1.24 shows several different display modes.

Working with Grids

By default, each viewport shows a grid, which you can use to position and align objects. The size of the grid is displayed in the lower-left corner of the interface. You can change the grid size or turn off the grid using the Display Options dialog box, which you can open using the Edit, Display Options menu command.

FIGURE 1.24
Display modes

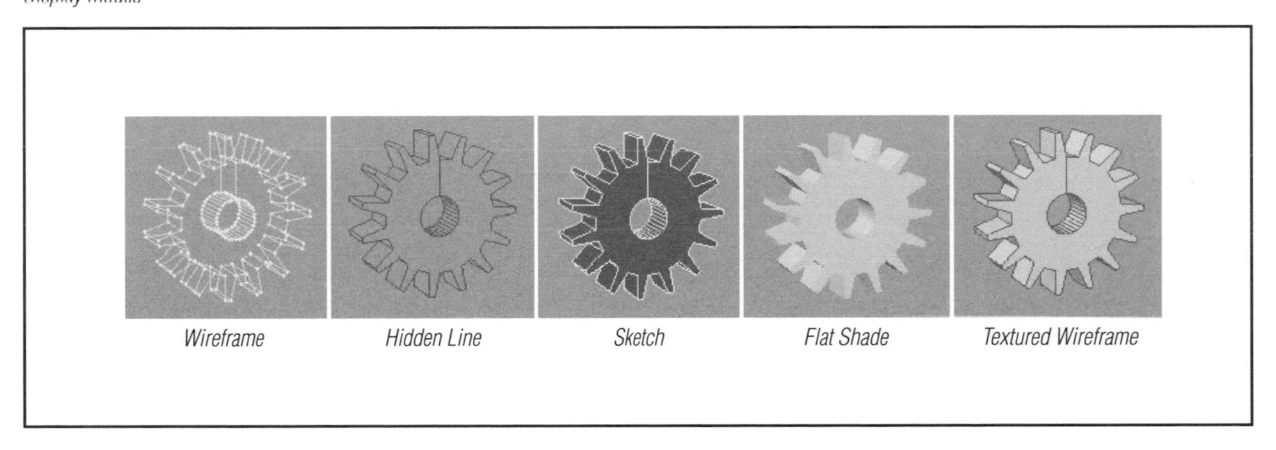

Navigate and maximize a viewport

1. Switch to the Modeler, if necessary.
2. Select the File, Load Object menu command, and then open the Gear.lwo file.

   LightWave loads a simple gear object.
3. Click the Move tool for the Top viewport, and then drag the gear until it is centered in the viewport.
4. Click the Move tool for the Right viewport, and then drag to zoom in on the gear.
5. Click the Zoom tool for the Perspective viewport, and then drag to center the gear.
6. Click the Max/Min button to increase the size of the Perspective viewport.

   The viewport is maximized, as shown in Figure 1.25.

FIGURE 1.25
Maximized viewport

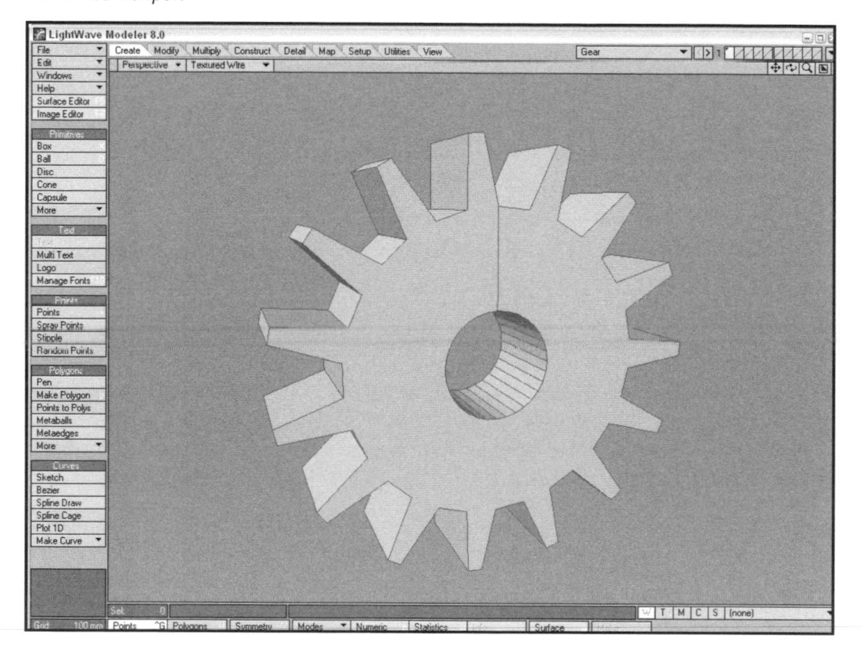

FIGURE 1.26
Altered view and display mode

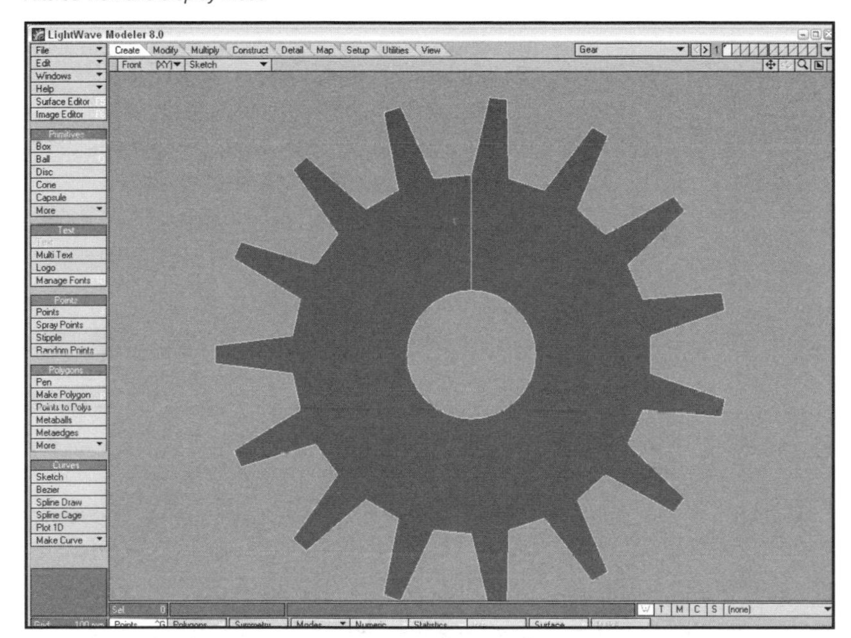

Change the viewport view and display mode

1. With the maximized Perspective viewport still visible, click the viewport title at the top of the viewport, and then select the Front viewport view.

   The point of view of the viewport changes to show the front of the gear.

2. In the viewport display mode list, click Sketch.

   The gear object is rendered using the new display mode, shown in Figure 1.26.

Turn the grid off

1. Click Edit, and then click Display Options.

   The view of the viewport now shows the front of the gear.

2. In the Layout panel, clear the Show Grid option.

   The default grids for all viewports are hidden.

LESSON 6

What You'll Do

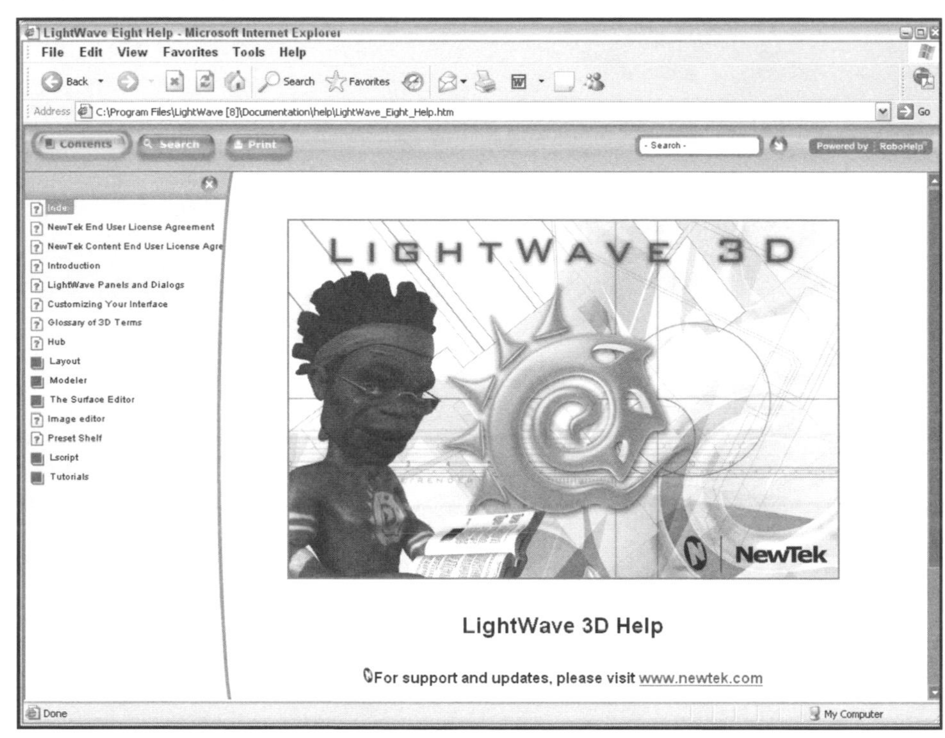

In this lesson, you'll learn how to get help as you work with LightWave.

The Help menu includes a command for opening the online reference in a Web browser. This reference lets you look up topics by subject or by searching the Help system using specific topics or keywords. Another place to get help is the Help Line, located at the bottom of the LightWave window.

> **CAUTION**
>
> The LightWave Help reference runs in a Web browser and uses active content. If the top menu bar buttons are visible, you need to disable your pop-up blocker software.

Accessing the Online User Reference

Selecting the Contents command from the Help menu opens the online reference, shown in Figure 1.27, in a Web browser. The list to the left displays the Help topics. Clicking a topic opens information about that topic in the pane on the right. You can also search the reference using the Search button.

TIP

You can also open the online reference by pressing F1.

Viewing the Help Line

A Help Line is located at the bottom of both the Layout and Modeler windows. It displays useful information, depending on what LightWave expects you to do next.

FIGURE 1.27
LightWave's online reference

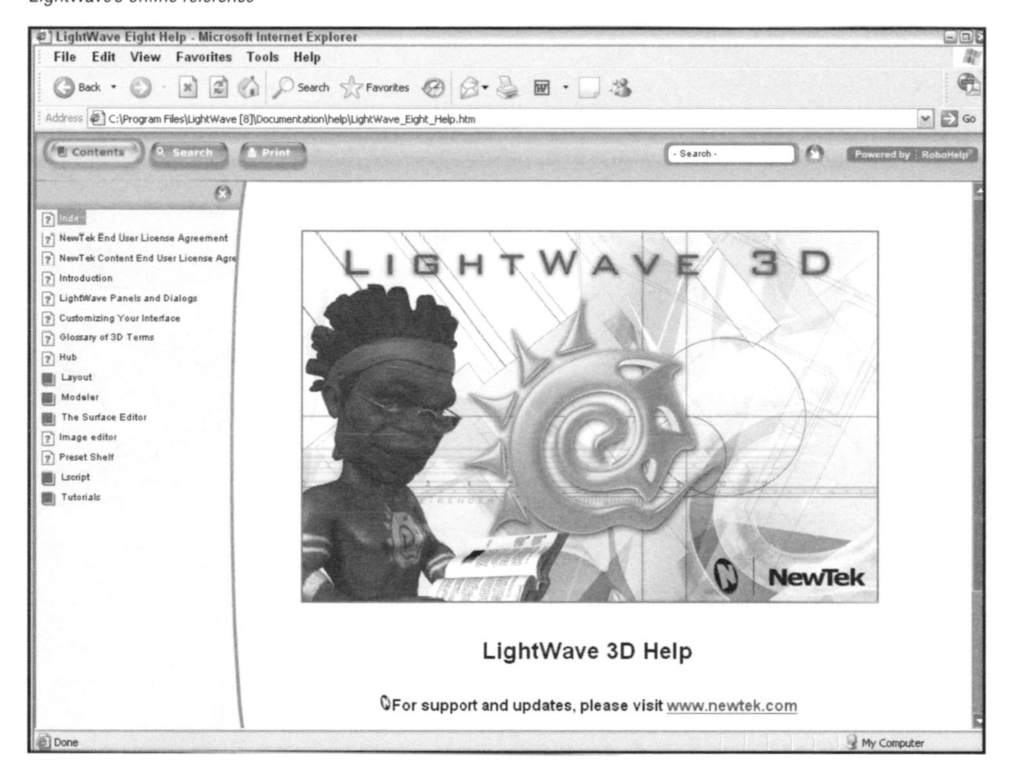

Access the online reference

1. Select the Help, Contents menu command.

   The online reference opens in a Web browser.

2. Click one of the topics in the list on the left. Information on the selected topic is displayed on the right, as shown in Figure 1.28.

3. To search the online reference, click the Search button and enter the words to search for.

FIGURE 1.28

Searched topic

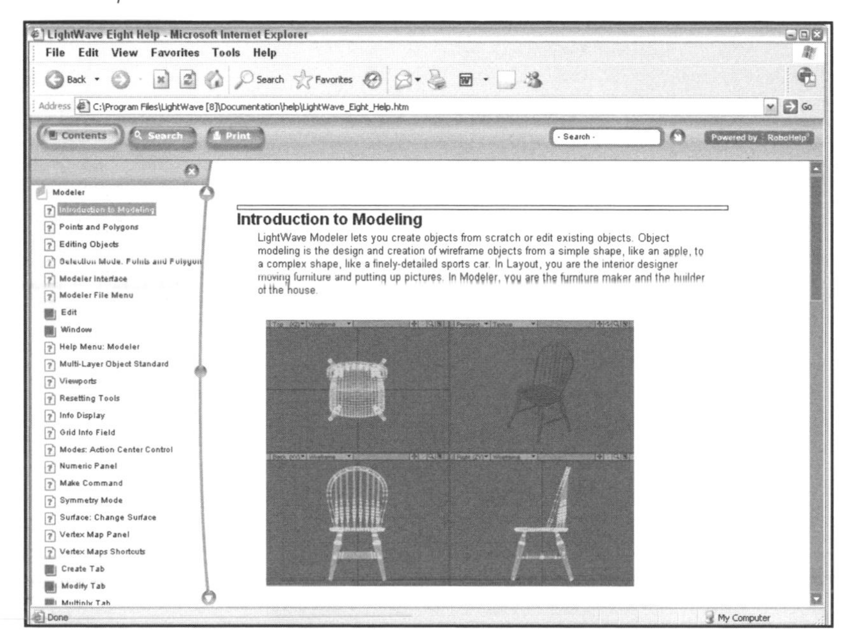

CHAPTER SUMMARY

This chapter introduced LightWave's two main interfaces: Modeler and Layout. Learning to use these two main interfaces effectively is the key to creating 3D scenes with LightWave. This chapter also covered the main interface elements that are available in each interface, including menus and viewports. The File menu was presented as a way to load and save files, and the Edit menu included options for customizing the interface and display options. Finally, this chapter covered the help options that are available.

What You Have Learned

- How to launch LightWave's Modeler and Layout interfaces and how to switch between them.
- What the main interface menus are that are common between both interfaces.
- How to work with the File menu to load, save, import, and export files.
- How to customize the display options, keyboard, and menu settings.
- How to control the viewports to change the view and shading type.
- How to get help from the online reference documentation.

Key Terms from This Chapter

- **Modeler.** A LightWave interface that is used to build objects.
- **Layout.** A LightWave interface that is used to position, animate, and render scenes.
- **LightWave Hub.** A background program that manages memory usage and interface processes.
- **keyboard shortcut.** A key or set of keys on the keyboard that you can press to execute an interface command.
- **menu tabs.** A set of tabs positioned along the top of the interface that access a different set of menu buttons in the toolbar when selected.
- **LWO, LWS.** File extensions that save LightWave objects and LightWave scenes.
- **Content Directory.** A designated directory that opens whenever you access a File dialog box.
- **viewport.** The center workspace that displays a view of the current scene or object.

CHAPTER 2

CREATING AND SELECTING OBJECTS

1. Create primitive objects.
2. Create text.
3. Create points and polygons.
4. Create curves.
5. Select objects.
6. Use layers and hide objects.

CHAPTER 6

CREATING AND SELECTING OBJECTS

After you are comfortable with the LightWave user interface, you are ready to begin building objects. You build objects in the Modeler interface using both **primitive objects** and parts. LightWave includes many default primitive objects, which you create by simply dragging in the viewports. You can set various options for these primitive objects using the **Numeric panel.** Other basic objects include text, points, polygons, and curves.

You can create text using a loaded system font. Extruded text is called **logo text** in LightWave. You use the Multi Text tool to enter multiple lines of text at once.

You can also create objects manually, using points and polygons. LightWave includes several different ways to create points, both random and specific. You can turn a selection of points into a polygon, or you can create a polygon by clicking where its points are to be located.

You can create curves using the Sketch tool. You can also use the Bezier and Spline Draw tools to create precise, smooth curves. You can also form a curve using a series of selected points.

LightWave includes two unique selection modes for selecting objects: points and polygons. Using these modes along with the commands in the View menu, you can quickly and easily select points or polygons by dragging over them, encircling them with a lasso, or by automatically selecting all connected points or polygons.

You can divide objects you create into **layers** using the layer icons in the upper-right corner of the interface. With these icons, you can quickly view just the objects on the current layer. You can also hide objects using the View menu.

Tools You'll Use

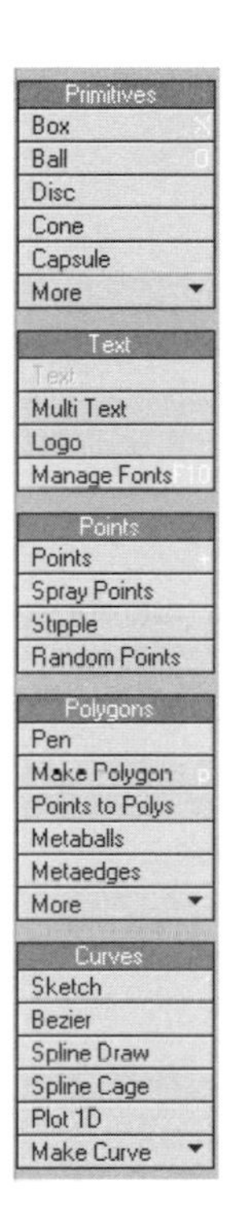

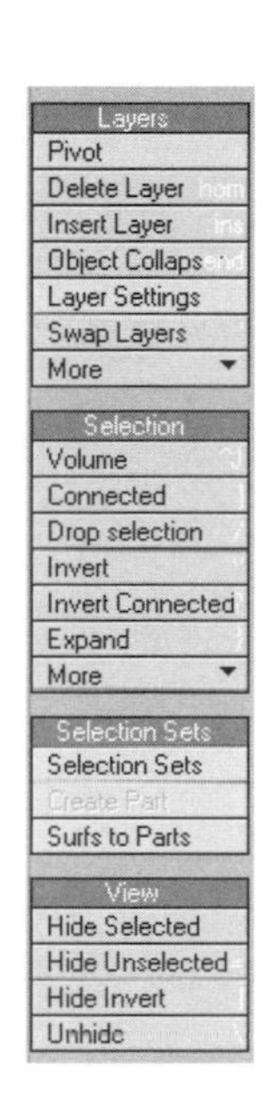

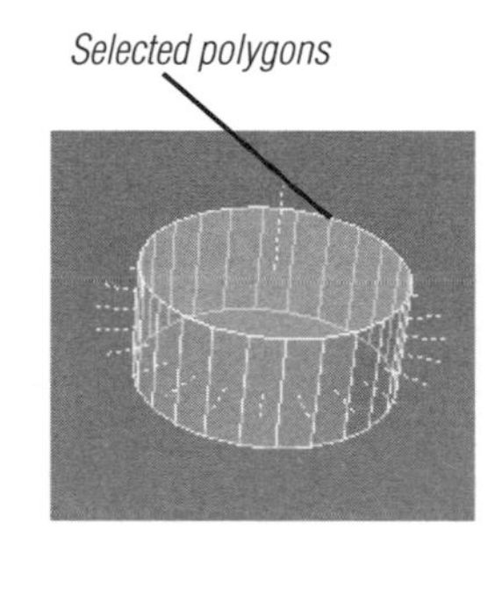

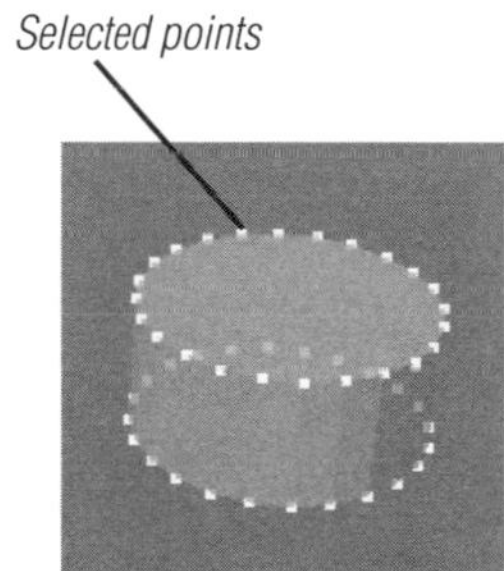

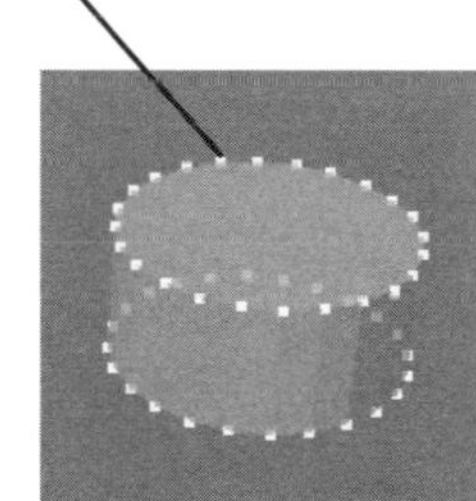

LESSON 1

CREATE PRIMITIVE OBJECTS

What You'll Do

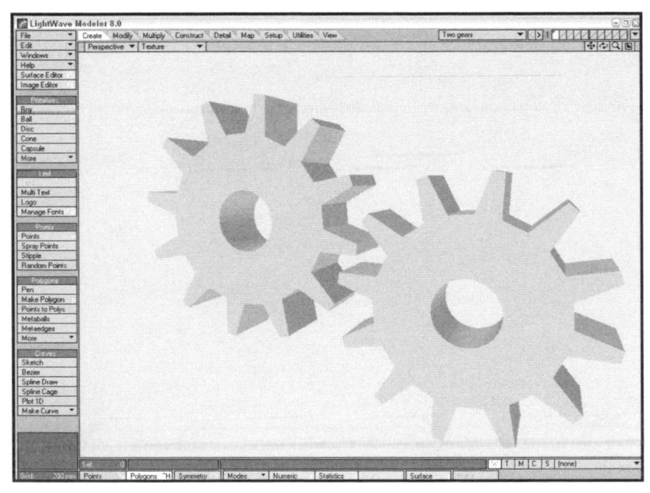

In this lesson, you'll learn how to create primitive objects.

You can start many modeling tasks using a set of basic objects called primitives. You can create and position these objects precisely using parameters found in the Numeric panel. There are five basic primitives in the Create tab, and several additional primitives are available on the More submenu.

Creating Primitive Objects

If you select the Create menu tab, several primitive objects menu buttons appear in the toolbar including Box, Ball, Disc, Cone, and Capsule. To create one of these primitives, click its button and then drag twice in the viewports. Drag in a viewport to first define the primitive's cross section, and then drag again in another viewport to set its height. Figure 2.1 shows each of the basic primitive objects.

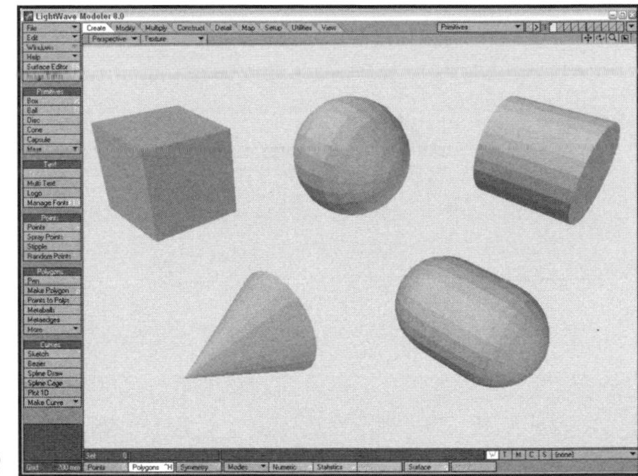

FIGURE 2.1
Basic primitive objects: Box, Ball, Disc, Cone, and Capsule

TIP

Holding down Ctrl before clicking in the viewport constrains the cross section to a perfect square or circle.

Modifying New Objects

After you select a primitives object button from the toolbar, its button turns white, indicating that the interface is in creation mode. After you drag to create an object, the object is surrounded by light blue handles, shown in Figure 2.2. Dragging these handles lets you modify the dimensions of the new object. Dragging the center handle moves the entire object. Dragging the edge or corner handle resizes the object. Once you finish modifying an object, click the Make button at the bottom of the interface, press Enter, or click the menu button again to exit creation mode.

TIP

In creation mode, you can use the arrow keys to increase and decrease the number of primitive segments.

FIGURE 2.2
Dragging handles changes the size of the object

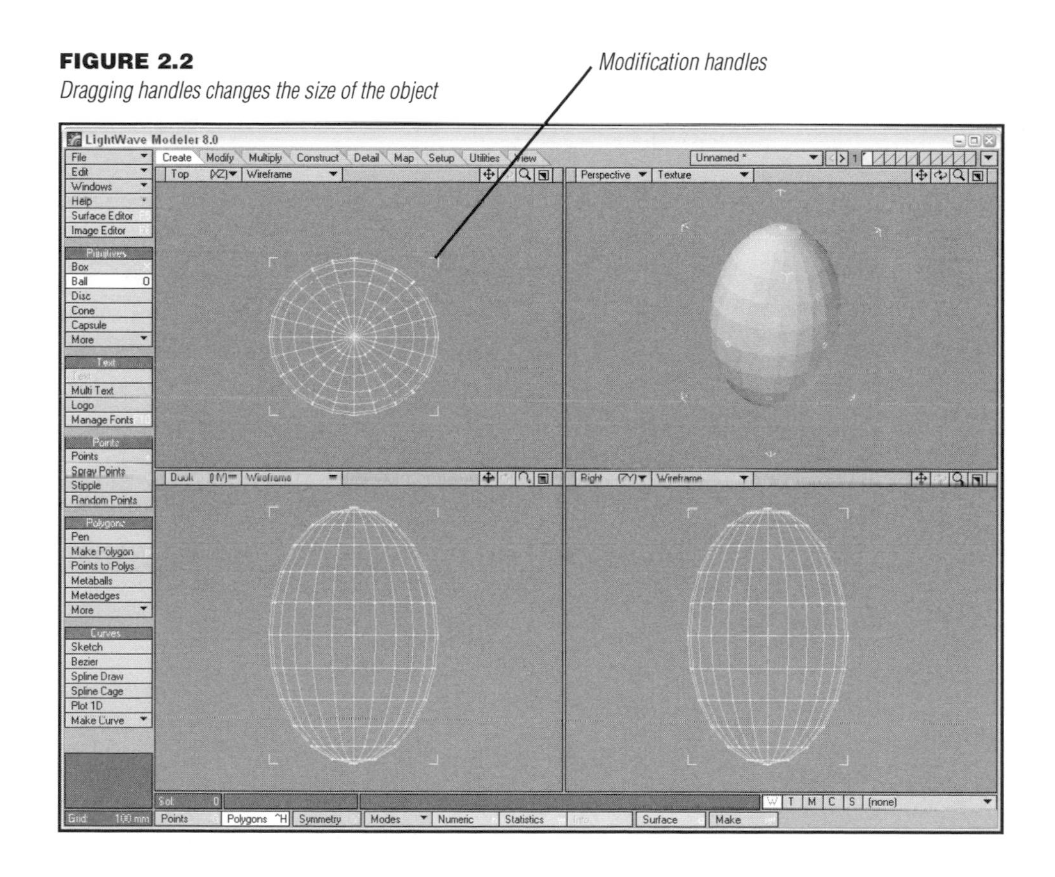

Creating Accurate Objects with the Numeric Panel

At any time during the creation of a primitive object, you can click the Numeric button at the bottom of the interface (or press N) to open a dialog box of options for the selected primitive object. Figure 2.3 shows the Numeric panel for the Ball object. These options let you change the dimensions of the object by entering values. You can also change the number of segments that make up the object and change its center location. Any value changes you make to the Numeric panel will be used the next time you create the same kind of object. You can reset the Numeric panel values to their defaults using the Reset option in the Actions menu.

FIGURE 2.3
Numeric panel

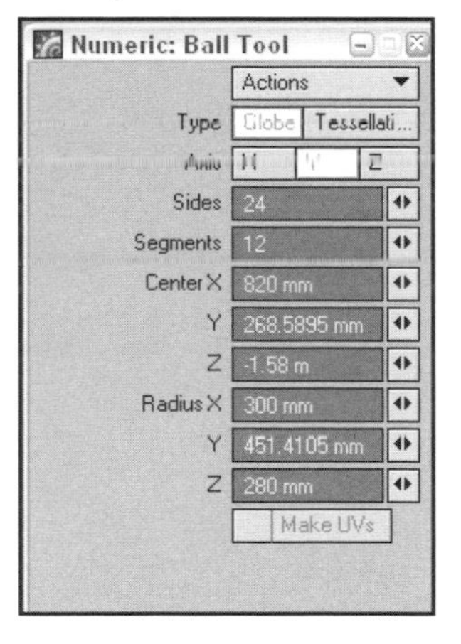

Creating More Objects

At the bottom of the Primitives menu in the toolbar is the More button. Use this button to open an additional menu of primitive objects. You use different methods to create the primitive objects in the More submenu. Some commands immediately open the Numeric panel and others require that you click and drag in the viewports.

- **Platonic Solid Tool.** Creates solid geometric shapes including tetrahedrons, octahedrons, cubes, cubeoctahedrons, icosahedrons, dodecahedrons, and icosidodecahedrons.
- **Toroid.** Creates a doughnut-shaped object with a circular cross section.
- **Wedge.** Creates a donut-shaped object with flat sides called an annulus. You can also use this object to create a wedge shape, similar to a piece of a pie.

FIGURE 2.4
More primitive objects

- **Gear/Gears.** Creates both simple and complex gears for which you can specify the number of teeth.
- **Gemstone.** Creates a diamond-shaped crystal object.
- **SuperQuadric Tool.** Creates quadric objects such as ellipsoids or toroids.
- **ParametricObj.** Creates a 3D object using mathematical equations.
- **Plot 2D.** Creates a flat 2D plane object with its height determined by an equation.
- **Equilateral Tri.** Creates a triangle with equal length sides.
- **Bubbles.** Creates a set of particles that are selected together as a single object.
- **Star Sphere.** Positions up to nine levels of single point polygons of differing magnitude in a spherical shape to be used as a starfield.
- **Teapot.** Creates a simple teapot object.

Figure 2.4 shows several of these primitive objects.

NOTE

The teapot object has been traditionally used in computer graphics to test rendering algorithms and is included as a popular benchmark.

Compare ball types

1. Open the Modeler, and then click the Create tab.
2. Click the Ball button.

   The Ball button turns white to indicate that you are in Ball creation mode.
3. Drag in the Top viewport to create the cross-section of a ball object, and then drag in the Right viewport to specify the ball height.
4. Click the handle at the center of the ball and drag the ball to the left side of the Top viewport.
5. Click the Make button at the bottom right of the interface.

   Clicking the Make button makes the ball object permanent and exits creation mode.
6. Repeat steps 2–3 to create another ball object to the right of the first ball in the Top viewport.
7. Click the Numeric button at the bottom of the interface (or press the n key).

   The Numeric panel displays several options for the ball object.
8. In the Numeric panel, click the Tessellation button.

   Setting the Ball Type to Tessellation in the Numeric panel causes the ball to be made of equal-sized triangles, as shown in Figure 2.5. These triangles are equally spread over the entire surface of the ball instead of having many small polygons bunched at each end of the ball object.
9. Click the Make button to exit creation mode.
10. Select the File, Save As menu command, and save the file as Two spheres.lwo.

FIGURE 2.5
Two spheres of different types

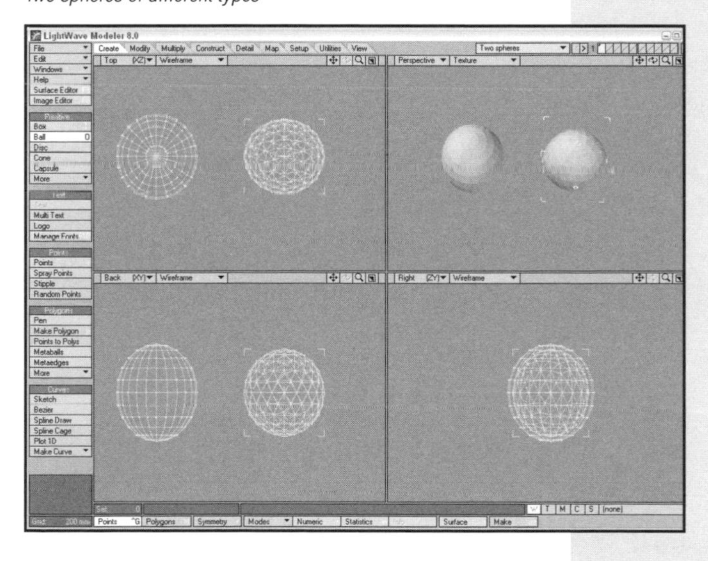

Use the Platonic Solid Tool

1. Click the Create menu tab.
2. Select the More, Platonic Solid Tool menu command from the Primitives section of the Create menu tab.
3. Drag in the Top viewport to create a tetrahedron object.
4. Click the Numeric button at the bottom of the interface (or press the n key), and then enable the Shape option.

   The Numeric panel displays several options. The Shape option changes the type of hedra that is created.
5. Click the Make button (or press Enter) to make the object permanent.
6. Repeat steps 2–5 for each shape type.

   Each of the available shape types is displayed in the viewport, as shown in Figure 2.6.
7. Click File on the menu, click Save Object As, and then save the file as Platonic solids.lwo.

FIGURE 2.6
Platonic solids

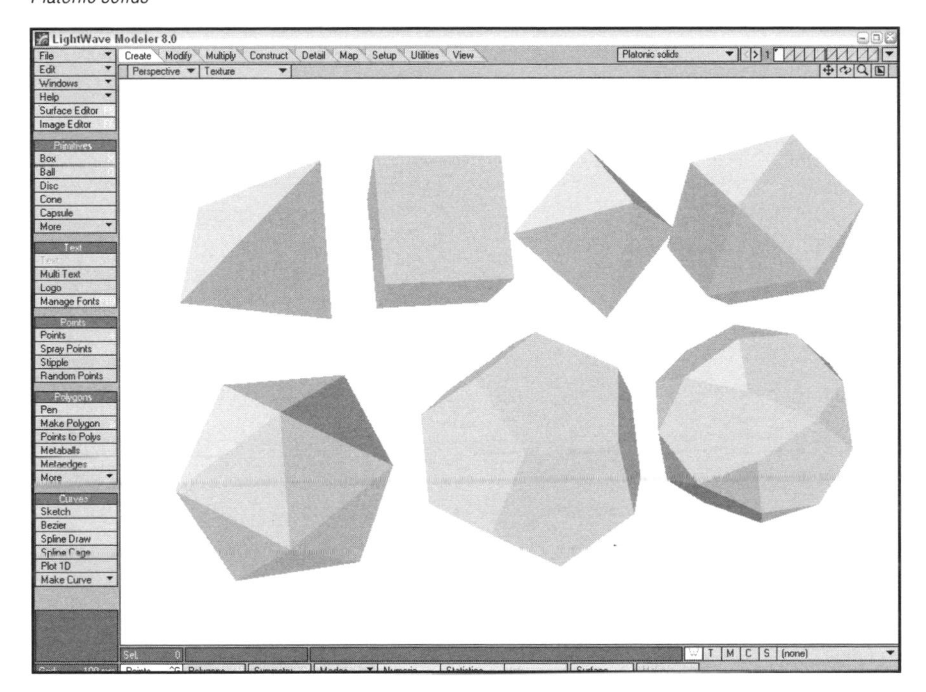

FIGURE 2.7
Gear objects

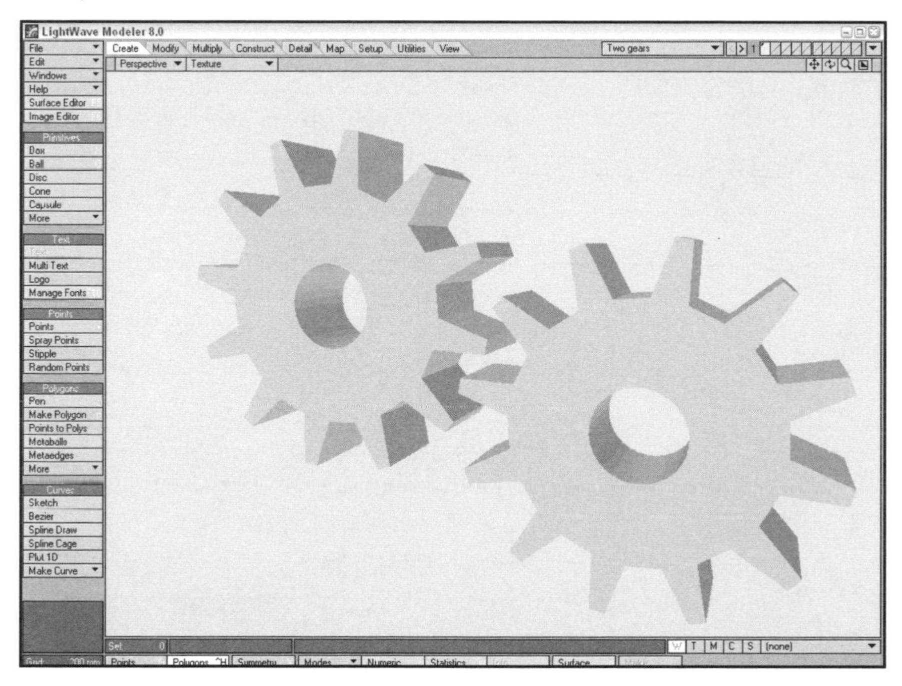

Create gears

1. Click the Create menu tab.
2. Select the More, Gears menu command from the Primitives section of the Create menu tab.

   The Gear dialog box opens.
3. In the Gear dialog box, set the Number of Teeth to 12, and then click the OK button.

   A gear is created and displayed in the viewports.
4. Repeat steps 2–3 with the Center X-axis value of 1.9 m in the Gear Options dialog box.

   A second gear is created and positioned next to the first one, as shown in Figure 2.7.
5. Select the File, Save Object As menu command and save the file as Two gears.lwo.

CREATE TEXT

What You'll Do

In this lesson, you'll learn how to create and modify text objects.

You can add text to a scene using the Text tool. The Text tool uses a specified font. You can create text as a 2D object or as an extruded (with depth) 3D object called a Logo in LightWave.

Loading Fonts

Before you can add text to a model, you need to select a text font. To do this, use the Manage Fonts menu button, which opens the Edit Font List dialog box, shown in Figure 2.8. This dialog box lets you add True-Type and Type-1 fonts. The loaded fonts appear in the Font list. Only one font is active at a time.

FIGURE 2.8
Edit Font List dialog box

Edit Font List
Font: Arial Black 400
Add True-Type | Load Type-1 | Clear List | Clear Entry
OK | Load List | Save List

Adding Text

After you load a font, the Text tool button in the toolbar is active. To add the text, click this button and click in the viewport where the lower-left corner of the text should start. Then you can type the text that you want to appear, as shown in Figure 2.9.

FIGURE 2.9
Text in LightWave

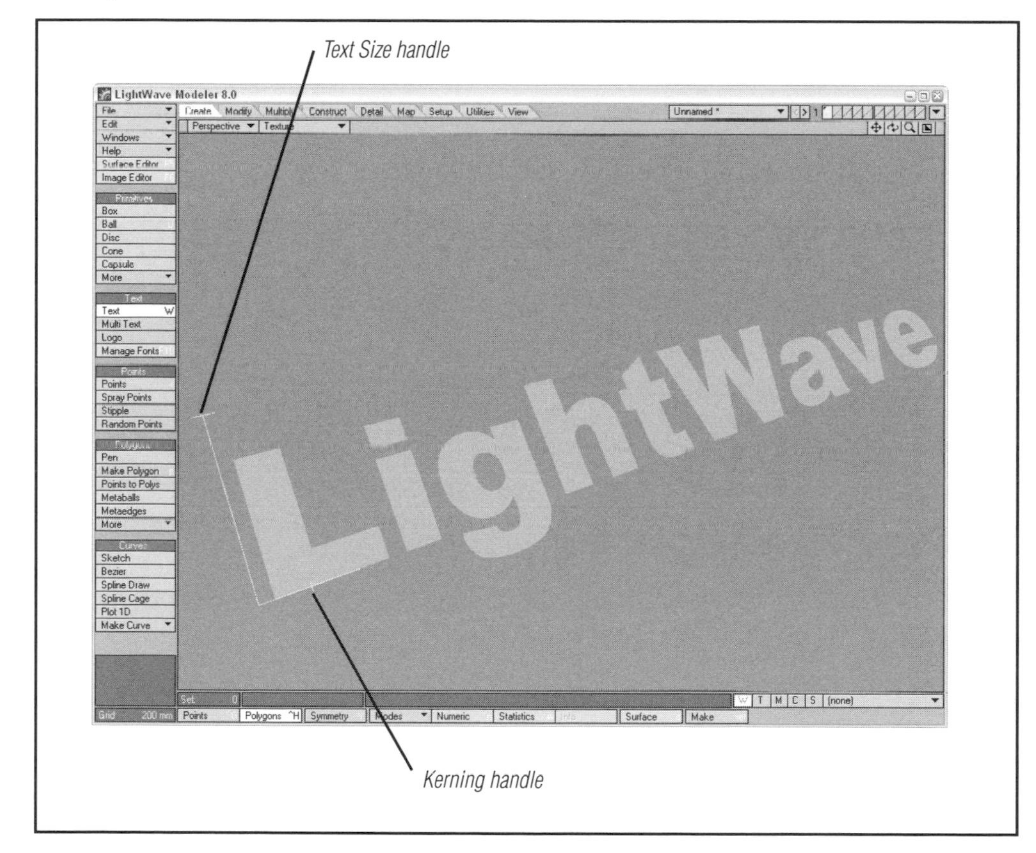

Manipulating Text

If you click the Numeric button at the bottom of the LightWave interface, a dialog box opens, as shown in Figure 2.10. Using these options, you can change the text, font, alignment, scale, position, and **kerning** of the text. While in text creation mode, you can also change the text size and kerning using the light blue handles that surround the text object.

> **TIP**
>
> Pressing Tab toggles between the right, center, and left alignment options.

FIGURE 2.10
Text Tool options

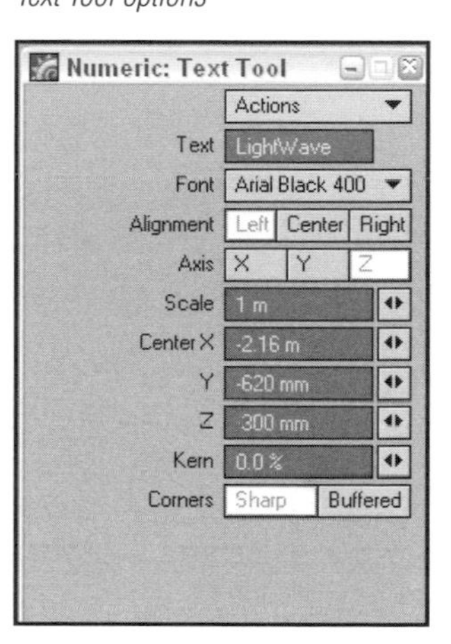

Using the Multi Text Tool

The Multi Text command opens a dialog box, shown in Figure 2.11, where you can enter several lines of text. You can also load simple text files into the dialog box.

Creating Logo Text

The Logo command creates extruded text that has depth, like the text shown in Figure 2.12. Clicking the Logo command opens a simple dialog box where you can set the logo text, the extrusion depth, and the font.

FIGURE 2.11

Make Multi Text Strings dialog box

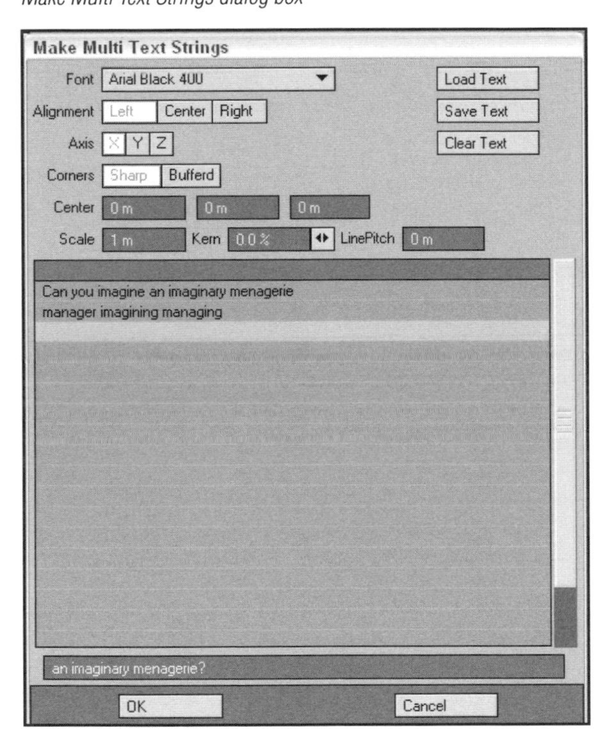

FIGURE 2.12

Logo text

FIGURE 2.13
Modified text

Create text

1. Click the Create menu tab.
2. Click the Manage Fonts menu button in the Text section of the Create menu tab.

   The Edit Font List dialog box appears.
3. Click the Add True-Type button, select the Arial Black font from the Font dialog box, and then click OK.

   The selected font is displayed in the Font field.
4. Click the Text button (or press Shift+W).
5. Click the Top viewport, and then type **Hello**.

   The typed text appears in the viewport.
6. Drag in the viewport to reposition the text: Drag upward on the text size handle to increase the text size, and then drag the kerning handle to the left to tighten the kerning.
7. Click the Make button to make the text permanent and maximize the Perspective viewport.

   The text size is increased and the tightening of the kerning pulls the text letters closer together, as shown in Figure 2.13.
8. Select the File, Save Object As menu command and save the file as Hello text.lwo.

Create Multiline text

1. Click the Create menu tab.
2. Click the Multi Text button in the Text section of the Create menu tab.

   The Make Multi Text Strings dialog box appears.
3. Click the text field at the bottom of the dialog box, enter a single line of text, and then press Enter to make the text appear in one of the lines in the dialog box.
4. After entering all the lines of text, click OK.

   The text appears within the viewport, as shown in Figure 2.14.
5. Select the File, Save Object As menu command and save the file as Multi line text.lwo.

Create logo text

1. Click the Create menu tab.
2. Click the Manage Fonts button in the Text section of the Create menu tab.

   The Edit Font List dialog box appears.
3. Click the Add True-Type button, select the Wingdings font from the Font dialog box, and then click the OK button. Click the OK button again to close the Edit Font List dialog box.

FIGURE 2.14
Multiline text

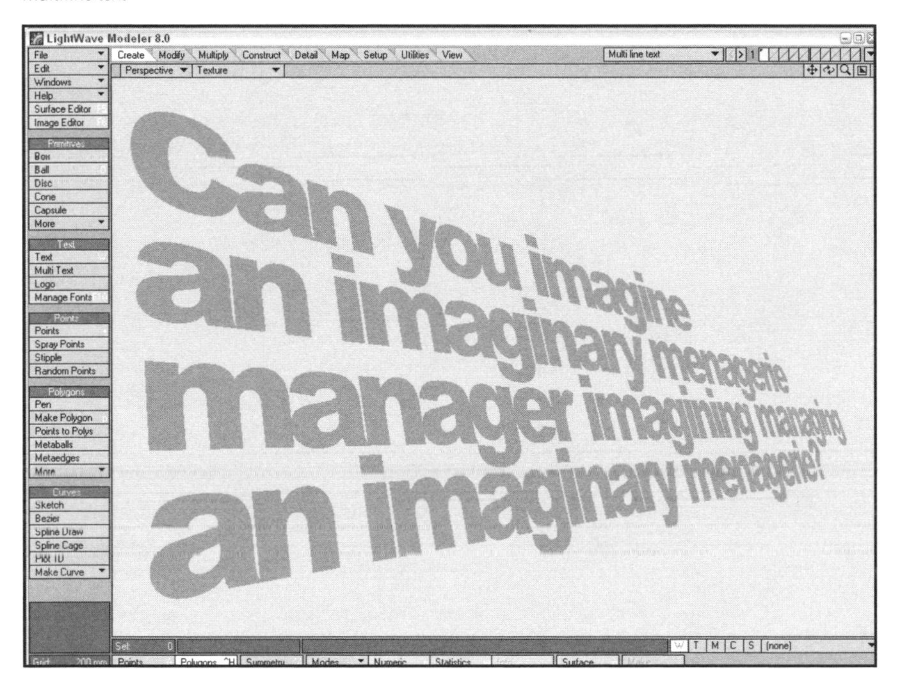

FIGURE 2.15
Extruded logo text

4. Click the Logo button in the toolbar.

   The Logo Maker dialog box opens.

5. Type the capital letters **J**, **K**, and **L** in the Logo Text field, select Wingdings 400 from the Font list, and then click the OK button.

   The extruded text symbols appear in the viewport, as shown in Figure 2.15.

6. Select the File, Save Object As menu command, and save the file as Symbol logo.lwo.

LESSON 3

CREATE POINTS AND POLYGONS

What You'll Do

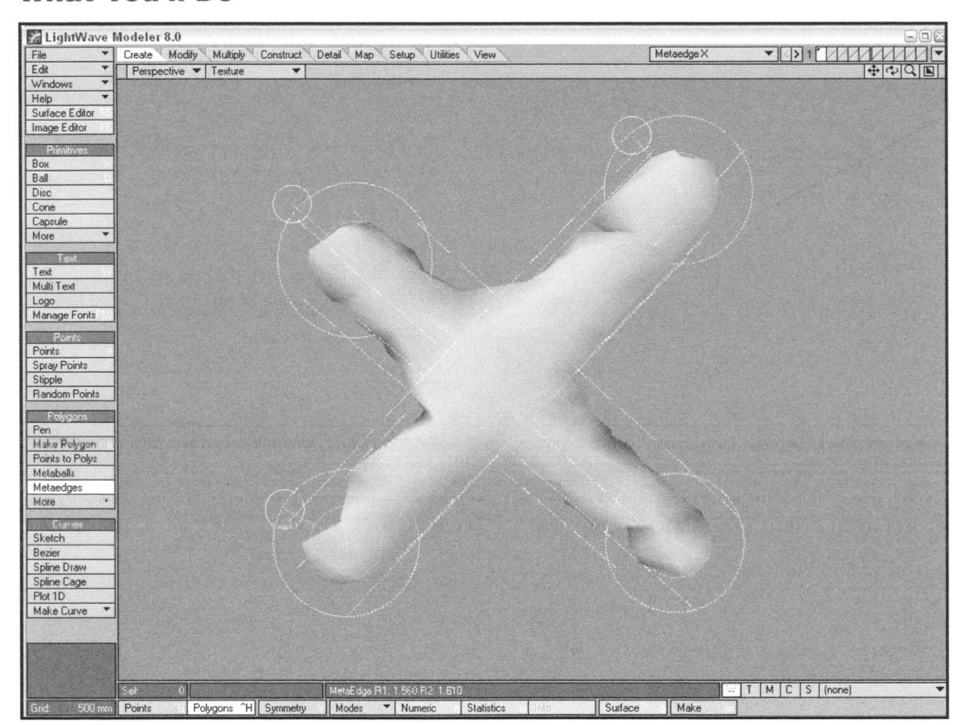

In this lesson, you'll learn how to create points and polygons using several different tools.

Every object in LightWave is made up of points and polygons. If the object you want to create isn't listed in the Primitives menu, you can create your own object manually by placing points and then connecting them. You use the Points and Polygons menus to manually create objects.

Using the Point Tool

Use the Point tool to create and manipulate single points. Clicking in the viewport creates a point and dragging lets you move the point about. Right-clicking in the viewport creates additional points. To precisely position a point, use the Numeric dialog box.

Spraying Points

To create multiple random points, you can use the Spray Points tool. You can use the Numeric panel for this tool to define a radius and a rate that determine the density of the points. Right-clicking and dragging on the circle's edge changes the radius of the Spray Points tool. Figure 2.16 shows an assortment of points created with the Spray Points tool.

Adding Points to an Object and Randomly Placing Points

You can use the **Stipple** menu button to add points to objects at regular intervals. After you click this command, the Regular Surface Points dialog box opens, where you can specify the distribution of the points. Figure 2.17 shows how the Stipple command added regularly spaced points to a cube object. Clicking the Random Points command opens a dialog box where you can specify the number of points and the volume shape (either square or sphere) within which to place the random points.

Creating Polygons with the Pen Tool

Use the Pen tool to create a polygon manually by clicking in the viewport to add points. As you create the points, edges are automatically attached between the points. By right-clicking, you can begin a new polygon that is detached from the previous polygon.

Making Polygons from Selected Points

If several (three or more) points are selected, clicking the Make Polygon command connects these points to form a polygon. Clicking the Points to Polys command changes all selected points to a specialized single point polygon called a **particle**, useful for creating stars.

FIGURE 2.16
Spray Points tool

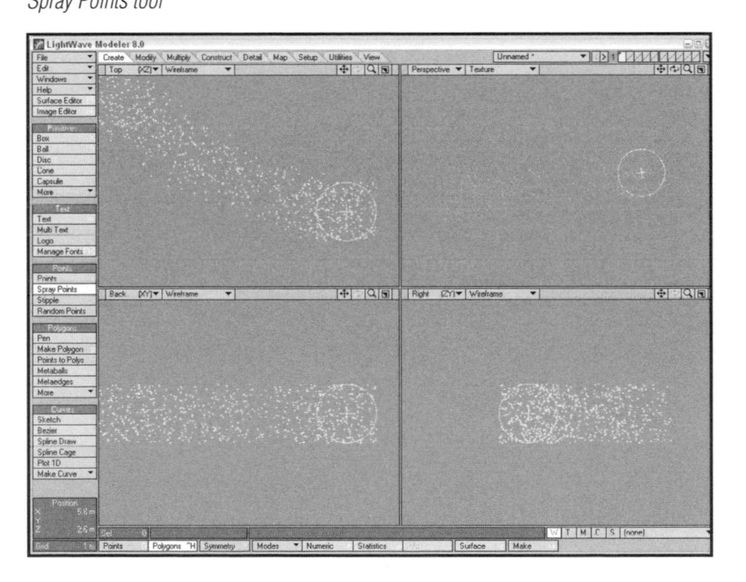

FIGURE 2.17
Stipple tool

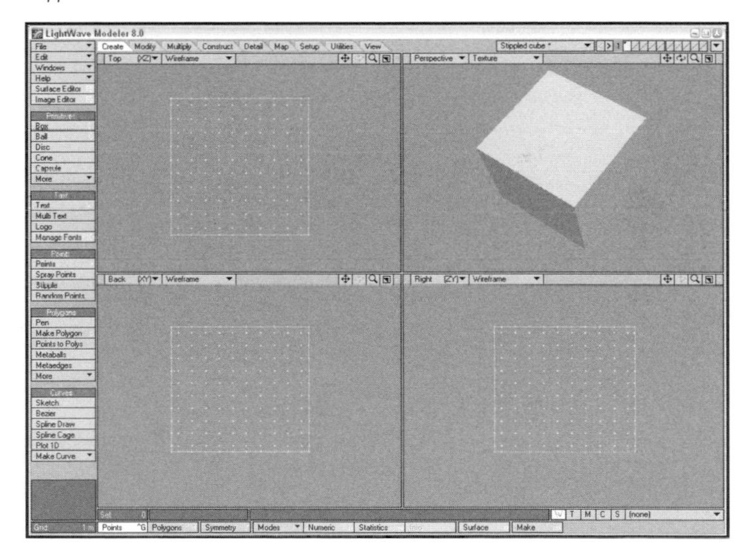

Creating Metaballs and Metaedges

Metaballs are single-point objects that act like simple spheres when separated, but flow into one another if two or more are placed close to each other, as shown in Figure 2.18. This makes them useful for creating soft-flowing objects like plants. **Metaedges** are similar to metaballs, except that metaedges include two points created by dragging the edge in the viewport.

Triangulating Polygons

One potential problem with manually created polygons is that they are flat, and if the polygon includes more than three points, the rendering engine has no way to smooth the polygon. As a result, the entire polygon will be colored the same color, which makes it appear flat. To fix this problem, you can divide the entire polygon into triangles using the Make Triangle Fan or Make Triangle Strip commands found in the Polygons, More menu. **Triangulated** polygons are shown in Figure 2.19.

FIGURE 2.18
Metaballs flow into one another

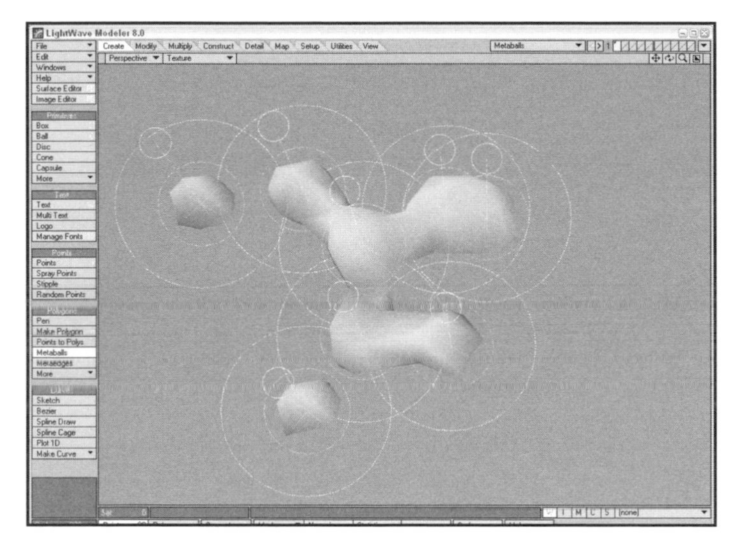

FIGURE 2.19
Triangulated polygons

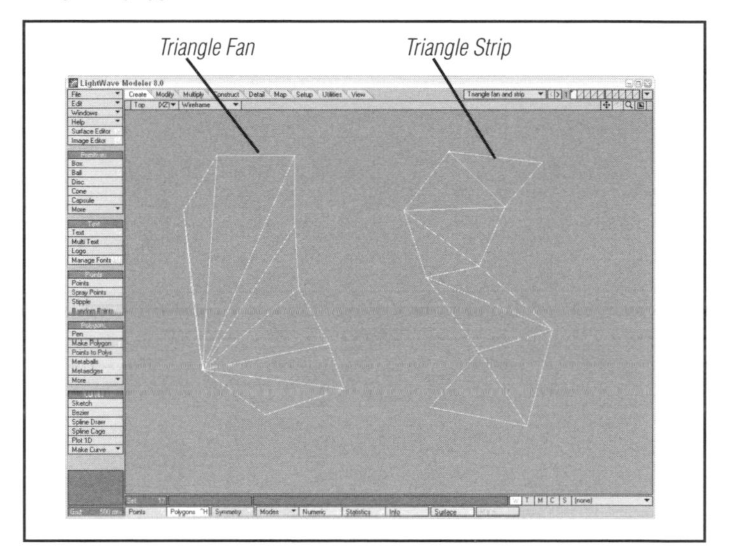

FIGURE 2.20
New mushroom-shaped polygon

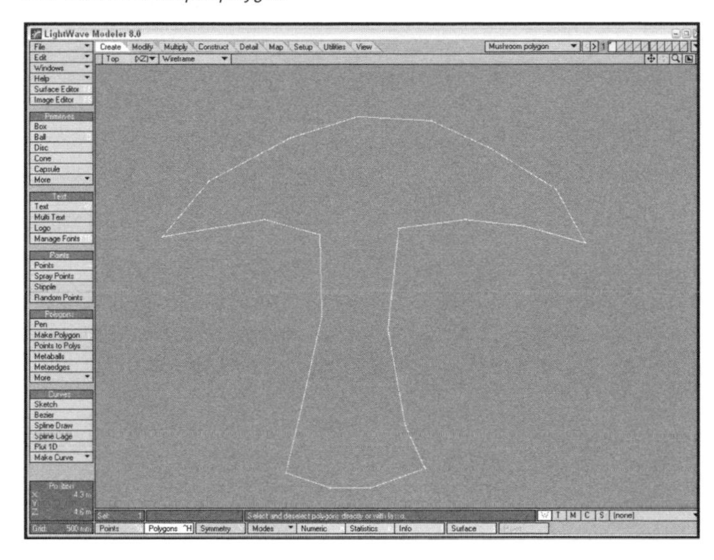

FIGURE 2.21
House-shaped polygon

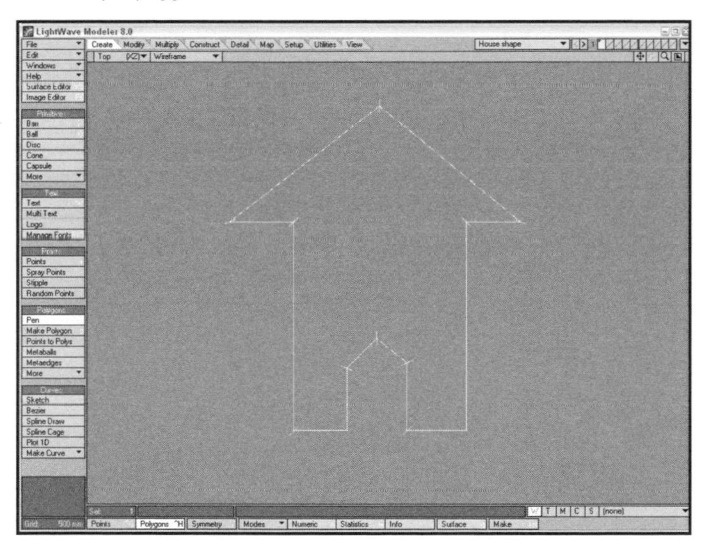

Manually create a polygon

1. Click the Create menu tab.
2. Click the Points button (or press the + key).
3. Click in the Top viewport to create the first point, and then right-click at the location of every other polygon corner. Create the points in the shape of a mushroom.
4. Click the Points button again after you've placed all the points.
5. Click the Make Polygon button.

   All points are connected in the order they were created to produce a new polygon, as shown in Figure 2.20.
6. Select the File, Save Object As menu command and save the file as Mushroom polygon.lwo.

Draw polygons with the Pen tool

1. Click the Create menu tab.
2. Click the Pen button, and then click in the Top viewport at each corner location to create a simple house-shaped outline.
3. After creating all the points, click and drag the created points to straighten the lines.
4. Click the Pen button again after you've straightened all the lines.

   The new polygon is created as you place the points, as shown in Figure 2.21.
5. Select the File, Save Object As menu command and save the file as House shape.lwo.

Work with Metaballs and Metaedges

1. Click the Create menu tab.
2. Click the Metaedges button, and then drag in the Perspective viewport twice to create two intersecting Metaedge objects.
3. While still in creation mode, drag the center of the smaller circle to increase the size of each corner.
4. Click the Metaedges button again to exit creation mode.

   The Metaedge objects run together where they intersect as if they were made of liquid, as shown in Figure 2.22.
5. Select the File, Save Object As menu command and save the file as Metaedge X.lwo.

FIGURE 2.22
Shape made from Metaedge objects

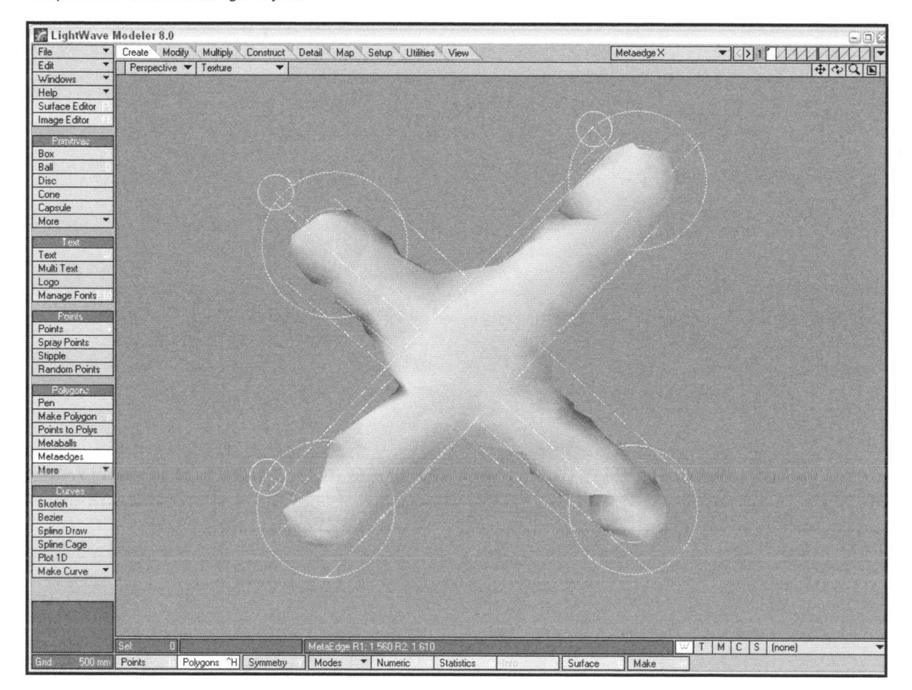

LESSON 4

CREATE CURVES

What You'll Do

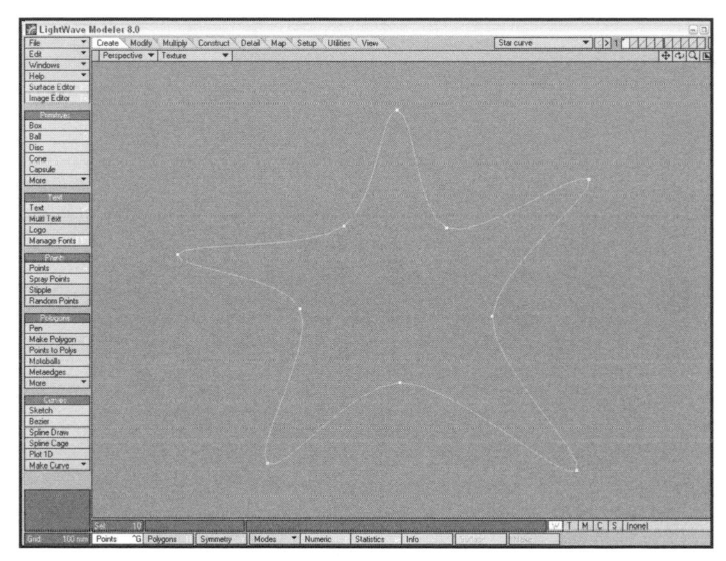

In this lesson, you'll learn how to create curve segments.

Curves are another common modeling piece. You can sketch or draw a curve, and then use that curve to create a polygon or another object.

Sketching Curves

The easiest way to create a curve is with the Sketch tool. With this tool selected, you simply draw the curve in the viewport. LightWave automatically inserts the correct number of points needed to represent the curve, as shown in Figure 2.23. You

FIGURE 2.23
Line drawn with the Sketch tool

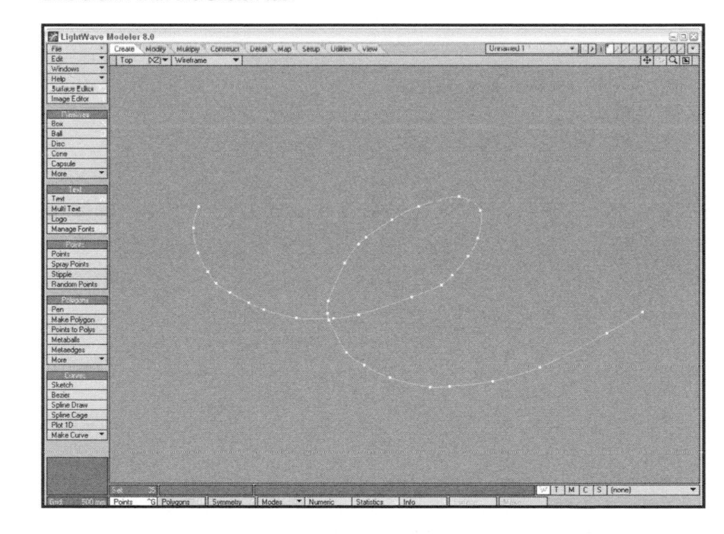

FIGURE 2.24
Bezier curve

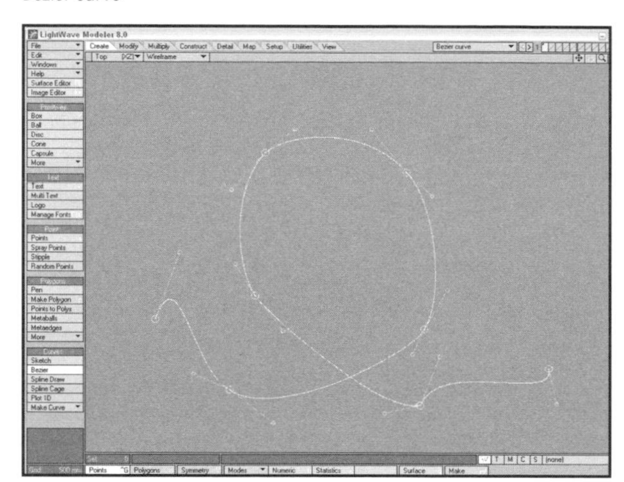

FIGURE 2.25
Spline curve

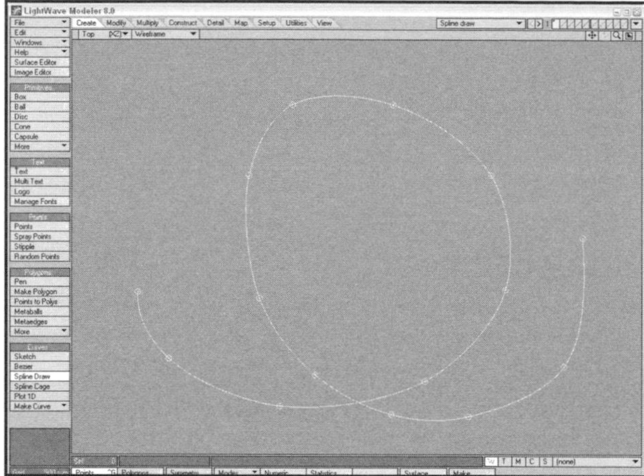

can also use the Sketch tool to create polygons by selecting the Face option in the Numeric dialog box.

Using the Bezier Tool

A **Bezier curve** is a unique type of curve that has tangent handles that control how the curve bends as it moves through a point. You create Bezier curves with the Bezier tool. After clicking in the viewport to place the curve points, you can drag the handles to change the curve point's location or the degree to which it bends. Figure 2.24 shows a simple Bezier curve with eight points.

Drawing Splines

A spline is another type of curve in which the curve moves through the center of each point while maintaining its smoothness. To create a spline curve, simply click in the viewports where each spline point should be located. Figure 2.25 shows a spline curve.

NOTE

The benefit of Bezier curves and splines is that you can use them to construct complex curves with a minimal number of points.

Creating a Spline Cage

The Spline Cage command opens a dialog box where you can specify the dimensions used to make a cylindrical cage of interconnected splines. Spline cages make it easy to create specialized surfaces.

Creating a Curve from an Equation

The Plot 1D command opens a dialog box, shown in Figure 2.26, where you can enter a mathematical equation. LightWave plots this equation between the designated minimum and maximum values to create a single curve.

Making a Curve from Selected Points

If several points are selected, you can make a curve from these points that follows the order in which the points are selected. To do so, use the Curves, Make Curves, Make Open Curve, or Make Closed Curve command. Closed curves are different from open curves in that the last and first points are connected.

FIGURE 2.26
Plot 1D dialog box

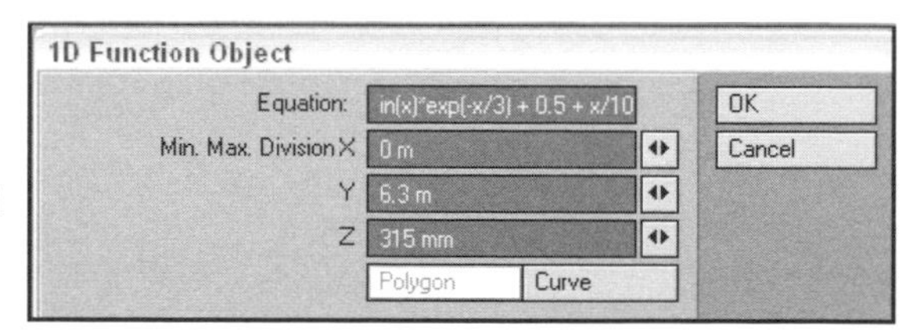

FIGURE 2.27
Spiral curve

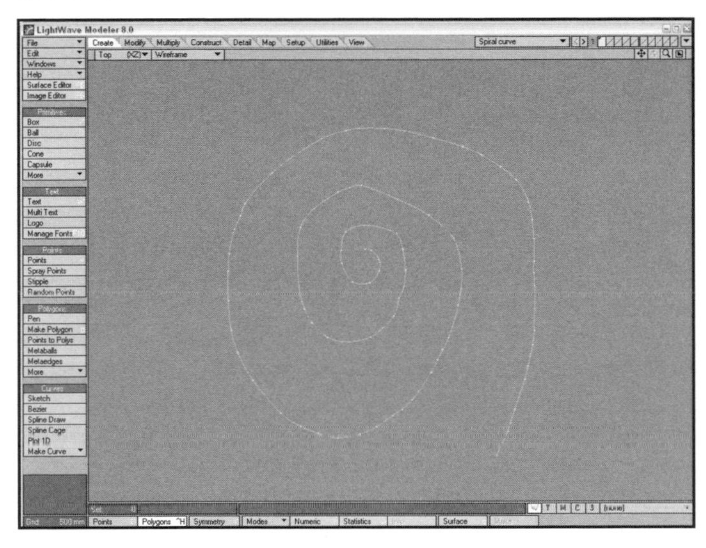

FIGURE 2.28
Bezier and Spline curves

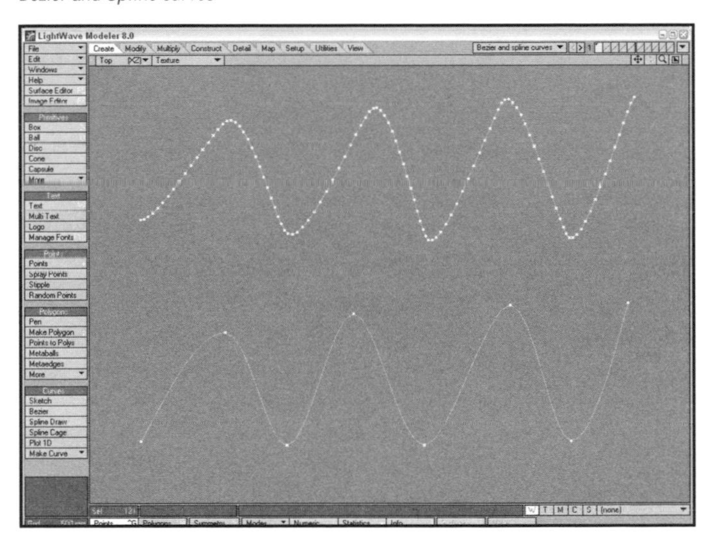

Sketch a curve

1. Click the Create menu tab.
2. Click the Sketch button and drag in the Top viewport to create a spiral.
3. Click the Make button at the bottom of the interface to finish the curve.

   The curve follows where the mouse is dragged, as shown in Figure 2.27.
4. Select the File, Save Object As menu command and save the file as Spiral curve.lwo.

Compare Bezier and spline curves

1. Click the Create menu tab.
2. Click the Bezier button, and then click in the Top viewport to create a zigzagging line.
3. Click the Spline Draw button below the Bezier curve in a similar zigzag path.
4. Click the Make button at the bottom of the interface to finish the curve.

   The Bezier curve, at the top of Figure 2.28, includes many more points than the spline curve.
5. Select the File, Save Object As menu command and save the file as Bezier and spline curves.lwo.

Create a star-shaped curve

1. Click the Create menu tab.
2. Click the Points button (or press the + key).
3. Click in the Top viewport to create the first point, and then right-click at the location of every other polygon corner needed to create a star.
4. Click Make Curve, and then click Make Closed Curve.

   All points are connected in the order they were created to produce a new star, as shown in Figure 2.29.
5. Select the File, Save Object As menu command and save the file as Star curve.lwo.

FIGURE 2.29
Star-shaped curve

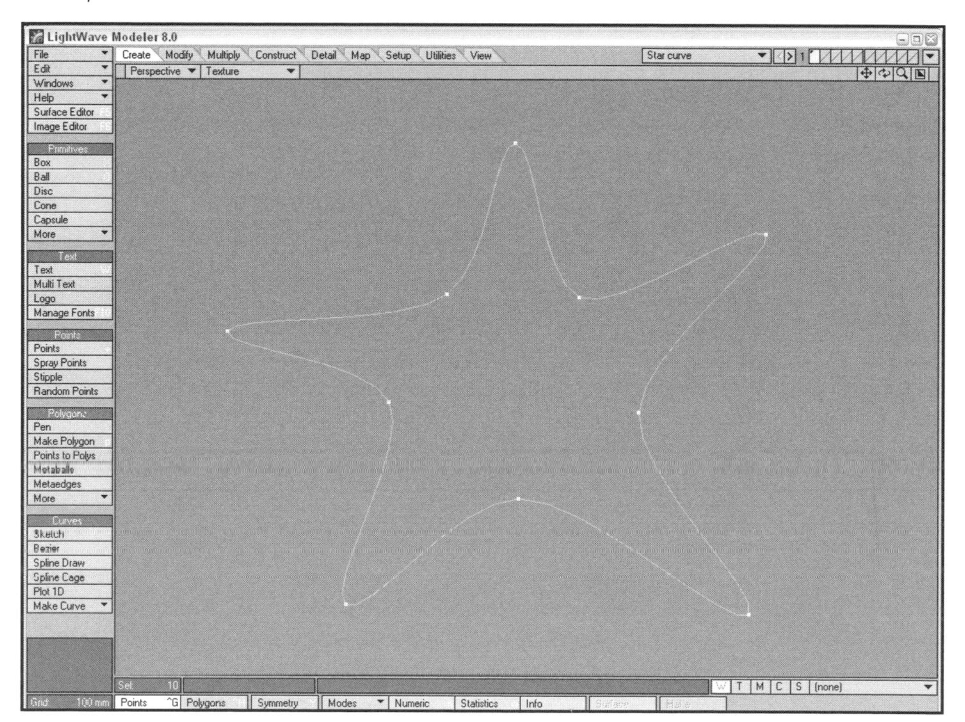

LESSON 5

SELECT OBJECTS

What You'll Do

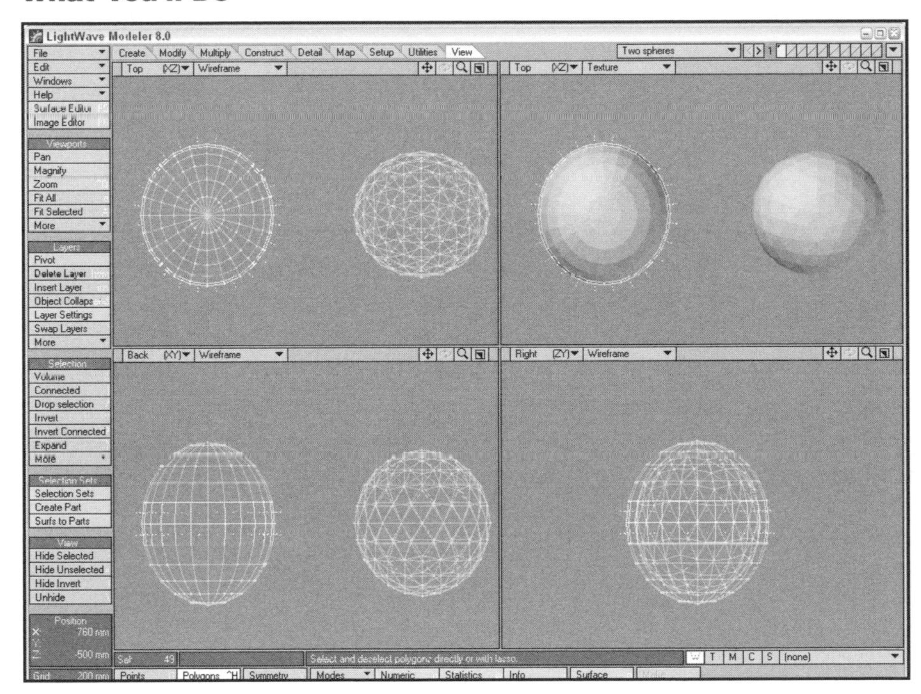

In this lesson, you'll learn how to select objects, points, and polygons.

After you have created objects, you can edit and modify them as needed. However, before you can modify an object, you need to select it. You can select objects and object parts using two different selection modes: points and polygons. With these two modes, you can accurately select exactly what you want to modify. The View menu tab also includes several commands you can use to select objects and object parts.

Using the Selection Modes

You can select points when the LightWave is in points mode, and select polygons when LightWave is in polygons mode. To access points mode, click the Points button at the bottom left of the interface (or press Ctrl+G). To access polygons mode, click the Polygons button (or press Ctrl+H). The selected mode is highlighted in white.

Selecting Points and Polygons

In points or polygons mode, select points or polygons by dragging the mouse over the points or polygons to be selected. After you release the mouse button, you can add points or polygons to the selection by holding down Shift while selecting more points or polygons. You can also drag over points or polygons with the middle mouse button. To remove points or polygons from the current selection, drag over the selected points or polygons after releasing the mouse button, or hold down Ctrl and drag over the points or polygons to remove them. Selected points or polygons are highlighted yellow in the viewports and the number of selected object parts appears in the information box directly above points mode, as shown in Figure 2.30.

FIGURE 2.30
Number of selected parts

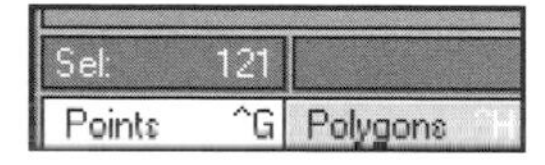

Selecting with a Lasso

Using the right mouse button in points or polygons mode, you can drag a lasso outline in the viewport. All points or polygons within the lasso area are selected.

Deselecting All

You can drop the current selection in several ways. You can click the toolbar away from all menu buttons when no tool is selected; you can select the View, Drop Selection command (or press /); or you can click the number in the information box directly above the points mode button.

Selecting Entire Objects

If a single object part is selected, you can choose the View, Selection, Connected command (or press the bracket key (])), and all parts of the object that are connected to the current selection are selected.

> NOTE
>
> If no part is selected, the entire object is selected by default.

Using the View Menu to Select Object Parts

The Selection section of the View menu tab includes several additional ways to select object parts. The Volume command lets you select object parts using a dragged volume that you can position in the viewports. You can toggle the Volume command between Exclude, which doesn't include polygons touching the volume, and Include, which does.

Other menu buttons in this section include Invert and Invert Connected. Clicking the More button accesses a pop-up menu with Expand Selection and Contract Selection options, which are useful for increasing and decreasing the selection set. The More menu button in the Selection section of the View menu tab also includes another More option in its pop-up menu. This includes commands such as Select Loop, Select Outline, and Select Switch, which changes the selected points into selected polygons and vice versa.

Using Selection Sets and Parts

A selection set is a group of selected points, and a part is a group of selected polygons. You can create and name both using the View, Selection Sets menu. Any selection sets and parts you create then show up in the Statistics panel, where you can select and reuse them.

FIGURE 2.31

Selected polygons

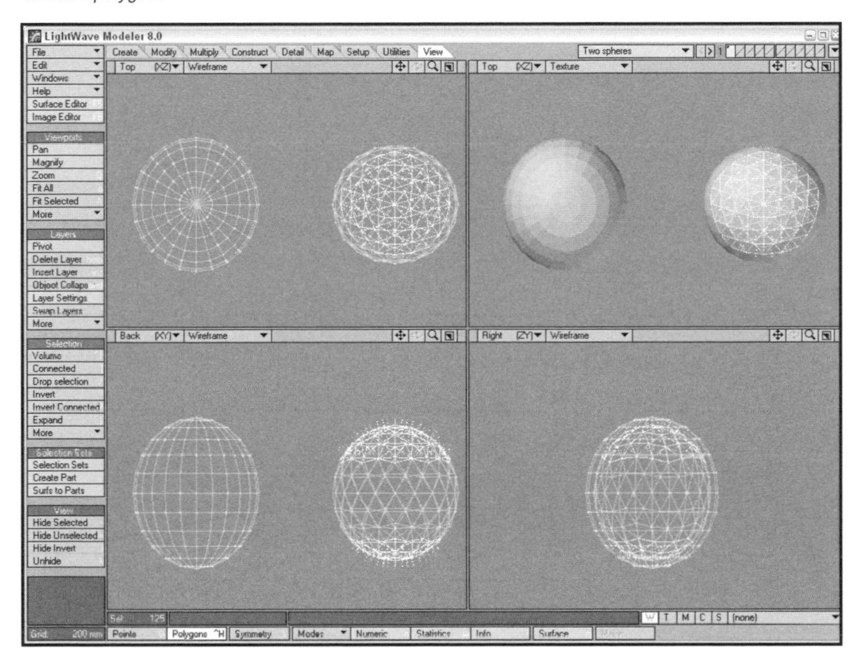

Select points and polygons

1. In the Modeler, select the File, Load Object menu command, and then open the Two spheres.lwo file.
2. Click the Points button at the bottom of the interface, and then drag over the points in the left sphere.

   The selected points are highlighted light yellow.
3. With several points selected, select the View, Connected menu command (or press the] key).

   All points on the left sphere are selected.
4. Click the Polygons button at the bottom of the interface, drag over the several polygons in the lower half of the right sphere, and release the mouse.

   The selected polygons are highlighted light yellow.
5. Hold down the Shift key, and then select several more polygons in the right sphere.

   The newly selected polygons are added to the selection.
6. Still holding down the Shift key, draw an outline over the top half of the right sphere with the right mouse button.

   The enclosed polygons are added to the selection, as shown in Figure 2.31.

Select a loop of polygons

1. With the sphere's file still open, select the View, Selection, Drop Selection menu command (or press the / key).

   The current selection is cleared.

2. While still in Polygons mode, select a single polygon at the middle of the left sphere.
3. Select the View, Selection, More, More, Select Loop menu command.

   All polygons that make up the center band of the left sphere are selected, as shown in Figure 2.32.

Designate a part

1. With the sphere's file still open and the middle band of polygons selected, select the View, Selection Sets, Create Part menu command.

   The Change Part Name dialog box opens, where you can name the part.

2. Type **Mid ring** for the part name, and then click the OK button.
3. Click the Statistics button at the bottom of the interface (or press the w key), and then, in the Part field, select the Mid ring part and click the plus sign to the left of the part field.

   The Statistics panel is displayed, as shown in Figure 2.33. Clicking the plus sign selects the part.

4. Select the File, Save Object As menu command and save the file as Selected ring part.lwo.

FIGURE 2.32
Selected loop of polygons

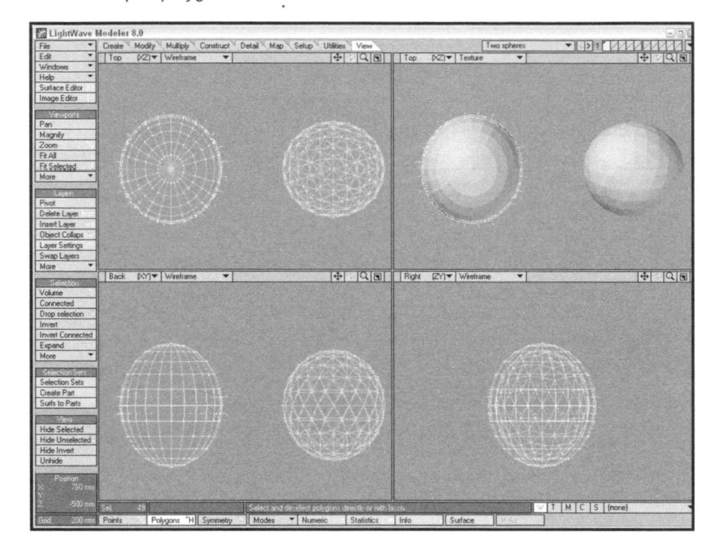

FIGURE 2.33
Statistic panel

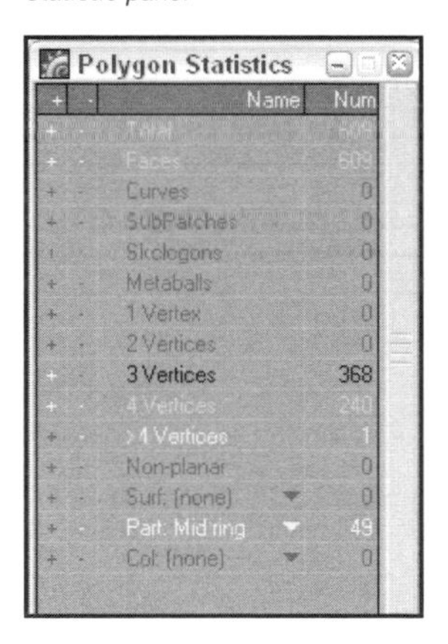

LESSON 6

USE LAYERS AND HIDE OBJECTS

What You'll Do

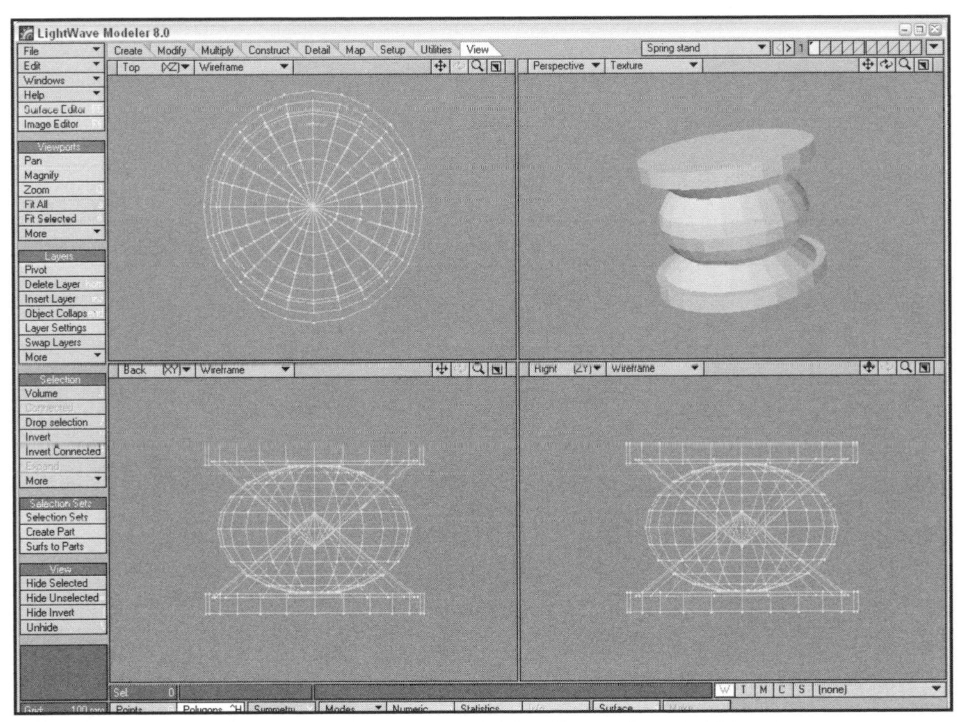

In this lesson, you'll learn how to use layers in LightWave and how to hide objects.

You can use layers to divide all the objects that make up a model into separate groups. By default, each file includes 10 different layers that you can select using the icons at the top right of the interface. Additional commands for working with layers are on the View, Layers menu. Using layers make it easy to hide groups of objects quickly, so that you can focus on the objects you're working on. Another way to hide objects is to use the Hide commands on the View menu.

Viewing an Object Name

You can have several objects open in the Modeler at the same time. The names of all open objects are listed in the drop-down list at the top right of the interface.

TIP

If you made changes the selected object without saving it, a small asterisk (*) appears next to the object name.

Selecting a Layer

Each of the 10 small square icons at the top-right corner of the interface, shown in Figure 2.34, represents an available layer. To select a layer, simply click the square icon. If an object exists on the layer, a small black triangle is displayed in the upper-left corner of the layer icon.

Showing Layer Objects as Background

You can only select one layer at a time, but clicking the lower half of the layer icon makes all the objects on that layer appear as background objects. Some features, such as the Boolean feature, require that objects involved in the operation are placed on the background layer.

Moving Between Layer Sets

Each layer set holds 10 layers. To move through the various layer sets, click the arrow icons to the right of the object name.

Moving Objects Between Layers

To move an object from one layer to another layer, select the layer that contains that object and choose the Edit, Cut command. Then select the new layer and choose Edit, Paste to move the object to the new layer. By moving objects between layers, you can control which objects are operated on and which act as operators.

Hiding Objects

The View menu contains commands that let you hide the current selection, hide all the unselected parts, invert the hidden parts, and unhide all parts. Hidden objects don't get in the way when you are working on other objects.

> CAUTION
>
> You cannot hide selected points. You can only hide polygons using the View menu commands.

FIGURE 2.34
Layer icons

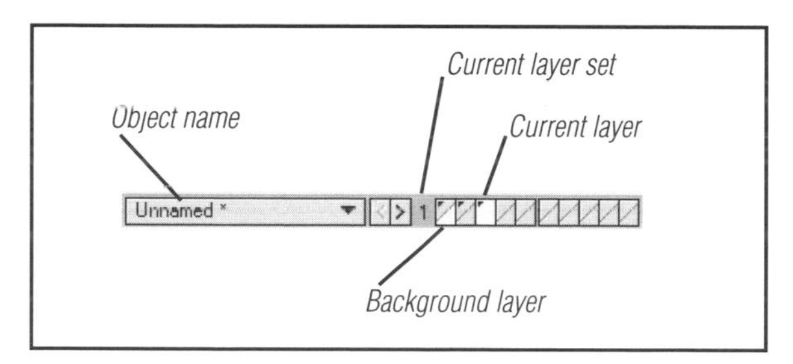

FIGURE 2.35
Layered objects

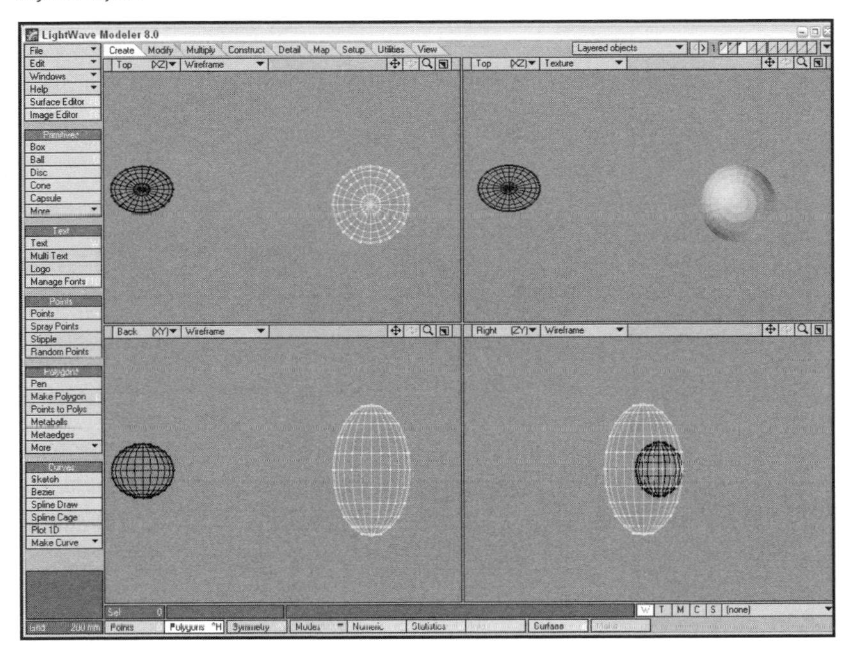

Access a new layer

1. Open the Modeler, select the Create, Ball menu button, and then drag in the Top viewport and again in the Back viewport to create a new ball object.
2. Click the icon for the second layer (the second box to the right of the Object Name drop-down menu in the upper right of the Modeler), and then create two new ball objects in the middle of the Top viewport.
3. Switch between the two layers by clicking the icon for each layer.
4. Click the second layer icon, and then, in Polygons mode, select some of the second ball's polygons. Press] to select the entire ball.
5. Select the Edit, Cut menu command (or press Ctrl+x).

   The selected sphere is cut and removed from the viewport.
6. Click the third layer icon in the upper-right corner of the interface to select the third layer.
7. Select the Edit, Paste menu command (or press Ctrl+v).
8. Click the third layer icon and the bottom half of the first layer.

   The ball object on the third layer is visible and the ball object on the first layer is visible as a darkened background object, as shown in Figure 2.35.
9. Save the file as Layered objects.lwo.

Hide objects

1. In the Modeler, select the File, Load Object menu command, and then open the Spring stand.lwo file.

   The selected sphere is hidden from the viewport.

2. Select the View, Unhide menu button from the View menu tab to see the ball object again, as shown in Figure 2.36.

FIGURE 2.36
Unhidden object

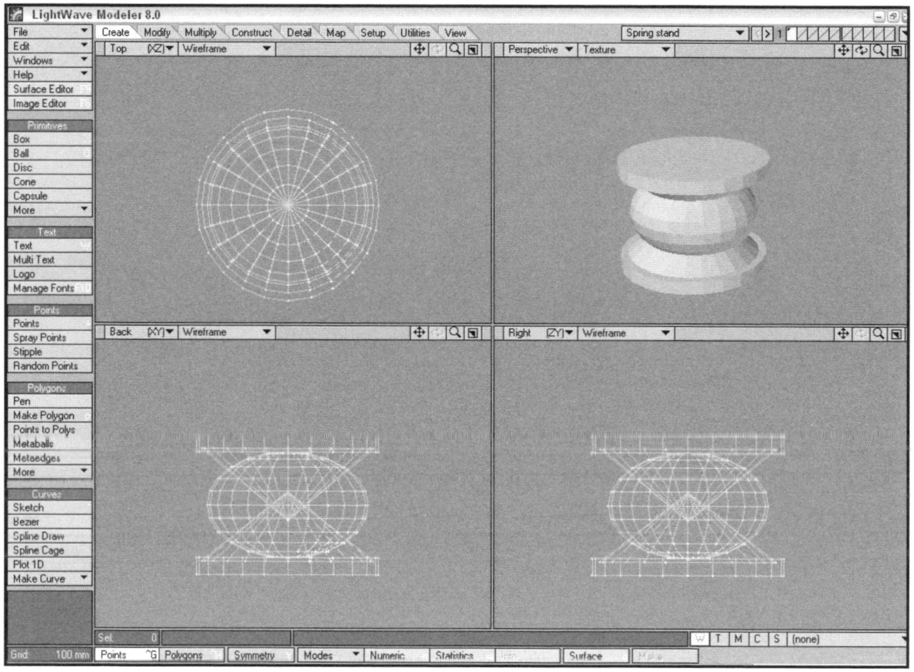

CHAPTER SUMMARY

This chapter delved into the Modeler interface and explained how to create many of the most basic fundamental objects, including primitives, text, points, polygons, and curves. You can find the menu buttons to create all of these basic objects under the Create menu tab. This chapter also covered selecting object points and polygons and using layers as a way to divide and organize objects.

What You Have Learned

- How to create an assortment of primitive objects including Box, Ball, Disc, Cone, and Capsule.
- How to use the Numeric panel to edit object parameters as they are being created.
- How to load system fonts and create text and logo objects.
- How to use different commands for creating points, polygons, meatballs, and metaedges.
- How to create curves by placing points, drawing curves, and using the Bezier tool.
- How to access the Points and Polygons selection modes for selecting objects.
- How to use layers and hide objects.

Key Terms from This Chapter

- **Primitive objects.** Prebuilt basic objects that can be created by dragging in the viewports.
- **Numeric panel.** A panel holding the parameters for the current object.
- **kerning.** A text parameter that controls the spacing between adjacent letters.
- **logo text.** Text that is extruded to form a 3D object.
- **Stipple.** A tool used to place points at regular intervals on the surface of an object.
- **particle.** A single point that is treated as an entire object.
- **metaball/metaedge.** A specialized object type consisting of a single point or an edge that is surrounded by a surface that flows seamlessly into like objects.
- **triangulate.** A process of simplifying polygons by dividing them into triangles.
- **Bezier curve.** A special curve type that creates curves by placing control points that define how the curve bends.
- **layer.** A division of objects that you can select easily.

CHAPTER 3

TRANSFORMING OBJECTS

1. Translate objects.
2. Center, align, and snap objects.
3. Use the Falloff options.
4. Rotate objects.
5. Size and stretch objects.
6. Transform and distort objects.

CHAPTER 3
TRANSFORMING OBJECTS

When you create a primitive object, you can always modify it before you click the Make button; however, after you click the Make button, you need to go to the Modify menu tab if you want to make changes to the primitive you created. The Modify menu tab includes commands to transform the selected object. Transformations can be as simple as moving or rotating an object, or as complex as **shearing** or **tapering** an object.

The commands on the Modify menu tab are divided into three categories: **Translate**, Rotate, and Transform. Translation involves moving an object or a portion of the object. Rotation involves spinning the object or its parts about an axis. Transformation is a general term that involves all other types of object modification and movement, including scaling and stretching an object (also called resizing).

You can open the Numeric panel whenever a transformation tool is selected. The Numeric panel includes options for the selected tool. One of these options is **Falloff**. Using the Falloff controls, you can define the movement of the selected portion relative to rest of the selection. For example, you can specify that when you move the selected polygons, the adjacent polygons only move half as far.

You can apply all the commands on the Modify menu tab to a selection of points or polygons that make up an object, or to an entire object.

Tools You'll Use

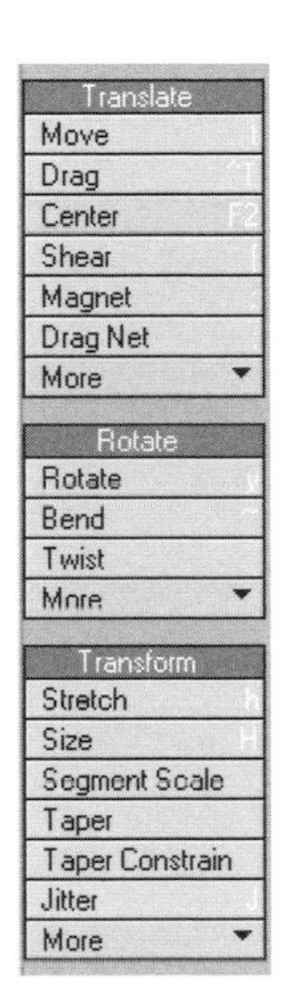

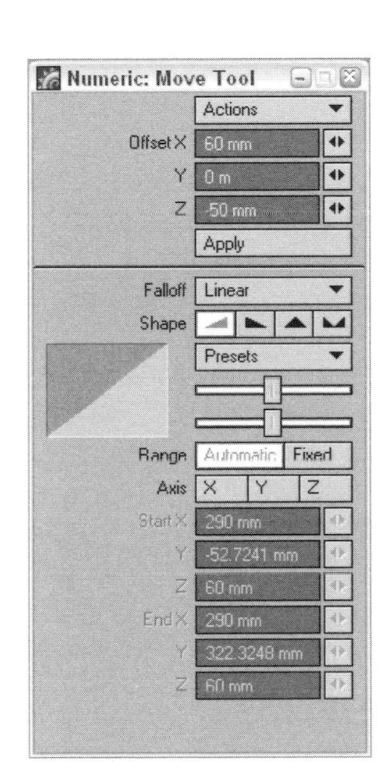

LESSON 1

TRANSLATE OBJECTS

What You'll Do

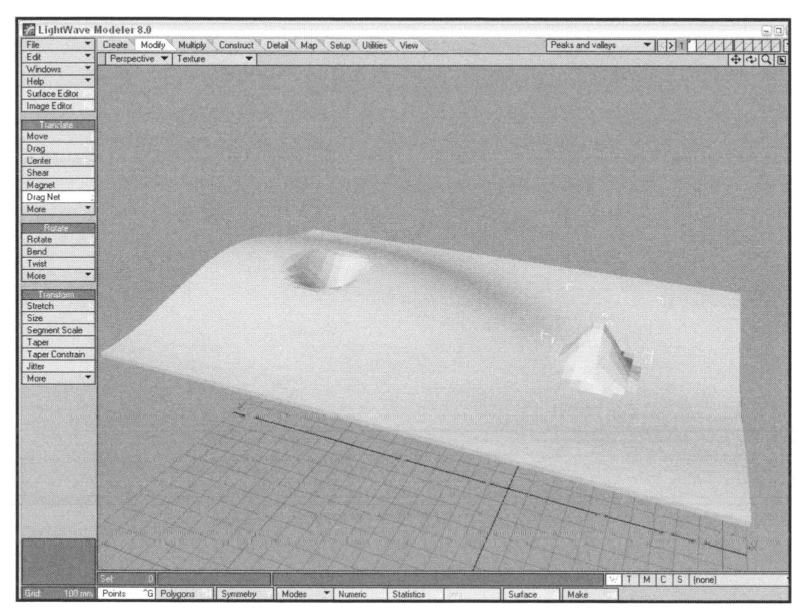

In this lesson, you'll learn how to move objects using the Modify, Translate menu commands.

The Modify, Translate menu includes several ways to move the current selection. If you move the selection of points or polygons, the polygons that are connected to the moved selection are deformed as needed to stay connected to the selection.

Moving Objects

To move objects about the viewports, use the Move tool (keyboard shortcut: t). When you select this tool, the mouse cursor changes to a four-arrow icon. Holding down Ctrl while dragging an object in the viewport constrains the movement to a single axis. You can also use the Numeric panel, shown in Figure 3.1, to enter precise offset values. After entering an offset value, click the Apply button in the Numeric panel to apply the offset value. Negative values are allowed.

FIGURE 3.1
Numeric panel for the Move tool

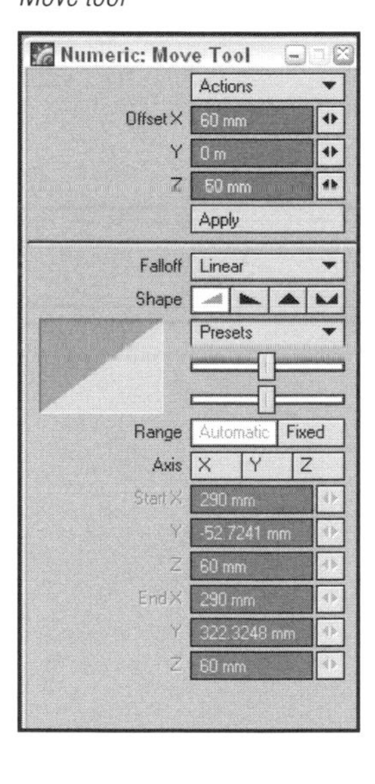

Moving Objects with Falloff

If you open the Numeric panel when the Move tool is selected, you can select a falloff type. Falloff type options include None, Linear, Radial, Point,

Polygon, Point Radial, and Weight Map. These options and the Shape determine how the polygons immediately adjacent to the selection move when the selection is moved. More details on using Falloff are presented in the "Using the Falloff Options" lesson later in this chapter.

Dragging Points

The Drag tool (keyboard shortcut: Ctrl+t) uses the Point Falloff method. This tool lets you select and drag a single point in a group of selected points. You can use the Drag tool to move points even if several polygons are selected. It is useful if you need to make a quick, subtle change. Clicking in the middle of a polygon has no effect; you need to click right on a point to select and move it.

Shearing Objects

You use the Shear tool (keyboard shortcut: [ ) to move the top edge of the selection in one direction while leaving the opposite edge unmoved, causing the selection to be slanted. With the Shear tool, the Linear falloff method is selected by default. Figure 3.2 shows a sphere object that was sheared to the right in the Back viewport.

Using the Magnet and DragNet Tools

The Magnet tool (keyboard shortcut: colon) moves the objects closest to the cursor the greatest distance, while all attached polygons are smoothly moved a partial distance. This tool effectively pushes and pulls the surface to form small hills and valleys. The DragNet tool (keyboard shortcut: semicolon) is similar, except that it includes a radial area of influence that controls how many points are moved along with the target points. With the right mouse button, you can change the DragNet tool's radial area widget (or control device). The Magnet tool uses the radial falloff and the DragNet tool uses the Point Radial tool. Figure 3.3 shows a selection on the top of a box object that was lifted from the surface using the Magnet tool.

FIGURE 3.2
Sheared object

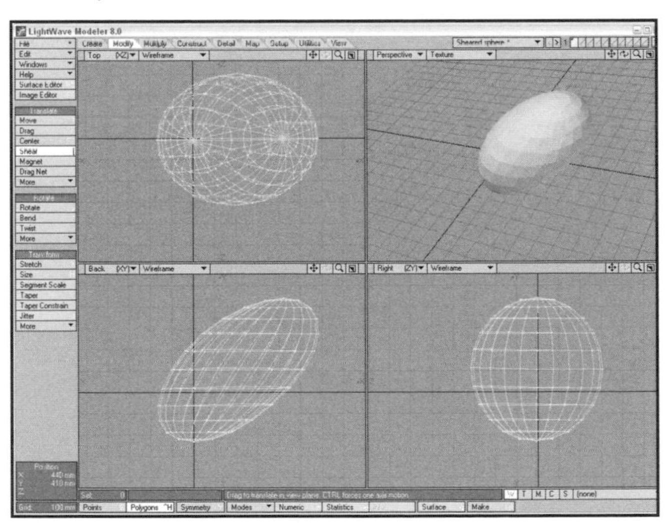

FIGURE 3.3
Selection raised with the Magnet tool

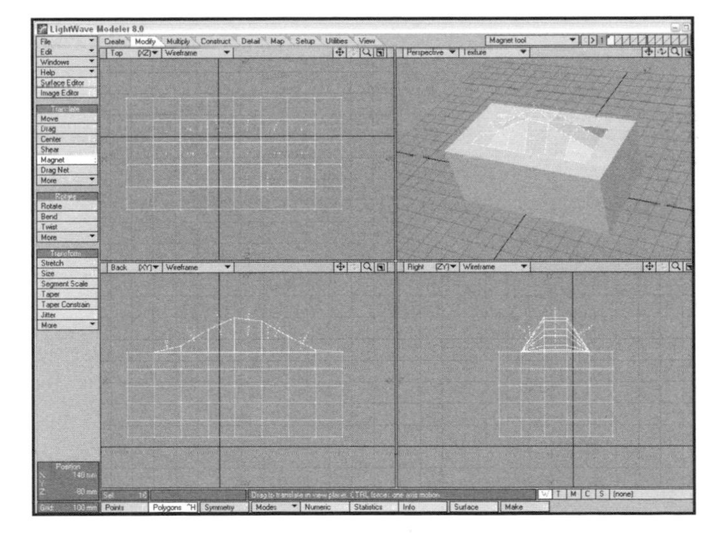

Using the Rove Tool

The Rove tool lets you move and rotate a selection with a single command. This tool places a light blue widget in the center of the viewport, as shown in Figure 3.4. Dragging on the axes moves the selection and dragging on the circle rotates the selection.

Moving Along Normals

The Move Plus tool on the More submenu works the same as the Move tool, except that dragging with the right mouse button moves the polygons along their normals. A normal is a vector that extends from the center of a polygon and specifies which way the polygon is facing. The Translate Plus tool lets you move, rotate, and scale the selection with a single tool. You can also move a polygon along a normal using the Point Normal Move tool, also found in the More submenu, as shown in Figure 3.5.

FIGURE 3.4

Rove tool moves and rotates objects

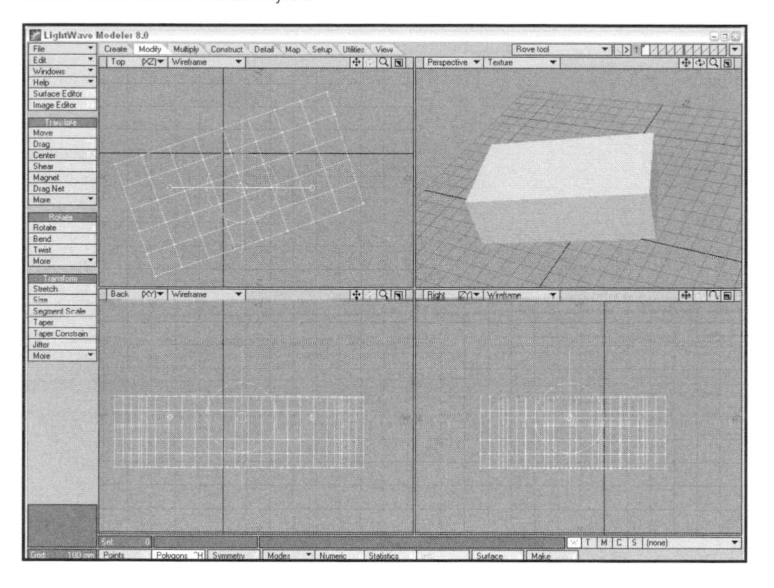

FIGURE 3.5

Polygons moved in the direction of their normals

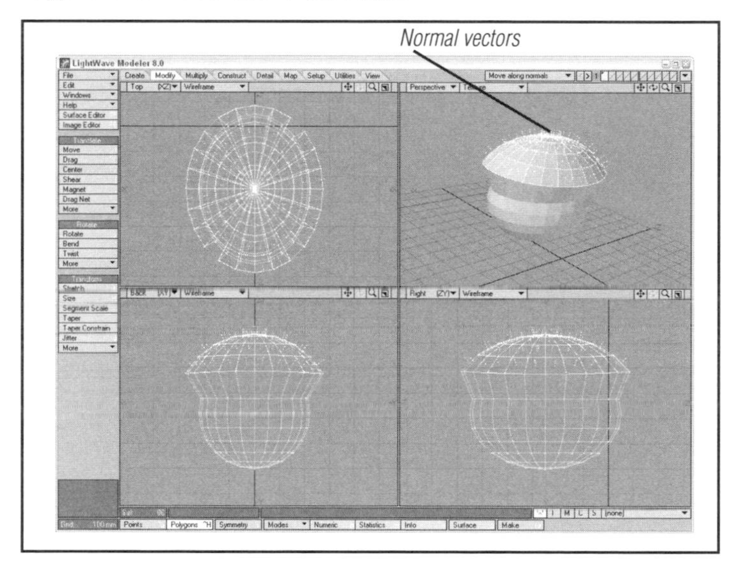

FIGURE 3.6
Pyramid of spheres

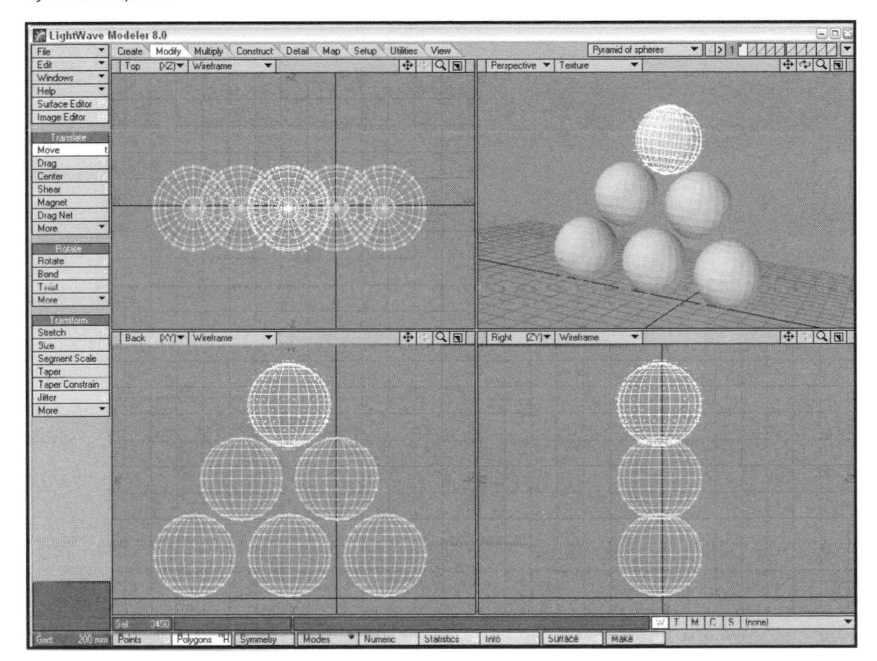

Move objects

1. Open the Modeler, and then click the Create menu tab.
2. Click the Ball button (or press Shift+O). Then drag in the Top viewport to create the ball's cross section and in the Back viewport to define the ball's height. After that, click the Polygons mode button and select all the polygons of the ball object.
3. Click the Modify menu tab.
4. Click the Move button (or press t), and then drag the sphere object into the lower corner position of a simple stacked pyramid of ball objects.

   The cursor changes to show that you're in move mode.
5. Copy and paste the ball object to create a duplicate ball object.
6. Repeat steps 4 and 5 until the pyramid is complete, as shown in Figure 3.6.
7. Select the File, Save As menu command and save the file as Pyramid of spheres.lwo.

Move points

1. Click the Create menu tab, if necessary.
2. Click the Box button (or press Shift+X) and drag in the Top and Back viewports to create a box object.
3. Click the Points mode button, and then select the two bottom points in the Top viewport.
4. Click the Modify menu tab.

5. Click the Drag button (or press Ctrl+T), and then drag the bottom two points halfway toward the center of the face

   As the points are moved, the edges follow to reshape the object. The resulting shape is shown in Figure 3.7.

6. Select the File, Save As menu command and save the file as Brick object.lwo.

Shear text

1. Click the Create menu tab, if necessary.
2. Click the Text button (or press Shift+W), click in the Top viewport, and then type **Speed**.
3. Click the Modify menu tab.
4. Click the Shear button (or press [), and then drag to the left in the Back viewport.

   The text is slanted to the right, as shown in Figure 3.8.

5. Select the File, Save As menu command and save the file as Slanted text.lwo.

Use the Magnet tool

1. Click the Create menu tab, if necessary.
2. Click the Box button (or press Shift+X), and then click in the Top and Back viewports to create a box that is long and wide, but not very high. Press the arrow keys on the keyboard to increase the number of horizontal and vertical segments.

> TIP The more polygons that make up the box object, the smoother the deformation.

FIGURE 3.7
Brick object

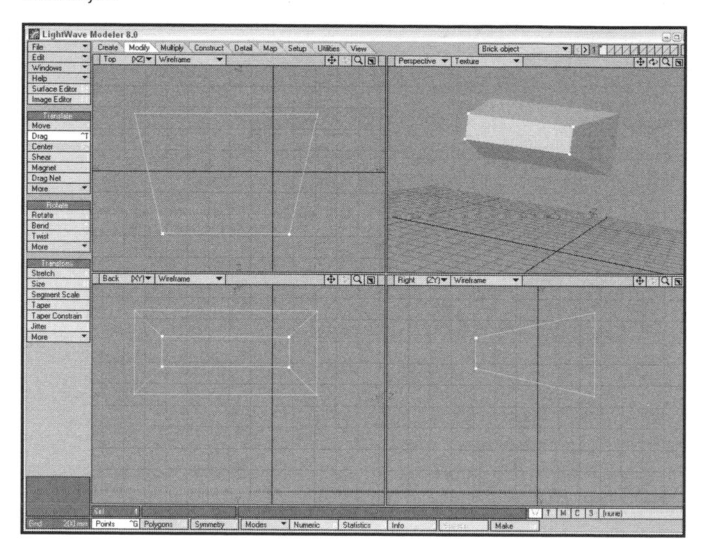

FIGURE 3.8
Slanted text

FIGURE 3.9

Peaks and valleys created with the Magnet tool

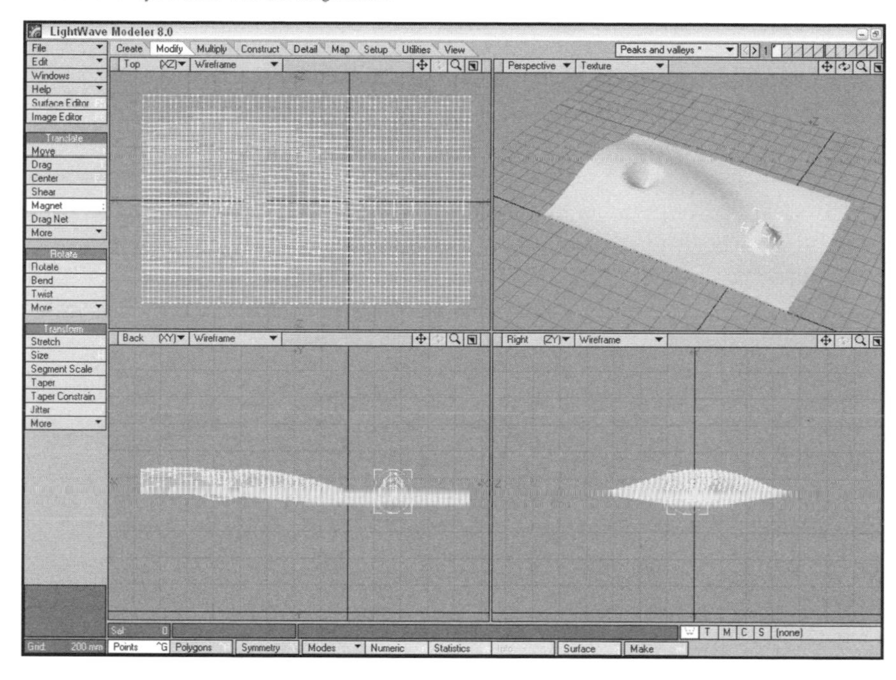

3. Click the Modify menu tab.
4. Click the Magnet button (or press :), and then drag the left portion of the box upward and the right portion downward in the Back viewport.

   Dragging in the Back viewport causes one surface to rise up and the other to sink
5. With the Magnet button still selected, right-click on the box object in the Top viewport to make the widget appear.
6. In the Back viewport, drag with the right mouse button to resize the widget into a box that cuts through the center of the box object. Then drag the widget upward in the Top viewport.

   The surface is altered using the size of the Magnet tool's widget, as shown in Figure 3.9.
7. Select the File, Save As menu command and save the file as Peaks and valleys.lwo.

LESSON 2

CENTER, ALIGN, AND SNAP OBJECTS

What You'll Do

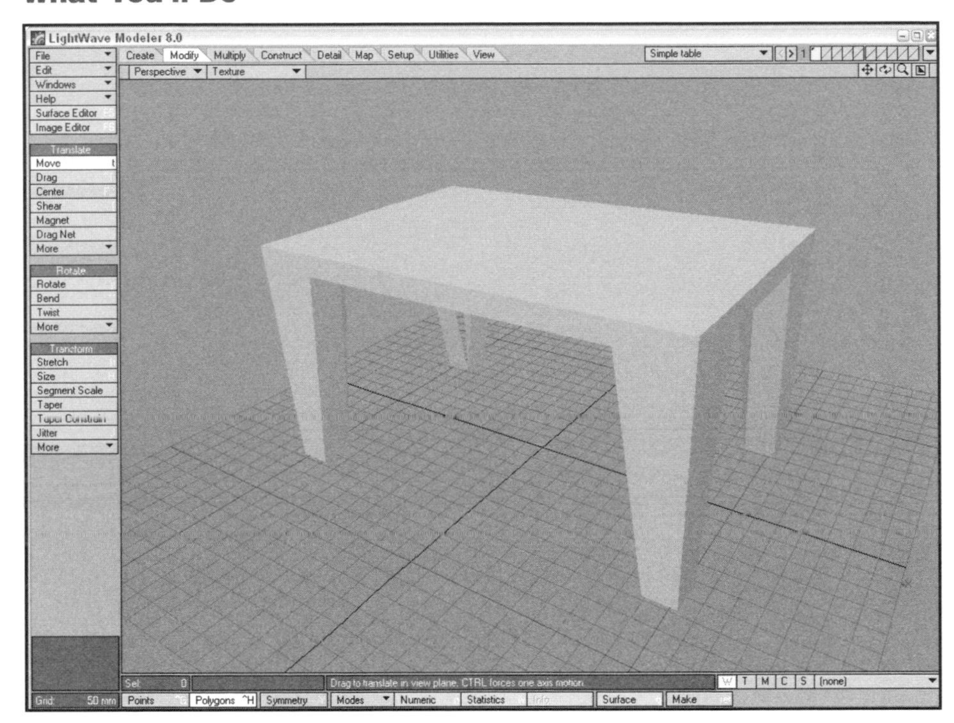

In this lesson, you'll learn how to center objects on the grid, align objects with other objects, and snap points to the same location.

The Modify, Translate menu also includes several commands that automatically move and orient objects to the viewport center, allowing you to align an object to another object, or snap a specific point to the same location as another point.

Centering Objects

The Modify, Center command (keyboard shortcut: F2) moves the current selection to the center of the viewport where the grid originates. The coordinates of this origin are 0,0,0. The Translate, More submenu includes the Center 1D command, which lets you center an object on a single axis. Selecting this command opens a dialog box where you can specify whether to center the object about the X, Y, or Z axis.

Aligning Objects

You can also use the Aligner to align objects with other objects within the viewport. The Aligner is located on the Translate, More submenu. Selecting the Aligner opens the Aligner dialog box, shown in

Figure 3.10. This dialog box includes several alignment modes: World, Foreground to Background, Background to Foreground, and Absolute. For each axis, you can select an icon to set where the object lies. The options are off, centered, negative side of axis, or positive side of axis.

Using the Snap Drag Tool

You can use the Snap Drag tool (keyboard shortcut: G) to move a point and drop it exactly on top of another selected point or on a grid intersection. This command is located on the Translate, More submenu. By snapping points together, you can make sure that they are in the same place, which is required for certain operations such as making patches.

Moving Polygons to the Ground Plane

Using the Rest on Ground tool (keyboard shortcut: F3), located on the Translate, More submenu, moves the selected polygons to the ground plane or the rest axis. Selecting this tool opens a dialog box, shown in Figure 3.11, where you can select which ground plane to move the selection toward.

FIGURE 3.10
Aligner dialog box

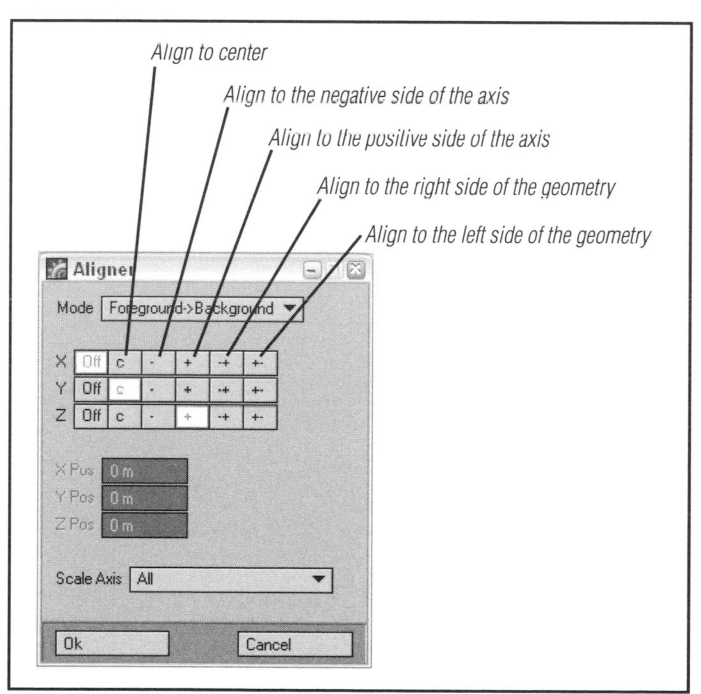

FIGURE 3.11
Rest on Ground dialog box

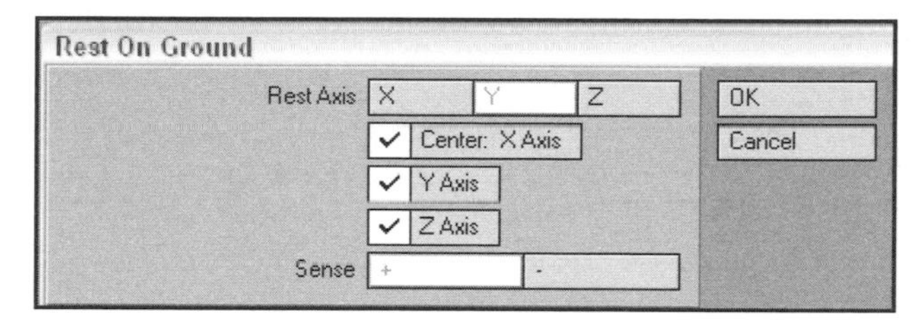

Align objects

1. Open the Modeler, click File, Load Object, and then open Snowcone.lwo.

   This file includes a cone object in one layer and a ball object in another layer.

2. Select layer 2 (the layer with the ball object) as the foreground layer and layer 1 (the layer with the cone object) as the background layer.
3. Click Modify, click More from the Translate category, and then click Aligner.

   The Aligner dialog box appears.

4. With the ball layer selected and the cone layer visible as a background, select the Foreground to Background mode in the Aligner dialog box, select to center the X and Z axes, turn the Y axis off, and then click OK.

   The ball object is aligned with the cone object, as shown in Figure 3.12.

5. Select the File, Save As menu command and save the file as Snowcone aligned.lwo.

Create a pyramid object

1. Click the Create menu tab, if necessary.
2. Click the Box button (or press Shift+X), and then drag in the Top and Back viewports to create a box object.
3. Click the Points mode button, and then select the two top points in the Top viewport.
4. Click the Modify menu tab.

FIGURE 3.12
Aligned snowcone

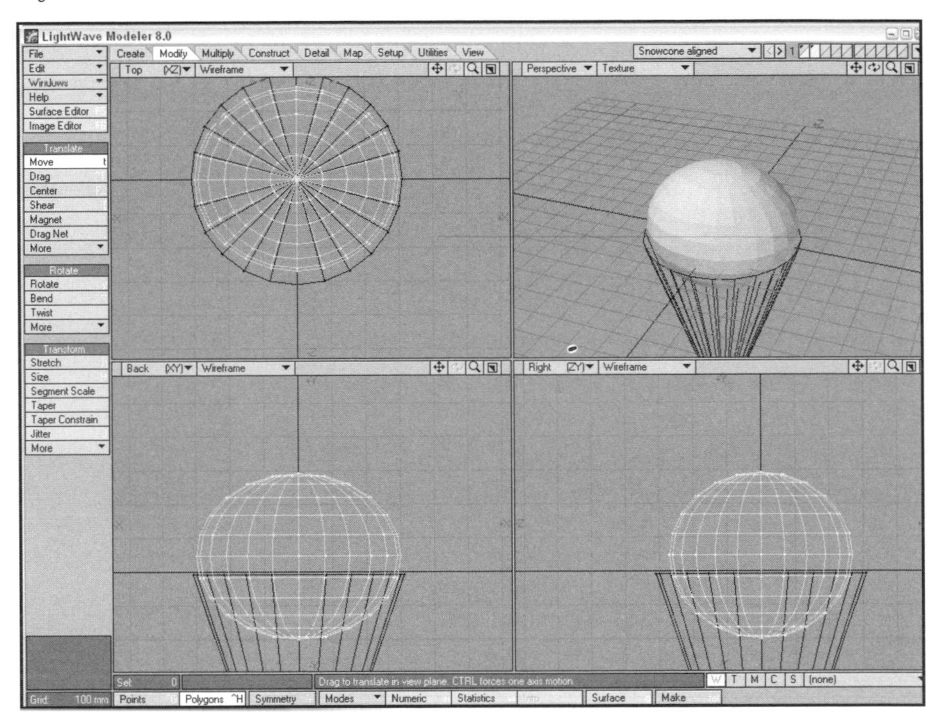

FIGURE 3.13
Pyramid object

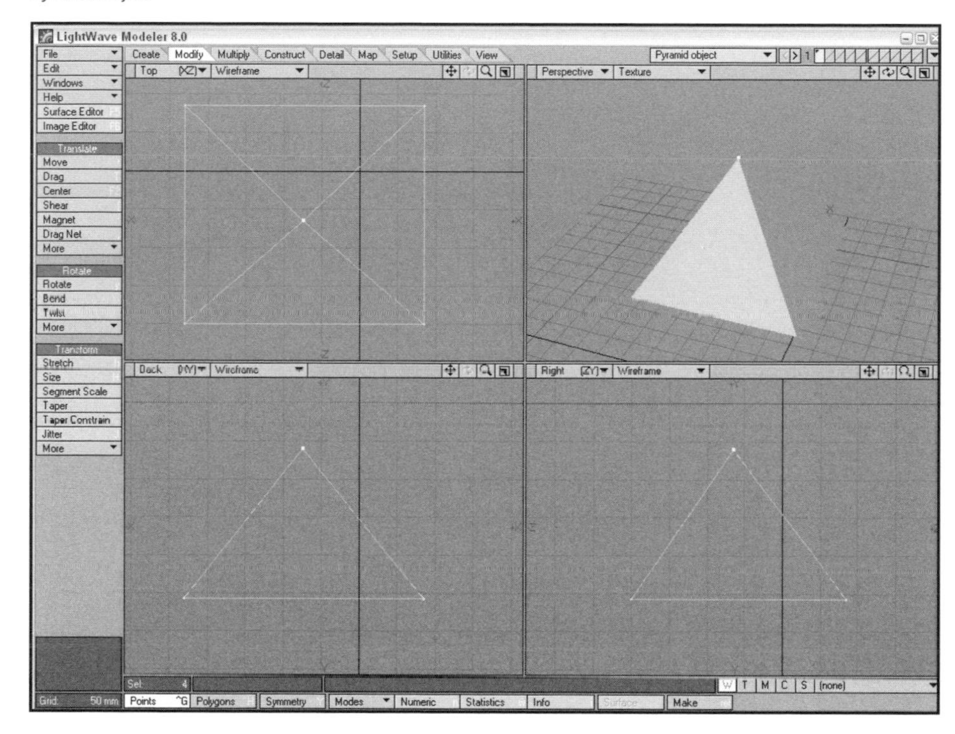

5. Click the More, Snap Drag menu command from the Translate section (or press G), and then drag each point toward the center of the face in the Top viewport.

   After you move the first point to the center, successive points snap to the centered point as they approach it. After you move all the corner points, a pyramid object is created, as shown in Figure 3.13.

6. Select the File, Save As menu command, save the file as Pyramid object.lwo, and then close the file.

Create a table

1. Click the Create menu tab, if necessary.
2. Click the Box button (or press Shift+X), and then click in the Top and Back viewports to create a box that is long and wide, but not very high. Press the arrow keys on the keyboard to set the number of horizontal and vertical segments so that the corner polygons can be used as table legs.
3. Click the Modify menu tab.
4. Click the Center button (or press F2).

   The box object is moved and centered on the origin.

5. Click the Move tool (or press t) and move the box object upward in the Back viewport.
6. Click the Polygons mode button, and then select the downward facing polygons at each corner. Make sure the normal vectors are pointing downward.
7. Click More in the Translate section, and then click Rest on Ground (or press F3).

   The Rest on Ground dialog box opens.
8. Select Y as the Rest Axis, and then click OK.

   Each corner polygon moves downward to rest on the ground plane, as shown in Figure 3.14.
9. Select the File, Save As menu command and save the file as Simple table.lwo.

FIGURE 3.14
Simple table

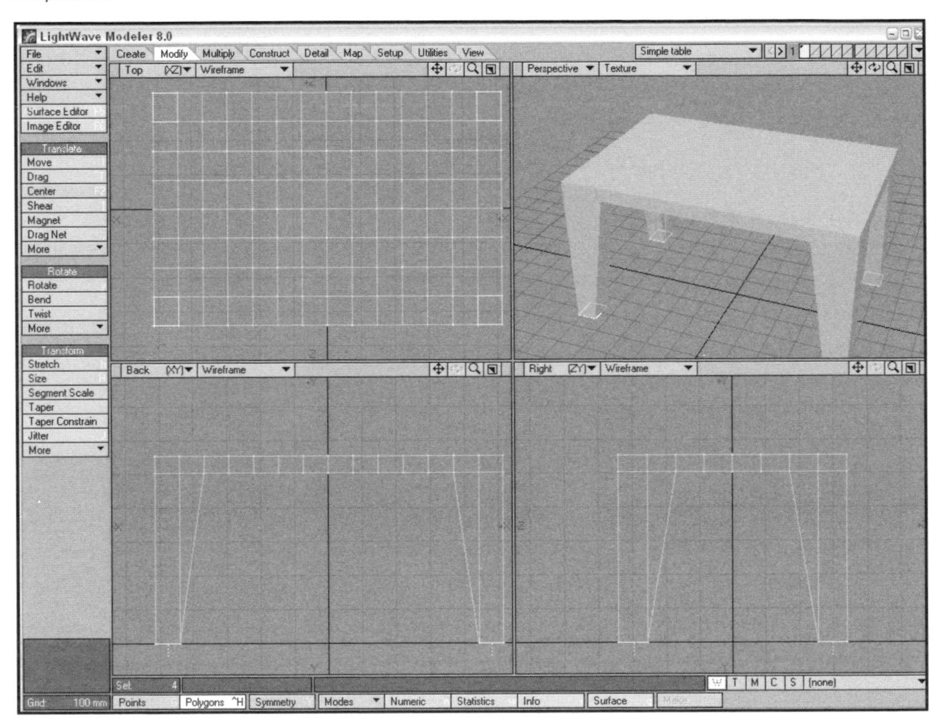

LESSON 3

USE THE FALLOFF OPTIONS

What You'll Do

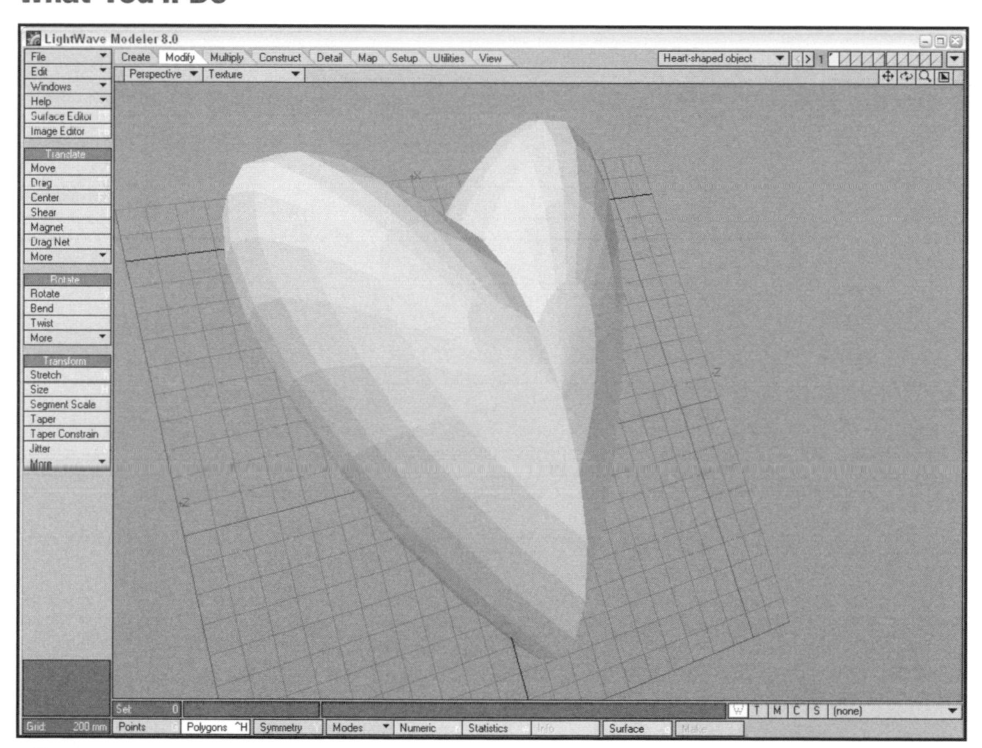

In this lesson, you'll learn how to use the various Falloff options available in the Numeric panel.

The Falloff controls let you define the movement of the selected portion relative to rest of the selection. For example, you can specify that the selected polygons move the full amount and adjacent polygons only move half as far. Almost all of the commands on the Modify menu tab include falloff options. You can access these options using the Numeric panel, which you open by clicking the button at the bottom of the interface (or by pressing N). Falloff options include None, Linear, Radial, Point, Polygon, Point Radial, and Weight Map. Each of the Modify tools has a different falloff method applied by default. For example, the Drag tool is set to use the Point falloff method and the Shear tool uses the Linear falloff method.

Using Linear Falloff

By default, the Linear falloff method causes the top edge of the selection to move a full amount of the translation value while the opposite edge does not move at all. All polygons between the two extreme edges move linearly based on their distance from the edge. You can use the Shape buttons to change the linear shape that is applied to the moved selection. Using the slider controls under the Presets list, you can change how smooth each transition is. Figure 3.15 shows the centered peak shape that was smoothed by dragging the sliders. The Presets drop-down list includes several smoothed variations of the selected shape. You can set the Range to Automatic or Fixed. Specifying Automatic sets the falloff center based on where you click in the viewport; specifying Fixed sets the falloff center as the point halfway between the listed Start and End values. If you select the Fixed range option, a widget that shows the specified limits appears in the viewports.

FIGURE 3.15

Smoothed falloff using the Shear tool

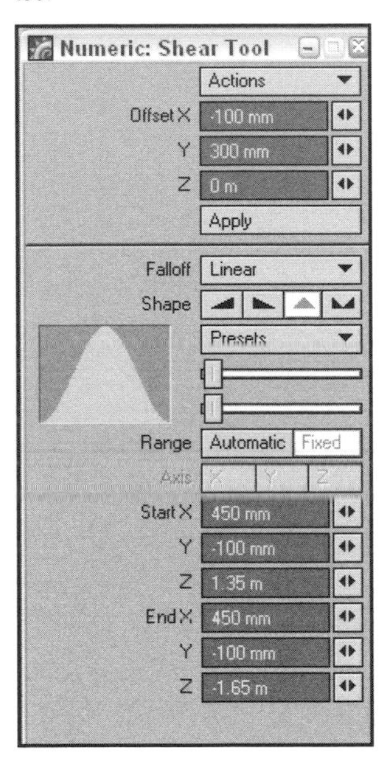

Using Radial and Point Radial Falloffs

The Radial falloff method moves those points closest to the mouse cursor the maximum distance and, while following the radial curve, gradually moves the points next to the selection to a lesser extent. Using the slider controls, you can change the shape's curve. The Range, like the Linear method, can be Automatic or Fixed. This falloff type is used by the Magnet tool. The Point fallout is similar to the Radial falloff, except that the falloff is centered about a point. The options shown in Figure 3.16 let you set a Radius value, which is the area around the selected point that is influenced. The Point Radial falloff is used by the DragNet tool.

FIGURE 3.16

Point Radial Falloff options

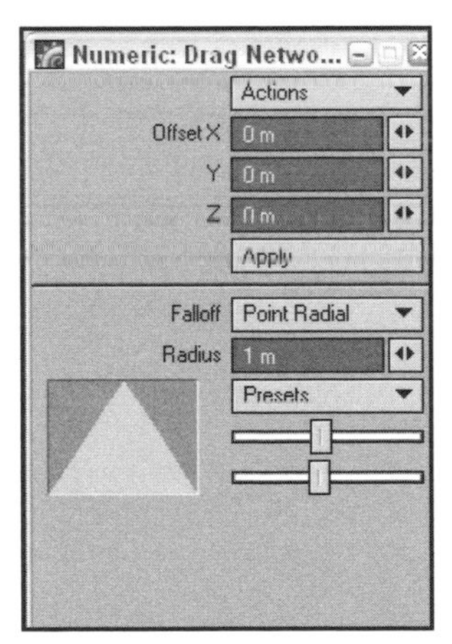

Using Point and Polygon Falloffs

The Point and Polygon falloff methods have no options, but they restrict the movement of objects with the transformation tools to only point objects or only polygon objects. The Drag tool uses the Point falloff method.

FIGURE 3.17
Heart-shaped object

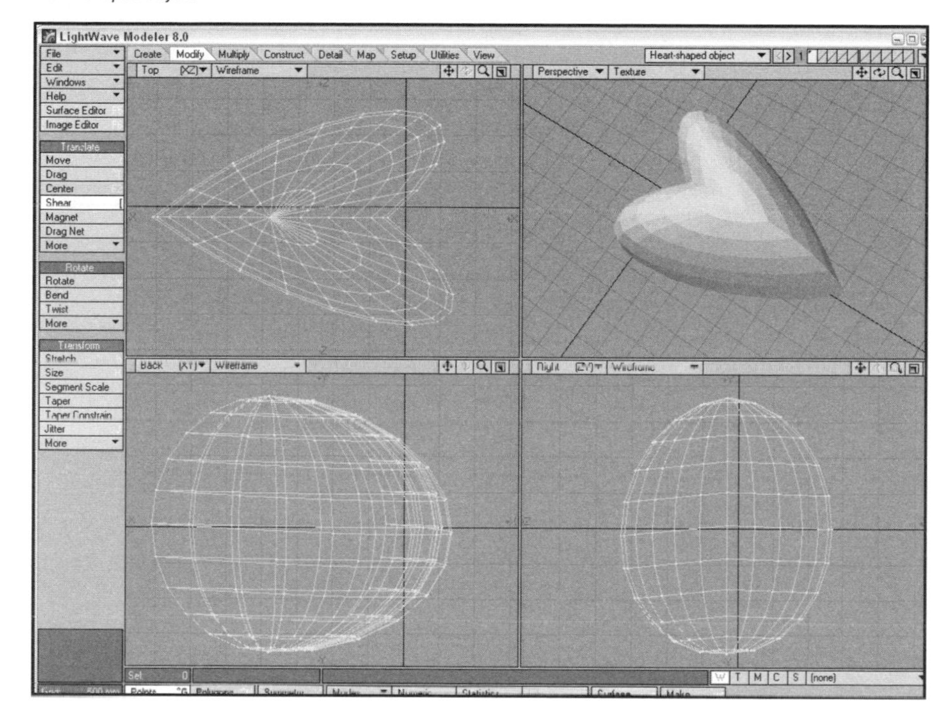

Create a heart-shaped object

1. Open the Modeler, if necessary, and then click the Create menu tab.
2. Click the Ball button (or press Shift+O), and then drag in the Top and Back viewports to create a ball object.
3. Click the Modify menu tab.
4. Click the Shear button (or press [), and then open the Numeric panel by clicking the button at the bottom of the interface (or by pressing n).

   The Numeric panel displays the Linear falloff method.
5. Choose the Linear falloff option. Select the center peaked Shape icon (the third one over), and then click on your ball object in the Back viewport and drag thc objcctuntil the object resembles a heart shape in the Perspective viewport.

   Dragging the Shear tool with the center peak shaped linear falloff causes the center of the ball object to move while either end stays put. This creates the heart-shaped object shown in Figure 3.17.
6. Select the File, Save As menu command and save the file as Heart-shaped object.lwo.

Move a selection with Falloff

1. Click the Create menu tab, if necessary.
2. Click the Box button, and then drag in the Top and Back viewports to create a wide, long box with little height and many segments. More segments can be added to the object by using the arrow keys on the keyboard.
3. Select the Polygons mode by clicking on the Polygons button at the bottom of the interface, then select an interior selection of polygons in the Top viewport.
4. Click the Modify button, click the Move button, and then open the Numeric panel.

   The Numeric panel displays the Linear falloff method.
5. Click the linear ramp Shape icon (the first one). In the Right viewport, drag upward on the selected polygons in the object.

   Dragging with the Move tool with the ramp-shaped linear falloff causes one end of the selection center to move while either end stays put, creating a ramp, as shown in Figure 3.18.
6. Select the File, Save As menu command and save the file as Ramp.lwo.

FIGURE 3.18

Creating a ramp

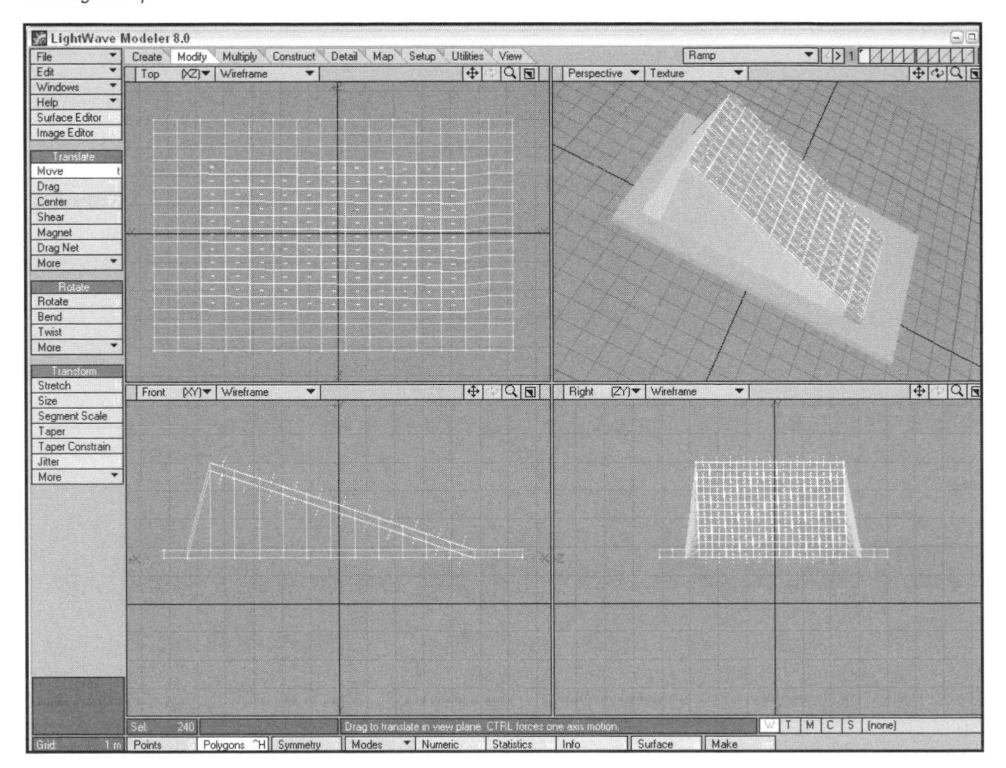

ROTATE OBJECTS

What You'll Do

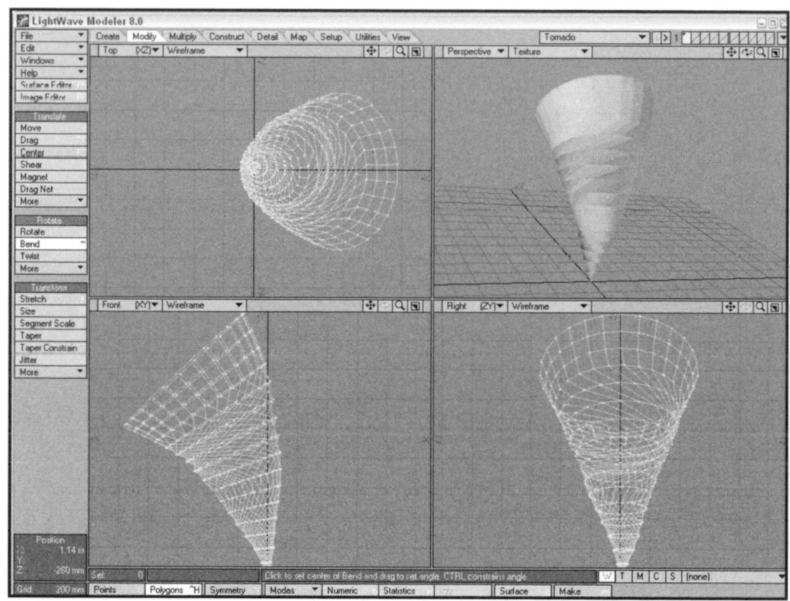

In this lesson, you'll learn how to rotate objects about their centers or about a specific axis.

To rotate objects, use the Modify, Rotate menu commands. The center about which an object is rotated is determined by the **Action Center,** which can be set through the Modes button at the bottom of the interface. You can set the Action Center to Mouse, Origin, Pivot, or Selection. The Modify, Rotate menu also includes tools for rotating a portion of the selection.

Setting the Action Center

The Action Center defines the point about which an object is rotated. You can set it using the Modes button at the bottom of the LightWave window. The options shown in Figure 3.19 are as follows:

- **Mouse (Shift+F5).** Rotates about the point where the mouse is clicked.
- **Origin (Shift+F6).** Rotates about the center of the viewport at 0,0,0.
- **Pivot (Shift+F7).** Rotates about the object's pivot point.
- **Selection (Shift+F8).** Rotates about the center of the selection.

FIGURE 3.19
Action Center modes/Modes drop-down menu

✓Action Center: Mouse +F5
Action Center: Origin +F6
Action Center: Pivot +F7
Action Center: Selection +F8

Rotating Objects

Use the Rotate (y) tool to rotate the selected object about the defined Action Center. You can also use the Falloff options in the Numeric panel in conjunction with the Rotate tool.

> TIP
>
> Hold down Ctrl to constrain the rotation to 15-degree increments.

Bending and Twisting Objects

Use the Bend tool (keyboard shortcut: ~) to rotate the top area of the selected object while keeping the bottom area stationary. The Twist tool is similar to the Bend tool, except that you use the Twist tool to rotate the top half of the selection in one direction and the bottom half in the opposite direction. Figure 3.20 shows an example of a box object that was bent and a box that was twisted.

Using the Dangle and Vortex Tools

Using the Dangle tool (under Rotate, More) allows you to rotate the selected object relative to the rotation center determined by the selected Action Center. You can use the options in the Dangle dialog box to select the precise absolute or relative rotation amount. Use the Vortex tool (under Rotate, More) to rotate the selection along a predefined, spiral-like path.

Rotating About Other Axes

The Rotate, More submenu includes several other commands for rotating a selected object about a unique location. Use the Rotate Any Axis command to select any two-point polygon as an axis to rotate an object about. Use the Rotate HPB command to specify a rotation in terms of Heading, Pitch, and Bank values. To rotate a polygon about its normal, use the Rotate About Normal command. Use the Rotate to Ground command (keyboard shortcut: F4) to rotate the selected object about the ground plane.

FIGURE 3.20
Bent and twisted objects

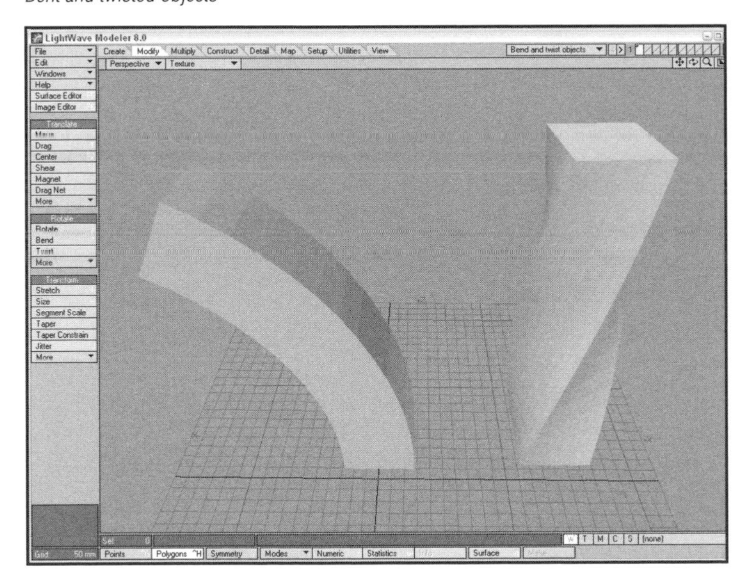

FIGURE 3.21

Twisted and rotated fan blades

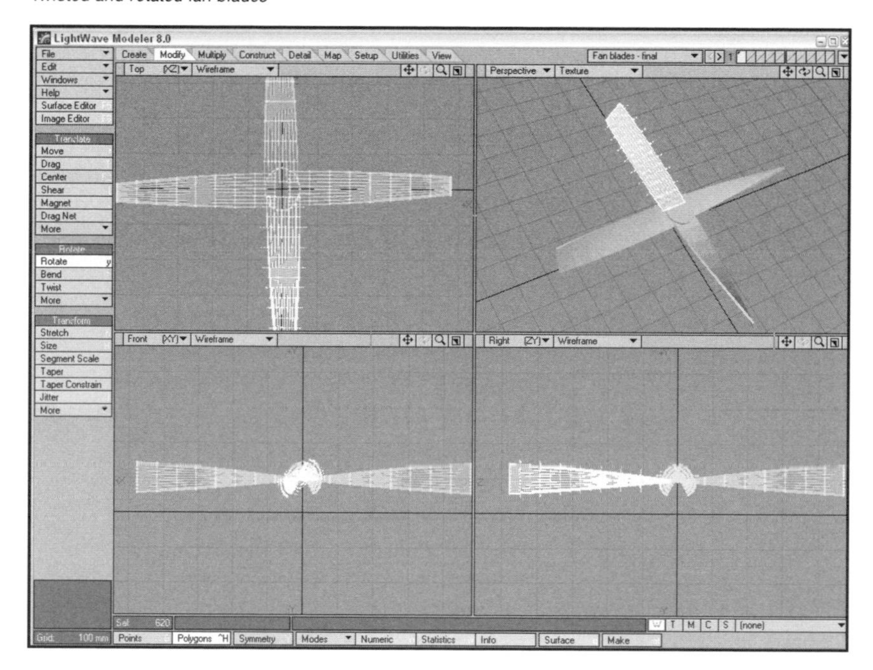

Create fan blades

1. Choose the File, Load Object menu command to open the Fan blades.lwo file.
2. Select the Polygons selection mode using the button at the bottom of the interface, drag over some of the polygons on the box object, and then press] to select the entire object.
3. Click the Modify menu tab, click the Twist button on the Rotate menu, and then drag to the right in the Right viewport to twist the box object about 60 degrees.

   The box object is twisted about its center axis.
4. With the box object still selected, choose the Action Center: Origin mode from the Modes button at the bottom of the interface.

   The box object is centered about the origin point, which means you can rotate it about the origin.
5. Click Edit, click Copy and Edit, and then click Paste to create a duplicate of the box object.
6. Click the Rotate button (or press y), and then drag the box object in the Top viewport until the new box object is vertically aligned.
7. Repeat steps 5 and 6 two more times until there are four blades all at right angles to each other, as shown in Figure 3.21.
8. Select the File, Save As menu command and save the file as Fan blades - final.lwo. Then close the file.

Create a tornado

1. Click the Create menu tab, if necessary.
2. Click the Cone button and drag in the Top and Back viewports to create a cone object with many horizontal and vertical segments. You can add more horizontal and vertical segments by using the arrow keys on the keyboard.
3. Click the Modify button, click the Rotate button, and then rotate the cone object 180 degrees in the Back viewport so that the cone is pointing down. You can do this easily by choosing the Action Center: Mouse option from the Modes button located at the bottom of the interface and then clicking on the point of the cone in the Back viewport and dragging it down to the bottom.
4. Click Rotate, More, Vortex Tool, and then drag in the Top viewport to the right.

   The Vortex tool causes the cone polygons to rotate about their vertical axes.
5. Click the Rotate, Bend button (or press ~), and then drag in the Front viewport to the left.

   The Bend tool causes the cone to bend slightly to the left, as shown in Figure 3.22.
6. Select the File, Save As menu command and save the file as Tornado.lwo.

FIGURE 3.22
Tornado

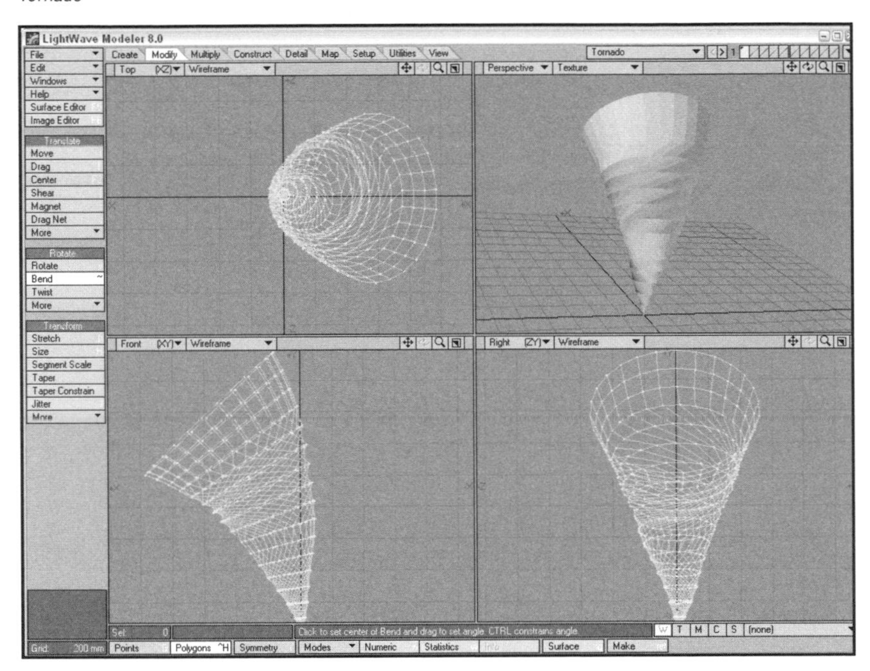

LESSON 5

SIZE AND STRETCH OBJECTS

What You'll Do

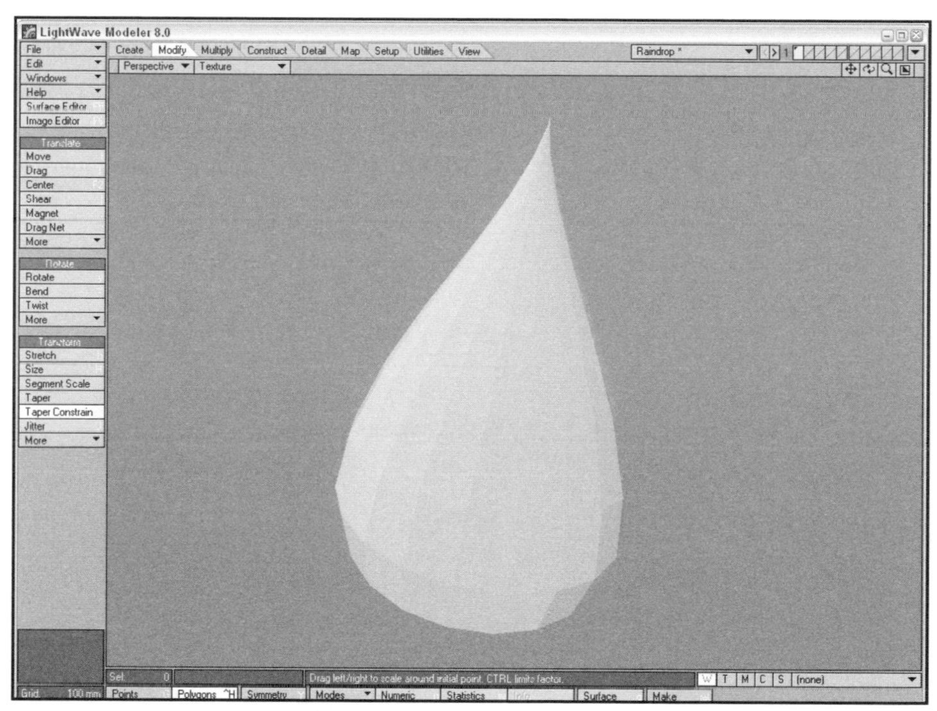

In this lesson, you'll learn how to resize objects using the Size and Stretch tools.

Sizing an object is the same as resizing it. Stretching an object is similar, except that the size is changed along only a single axis, resulting in a distortion of the original object. The Size and Stretch commands are located on the Modify, Transform menu. This menu also includes commands for changing the size of an object or portion of an object.

Resizing an Object

Use the Size tool (keyboard shortcut: H) to change the size of an object equally along all axes. When you use this command, the object is scaled uniformly.

Stretching an Object

Use the Stretch tool (keyboard shortcut: h) to change the size of an object along a single axis. Hold down Ctrl to constrain the stretching to a single axis so that the object is stretched only vertically or only horizontally.

Scaling Edge Segments

Use the Segment Scale tool to scale selected individual points along their attached edge. You can use the Numeric panel to specify the direction in which to scale the points, which is shown by a light blue line in the viewports. You can also specify that the scaling is Centered, along Side 1 Only, or along Side 2 Only. Figure 3.23 shows the center polygon of a box object that was scaled.

Tapering an Object

Use the Transform, Taper tool to make one end of the object smaller while not changing the size of the opposite end of the object. You can taper each axis to a different degree, or you can use the Transform, Taper Constrain tool to taper both axes in a plane equally, which results in a tighter point at the end of the object.

FIGURE 3.23
Scaled polygon

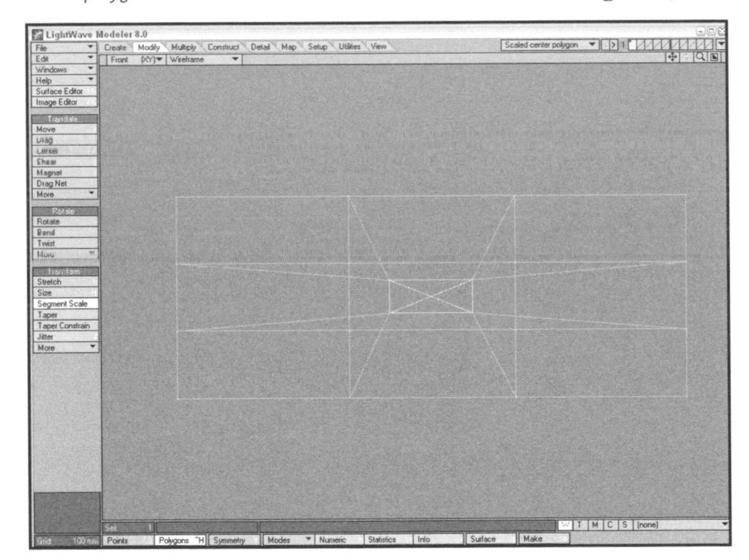

> **TIP**
>
> Use the Taper Constrain tool to taper an object to a fine, sharp point.

Scaling an Object with Precision

You can use the Stretch and Size tools to interactively scale objects by dragging in the viewports, but to precisely enter a scaling factor, use the Transform, More, Absolute Size tool. In the Absolute Size dialog box (shown in Figure 3.24), you can choose the Independent option to scale each axis separately, or the Locked option to make all scaling uniform.

Scaling and Smoothing Polygons

Use the Transform, More, Smooth Scaling tool to automatically smooth any scaled polygons. Using this tool helps maintain the smooth look of an object as you move a selection of polygons.

Scaling About an Object's Center

Use the Transform, More, Center Scale tool to open a dialog box where you can enter a scaling factor. When you specify a scaling factor, the entire object is scaled about its center using this value. You can also use the Transform, More, Center Stretch tool to open a dialog box where you can specify the scaling factor for each axis independently.

FIGURE 3.24
Absolute Size dialog box

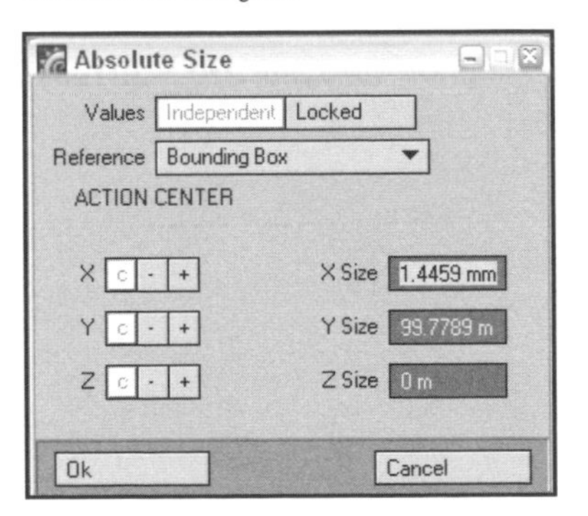

FIGURE 3.25
Creating a raindrop with the Taper tool

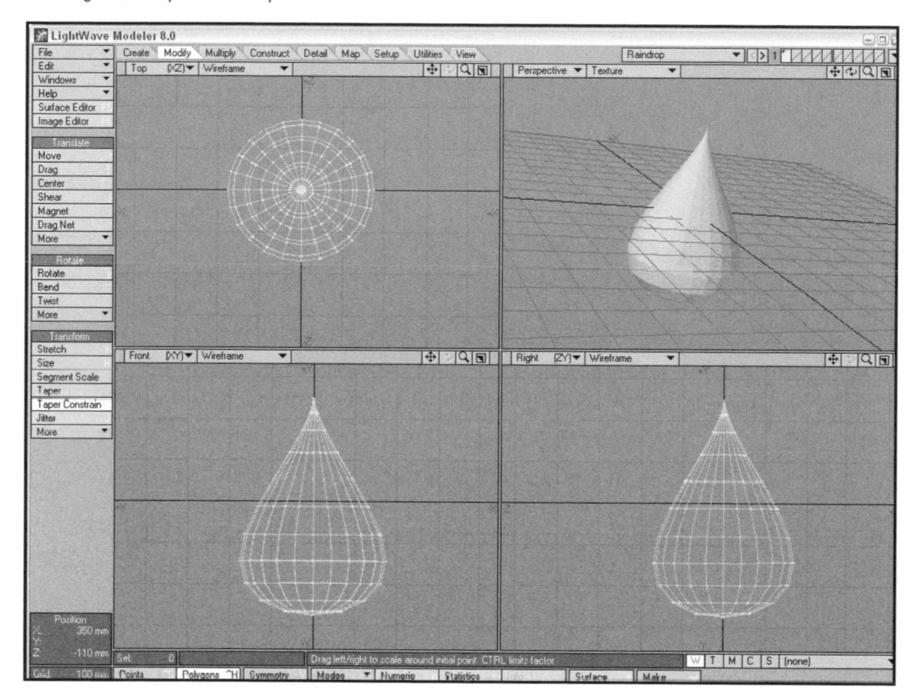

Create a raindrop

1. Open the Modeler, if necessary, and then click the Create menu tab.
2. Click the Ball button (or press Shift+O) and drag in the Top and Back viewports to create a ball object.
3. Click the Modify menu tab.
4. Click the Taper Constrain button, and then clicking at the center of the ball, drag left in the Top viewport.

   A sharp point is formed at the center of the ball object, as shown in Figure 3.25.
5. Select the File, Save As menu command and save the file as Raindrop.lwo, and then close the file.

LESSON 6

TRANSFORM AND DISTORT OBJECTS

What You'll Do

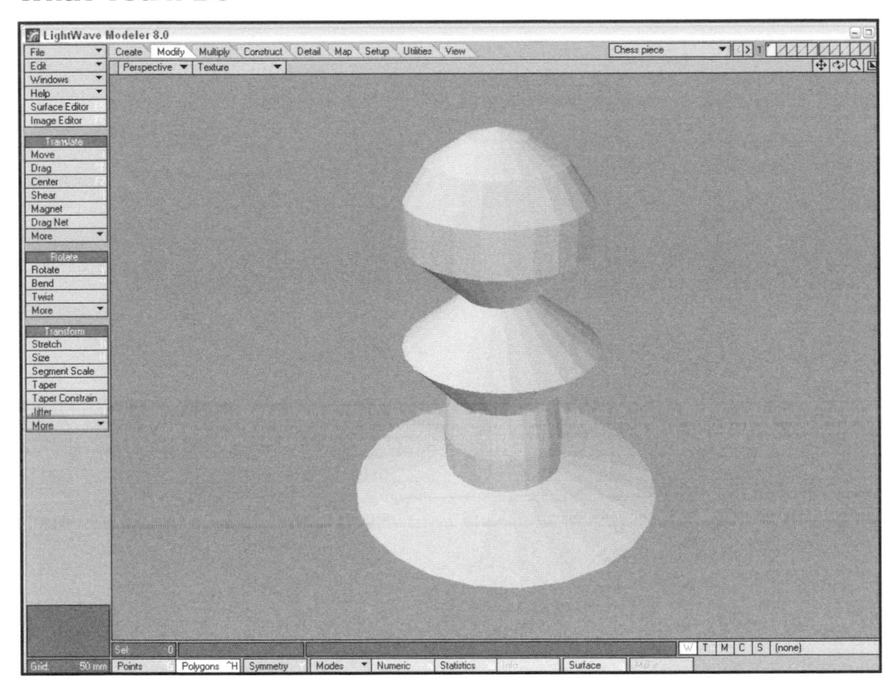

In this lesson, you'll learn how to distort objects using the tools in the Transform menu.

In addition to the stretch and scaling tools, the Modify, Transform menu also includes several tools for distorting and deforming objects. The menu includes tools to **jitter** (or roughen) the surface of an object, and the Transform, More, Smooth tool. Other tools include the Pole tool, which you can use to poke and pull objects to deform them along an axis, and the Spline Guide tool, which adds a widget alongside the object so that you can deform the object by moving its points.

Adding Roughness

When you want to add some roughness to an area of your object, you can randomly move the points that make up the area but this is difficult to do when you have an object with a large number of points. The Jitter tool simplifies this process. To use it, select the Jitter command from the Modify, Transform menu to open a dialog box where you can specify the type as Uniform, Gaussian, Normal, Radial, and Scaling. You can also specify the jitter range and distance. Figure 3.26 shows four spheres that had different degrees of the Jitter command applied to them.

Smoothing Objects

Just as you can make objects rough using the Jitter tool, you can also smooth objects with the Smooth tool. To smooth an object, LightWave takes the average position of all the points and moves them closer to this average. You can use the Numeric panel to specify the Strength and Iterations or the smoothing tool. Figure 3.27 shows a plane object with several polygons that were moved upward and the same plane object after it was smoothed.

Distorting Along an Axis

Use the Transform, More, Pole tool to distort an object along a horizontal or vertical axis. You can drag in the viewports to pull or push the selected area along a single axis. In the Numeric panel, you can set the Horizontal and Vertical Factor values. You can also use the Transform, More, Pole

FIGURE 3.26
Jittered spheres

FIGURE 3.27
Smoothed plane objects

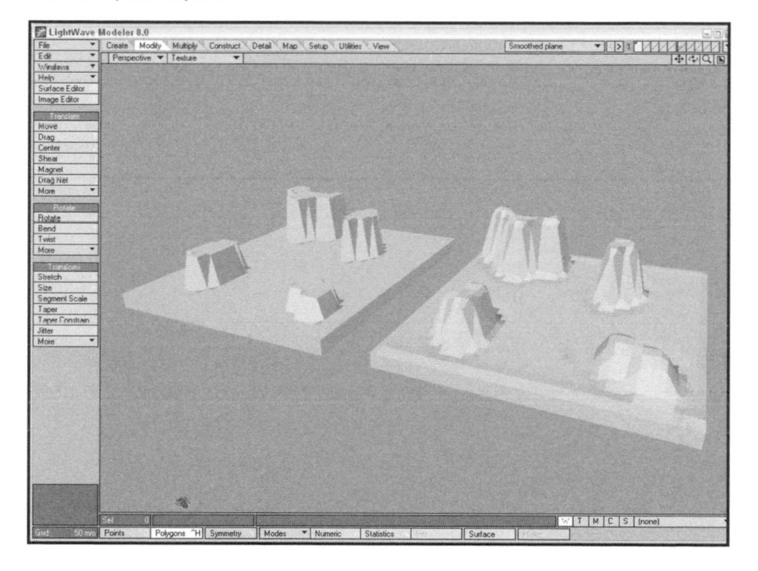

Evenly tool to uniformly distort an object along an axis, with equal horizontal and vertical factors. Figure 3.28 shows a sphere that was pushed into and stretched using the Pole Evenly tool.

Distorting with a Spline Guide

The Transform, More Spline Guide tool places a light blue widget next to an object. By moving the points of this widget, you can deform the object's surface. This means that you can make changes with this tool that would be difficult to accomplish using the other tools. In the Numeric panel, shown in Figure 3.29, you can specify the number of points used to create the spline guide and the Operation option that occurs when you move the points. The available operations are Scale, Stretch, Twist, Bend, and Weight Map. Figure 3.30 shows a spline guide to the side of the object. In the Right viewport, you can see how the spline guide points were moved to change the shape of the object.

FIGURE 3.28

Pole tool

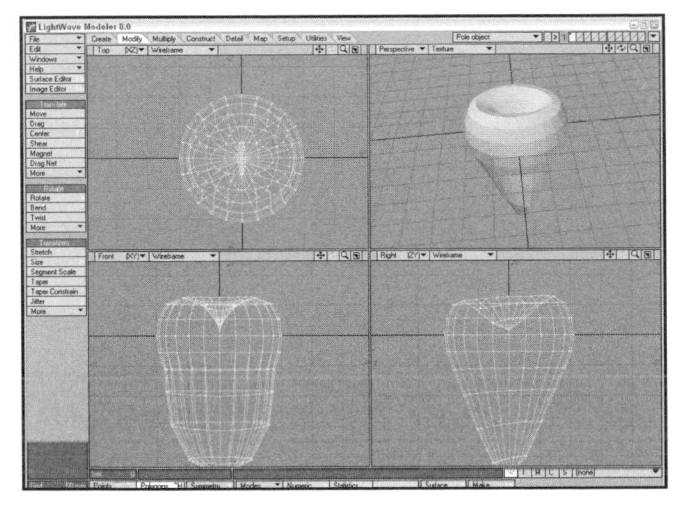

FIGURE 3.29

Spline guide numeric panel

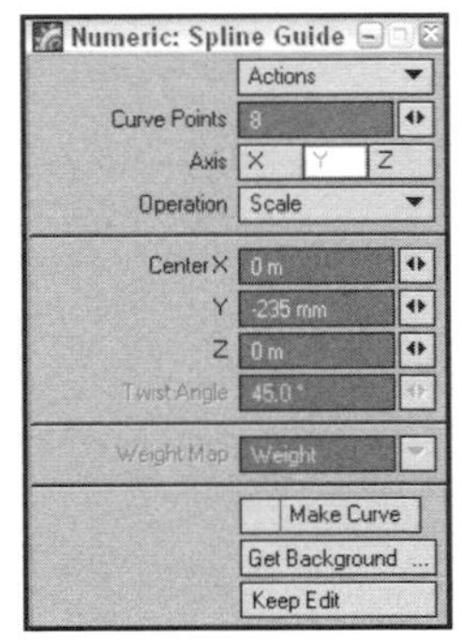

FIGURE 3.30

Spline guide

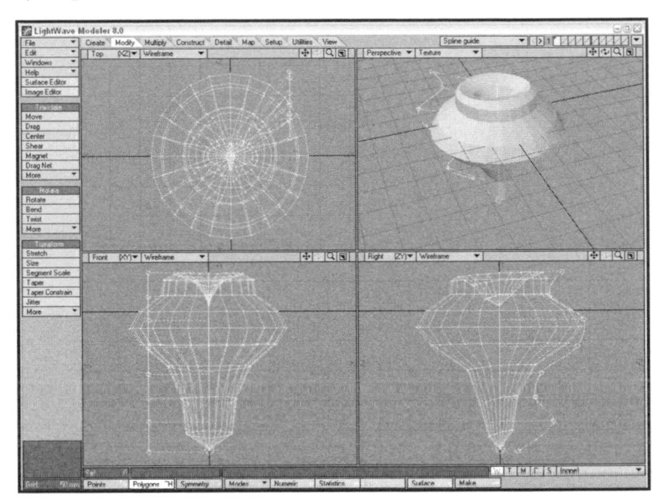

FIGURE 3.31
Stone block

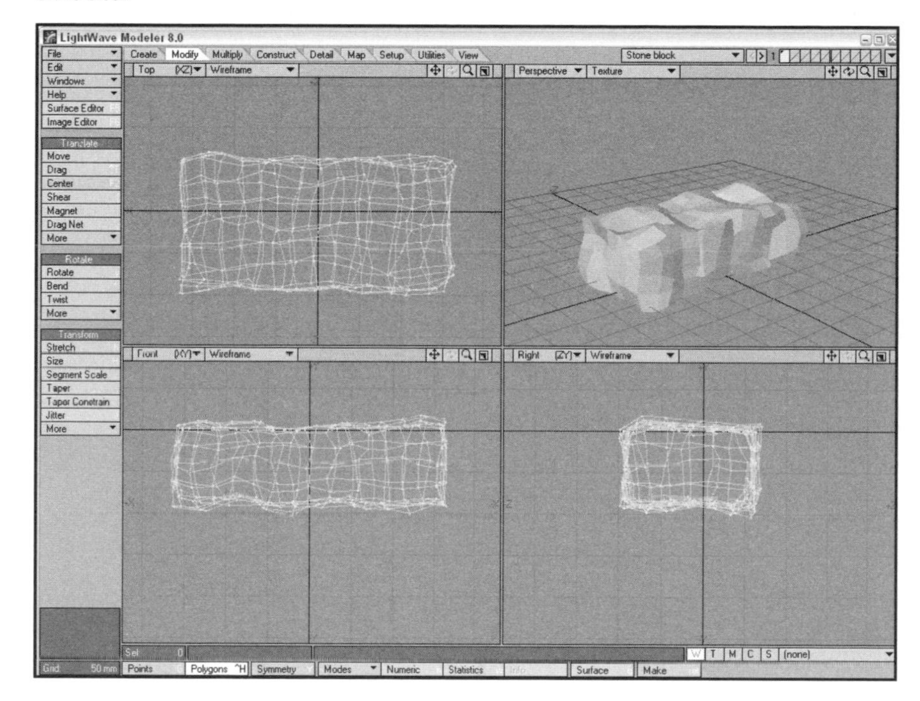

Create a block of stone

1. Open the Modeler, if necessary.
2. Click the Create menu tab and select the Box button in the Primitives section.
3. Drag in the Top and Front viewports to create a new box object with several segments.
4. Click the Modify menu tab, click the Jitter button (Shift+J), and then enter values of **20 mm** for each axis in the dialog box and click the OK button.

   The polygons that make up the box object are moved randomly.
5. Click More in the Transform menu, click Smooth, and then enter **2.0** for the Strength value and **3** for the Iterations option. Then click the OK button.

   The Smooth command smoothes the rough portions of the box object, creating a general roundness, as shown in Figure 3.31
6. Select the File, Save As menu command and save the file as Stone block.lwo.

Create a flower

1. Open the Modeler, if necessary.
2. Click the Create menu tab. Then from the Primitives section, click the Ball button, and drag in the Top and Front viewports to create a new ball object.
3. Click the Modify menu tab and select the Action Center: Origin option from the Modes button at the bottom of the interface.

4. Click More on the Transform menu and then click Pole Evenly Tool.
5. Drag each side of the sphere away from its center in the Front and Right viewports, and then drag the top and bottom sphere edges in the Front viewport downward.

   The sphere is divided into four parts that extend from the center, as shown in Figure 3.32.
6. Select the File, Save As menu command and save the file as Flower.lwo.

Create a chess piece

1. Open the Modeler, if necessary.
2. Click the Create menu tab, click Ball in the Primitives menu, and then drag in the Top and Front viewports to create a new ball object.
3. Click the Modify menu tab. Click More on the Tranform menu, click Spline Guide, and then click the sphere object in the Front viewport.

   A spline guide appears along the profile of the sphere object.
4. Open the Numeric panel and set the number of curve points to 12.
5. Manipulate the points in the spline guide to create a chess piece profile.

   By moving the points of the spline guide, you can control the shape of the object, as shown in Figure 3.33.
6. Select the File, Save As menu command and save the file as Chess piece.lwo.

FIGURE 3.32
Flower

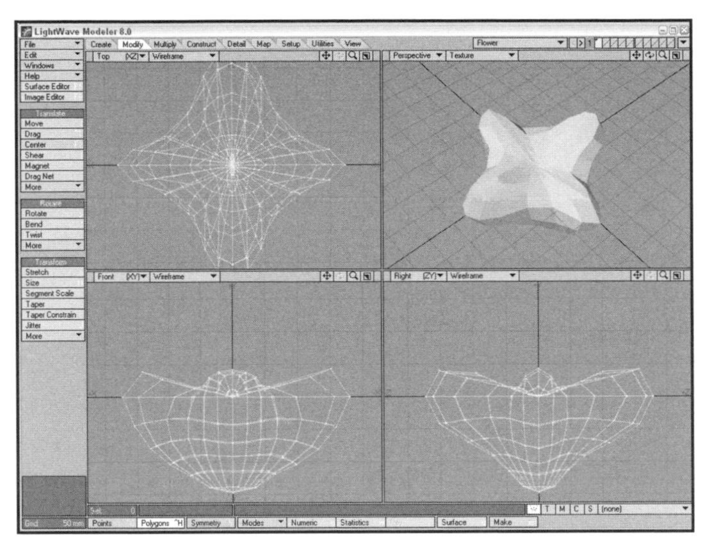

FIGURE 3.33
Chess piece

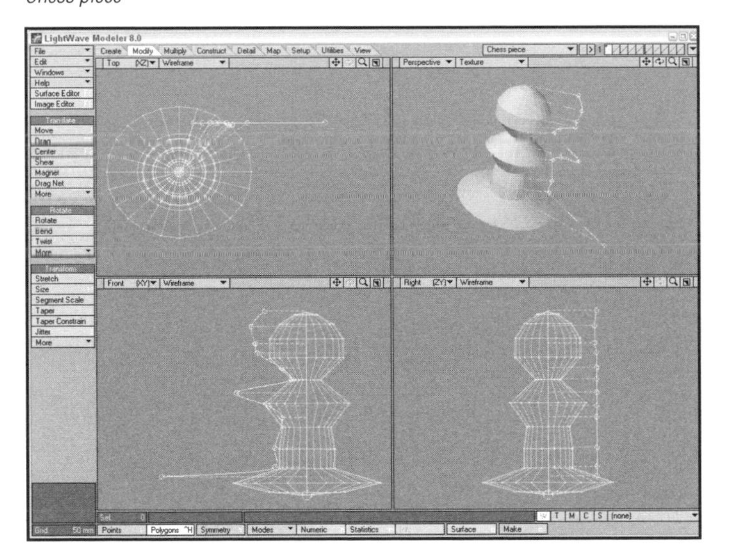

CHAPTER SUMMARY

This chapter covered the basic transformation commands available in the Modify menu tab. Using these commands, you can translate, rotate, scale, and stretch the currently selected object. This chapter also covered the Falloff options that enable only a portion of a selection to be moved to the full extent.

What You Have Learned

- How to move objects, points, and polygons using the Move, Drag, Magnet, and DragNet tools.
- How to use the commands in the Translate, More menu to center, align, and snap objects.
- How the various Falloff options are used.
- How to rotate objects about different object centers.
- How to scale and stretch objects to change their sizes.
- How to use transform commands to distort objects using the jitter and smooth tools.

Key Terms from This Chapter

- **translate.** A process of moving an object.
- **shear.** A process of diagonally deforming an object by moving only its top edge and leaving its bottom edge unmoved.
- **Falloff.** A parameter option for moving the selected portion of an object a relative distance to the adjacent points and polygons.
- **Action Center.** The point about which objects are rotated and scaled.
- **taper.** The process of scaling one end of an object while leaving the other end unchanged.
- **jitter.** The process of randomly moving the points of an object to add variety to the object.

CHAPTER 4

EXTENDING, DUPLICATING, AND SUBDIVIDING OBJECTS

1. Bevel faces and edges.
2. Extrude and lathe shapes.
3. Create specialized objects.
4. Duplicate objects.
5. Work with arrays.
6. Subdivide objects.

CHAPTER 4 EXTENDING, DUPLICATING, AND SUBDIVIDING OBJECTS

So far we've covered the interface and how to create, select, and move objects, but you are still limited to creating models using the primitive objects. The next, critical part of the modeling process is editing the primitive objects in unique ways to create new objects. LightWave includes interesting features you can use to alter and edit objects and some of them are just plain fun.

This chapter covers the various features you can access from the Multiply menu tab. The name of the tab refers to the different ways that you can edit existing points, edges, and polygons to multiply the total number of points, edges and polygons. This Multiply menu tab includes features categorized under Extend, Duplicate, and Subdivide lists. From this tab, you can do things like bevel, extrude, duplicate, cut, and separate objects.

Before continuing, be advised that multiplying the total number of points and polygons is not always a good idea. For example, if you subdivide an object 10 or more times, you are likely to produce polygons that are so small, you have to zoom in to even see that they are there. Furthermore, if you overuse these tools, you might find it increasingly difficult to work with your objects. You could encounter problems with file sizes and memory issues, and even an unstable system.

It's also important to know that there are often several different ways to accomplish the same task. For example, you can cut a polygon in half using the Subdivide button, the **Knife tool**, or the Cut dialog box. You'll need to determine which method makes the most sense, and best use of available features, to accomplish your tasks.

Several features found in the More menus are earlier versions of a tool that has been improved with additional functionality. But the older tools remain in the More menu for backward compatibility only, and it is advised that the new versions be used. For example, the Band Saw Pro tool has replaced the More, Band Saw tool.

Tools You'll Use

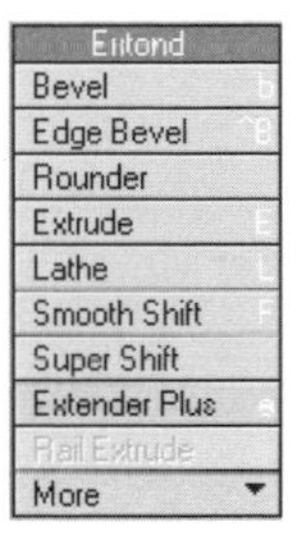

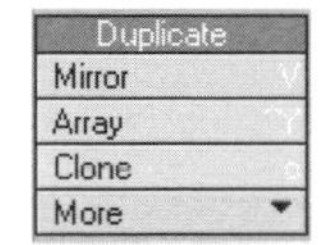

LESSON 1

BEVEL FACES AND EDGES

What You'll Do

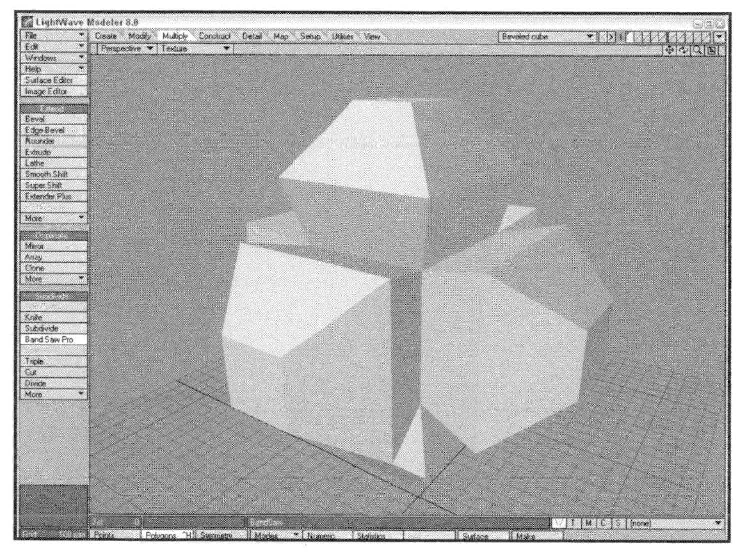

In this lesson, you'll learn how to bevel object faces and edges using the Rounder, Smooth Shift, Magic Bevel, and Router tools.

Beveling is the process of moving a selected polygon outward from its original position while connecting the face with edges attached to the corners. If the new object is an edge, new vertices appear at each corner. Use the first two commands in the Extend category of the Multiply menu tab to bevel selected faces or edges.

Figure 4.1 shows two cube objects. The left cube was beveled along its edge; the right cube was beveled on its face.

Beveling a Face

When you select several polygons or an entire object, the Extend, Bevel (keyboard shortcut: b) command is active. Using this command, you can drag in the viewports

FIGURE 4.1
Edge and face beveling

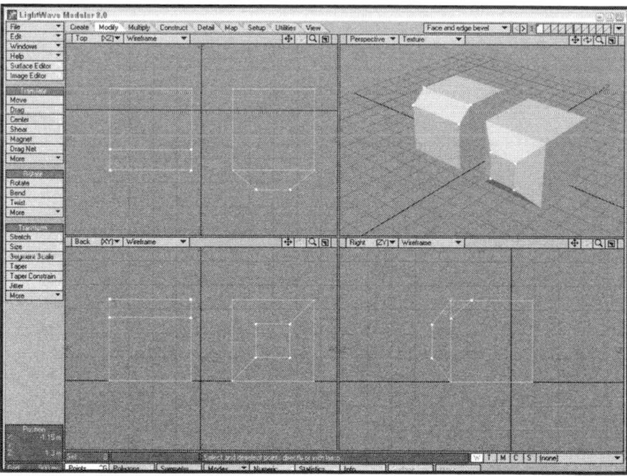

to change the shape of the bevel. Dragging up and down changes the distance the face is pushed from its original location (known as the Shift value in the Numeric panel, shown in Figure 4.2). Dragging side to side changes the size of the face (known as the Insert value in the Numeric panel). You can hold down the Shift key while dragging to constrain the change to a single value. If you enter a negative shift value, the face is pushed within the object. If you enter a negative inset value, the face size increases in size so that it is larger than the original face. Use the +/- setting in the Numeric panel if you want to set a range of randomness for the bevel feature.

Beveling Edges

Use the Extend, Bevel Edges (keyboard shortcut: Ctrl+b) menu command to bevel the edges of the selected polygon or the edges between all selected vertices.

Using the Rounder Tool

Use the Rounder tool to both bevel and smooth an object. You can use it on selected points, edges, polygons, or entire objects. You can use the Numeric panel to specify that you only round points or edges. You can also specify the number of rounding polygons to include. If you specify more rounding polygons, the result is a smoother edge. The Inset distance determines how much the rounded polygons encroach on the original face. Figure 4.3 shows the result of rounding the previously beveled objects using the Rounder tool with the number of rounding polygons set to 4.

Beveling Multiple Polygons as a Group

When you bevel multiple polygons with the Bevel tool, each individual polygon is copied and moved independently. To move all the selected polygons outward as a group, use the Smooth Shift tool. Using the

FIGURE 4.2
Bevel tool

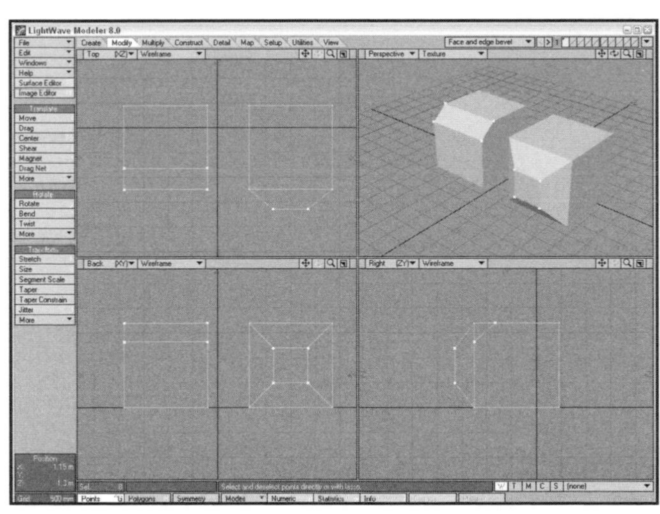

FIGURE 4.3
Objects rounded with the Rounder tool

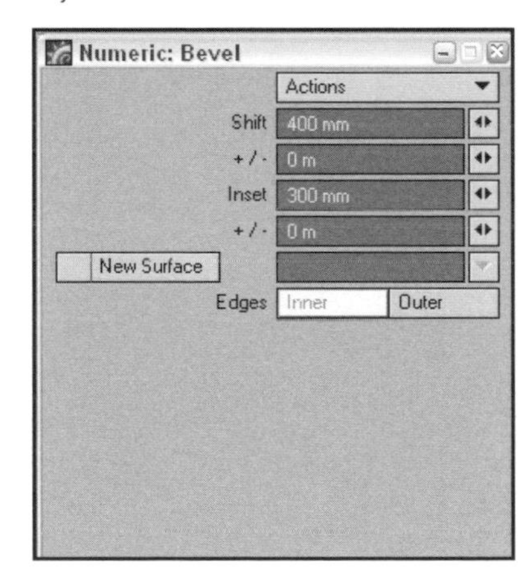

Smooth Shift tool moves each polygon along its normal, but maintains the edges between the polygons in the group. The Offset value is the amount the polygon group is moved and you can use the Scale value in the Numeric panel to scale the polygon group. Figure 4.4 shows the difference between the Smooth Shift and Bevel tools. Several polygons on each sphere were moved with each tool.

If you want to move just the vertices without creating a new face, use the Multiply, Extender Plus (keyboard shortcut: e) tool to clone the selected points. The attached edges won't be visible until you move the selected points.

You can also use the Super Shift tool to move polygons as a group away from the main object. unlike the Smooth Shift tool, you can also change the Inset value. The Super Shift tool isn't restricted to moving polygons only along their normals.

Using the Magic Bevel Tool

If you need more control over the path of the beveled polygon, try using the Multiple, Extend, More, Magic Bevel tool. When you select this tool, a light blue circular handle is displayed on the center of each polygon of the current object. You can drag this handle to bevel the selected polygon following a dragged path. In the Numeric panel, you can select from multiple operations including Extrude, Edit Path, Delete Knot, Delete Path, Uniform Spans, and Straight. By default, the Extrude operation is selected. Use this operation to click on a polygon handle and extrude it by dragging a path for the extrusion to follow. Use the Edit Path operation to edit any existing extrusions. You can use the Delete Knot and Delete Path operations to delete any knot or path that you click on. Using the

FIGURE 4.4

Left sphere shows the Smooth Shift tool; right sphere shows the Bevel tool

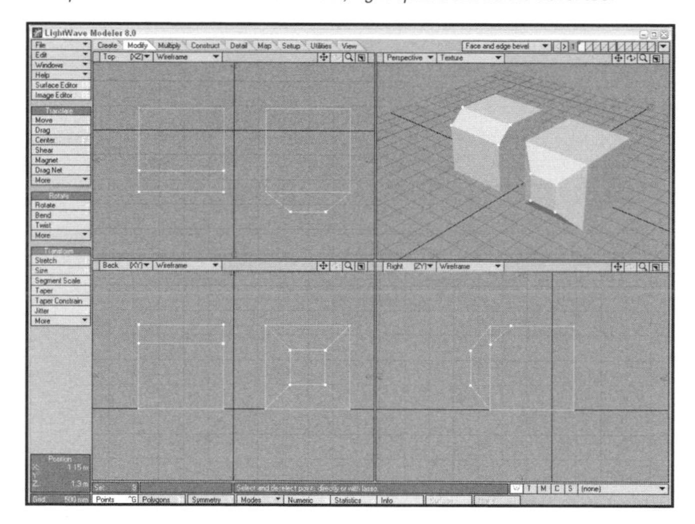

Uniform Spans operation changes the selected extrusion so that it has equally spaced segments. Using the Straight operation makes the selected extrusion run straight along its normal. There is also a Symmetry option, which you can use to enable extrusions to be symmetrical about the specified axis. Figure 4.5 shows a simple sun object created by beveling the sides of a disc object with the Magic Bevel tool.

Beveling Along a Rail

If you have a curve that you want the bevel to follow, you can use the Multiply, Extend, More, Bevel Rail tool. To use this tool, you need to place the curve on the background layer and position the shape to bevel on the foreground layer perpendicular to the curve. After you select this tool, a dialog box opens where you can set the number of Segments and Knots, and the Strength value, which determines how closely the shape hugs the rail.

Using the Router Tool

Use the Multiply, More, **Router tool** to bevel edges using one of three profile curves: Round, Hollow, and Stair Step. You can select these profile curves from the Numeric panel. You can also set the Depth, Edge Width, and Steps values. Figure 4.6 shows each of the options.

FIGURE 4.5

Sun object created with the Magic Bevel tool

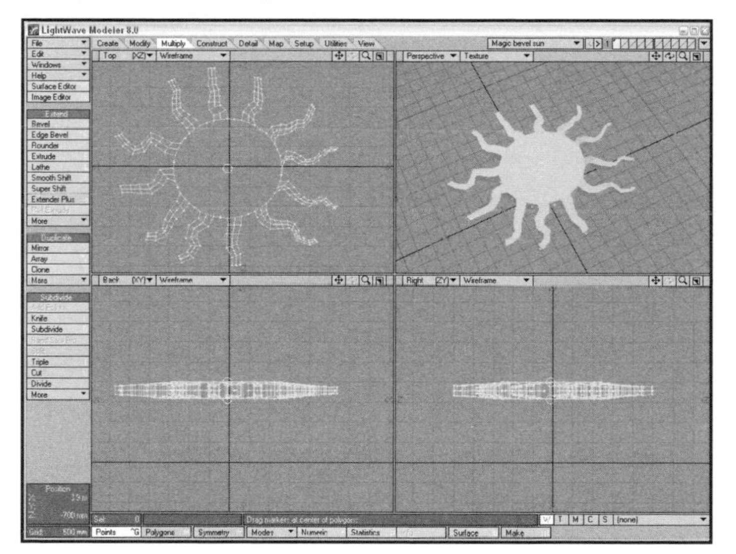

FIGURE 4.6

Router tool includes three profile curves: Round, Hollow, and Stair Step

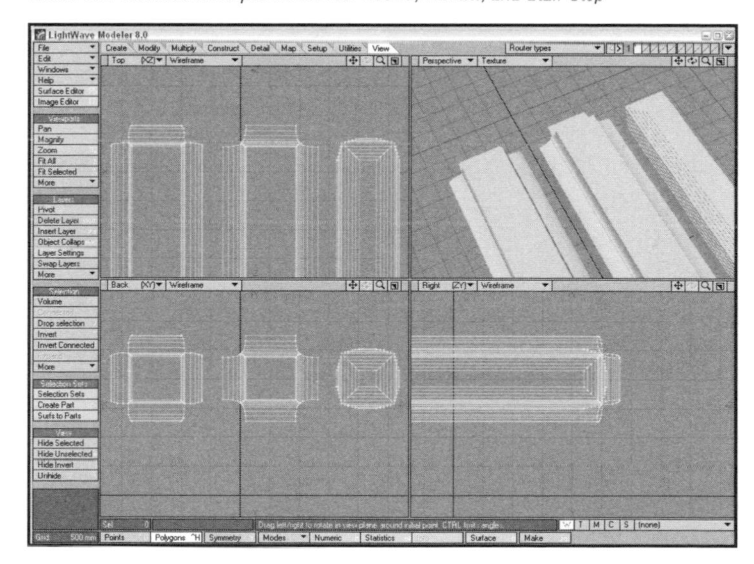

Bevel cube faces

1. Open the Modeler and select the Create menu tab.
2. Click the Box button (or press Shift+X) and drag in the Top and Back viewports to create a box object.
3. Click the Multiply menu tab, select the Bevel menu button from the Extend section, and then drag in the Top viewport to move each face out from its original location.

   The cursor changes to show that you're in bevel mode.
4. Open the Numeric panel and set the Shift value to **400** and the Inset value to **–100**.

   The bevel operation with a negative Insert value increases the size of the cube faces.
5. Click the Polygon mode button at the bottom of the interface and select just the outermost faces.
6. Click the Multiply, Extend, Bevel menu button and drag in the Top viewport again to move the selected faces out from the center of the object.
7. Open the Numeric panel and set the Shift value to **400** and the Inset value to **300**.

   The second bevel operation with a positive Insert value decreases the size of the cube faces, resulting in the object shown in Figure 4.7.
8. Select the File, Save Object As menu command and save the file as Beveled cube.lwo.

FIGURE 4.7
Beveled cube

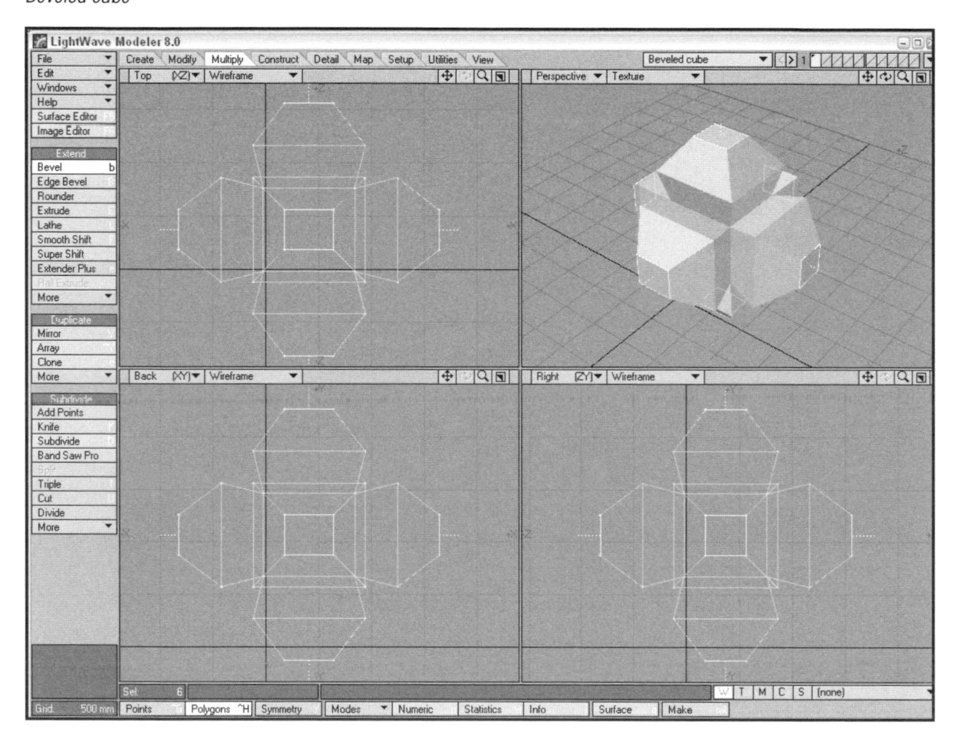

FIGURE 4.8
Beveled disc edges

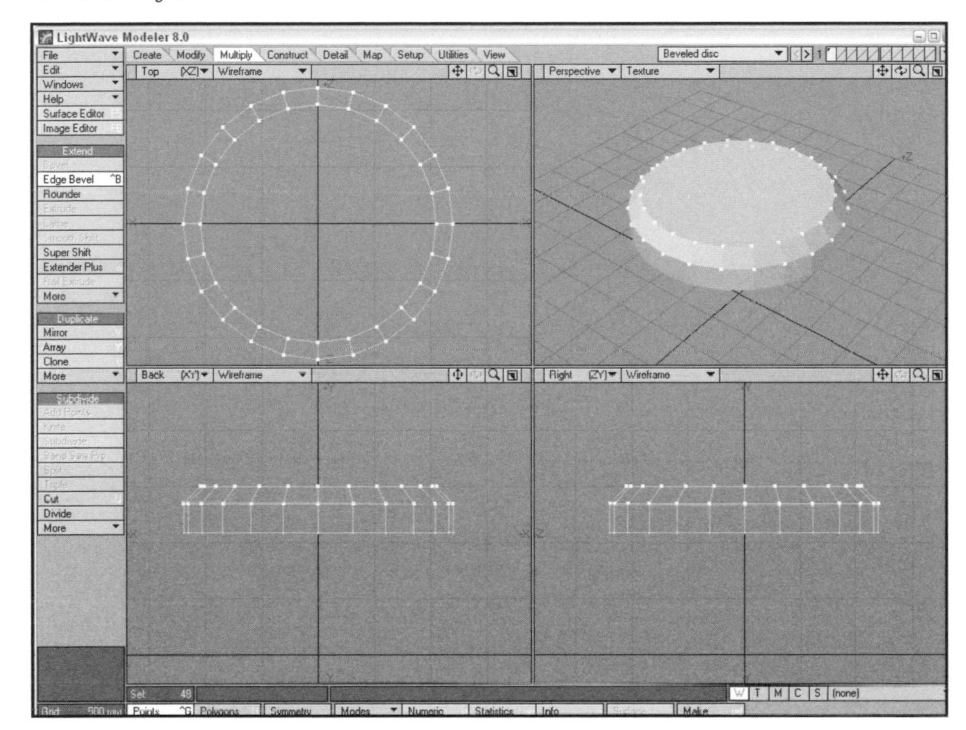

Bevel disc edges

1. Open the Modeler and select the Create menu tab.
2. Click the Disc button in the Primitives section and drag in the Top and Back viewports to create a disc object.
3. Click the Points mode button at the bottom of the interface and select the top row of vertices in the Back viewport.
4. Click the Multiply menu tab, click the Edge Bevel menu button in the Extend section, and drag in the Top viewport to bevel the top edge of the disc object.
5. Open the Numeric panel and set the Move value to **150**.

   The top edges of the disc object are beveled, as shown in Figure 4.8.
6. Select the File, Save Object As menu command and save the file as Beveled disc.lwo.

Round box edges

1. Open the Modeler and select the Create menu tab.
2. Select the More button from the Primitives section, and then click Wedge. Set the number of Sections to **4** and click OK to create a square box with a square hole in its center.

3. Click the Multiply menu tab, and then click the Rounder button in the Extend section to access the Rounder tool.
4. Open the Numeric panel and set the Rounding Polygons value to **2** and the Inset Distance to **60**. Then close the Numeric panel.

   All edges of the Wedge object are rounded with two polygons as shown in Figure 4.9.
5. Select the File, Save Object As menu command and save the file as Rounded wedge.lwo.

FIGURE 4.9
Rounded wedge

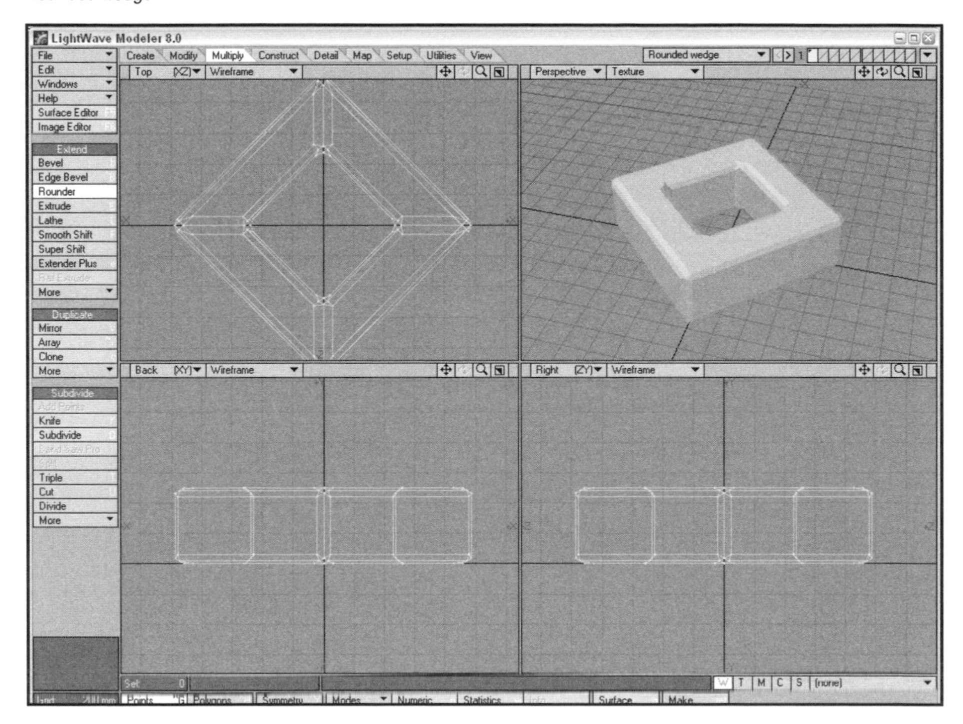

LESSON 2

EXTRUDE AND LATHE SHAPES

What You'll Do

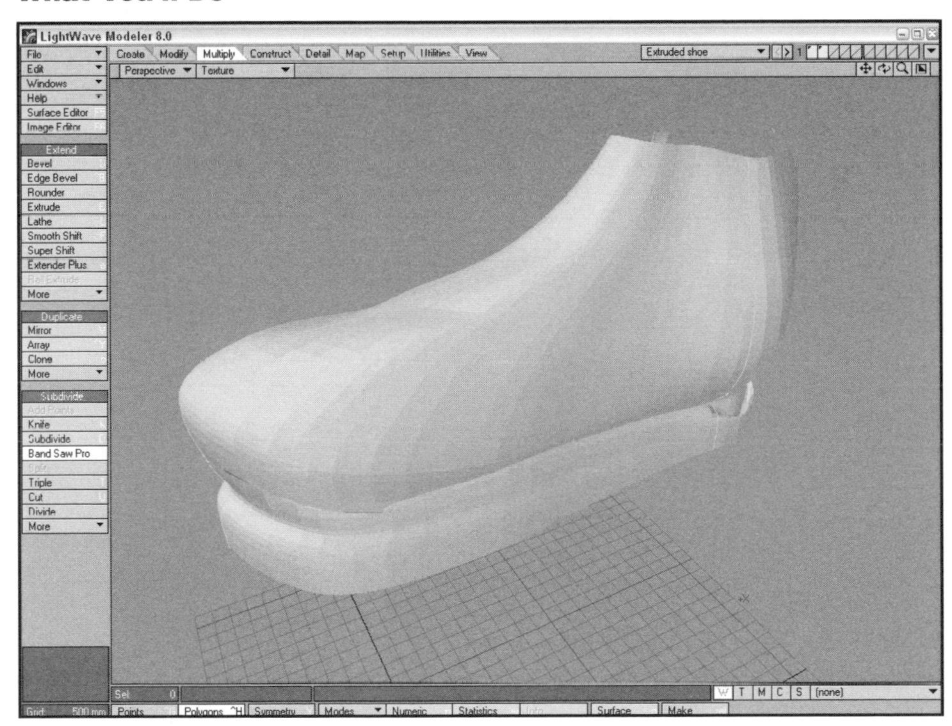

In this lesson, you'll learn how to extrude shapes, lathe curves, and extrude along a rail.

The Extrude and Lathe functions are typically used to make a 2D shape into a 3D shape using two uniquely different methods. **Extruding** works by copying the selected shape and moving it perpendicular to itself with its edges remaining attached to the original shape. The result adds depth to the shape. For example, extruding a simple square results in a cube object.

Lathing works differently than extruding. To lathe a shape, you spin the shape about an axis, making copies of the shape at regular intervals. Each copy is attached by edges to the previous one, thereby creating a 3D object that is symmetrical about its center axis. A baseball bat is a good example of an object that you can create using a lathing process.

Extruding Shapes

Use the Multiply, Extend, Extrude (E) menu command to extrude the selected polygon by dragging in the viewport. The

FIGURE 4.10
Extruded text

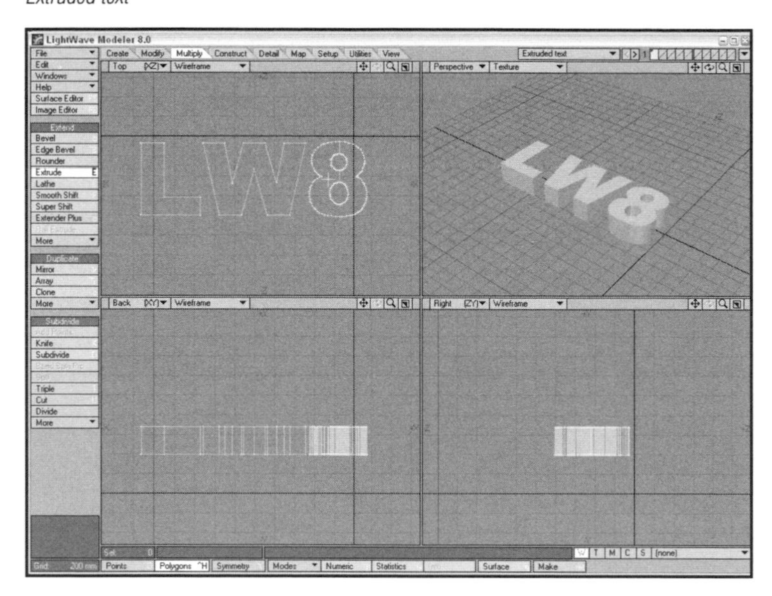

FIGURE 4.11
Lathed vase

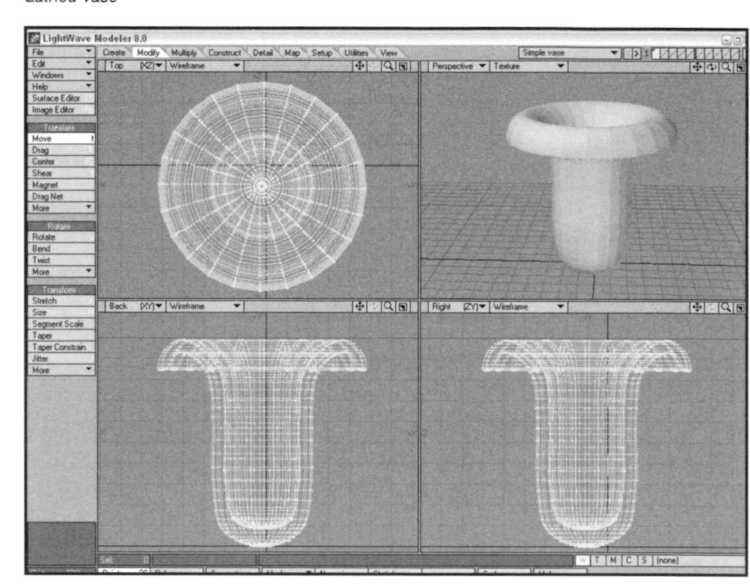

object's depth depends on the distance that you drag or the values you specify in the Numeric panel. The Numeric panel also includes a setting for the number of sides to divide the extruded section into. Figure 4.10 shows a sample text object that was extruded.

Lathing Curves

Use the Multiply, Extend, Lathe (L) menu command to revolve a selected curve or shape about an axis to create a cylindrical shaped object, like the vase in Figure 4.11, which was created by drawing a simple curve and revolving it about the Z-axis. When you click in the viewport, the point where you first click is the center about which the curve is revolved and dragging defines the axis about which the curve is revolved. You can use the Numeric panel for the Lathe tool, shown in Figure 4.12, to specify the number of sides that make up the lathed object, the axis to revolve about, and the start and end angles. You can use the left and right arrow keys to change the number of sides. Most lathed objects are revolved 360 degrees about an axis, but you can use the Start and End Angle values to revolve only portion of the way around. You can interactively change the Start and End Angle values by dragging on the handles near the center of the lathed object. You can also use the Center and Offset values to specify the center of the lathe.

FIGURE 4.12
Numeric panel for the Lathe tool

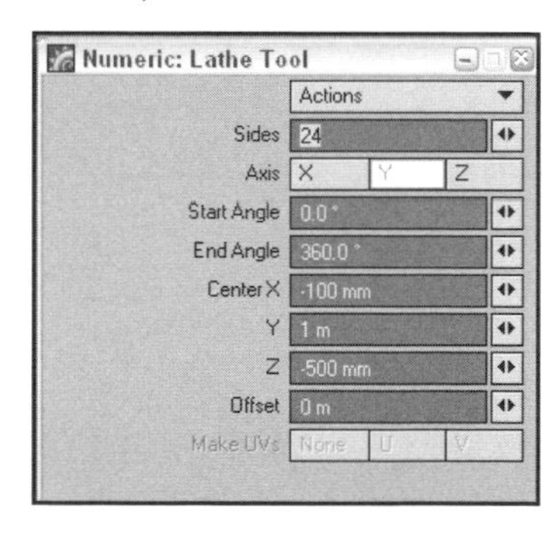

TIP

If the lathed object appears to be transparent in the Perspective view, you probably created the object in such a way that the normals are inverted and pointing inward. To correct the problem, select the object and choose the Detail, Polygons, Flip command to switch the direction of the normals.

Extruding Along a Rail

You can use the Multiply, Extend, Rail Extrude tool to add depth to a selected polygon. This tool is similar to the Extrude tool, but instead of moving perpendicular in a straight line, when you use the Rail Extrude tool, you can specify a **rail curve** for the extrusion to follow. To use this tool, the rail curve should be in the background layer and the selected shape in the foreground layer. Figure 4.13 shows a heart shape extruded along a rail. If multiple rail curves are in the background layer, each curve is included to create the final object.

FIGURE 4.13

Rail extrusion

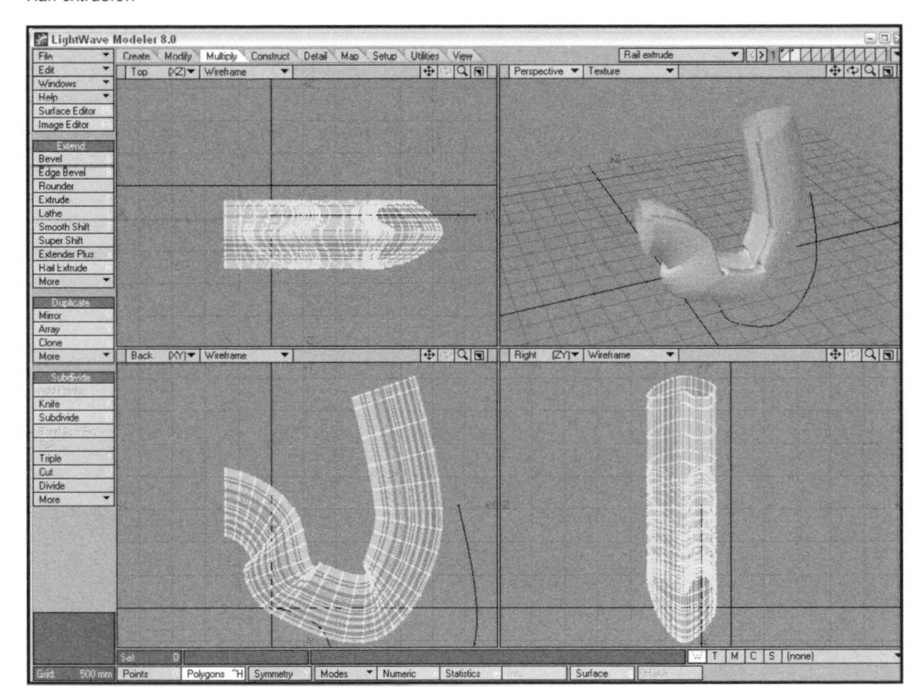

Extrude a plus sign shape

1. Choose the File, Load Object menu command and open the Plus sign.lwo file.

   This file includes a simple polygon in the shape of a plus sign.

2. Click the Polygons selection mode button at the bottom of the interface and drag over the polygon shape to select it.
3. Click the Multiply menu tab and select the Extrude menu button from the Extend menu. Then drag downward in the Back viewport.

   The polygon shape is extruded, as shown in Figure 4.14.

4. Select the File, Save Object As menu command and save the file as Extruded plus sign.lwo.

Lathe a curve to create a rolling pin

1. Choose the File, Load Object menu command and open the Rolling pin curve.lwo file.

   This file includes a simple curve that shows the profile of a rolling pin.

2. With none of the curve's points selected, click the Multiply menu tab and select the Lathe menu button from the Extend section.

FIGURE 4.14
Extruded shape

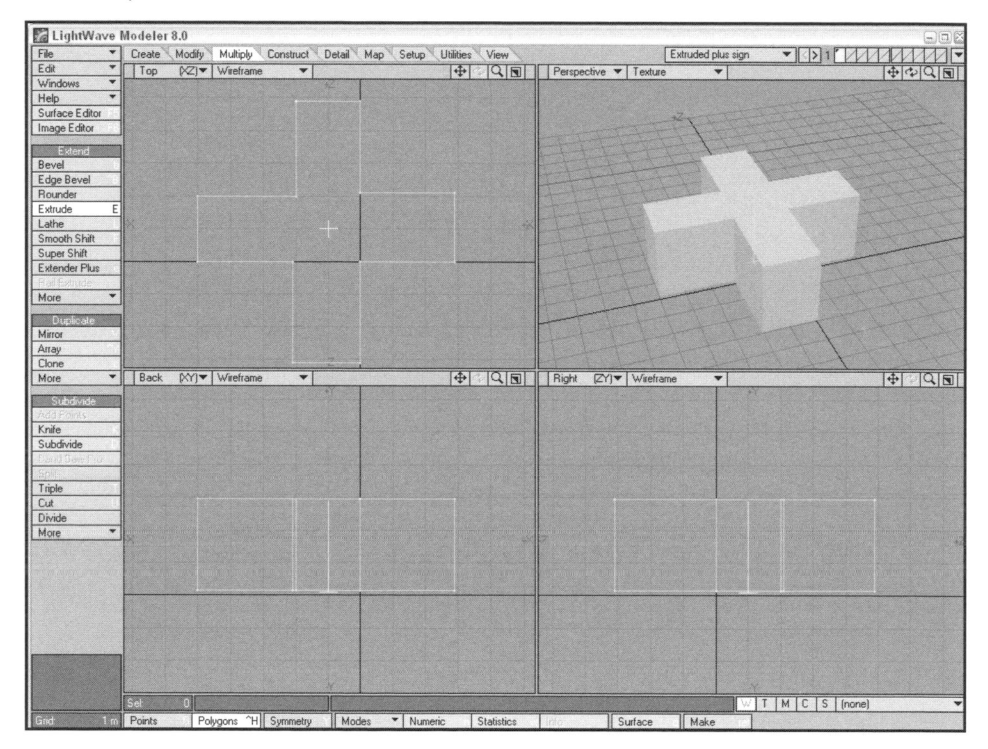

FIGURE 4.15
Rolling pin

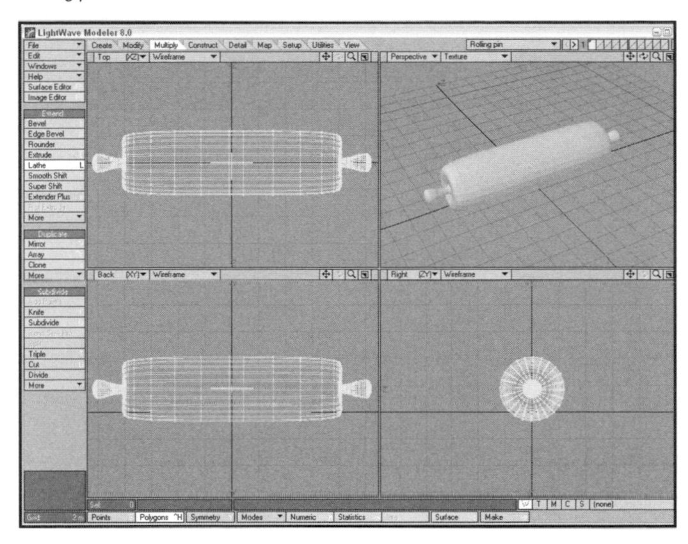

FIGURE 4.16
Extruded shoe created with Rail Extrude

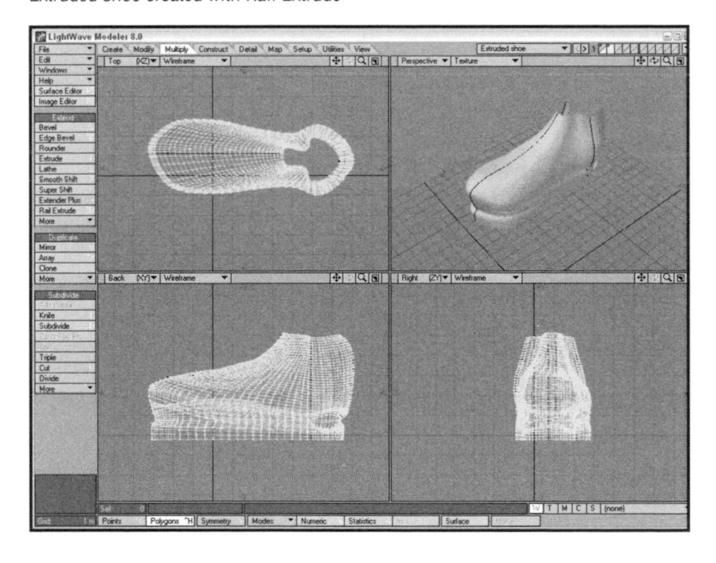

3. Drag horizontally to the left in the Top viewport to define the revolving axis.

   The rolling pin is created with six sides.

4. Open the Numeric panel and set the number of sides to **24** to create the object shown in Figure 4.15.

5. Select the File, Save Object As menu command and save the file as Rolling pin.lwo.

Create a shoe with Rail Extrude

1. Choose the File, Load Object menu command and open the Shoe extrusion curves.lwo file.

   This file includes an outline of a shoe footprint in the foreground layer and four profile curves in the background layer.

2. Make sure that the curves are on the background layer and the shoe object is on the foreground layer. Click the Multiply menu tab and select the Rail Extrude menu button on the Extend section.

   The Rail Extrude: Multiple dialog box appears.

3. Select the Length and Automatic buttons with a Strength value of **2.0** and click OK.

   The polygon is extruded following the curves on each side to create the shoe shown in Figure 4.16.

4. Select the File, Save Object As menu command and save the file as Extruded shoe.lwo.

LESSON 3

CREATE SPECIALIZED OBJECTS

What You'll Do

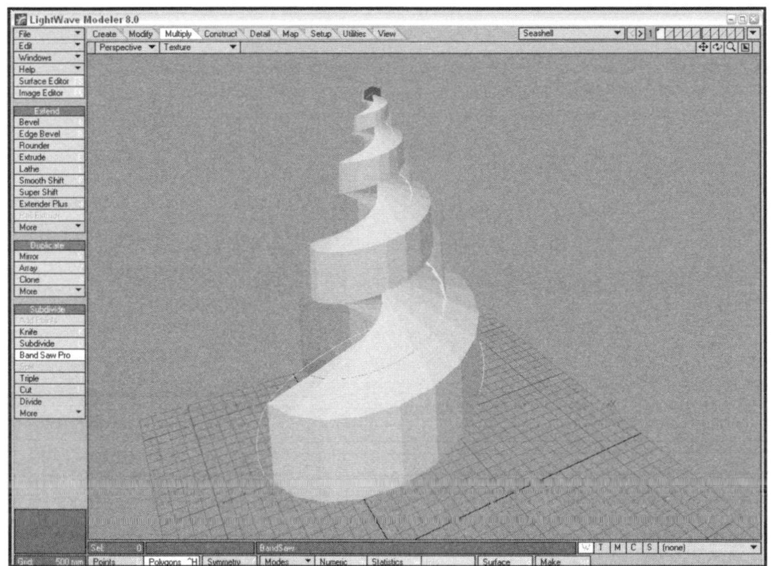

In this lesson, you'll learn how to create unique objects like seashells, and spiked and skinned objects.

The Extend, More menu includes several tools you can use to create specialized object types like seashells, spiky objects, skins, and **morphs**. You can create these unique object types using other means, but using these tools will save you time.

Using the Seashell Tool

Use the Extend, More, Seashell tool to make, you guessed it, seashells. It can be tricky to manually model seashells with their intricate spiraling patterns. The seashell object starts as a single polygon that defines the cross section of the seashell. You can use the Numeric panel, shown in Figure 4.17, to specify the spiral axis, number of loops, and the sides, shift, and scale per loop.

FIGURE 4.17
Seashell Numeric panel

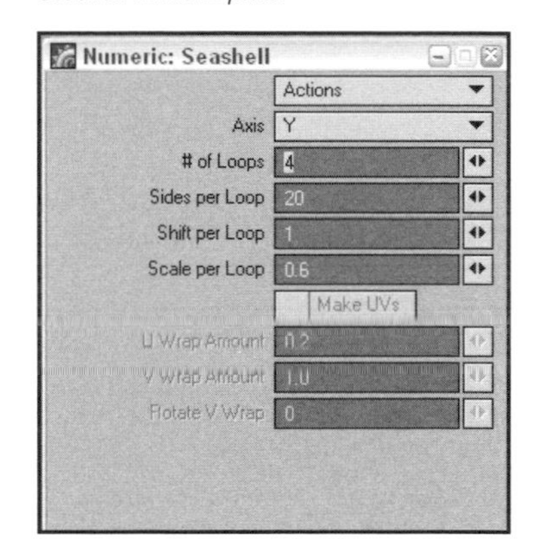

Making Objects Spikey

Using the Multiply, Extend, More, Spikey tool places a vertex at the center of the selected polygons and extrudes these center points to create spikes for all selected polygons. You can specify a Spike Factor, which determines the length of the spikes, in the Numeric panel. Figure 4.18 shows a simple disc object that has a Spike Factor of 60 percent.

Creating Skin Objects

You can create skin objects by connecting several polygon shapes using the Multiply, Extend, More, Create Skin menu command. The shapes can be different and do not need to have the same numbers of points. The order that the skin follows depends on the order in which you created the polygon shapes. Figure 4.19 shows a skin object created from two dissimilar polygon shapes.

Creating Objects by Morphing Polygons

You can also create objects by morphing between two polygons using the Multiply, Extend, More, Morph Polygon tool. This tool requires that the polygons that are included in the morphing operation have the same number of points. It is best to create a duplicate of one of the polygons and

FIGURE 4.18
Spikey disc object

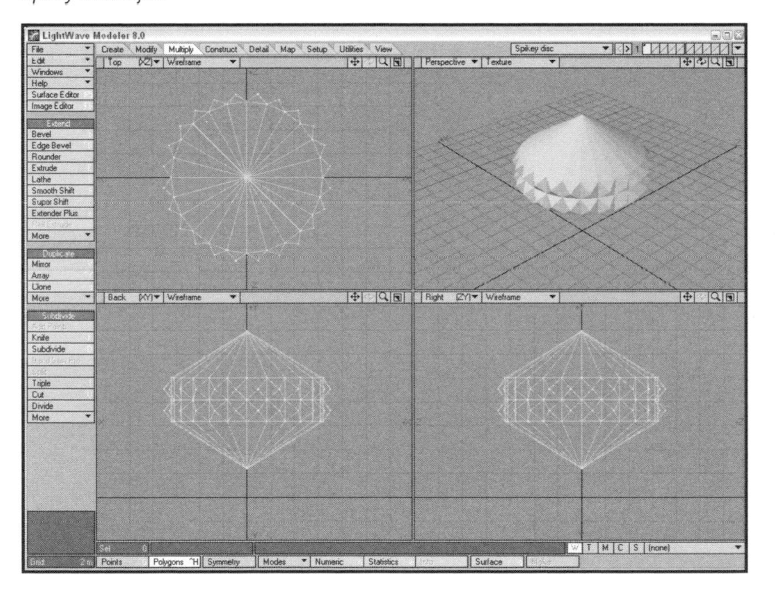

FIGURE 4.19
Skin object

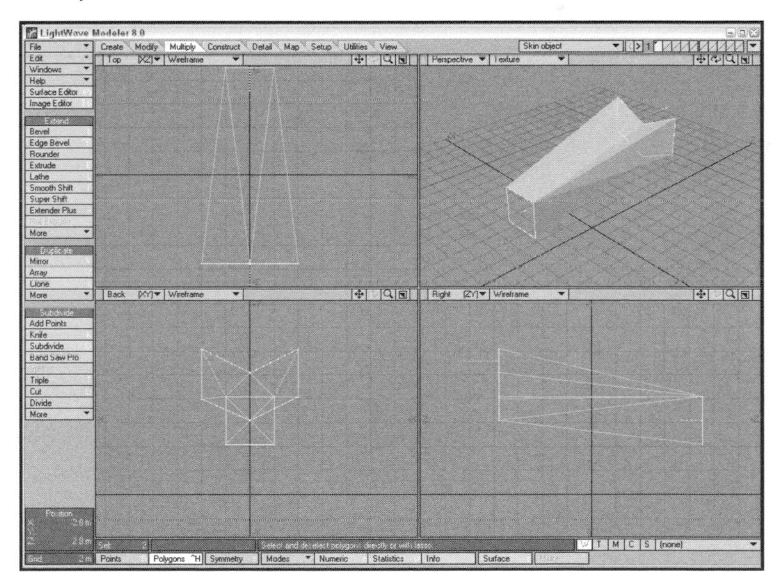

make changes by moving the duplicate's points. After you select this tool, a dialog box opens where you can specify the number of segments to use to create the surface. Figure 4.20 shows a simple polygon morph object created by morphing together two polygons with the same number of points.

FIGURE 4.20
Polygon morph object

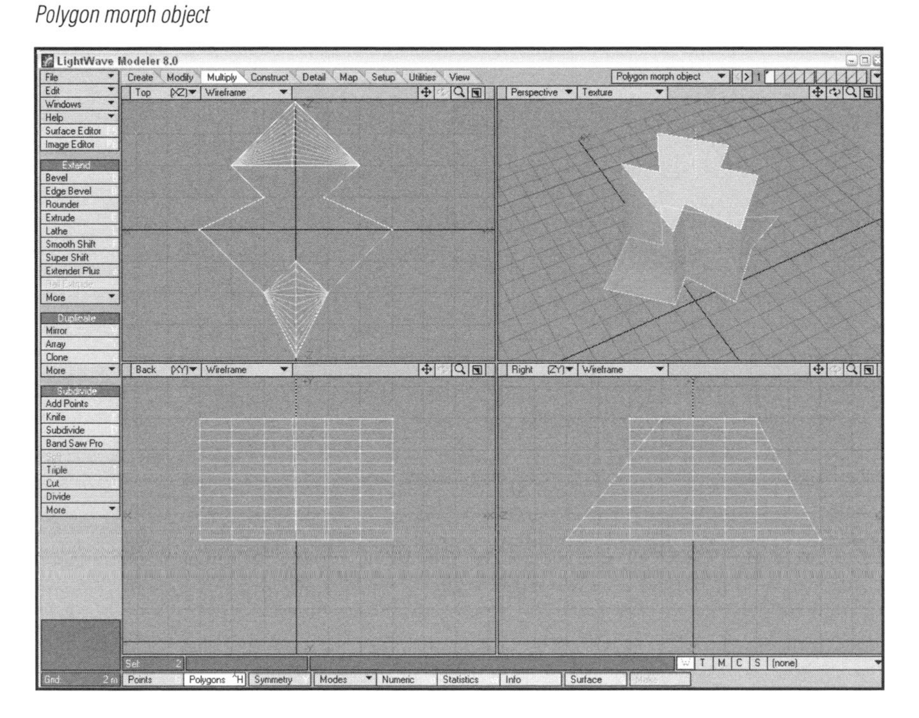

FIGURE 4.21
Seashell

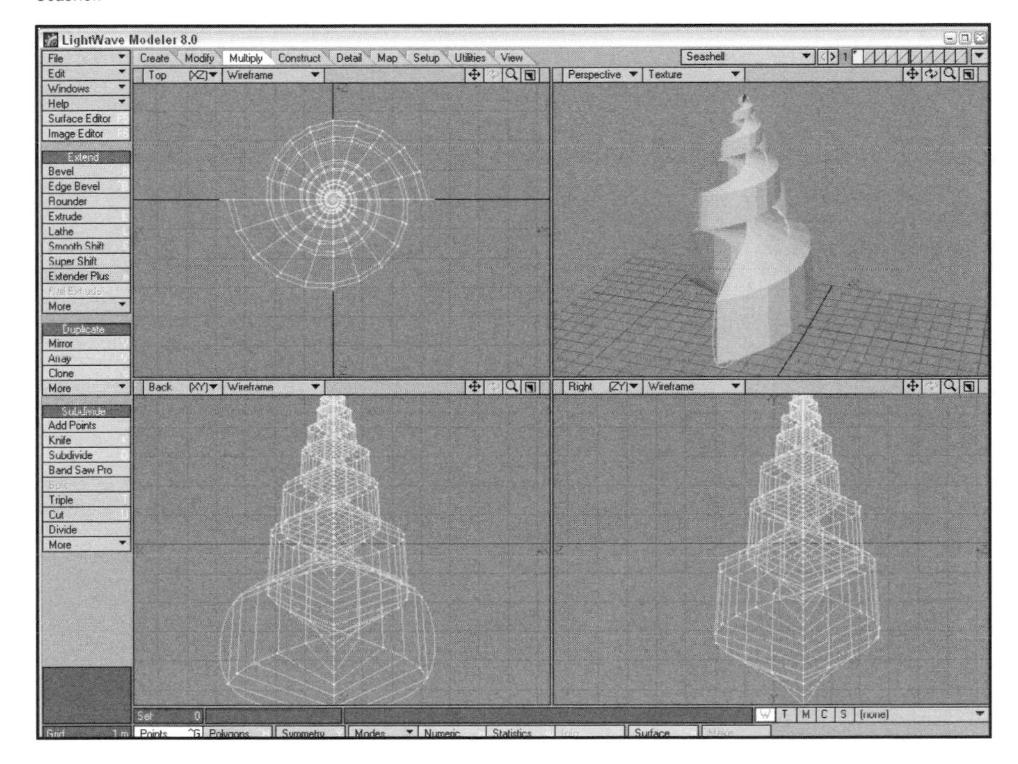

Create a seashell object

1. Open the Modeler and select the Create menu tab.
2. Click the Spline Draw button on the Curves menu and create a simple closed ellipse in the Back viewport. Press Enter.

   The Seashell feature needs a cross section polygon shape to start with.
3. With the cross section polygon selected, click the Multiply menu tab and select the More, Seashell menu command from the Extend menu.
4. Open the Numeric panel, set the Axis to **Y**, the number of Loops to **4**, and the Shift per Loop to **8**.

   The resulting seashell is shown in Figure 4.21. Note that the actual seashell might look much different from the one in the figure, depending on the original ellipse.
5. Select the File, Save Object As menu command and save the file as Seashell.lwo.

Create a spikey ball

1. Open the Modeler and select the Create menu tab.
2. Click the Ball button and drag in the Top and Back viewports to create a ball object.

3. Open the Numeric panel and set the number of Sides to **12** and the number of Segments to **6**. Then close the Numeric panel.
4. Select the Polygons mode button from the bottom of the interface and select all the center polygons that make up the middle of the ball object, without selecting the end polygons.
5. Click the Multiply menu tab and select the More, Spikey Tool from the Extend menu Then drag to the right in any of the viewports to extend the spikes from the selected polygons.

   The resulting spikey ball object is shown in Figure 4.22.
6. Select the File, Save Object As menu command and save the file as Spikey ball.lwo.

Create a megaphone skin

1. Choose the File, Load Object menu command and open the Megaphone cross sections.lwo file.

   This file includes several cross section curves positioned to create a megaphone object.

FIGURE 4.22
Spikey ball

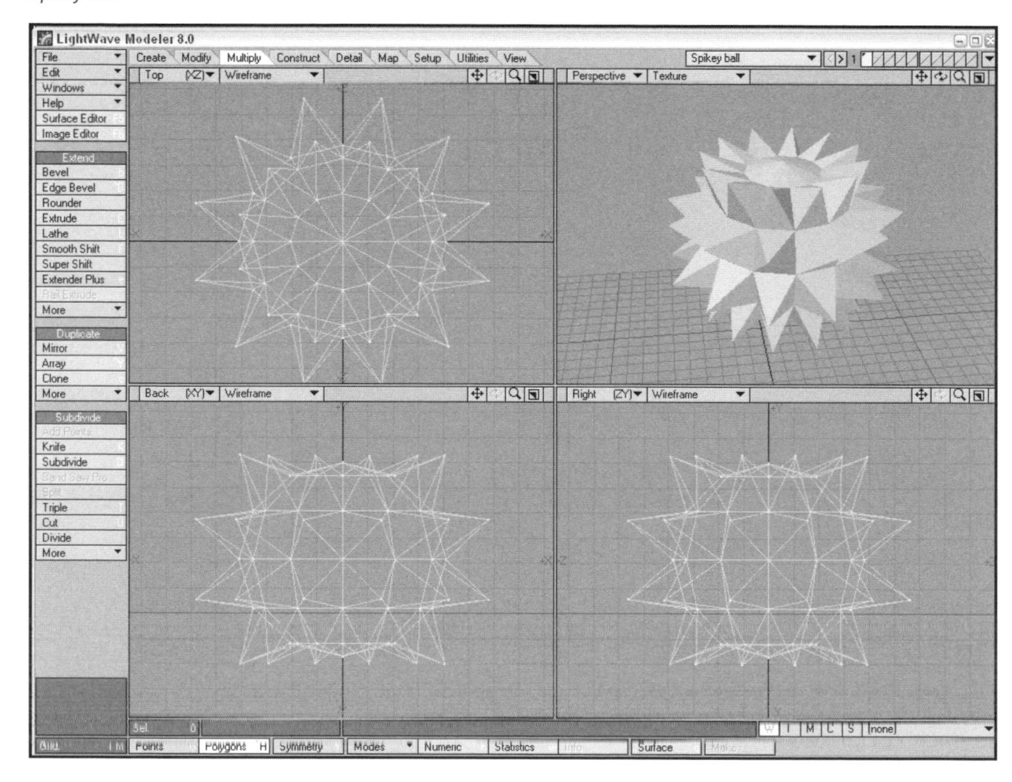

FIGURE 4.23

Megaphone created by skinning curves

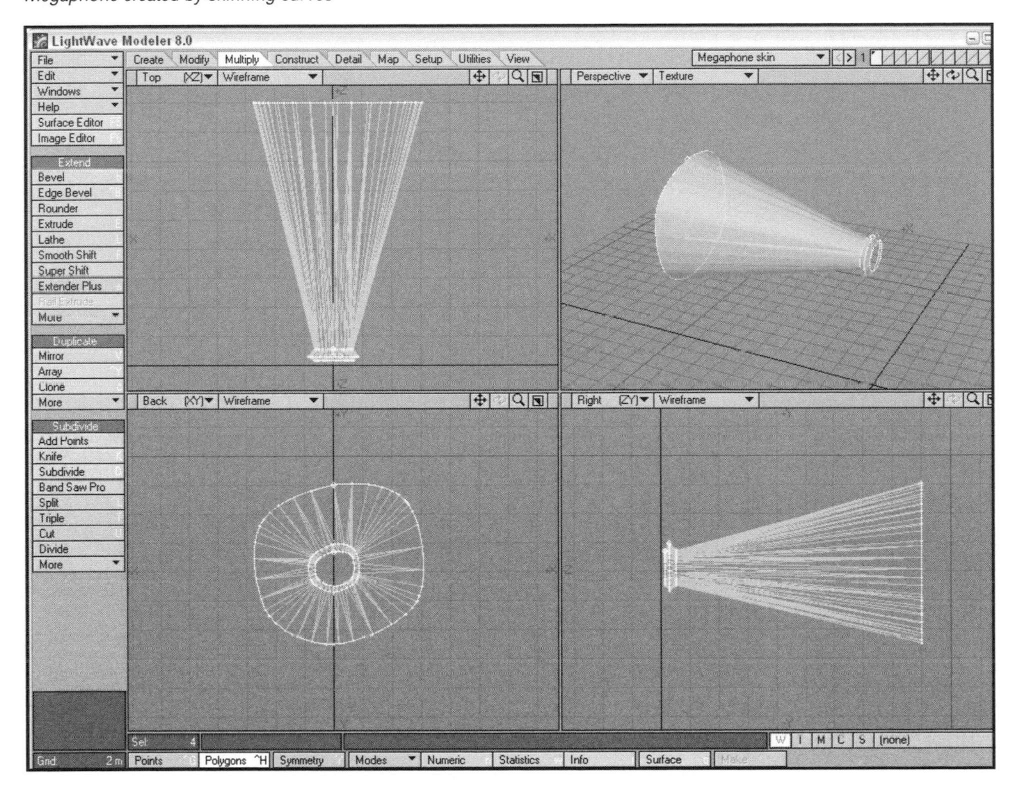

2. Select all of the polygons, click the Multiply menu tab and select the More, Create Skin menu command from the Extend menu.

   The curves are skinned in the order they were created producing a megaphone object, shown in Figure 4.23.

3. Select the File, Save Object As menu command and save the file as Megaphone skin.lwo.

LESSON 4

DUPLICATE OBJECTS

What You'll Do

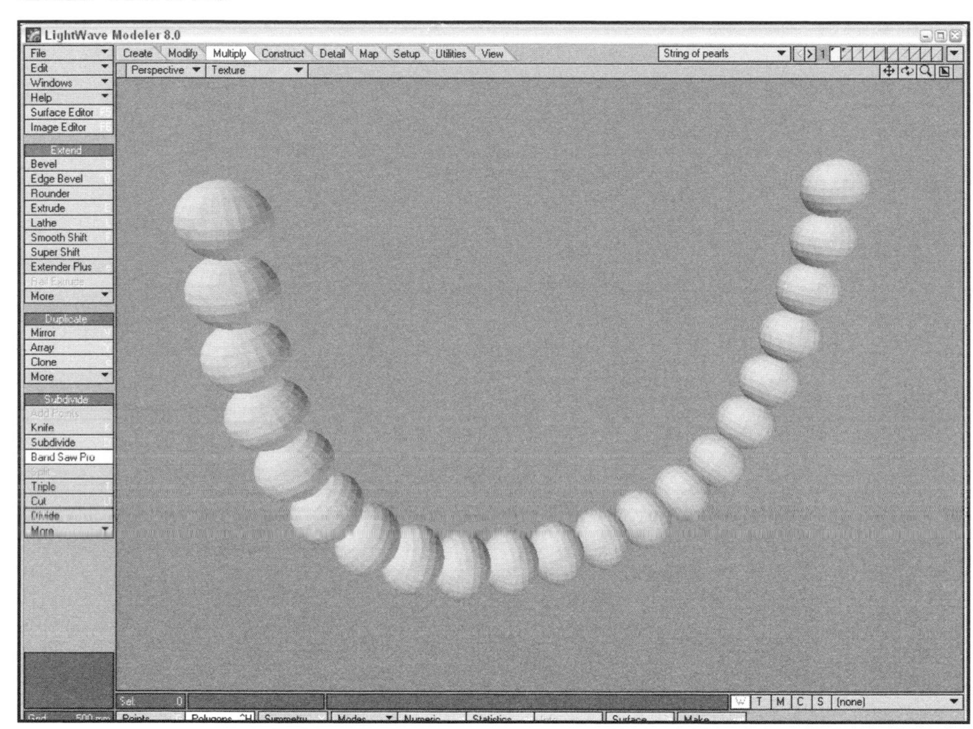

In this lesson, you'll learn how to mirror and clone objects along a rail.

They say that you can never have too much of a good thing, and with LightWave's Duplicate features, creating more of a good thing is easy. LightWave includes several different ways to create duplicate objects, including mirroring and cloning. You can also clone objects using the Edit, Cut, Copy, and Paste menu commands.

Mirroring Objects

The first available command in the Duplicate section of the Multiply menu tab is Mirror (keyboard shortcut: V). When you select this tool, you can click and drag in the viewport to set the mirror axis. After drawing the axis, you can select it and move it about to position the mirrored objects. If you selected the Free Rotation option in the Numeric panel, you can rotate the mirror axis. To constrain the rotation to 15 degree increments, hold down the Ctrl key. If you want to merge points that overlap along the midsection, use the Merge Points option. For objects that have symmetry, such as a human character or a robot, you can use the Mirror tool to save half the time. Figure 4.24 shows a simple curve mirrored about its center axis.

Cloning Objects

Using the Multiply, Duplicate, Clone tool (keyboard shortcut: c) opens a dialog box, shown in Figure 4.25, where you can specify the number of clones to create and the Offset, Scale, Rotation, and Center values for the clone for each axis. Use this dialog box, which is similar to the Array dialog box, to create an **array** of objects that grow smaller or larger, rotate about an axis, or move gradually to a new position like a set of stairs. If you want each clone to be on a different layer, use the Multiply, Duplicate, More, Clone to Layer tool.

> **NOTE**
>
> Cloned objects that you do not move to a different location appear directly on top of the existing object, which can make it difficult for you to select them.

FIGURE 4.24

Use the Mirror command to mirror curves or polygons

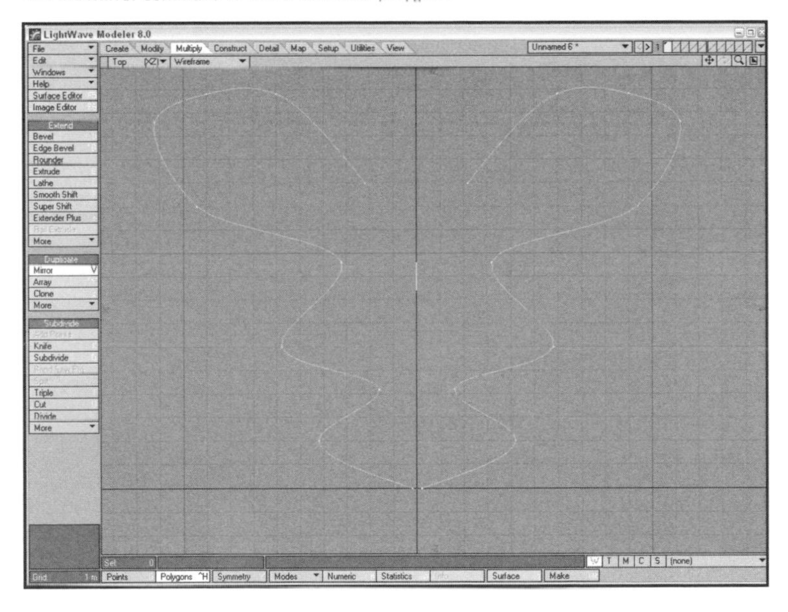

FIGURE 4.25

Clone dialog box

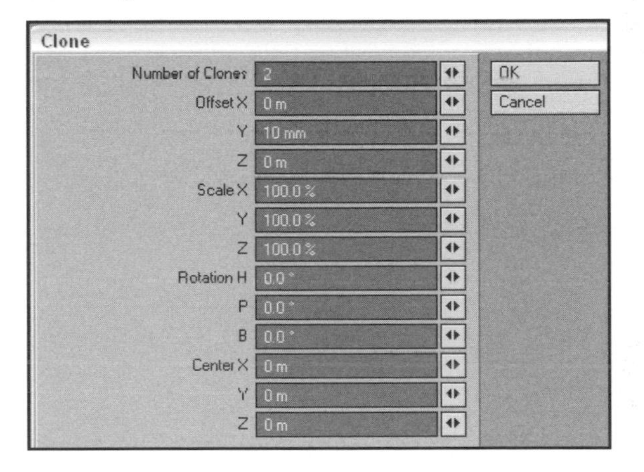

Replacing Points with Objects

The Multiply, Duplicate, More, Particle Clone tool is an interesting tool that you can use to create a neat effect. Use this tool to replace the points of any object in the background layer with the object in the foreground layer. Figure 4.26 shows the result of a small ball object replacing the points of a box object.

Cloning Along a Rail

The Multiply, Duplicate, More, Rail Clone tool works just like the Rail Extrude tool, except each clone along the path is separate. The rail curve to follow must be in the background layer and the object to clone must be in the foreground layer. If multiple rail curves are on the background layer, then the first curve is followed to create the clones and the other curves shape the object being cloned.

FIGURE 4.26

Particle clone object

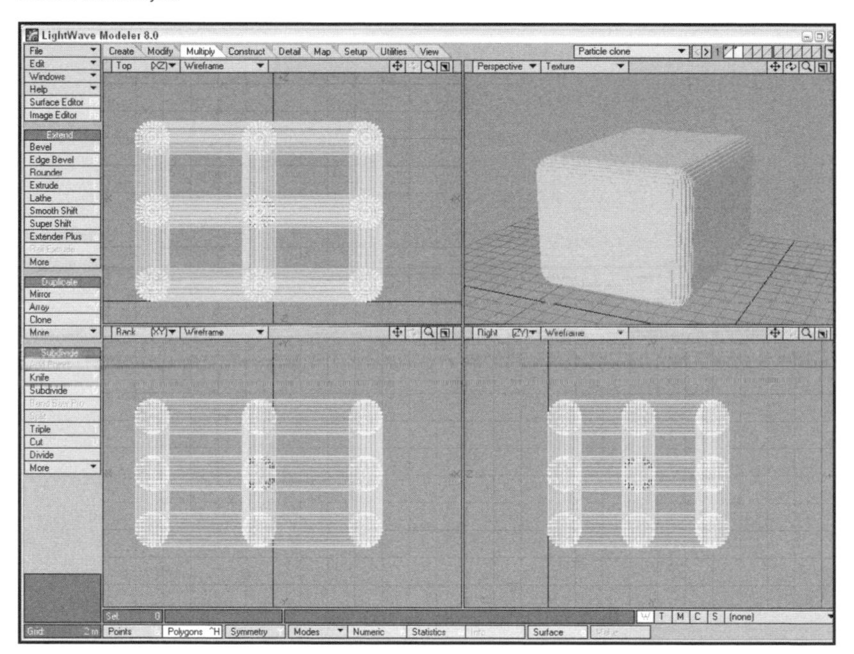

FIGURE 4.27
Mirrored shoes

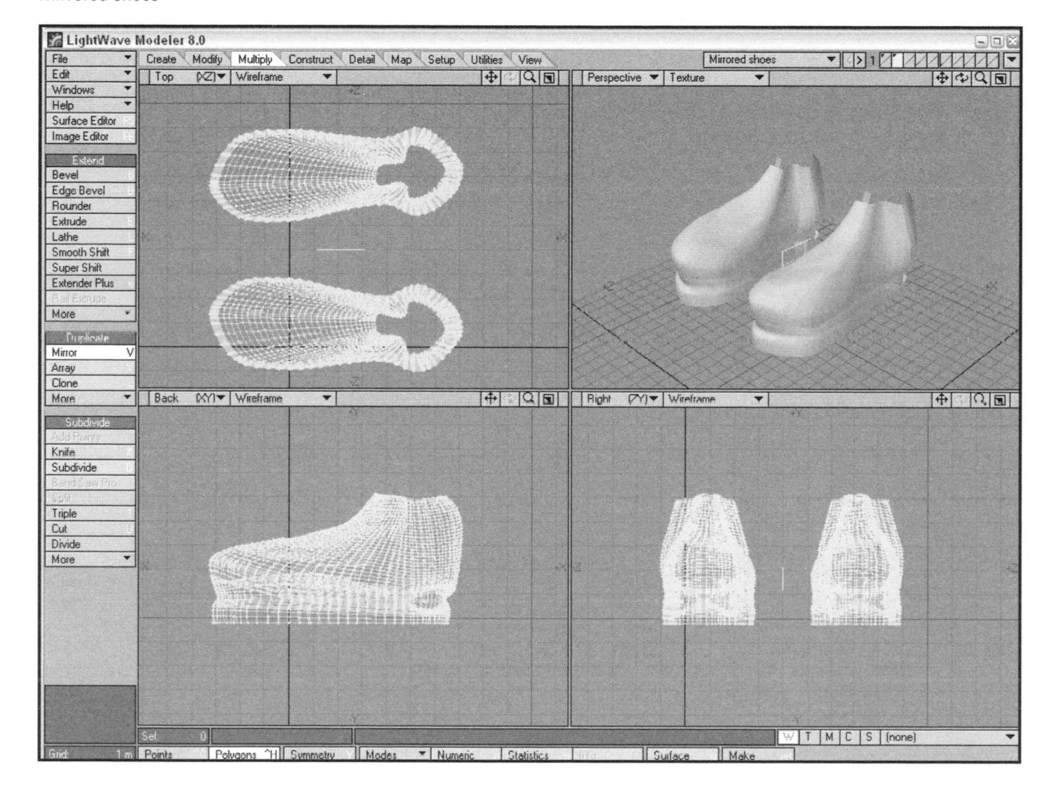

Mirror shoes

1. Choose the File, Load Object menu command and open the Extruded shoe.lwo file.
2. Select the Multiply menu tab and click the Mirror menu button on the Duplicate menu.
3. Drag horizontally in the Top viewport above the shoe.

   A mirrored duplicate of the shoe is created, as shown in Figure 4.27.
4. Select the File, Save Object As menu command and save the file as Mirrored shoes.lwo.

Create a set of stairs

1. Open the Modeler interface and select the Create menu set.
2. Click the Box button and drag in the Top and Back viewports to create a long thin box object that looks like a single stair.
3. Click the Multiply menu tab, and then select the Clone button on the Duplicate menu.

   The Clone dialog box opens.

4. In the Clone dialog box, set the number of Clones to **12**, the Y Offset to **1 m**, and the Z Offset to **2 m**. Then click OK.

   The single box object is cloned 12 times and the position is moved for each, as shown in Figure 4.28.

5. Select the File, Save Object As menu command and save the file as Stairs.lwo.

Create a string of pearls

1. Choose the File, Load Object menu command and open the Rail clone path.lwo file.

   This file includes a simple ball object in the foreground layer and a spline path in the background layer.

2. Select the Multiply menu tab and click the More, Rail Clone menu button on the Duplicate menu.

   The Rail Clone: Single dialog box opens.

3. Click OK.

   The foreground ball object is cloned along the rail curve, as shown in Figure 4.29.

4. Select the File, Save Object As menu command and save the file as String of pearls.lwo.

FIGURE 4.28
Stairs

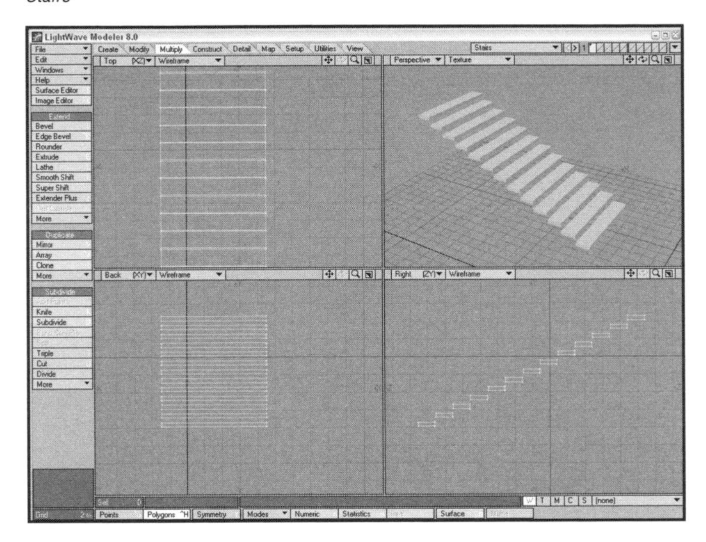

FIGURE 4.29
String of pearls

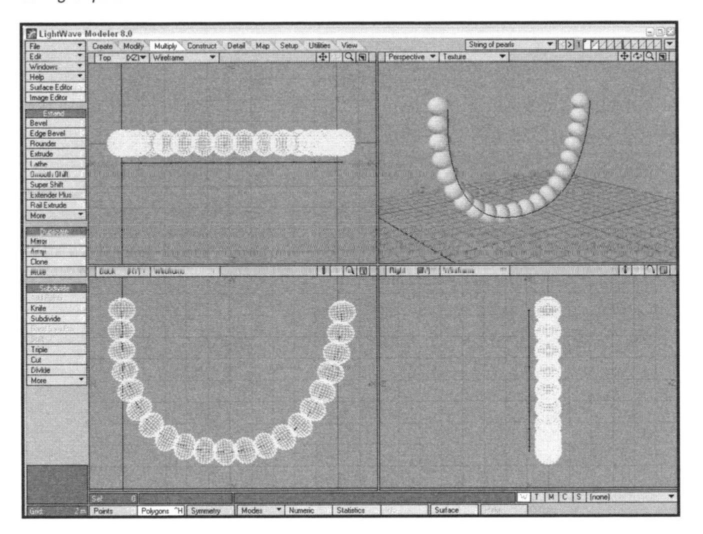

WORK WITH ARRAYS

What You'll Do

In this lesson, you'll learn how to create a rectangular and radial array of objects.

Using the Array dialog box, you can create an array of objects using all three dimensions. You can use this feature to create a huge number of regularly spaced objects and add some variety to the created objects using the Jitter commands.

Creating a Rectangular Array

If you need to create a lot of objects quickly, use the Multiply, Duplicate, Array tool (keyboard shortcut: Ctrl+y) to open the Array dialog box, shown in Figure 4.30. You can use the Array tool to create rectangular and radial type arrays. For Rectangular type arrays, you can specify the number of objects for each dimension, a Jitter value for creating some randomness, and the Scale value (for the Automatic setting) or Offset values (for the Manual setting). If you use the Automatic setting and set all dimensions to 100% scale, the object will be positioned end to end throughout the entire array.

Creating a Radial Array

You can use the Array tool to create radial arrays by selecting the Radial button at the top of the dialog box. When you use the Radial array type, you can specify the number of elements to include, the axis, and the radial center point.

FIGURE 4.30
Array dialog box

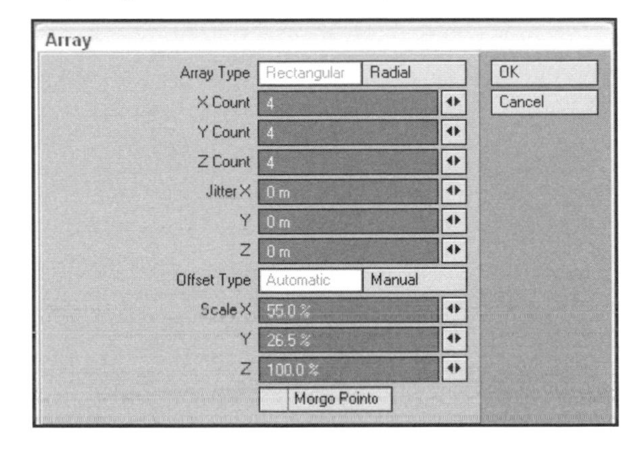

FIGURE 4.31
Array of boxes

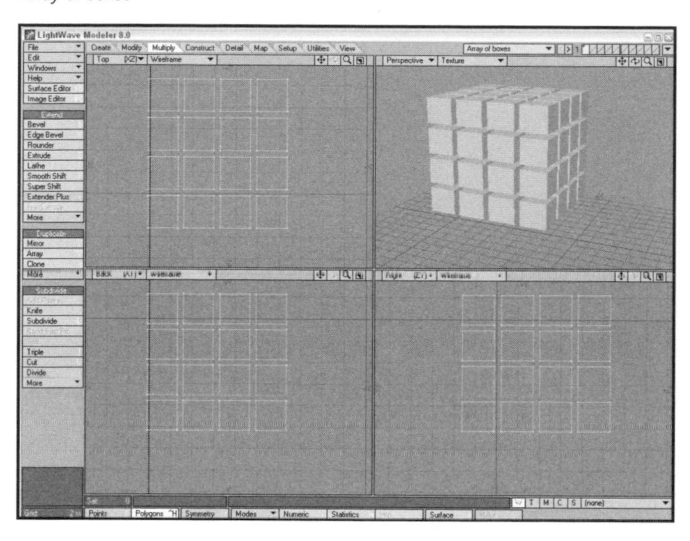

FIGURE 4.32
Radial array

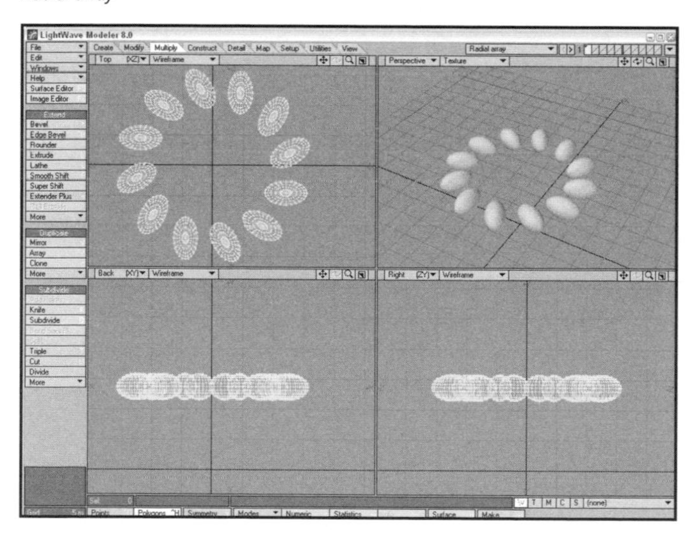

Create an array of boxes

1. Open the Modeler and select the Create tab.
2. Click the Box button and drag in the Top and Back viewports to create a box object.
3. Select the Multiply menu tab and click the Array menu button from the Duplicate menu.

   The Array dialog box opens.
4. In the Array dialog box, set the X, Y, and Z Count values to **4** and the X, Y, and Z Scale values to **120%**. Then click OK.

   An array of boxes is created, as shown in Figure 4.31.
5. Select the File, Save Object As menu command and save the file as Array of boxes.lwo.

Create a radial array

1. Open the Modeler and select the Create menu set.
2. Click the Ball button and drag in the Top and Back viewports to create a ball object that is elliptical.
3. Select the Multiply menu tab and click the Array menu button on the Duplicate menu.

   The Array dialog box opens.
4. In the Array dialog box, click the Radial button, set the Number value to **12**, and click OK.

   An array of ball objects is created, as shown in Figure 4.32.
5. Select the File, Save As menu command and save the file as Radial array.lwo.

LESSON 6

SUBDIVIDE OBJECTS

What You'll Do

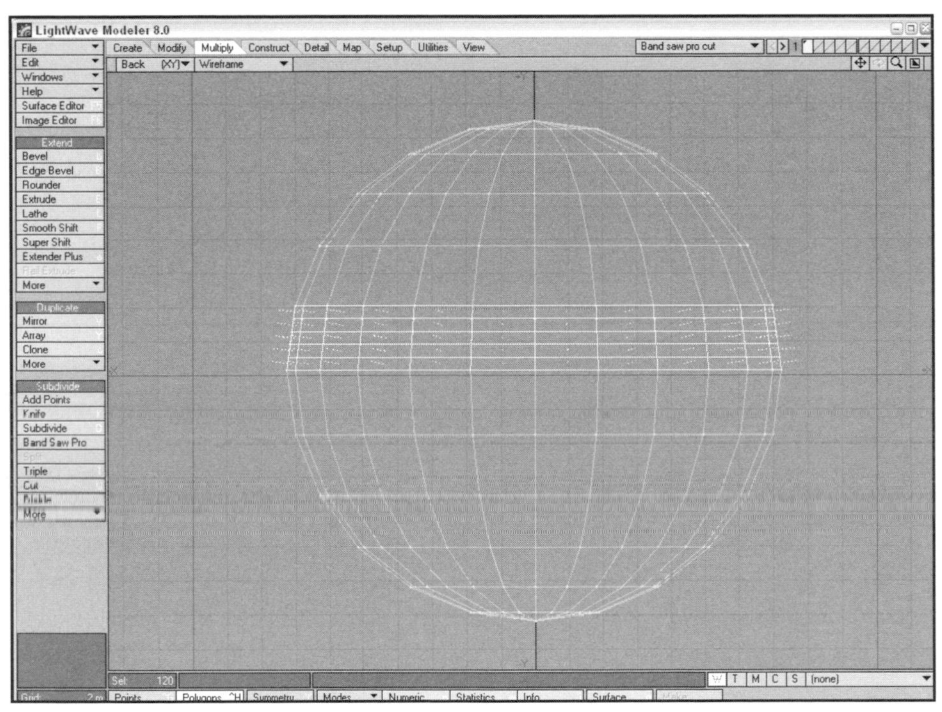

In this lesson, you'll learn how to subdivide objects using the Knife tool, the Subdivide feature, the Band Saw Pro tool, and the Cut tool.

As you model, there are many occasions where you'll need to subdivide the selected polygons. For example, you might need to add new points, cut a polygon in half, or increase the overall resolution. The commands on the Multiply, Subdivide menu can help.

Adding Points to a Polygon

Points are closely tied to polygons and adding a new point in the exact place you need it is a common task. You can do this with the Multiply, Subdivide, Add Points tool. Note that you can only add points to edges with this tool. Before you can use this tool, you need to select both polygons that make up the polygon edge. Then simply click where you want the new point to go. Another way to add points to the midpoint of every selected polygon or between every set of adjacent points is to use the Divide tool.

Using the Knife Tool

You can use the Knife tool to set a slice plane that cuts through the entire object or only through the selected polygons. After you select the Knife tool (keyboard shortcut: K), drag in the viewports to position the tool. You can drag the handles on either end of the tool to reposition it. Press Enter to perform the slice operation and add a new edge wherever the Knife tool intersects a polygon. This tool is handy for adding new segments to an object. Figure 4.33 shows the Knife tool in action. The ellipse in the Right viewport shows a preview of where the cuts will be.

FIGURE 4.33
The Knife tool

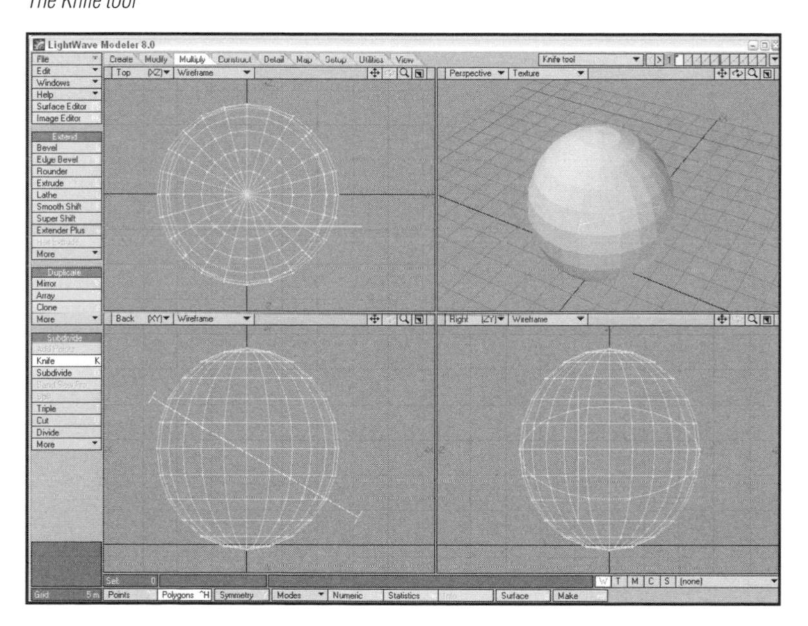

Subdividing Polygons

When you subdivide a polygon, the single polygon is broken down into several polygons, increasing its resolution. Use the Multiply, Subdivide, Subdivide menu command to open the dialog box, shown in Figure 4.34, where you can select from three different subdivision methods: Faceted, Smooth, and Metaform. The Faceted method simply adds new faces without altering the shape of the object. The Smooth method positions the subdivided polygons to make the object smoother following the existing curvature of the object. The Metaform method adaptively subdivides the areas of greater detail more aggressively than it does for areas of little change. The Subdivide Polygons dialog box also includes a Fractal value that you can use to randomly distort the center point's location.

NOTE

Another way to subdivide polygons is with the Multiply, Subdivide, Triple command, which divides all polygon faces into triangular faces, which can't be nonplanar.

FIGURE 4.34
Subdivide Polygons dialog box

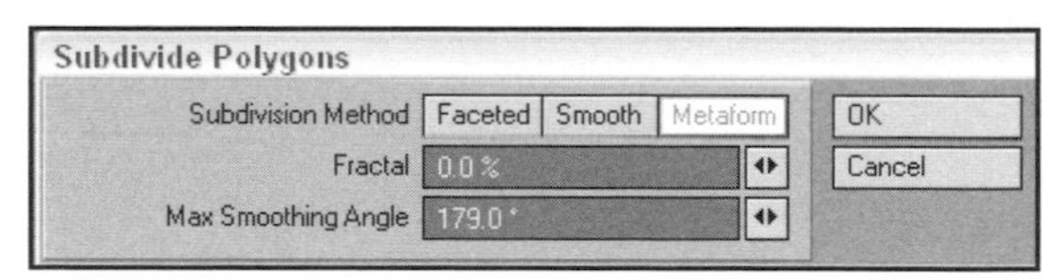

Using the Band Saw Pro Tool

Use the Band Saw Pro tool to select and divide an entire row or column of polygons at once. To use this tool, select two polygons and click the Multiply, Subdivide, Band Saw Pro tool. All contiguous four-sided polygons are selected. Then you can use the Numeric panel, shown in Figure 4.35, to divide the polygons by enabling the Enable Divide option. The resulting slices are displayed in the Divide pane in the middle of the dialog box. You can select the Add option from the Operation list to add more slices to the Divide pane. Use the Edit operation to move the slices and the Delete operation to delete them. You can also use the Uniform, Mirror, Reverse, and Clear buttons to realign the slices within the Divide pane.

Splitting Curves and Polygons

Use the Multiply, Subdivide, Split command to split a selected curve into two curves. If you select two nonadjacent points, the polygon dividing them is split when you select this command.

Cutting Selected Polygons

You can use the Multiply, Subdivide, Cut tool to cut selected polygons using the same interface as in the Band Saw Pro dialog box. After you select the polygons to cut, select the Cut tool to open the dialog box shown in Figure 4.36. Use the options at the top of the dialog box to set restrictions to the cuts, such as maintaining quads. Any changes you make to the dialog box are interactively shown in the viewport. Click the Continue button to make the cuts permanent.

FIGURE 4.35
Numeric panel for the Band Saw Pro tool

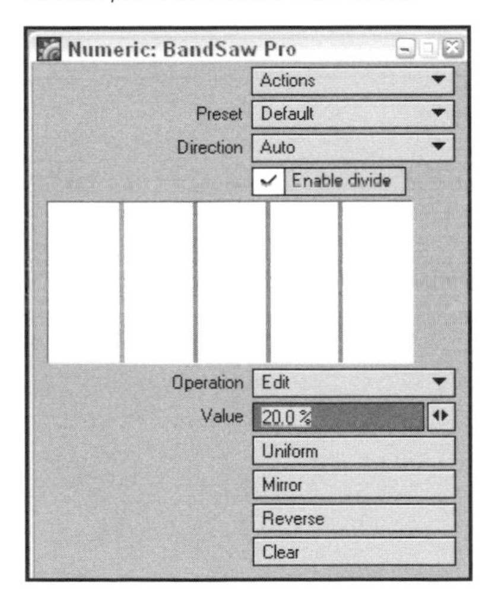

FIGURE 4.36
Numeric panel for the Cut tool

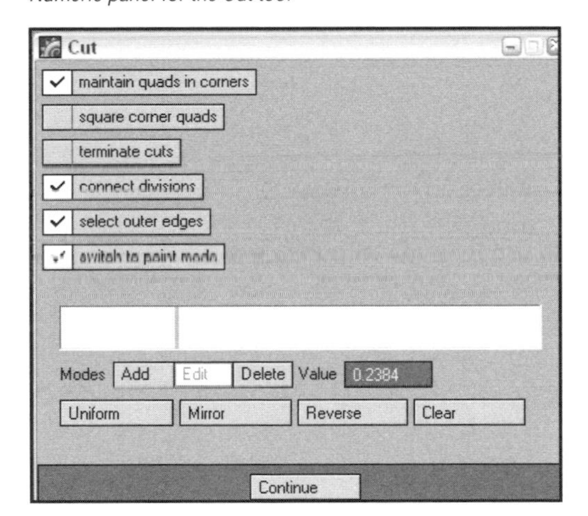

FIGURE 4.37

Knife slice

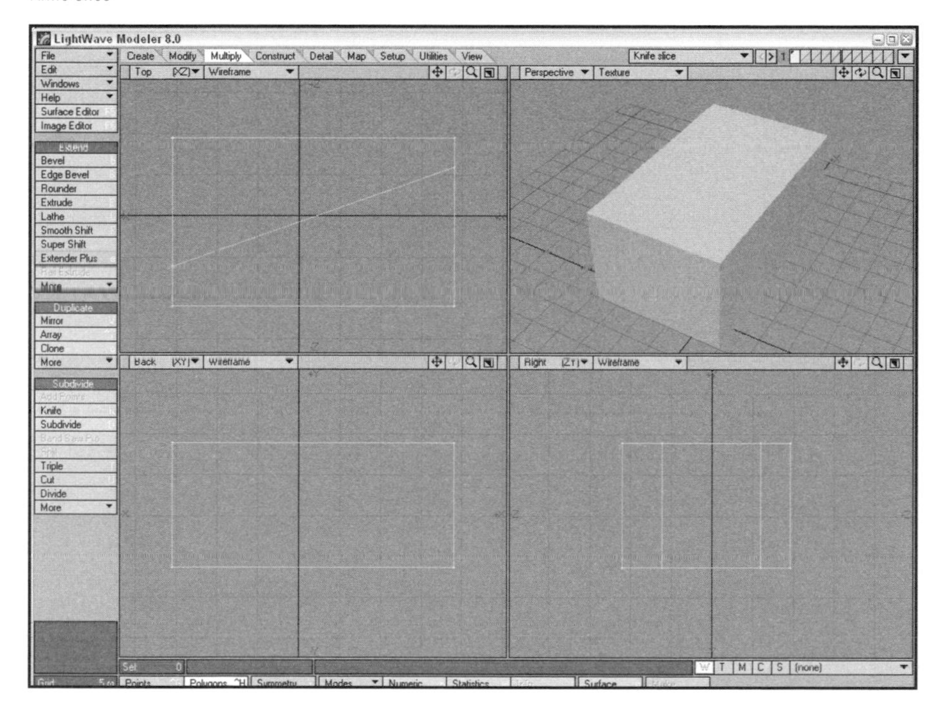

Use the Knife tool

1. Open the Modeler and select the Create menu set.
2. Click the Box button and drag in the Top and Back viewports to create a box object.
3. Select the Multiply menu tab and click the Knife menu button on the Subdivide menu.
4. Drag in the Top viewport over the box object to define a slice plane and press Enter.

   The box object is sliced and new points are added wherever the slice plane intersects an edge, as shown in Figure 4.37.
5. Select the File, Save Object As menu command and save the file as Knife slice.lwo.

Use the Band Saw Pro tool

1. Open the Modeler, click the Create menu tab, and then click the Ball menu command. Then drag in the Top and Front viewports to create a new ball object.
2. Click the Polygons mode button at the bottom of the interface and select two adjacent polygons.
3. Select the Multiply menu tab and click the Band Saw Pro tool on the Subdivide menu.

   The entire row of polygons that contain the selected polygons is selected.
4. Open the Numeric panel and change the Operation to Add, and click in the center Divide pane to create four lines. Then click the Uniform button to evenly separate the lines.

   The selected polygons are cut along the lines that are in the Numeric panel, as shown in Figure 4.38.
5. Select the File, Save Object As menu command and save the file as Band saw pro cut.lwo.

FIGURE 4.38
Band Saw Pro cut

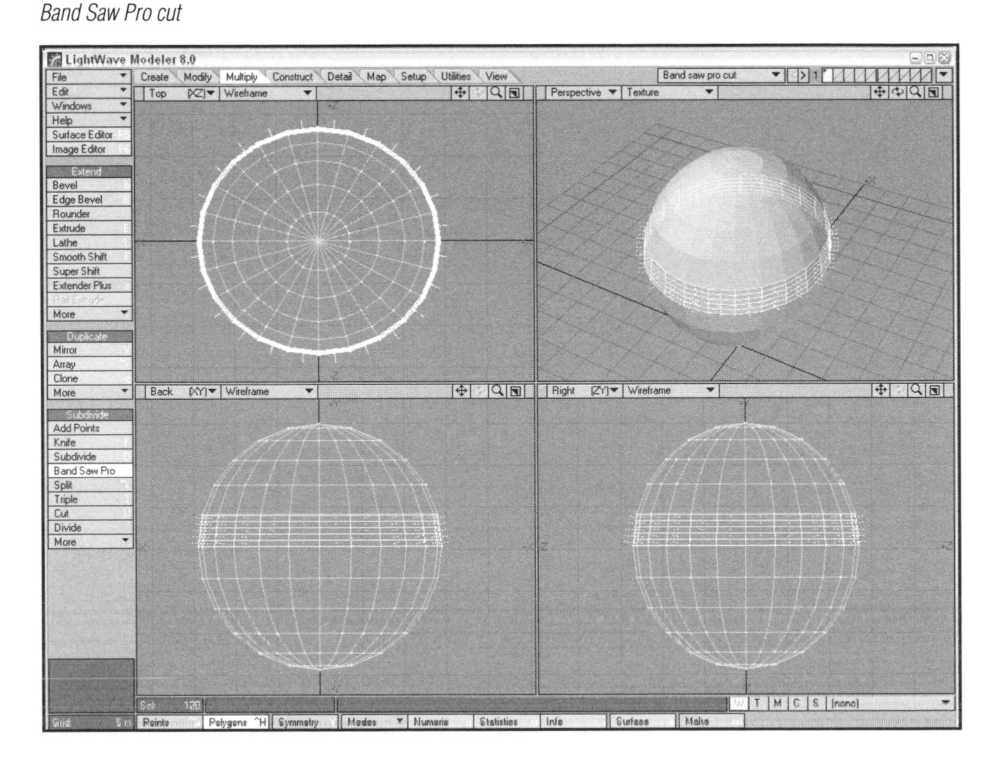

CHAPTER SUMMARY

This chapter covered the basic commands available in the Multiply menu tab of the Modeler interface. With these commands, you can add new edges, polygons, and points to an object using commands such as Bevel, Extrude, and Lathe. You can use many of these tools to create new objects using specialized features. Other commands enable you to duplicate, subdivide, and create object arrays.

What You Have Learned

- How to add new faces to an object using the Bevel tool.
- How to make new objects by adding depth to a shape with the Extrude tool and by rotating a spline about an axis with the Lathe tool.
- How to create several specialized objects, such as seashells and a spikey ball.
- How to duplicate objects in various ways, including mirroring and cloning.
- How to create an array of objects using the Array dialog box.
- How to subdivide an object by cutting and splitting points and polygons.

Key Terms from This Chapter

- **bevel.** The process of replacing the selected face or edge with a new face that is connected with new faces to the original edges.
- **rail curve.** A curve used as a guide that a face is moved along to create a new object.
- **router tool.** A tool used to replace an object's edge with a curved face.
- **extrude.** The process of adding depth to a selected shape.
- **lathe.** The process of revolving a curve about an axis to create a new symmetrical object.
- **morph.** The animating process of gradually changing one object to resemble another.
- **array.** The group of objects that is duplicated a given number of times in a regularly repeating pattern. Can include a rectangular or radial pattern of objects.
- **Knife tool.** A tool used to create a slice plane that cuts through all intersecting polygons.

CHAPTER 5

CONSTRUCTING AND DETAILING OBJECTS

1. Reduce and remove objects.
2. Combine objects.
3. Convert object types.
4. Weld points.
5. Align polygons.
6. Adjust curves and edges.
7. Use the Measure tool.

CHAPTER 5

CONSTRUCTING AND DETAILING OBJECTS

This chapter is the last of the modeling chapters that focus on changing the geometry of objects. From here, we move onto mapping and the Layout interface. So, before we leave modeling, there are several additional features and techniques that we need to cover.

Using the commands on the Multiply menu tab can leave you with objects that include many more points and polygons than you actually need, which can weigh down your file sizes and require additional memory usage. To address these issues, you can use commands on the Construct menu tab to reduce and eliminate unwanted points and polygons.

The Construct menu tab also includes commands to combine two or more objects to create new objects. You can also use the Boolean operations available with these commands, which only affect the overlapping areas between objects so that you can add, subtract, and intersect areas. Using the drill features, you can use an object or a polygon to cut a hole in another object. To create a tunnel of polygons that connects two selections of polygons on two different objects, use the Bridge command.

Finally, the Construct menu tab includes commands you can use to create patch surfaces and to convert between different object types. In particular, the Convert to Subpatches command provides an option for creating smooth subpatch objects based on a low polygon object. Using subpatches is the key to creating organic-looking, smooth-flowing objects.

This chapter also covers another key menu tab: the Detail menu tab. The Detail menu tab includes sections of commands you can use to work with individual points, polygons, curves, and edges. Using commands in its points section, you can weld and merge several points. The Polygons section includes commands for merging and flipping polygon normals. The Curve and Edges sections include commands for smoothing adjacent curves and adding, reducing, and removing edges.

The Detail menu tab also includes several measure tools you can use to get real-time feedback on the distance between points. After completing this chapter, you should have all the tools you need to complete any modeling task.

Tools You'll Use

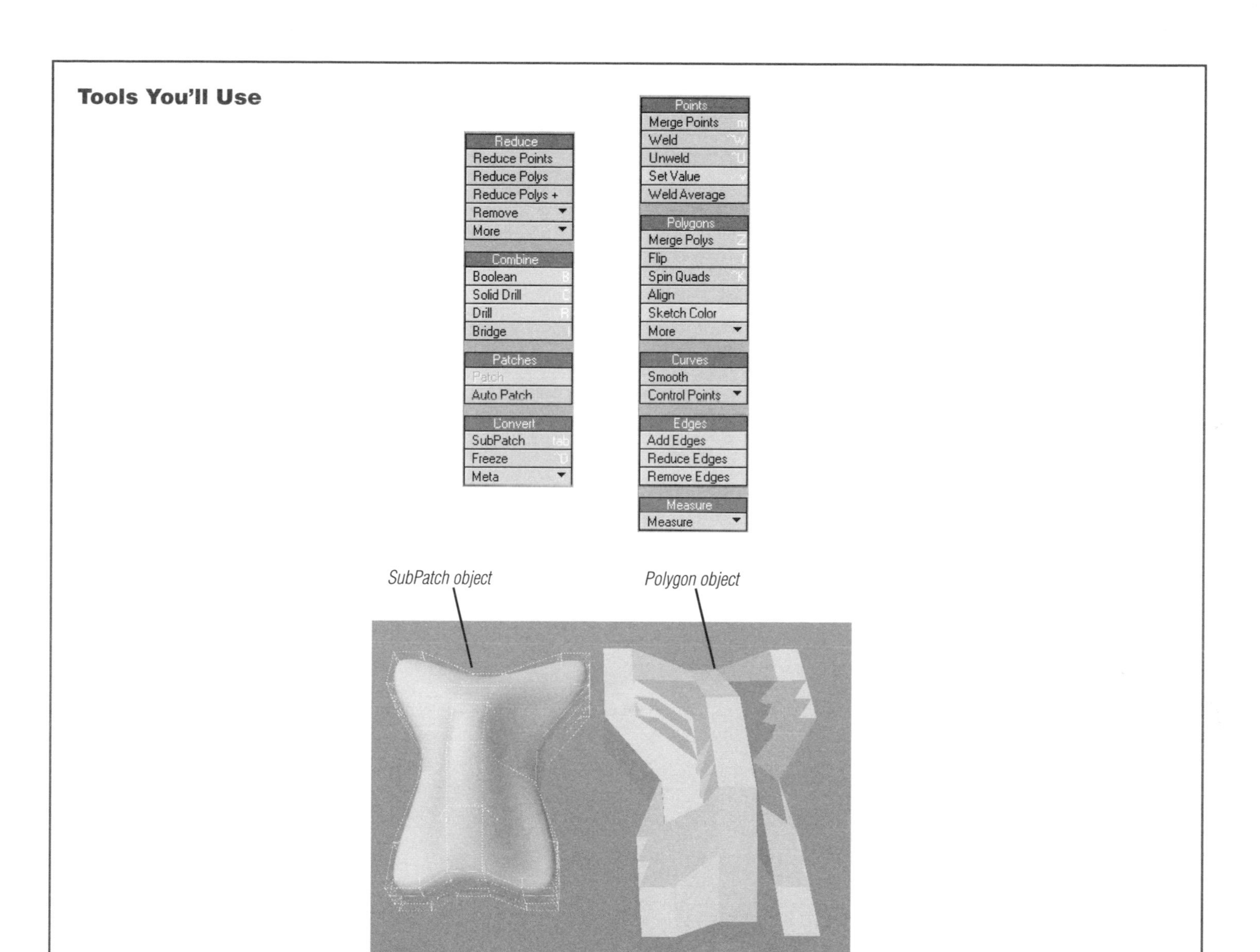

LESSON 1

REDUCE AND REMOVE OBJECTS

What You'll Do

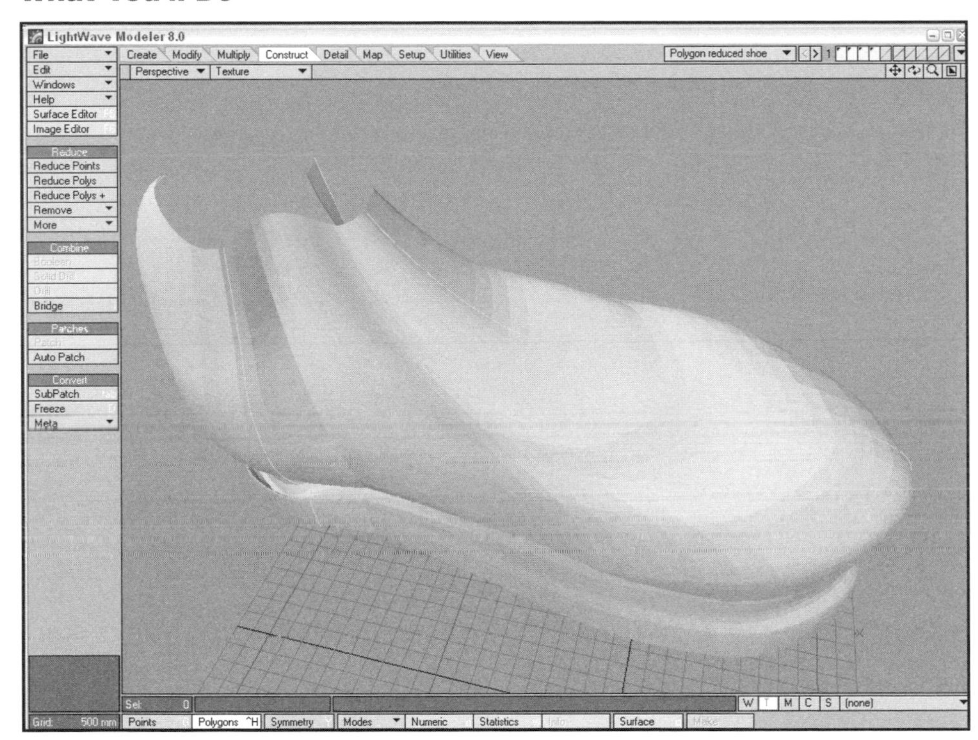

In this lesson, you'll learn how to reduce and delete points and polygons to simplify objects.

When you create some objects or perform an operation (for example, an extrusion) on a set of points or polygons, the resulting object might contain many more points or polygons than is necessary. The overhead that these items add can increase the file size and the memory requirements, and thus make it difficult for you to work with that object.

Reducing Points

You can use the first button in the Construct menu tab, the Reduce Points button, to reduce the total number of points. Select the Construct, Reduce, Reduce Points button to open a dialog box, like the one in Figure 5.1, where you can set the Point Reduction Threshold. The dialog box also includes several threshold presets including Low, Medium, High, Max, and Custom. These buttons set the Degrees value, which is the angle between adjacent points. You can also click the Delete Points option, which is especially useful for deleting unnecessary points in text objects. Text objects are notorious for adding more points than necessary.

CAUTION

Reducing the number of points or polygons changes the shape of the object.

Reducing Polygons

The Construct, Reduce section includes two buttons for reducing the total number of polygons: Reduce Polys and Reduce Polys +.

Using the Reduce Polys feature combines all **co-planar polygons** (or those that are within the Polygon Reduction threshold value) into a single polygon face. For example, if you create a box object with Segment values that are greater than one, the box will be divided into several polygons, all of which are co-planar (existing in the same plane) across each face. Using the Reduce Polys command on such a box would reduce the polygons on each face to 1. The Reduce Polys command also removes any interior points.

The Reduce Polys + feature uses an adaptive algorithm to reduce as many polygons as possible without radically changing the shape of the object. Clicking on the Reduce Polys + button opens a dialog box, shown in Figure 5.2, where you can set the target Goal value. LightWave uses this setting to determine how aggressively to alter the object. This command is useful for high-resolution models you need to reduce so that you can include them in a game or in a real-time simulation. The Reduce Polys + dialog box also includes settings you can use to specify that the surface and boundary points stay in place. When you set the Surface Border and Boundary Preservation Weight values to 100, points along the surface and at the boundaries are protected from moves or alterations. Figure 5.3 shows a simple sphere that was reduced using a Goal value of 0.5.

FIGURE 5.1
Point Reduction dialog box

Point Reduction
Point Reduction Threshold Setting
Low | Medium | High | Max | Custom
Degrees 0.0 | Delete Points
OK | Cancel

FIGURE 5.2
Reduce Polys + dialog box

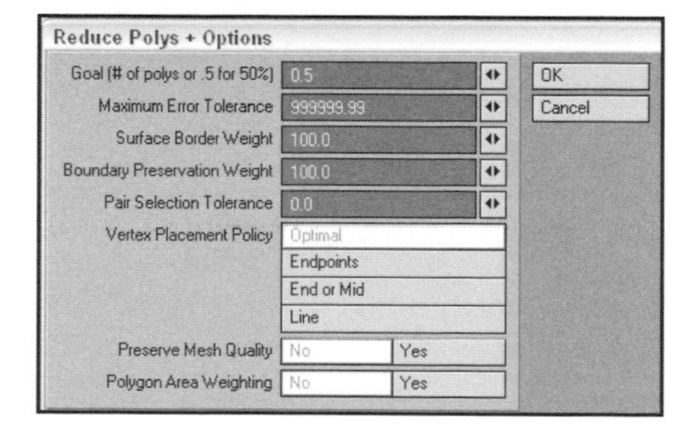

FIGURE 5.3
Sphere and reduced polygon sphere

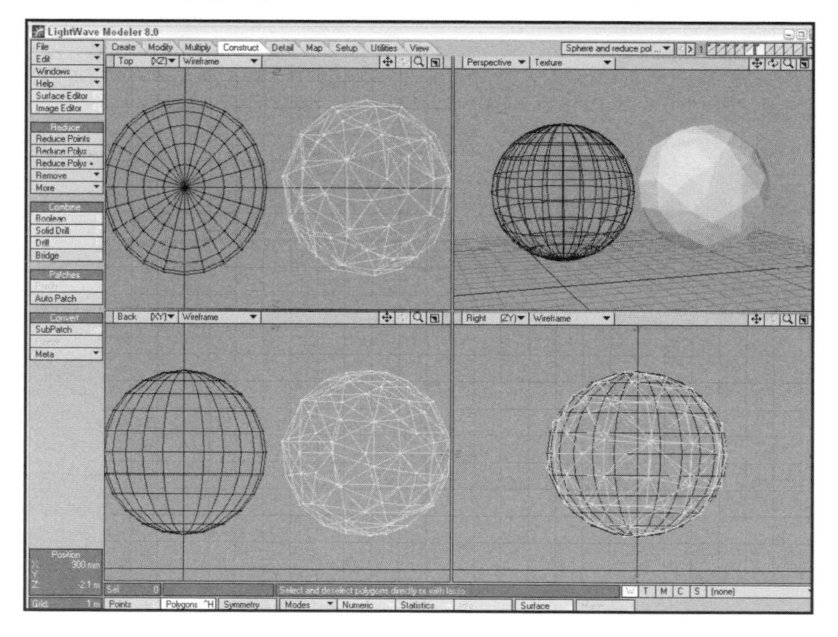

Viewing Statistics

Use the Statistics button at the bottom of the interface to open the Statistics panel, shown in Figure 5.4, where you can view the total number of points or polygons. Use the + icons to select an item, or the – icons to clear an item.

Deleting Points and Polygons

You can easily remove selected points and polygons by using the Delete key, but if you want to remove the polygons while preserving the points, use the Construct, Remove, Remove Polygons menu command (keyboard shortcut: k).

Collapsing Several Polygons to a Point

Using the Construct, Reduce, More, Collapse Polygons menu command replaces all selected polygons with a single point located at the center of the selection. Figure 5.5 shows a sphere object where several polygons were selected and then collapsed.

FIGURE 5.4
Statistics panel

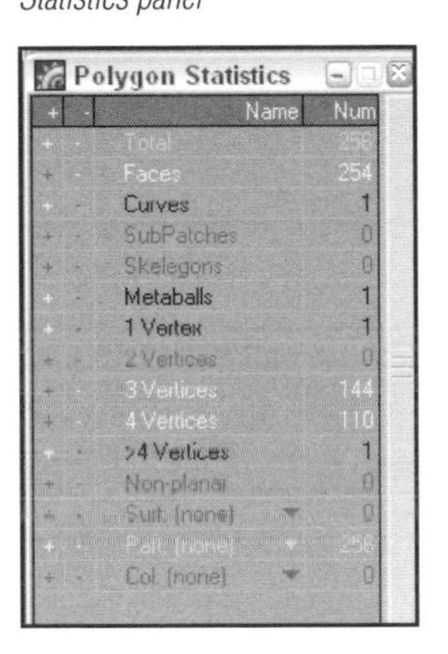

FIGURE 5.5
Collapsed polygons

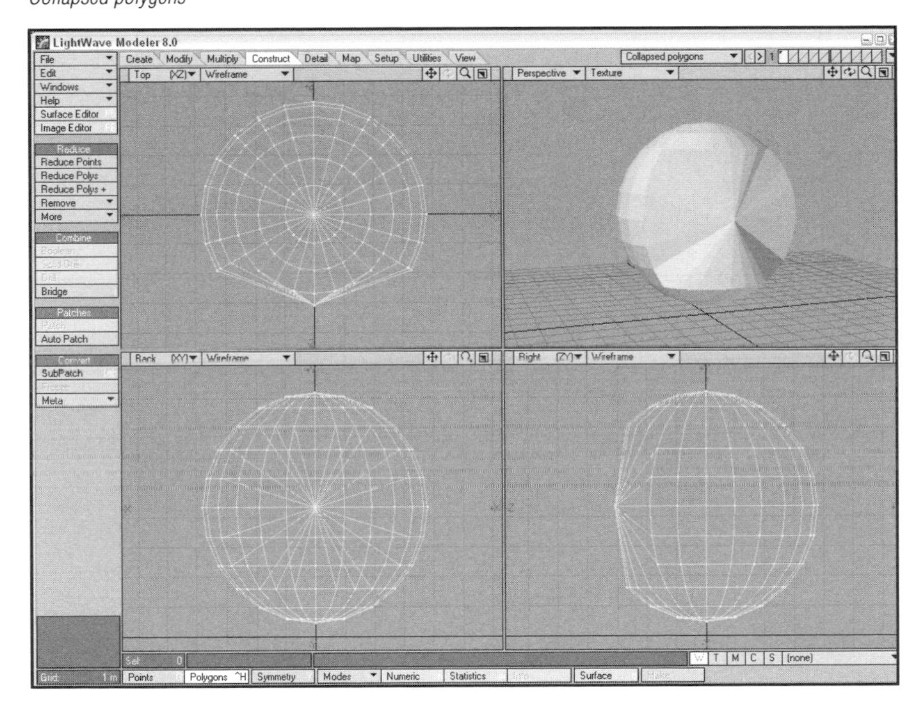

Combining Rows and Columns of Polygons

When you select two or more contiguous polygons, you can use the Reduce, More, Band Glue menu command to combine the selected polygons for the entire row or column. This operation is the opposite of the Band Saw Pro tool in the Multiply, Subdivide section. Figure 5.6 shows what happens when you use the Band Glue tool on a selection of the polygons in the front of a sphere. Notice how the entire column of polygons was combined.

FIGURE 5.6

Columns of polygons combined using the Band Glue tool

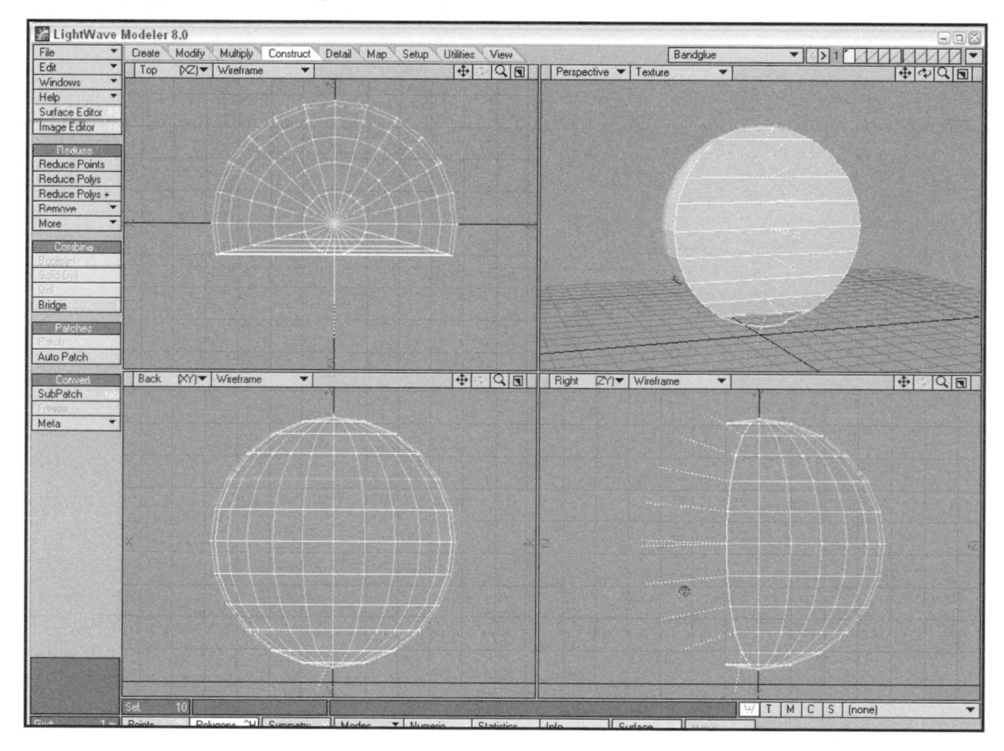

Reduce points on a text object

1. Open the Modeler and select the Create menu tab.
2. Click the Text button and then click in the Top viewport to create a text object.
3. Type the numbers **1–5** and press Enter.

   The typed numbers appear in the Top viewport.
4. Click the Text button again and click in the Top viewport beneath the first text object. Then press the Backspace key to delete the existing numbers and type the numbers **6–0**. Then press the Enter key.
5. Click the Polygons mode button at the bottom of the interface and drag over the entire lower set of numbers to select them all.
6. Select the Construct menu tab and click the Reduce Points button.

   The Point Reduction dialog box opens.
7. Click the Max button, enable the Delete Points option, and then click OK.

   Points are aggressively deleted, as shown in Figure 5.7, and a small dialog box appears stating the number of deleted points.
8. Select the File, Save Object As menu command and save the file as Reduce pointsnumbers.lwo.

FIGURE 5.7

Text numbers with reduced points

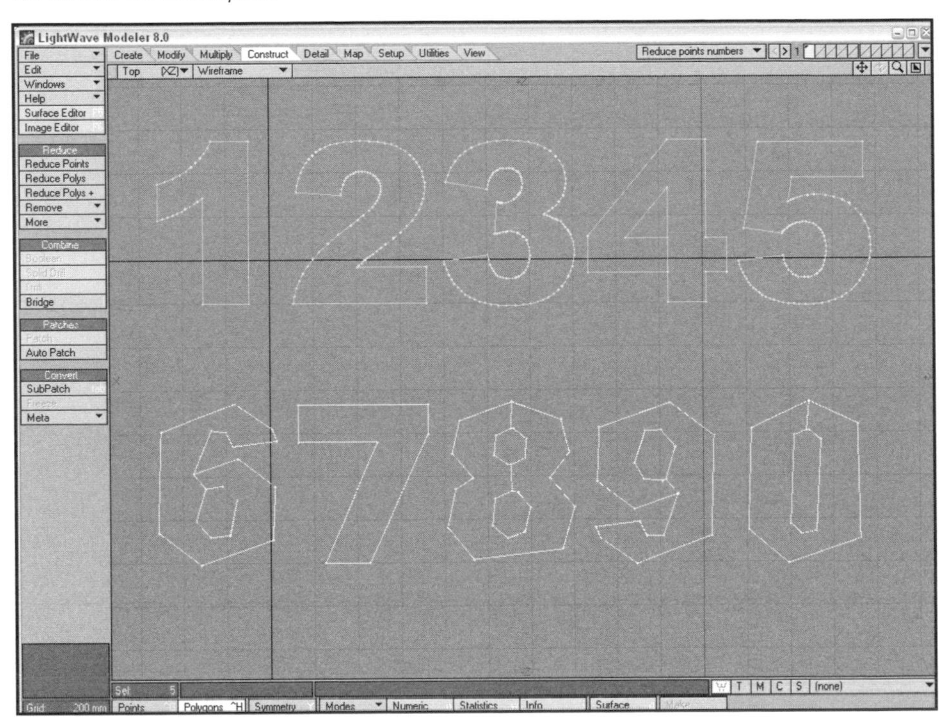

FIGURE 5.8
Polygon reduced shoe

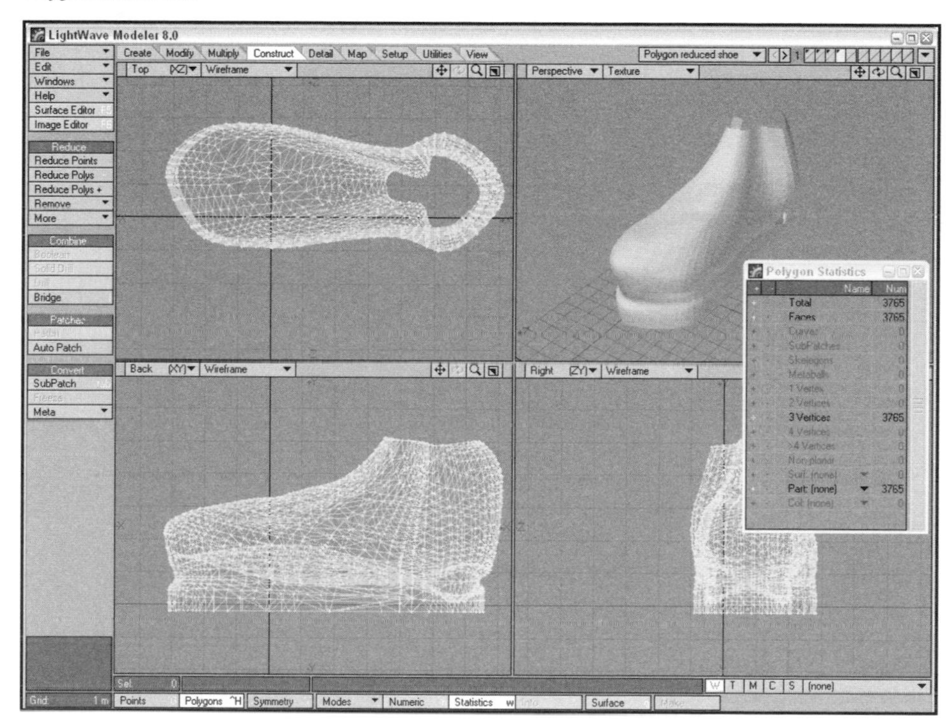

Reduce polygons

1. Choose the File, Load Object menu command and open the Extruded shoe.lwo file.
2. Select the Polygons button and click the Statistics button at the bottom of the interface to open the PolygonStatistics panel.

   Note that the total number of polygon faces is 11,289.
3. Click the Construct menu tab and click the Reduce Polys + button in the Reduce section.

   The Reduce Polys + dialog box opens.
4. Set the Goal value to **0.5**, and the Surface Border Weight and Boundary Preservation Weight values to **100**. Then click OK.

   The total number of polygons is reduced while maintaining the surface and boundaries, as shown in Figure 5.8. In the Statistics panel, notice how the total number of polygon faces was reduced to 5648.
5. Select the File, Save Object As menu command and save the file as Polygon reduced shoe.lwo.

Collapse polygons

1. Open the Modeler and select the Create menu tab.
2. Click the Box button, and then click in the Top and Back viewports to create a box object.

3. Open the Numeric panel and set the X, Y, and Z Segments values to **4**.
4. Click the Polygons button at the bottom of the interface and drag over all the polygons on the top of the box. Then hold down the Ctrl key and select all the side polygons in the Back viewport to remove them from the selection.
5. Click the Construct menu tab and select the More, Collapse Polygons command from the Reduce section.

   All the selected polygons along the top of the box are combined and replaced with polygons that meet at a point placed in the center of the polygon, as shown in Figure 5.9.
6. Select the File, Save Object As menu command and save the file as Collapsed box polygons.lwo.

FIGURE 5.9
Collapsed box polygons

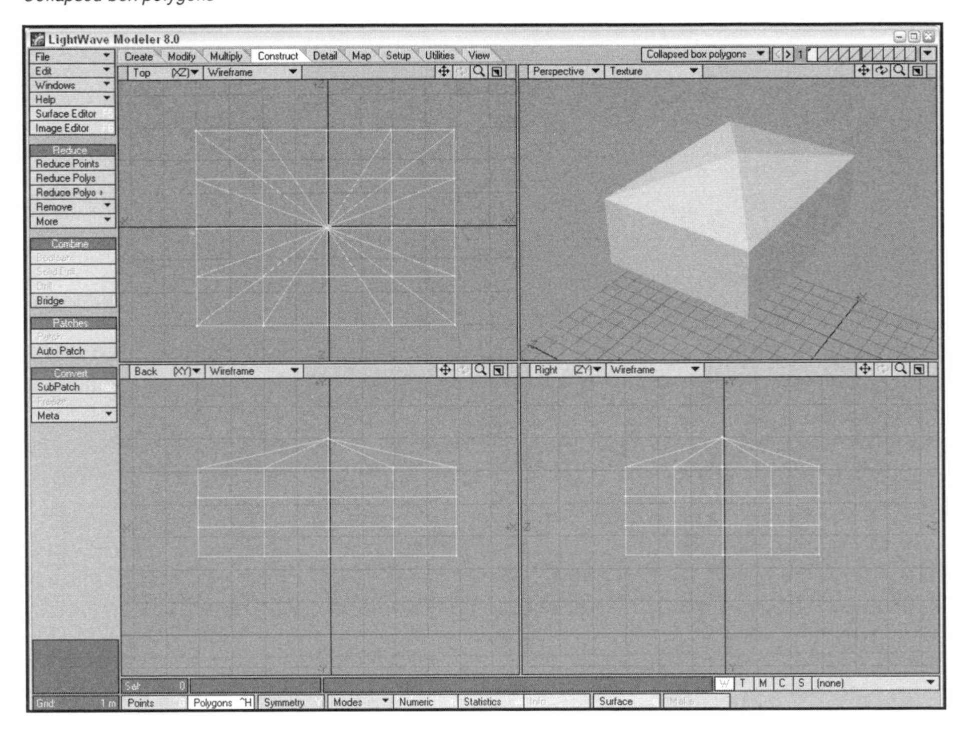

LESSON 2

COMBINE OBJECTS

What You'll Do

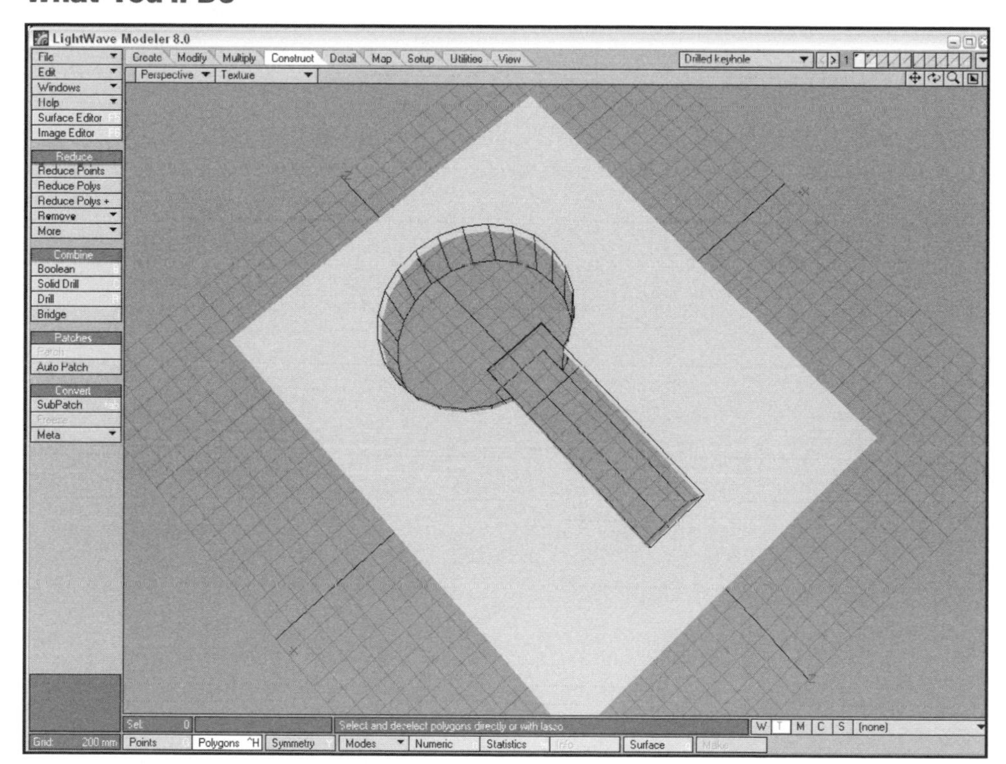

In this lesson, you'll learn how to combine two or more objects using Boolean, drilling, and bridge operations.

The Combine section of the Construct menu tab includes several different features for combining overlapping objects. Before you can perform many of these operations, you need to place one object on the background layer and one object on the foreground layer.

> TIP
>
> You can quickly switch between the background and foreground layers using the ' (apostrophe) key.

Using Boolean Operations on Objects

Use the **Boolean** command, the first button in the Combine section of the Construct menu tab, to open a simple dialog box where you can select Boolean commands to perform. This command is only available when an object in the foreground layer overlaps an object in the background layer. The available Boolean commands include Union, Intersect, Subtract, and

Add. Use the Union command to combine the two objects and eliminate any overlapping polygons. To remove all portions of both objects and leave only those portions that overlap, use the Intersect command. Using the Subtract command removes the background object that overlaps the foreground object. You can use the Add command to combine the two objects, without removing any polygons. Figure 5.10 shows each of the available Boolean objects.

Drilling Objects

The Combine section of the Construct menu tab includes two drill commands: Solid Drill and Drill. You can use the Solid Drill command with 3D objects, and it only affects the intersecting portions of the two objects. The Drill command is similar, but you use it with 2D shapes to infinitely extend those shapes to bore through an entire object. To enable these commands, make sure that the drilling object is on the background layer and the object to drill is on the foreground layer. Both commands open a dialog box with four options: Core, Tunnel, Stencil, and Slice. When you select the Core option, the portion outside of the drill object is deleted. With the Tunnel option, the portion inside the drill object is deleted. Use the Stencil option to mark the edges where the two objects intersect on the surface of the foreground object and give the shape a name. The Slice option is similar to the Stencil option, except the Slice option doesn't name the shape. Figure 5.11 shows a sphere object that was drilled by a background object using the Tunnel option.

FIGURE 5.10
Boolean objects

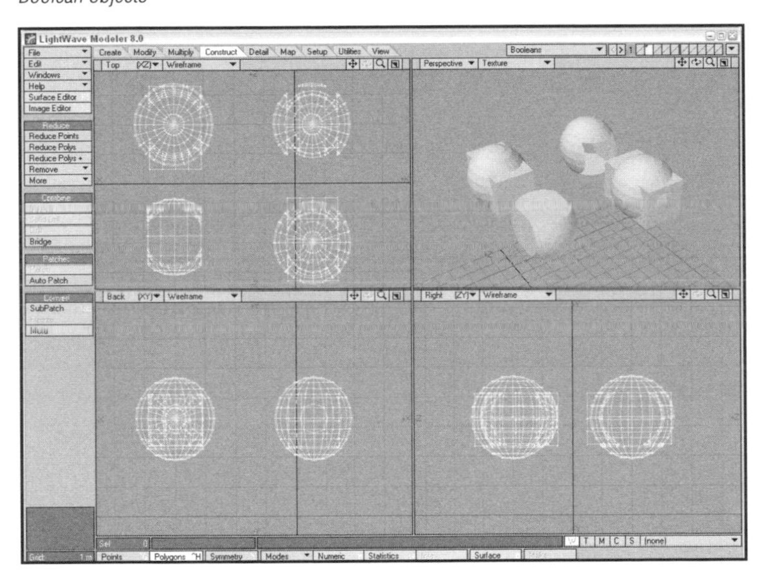

FIGURE 5.11
Drilled objects

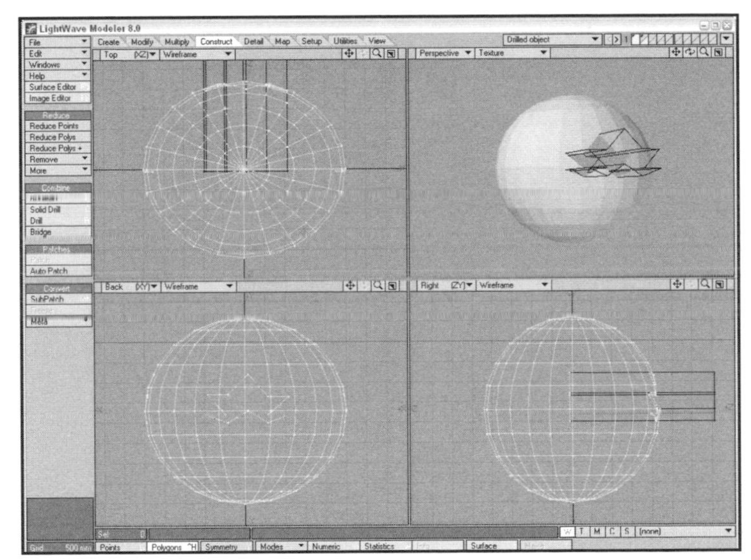

Using the Bridge Tool

You can use the **Bridge tool** to connect selected polygons between two different objects. For example, you can create a forearm using the Bridge tool by selecting the polygons on the hand and the polygons on the upper arm. The Bridge tool doesn't require that the selected polygons have the same number of points. Figure 5.12 shows a polygon from a sphere bridged to polygons from a box object.

Creating Patches from Curves

Patches are a unique modeling type that you can make by stretching a mesh of polygons over a set of at least three curves. You need to place these curves end to end in a closed loop. Once the curves are in place, simply choose the Patches, Patch command in the Construct menu tab. In the dialog box that opens, you can specify the number of Perpendicular and Parallel divisions to use. Using the Auto Patch command automatically detects and creates a patch object from any available sets of curves without you having to select them. Figure 5.13 shows a path with four rows and columns created using the Auto Patch command.

TIP

You can use the Merge Points or Weld commands in the Detail menu tab to ensure that the end points or adjacent curves are connected.

FIGURE 5.12
Bridged objects

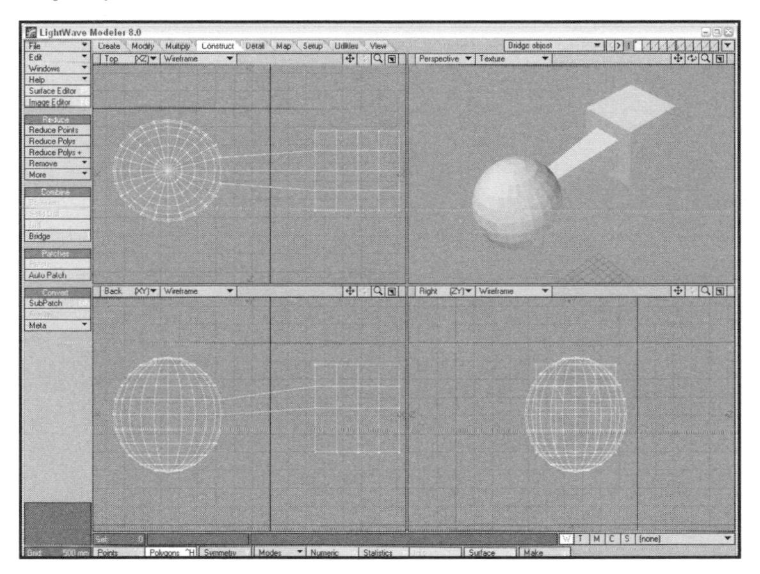

FIGURE 5.13
Auto Patch

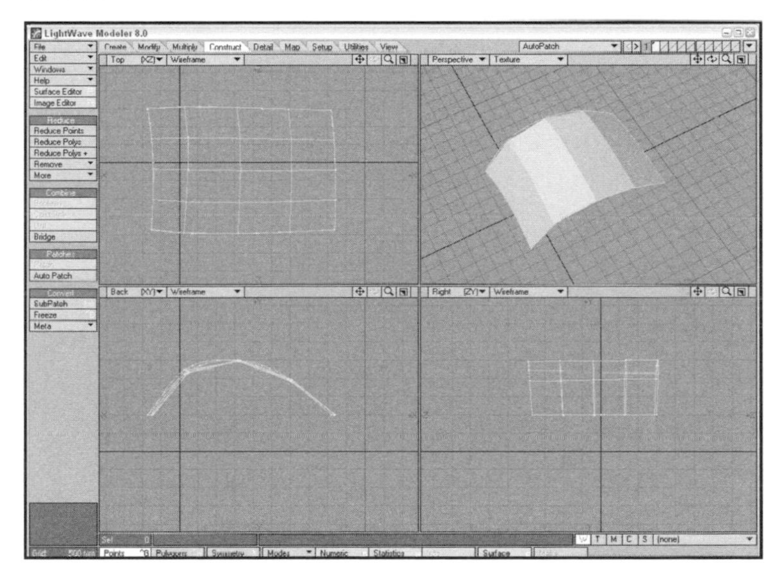

Use a Boolean operation

1. Click the File, Load Object menu command and open the Boolean holes in box.lwo file.

   This file includes a box object that is intersected by an array of 24 smaller boxes.

2. Using Polygons mode, select all the smaller box objects.

3. Click the Edit, Cut menu command. Select the second layer in the upper-right corner and then click the Edit, Paste menu command.

   The smaller boxes are pasted onto a different layer.

4. In the upper-right corner of the window, select the first layer as the foreground and enable the second layer as the background layer.

   The smaller boxes are outlined in black because they are on the background layer.

5. Click the Construct menu tab and then click the Boolean button in the Combine section.

   The Boolean CSG dialog box opens.

6. Click the Subtract button in the Boolean dialog box and click OK.

   All the smaller boxes are removed from the larger box, creating a set of holes in the box object, as shown in Figure 5.14.

7. Select the File, Save Object As menu command and save the file as Boolean holes.lwo.

FIGURE 5.14
Boolean holes

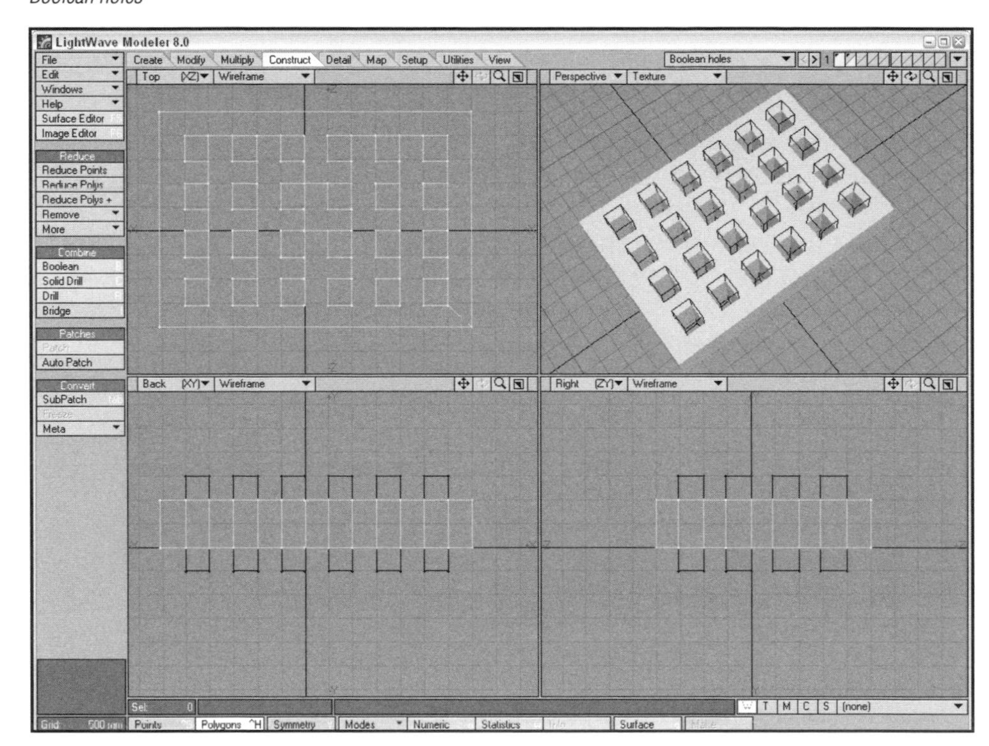

Drill holes in an object

1. Click the File, Load Object menu command and open the Keyhole objects.lwo file.

   This file includes a box object that is intersected by a disc and box object in the shape of a keyhole.

2. Using Polygons mode, drag over some polygons of the disc object and then press the] key to select the entire object.

3. Click the Edit, Cut menu command. Select the second layer in the upper-right corner, and then click the Edit, Paste menu command.

4. In the upper-right corner of the window, click the upper-left corner of the first layer to select it as the foreground layer, and then click the lower-right corner of the second layer to select it as the background layer.

   The objects on the background layer appear in black.

5. In Polygons mode, select some polygons on the small box object and press the] key to select the entire object. Click the Construct menu tab and then click the Boolean button in the Combine section.

6. In the Boolean dialog box, click the Union button and click OK.

   The small box and the disc objects are combined to make one object.

7. Select the union Boolean object and click the Edit, Cut menu. Select the background layer and delete the disc object that is there. Then click the Edit, Paste menu command to paste the unioned Boolean object to the background layer.

8. Select the foreground layer, click the lower-right corner in the background layer so the union Boolean object appears highlighted in black, and then choose the Solid Drill button in the Combine section. Select the Tunnel button in the Solid Drill dialog box and click OK.

   The union Boolean object is removed from the box object, as shown in Figure 5.15.

9. Select the File, Save Object As menu command and save the file as Drilled keyhole.lwo.

FIGURE 5.15
Drilled hole

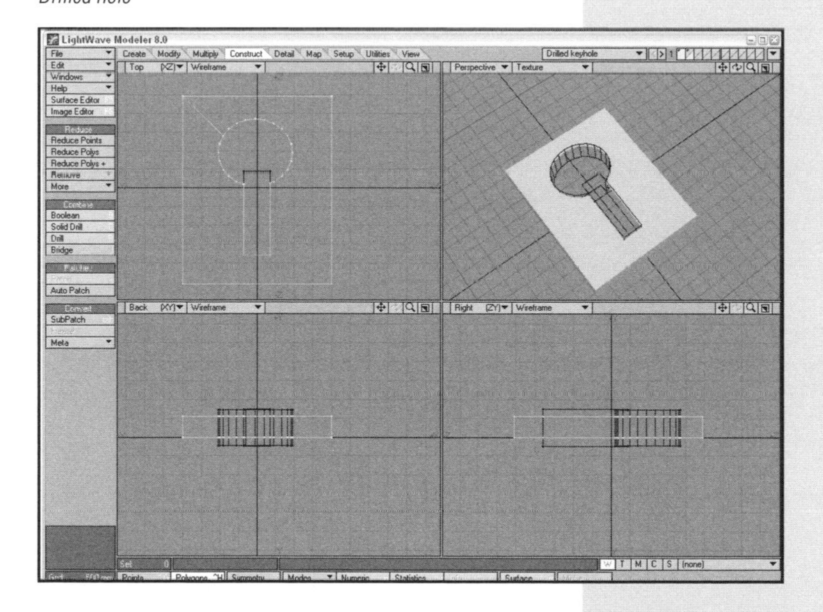

Create a barbell with the Bridge tool

1. Open the Modeler and select the Create menu tab.
2. Click the Disc button, and then click in the Top and Back viewports to create a disc object.
3. In Polygons mode, choose one of the circular end polygons. Select the Multiply menu tab, and click the Bevel button in the Extend section.
4. In the Numeric panel, set the Shift value to **0** and the Inset value to **2** to create a small polygon in the center of the circular polygon.
5. Select the entire polygon and click the Mirror button in the Duplicate section, and then drag from the center of the Top viewport to the right to create a mirrored copy of the disc object.
6. Select the two small centered polygons in each disc object and click the Construct menu tab. Then, click the Bridge button in the Combine section.

   The Bridge command connects the two polygons, as shown in Figure 5.16.
7. Select the File, Save Object As menu command and save the file as Barbell.lwo.

FIGURE 5.16
Simple barbell created with the Bridge tool

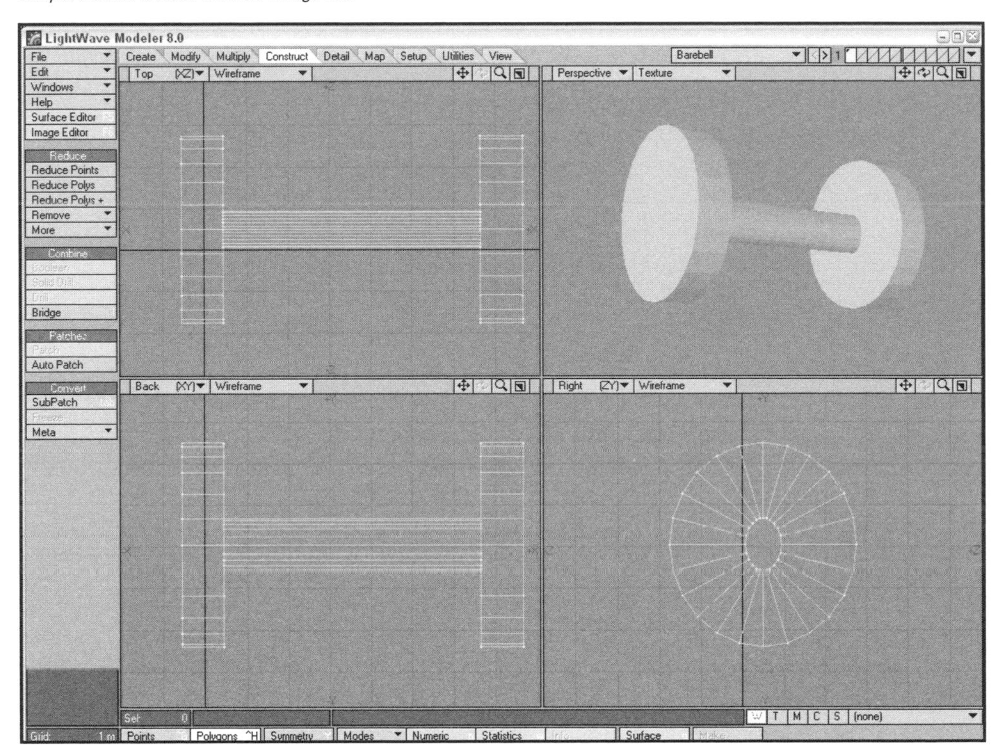

LESSON 3

CONVERT OBJECT TYPES

What You'll Do

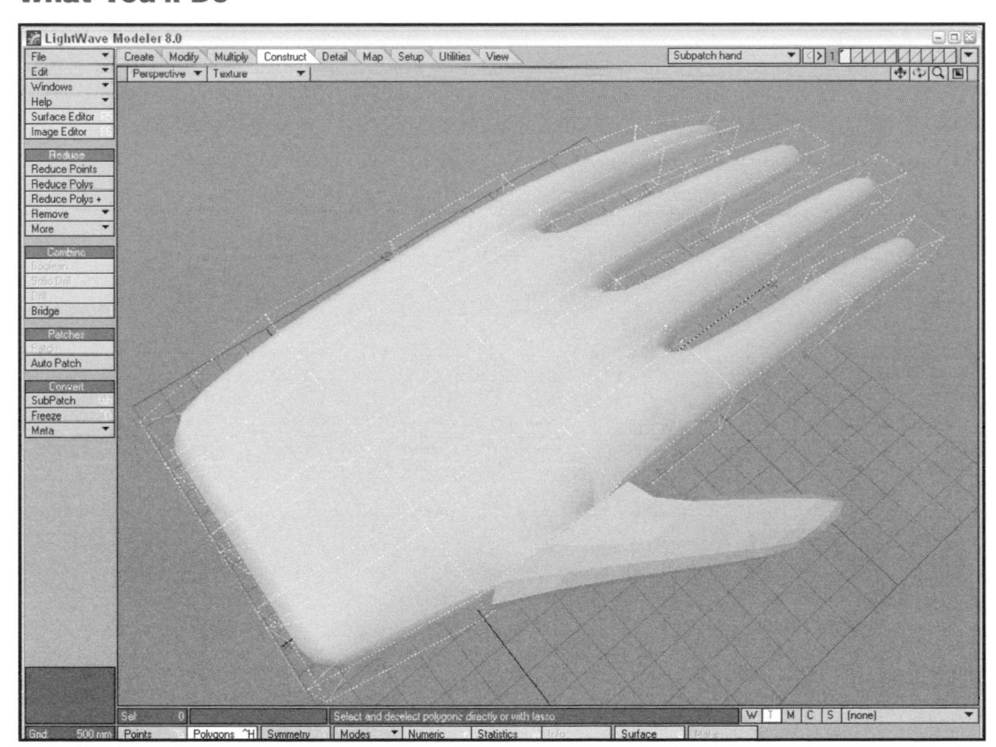

In this lesson, you'll learn how to convert objects from one object type to another and learn how to use subpatches, which can smooth polygon surfaces.

The Modeler includes several different object types for modeling objects, including polygons, subpatches, and Metaballs. If you need to convert between these different types, use the commands on the Construct menu tab.

Smoothing Objects with Subpatches

Polygon modeling is rather intuitive, but it doesn't always yield the smoothest of objects. To create smooth, organic-looking objects that flow in a more natural way, you can convert polygon objects into subpatches using the Construct, Convert, Subpatch command (keyboard shortcut: the Tab key). Converted objects retain a polygon cage that surrounds them, and you can select and edit this cage as needed. Figure 5.17 shows a typical polygon object and a copy of the object that was converted into a subpatch object.

CAUTION

Subpatch conversion only works on three- and four-sided objects. If an object has a polygon with more than four sides, use the Subdivide or Triple commands in the Multiply menu tab to reduce its number of sides.

Converting Curves to Polygons

You can convert curves into polygons using the Construct, Convert, Freeze menu button. You can do this with both open and closed curves. The beginning and end points of an open curve are connected before they are converted into a polygon.

NOTE

Each time you convert between different modeling types, the resolution of the polygon mesh increases.

Converting Subpatches to Polygons

You can also use the Construct, Convert, Freeze command on subpatch objects to convert the selected polygon cage items to polygons. This conversion will maintain the smoothness of the subpatch surface by increasing the number of polygons to create a smooth surface. Figure 5.18 shows a subpatch object with a front section that was converted to polygons.

Converting and Editing Metaballs, Metaedges, and Metafaces

The Construct, Convert, Meta menu button includes several commands for converting

FIGURE 5.17

Polygon and subpatch objects

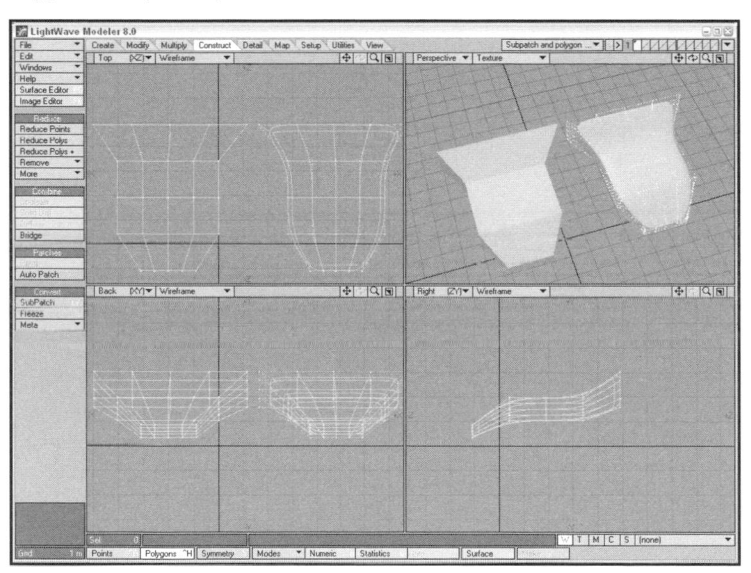

FIGURE 5.18

Subpatch converted to polygons

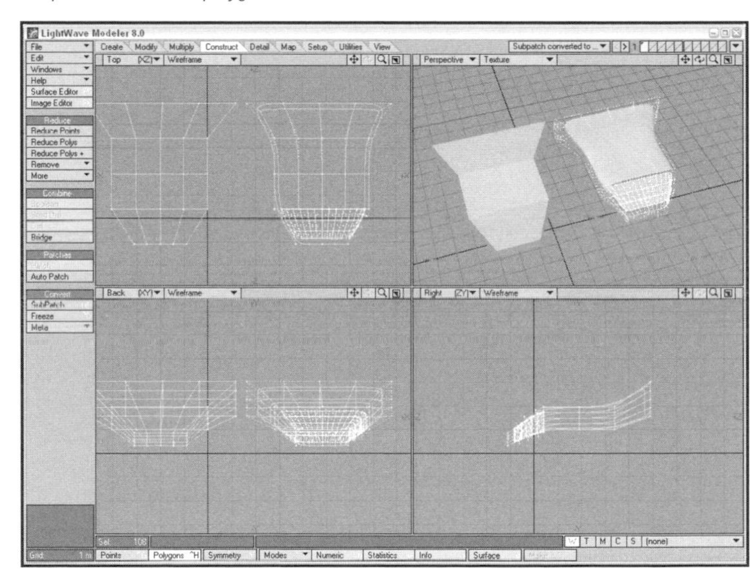

points, curves, and polygons to Metaballs, Metaedges, and Metafaces. When a Metaball object is selected, you can select the Construct, Convert, Meta, Edit Metaballs menu command to edit the Radius and Influence values for the selected Metaball object.

Because it takes a while to redraw Metaballs in the viewport, you can use the Toggle Metamesh command to turn off the display of Metamesh object. Figure 5.19 shows two crossing box objects that were converted into Metaface objects.

NOTE

Although the Create menu tab includes buttons for creating Metaballs and Metaedges, you can only create Metafaces using the Convert command.

FIGURE 5.19
Metaface object

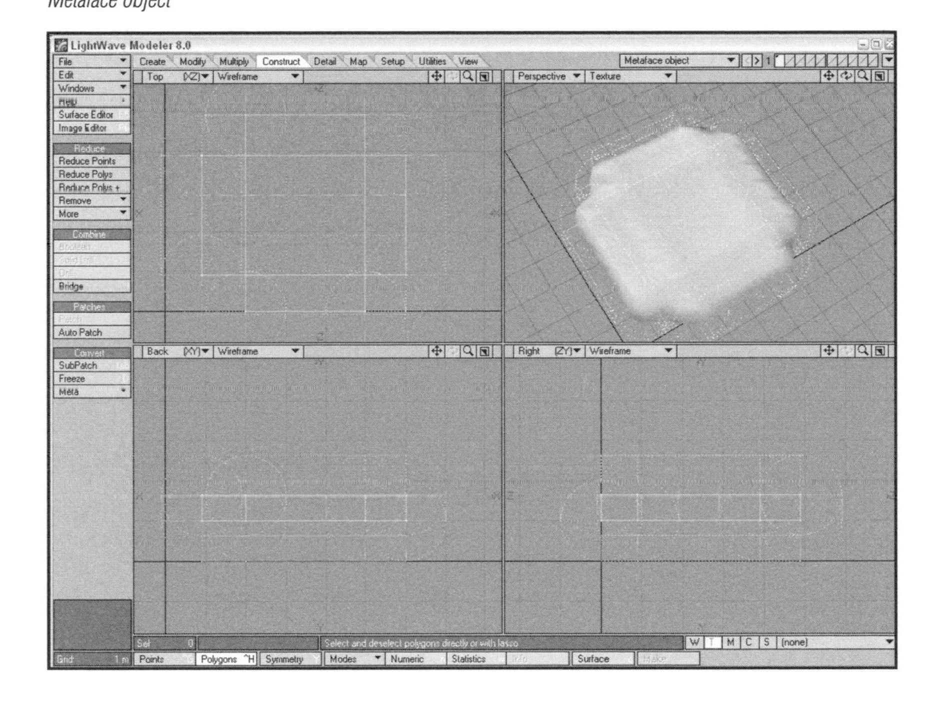

Create a subpatch hand

1. Click the File, Load Object menu command and open the Polygon hand.lwo file.

   This file includes a simple hand object made by extruding polygons from the end and side of a box object.

2. Click the Construct menu tab and then click the SubPatch button in the Convert section.

   The hand is smoothed to look more natural.

3. Select the polygons that make up the thumb and click the Freeze command from the Convert section.

   The selected thumb subpatches are converted back to polygons, as shown in Figure 5.20.

4. Select the File, Save Object As menu command and save the file as Subpatch hand.lwo.

Create a Metaface

1. Click the File, Load Object menu command and open the Extruded polygon.lwo file.

2. Click the Construct menu tab and then click the Meta, Convert Metafaces command in the Convert section.

   The entire object is converted to a Metaface object, as shown in Figure 5.21.

3. Select the File, Save Object As menu command and save the file as Converted metaface object.lwo.

FIGURE 5.20
Subpatch hand object

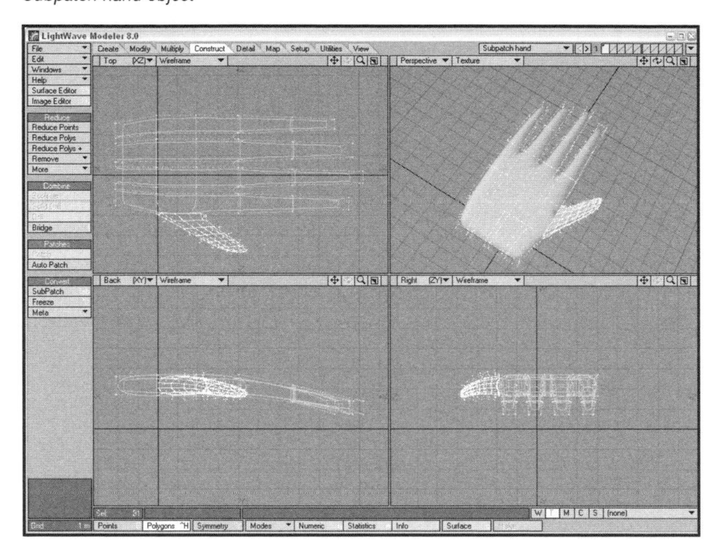

FIGURE 5.21
Metaface object

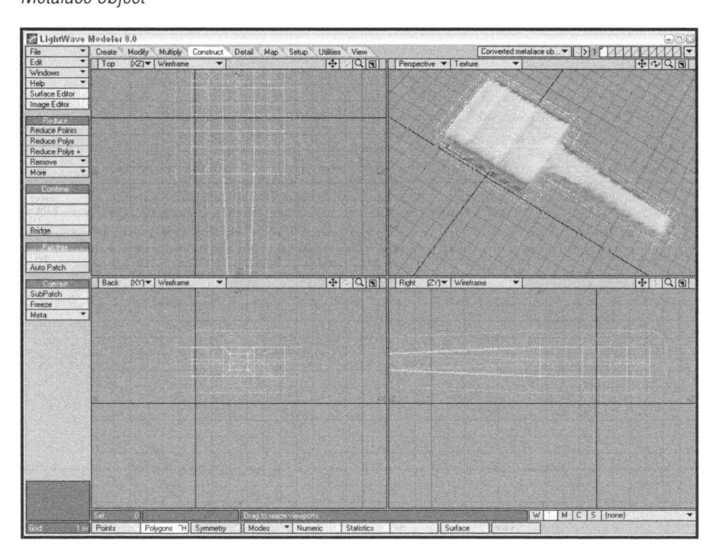

LESSON 4

WELD POINTS

What You'll Do

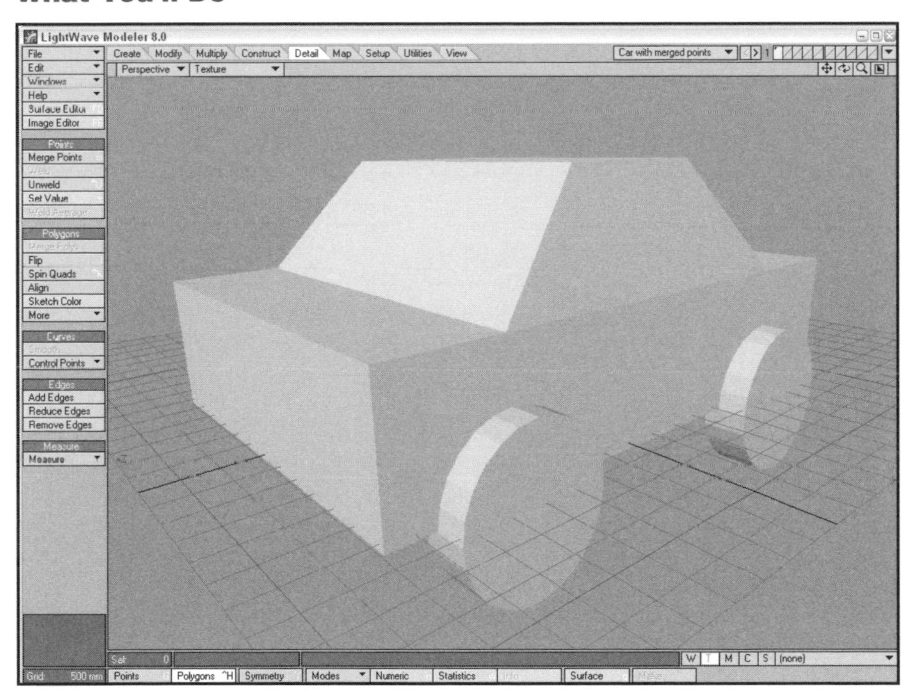

In this lesson, you'll learn how to combine points by welding and merging.

As you model, you will want to combine, reduce, and precisely place points. You can work specifically with points to accomplish these tasks by using the commands in the Points section of the Detail menu tab.

Merging Points

You can use the Detail, Points, Merge Points command to quickly clean up any extra points that occupy the same location. For example, when you mirror an item and place the mirrored portion next to the original, all the points along the mirror axis are duplicated. You can use the Merge Points command to eliminate the extra points. When you click this command, the Merge Points dialog box, shown in Figure 5.22, opens, where you can select either the Automatic or Fixed merging method.

FIGURE 5.22
Merge Points dialog box

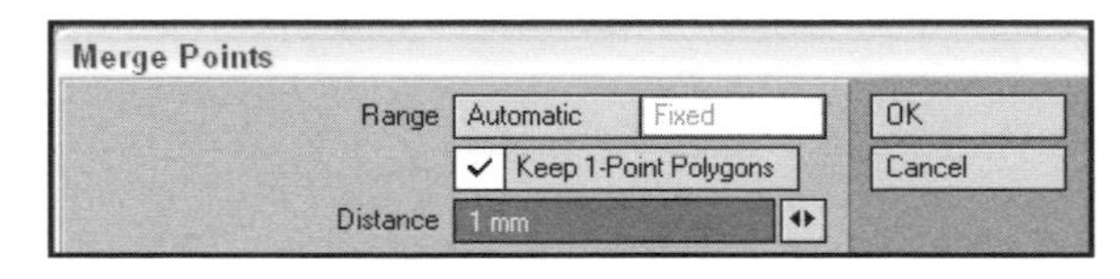

Using the Automatic option selects which points are merged; using the Fixed option merges only points with the specified Distance value.

Welding Points

When you select two or more points and **weld** them with the Detail, Points, Weld Points command, all the points are combined and moved to the location of the last point selected. After you execute this command, a dialog box opens to tell you how many points were welded together. If you're welding together a large number of points, you'll probably want to use the Detail, Points, Weld Average command. This command is similar to the Weld command, except that it combines all points to a location that is the average of all the selected points. Figure 5.23 shows three box objects. The first object hasn't been welded, the last row of points for the middle box were welded with the Weld command, and the last row of points for the third box were welded using the Weld Average command.

Unwelding Points

The opposite of welding points is unwelding them with the Detail, Points, Unweld button. Using this command splits the selected points into separate points, one for each polygon.

Setting Point Values

Clicking the Detail, Points, Set Value button opens a dialog box, shown in Figure 5.24, where you can specify a precise X, Y, or Z location value for the selected points.

FIGURE 5.23
Welded points

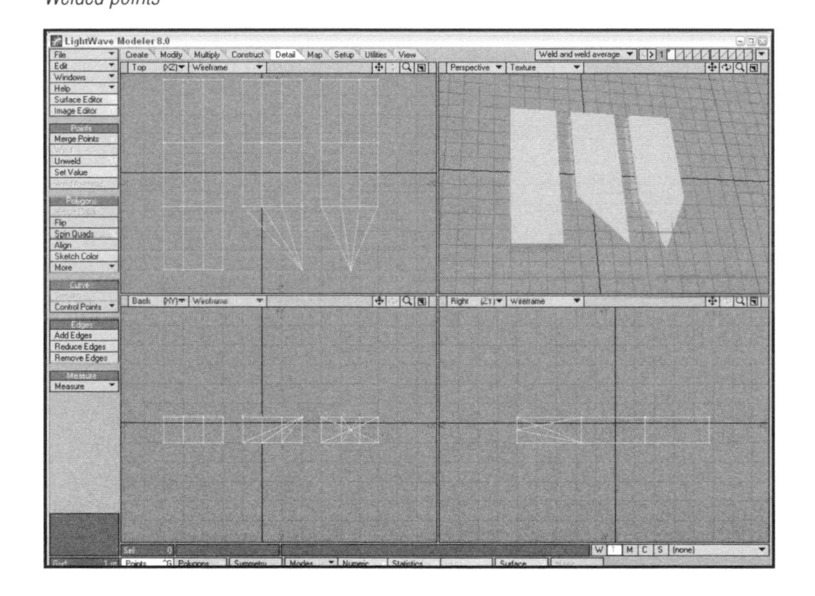

FIGURE 5.24
Set Value dialog box

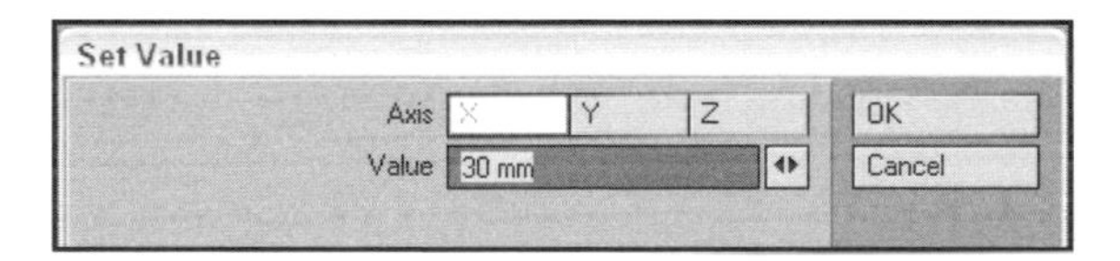

FIGURE 5.25
Car with merged points

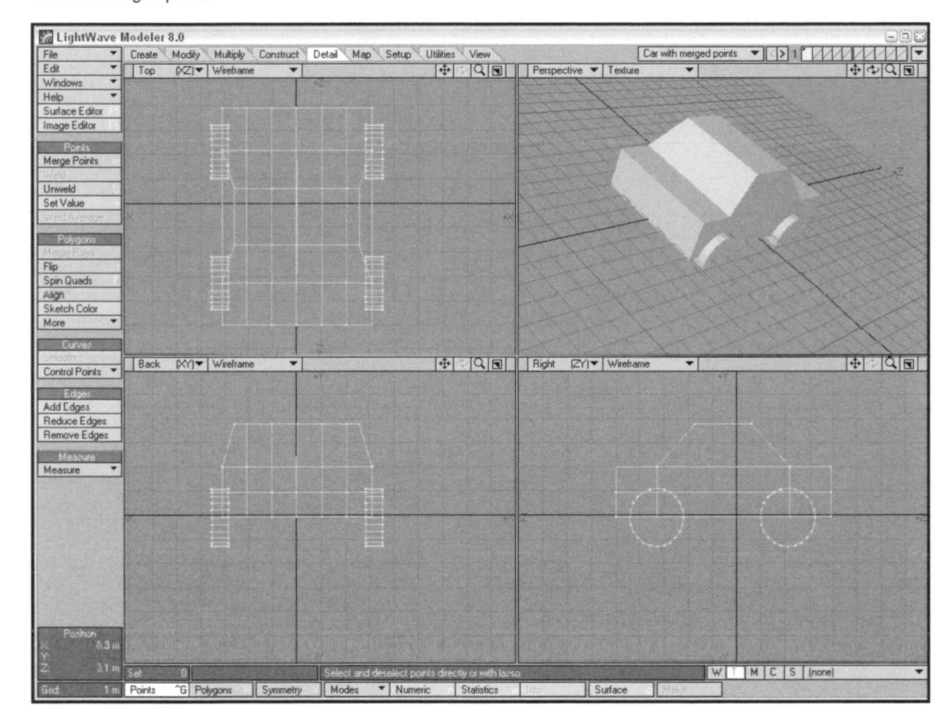

Merge points

1. Click the File, Load Object menu command and open the Half a car.lwo file.
2. Click the Multiply menu tab and then click the Mirror button in the Duplicate section. Drag from the center line outward in the Top viewport to create the other half of the car.
3. With the Points selection mode active, drag over all the points along the center line of the car.
4. Click the Detail menu tab and select the Merge Points button in the Points section. In the Merge Points dialog box, click the Fixed button, set the Distance value to **50mm**, and then click OK.

   A dialog box opens and notifies you that 14 points were eliminated. The car with the eliminated points is shown in Figure 5.25.
5. Select the File, Save Object As menu command and save the file as Car with merged points.lwo.

Weld points

1. Click the Create menu tab and then click the Disc button. Drag in the viewports to create a disc object.
2. Select the two end polygons and click the Multiply menu tab, and then click the Bevel tool in the Extend section. Drag in the Top viewport to create an inset circle with a smaller radius.

3. Select Points from the bottom of the screen, select a point in the Top viewport on the outer radius of the disc object, hold down the Shift key, and then select the adjacent point on the inner radius.
4. Click the Detail menu tab and then click the Weld button in the Points section.

   A dialog box opens and notifies you that four points were welded.
5. Continue around the disc object, repeating steps 3 and 4.

   A star shape appears after the points are welded around the outer disc, as shown in Figure 5.26.
6. Select the File, Save Object As menu command and save the file as Welded star.lwo.

FIGURE 5.26
Welded star

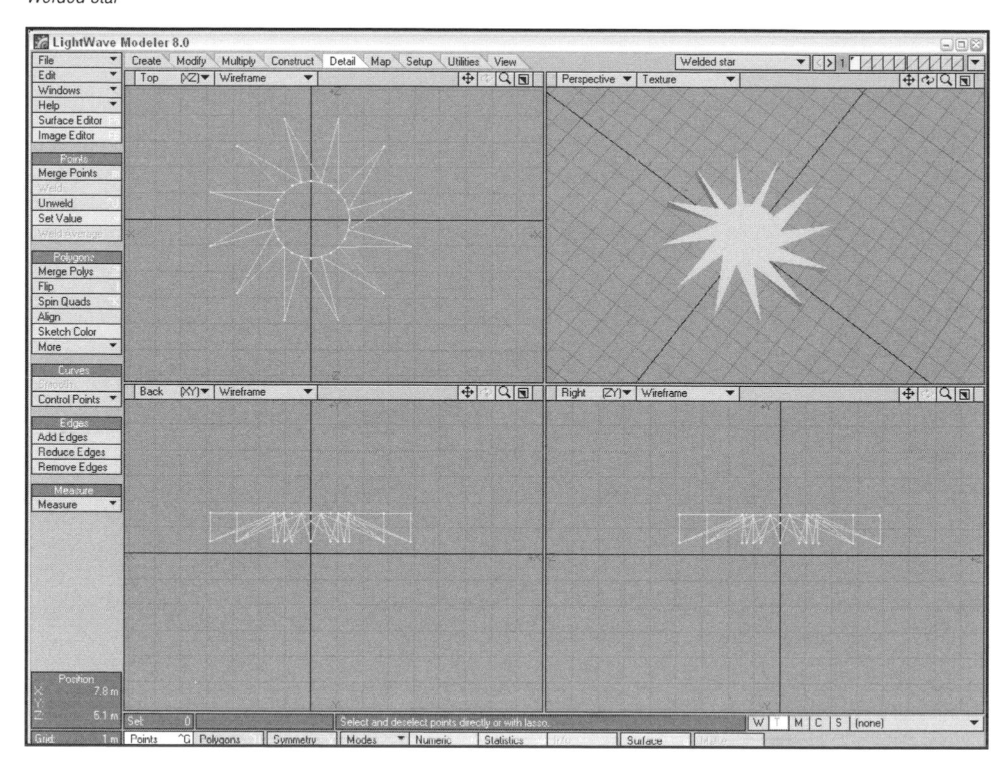

LESSON 5

ALIGN POLYGONS

What You'll Do

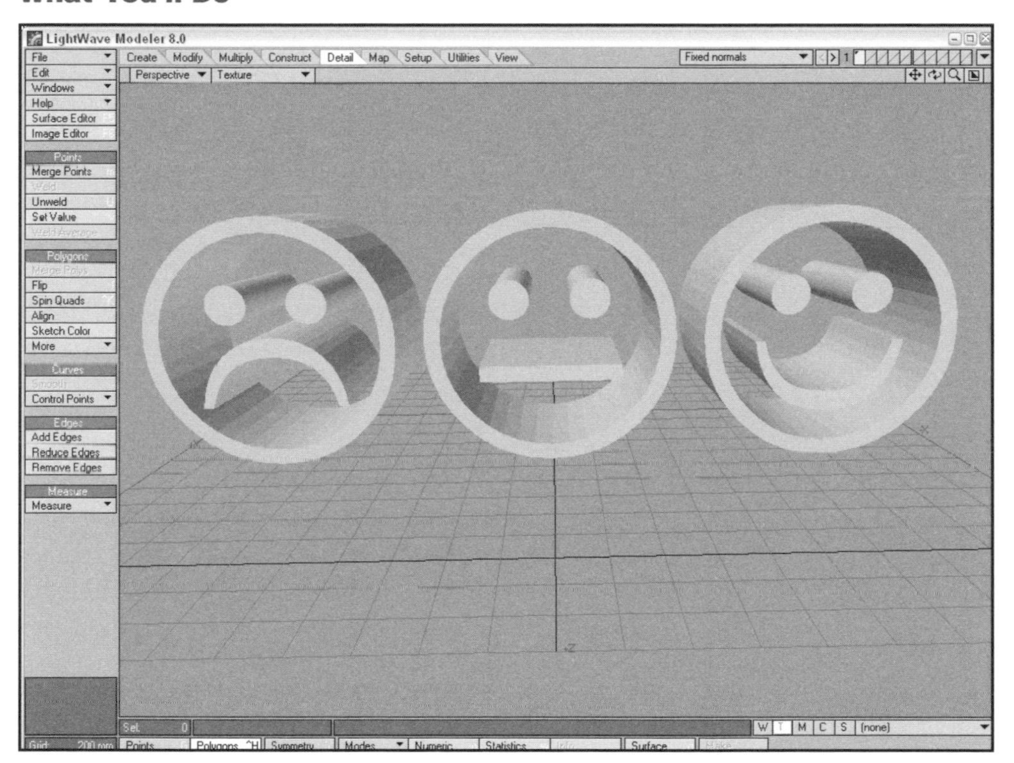

In this lesson, you'll learn how to combine polygons by merging, flipping, and spinning their elements.

The Detail menu tab includes a set of commands for working with polygons. This lesson also explains what normals are and how to work with them.

Merging Polygons

Just as you can merge points, you can also merge any adjacent polygons you select that share an edge using the Detail, Polygons, Merge Polys button. Using this command eliminates the edge between the two polygons.

Flipping Polygons and Curves

When you select a polygon, a single line extends perpendicular from the polygon face. This line is called a **normal**, and it is used to tell which way the polygon faces. If a polygon normal faces away from the camera's view, its backside is facing the camera, typically making it invisible.

Figure 5.27 shows two boxes. The one on the left has flipped normals. Notice how all the normal vectors are pointing inward. The box on the right has outward facing normals. To fix this condition, select the Detail, Polygons, Flip button. You can also use this command on curves to change the ending point to the starting point, and vice versa. If all the normals for an object point every which way, you can use the Detail, Polygons, Align button to align all the normals so they point in the same direction.

Spinning Quads

Another potential polygon problem happens when several polygons with parallel edges are smoothed in a way that shows bands. To break up the polygons so they are smoothed correctly, you can use the Detail, Polygons, Spin Quad button. You can use this button when you select two adjacent polygons. Using this command combines the two polygons and then separates them by adding an edge that runs diagonally. If an edge already runs diagonally across the two selected polygons, using this command switches the direction that the edge runs.

Creating Double-Sided Polygons

If you have a hole in an object through which you can see inside to the back side of the polygons on the opposite side of the object, the polygons won't be visible, because their normals are pointing away from the camera view. If you want to make the backside of a polygon visible, you can make it double sided using the Detail, Polygons, More, Double Sided command. **Double-sided polygons** have a normal pointing away from both sides.

FIGURE 5.27

Box with flipped normals

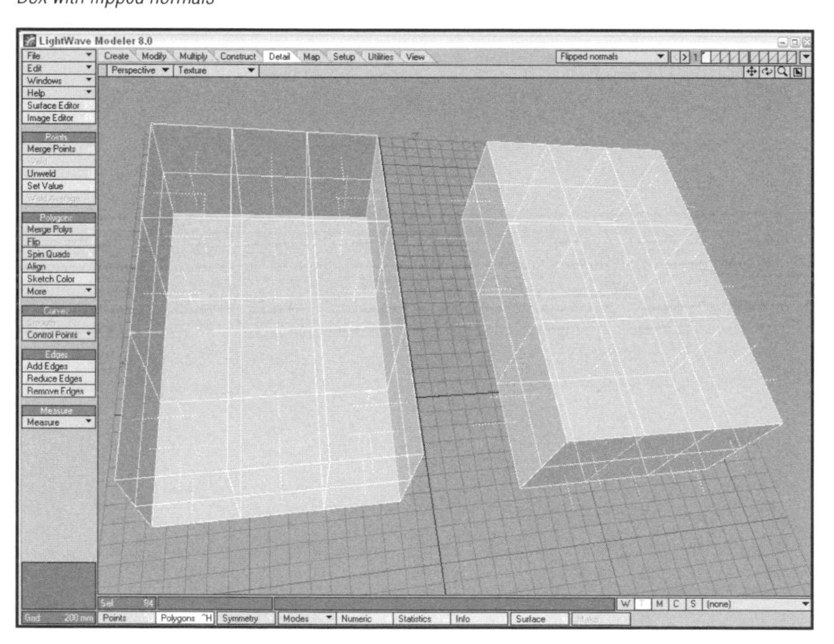

FIGURE 5.28
Fixed normals

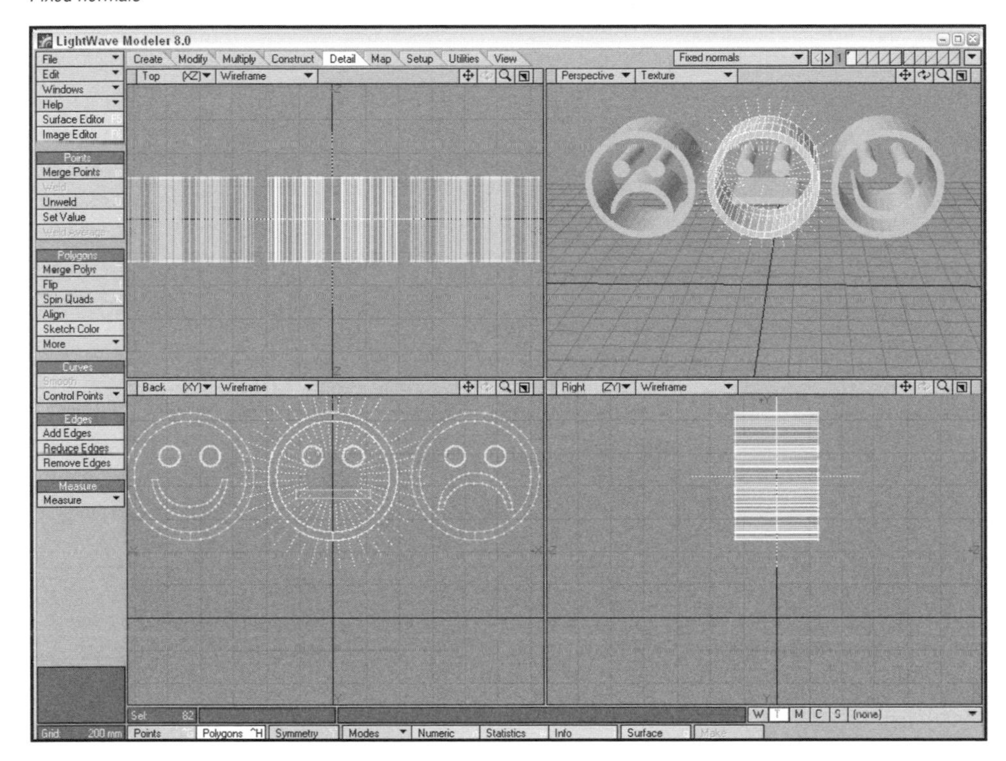

Flip normals

1. Click the File, Load Object menu command and open the Flipped normal.lwo file.
2. Look in the Perspective viewport and try to figure out which object has flipped normals.
3. With the Polygons selection mode active, drag over the polygons in the Back viewport to verify the direction of the normals.

   The middle cylinder has flipped normals. You can tell this by looking in the Perspective viewport, where you can see the backside of the object, and by selecting the polygons in the Back viewport to see which way the normals point.
4. Select all polygons that make up the center cylinder object. Click the Detail menu tab and then click the Flip button in the Polygons section.

   The view in the Perspective viewport is now correct, as shown in Figure 5.28.
5. Select the File, Save Object As menu command and save the file as Fixed normals.lwo.

LESSON 6

ADJUST CURVES AND EDGES

What You'll Do

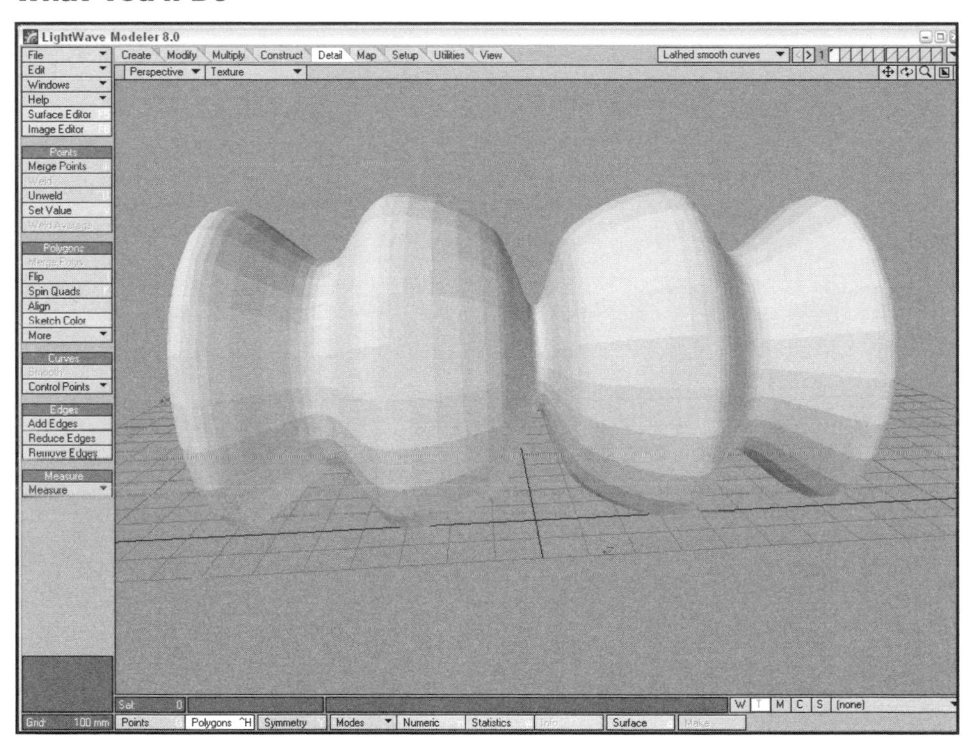

In this lesson, you'll learn how to adjust curves and edges.

Curves and edges are similar in some ways, but different in others. Curves are independent of polygons and you can use them in certain operations like lathing. You use edges to create polygons.

Smoothing Two Adjacent Curves

If two separate curves share an end point, you can smooth the connection between these two curves using the Detail, Curves, Smooth button. After using this command, the two curves will still be separate curves, but they are adjusted so there is a smooth connection between them. Figure 5.29 shows two curves that meet in the center of the screen before and after the Smooth command.

Adjusting Curve Ends

Use the Detail, Curves, Control Points button to add a dashed line to the end of the selected curve. When you drag this dashed line, you adjust the curvature of the end point of the curve.

Adding Edges

When you click the Detail, Edges, Add Edges button, you open a tool you can use to add edges to an object. When this tool is active, blue handles appear at the midsection of each edge of the selected polygons. You can drag these edges to specify where the new edge starts. After dragging the edge markers to their correct locations, click on each to create the new edge. Figure 5.30 shows a new edge being created toward the bottom of this box object.

Reducing and Removing Edges

To reduce edges, you again need to select the edge markers for the edges that you want to reduce. You can use the Remove Edge button to select the mid-edge marker of the edge that you want to select, and press Enter to remove the edge.

FIGURE 5.29
Smoothed curves

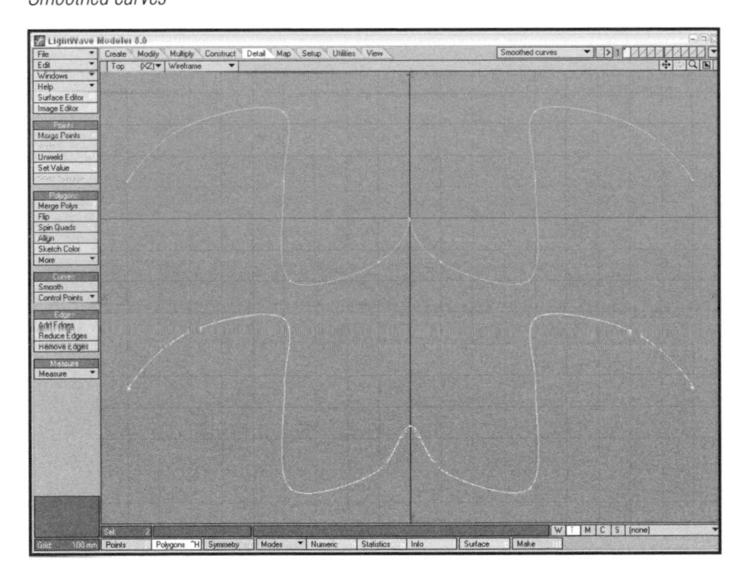

FIGURE 5.30
Creating a new edge

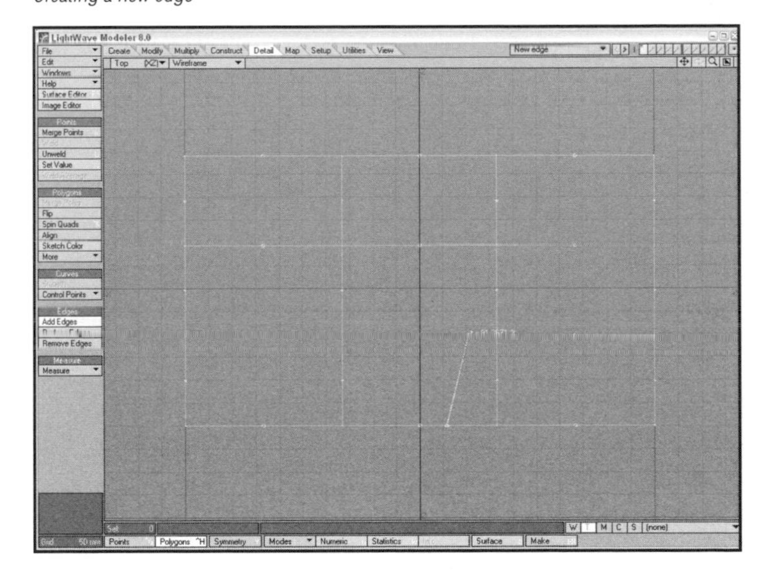

Lathe a smooth curve

1. Click the Create menu tab and then click the Spline Draw button in the Curves section. Click several times in the Top viewport to create a curve object.
2. Click the Multiply menu tab and then click the Mirror button in the Duplicate section. Drag in the Top viewport on the curve's right end point.

   This creates a mirrored curve that is connected to the first curve.
3. Select both curves, click the Detail menu tab, and then click the Smooth button in the Curves section.

   Clicking the Smooth button causes the curves to be smoothed where they are connected.
4. Select the first curve and click the Flip button in the Polygons section.

   The Flip button switches the curve's start and end points so that the normals are correct when the curves are lathed.
5. Select both curves again, click the Multiply menu tab, and then click the Lathe button in the Extend section. Click in the Top viewport where the highest point is located and drag to the left.

   The curves are revolved about their axis, as shown in Figure 5.31. Notice how the point where the curves meet is smooth.
6. Select the File, Save Object As menu command and save the file as Lathed smooth curves.lwo.

FIGURE 5.31
Lathed smooth curves

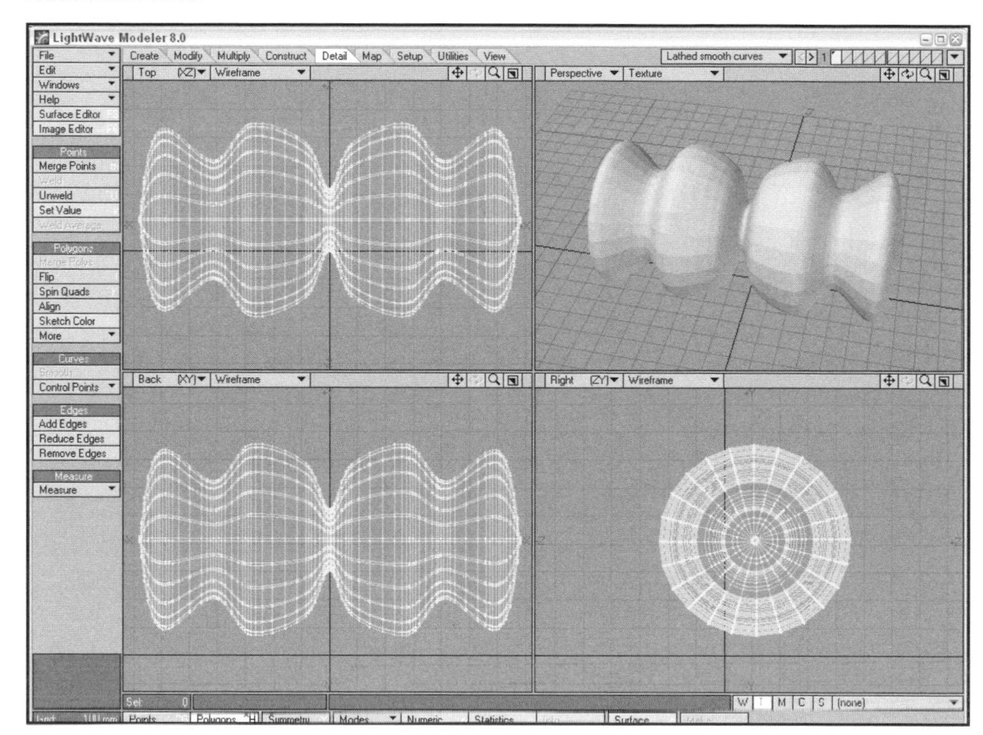

FIGURE 5.32

New and removed edges

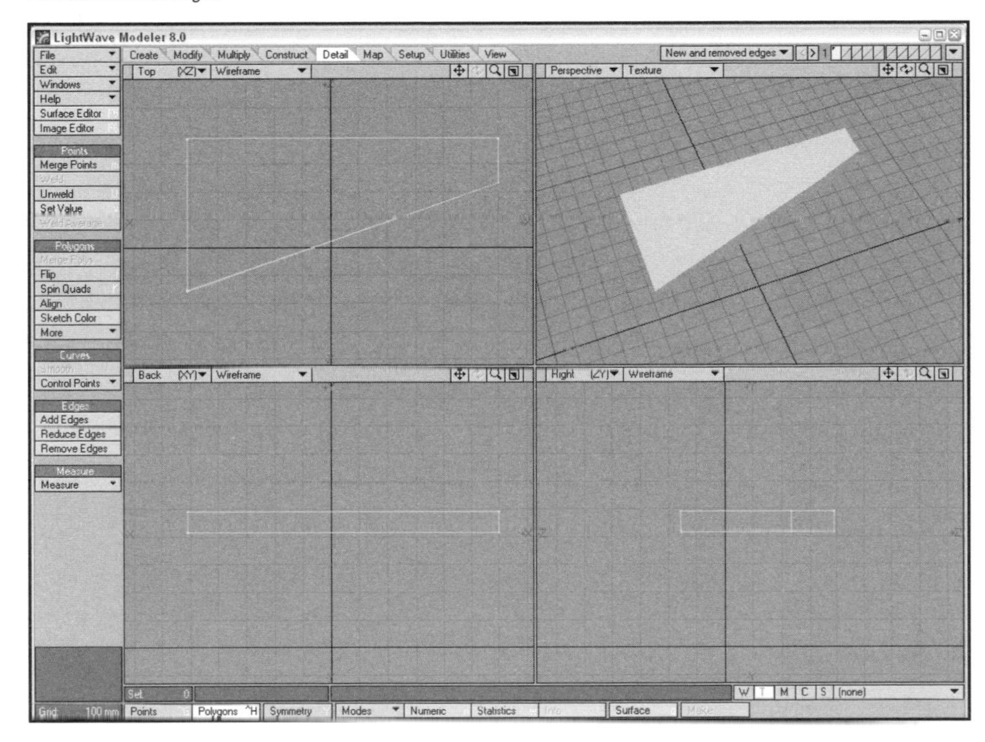

Remove an edge

1. Click the Create menu tab and then click the Box button. Click in the Top and Back viewports to create a box object. Press the left and down arrow keys until the box includes only one segment.
2. Click the Detail menu tab and then click the Add Edges button in the Edges section.

   Markers appear at the middle of each edge.
3. Click the right edge marker in the Top viewport and drag it halfway toward the top-right corner. Click the opposite edge marker and drag it halfway toward the lower-left corner.

   A new edge between these two dragged points is created.
4. Click the lower middle marker in the Right viewport and drag to the left until a new vertical edge is created.
5. Click the right marker again in the Top viewport and drag to the same first point to create a new edge on the backside of the box object.
6. Complete the cut by clicking on the top middle marker in the Right viewport.

   The new edges now cut all the way around the box object.
7. Click the Remove Edges button and select the lower-middle marker in the Top viewport.
8. Repeat step 7 for all the edges below the new edges.

   With all the edges below the new edges removed, the box object looks like the one in Figure 5.32.
9. Select the File, Save Object As menu command and save the file as New and removed edges.lwo.

LESSON 7

USE THE MEASURE TOOL

What You'll Do

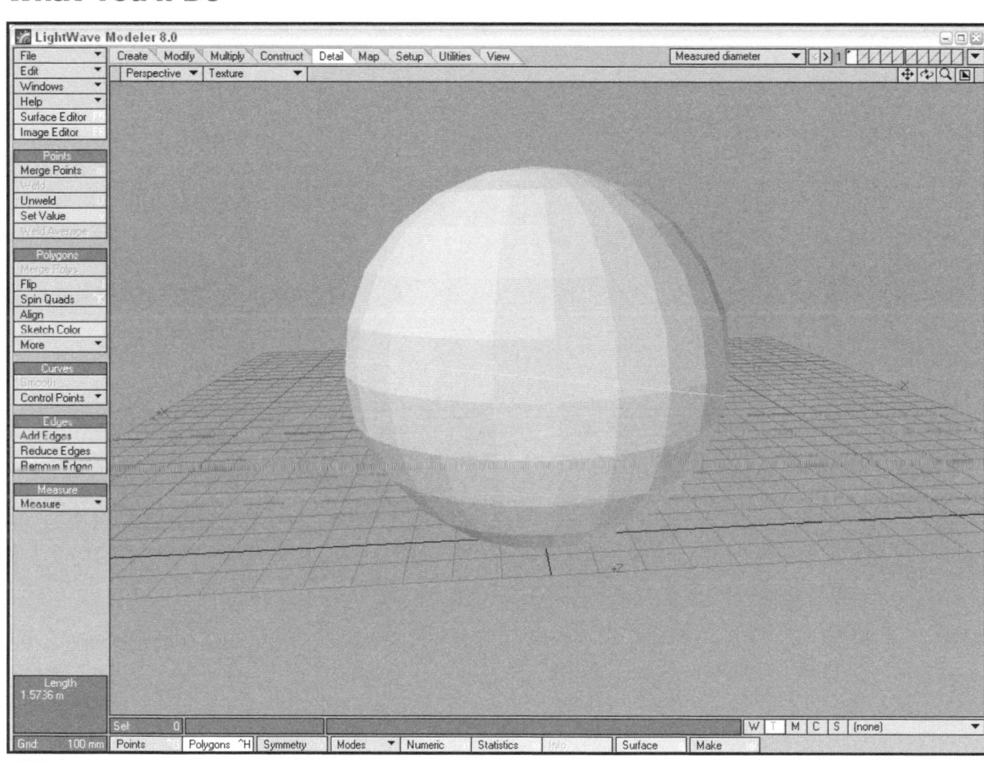

In this lesson, you'll learn how to measure distances and angles.

The Detail, Measure, Measure button includes several tools for measuring precise distances, angles, and center points.

Measuring Distance

You can measure distances using the Detail, Measure, Measure, Measure Tool. Select the Measure tool, click on the first point, and then drag in the viewport to the end point. The Length value is shown as you drag in the lower-left corner of the window, as shown in Figure 5.33.

FIGURE 5.33
Measure tool value

Length
433.2436 mm

Measuring Angles

The Detail, Measure, Measure, Angle Tool command works just like the Measure tool, except you click and drag once to create a baseline and a second time to set the angle. The angle's value is displayed in the lower-left corner of the window.

Locating the Center of a Polygon

To find the center of the selected polygon, use the Detail, Measure, Measure, Find Center command. Executing this command places a point in the center of the selected polygon.

Measure diameter

1. Click the Create menu tab and then click the Ball button. Click in the Top and Back viewports to create a ball object.
2. Click the Detail menu tab and select the Measure, Measure Tool command in the Measure section.
3. Drag in the Top viewport from one side of the ball object to the other.

   The Measure tool is displayed in blue and the diameter of the ball object is displayed in the lower-left corner of the interface while the mouse button is held down, as shown in Figure 5.34.
4. Select the File, Save Object As menu command and save the file as Measured diameter.lwo.

FIGURE 5.34
Measured diameter

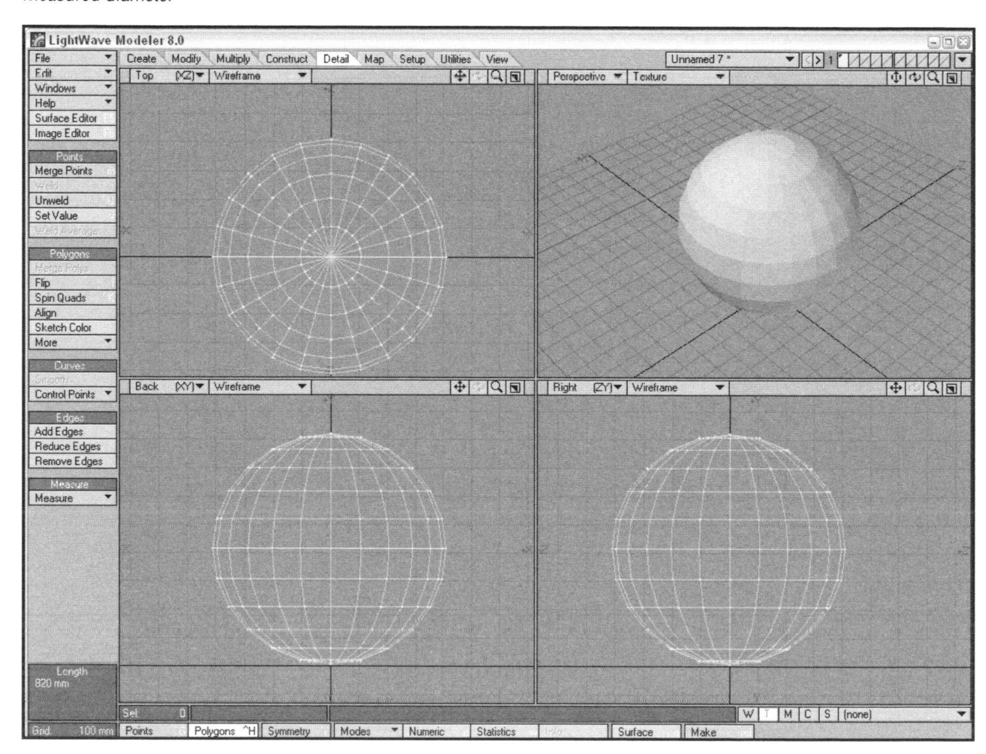

CHAPTER SUMMARY

This chapter covered all the remaining commands and tools used to modify geometry. These commands include features that reduce the number of points and polygons in an object, features to combine several objects using Boolean operations, commands to drill portions of an object, and the Bridge command to build a connection between objects. This chapter also covered commands in the Detail menu tab, welding points, merging and flipping normals, smoothing curves, and measuring distances.

What You Have Learned

- How to simplify an object by reducing its total number of points and polygons.
- How to combine objects using Boolean operations for Union, Subtract, Intersect, and Add.
- How to use the Drill commands to create holes in geometry.
- How to convert objects to subpatches for smooth, flowing surfaces.
- How to merge and weld points together to simplify polygons.
- How to work with normals to flip polygon faces.
- How to flip curves and extend curve lengths.
- How to use the Measure tool to determine the distance between two points.

Key Terms from This Chapter

- **co-planar points.** Points that exist within the same plane.
- **surface border.** A line or edge where a defined surface material ends and a new one begins.
- **Boolean.** Several methods for combining overlapping geometry sections, including Union, Subtract, Intersect, and Add.
- **Bridge tool.** A tool that creates a polygon tunnel joining two object holes.
- **patch.** A modeling construct created by stretching a polygon mesh over a set of curves.
- **converting.** The process of changing one modeling type to another.
- **subpatch.** A modeling type created by converting a polygon model to create a smooth organic-looking object.
- **welding.** The process of combining two points to make one.
- **normal.** A vector that is projected perpendicular from the center of a polygon face. It determines which polygon face is pointing outward.
- **double-sided polygon.** A polygon object that has two visible sides.

CHAPTER 6

SURFACING OBJECTS AND MAPPING TEXTURES

1. Apply a surface.
2. Use the Surface Editor.
3. Set surface properties.
4. Use the Texture Editor.
5. Use environment settings and shaders.
6. Use vertex maps.
7. Work with vertex color and UV texture maps.

CHAPTER 6 SURFACING OBJECTS AND MAPPING TEXTURES

Now that you have modeled objects, there is another key feature to learn in the Modeler before moving on to the Layout interface. This chapter describes surfacing objects, which is the process of adding color, transparency, and textures to objects.

Each polygon has a **surface** applied to it by default, but by selecting polygons and using the Surface button at the bottom of the interface, you can give a specific selection of polygons a different surface name. You can alter the properties for that surface using the Surface Editor.

The Surface Editor includes physical property values you can set to define the look and feel of the surface. These properties can include color, transparency, texture, glow, and reflection. You can also use the Surface Editor to define images used in the environment for reflection and refraction maps. Within the Surface Editor, you can assign textures to any of the available properties using the Texture Editor.

Using the Texture Editor, you can load bitmap images, select a grayscale **procedural texture**, or create a gradient. You can apply these textures to many different surface properties to create effects like blotchy highlights and surface bumps.

You can use **vertex maps** to apply information to the vertices of objects. For example, you can apply weight information to specify which vertices have more pull and which shouldn't be moved when an object is converted to subpatches. Vertex maps can also hold color information applied at the vertex level.

To apply weights and colors, use the Vertex Paint dialog box, which includes a sizable brush for painting directly onto objects. Another common use of vertex maps is to apply a UV texture map to objects that can't be mapped using one of the normal projection methods.

Tools You'll Use

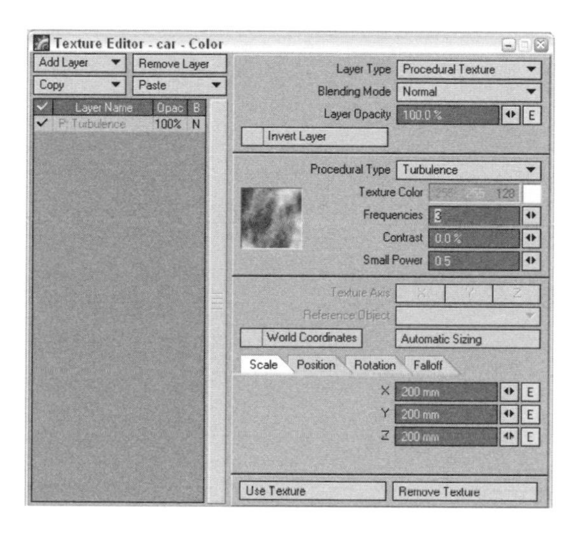

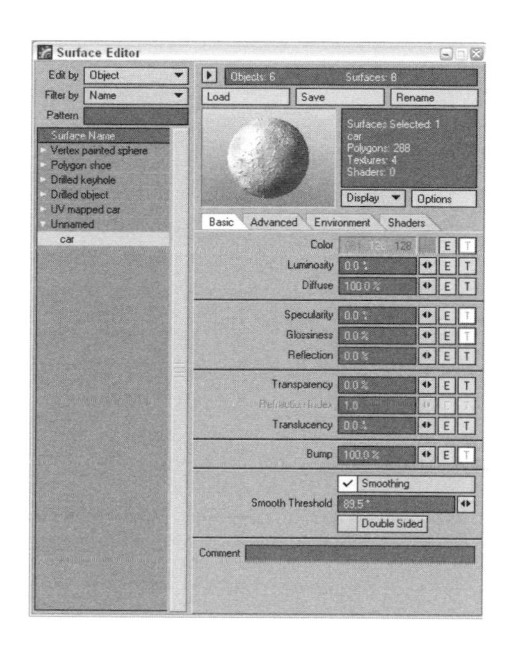

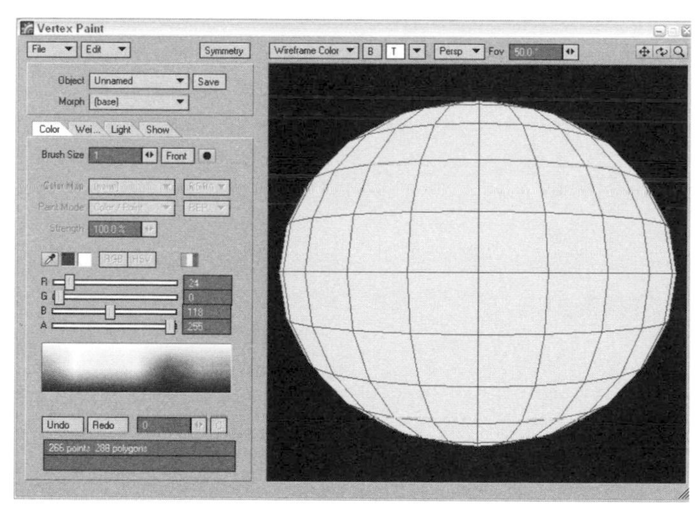

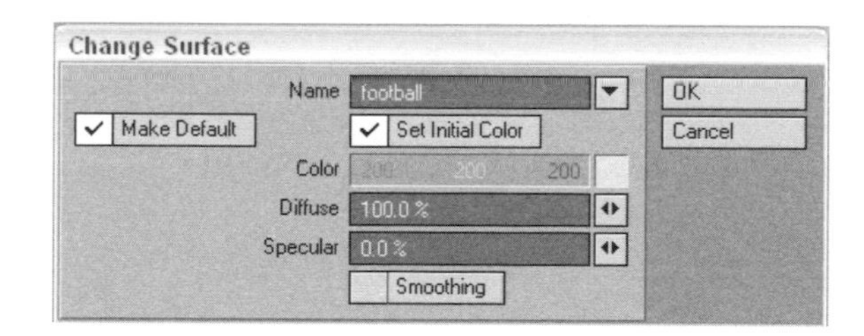

LESSON 1

APPLY A SURFACE

What You'll Do

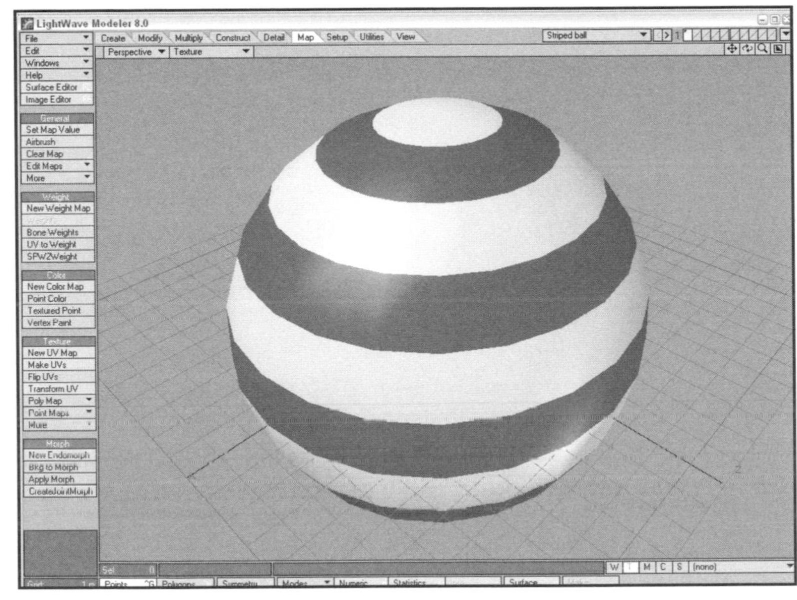

In this lesson, you'll learn how to apply surfaces to an object using the Change Surface dialog box.

Use the Surface button (keyboard shortcut: q) at the bottom of the interface to name a surface and apply it to the selected set of polygons. When you click this button, the Change Surface dialog box, shown in Figure 6.1, opens.

Naming Surfaces

Use the Change Surface dialog box to name the surface for the selected polygons. This name should reflect the type of surface you intend to apply to the selection; for example, blue rubber, shiny red, or yellow cloth. You can select a surface name from the drop-down list or type a new name, and then later apply that surface name to selected polygons. This name will also appear in the Surface Editor, where you can define exactly how the sur face looks.

FIGURE 6.1
Change Surface dialog box

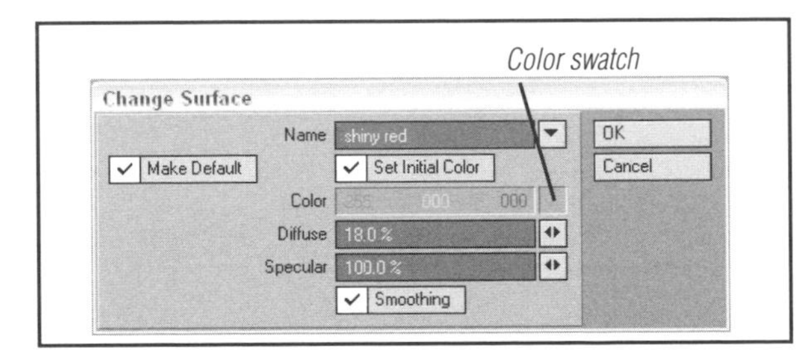

NOTE

You can change surface names in the Surface Editor by clicking the Rename button.

Selecting an Initial Color

After you name an object, you can click on the Set Initial Color options to enable the Color property. Clicking the color swatch opens the Color Selector dialog box, shown in Figure 6.2, where you can select a color. You can also change the color by changing the Red, Green, and Blue color values. This color, along with the Diffuse and Specular values, is used to shade the objects in all viewports that are set to display texture. If you already applied a surface to the selected polygons, only the Name field is active. To define the default surface that is applied to all new objects, click the Make Default option.

Changing the Diffuse and Specular Values

The **Diffuse** value controls how saturated the color is. A Diffuse value of 100% shows the pure color, and a Diffuse value of 10% is almost black. The Specular value determines the amount of highlights that shine off the object as the light hits it. The Smoothing option causes all polygons to be smoothed across the surface. When you disable this option, each polygon face is visible. Figure 6.3 shows several examples of the Diffuse, Specular, and Smoothing properties.

FIGURE 6.2
Color dialog box

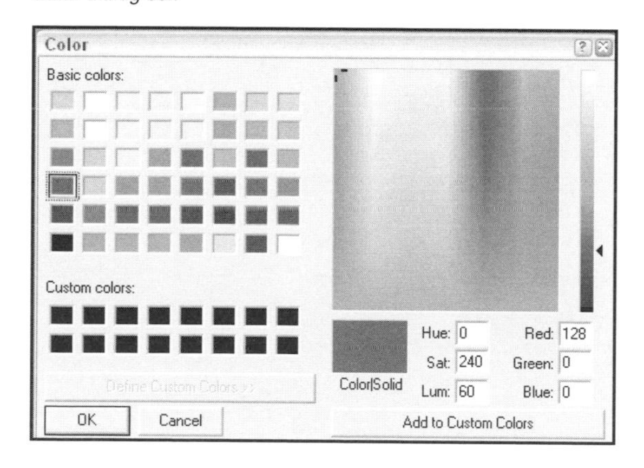

FIGURE 6.3
Spheres with varying Diffuse, Specular, and Smoothing values

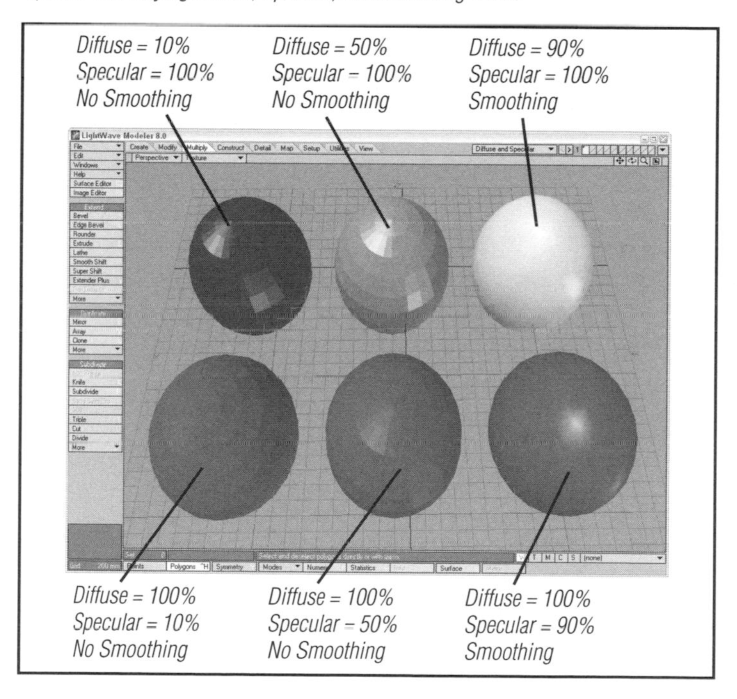

Apply a surface

1. Click the Create tab, select the Ball button, and then drag in the Top and Back viewports to create a ball object.
2. Click the Surface button at the bottom of the interface.

   The Change Surface dialog box opens.
3. Type **ball** for the name, enable the Set Initial Color option if necessary, and then click the color swatch button. Select a light blue color and click OK to close the Color dialog box. Set the Diffuse and Specular values to 100% and enable the Smoothing option. Then click OK to close the Change Surface dialog box.

   The ball object in the Perspective viewport is updated with the surface changes, displaying a light blue, smooth surface with highlights.
4. Click the Polygons button and, while holding down the Shift key, select every other row of polygons in the Back viewport.
5. Click the Surface button at the bottom of the interface again.
6. Type **stripes** for the name, select a dark blue color from the color swatch, and click OK twice.

   The selected stripes are now dark blue, as shown in Figure 6.4.
7. Select the File, Save Object As menu command, and save the file as Striped ball.lwo.

FIGURE 6.4
Striped ball

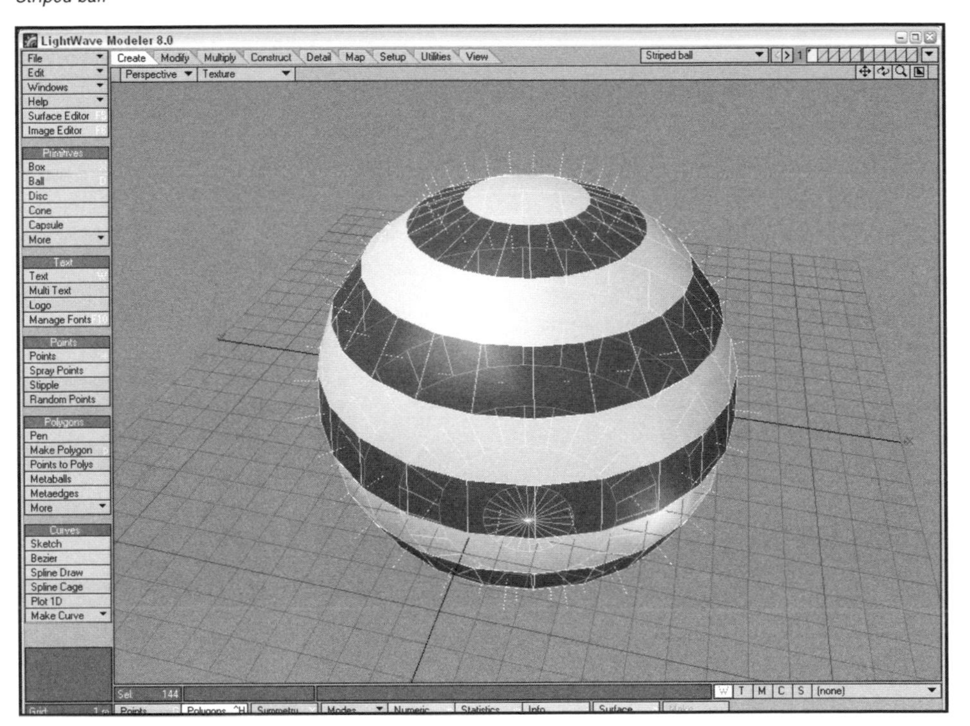

LESSON 2

USE THE SURFACE EDITOR

What You'll Do

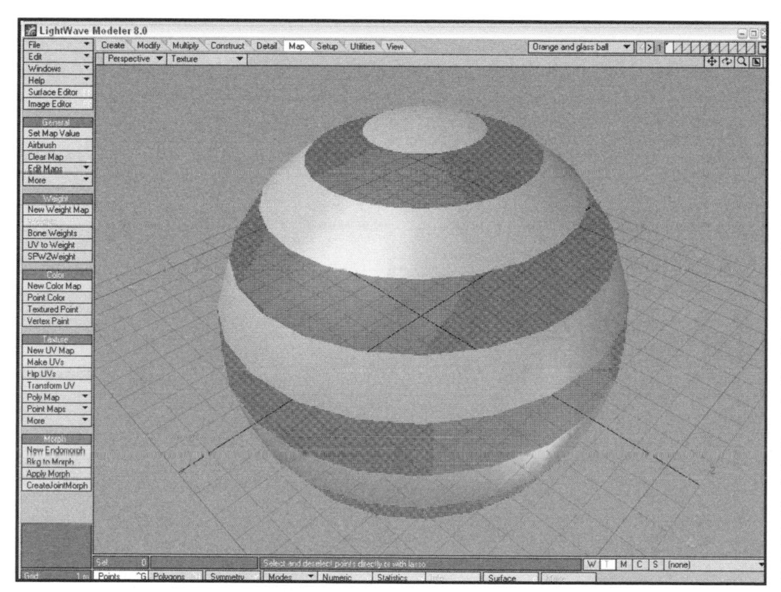

In this lesson, you'll learn how to use the Surface Editor to manage object surfaces.

The purpose of the Change Surface dialog box is to let you name and set the initial color for the selected polygons, but if you need to create advanced surfaces, use the Surface Editor, shown in Figure 6.5. To open the Surface Editor, click the Surface Editor button in the toolbox or press F5. All surface names you applied in the Change Surface dialog box are listed in the left pane of the Surface Editor. If you select a surface name and change its properties, the polygons that have that surface are automatically updated. The Surface Editor dialog box is common between the Modeler and the Layout interfaces.

FIGURE 6.5

Surface Editor

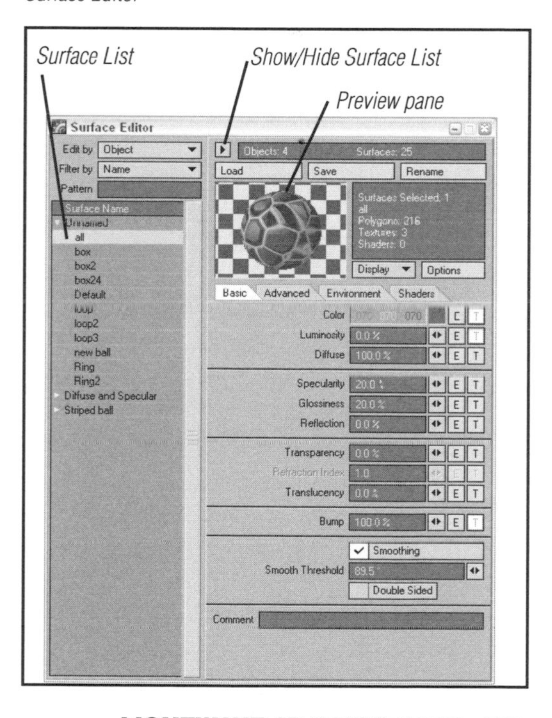

Saving and Loading Surfaces

You can save edited surfaces to your hard disk for later recall using the Save button at the top of the Surface Editor. When you click this button, the Save Surface dialog box, shown in Figure 6.6, opens. Use this dialog box to name and select the folder where you want to save the surface. Saved surfaces have the SRF extension. To open a saved surface into the Surface Editor, click the Load button.

> NOTE
>
> Compared to object files, surface files are quite small.

FIGURE 6.6

Save Surface dialog box

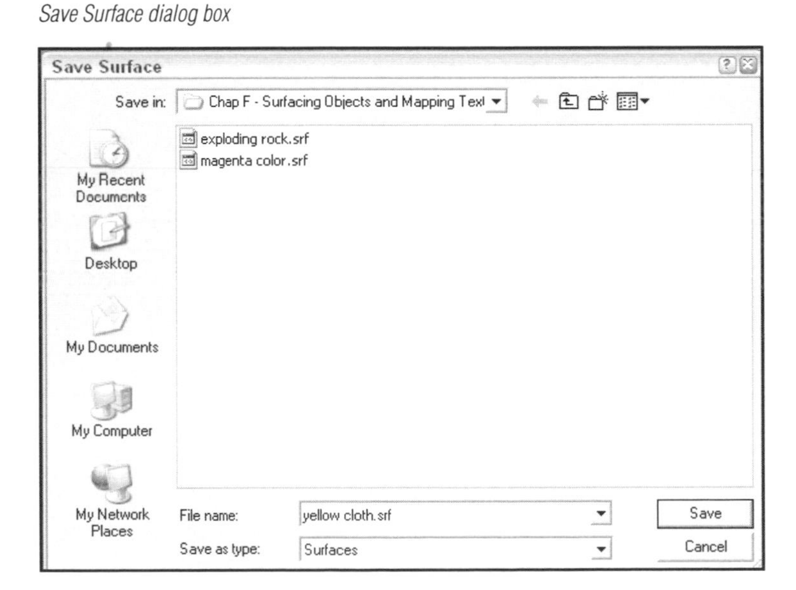

Loading Surface Presets

To give you a head start, the default installation of LightWave includes many preset surfaces that you can access. These surfaces are contained with the Surface Preset dialog box, shown in Figure 6.7, which you can open using the Windows, Presets Panel menu command (keyboard shortcut: F9). You can use the drop-down list at the top of the Surface Preset dialog box to select from several categories, including Fabric, Glass, Metal, Nature, and Rock. To load a preset surface into the Surface Editor, simply double-click it and select Yes in the Confirmation dialog box that opens.

Changing Edit Mode

The Edit By drop-down list in the Surface Editor includes two options: Object and Scene. Using Object mode restricts any surface property changes to the current loaded object, but in the Layout interface, many different objects might share a specific named surface. Using Scene edit mode lets you change the surface properties for all objects that use the named surface within

FIGURE 6.7

Surface Preset dialog box

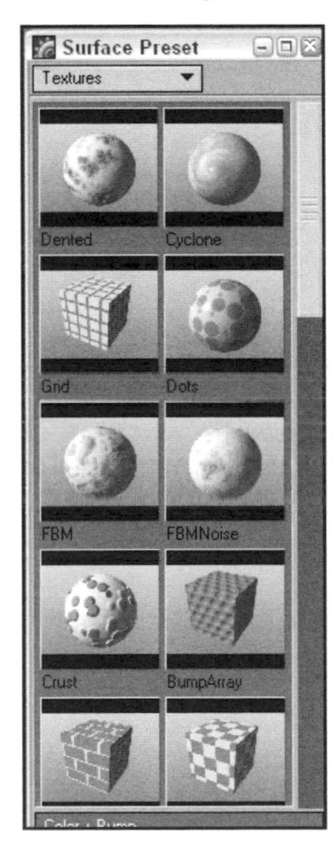

the entire scene and is useful for making global changes to surfaces.

Using the Surface List

All available named surfaces are listed in the left pane of the Surface Editor is the Surface List. You can filter this list using the options in the Filter By drop-down list, or hide the list by clicking the arrow icon above the Load button. The current surface is displayed in the preview pane and is highlighted in the Surface List. You can select multiple surfaces by simultaneously pressing the Ctrl and Shift keys.

Copying and Pasting Surface Properties

If you right-click on the selected surface in the Surface List, a pop-up menu opens, from which you can then click Copy to copy the surface attributes. If you select another surface name, right-click on it, and then click Paste, you paste the copied attributes onto the selected surface.

Changing Preview Options

When you click the Options button, the Preview Options dialog box opens, as shown in Figure 6.8. Using these settings, you can change the sample size of the preview object, whether it is a sphere or a cube, its background, whether it is antialiased, and its refresh rate. These same options are available when you right-click on the preview pane. If you want to see just one surface property channel, use the Display drop-down list to select the specific properties that are viewed in the preview pane. Display options include Render Output, Color Channel, Luminosity Channel, Specular Channel, and Mirror Reflection.

FIGURE 6.8
Preview Options dialog box

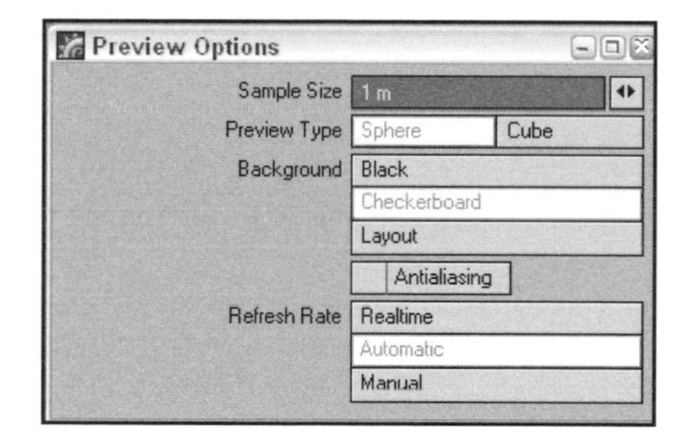

Load surface files and use preset surfaces

1. Click the File, Open Object menu command and then open the Striped ball.lwo file.
2. From the toolbox, click the Surface Editor button.

   The Surface Editor dialog box opens.
3. In the Surface Name List, select the ball surface.
4. At the top of the Surface Editor, click the Load button, locate the Orange rind.srf file, and click OK.

   The surface of the ball object is updated with the loaded surface.
5. In the Surface List, select the stripes surface.
6. From the main interface, click the Windows, Presets Panel menu command.

   The Surface Preset dialog box opens.
7. In the Surface Preset dialog box, select the Glass category from the drop-down list at the top of the dialog box, and then double-click on the Glass_Outside surface. Click Yes in the confirmation dialog box. Close the Surface Preset dialog box.

   The stripes surface is updated in the Perspective viewport, as shown in Figure 6.9.
8. Select the File, Save Object As menu command and save the file as Orange and glass ball.lwo.

FIGURE 6.9
Orange and glass ball

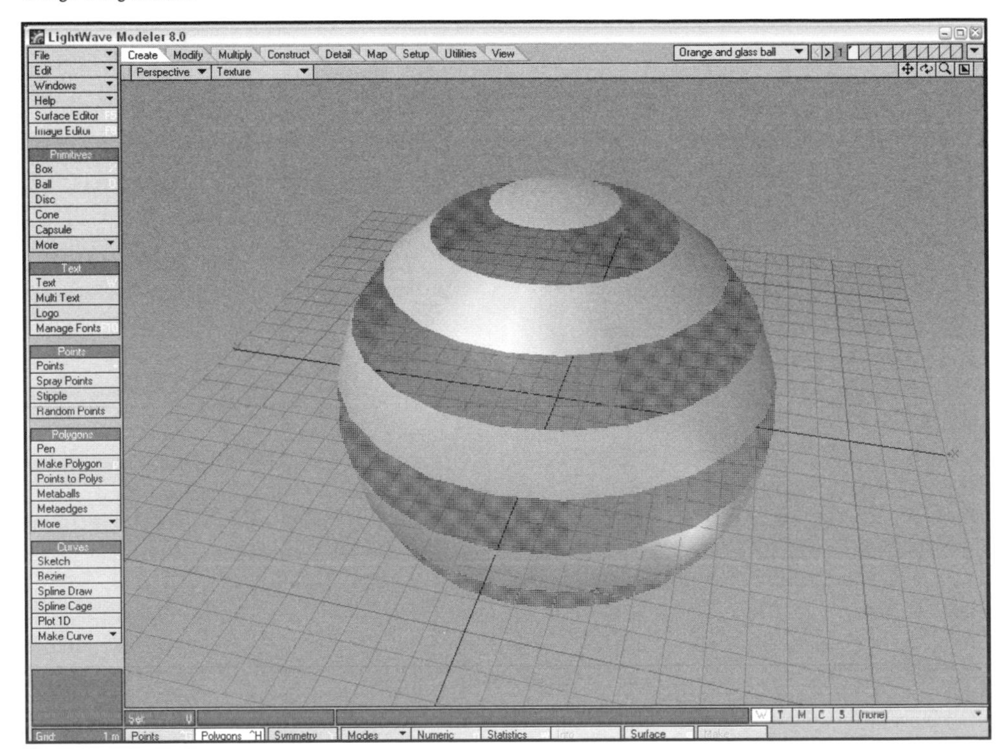

LESSON 3

SET SURFACE PROPERTIES

What You'll Do

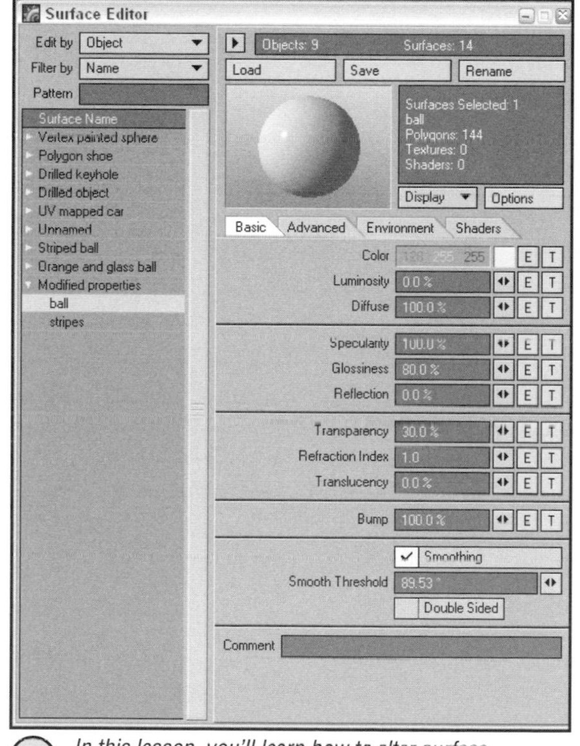

In this lesson, you'll learn how to alter surface characteristics by changing properties.

The first two tabbed panels in the Surface Editor include a variety of surface properties, which are divided into two categories: Basic and Advanced. Buttons for changing the value, and for accessing the Envelope and Texture Editors, as shown in Figure 6.10, are located to the right of each property.

NOTE

You can use envelopes to change a value over time. Envelopes are covered in a later chapter on animation.

FIGURE 6.10

Property icon buttons

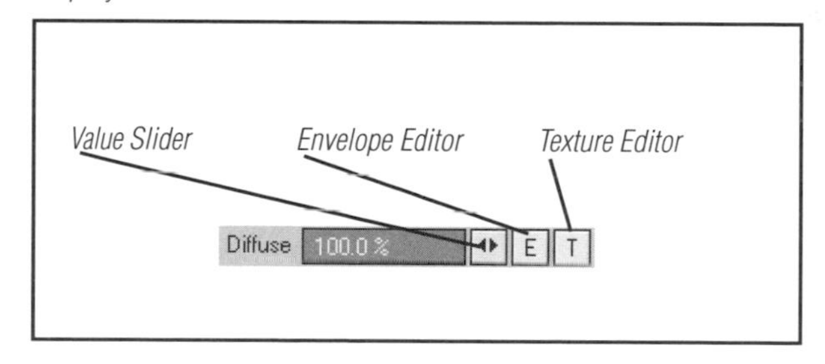

Setting Basic Surface Properties

The Basic panel in the Surface Editor dialog box includes common properties such as Color and Transparency. Other properties, such as Diffuse, Glossiness, and Bump, are more vague. Table 6.1 describes each of these surface properties. Most of these properties accept both positive and negative values.

CAUTION

Although all surface properties are visible in the Preview pane, not all surface properties will be visible in the viewport. Properties such as Reflection and Bump are only visible when a surface is rendered.

TABLE 6.1: BASIC SURFACE PROPERTIES

Property Name	Description
Color	Sets the surface color using values for Red, Green, and Blue, or using a color selector in the color swatch.
Luminosity	Defines how bright a color is. Light bulbs have a high Luminosity value because they emit light. Strong Luminosity values reduce the shadows on the surface.
Diffuse	Defines the saturation of the color. Low Diffuse values turn black, and high Diffuse values show full color.
Specularity	Defines the shininess of the surface. Surfaces with high Specularity values, like glass, have a bright highlight where the light hits them. Cloth and dirt have low Specularity values.
Glossiness	Determines how the specular highlights spread out over the surface. Clear glass has a high Glossiness value, and frosted glass has a low Glossiness value.
Reflection	Specifies how surroundings are reflected. A mirror has a maximum Reflection value.
Transparency	Specifies the transparency of the surface. Transparent objects are objects you can see through, like glass.
Refraction Index	Specifies how light is bent as it passes through transparent objects like glass. A thin layer of glass does not refract the light much, but thick glass would bend it more. Different types of materials bend the light to different degrees.
Translucency	Specifies the translucency of the surface. A Translucent object is one that allows light from behind to shine through it, such as a projector screen or a leaf.

Setting Advanced Surface Properties

The Advanced panel includes properties for creating certain effects, such as glowing objects. Each of these surface properties is explained in Table 6.2.

TABLE 6.1: BASIC SURFACE PROPERTIES

Property Name	Description
Bump	Specifies bump values. You use **bump maps** to add small textures to a surface, such as an orange rind. You typically apply a bump map as a grayscale texture, which causes the dark areas to rise and lighter areas to be inset in the surface.
Smooth Threshold	Specifies values for the Smoothing option, which causes all polygons whose adjacent normals form an angle less than the Smooth Threshold to be smoothed. Adjacent polygons that have an angle that exceeds the Smooth Threshold aren't smoothed.
Double Sided	Specifies whether both sides of a surface are visible.
Comment	Provides a text box where you can add comments about the defined surface. These comments are visible when the surface is enabled.

TABLE 6.2: ADVANCED SURFACE PROPERTIES

Property Name	Description
Alpha Channel	Specifies how the selected surface is saved to the alpha channel when you select the Save Alpha Image option in the Rendering Options dialog box. Alpha channels are typically used to mark the opaque areas of the object. The options include Unaffected by Surface, Constant Value, Surface Opacity, and Shadow Density.
Glow Intensity	Specifies how the object color radiates from the surface. This glow shines onto all surrounding objects.
Render Outlines/ Line Size	Renders the polygons edges instead of the polygon face. Use this option to create a rendered wireframe of the object. The Line Size defines how thick the edges are.

(continued on next page)

TABLE 6.2: ADVANCED SURFACE PROPERTIES (CONTINUED)

Property Name	Description
Vertex Color Map/ Vertex Coloring	Specifies a map to use for vertex colors and whether to use the vertex coloring feature, which lets you color the surface by coloring its vertices instead of its face. Vertex coloring is a memory-efficient way to color objects and is typically used for game objects.
Color Highlights	Mixes the light color with the surface color to change the color of the highlights.
Color Filter	Defines how much the objects seen through the surface are tinted by the object's color. This option is only relevant for transparent objects.
Additive Transparency	Adds the brightness of the color behind a transparent surface to the surface color, causing the transparent surface to become brighter.
Diffuse Sharpness	Causes the shadow line on a surface to become more pronounced and distinct.

FIGURE 6.11
Updated basic properties

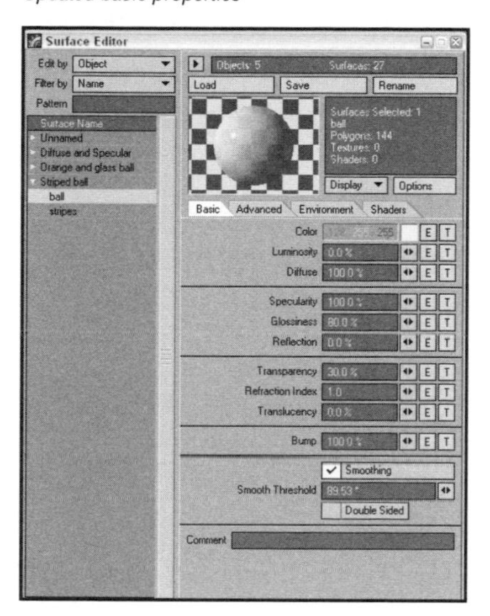

FIGURE 6.12
Updated advanced properties

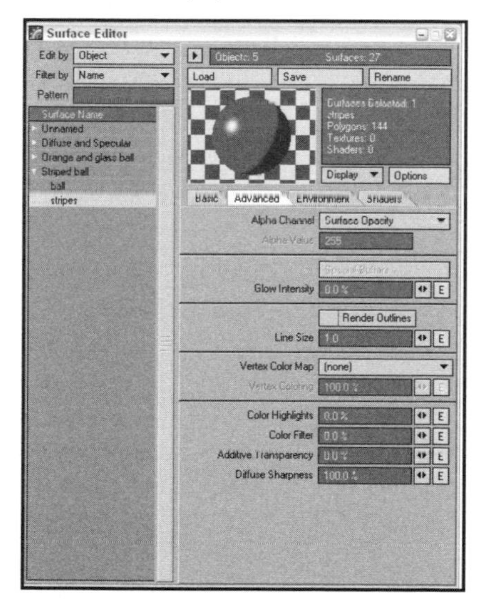

Explore surface properties

1. Choose the File, Load Object menu command and open the Striped ball.lwo file.
2. From the toolbox, click the Surface Editor button.
3. In the Surface Name List, select the ball surface.
4. In the Basic panel of the Surface Editor, set the Specularity value to **100%**, the Glossiness value to **80%**, and the Transparency value to **30%**.

   The Preview pane shows the updated surface, which is now semi-transparent with a small, sharp, specular highlight, as shown in Figure 6.11.
5. In the Surface List, select the stripes surface.
6. Click the Advanced tab in the Surface Editor dialog box.
7. In the Advanced panel of the Surface Editor, set the Diffuse Sharpness value to **100%**.

   With the Diffuse Sharpness value set to **100%**, the object appears like it is in a harsh light, as shown in Figure 6.12.
8. Select the File, Save Object As menu command and save the file as Modified properties.lwo.

LESSON 4

USE THE TEXTURE EDITOR

What You'll Do

In this lesson, you'll learn how to use the Texture Editor.

When you click the T icon to the right of one of the surface properties on the Basic tab in the Surface Editor, the Texture Editor dialog box opens, as shown in Figure 6.13. Using this dialog box, you can apply textures to the selected property. If you apply the texture to the Color property, the texture is wrapped to the surface; if you apply the texture to any other property, the image's brightness is used to set the value at each pixel, with pure white representing a 100% value and black representing a 0% value. These textures can be Image Maps, Procedural Textures, or a Gradient. When you apply a texture to a surface property, the Texture icon is highlighted and the Property value is disabled. To remove a texture from a surface property, open the Texture Editor and click the Remove Texture button at the bottom of the dialog box.

> **TIP**
>
> If you hold down the Shift key and click on the Envelope or Texture icon buttons, the envelope or texture is removed.

Layering Textures

Use the left pane of the Texture Editor to layer several different textures. To add the various texture types as a new layer, click the Add Layer button. You can also copy and paste layers in the layer pane. Use the check mark to the left of each layer name in the layer list to turn on and off the texture layer. The Opacity setting is located to the right of the layer name. Any layers underneath a layer with an Opacity value of 100% won't show through. The final column in the Layer list denotes the Blending Mode, which you can set using the drop-down list under the Layer Type field. Use the Blending Mode option to specify how the image is blended with the layers below it. Options include Normal, Additive, Subtractive, Multiply, and Alpha.

Loading an Image Map

When you first open the Texture Editor, the Image Map option is selected by default as the layer type. You can use this option to load a bitmap image using the Load Image option in the Image drop-down list. The Load Clip or Still dialog box, shown in Figure 6.14, opens, and here you can select the image file to load. After you load an image, it appears in the image pane beneath the Image field and its name appears in the Image drop-down list.

FIGURE 6.13

Texture Editor dialog box

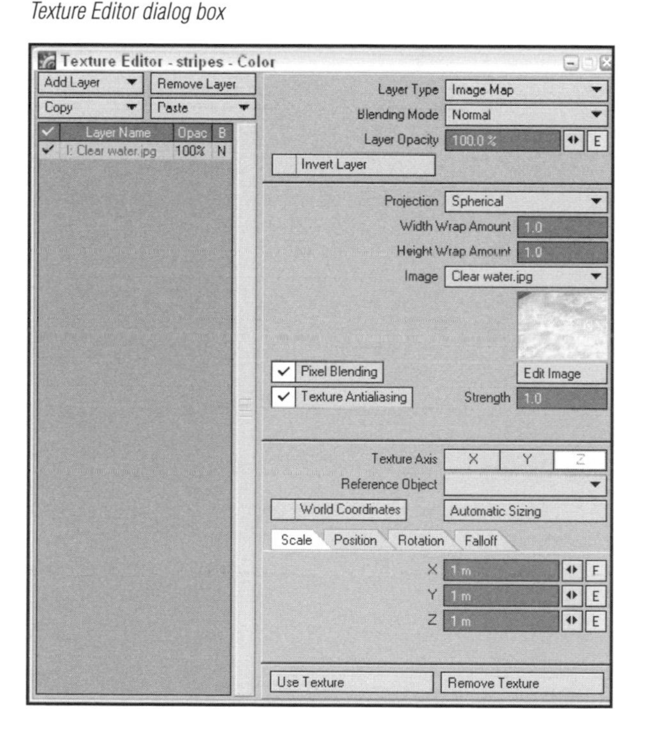

FIGURE 6.14

Load Clip or Still dialog box

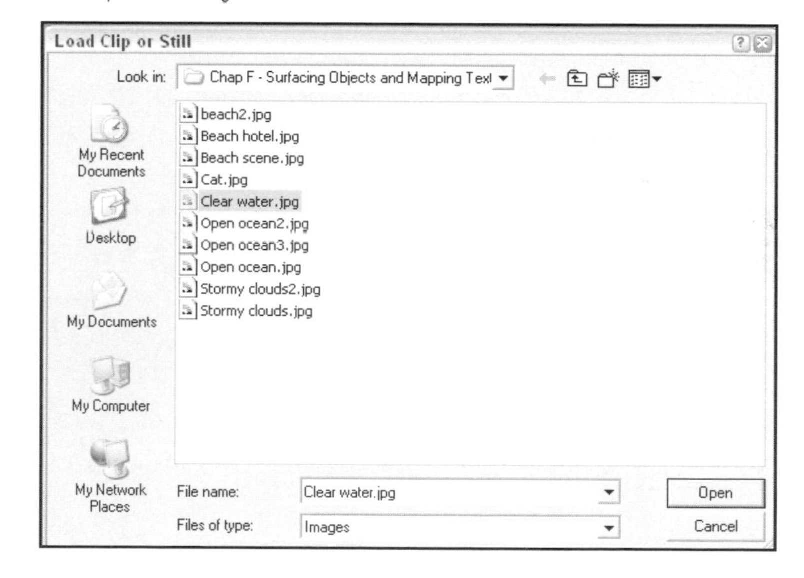

Editing an Image Map

After you load an image map into the Texture Editor, you can use a number of settings to specify how the image appears on the surface. The Projection options set how the image is wrapped about the surface. The Projection options include Planar, Cylindrical, Spherical, Cubic, Front, and UV. You can select how the many times the image wraps around the width and height of the surface. Using the Pixel Blending option smoothes the image to prevent any raster effects, and the Texture Antialiasing option, along with the Strength value, reduce any jagged edges that appear. When you click the Edit Image button, the image opens in the Image Editor, shown in Figure 6.15. You can also open the Image Editor by pressing F6. You can use the Image Editor to work with still images, video, and animation sequences. Using the Image Editor, you can control image properties, such as interlacing, and video properties, such as frame rate. The Editing panel includes controls for changing properties such as Brightness, Contrast, Hue, Saturation, and Gamma.

TIP

Use the projection type that closely matches the object. For irregularly shaped surfaces, you can use **UV coordinates**, which are covered in a later lesson.

Positioning Images

The bottom section of the Texture Editor includes controls and panels for specifying how the image is positioned on the surface. The Texture Axis sets the axis that is used to apply a Planar projection. The Scale panel includes scale settings for the X, Y,

FIGURE 6.15
Image Editor dialog box

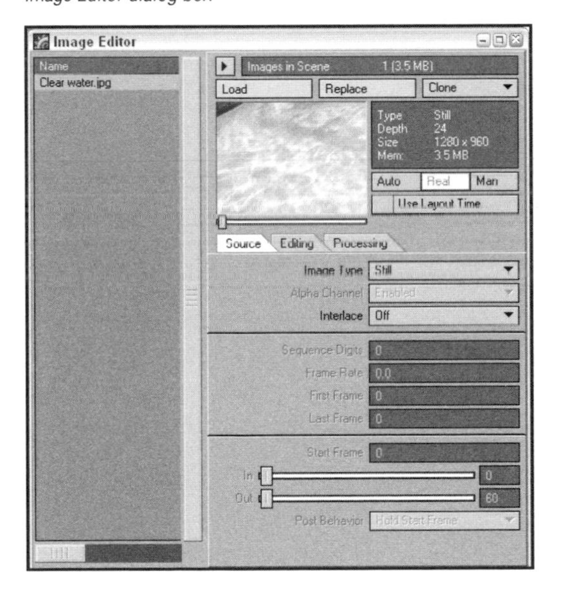

and Z dimensions. If you click the Automatic Sizing button, these dimensions are automatically set to values that correspond to the size of the surface object. Using the Position panel sets the precise location of the starting corner of the image map. Use the Rotation panel to rotate the image map about three axes.

Using Procedural Textures

Procedural textures, shown in Figure 6.16, are like predefined grayscale bitmaps that you can apply to surface properties. Using the Procedural Type drop-down list, you can select from an assortment of texture types, including Brick, Smoky, Honeycomb, Ripples, Veins, and Clouds. Each procedural texture has its own settings that you can control.

> NOTE
>
> The Procedural Type drop-down list is available only when the Procedural Texture option is selected as the layer type.

Creating Gradients

A **gradient** is a series of colors that slowly transition between colors. By selecting the Gradient option in the Layer Type drop-down list in the Texture Editor, you can select exactly which colors are included in the gradient and how quickly the transitions between the colors happens, as shown in Figure 6.17. To change the gradient colors, click the Gradient ramp. A bar appears that crosses the ramp. Dragging the icon on the left side of the ramp lets you drag to move the color bar. Clicking the right icon removes the color bar. You can use the Input Parameter drop-down list to select the definition for the gradient.

FIGURE 6.16
Procedural textures

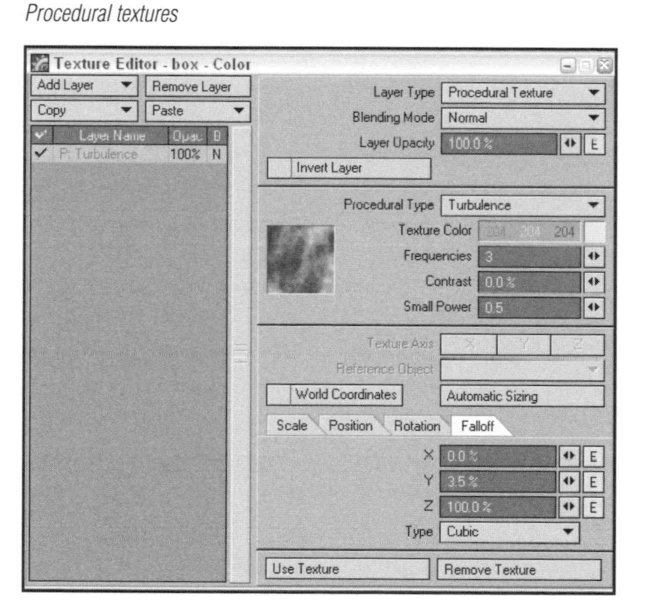

FIGURE 6.17
Creating a gradient

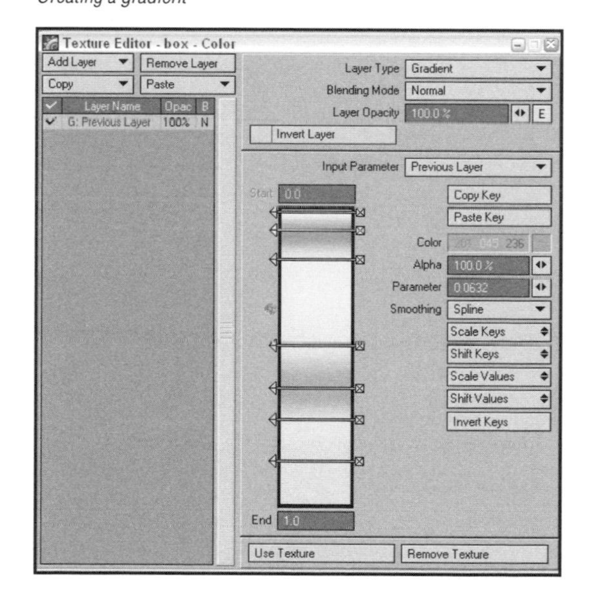

Apply an image map to an object

1. Click the Create tab, click the Box button, and then drag in the Back viewport, followed by the Top viewport, to create a box object that fills most of the Back viewport. Change the shading method for the Perspective viewport to Texture.
2. Click the Surface button at the bottom of the interface.
3. Type in the name **Box** and click OK to close the Change Surface dialog box.
4. From the toolbox, click the Surface Editor button to open the Surface Editor dialog box, and then select the box surface.
5. Click the Texture button to the right of the Color property.

   The Texture Editor opens.
6. In the Texture Editor, click the Image button and select the Load Image option.

   The Load Clip or Still dialog box opens.
7. In the Load Clip or Still dialog box, load the Beach hotel.jpg file.

   The loaded image appears in the Texture Editor dialog box.
8. Select the Planar option from the Projection drop-down list, and then enable the Pixel Blending and Texture Antialiasing options, if necessary.
9. Click the Edit Image button beneath the preview image.

   The Image Editor dialog box appears.
10. In the Image Editor dialog box, select the Editing tab and set the Brightness value to **–0.1**. Then close the Image Editor.

TIP Because 3D scenes include lights, you'll typically want to reduce the brightness of your mapped images to compensate for the increased light that the scene lights add.

11. Back in the Texture Editor, click the Automatic Sizing button, and click the Use Texture button.

    Clicking the Use Texture button closes the Texture Editor and updates the preview in the Surface Editor and the object in the viewport. After you close the Surface Editor, the image is mapped onto the box object, as shown in Figure 6.18.
12. Select the File, Save Object As menu command and save the file as Image mapped box.lwo.

FIGURE 6.18

Image mapped box

FIGURE 6.19
Bump mapped sphere

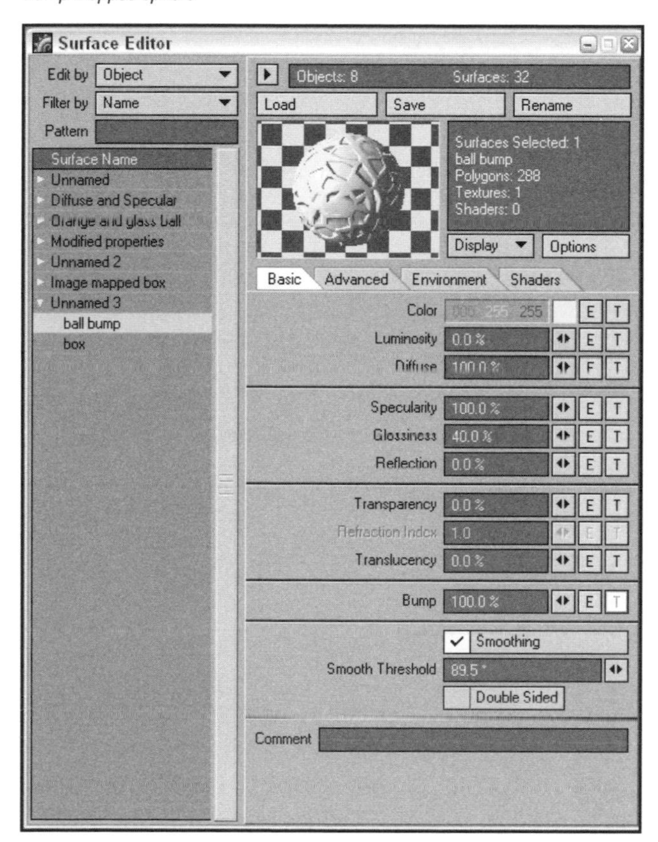

Use a Procedural Texture for a bump map

1. Click the Create tab, select the Ball button, and then drag in the Top and Back viewports to create a ball object.
2. Click the Surface button at the bottom of the interface and name the surface ball bump.
3. From the toolbox, click the Surface Editor button to open the Surface Editor dialog box, and then select the ball bump surface.
4. Click the Texture button to the right of the Bump property.
5. In the Texture Editor, click the Layer Type button and select the Procedural Texture option.

   The default Turbulence texture appears in the preview pane.
6. From the Procedural Type drop-down list, select the Veins texture and set the Texture Value to **60%**.
7. At the bottom of the Texture Editor, click the Scale tab and set the X, Y, and Z values to **200 mm**. Then click the Use Texture button to close the Texture Editor.

   The preview pane in the Surface Editor is updated with a bumpy texture, as shown in Figure 6.19. The viewport is not updated because you would need to render the ball to see the bumps.
8. Select the File, Save Object As menu command and save the file as Bumpy sphere.lwo.

LESSON 5

USE ENVIRONMENT SETTINGS AND SHADERS

What You'll Do

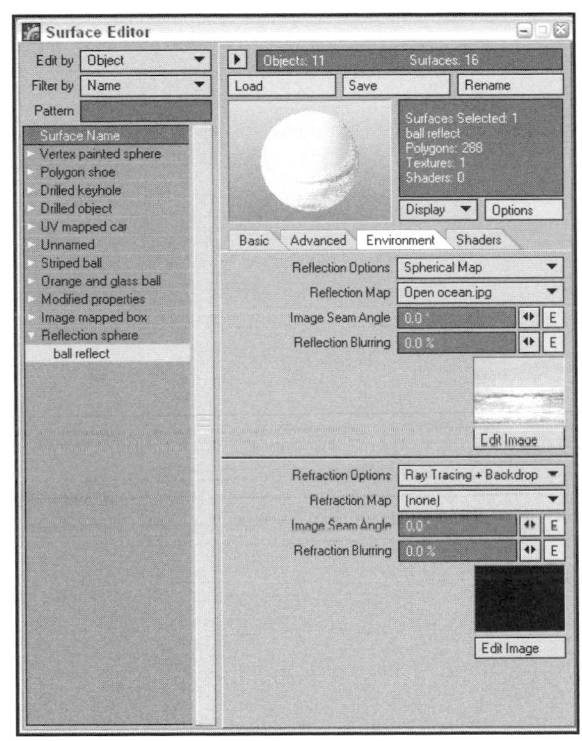

In this lesson, you'll learn how to add reflective maps and use shaders.

The final two tabs in the Surface Editor are the Environment and Shaders panels. Use the Environment panel to select environment settings, such as the image that is reflected off shiny surfaces. Use the Shaders panel to select and use different **shaders** to create specialized rendered effects.

Setting Reflection and Refraction Options

In the Environment panel of the Surface Editor, as shown in Figure 6.20, you can use the Reflection and Refraction options to specify what is reflected onto the object. The options include reflecting the backdrop, ray tracing along with the backdrop, a spherical map, or a spherical map along with ray tracing. With the Reflection and Refraction Map fields, you can load an image for use as a backdrop or as a spherical map. The Image Seam Angle sets where the seam of the loaded image appears.

FIGURE 6.20

Environment panel of the Surface Editor

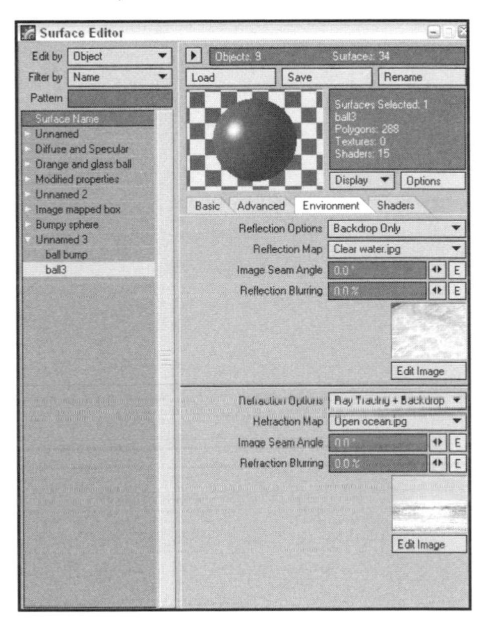

Understanding Shaders

The standard surface rendering method uses the surface attributes to realistically define how the surface should appear, but these definitions can be interpreted in different ways. A shader is a different interpretation of how surfaces should be shaded. You can program shaders and use shader plug-ins to render surfaces in different ways. For example, one surface shader called a Cel Shader renders all surfaces as if they were cartoons.

Selecting an Alternative Shader

To select one or more alternate shaders, click the Shaders panel in the Surface Editor (shown in Figure 6.21) and then click the Add Shader button. A list of available shaders is presented. If you select one, it appears in the list of shaders and becomes active. If you double-click on the shader's name, its properties are revealed in a dialog box.

FIGURE 6.21

Shaders panel of the Surface Editor

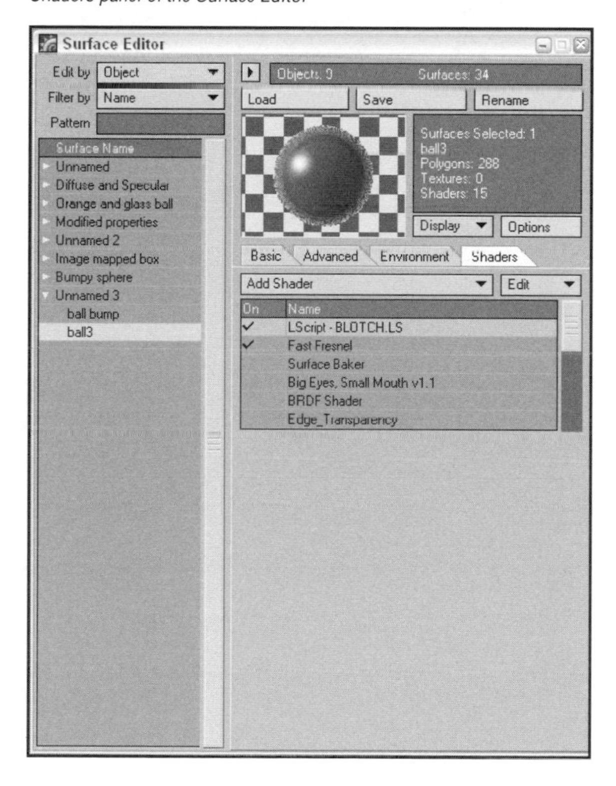

Enable a reflection map

1. Click the Create tab, select the Ball button, and then drag in the Top and Back viewports to create a ball object.
2. Click the Surface button at the bottom of the interface and name the surface ball reflect.
3. From the toolbox, click the Surface Editor button to open the Surface Editor dialog box, and then select the ball reflect surface. Click the Basic tab, if necessary. Increase the Reflection property to **60%**.
4. Click the Environment tab, set the Reflection Options to Spherical Map, and, from the Reflection Map drop-down list, click the Load Image option.
5. From the Load Clip or Still dialog box that appears, locate and select the ocean.jpg image file and click the Open button.

   The surface in the preview pane is updated to show the reflected image, as shown in Figure 6.22.
6. Select the File, Save Object As menu command and save the file as Reflection sphere.lwo.

FIGURE 6.22
Reflection sphere

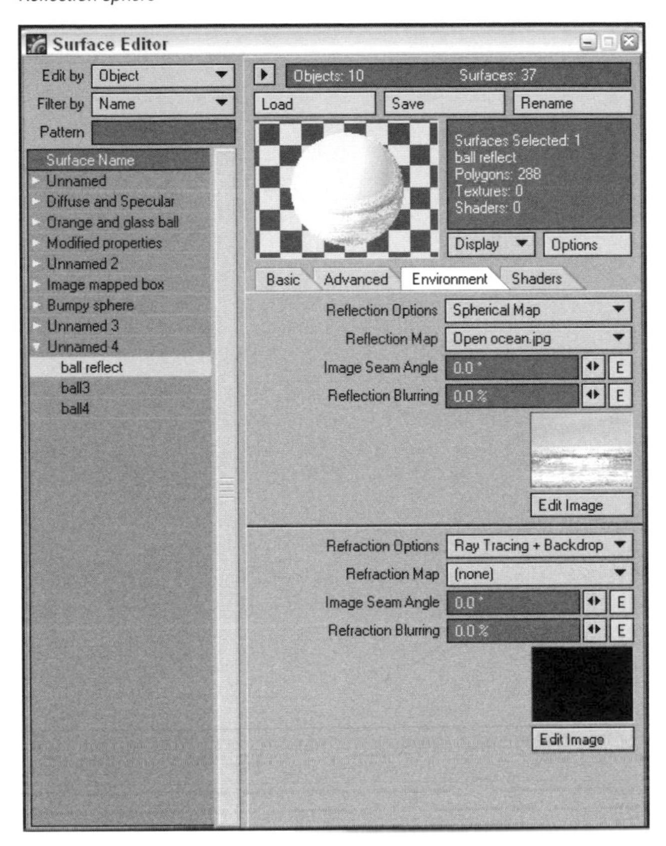

FIGURE 6.23
Halftone shader

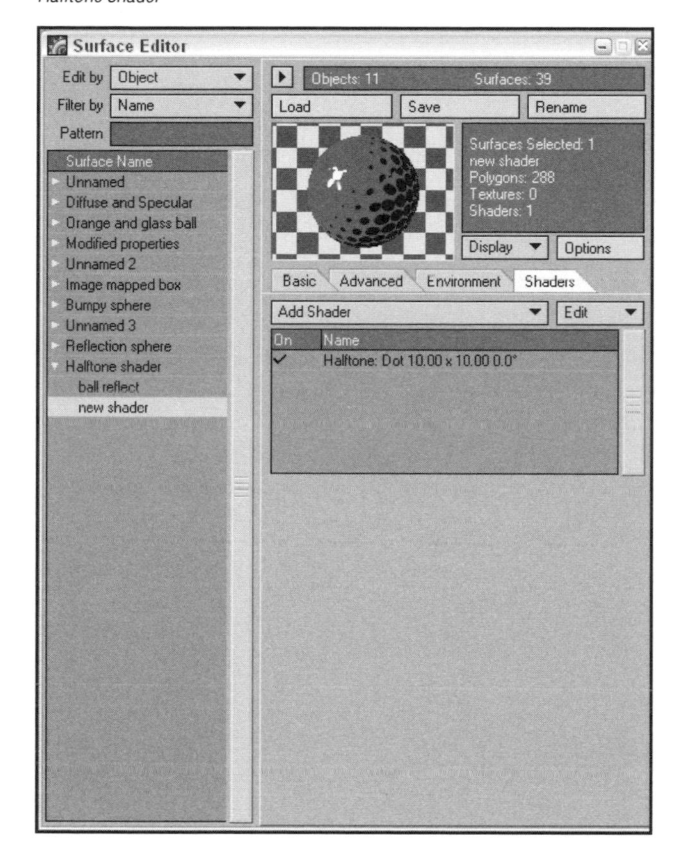

Select a different shader

1. Click the Create tab, select the Ball button, and then drag in the Top and Back viewports to create a ball object.
2. Click the Surface button at the bottom of the interface and name the surface new shader.
3. From the toolbox, click the Surface Editor button to open the Surface Editor dialog box, and then select the new shader surface.
4. Click the Shaders tab, click the Add Shader button, and then select the Halftone shader from the drop-down list.

   The surface in the preview pane is updated to show the surface rendered with the new shader, as shown in Figure 6.23.
5. Select the File, Save Object As menu command and save the file as Halftone shader.lwo.

LESSON 6

USE VERTEX MAPS

What You'll Do

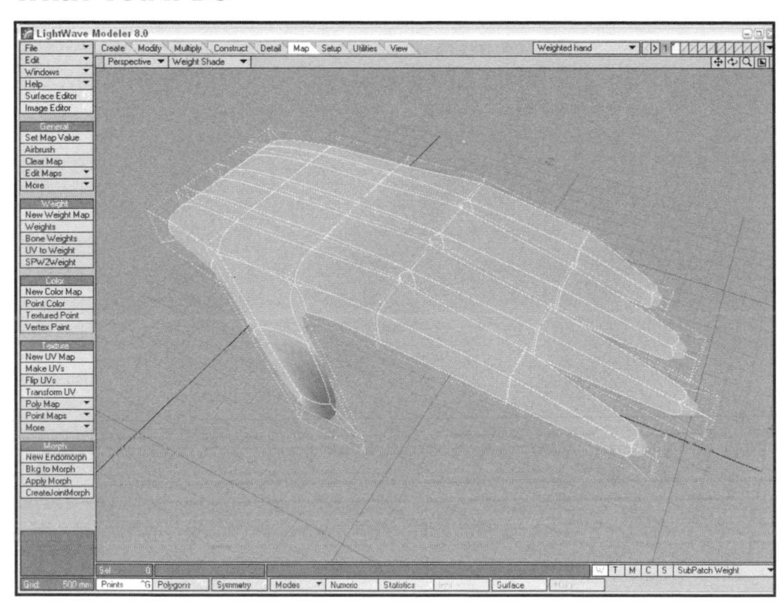

In this lesson, you'll learn how to create and use various vertex maps.

You can apply surfaces to polygons, but you might not yet know that you can also map information to points. A VMap is a collection of data that is applied to a selected set of points. There are five different available VMap types, indicated by the W, T, M, C, and S icon buttons in the lower-right corner of the interface, as shown in Figure 6.24. The VMap types correspond to Weight, UV Texture, Endomorph, Vertex Color, and Point Selection Set.

FIGURE 6.24
VMap icons

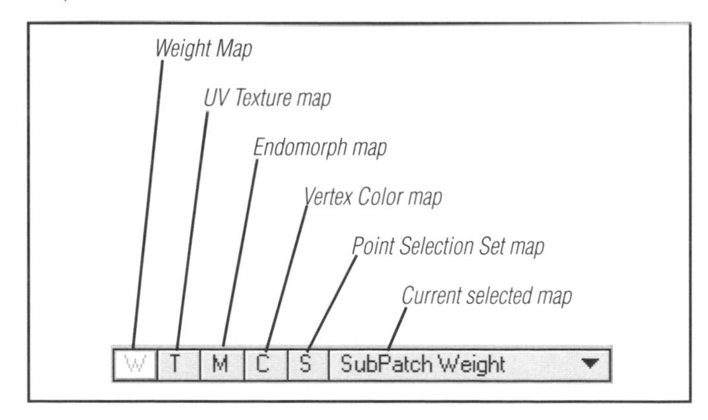

Creating New VMaps

To create a new map, click the icon of the map type you want to create and then either click the New option from the drop-down list to the right of the map icons or click one of the New Map buttons in the Map tab.

Setting Map Values

You can also set map values by selecting specific points and then clicking the Set Map Value button in the General section of the Map tab. Clicking this button opens the Set Vertex Map Value dialog box, shown in Figure 6.25. Using this dialog box, you can select the map from the top drop-down list and the values using the enabled Value fields. For example, Vertex Color maps include four values, each corresponding to color values for R, G, B, and Alpha values. If you did not select any points, the value you specify is applied to the entire object. If you make a mistake, you can reset all map values using the Clear Map button. To delete the entire map, click in the General section of the Map menu tab and click the More, Edit Maps, Delete Vertex Map menu command.

FIGURE 6.25
Set Vertex Map Value dialog box

Painting Map Values

Opening the Set Vertex Map Value dialog box for each point would be time consuming, so LightWave includes other tools that are useful for assigning vertex values. Using the Airbrush button in the General section of the Map tab, you can interactively paint vertex values in the viewports. By using the Numeric panel for a selected Vertex Color map, shown in Figure 6.26, you can select which map to paint, the brush Size and Strength, and the value that is painted.

Using Weight Maps

When you smooth a polygon object by converting it to a subpatch object using the SubPatch button in the Construct tab, vertex weight values are used to determine how much the point moves. Vertices with a weight value of 100% don't move at all, and vertices with a weight value of 0% move the maximum distance. You can interactively set weight values using the Weights button in the Weight section of the Map tab. To see the weight values as colors, select the Weight Shade display type at the top of the viewport. With the Weights tool selected, drag to the right on a point to increase its weight value and color the vertex red. Drag to the left to decrease the vertex weight and color the vertex blue in the Weight Shade display view. Figure 6.27 shows a simple box that was converted to a subpatch. The vertices along the bottom of the box are weighted to 100% and the upper vertices are weighted to 0%.

FIGURE 6.26
Numeric panel for the Airbrush tool

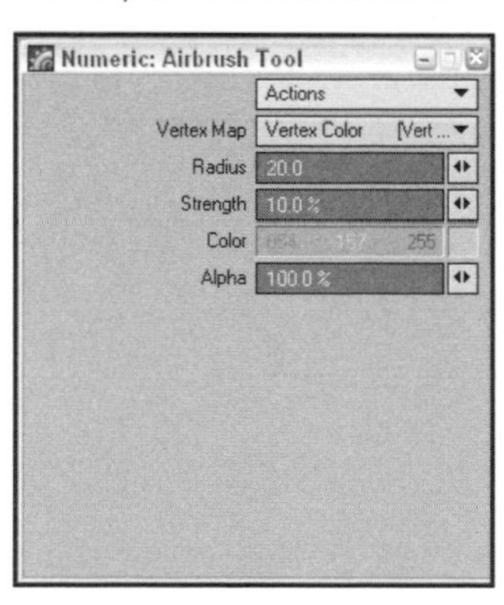

FIGURE 6.27
Box with weighted vertices

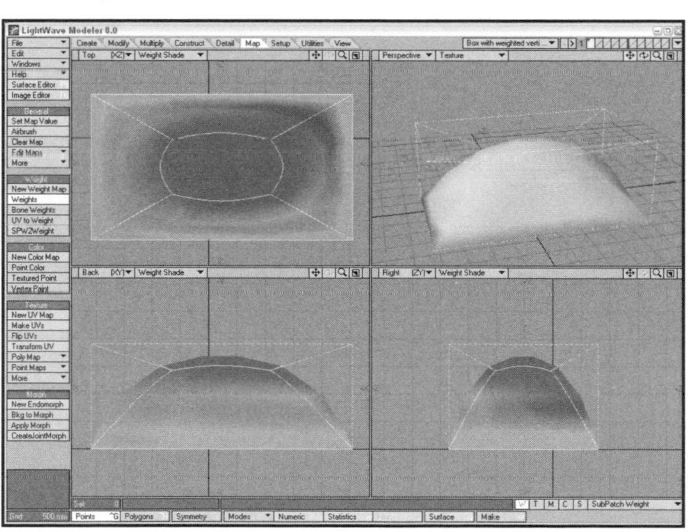

Edit a subpatch weight map

1. Click the File, Load Object menu command and open the Polygon hand.lwo file.
2. Click the Construct tab and click the Sub-Patch button in the Convert section.

   The entire hand is changed to a subpatch object.
3. In the lower-right corner of the interface, click the W icon and select the SubPatch Weight map from the drop-down list on the right.
4. In the top of the Top, Back, and Right viewports, select the Weight Shade display type.
5. Click the Map tab and select the Weights button in the Weight section. Drag in the Top viewport to the right, around the points near the first and second knuckles of the fingers, and drag to the left over the inside points on the tip of the thumb.

   Changing these weights expands the areas around the knuckles and tightens the tip of the thumb, as shown in Figure 6.28.
6. Select the FIle, Save Object As menu command and save the file as Weighted hand.lwo.

FIGURE 6.28
Weighted hand

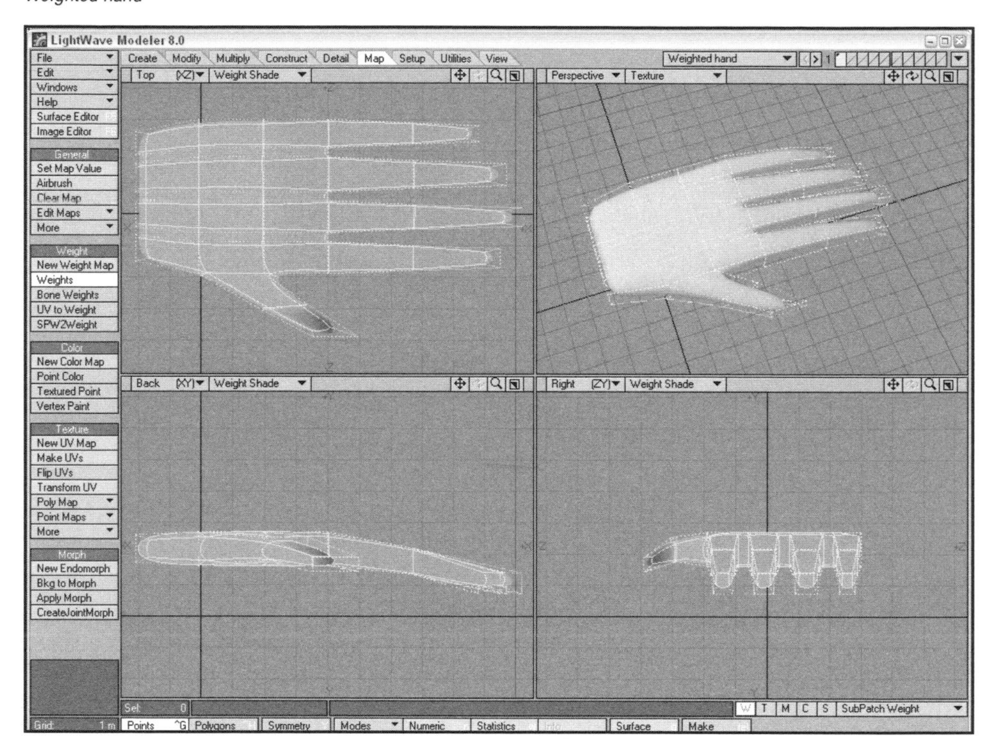

LESSON 7

WORK WITH VERTEX COLOR AND UV TEXTURE MAPS

What You'll Do

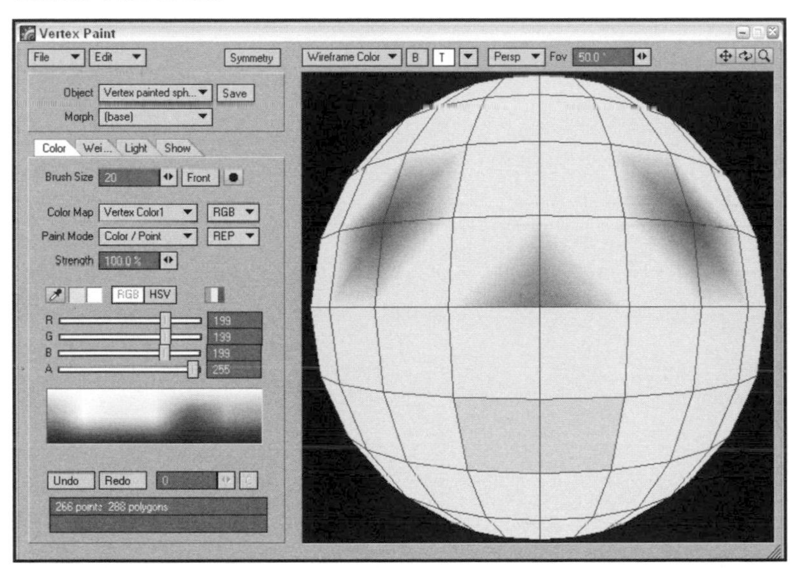

In this lesson, you'll learn how to add vertex color and UV texture maps to an object.

Two additional key vertex map types are the Vertex Color and UV Texture maps. Vertex colors offer a way to efficiently apply colors to objects because the object only needs to remember a single R, G, and B value at each vertex, which means that less data is involved than with textures. UV Texture maps provide a way to map textures onto irregular shaped objects by manipulating UV coordinates.

Coloring Points

If you create a Vertex Color map and select it in the Vertex Color Map field of the Advanced tab of the Surface Editor, you can add color to individually selected points using the Point Color button in the Color section of the Map tab. Clicking this button opens the RGBA Vertex Map dialog box, shown in Figure 6.29. Using this dialog box, you can select a Vertex Color map, RGB and Alpha values, and a Color Mode for the selected points. In addition to color, you can also use the Textured Point button to add luminosity to an applied texture.

FIGURE 6.29
RGBA Vertex Map dialog box

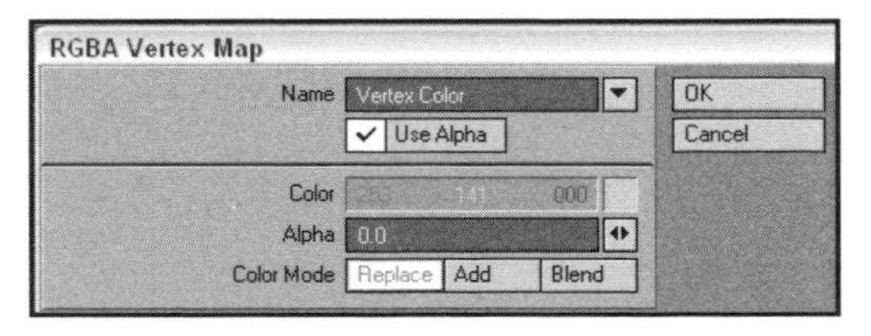

Using Vertex Paint

Clicking the Vertex Paint button in the Color section of the Map tab opens the Vertex Paint dialog box, shown in Figure 6.30. Use this dialog box to interactively color vertices by dragging over them. The left section of the dialog box includes controls for selecting an object to paint on, a color map, and a color palette. There are also three different Paint Modes: Color/Point, which surrounds the point with color; Color/Polygon, which colors the entire polygon; and Color/Index, which colors only one polygon touching a point. The right half of the dialog box displays the object and includes controls for manipulating the object, similar to the viewports.

> **TIP**
>
> You can also use the Vertex Paint dialog box to paint weights.

Adding UVs

After you create a UV Texture Map, you can add UVs to it using the Make UVs button in the Texture section of the Map tab. Clicking this button opens the Assign UV Coordinates dialog box, shown in Figure 6.31. Use this dialog box to select a Map Type as Planar, Cylindrical, Spherical, or Atlas. The Atlas projection method simply spreads the UV coordinates out on the map. Each of these projection methods provide just a place to start. To see the mapped texture in the viewports, you need to select the UV Texture map by name and select the UV Projection method in the Texture Editor.

FIGURE 6.30
Vertex Paint dialog box

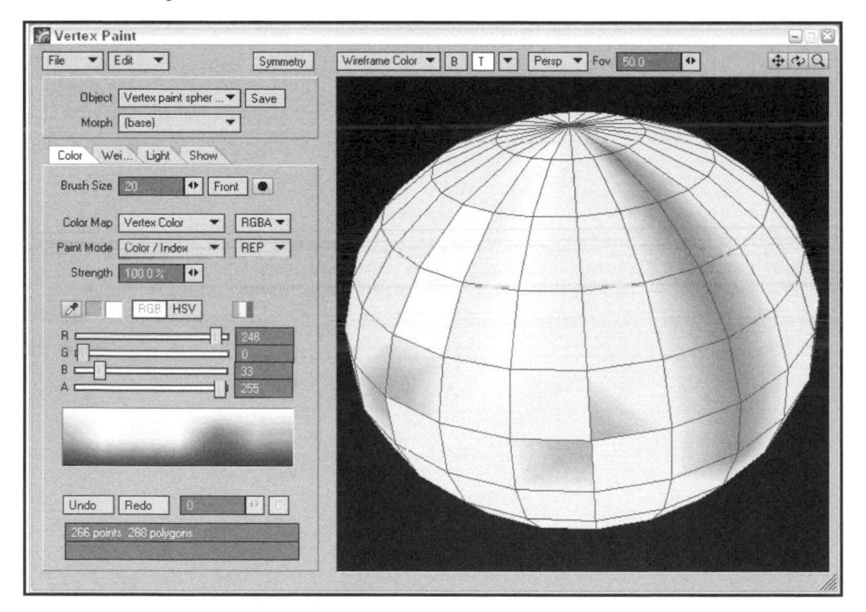

FIGURE 6.31
Assign UV Coordinates dialog box

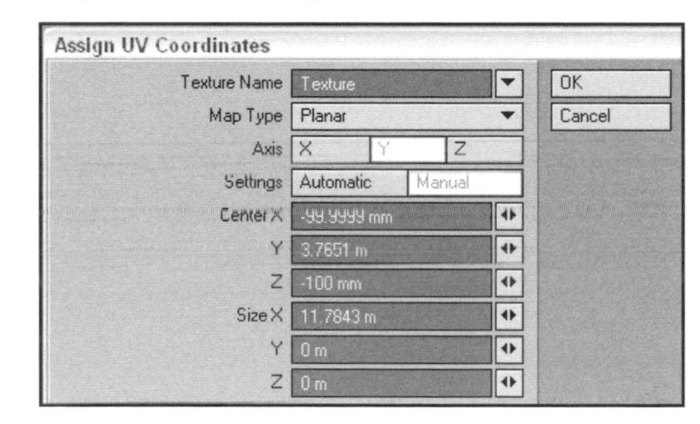

Viewing UV Texture Maps

You can view UV texture maps in the viewports by selecting UV Texture as the viewport view from the top of the viewport. The maps are two dimensional and cannot be rotated, but selecting points in any view also selects them in the UV Texture view, which makes it easy for you to see the association between the two dimensional texture map and the actual three dimensional object. Figure 6.32 shows a simple disc object that was mapped using the Atlas Map Type.

Adjusting UVs

You can select, move, and scale UV coordinates shown in the UV texture view, just as you can do with objects in the other views. You can use the Flip UVs and Transform UVs buttons in the Texture section of the Map tab to adjust the position of UVs.

FIGURE 6.32
UV texture map in the viewport

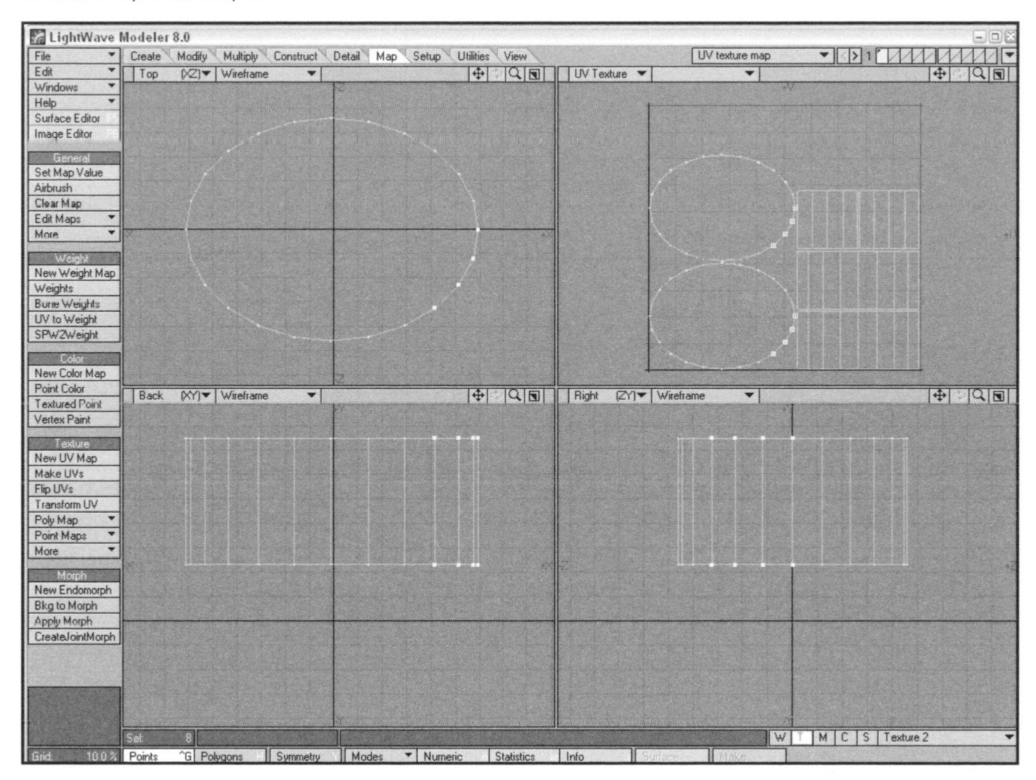

Paint vertices

1. Click the Create tab, select the Ball button, and then drag in the Top and Back viewports to create a ball object.
2. Click the Surface button at the bottom of the interface and name the surface vertex paint.
3. Click the C icon in the lower-right corner of the interface and select New from the drop-down list to its right. In the Create Vertex Color Map dialog box, type the name, **Vertex Color1**, and select vertex paint from the Apply to Surface drop-down list. Then click OK.

   If you look at the Advanced panel of the Surface Editor, you'll see that the Vertex Paint1 map is selected for the vertex paint surface.
4. Select two points in the Back viewport, click the Map tab, and select the Point Color button from the Color section. In the RGBA Vertex Map dialog box, select the Vertex Color1 map and choose a blue color. Then click OK twice.
5. Click the Vertex Paint button in the Color section.

   The Vertex Paint dialog box opens and displays the ball object with the two selected vertices colored blue.
6. From the color palette of the Vertex Paint dialog box, select a dark red color, select the Color/Index paint mode, and then drag over two polygons positioned between the two colored polygons.
7. From the color palette of the Vertex Paint dialog box, select a green color, select the Color/Polygon paint mode, and then drag over two polygons positioned underneath the last two colored polygons.
8. Select the File, Save to Modeler menu command in the Vertex Paint dialog box. Then close the Vertex Paint dialog box.

   The vertex colors appear in the Vertex Paint dialog box, as shown in Figure 6.33.
9. Select the File, Save Object As menu command and save the file as Vertex painted sphere.lwo.

FIGURE 6.33
Vertex painted sphere

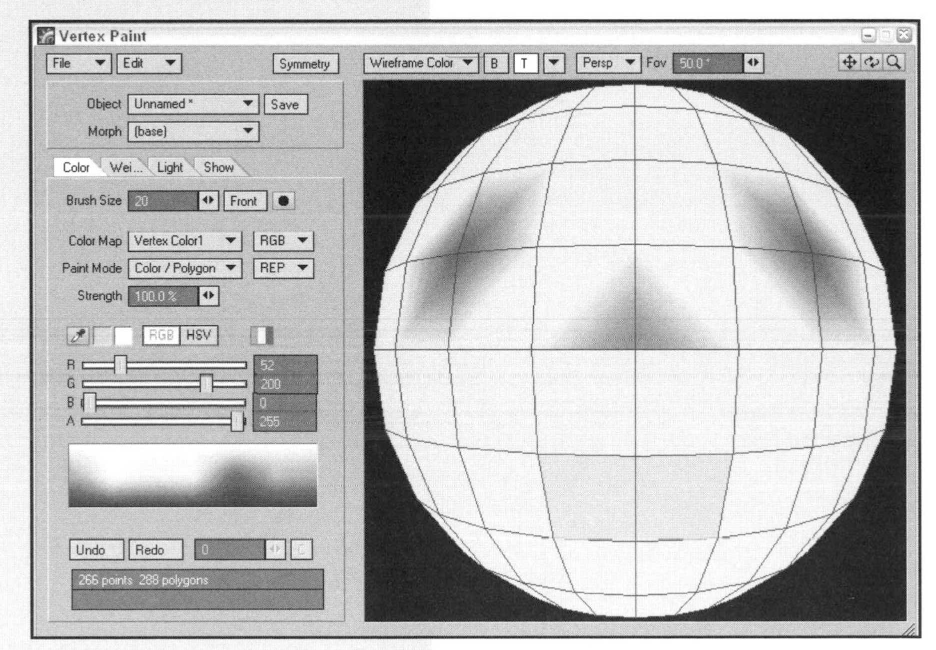

Use a UV texture map

1. Choose the File, Load Object menu command and open the Simple car.lwo file.
2. Click the T icon in the lower-right corner of the interface and select the New option from the drop-down list to its right. In the Create UV Vertex Map dialog box, type the name, **Car details**, select the Initial Value option, and then select the Atlas Map Type with a Relative Gap Size set to 100%. Click OK.

   A UV texture map is created.
3. Click the Surface button at the bottom of the interface and enter the name **car** in the Change Surface dialog box. Then click OK.
4. Open the Surface Editor and select the car surface from the list on the left. Click the Basic tab if necessary. Click the T icon to the right of the Color property to open the Texture Editor.
5. In the Texture Editor, select the UV Projection type, the Car details UVMap, and then load the Car details.tif image file into the Image field. Click the Use Texture button to close the Texture Editor.
6. Close the Surface Editor. Maximize the Perspective viewport, and then select the UV Texture view and Car details.tif display option.

   The UV Texture map with its Atlas projection appears along with the texture image in the viewport.

7. Select the four circle shapes and position them so they surround the circle images. Then move the door coordinates so they align with the door handles.

   After aligning the coordinates with the car objects, look in the Perspective view with the Texture shading option selected to see the details mapped to the car, as shown in Figure 6.34.

8. Select the File, Save Object As menu command and save the file as UV mapped car.lwo.

FIGURE 6.34
UV mapped car

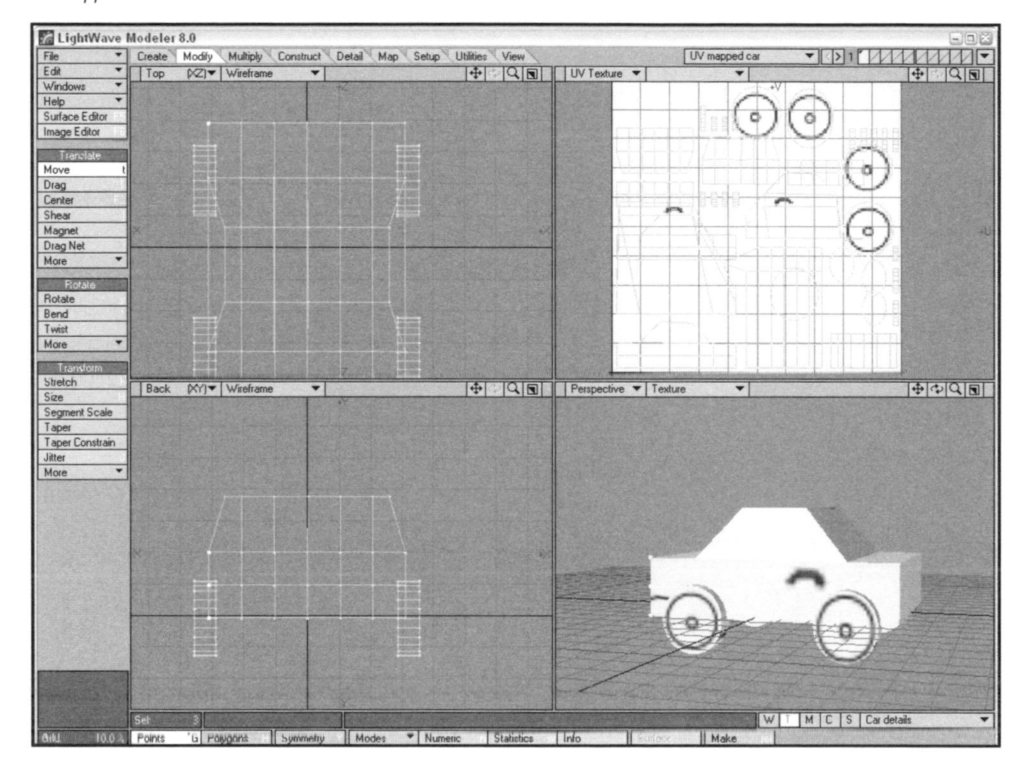

CHAPTER SUMMARY

This chapter covered all the features found in the Surface and Texture Editor windows. Using these windows, you can apply surfaces to selected polygons that add materials with an array of properties. These surface properties can include color, transparency, glossiness, reflections, and so on. In addition to surface properties, you can apply bitmap images to surfaces.

What You Have Learned

- How to name and define surface areas using the Change Surface dialog box.
- How to use the Surface Editor to set the properties for the created surfaces.
- How to access the available surface presets.
- How to use the Texture Editor to load bitmap images into the various surface properties.
- How to use the Texture Editor to access Procedural Textures and gradients.
- How to set environment settings for reflection and refraction.
- How to create vertex maps as an efficient way to save colors with the geometry, including vertex colors and weight maps.

Key Terms from This Chapter

- **surface.** A designated polygon area that has a unique set of material properties assigned to it.
- **diffuse color.** The default color of a surface.
- **specularity.** The highlights reflecting off a surface where the reflected light is most intense.
- **luminosity.** A surface property defining the brightness and saturation of the surface color.
- **glossiness.** A surface property that defines how wide the specular highlights are.
- **bump map.** A surface property that creates a relief-texture to the surface.
- **opacity.** A surface property that determines whether you can see through a surface. The opposite of transparency.
- **Procedural Texture.** Grayscale images where the bright portions represent a maximum value and the dark areas represent a minimum value.
- **gradient.** A band of colors that gradually runs from one distinct color to another over a given area.
- **shader.** A programmed definition of how a material surface looks.
- **vertex map.** A data mapping that includes one piece of information for each vertex in a geometry object. This information can be a vertex color, a vertex weight, and so on.
- **UV coordinates.** A set of coordinates that positions bitmap images on the surface of an object.

CHAPTER 7

USING OBJECTS, CAMERAS, AND LIGHTS IN THE LAYOUT INTERFACE

1. Load and save scenes.
2. Use the Layout viewports.
3. Work with objects.
4. Add lights and cameras.
5. Set object properties.
6. Set camera properties.
7. Set light properties.

CHAPTER 7 USING OBJECTS, CAMERAS, AND LIGHTS IN THE LAYOUT INTERFACE

After using the Modeler to create all the objects you need for a scene, you are finally ready to load the Layout interface. In the Layout interface, you can load, position, and prepare the scene for animation or rendering. The Layout interface is where you combine items and set up interactions between multiple objects, cameras, and lights.

Although most of the interface elements in the Layout interface are identical in function to the Modeler interface, there are several subtle differences, particularly with the viewports and what they can show. Viewports in the Layout interface can show a scene from a light's or camera's perspective.

Adding lights and cameras to the Layout interface is a straightforward process, and you can manipulate lights and cameras just as you manipulate objects. You'll see the differences between objects and lights and cameras when you open the Properties dialog box. The options in the Properties dialog boxes are different for each type of item.

The Object Properties dialog box includes options specific to objects, such as the **level of detail** feature.

The Camera Properties dialog box includes typical camera settings such as resolution, aspect ratio, and aperture height. This dialog box also includes properties that are unique to a rendering environment such as **antialiasing**, which you can use to reduce the jaggies at the object edges. You can also use the Camera Properties dialog box to enable several camera effects such as motion blur, depth of field, and camera masks.

The Light Properties dialog box includes options for changing the light's color, intensity, and falloff. You can also enable several light-specific effects such as lens flares, volumetric lighting, shadows, and projected images. You can use the Global Illumination dialog box to control all lights at once and enable radiosity and caustics.

Tools You'll Use

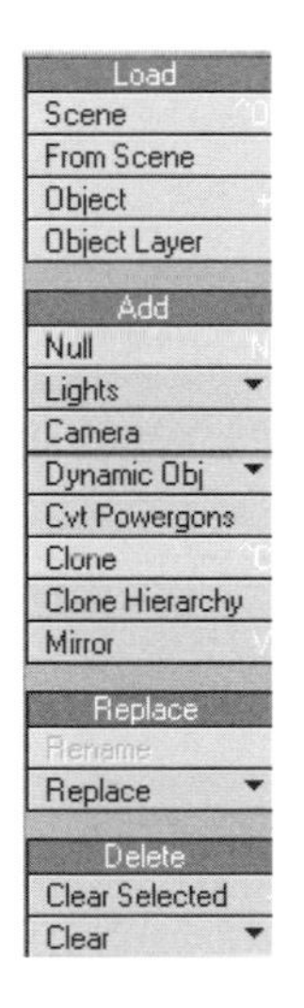

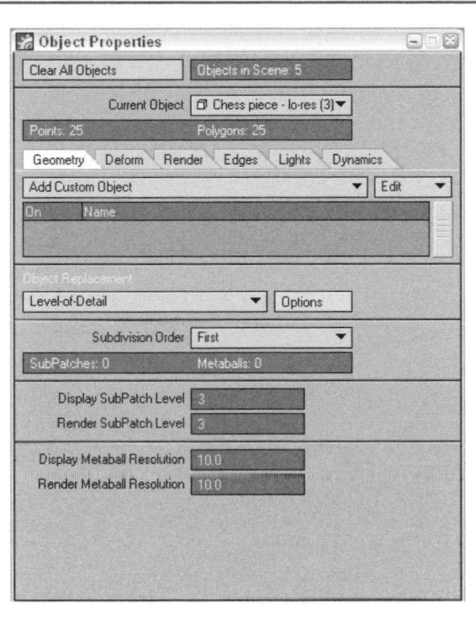

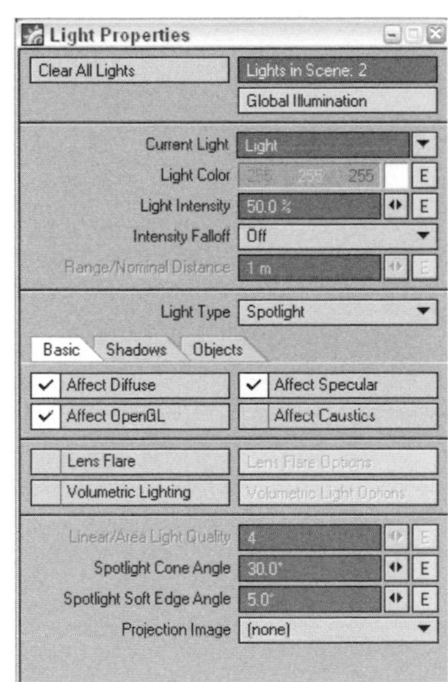

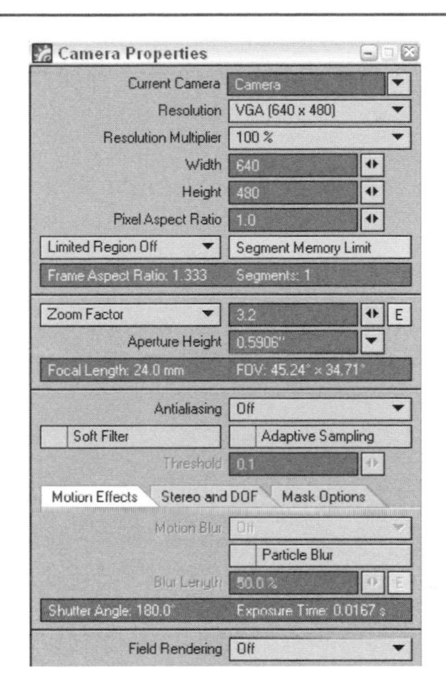

LESSON 1

LOAD AND SAVE SCENES

What You'll Do

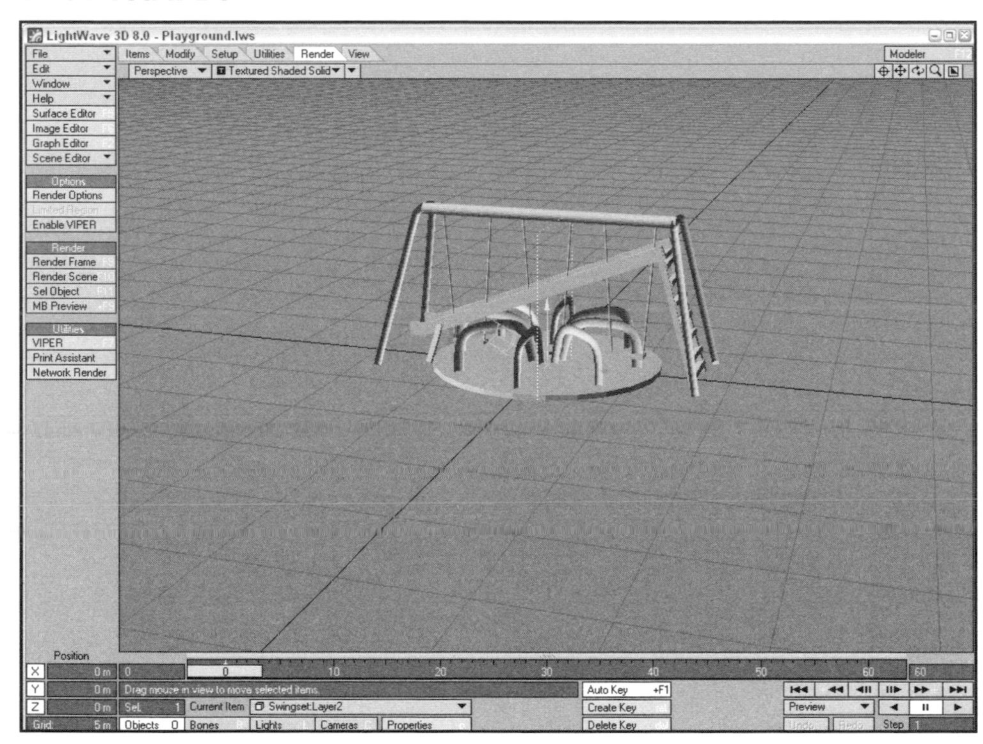

In this lesson, you'll learn how to load objects and save scenes.

Most of the interface controls in the Layout interface work the same as those in the Modeler. The Layout interface also includes menu buttons in the toolbar, which are positioned to the left of the interface, and menu tabs, which are located along the top of the interface. The center viewport also includes the same controls in its upper-right corner, but the controls along the bottom of the interface are different.

Using the Toolbar

The top section in the menu toolbar—including the File, Edit, Window, and Help menu buttons—is always available. The File menu includes commands for loading, saving, importing, and exporting files. Several Editor buttons under these menu buttons are also always available. The Surface and Image Editors work exactly the same as those in the Modeler, which were covered in Chapter 6. The Graph Editor and animation are described in Chapter 9.

Loading Scenes

The File, Load menu includes options for loading a scene, loading a recent scene, loading items from a scene, and loading an object. When you select any of these commands, the Load Scene dialog box opens, as shown in Figure 7.1. Using this dialog box, you can select the folder and file name to load. The File, Load, Recent Scene menu command lists all the recently opened files. Use the File, Load, Load Items from Scene menu command to load all the objects from another scene file into the current scene. When you use this command, a dialog box also opens, where you can load the scene lights along with the objects. If you want to clear the current scene contents, select the File, Clear Scene menu command.

> TIP
>
> You can also access all of the Load menu commands from the Load section in the Items tab.

Loading Objects

The File, Load menu also includes commands to load individual objects into the current scene. Use the File, Load, Load Object command to select a single object file to load and the File, Load, Load Object Layer menu command to open a dialog box where you can select the layer number to load. Clicking the File, Load, Load Multiple menu command opens the Multiloader dialog box, shown in Figure 7.2. Use this dialog box to open objects from a scene, individual objects, or lights from a scene file. You can also select the number of copies of the specific objects to open.

> TIP
>
> Loading an object with the File, Load, Load Object menu command loads all layers as separate objects into the Layout interface. To load a single layer, use the File, Load, Load Object Layer menu command.

FIGURE 7.1
Load Scene dialog box

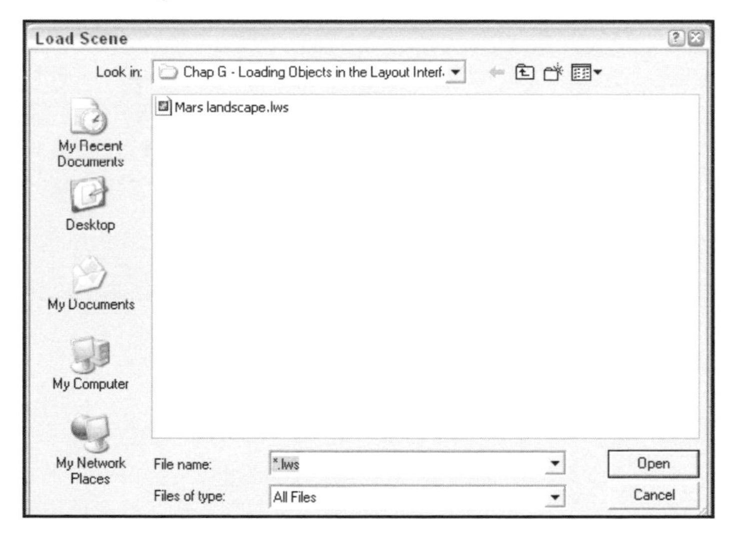

FIGURE 7.2
Multiloader dialog box

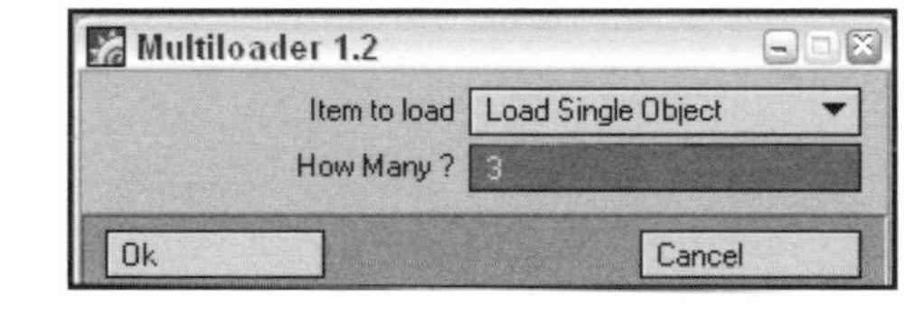

Saving Scenes and Objects

The File, Save menu includes options to save the current scene or the selected object. Object files have an LWO extension and scene files have an LWS file extension. For objects and scenes, the File, Save menu command includes options to save a copy or save an increment, which appends an incremented number on the end of the file each time you use the Save Increment menu command. The File, Save menu also includes options to save transformed objects, endomorphs, lights, and motion paths. When you save a scene, its file name appears in the title bar.

CAUTION

When saving scene files with the File, Save, Save Scene As menu command, but sure to add the LWS extension on the end of the file name. LightWave will not add the extension by default, and if it is missing, the Load Scene dialog box won't recognize the files.

Importing and Exporting

LightWave can import files from two different formats: BioVision Motion Capture and LightGen files. You can also export LightWave files to these formats: LightWave 5.6, VRML97, Shockwave 3D, and Image List. When exporting to the VRML97 or the Shockwave 3D formats, dialog boxes prompt you to specify exactly which objects to export. Figure 7.3 shows the Export dialog box for the Shockwave 3D format. If you use the Image List option, LightWave exports a text file that lists all the files used in the scene, and their file locations.

Using the Content Manager

Using the File, Content Manager menu command opens a dialog box, shown in Figure 7.4, where you can see all the objects and images that are used within a scene. For each item, you can see its Status, Source, and Destination. If you select an item and click the Set Path button, you can change the path for the selected object. Clicking the Options button opens a dialog box where you can select Consolidate Only or Export Scene mode. Clicking the Externals button displays only items that are externally referenced. If you click OK, all items are exported to a specific location. This option is great for making sure that you have all the items used in a scene.

FIGURE 7.3
Shockwave 3D Export dialog box

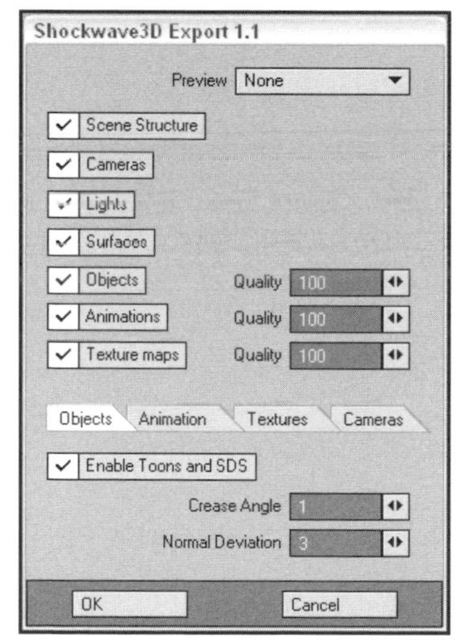

FIGURE 7.4
Content Manager dialog box

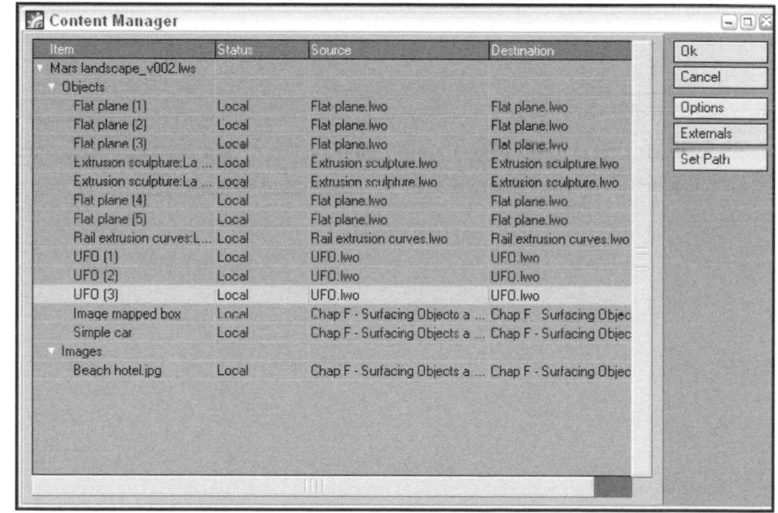

FIGURE 7.5

Playground scene of loaded objects

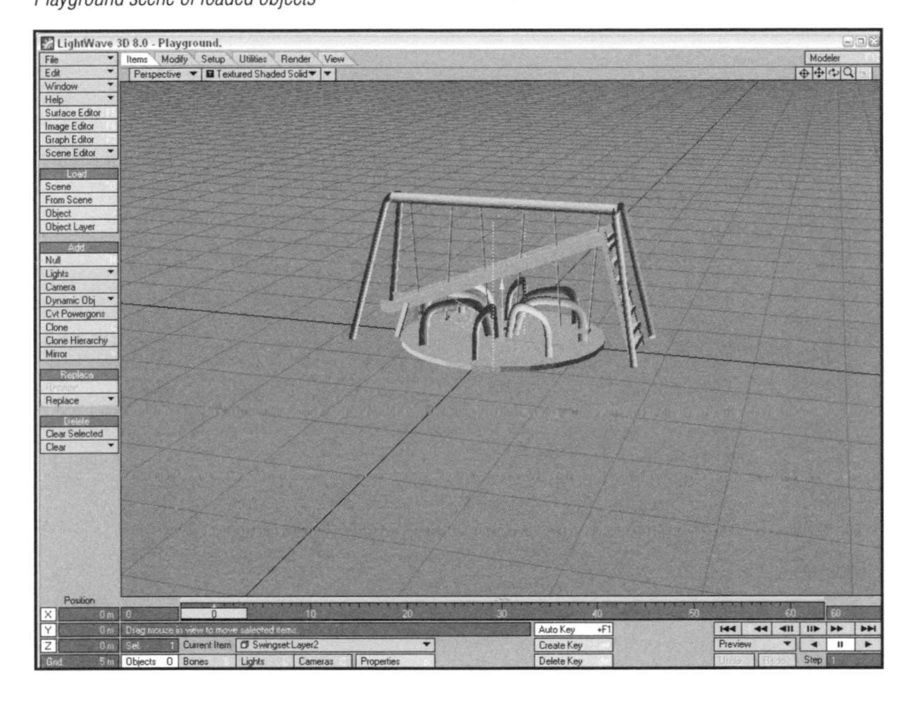

FIGURE 7.6

Content Manager dialog box for the current scene

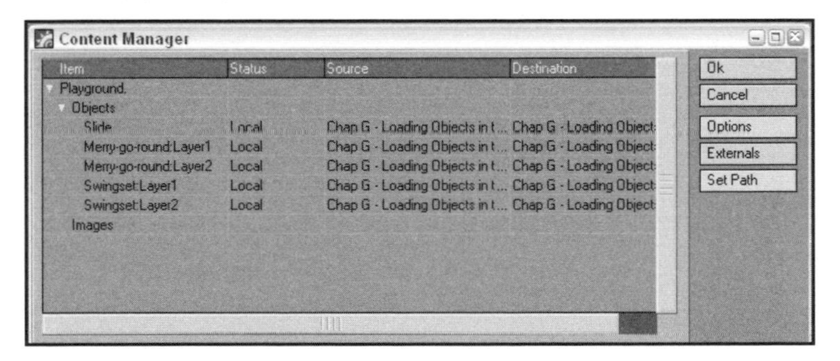

Load objects and save a scene

1. Select the Start, All Programs, NewTek LightWave, LightWave program icon to open the Layout interface.
2. Select the File, Load, Load Object menu command. In the Load Object dialog box, select the Slide.lwo file and click OK.
3. Repeat step 2 for the Merry-go-round.lwo and Swingset.lwo objects.

   The objects appear centered about the scene origin in the center of the grid, as shown in Figure 7.5.
4. When all three objects are loaded, select the File, Save, Save Scene As menu command. In the Save Scene As dialog box, save the file as Playground.lws.

Use the Content Manager

1. With the Playground.lws file still open, select the File, Content Manager menu command.

   The Content Manager Options dialog box appears.
2. In the Content Manager Options dialog box, select the Consolidate Only option and click OK.

   The Content Manager dialog box opens to display all the objects included in the scene and their paths, as shown in Figure 7.6.
3. Click OK. A dialog box opens to ask if you want to save the modified objects. Click Yes. Another dialog box opens to ask if you want to save all objects. Click Yes.

LESSON 2

USE THE LAYOUT VIEWPORTS

What You'll Do

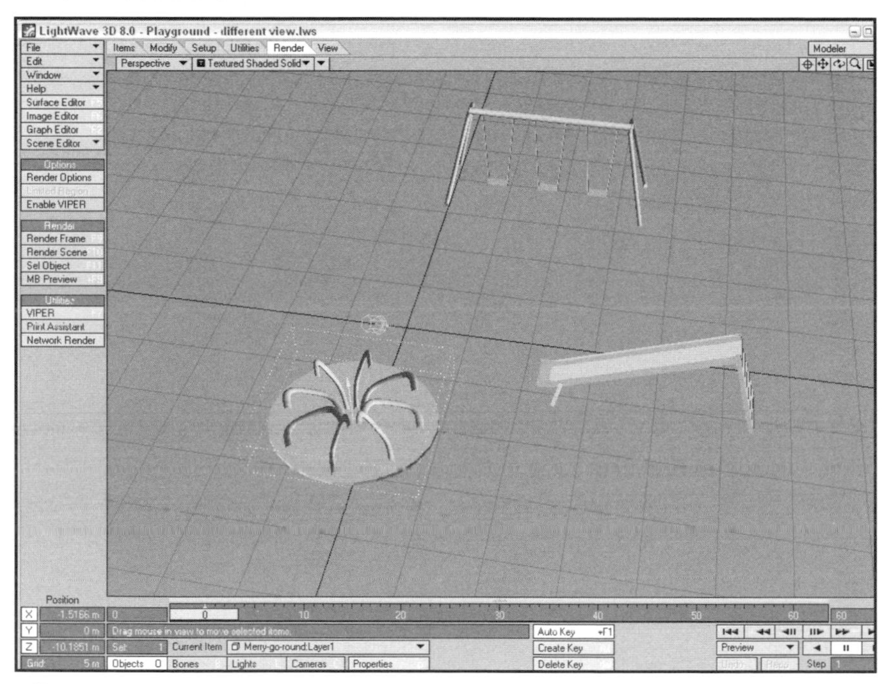

In this lesson, you'll learn how to use controls in the Layout viewports and how to use the Schematic view.

Although viewports in the Layout interface work mostly the same as viewports in the Modeler, there are some subtle differences that are only available in the Layout interface. Viewport controls are located along the top bar of the viewport and also in the Views tab.

Learning the Unique Layout Views

As in the Modeler, you can switch between standard viewport views (for example, Top, Left, Front, and Perspective) using the view drop-down list at the top of the viewport, but the Layout interface also includes several unique views including Light View, Camera View, and Schematic. In the Light and Camera views, you can view the scene from the selected camera's or light's view. In the **Schematic view**, all objects are shown as small rectangular nodes.

Using the Schematic View

When working with a scene of many small objects, it can be difficult to select the smaller objects when larger ones are in front of them. The Schematic view displays all objects as separate rectangular nodes, as shown in Figure 7.7. The Pan and Zoom tools still work in Schematic view. To help you easily recognize the various items, the nodes are color-coded. Purple indicates lights, green indicates cameras, and cyan indicates objects. You can right-click on a node to access a pop-up menu of options, including Clear, Clone, Rename, and Item Properties. Selecting the Edit, Schematic View Tools menu command opens a dialog box of options for the Schematic view, shown in Figure 7.8.

> NOTE
>
> When a node is selected in the Schematic view, the Rename button in the Replace section of the Items tab becomes active, allowing you to rename the object.

Setting the View's Position, Rotation, and Zoom

Another pop-up menu is located to the right of the display options on the viewport controls at the top of the viewport. Access this pop-up menu by clicking on the arrow icon, shown in Figure 7.9. This pop-up menu includes commands for setting and resetting the View Position, Rotation, and Zoom. When you click one of these options, a dialog box in which you can set the values for these settings opens.

FIGURE 7.7
Viewport controls

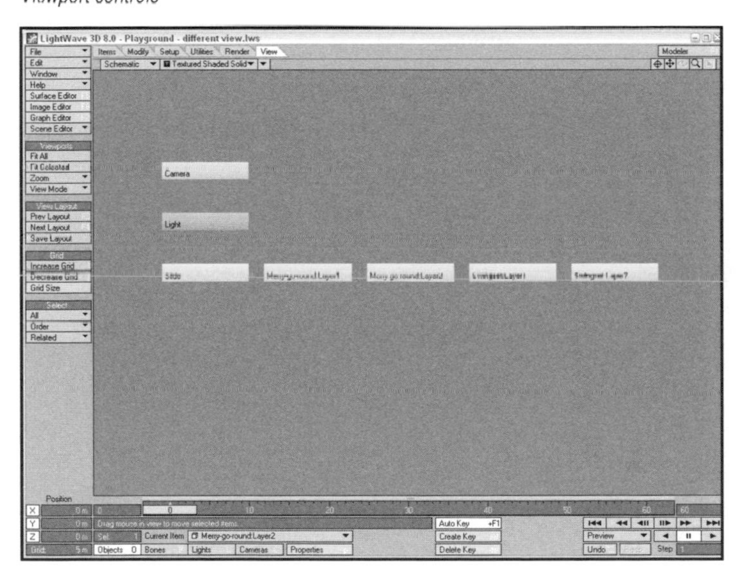

FIGURE 7.8
Schematic View Tools dialog box

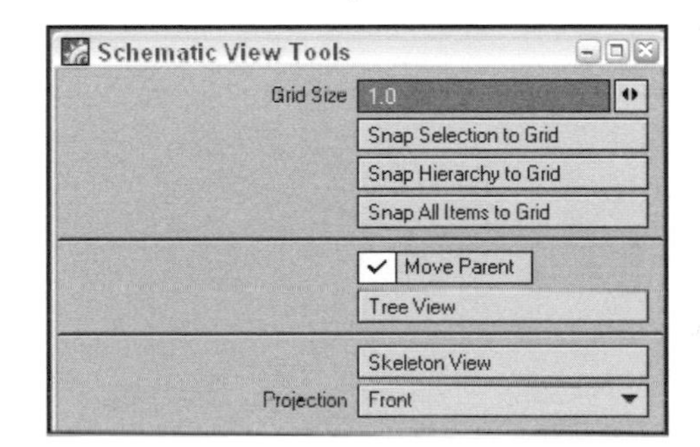

FIGURE 7.9
Viewport controls

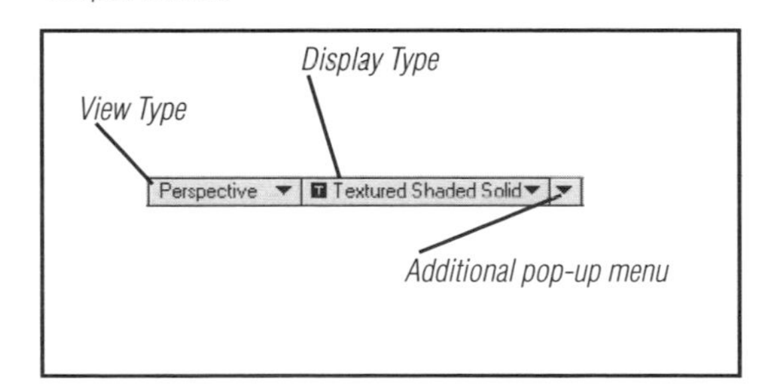

Panning About the Selected Object

As in the Modeler interface, the viewport controls in the upper-right corner of the viewport include the standard Pan, Rotate, Zoom, and Maximize buttons. The Layout interface includes an additional icon, the Pan About Selection button, shown in Figure 7.10. Click this button to pan all objects while keeping the selected object centered in the viewport.

Fitting Objects Within the Viewport

Within the View tab, the Viewports section includes buttons that automatically zoom and pan the viewport to fit all objects or selected objects within the available non-Perspective viewports. Figure 7.11 shows the slide object fit to the available views.

FIGURE 7.10

Additional viewport controls

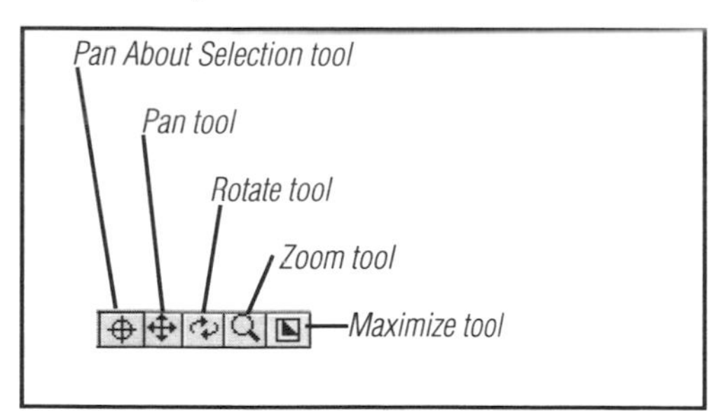

Changing Layouts

The default layout for the Layout interface shows a single perspective view, but you can use the Prev Layout and Next Layout buttons in the View tab to switch between the different available layouts, shown in Figure 7.12. You can also select these layouts from the Viewport Layout drop-down list in the Display Options panel of the Preferences dialog box. Use the Edit, Display Options menu command to open this dialog box, and look at the drop-down list. To save a unique layout, click the Save Layout button.

Changing Grid Size

Use the Increase and Decrease Grid buttons in the Grid section of the View menu tab to increase or decrease the grid in steps. To customize the grid size, click the Grid Size button and enter the desired grid size in the dialog box that opens.

FIGURE 7.11

Fitting selected objects within views

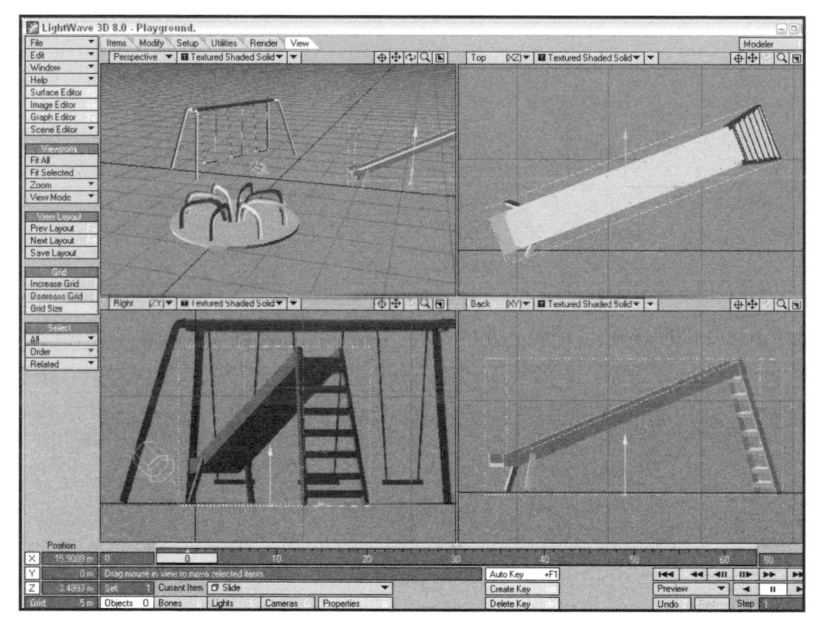

FIGURE 7.12

Available default layouts

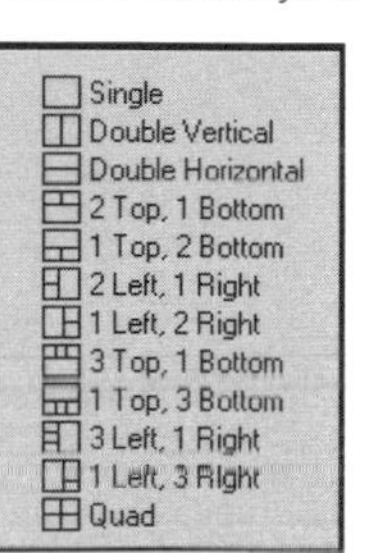

FIGURE 7.13
Schematic view

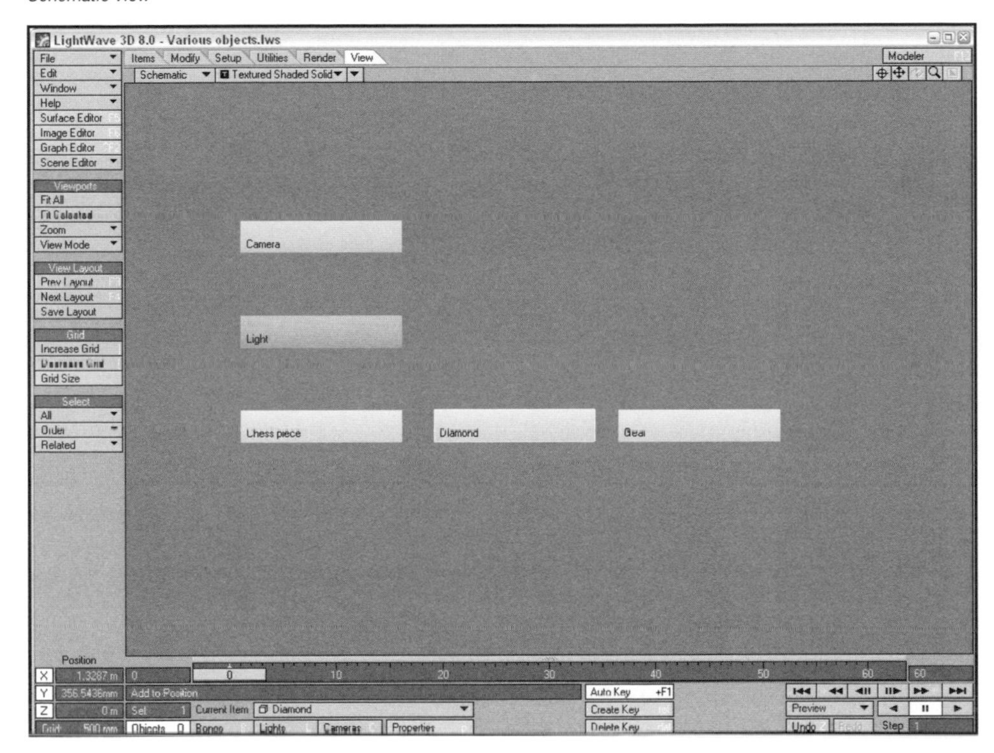

Use Schematic view

1. Click the File, Load, Load Scene menu command and open the Various objects.lws file.
2. Select Schematic from the View Type drop-down list at the top of the viewport.

   All scene items appear as rectangular labeled nodes.
3. Drag with the Zoom tool to make the nodes larger within the viewport.
4. Select the Edit, Schematic View Tools menu command to open the Schematic View Tools dialog box. Click the Snap All Items to Grid button to align all the nodes, as shown in Figure 7.13.
5. Select the File, Save, Save Scene As menu command and save the file as Schematic view.lws.

Change default view

1. Click the File, Load, Load Scene menu command and open the Playground.lws file.

   The scene is shown using a single Perspective viewport.
2. Click the Pan About Selected button in the upper-right corner of the viewport. Select the slide object and drag in the scene until the slide is separated from the other items. Repeat with the other objects until all objects are separate from the center of the viewport.

3. Click the pop-up menu to the right of the display options drop-down list on the viewport title, as shown in Figure 7.9, and select the Set View Rotation option.

   The Set View Rotation dialog box appears.

4. In the Set View Rotation dialog box, set the Pitch value to **45** and click OK.

   The alignment of the scene in the viewport is changed.

5. Select the Set View Zoom option in the same pop-up menu. In the Set View Zoom dialog box, change the Zoom value to **3.0** and click OK.

   The view is zoomed out so all the objects are visible, as shown in Figure 7.14.

6. Select the File, Save, Save Scene As menu command and save the file as Playground – different view.lws.

FIGURE 7.14
View altered playground

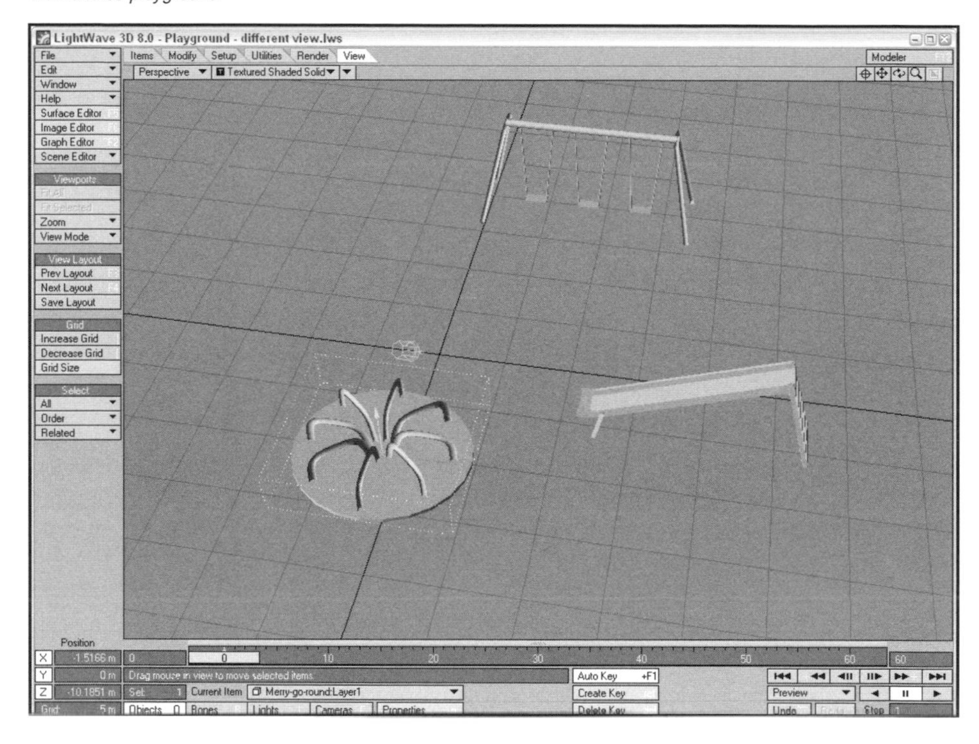

LESSON 3

WORK WITH OBJECTS

What You'll Do

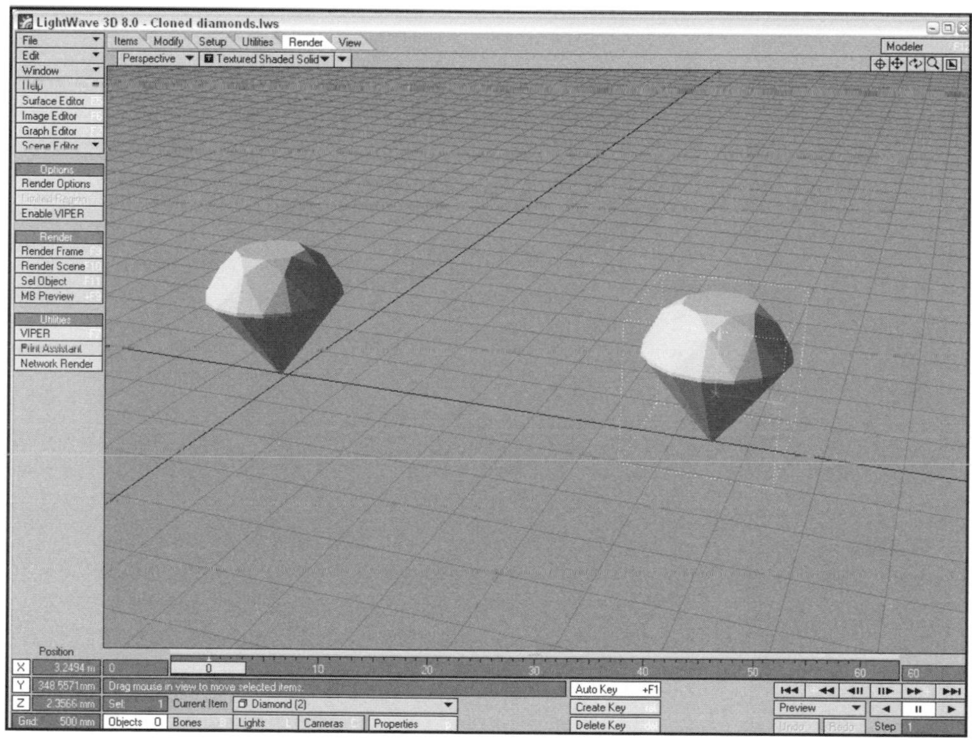

In this lesson, you'll learn how to select, clone, mirror, clear, and replace objects.

When working with objects in the Layout interface, the first thing to learn is how to select objects. After you select objects, you can clone, mirror, delete, or replace them. Many of these commands you need to accomplish these tasks are available when the Items tab is selected.

Selecting Objects

Selecting objects within the Layout interface is as simple as clicking on the object. The selected object is bounded with a light yellow dashed line, with its pivot point highlighted. When you select lights and cameras, they are highlighted yellow.

Selecting Multiple Objects

To select multiple objects, simply hold down the Shift key while clicking on each object. Each selected object is surrounded with a light yellow set of dashed lines. Figure 7.15 shows four chess pieces, with the first and third objects selected.

Selecting All Objects

The All drop-down-menu button in the Select section of the View tab includes menu commands for selecting all objects, all lights, or all cameras. It also includes a Search by Name command that opens a dialog box, shown in Figure 7.16, where you can locate and select objects by searching for the object's name. You can also select objects by moving through their listed order using the Select, Order, Select Previous Item and the Select, Select Next Item options, or by pressing the up and down arrows. Finally, the Related button includes commands to select objects within a hierarchy.

Cloning Objects

Selecting the Clone button in the Add section of the Items tab opens a simple dialog box where you can enter the number of clones that you want to create. The cloned objects occupy the same position as their original, so they are not visible until you move them.

FIGURE 7.15
Multiple selected objects

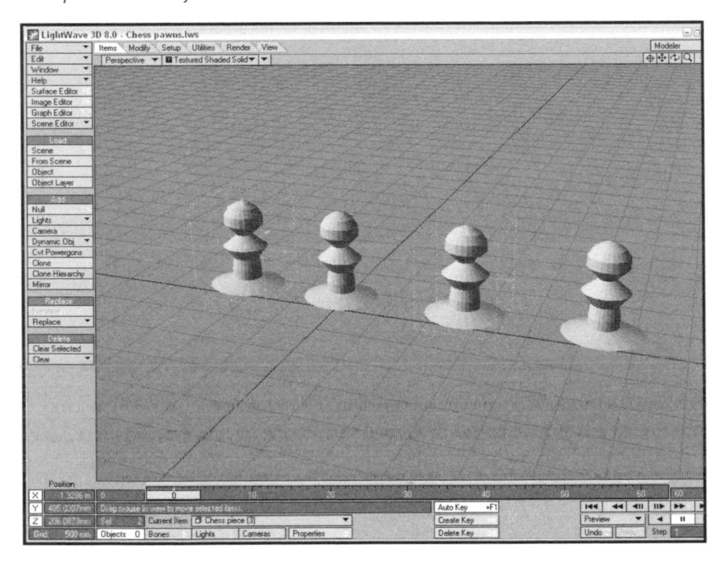

FIGURE 7.16
Search by Name dialog box

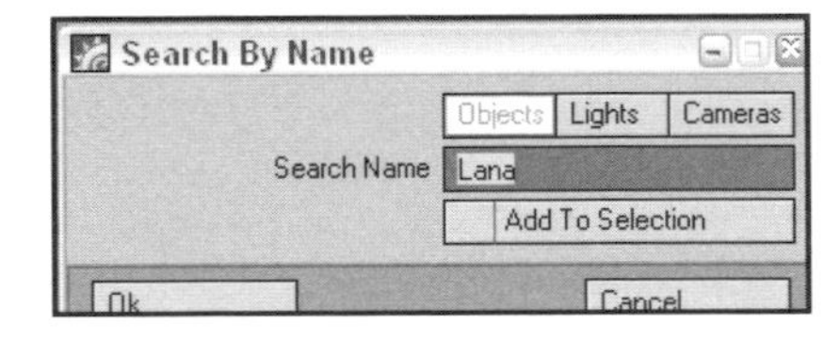

Mirroring Objects

The Add section also includes a Mirror command. Clicking this command also opens a dialog box, shown in Figure 7.17, where you can specify the Mirror Axis, Mirror Center, and the point about which the object is mirrored.

Clearing Objects

To delete an object from the scene, simply select it and click the Clear Selected button in the Delete section of the Items tab. Whenever the Clear Selected command is used, a confirmation dialog box opens that gives you the chance to cancel the command. The Delete section also includes a Clear menu with options to Clear All Objects, Clear All Bones, Clear All Lights, and Clear All Cameras.

NOTE

The keyboard shortcut for Clear Selected is the – (minus) key, not the Delete key. The Delete key is used to delete motion keys.

Replacing Objects

Three options are available when you click the Replace button. Clicking the Replace with Object option opens a file dialog box where you can select an object to replace the current selection. Clicking the Replace with Layer option opens a dialog box where you can select a single layer to replace the current selection. Clicking the Replace with Null option replaces the selected object with a **null object**.

FIGURE 7.17
Mirror dialog box

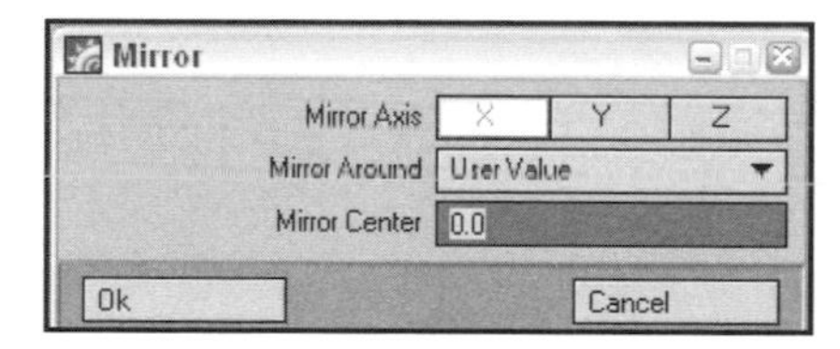

Select, clone, and clear objects

1. Click the File, Load, Load Scene menu command and open the Diamond.lws file.
2. Click the diamond object to select it.

   A dashed line surrounds the object when it is selected.
3. Click the Items tab, and select the Clone button in the Add section. In the Clone Current Item dialog box, enter the value of **3** and then click OK.

   Three new cloned objects are added to the scene in the same location as the original.
4. Click the Pan About Selected tool at the top-right corner of the viewport and then drag in the viewport to separate each of the cloned diamonds from the others.
5. Hold down the Shift key and click the two middle diamond objects. Then click the Clear Selected button. In the Clear Object dialog box that opens, click the Yes to All button.

   The middle two diamonds are deleted, as shown in Figure 7.18.
6. Select the File, Save, Save Scene As menu command and save the file as Cloned diamonds.lws.

FIGURE 7.18
Cloned objects

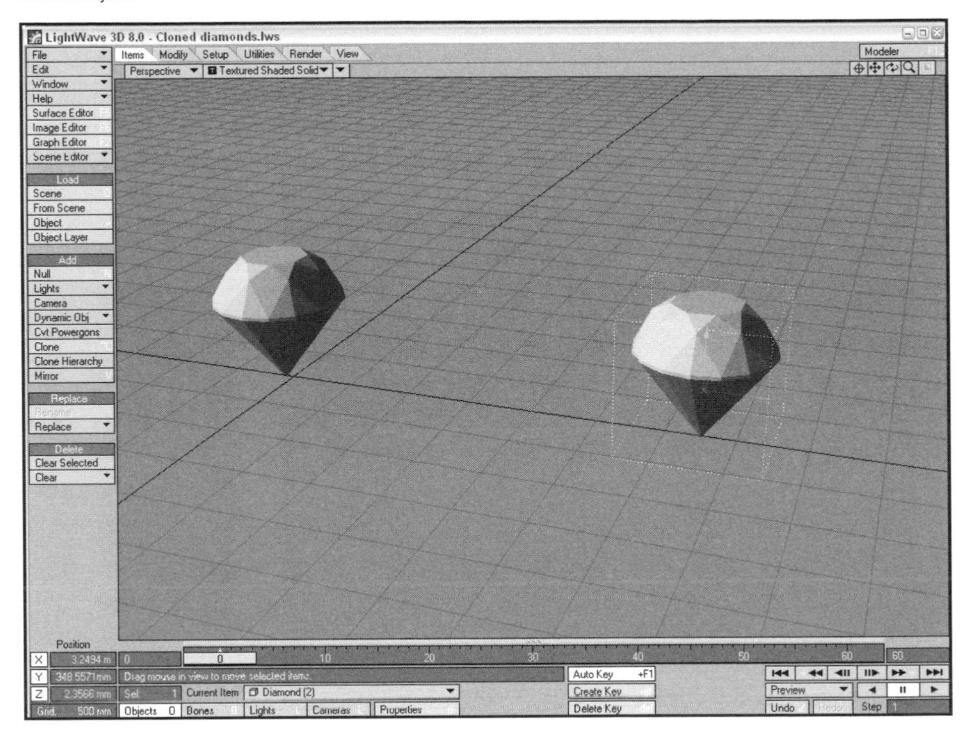

LESSON 4

ADD LIGHTS AND CAMERAS

What You'll Do

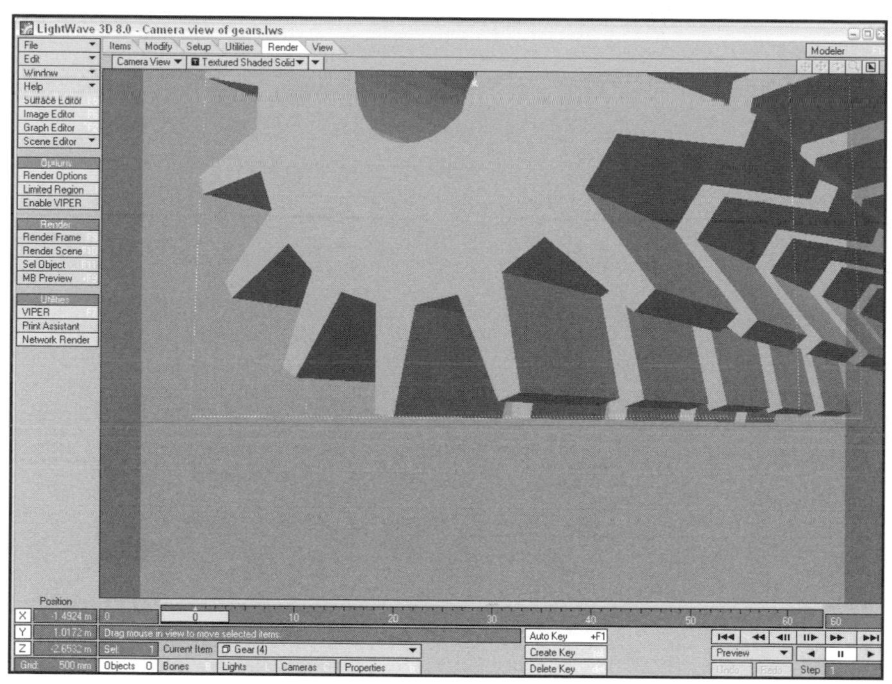

In this lesson, you'll learn how to add lights and cameras to a scene.

The Items tab includes an Add section with commands you can use to add items—including lights and cameras—to a scene.

Adding Null Objects

Null objects are simple objects that are recognized in the scene as objects but aren't rendered or even shaded in the viewport. The value of null objects is that you can use them as placeholders for other objects or controls that affect other objects when moved. To create a new null object, click the Null button in the Add section of the Items tab. The null object appears at the center of the scene.

Adding Lights

Several different lights are available in LightWave. Each of these light types is described in Table 7.1. You can select these options from the Lights button in the Add section of the Items tab. When you select one of these light types, a dialog box opens where you can give the new light a name. The icon for each light type is unique, as shown in Figure 7.19. All light icons are purple when not selected.

TABLE 7.1: LIGHT TYPES

Light Type	Description
Distant Light	Simulates a light source from a source so far away that all light rays are parallel. This type is good for lighting outdoor scenes so that the scene appears to be lit by the sun.
Point Light	Shines equally in all directions, much like a standard light bulb would. This type is good for indoor light sources and for general lighting purposes.
Spotlight	Focuses light within a cone that drops off around the edges of the cone. This type is good for focusing light on a specific object from a specific direction.
Linear Light	Emits light rays in all direction like a Point Light, except light is emitted from all points along a straight line. This type is good for simulating florescent lights.
Area Light	Emits lights from a two-dimensional surface and is good for bathing an entire area with equal light.

FIGURE 7.19
Light icons

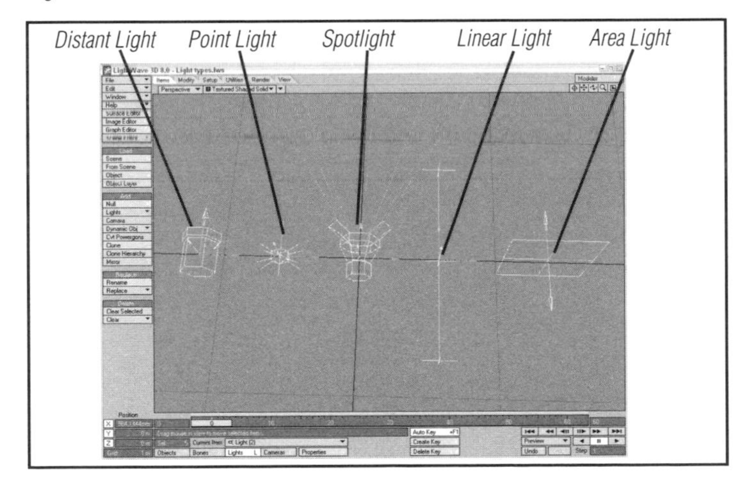

Adding Cameras

The default scene starts with one distant light and one camera, but you can add additional cameras to the scene using the Camera button in the Add section of the Items tab. When you click this button, a dialog box appears where you can name the camera. Camera icons are in green. Only one camera can be active at a time, and the active camera is used to render the scene.

Changing to a Camera or Light View

If you select the Camera View or Light View option from the viewport's View Mode drop-down list at the top of the viewport when a camera or light is selected, the view changes to show the scene from the camera's or the light's perspective. Figure 7.20 shows a camera view in the upper-left viewport. When you are in a camera view, the viewport controls in the upper-right corner are disabled.

FIGURE 7.20
Camera view

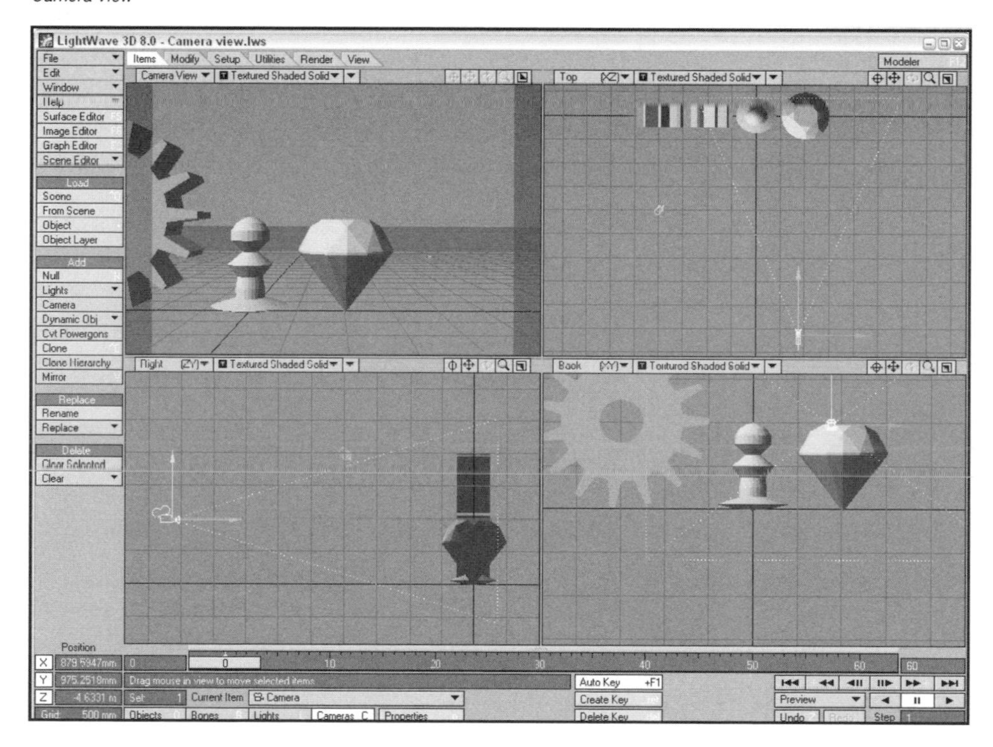

Add lights and a camera

1. Choose the File, Load, Load Scene menu command and open the Gears.lws file.
2. Click the Items tab, and then select the Lights, Area Light menu command from the Add section. In the Light Name dialog box, type the name **Area Light** and click OK. Then, position the Area Light icon above the gears.

   The lighting on the gears changes as the light is added and as it is moved.
3. Click the Camera button in the Add section to create a new camera. In the Camera Name dialog box, type the name **Camera02** and click OK.

   A new camera icon appears at the scene origin.
4. Drag the camera icon backward, away from the gears, and rotate it to face the gears.
5. With the new camera still selected, click the Camera View option from the View Type drop-down list at the top of the viewport.

   The gears are displayed from the camera's position, level with the bottom of the gears, as shown in Figure 7.21.
6. Select the File, Save, Save Scene As menu command and save the file as Camera view of gears.lws.

FIGURE 7.21
Camera view of gears

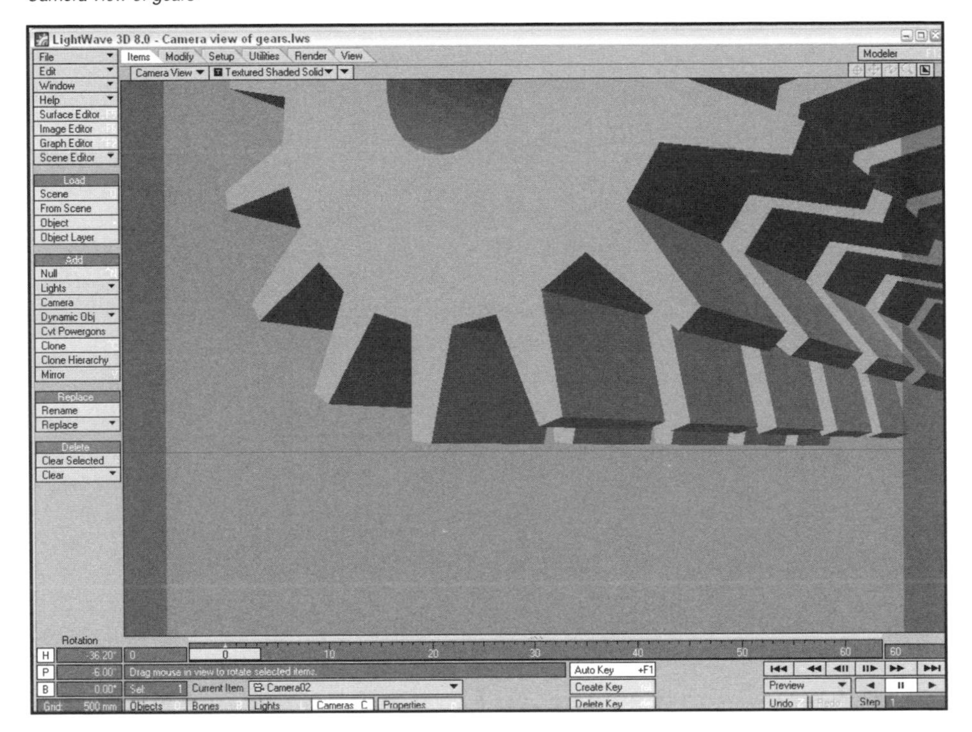

SET OBJECT PROPERTIES

What You'll Do

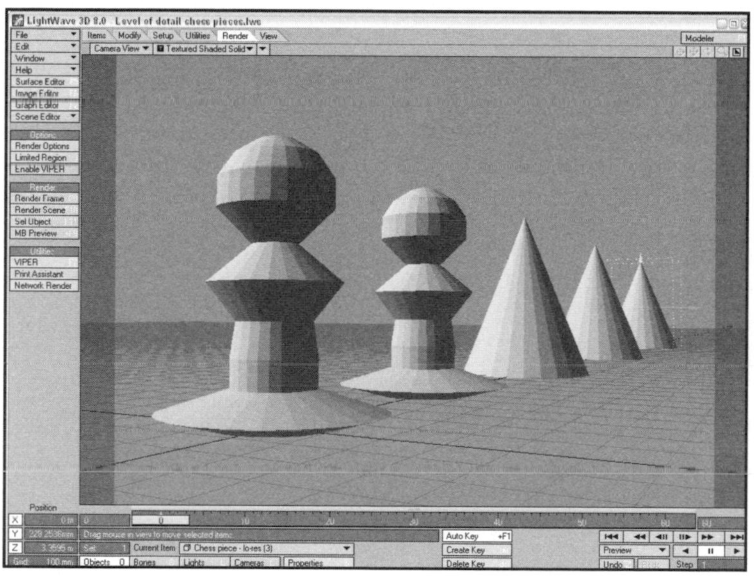

In this lesson, you'll learn how to change object properties.

You can set properties for all scene items by selecting the item in the viewport and then clicking the Properties button at the bottom of the interface. Doing so opens the Properties dialog box for the selected item type. The Object Properties dialog box, shown in Figure 7.22, includes lots of valuable information.

FIGURE 7.22
Object Properties dialog box

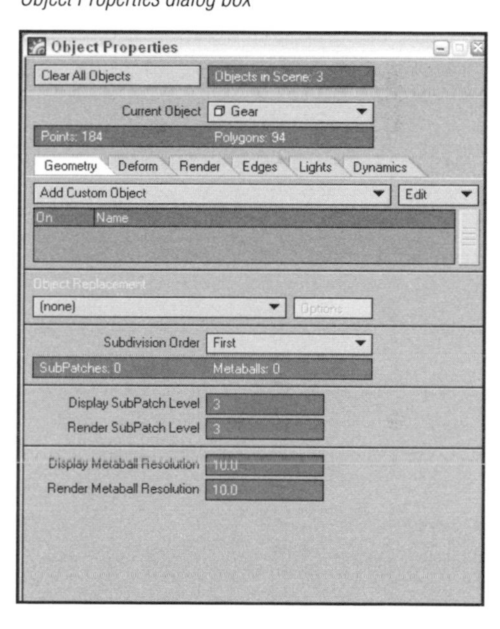

Selecting Objects

A field at the top of the dialog box lists the total number of objects in the scene and the name of the current object. From the Current Object drop-down list, you can select any of the other objects in the scene. Selecting an object in the Properties dialog box automatically selects the object in the viewports. Below the object name, the dialog box lists the number of points and polygons that make up the selected object.

Accessing the Tabbed Panels

Several tabbed panels are located in the middle of the Object Properties dialog box. Using the controls on these panels, you can add custom objects to the scene, selectively deform the selected object, set render options for the object, set the size and thickness of object edges, exclude the object from being lit by certain lights, or set the object to act as a dynamic object. Each of these panels is discussed in later chapters.

Adding Custom Objects

The Add Custom Object list in the Object Properties dialog box includes many different custom objects that you would typically use to replace a selected null object. The options include a variety of specialized objects such as a **Camera Mask** and a Frame Rate Meter. Other custom objects—like the Protractor, Ruler, and Sliders— are useful for measuring distances. Figure 7.23 shows a scene with three custom objects enabled: a Ruler, the Frame Rate Meter, and a Protractor.

FIGURE 7.23
Custom objects

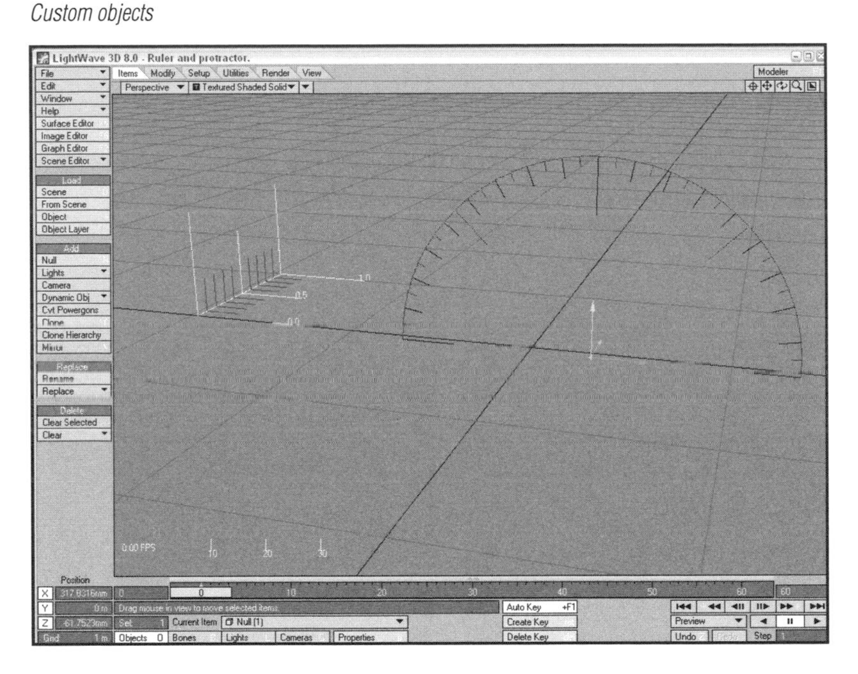

Enabling Level of Detail

When a scene includes a complex model, rendering the model can take a considerable amount of time, even if it is far away from the camera. To fix this problem, you can create low-resolution versions of the complex model that are visible at further distances. To enable this feature, select the Level-of-Detail Object Replacement option in the Object Replacement list in the Geometry panel of the Object Properties dialog box. Then click the Options button. This opens the Level-of-Detail Object Replacement dialog box, shown in Figure 7.24, where you can specify a Base Object and select different items to appear after the object is beyond a given distance.

FIGURE 7.24
Level-of-Detail Object Replacement dialog box

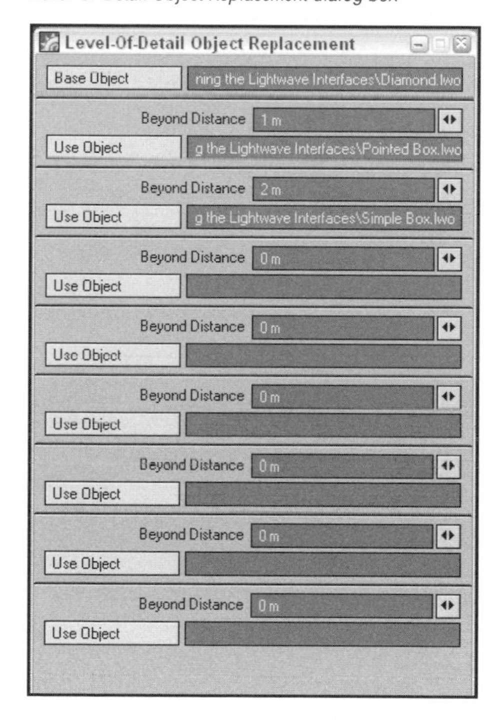

Enable level of detail

1. Click the File, Load, Load Scene menu command and open the Chess pieces.lws file.
2. Select the first chess piece and click the Properties button at the bottom of the interface.

   The Object Properties dialog box opens.
3. From the Object Replacement drop-down list, select the Level-of-Detail Object Replacement option, and then click the Options button.

   The Level-of-Detail Object Replacement dialog box opens. The Base Object should already be set to Chess piece.lwo.
4. In the Level-of-Detail Object Replacement dialog box, set the Beyond Distance value for the first entry to **2 m**, and click the first Use Object button.
5. In the Open dialog box that appears, select the Chess piece – lo-res.lwo object and click Open. Then close the Level-Of-Detail Object Replacement and Object Properties dialog boxes.
6. With the single chess piece selected, click the Clone button in the Items tab, enter **4** in the Clone Current Item dialog box that opens, and then click OK.
7. Select and drag the clones to space them in a straight line away from the first chess piece.

   Each cloned chess piece has the same Level-of-Detail Object Replacement settings as the first, but you need to render the scene before you can see the change.
8. Click the Render tab and then click the Render Frame button.

   The chess pieces are rendered and the objects that are farther away than 2 m are replaced with the low-resolution cone-shaped object. Once rendered, the replaced objects appear in the viewports, as shown in Figure 7.25.
9. Select the File, Save, Save Scene As menu command and save the file as Level-of-Detail chess pieces.lws.

FIGURE 7.25
Level-of-Detail chess pieces

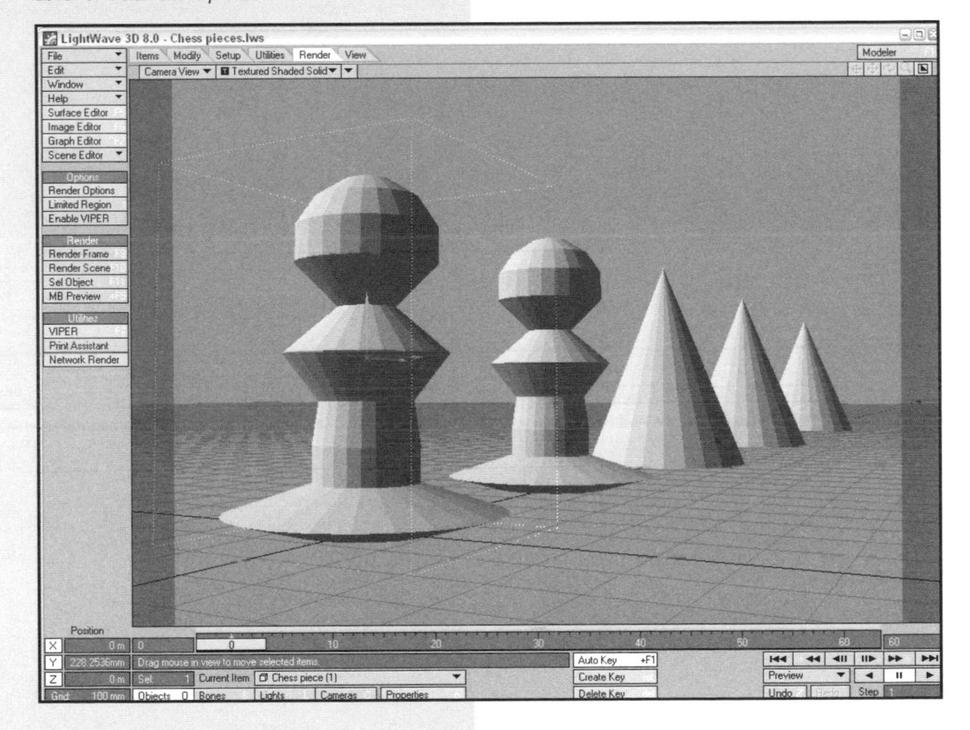

SET CAMERA PROPERTIES

What You'll Do

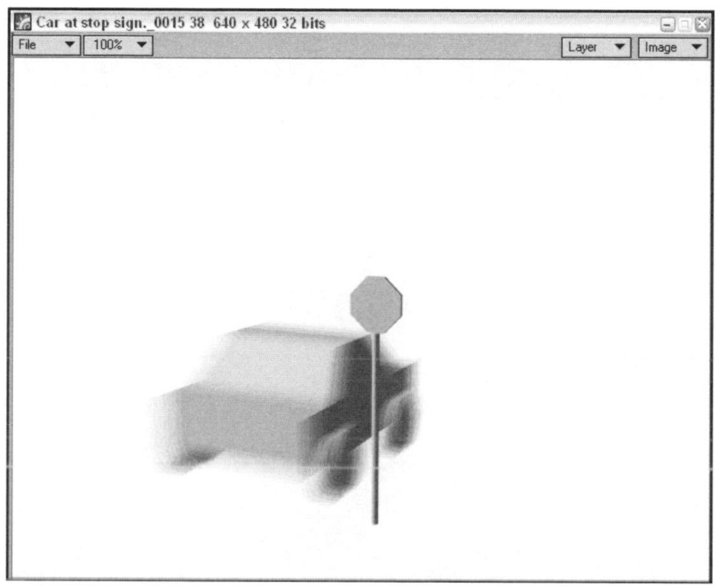

In this lesson, you'll learn how to set camera properties and enable camera effects.

Besides using the Properties button at the bottom of the interface to set object properties, you can also use it to set the properties of other scene items, such as cameras. The Camera Properties dialog box, shown in Figure 7.26, includes a list of all available scene cameras.

FIGURE 7.26
Camera Properties dialog box

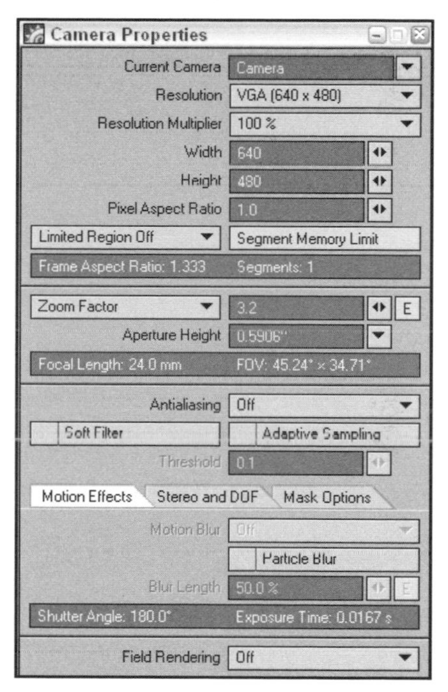

Setting Camera Resolution

From the Resolution list, you can select resolution presets or custom dimensions using the Width and Height fields. From the Zoom Factor drop-down list, you can change the Zoom Factor, the Lens **Focal Length**, Horizontal FOV, and Vertical FOV. The Aperture Height setting is right beneath this list. Each of these settings affect the Focal Length and Field of View values, which are displayed. The resolution of the camera is displayed in the viewports as a rectangular cone that is projected from the camera icon when the camera item is selected, as shown in Figure 7.27.

Enabling Antialiasing

Use the Antialiasing list to specify the amount of antialiasing to apply to the camera image. The options run from Off and Low to High and Enhanced Extreme. You can also enable Soft Filtering and Adaptive Sampling. Figure 7.28 shows a rendered image with and without these settings

FIGURE 7.27

Camera dimensions are projected when the camera is selected

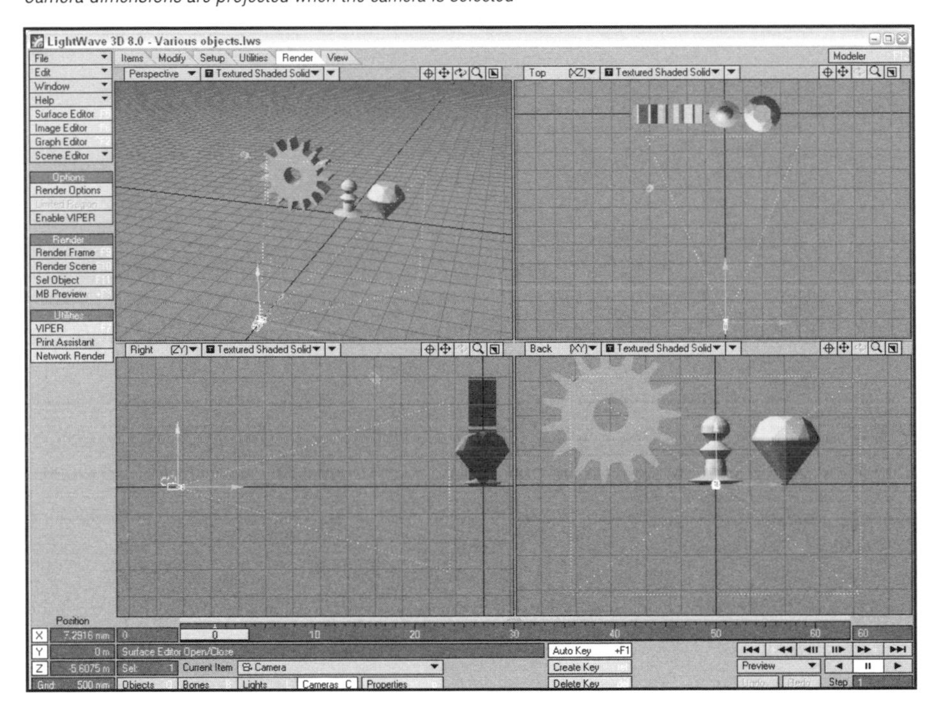

enabled. In the top half of the image, Antialiasing is turned off and the Soft Filter and Adaptive Sampling options are disabled. Notice the jagged lines at the object edges. In the lower half of the image, these options are enabled with an Extreme Antialiasing setting. The lower half of the image took considerably longer to render, but the results are noticeable.

Enabling Motion Blur

Three panels are located at the bottom of the Camera Properties dialog box. Use the options to enable different camera effects such as **Motion Blur**, Stereo, and Depth of Field. Using the Motion Blur effect causes objects moving quickly through the current frame to blur to show the illusion of motion. You can enable Motion Blur by selecting Normal or Dithered from the Motion Blur field. Using the Particle Blur effect enables the blurring of particles in the scene. You can also specify the Blur Length value. Figure 7.29 shows a simple scene with the center object animated moving vertically with the Motion Blur option enabled.

> NOTE
>
> You can only enable the Motion Blur and Depth of Field camera effects if the Antialiasing option is enabled.

FIGURE 7.28
Rendered image with and without antialiasing

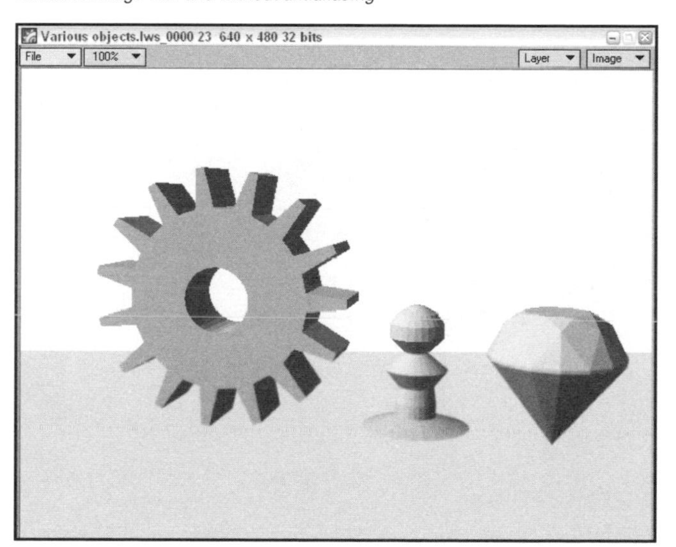

FIGURE 7.29
Motion Blur camera effect

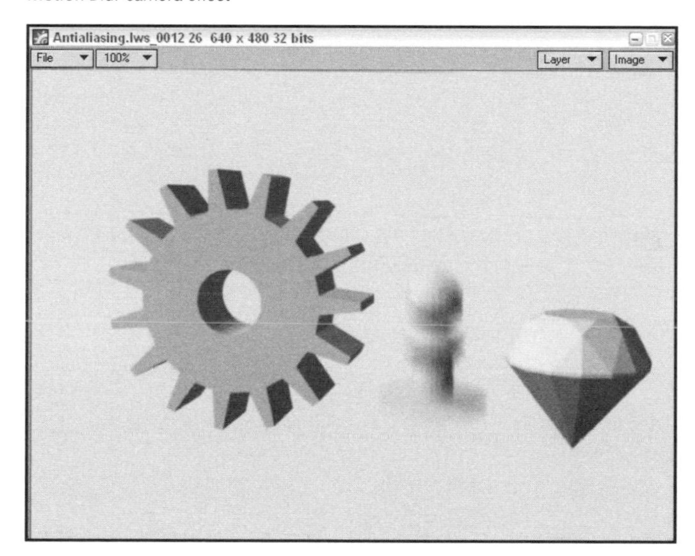

Enabling Depth of Field

Using the **depth of field** camera effect focuses the camera on a center point called the focal point and blurs all objects closer to or farther from the focal point. To enable the depth of field effect, click the Stereo and DOF panel in the Camera Properties dialog box, and then enable the Depth of Field option. The Depth of Field option can only be enabled if you set the Antialiasing option to Medium or higher.

Using the Focal Distance sets the focal point from the camera, and using the Lens F-Stop option sets how quickly the objects on either side of the focal point become blurry. Figure 7.30 shows a row of pawns with the focal point set at one of the middle pawns. Notice how the pawns on either side are blurred.

Using a Camera Mask

If you're trying to render an entire frame, but you only want to see a small portion of the rendered image, you can use a camera mask to render only part of the final image. The camera mask option is in the Mask Options panel of the Camera Properties dialog box. With the Use Mask option enabled, you can set the upper-left corner location of the area that you want to render and the Width and Height of the render area. The Mask Color is the color of the masked area. Figure 7.31 shows a rendered image with the camera mask enabled.

FIGURE 7.30
Depth of field camera effect

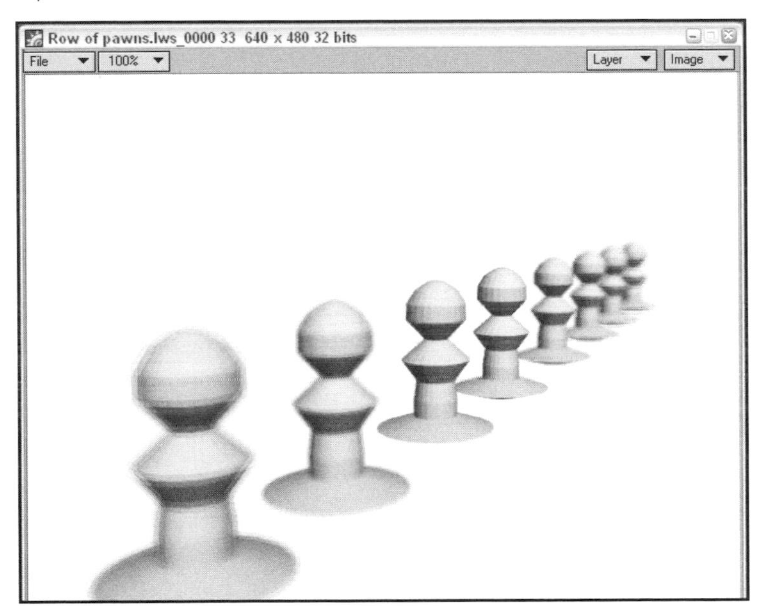

FIGURE 7.31
Camera mask

FIGURE 7.32
Motion Blur car

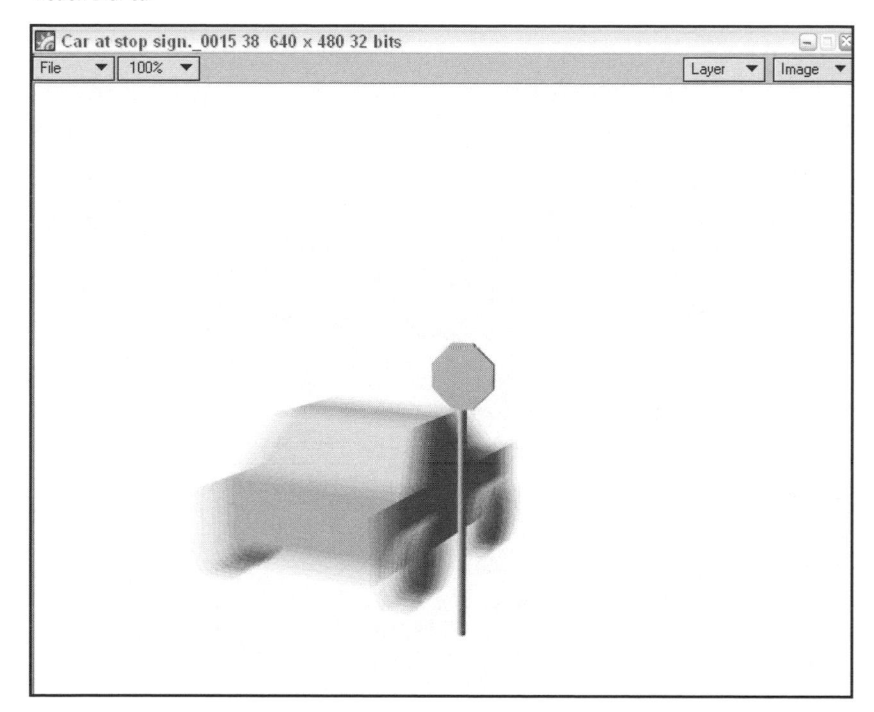

Set camera properties and enable motion blur

1. Click the File, Load, Load Scene menu command and open the Car at stop sign.lws file.

   This file includes a simple animated car running past a stop sign.

2. Select the camera object and click the Properties button at the bottom of the interface.

   The Camera Properties dialog box opens.

3. Select the VGA (640 x 480) option from the Resolution drop-down list. Select the Medium option from the Antialiasing drop-down list, and then enable the Soft Filter and Adaptive Sampling options.

4. In the Motion Effects panel at the bottom of the Camera Properties dialog box, select the Normal option in the Motion Blur drop-down list.

5. Click the Render tab in the main interface and select the Render Frame button.

   The car is blurred to show its motion but the stop sign is not blurred, as shown in Figure 7.32.

6. Select the File, Save, Save Scene As menu command and save the file as Motion blur car.lws.

SET LIGHT PROPERTIES

What You'll Do

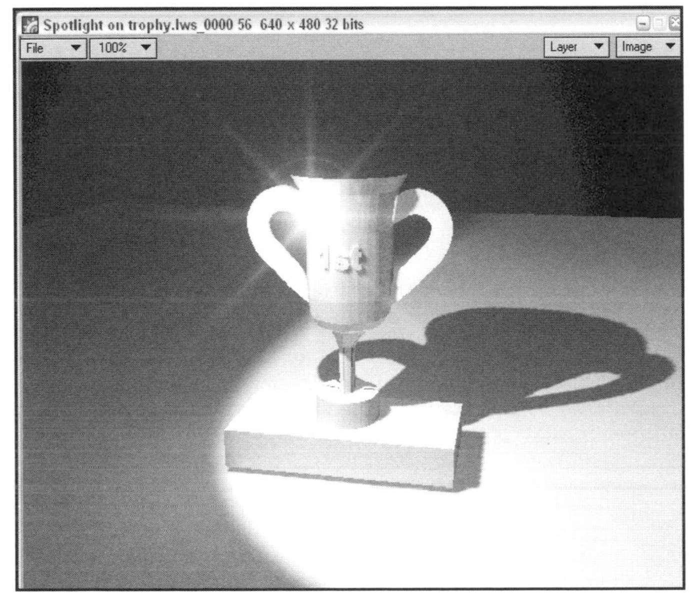

In this lesson, you'll learn how to set light properties and enable light effects such as lens flares, volumetric lighting, and projection maps.

Perhaps no single item can change the scene more than lights can. LightWave includes several different lights and the Light Properties dialog box includes many unique settings for controlling how they affect the scene. The Light Properties dialog box, shown in Figure 7.33, lists the total number of lights in the scene and you can select from available lights using a drop-down list. Use the Light Type drop-down list to change light types at any time.

FIGURE 7.33
Light Properties dialog box

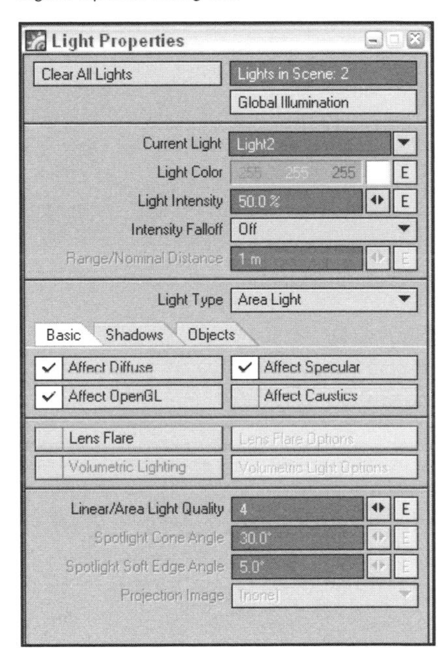

Setting Light Color and Intensity

Each light can have a color set using the color swatch, and an intensity value. With the Intensity Falloff option, you select from several different algorithms for computing how quickly the intensity decreases over distance. The options include Off, Linear, Inverse Distance, and Inverse Distance Squared.

Enabling Lens Flares

Lens flares are the circles, streaks, and glows that occur when light bounces off a particularly shiny object. You can enable lens flares for a given light by enabling the Lens Flare option in the Basic panel of the Light Properties dialog box. This makes the Lens Flare Options button active, which opens the Lens Flare Options dialog box, shown in Figure 7.34. Using these options, you can set the Flare Intensity and several other settings for controlling the glow, ring, streaks, and reflections. Figure 7.35 shows a rendered image with a lens flare enabled.

FIGURE 7.34
Lens Flare Options dialog box

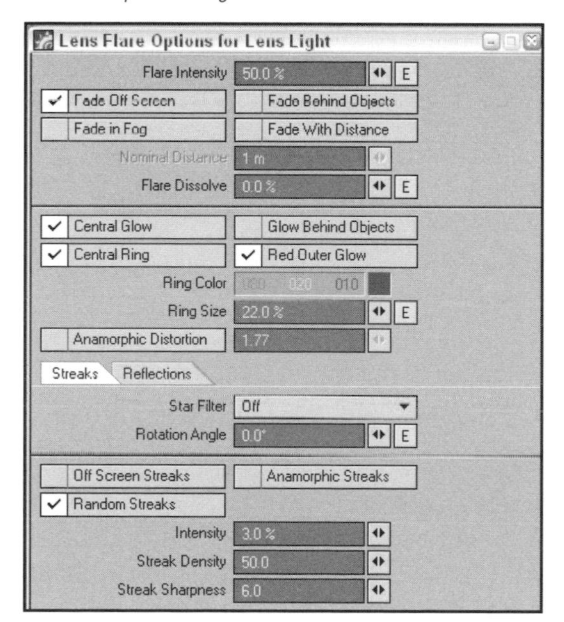

FIGURE 7.35
Rendered image with a lens flare

Enabling Volumetric Lights

Volumetric lights are lights that emit a glow around the center of the light as if the light were within a foggy environment. You can enable volumetric lighting for a given light by enabling the Volumetric Lighting option in the Basic panel of the Light Properties dialog box. This makes the Volumetric Light Options button active, which opens the Volumetric Options dialog box, shown in Figure 7.36. Using these options, you can set the Quality of the volumetric lights and the light's radius, luminosity, and opacity, along with several other settings, including its color. Figure 7.37 shows a rendered image with a volumetric light enabled.

FIGURE 7.36
Volumetric Options dialog box

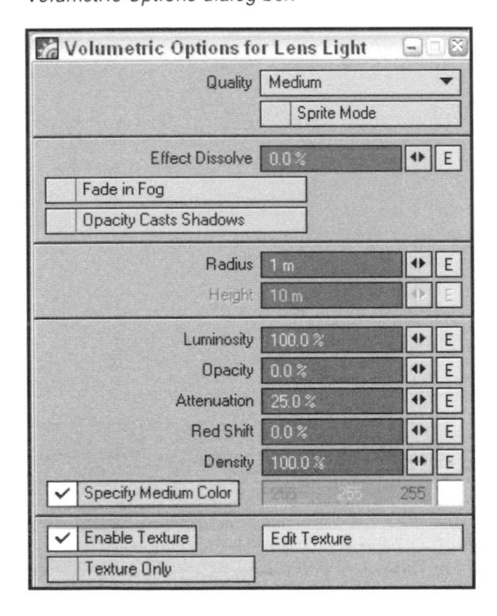

FIGURE 7.37
Rendered image with a volumetric light

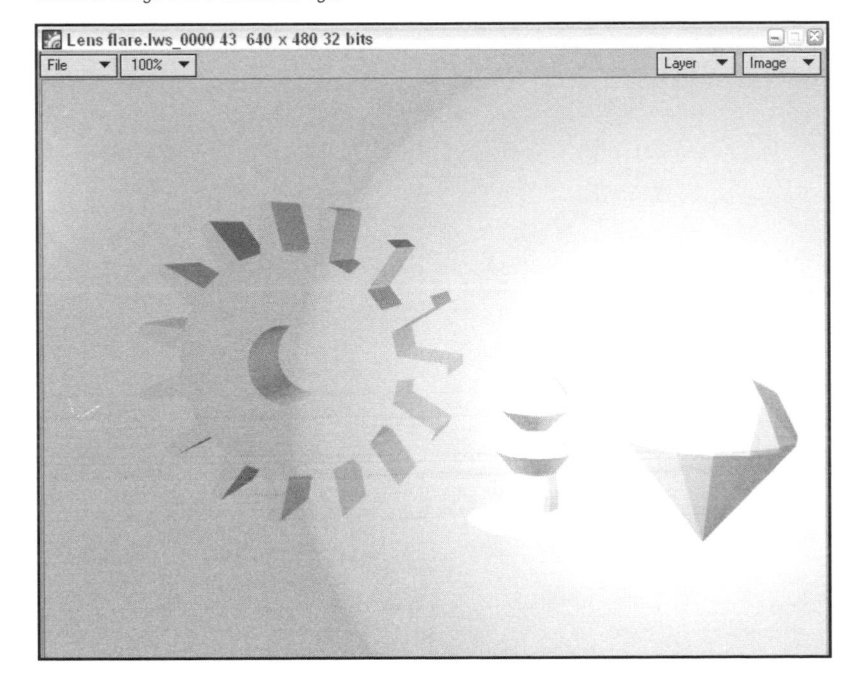

Enabling Shadows

All lights cast shadows, but in LightWave, you can control exactly which lights cast shadow and which don't. If your scene has many lights, you'll probably only want one of them to cast shadows. By clicking the Shadows panel in the Light Properties dialog box, you can enable two different types of shadows. Ray Trace shadows have clean edges, but if you are using a spotlight, you can enable a Shadow Map. Shadow Maps are much quicker to render than Ray Trace shadows, and with Shadow Maps, you can specify the degree of fuzziness of the edges. Figure 7.38 shows a simple rendered scene with shadows enabled.

Using Projection Maps

When you select a spotlight, the option to include a **projection map** is available. A projection map is an image that is placed in front of the light and projected onto the scene. To add a projection map, select the Load Image option from the Projection Image drop-down list in the Basic panel of the Light Properties dialog box. Figure 7.39 shows a rendered image with an image projected onto the scene.

FIGURE 7.38
Rendered image with shadows

FIGURE 7.39
Projected image

Enabling Global Illumination, Radiosity, and Caustics

The Global Illumination button is located at the top of the Light Properties dialog box. When you click this button, the Global Illumination dialog box, shown in Figure 7.40, opens. Use this dialog box to set the global lighting settings for the scene. You can use the Global Light and Global Lens Flare Intensity values to set the intensity for all lights and lens flares in the scene and provide a control for dimming all lights at once. Ambient light is the light that doesn't come from a light source, but is present everywhere. You can set its color and intensity. **Radiosity** is a lighting method that takes into account how light bounces off surfaces and provides much more realistic lighting for interior spaces. **Caustics** are those colorful lines of light that are seen at the bottom of a swimming pool and are caused by light that is refracted through a large body of water.

FIGURE 7.40

Global Illumination dialog box

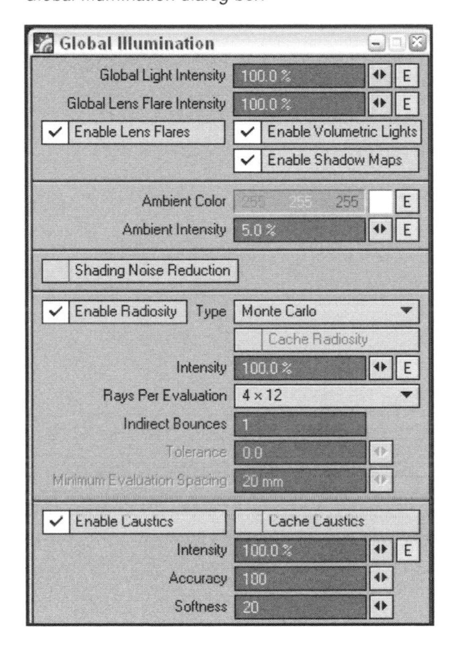

FIGURE 7.41
Trophy with shadows

Change light properties and enable shadows

1. Click the File, Load, Load Scene menu command and open the Trophy.lws file.
2. Select the light object and click the Properties button at the bottom of the interface.

   The Light Properties dialog box appears.
3. Select the Spotlight option in the Light Type drop-down list.

   The light is changed to the spotlight.
4. At the bottom of the Light Properties dialog box, change the Spotlight Cone Angle value to **45.0**.
5. Click the Shadows tab and select the Shadow Map option in the Shadow Type drop-down list. Then close the Light Properties dialog box.
6. Click the Render tab in the main interface and then click the Render Frame button.

   The trophy is rendered along with shadows, as shown in Figure 7.41.
7. Select the File, Save, Save Scene As menu command and save the file as Spotlight on trophy.lws.

Enable a lens flare

1. Click the File, Load, Load Scene menu command and open the Spotlight on trophy.lws file.
2. Click the Items tab and select the Lights, Point Light command from the Add section. Name the light **Lens flare** and click OK. Move the new light to the front of the trophy object.
3. With the Lens Flare point light selected, click the Properties button at the bottom of the interface.
4. Select the Basic tab, enable the Lens Flare option, and then click the Lens Flare Options button.
5. In the Lens Flare Options dialog box, set the Flare Intensity to 80%, and select the 8 Point option for the Star Filter drop-down list. Then close the Lens Flare Options and the Light Properties dialog boxes.
6. Click the Render tab in the main interface and then click the Render Frame button.

   The trophy is rendered along with shadows and a lens flare, as shown in Figure 7.42.
7. Select the File, Save, Save Scene As menu command and save the file as Trophy with lens flare.lws.

FIGURE 7.42
Trophy with lens flare

CHAPTER SUMMARY

This chapter introduced the Layout interface and explained how to load and save scene files. It also explained how the Layout viewports differ from the Modeler viewports. The Layout interface allows you to work with many different types of items, including lights and cameras. The properties for scene objects, lights, and cameras can be viewed and changed as needed using the Object Properties dialog box.

What You Have Learned

- How to load and save objects and scenes in the Layout interface.
- How to use the Layout interface's unique viewport features, including the Schematic view.
- How to select, clone, and manipulate objects in the Layout interface.
- How to add lights and cameras to a scene.
- How to access the camera properties for enabling resolutions, antialiasing, and motion blur.
- How to access the light properties for setting light color, intensity, lens flares, and shadows.

Key Terms from This Chapter

- **Schematic view.** A view that displays all scene items as simple rectangular nodes.
- **null object.** A simple nonrenderable object that marks a position within the scene.
- **level of detail.** A rendering technique that displays a high-resolution model of an object when it's close to the camera and a low-resolution version when the object is far from the camera.
- **focal length.** A distance from the camera where the camera is in focus.
- **antialiasing.** A rendering technique that smoothes the transitions between colors to eliminate jagged edges.
- **motion blur.** A rendering technique that blurs objects by degrees based on how fast they are moving in the scene.
- **depth of field.** A rendering technique that blurs scene objects by degrees based on their distance from a designated focal point.
- **camera mask.** A method of selecting only a portion of the scene to be rendered.
- **lens flare.** A bright highlight that reflects off shiny objects with circles, streaks, and glows when a camera is pointed at a light source.
- **volumetric lights.** A specialized light source that emits a glow about the center of a light as if it were in a foggy environment.
- **projection map.** A bitmap image that is placed in front of a light source and projected onto the scene.
- **radiosity.** A lighting method that computes light effects based on how light bounces off objects in the scene.
- **caustics.** A lighting method that produces random streaks of light caused by light passing through a body of water.

CHAPTER 8

MODIFYING LAYOUT OBJECTS

1. Translate, rotate, and transform objects.
2. Work with bones.
3. Work with Skelegons.
4. Morph objects.
5. Deform objects.
6. Add fur and hair.

CHAPTER 8
MODIFYING LAYOUT OBJECTS

Although the Modeler is where most of the object deformation takes place, there are several ways you can modify objects in the Layout interface. Some of these methods are useful for placing objects in their correct positions, and others take advantage of the rendering process to add certain effects.

The Modify menu tab includes several buttons for moving, rotating, and transforming objects. Using these buttons, you can position and orient objects within the Layout exactly where they need to be. You can also transform lights and cameras using these tools.

In preparation for animating characters, LightWave includes a robust bone creation system. By placing bones within a character, you can deform and mold a character's movements by controlling its underlying bones. This simplifies the process of animating characters. LightWave includes many tools for working with bones.

Or, instead of creating bones, you can use Skelegons in the Modeler interface. Skelegons are saved with the object and you can easily convert them into bones when you load the object into the Layout interface.

If animating characters with bones isn't as precise as you'd like, you can use morphing to change the exact point locations of an object between different states. The drawback of morphing is that it can only take place between two objects that have the same number of points in the same order. Using the Endomorph features in the Modeler, you can save several morph targets within a single object and access these morph targets using the Layout's Morph Mixer dialog box.

The Object Properties dialog box includes several deformation plug-ins that you can apply to Layout objects. You can even animate these deformations to create special effects. To control a deformation, you transform null objects in the scene.

Another interesting plug-in that you can access in the Layout interface is the Sasquatch Lite plug-in, which enables you to add fur and hair to objects and surfaces. To render an object with fur or hair, you'll need to add a Pixel Filter into the Image Processing panel of the Effects dialog box.

Tools You'll Use

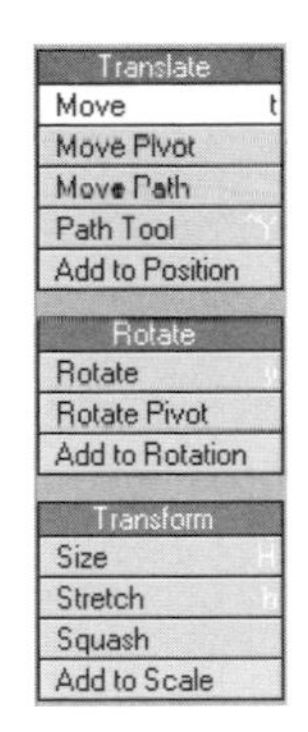

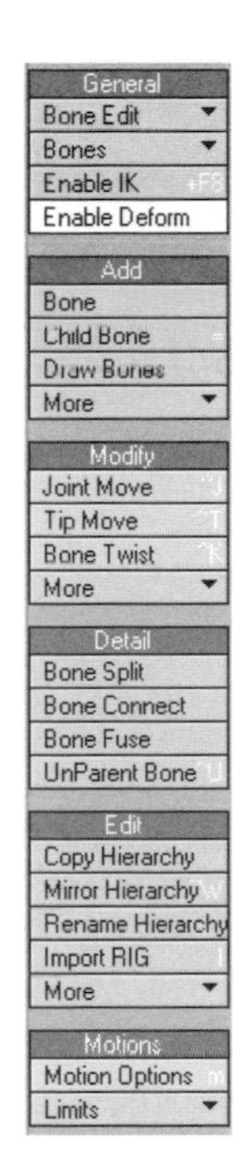

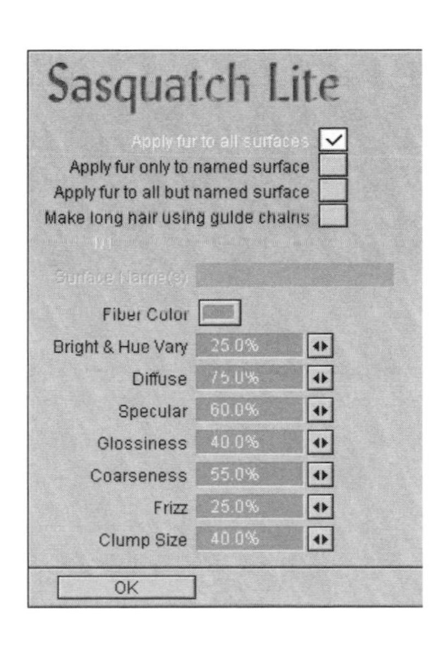

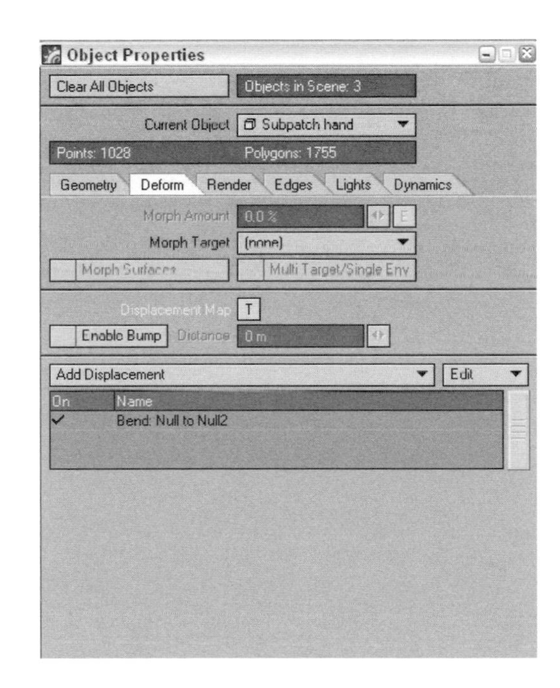

LESSON 1

TRANSLATE, ROTATE, AND TRANSFORM OBJECTS

What You'll Do

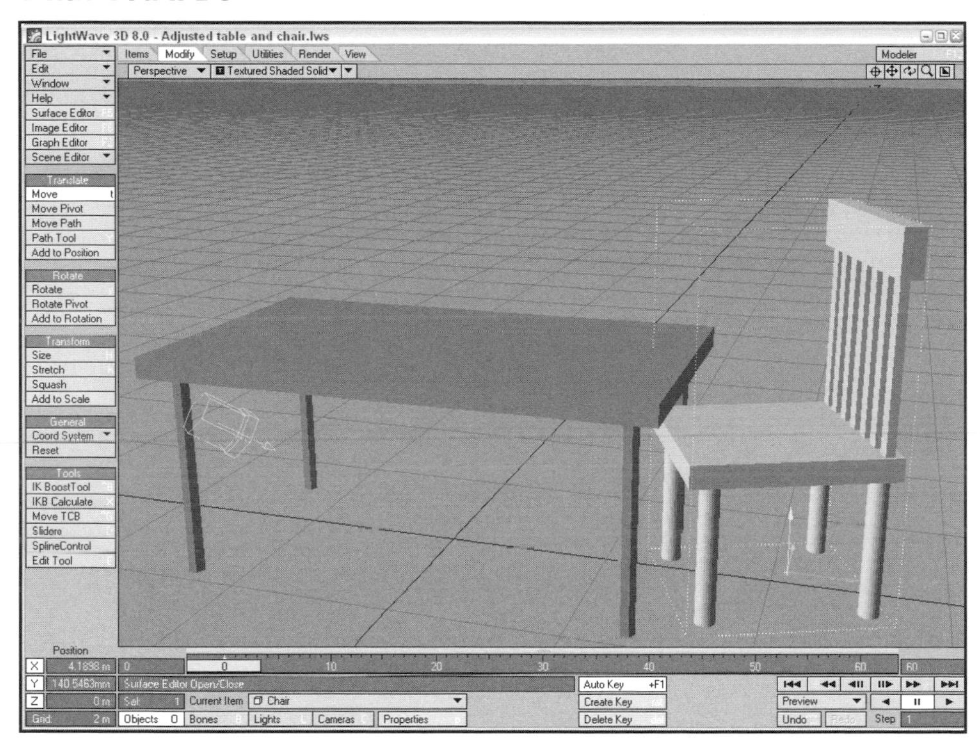

In this lesson, you'll learn how to change the position, orientation, and size of objects.

Although moving, rotating, and scaling objects in the Layout interface works much the same as in the Modeler interface, there are some unique differences. For example, in the Layout interface, you have the ability to move and rotate pivot points. All of the transformation commands are located in the Modify tab.

Moving Objects

When you first load an object into the Layout interface, the object is placed at the scene origin and the Move tool is selected by default. This is convenient because it lets you move the new object into its proper position immediately. When the Move tool is active, a red, green, and blue set of axes, shown in Figure 8.1, appears at the object's pivot point. Dragging on only one of these axes limits the object movement to that particular axis. You can enable the Move tool by clicking the Move button in the Translate section of the Modify menu tab (or by pressing t).

TIP

You can move objects in the Perspective viewport of the Layout interface by dragging the mouse. If you want to move the object up and down in the scene, hold down the right mouse key and drag.

Rotating Objects

The Rotate tool also uses a set of circular axes that you can use to limit the rotation to a single plane, as shown in Figure 8.2. Select the Rotate tool in the Rotate section of the Modify menu tab (or press y). The three rotation directions are known as heading, pitch, and bank, which correspond to rotating about the Y, X, and Z axes.

FIGURE 8.1
Move tool axes

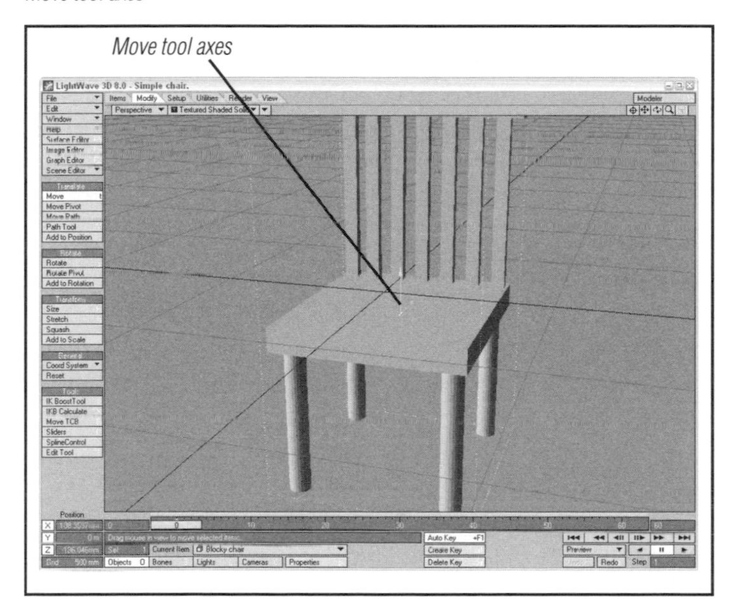

FIGURE 8.2
Rotate tool axes

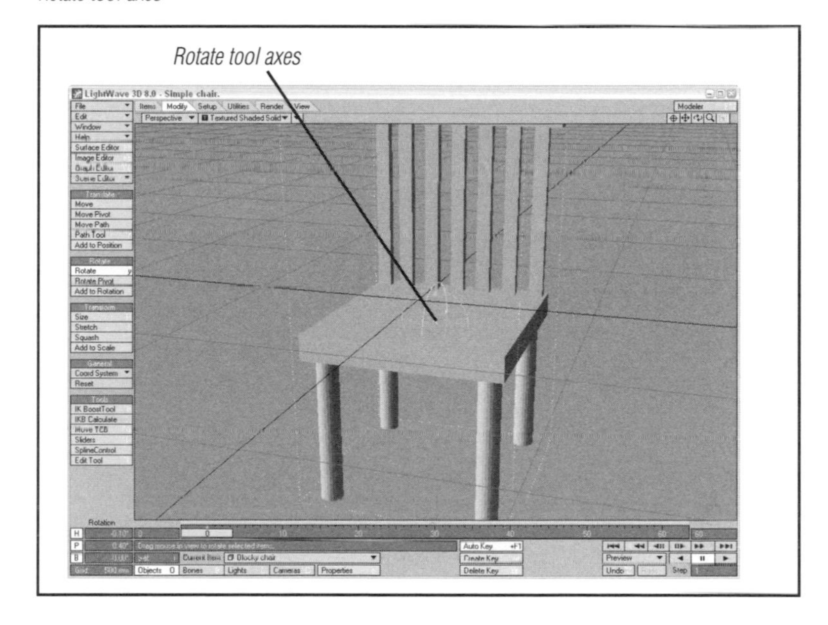

TIP

You can change an object's heading and pitch in the Perspective viewport of the Layout interface by dragging the mouse. To change the object's bank value, hold down the right mouse key and drag.

Moving and Rotating Pivots

When you select the Move or Rotate tool, their axes appear at the object's pivot. This is the point about which the object is rotated and can be anywhere in the scene. For example, imagine the moon circling the Earth. By setting the moon's pivot to the center of the Earth, it is easy to have the moon orbit the Earth. Selecting the Move Pivot or Rotate Pivot buttons in the Modify menu tab lets you alter the pivot's location. Figure 8.3 shows a chair rotated after moving its pivot to the base of the chair.

Sizing, Stretching, and Squashing Objects

Use the Size tool in the Modify menu tab to you uniformly change the size of an object. The Stretch button is a variation of the Size tool that you used to scale the object along a single axis. The Squash tool also scales the object along a single axis, but maintains the object's volume in the process. When you select the Stretch or Squash tools, a handle appears at the end of the axes about the pivot, as shown in Figure 8.4. Selecting and dragging one of the handles scales the object only along the selected axis.

Specifying Transform Offsets

After an object is in place, you can add a precise offset value to the object using the buttons named Add to Position in the Translate section, Add to Rotation in the

FIGURE 8.3
Rotating about the object's pivot point

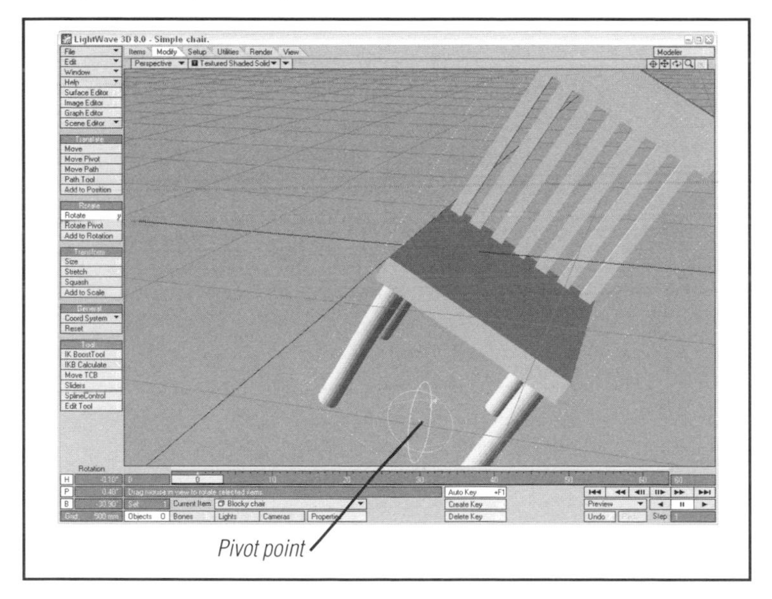

FIGURE 8.4
Stretch and Squash tool axes

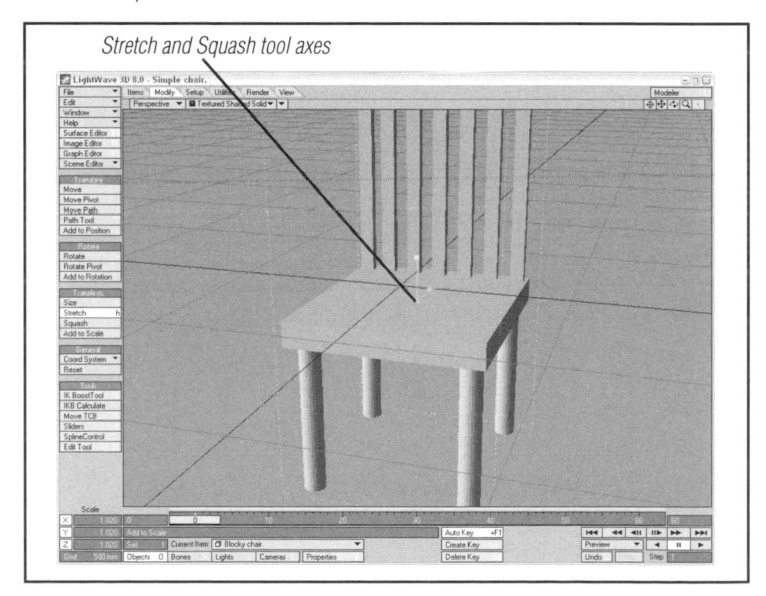

Rotate section, and Add to Scale in the Transform section of the Modify menu tab. Clicking these buttons opens a dialog box, like the one in Figure 8.5, where you can enter a precise coordinate offset value to move, rotate, or scale the object from its current position.

Using the Numeric Adjustment Controls

The lower-left corner of the interface contains three fields marked X, Y, and Z, as shown in Figure 8.6. These fields show the current global position for each dimension of the selected object. By entering a value in one of these fields, you can move the selected object to a different global position. If you click the X, Y, or Z buttons to the left of these fields, you can restrict the motion of the selected object in that direction. For example, if you click the X button so that it is inactive, and then drag the object in the viewport, the object only moves in the Y or Z directions.

FIGURE 8.5
Add to Position dialog box

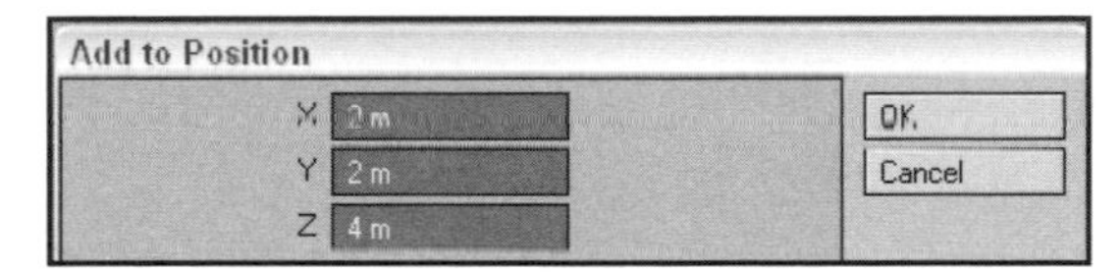

FIGURE 8.6
Numeric adjustment controls

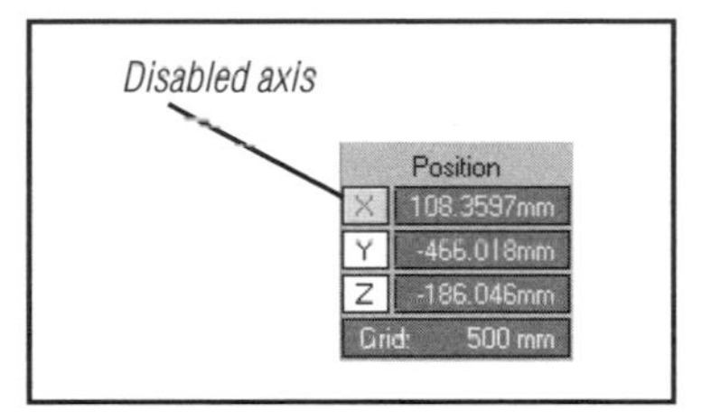

Move, rotate, and scale objects

1. Click the File, Load, Load Scene menu command and open the Table and chair.lws file.
2. Select the table, click the Move button in the Translate section of the Modify menu tab, and then drag upward with the right mouse button to move the table until its legs are aligned with the grid.
3. Click the Center Object icon in the upper-right corner of the viewport to readjust the Perspective viewport to the new table position.
4. With the chair object selected, click the Modify tab, click the Size button from the Transform section, and then drag in the viewport until the chair is the correct size relative to the table.
5. Click the Rotate button in the Rotate section and drag the red axis until the chair is aligned so that it faces the left end of the table.
6. Click the Move button in the Translate section and drag the chair object to the right end of the table.

   After the table and chair are moved, scaled, and rotated, they should look like Figure 8.7.
7. Select the File, Save, Save Scene As menu command and save the file as Adjusted table and chair.lws.

FIGURE 8.7
Adjusted table and chair

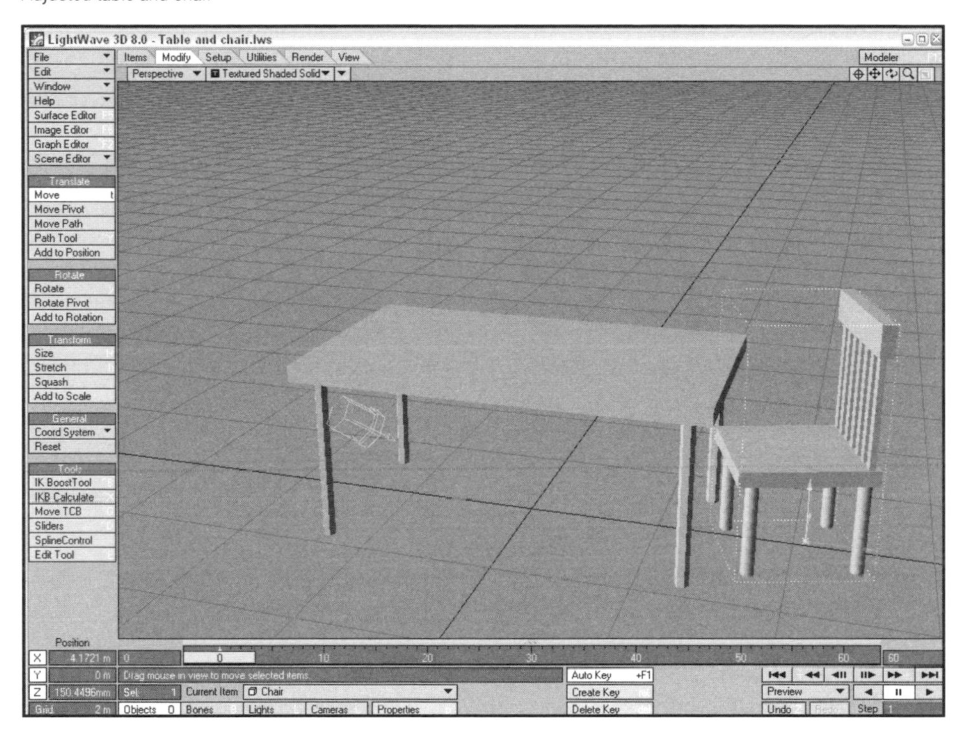

LESSON 2

WORK WITH BONES

What You'll Do

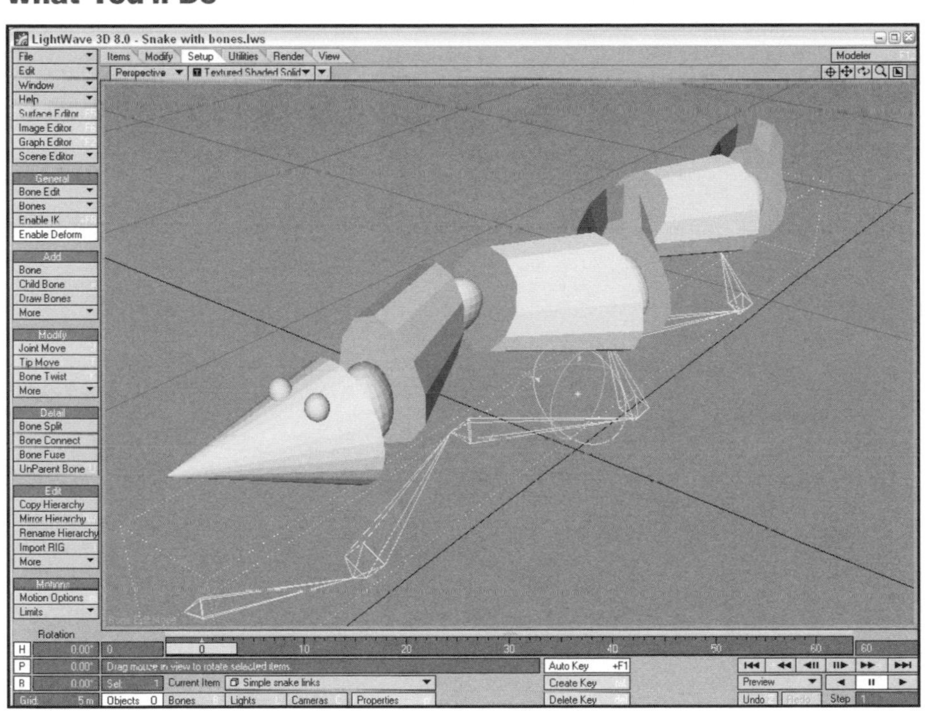

In this lesson, you'll learn how to create, edit, and position bones within an object.

Underneath our skin, we all have a structure of bones that help us as we move. In LightWave, you can build a structure of **bones** that you can use to drive the animation of the object attached to the bones. You can use bones to animate characters.

Using Bone Edit Mode

When you select the Bone Edit, Enter Bone Edit Mode menu command from the General section of the Setup tab, the viewports are outlined in red and text in the lower-left corner of each viewport indicates that you're in a special mode, see Figure 8.8. All objects, cameras, and lights—except for the current selection—are hidden. You don't have to use the Bone Edit mode to work with bones, but using this mode can simplify your work because there are no distractions. To exit this mode, select the Bone Edit, Exit Bone Edit Mode menu command (keyboard shortcut: D).

Creating Bones

Before creating any bones, you should select the object that the bone will drive. Then, click the Setup menu tab and click the Bone button in the Add section. Clicking this command opens the Bone Name dialog box, where you can name the bone. After you click OK, a single bone is added to the scene, along the object's Z-axis. When you select a bone, you can use the Child Bone button to add a child bone to the structure, which is connected to the first bone, as shown in Figure 8.9. Moving a parent bone moves all the children bones with it, but a child bone can also move independently of its parent.

Another way to create a bone is to draw one in an orthogonal viewport with the Draw Bones tool. Drawn bones are parented to the selected object and drawn from head to tail. You can use the More, Draw Child Bones tool to draw child bones.

> **CAUTION**
>
> You can't draw bones in the Perspective viewport.

FIGURE 8.8
Bone Edit mode

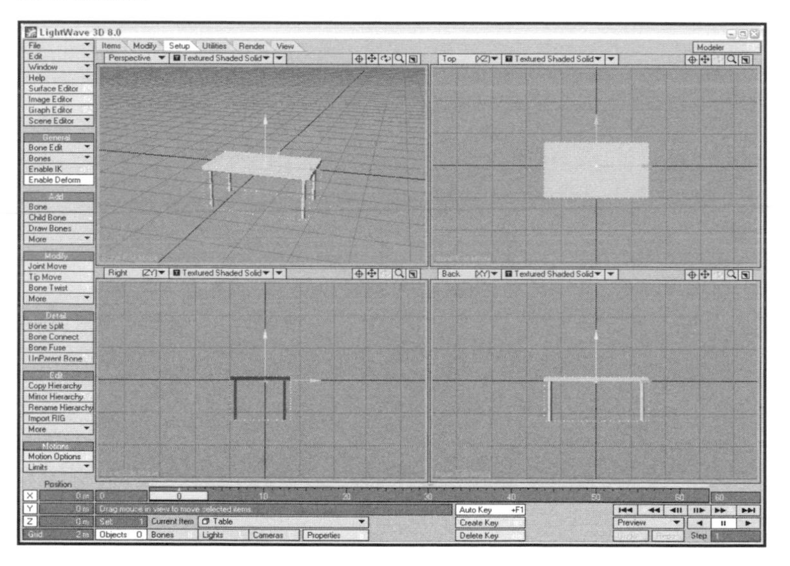

FIGURE 8.9
Parent and child bones

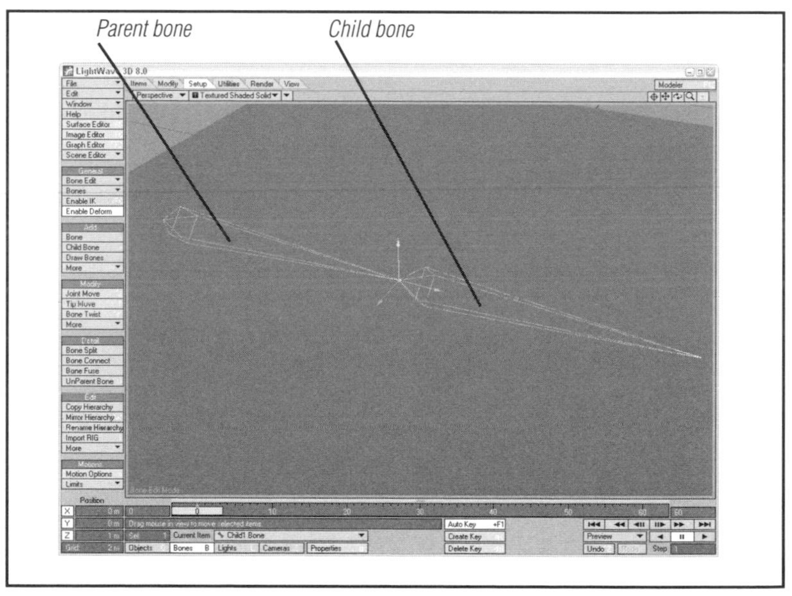

Selecting and Modifying Bones

After you create a structure of bones, you can easily select them by clicking the Bones button at the bottom of interface. In this mode, you can only select bones. With a bone selected, you can use the buttons in the Modify section of the Setup menu tab to change its position and orientation. Using the Joint Move tool places a red line through the center of the bone and a green cross at the end of the selected bone, which you can drag to a new location, as shown in Figure 8.10. When the joint is correctly oriented, press the Spacebar to update the bone's position. The Tip Move tool works just like the Joint Move tool, except that you can use it to move the entire hierarchy beneath the selected point along with the tip. Use the Bone Twist tool to rotate the bone about its center axis. Use the More, Scale Hierarchy command from the Modify section of the Setup menu tab to scale the entire hierarchy of bones by dragging on the center of the parent's axis.

Breaking and Fusing Bones

The Detail section of the Setup menu tab includes commands for dividing and combining adjacent bones. Clicking the Bone Split button opens a dialog box where you can specify the number of new bones to create. To select multiple bones at once, hold down the Shift key and then click the bones. When you select several bones, you can use the Bone Connect button to open a dialog box to define how to connect the bones. The options include snapping the parent tip to the child base, snapping the child base to the parent tip, and creating a new bone between the selected bones. Clicking the Bone Fuse button combines the selected bones to make a single bone.

Copying Hierarchies and Deleting Bones

The Edit section of the Setup menu tab includes buttons to Copy and Mirror Hierarchy. These options are useful if you've

FIGURE 8.10
Joint Move tool

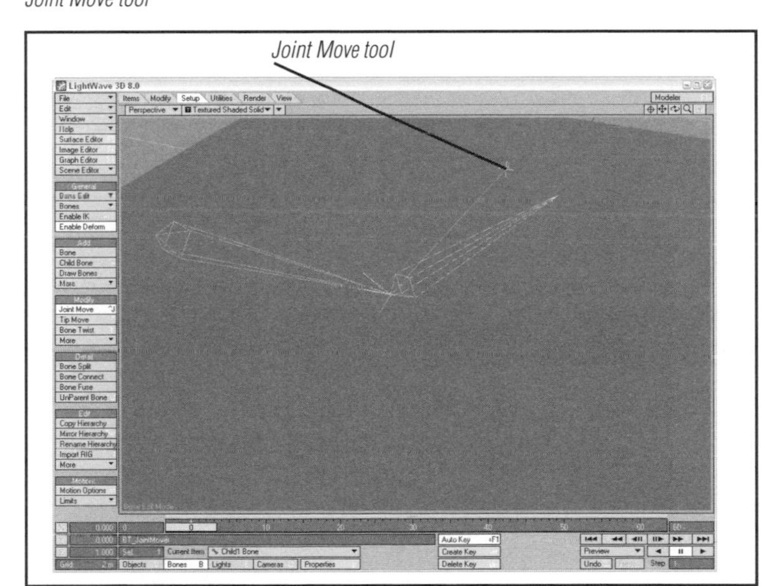

created a set of bones for an arm or a leg. You can use the Mirror Hierarchy button to create a similar hierarchy for the other arm or leg. The More, Delete menu in the Edit section includes commands for deleting an entire hierarchy or a single bone.

Enabling Bone Modes

To turn the bones on, select the Bones, Bones On menu command from the Setup menu tab in the General section. When the bones are enabled, they are shown with solid lines; when disabled, they are shown with dashed lines. Bones that are turned on can affect the geometry object that it controls. Bones can be turned off again by selecting the Bones, Bones Off menu command in the General section.

After you create a bone hierarchy, you can deform the attached object by the bone structure by clicking the Enable Deform button in the General section of the Setup tab. If this mode is disabled, the object remains unchanged as you move the bones. Clicking the Enable IK button activates the **Inverse Kinematics** controls, which you can use to make the children bones control their parents instead of vice versa. You can set up IK controls in the Motion Options dialog box (found in the Motions section of the Setup menu tab), which is discussed in Chapter 9.

Setting Bone Properties

When you select a bone, you can open its Properties dialog box, shown in Figure 8.11, to specify an number of bone settings, including joint constraints.

FIGURE 8.11
Bone Properties dialog box

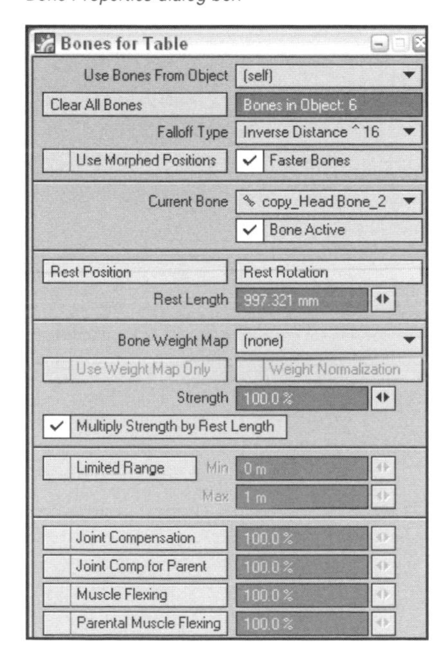

Create a bone structure

1. Click the File, Load, Load Scene menu command and open the Simple snake links.lws file.
2. With the snake object selected, click the Setup menu tab and then click the Bone Edit, Enter Bone Edit Mode menu command in the General section.

   The viewports are highlighted in red and all items are hidden except for the selected object.
3. Click the Draw Bones button in the Add section and drag from the front tip of the snake's head to its neck in the Top viewport.
4. Click the Bones button at the bottom of the interface, select the new bone, and then move it up in the Back viewport to align with the snake's head.
5. With the first bone still selected, click the Child Bone button in the Add section. In the Bone Name dialog box, name the new bone **Bone link1** and click OK.
6. Click the Joint Move button in the Modify section and drag the crosshair in the Top viewport to the middle of the next sphere in the snake's link. After positioning the crosshairs, press the Spacebar.
7. Repeat steps 5 and 6 for the remaining links, naming each one with an incremented number.
8. Select the first bone and rotate it in the Top viewport about 30 degrees to the side, and then alternate with each successive link. Click the Bones, Bones On menu command in the General section and click the Enable Deform button in the same section.

   The snake object is deformed to match the bones, as shown in Figure 8.12.
9. Select the File, Save, Save Scene As menu command and save the file as Snake with bones.lws.

FIGURE 8.12
Snake with bones

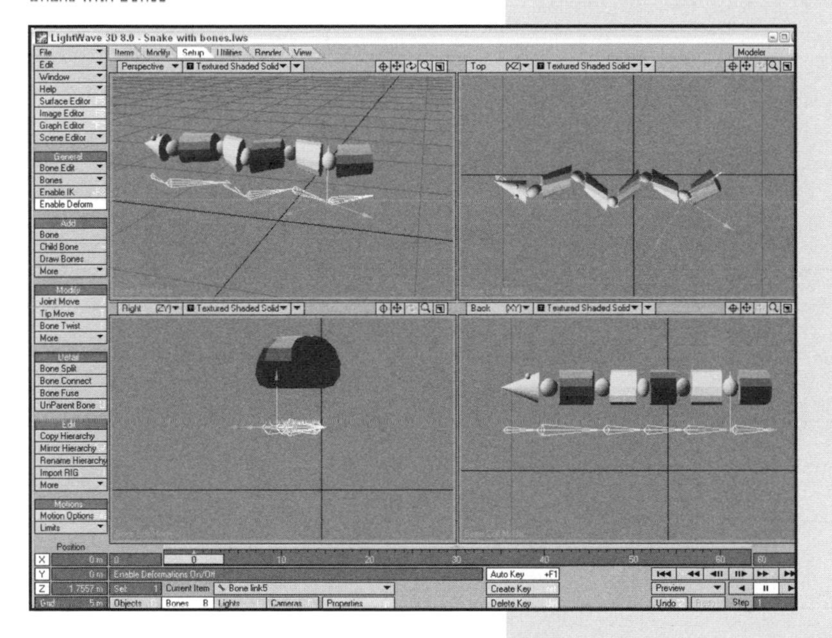

LESSON 3

WORK WITH SKELEGONS

What You'll Do

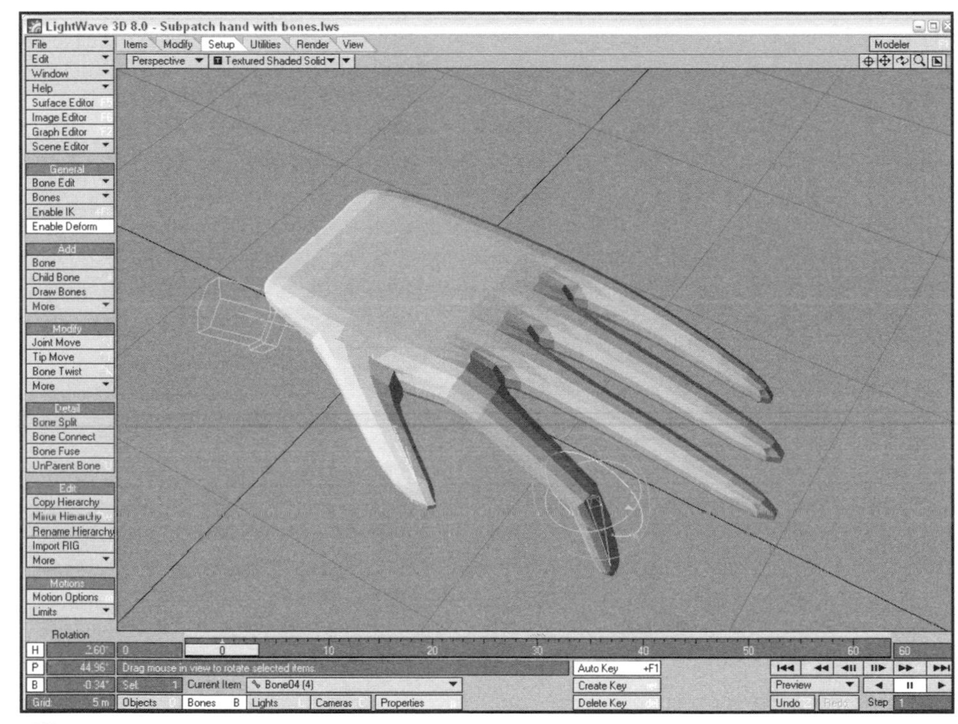

In this lesson, you'll learn how to create and edit Skelegons and convert them into bones.

Bones are created in the Layout interface, but you can add polygon-based versions of bones, called **Skelegons**, to an object in the Modeler. The advantage of using Skelegons is that you can precisely place them using the same points available for modeling. It is also helpful to have the bones saved with the object. When you load an object that includes Skelegons into the Layout interface, you'll need to convert the Skelegons to bones before you can use them to drive animation.

Adding Skelegons in the Modeler

To add Skelegons to an object in the Modeler, click the Create Skelegons button in the Skelegons section of the Setup tab. In this mode, you can draw Skelegons just as you would in the Layout interface, by dragging in a viewport from the Skelegon's base to its tip. After creating a single Skelegon, dragging again creates a child Skelegon object attached to the first. Click the Create Skelegon button again to exit this mode. While in Skelegon creation mode, you can specify a name and number value for each new Skelegon using the Numeric panel. After a Skelegon is created, you can rename it using the Rename Skelegon button, which opens a dialog box where you can type a new name.

Selecting and Editing Skelegons

Skelegons look just like bones, but you select them in the Modeler using Polygons mode. When you select a Skelegon, you can click the Edit Skelegons button to enter an editing mode. In this mode, the selected Skelegon and its children are highlighted with a cross at its base and a circle at each tip. You can drag this cross or circle to reorient the Skelegons. Figure 8.13 shows a object that consists of several attached spheres and a chain of Skelegons that are in edit mode that were moved above the spheres to be easily seen. In addition to Edit Skelegons mode, you can also access Rotate Skelegons mode, which places a circular handle in the center of the Skelegon that you can use to rotate the Skelegon and its children.

FIGURE 8.13
Skelegon chain in edit mode

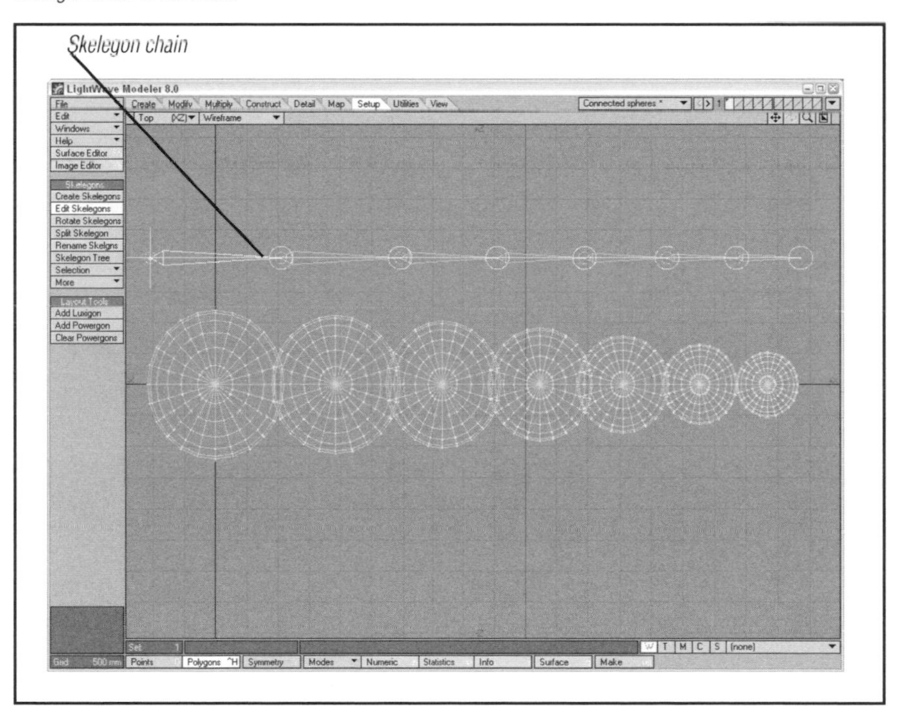

Restructuring a Skelegon Chain

Clicking the Skelegon Tree button opens the dialog box shown in Figure 8.14. This dialog box shows the hierarchical structure of the Skelegons. Using this dialog box, you can reorder the structure of the Skelegons and connect two different Skelegon chains to the same parent by dragging and dropping one bone on another. You can also use this dialog box to specify a weight map for each bone.

Converting Skelegons into Bones

After you load an object containing Skelegons into the Layout interface, you need to convert the Skelegons into bones before you can use them to control the object. To convert Skelegons, click the More, Convert Skelegons into Bones menu command in the Add section of the Setup tab. After conversion, a simple dialog box opens that tells you the number of Skelegons that were converted. After you convert Skelegons into bones, you can use the bones just like you use other bones. Figure 8.15 shows the row of spheres deformed using bones that were converted from Skelegons.

FIGURE 8.14
Skelegon Tree dialog box

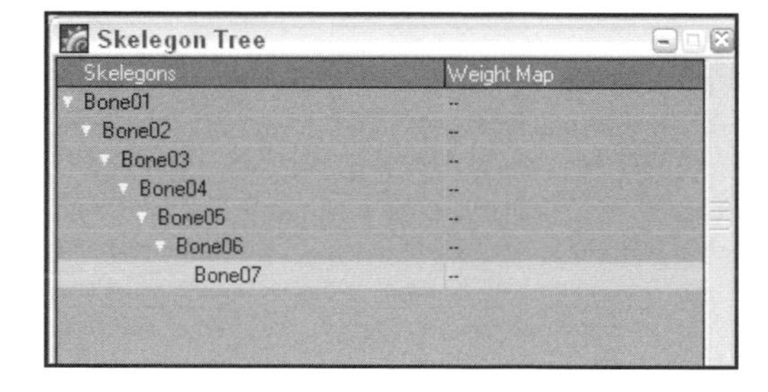

FIGURE 8.15
Skelegons converted to bones

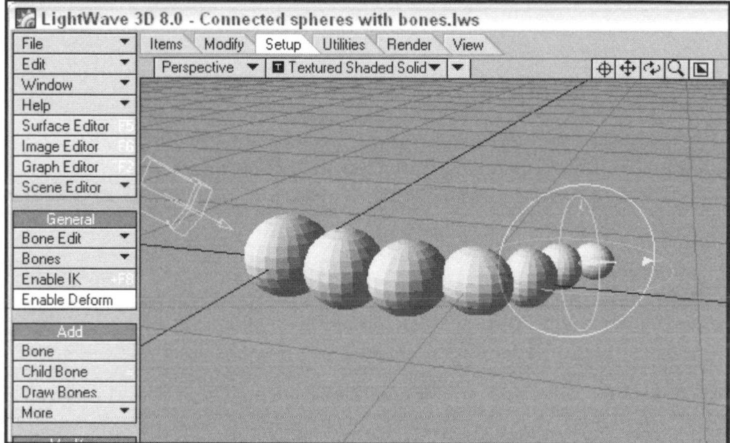

FIGURE 8.16
Restructured Skelegons

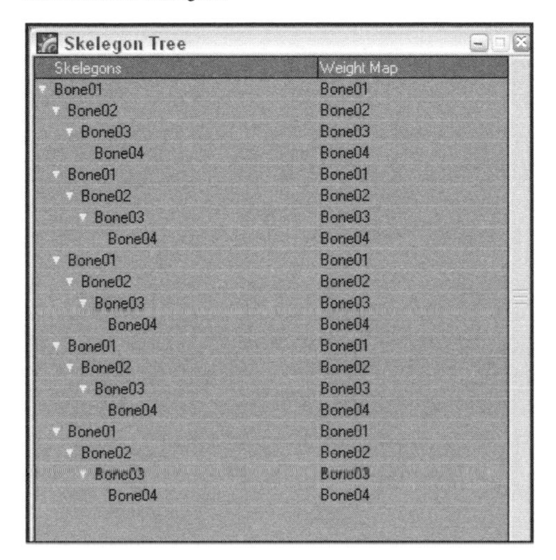

FIGURE 8.17
Subpatch hand with bones

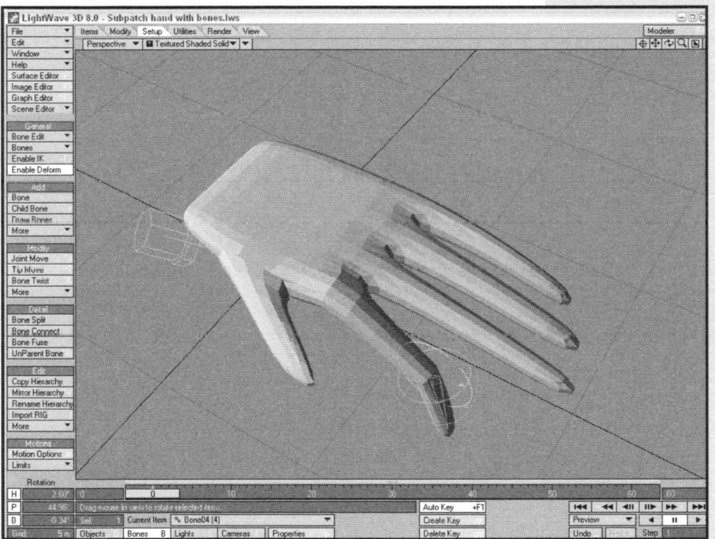

Create, edit, and convert Skelegons

1. In the Modeler, select the File, Load Object menu command and load the Subpatch hand.lwo file. Click the Polygons selection mode button at the bottom of the interface, if necessary.
2. Click the Setup tab, click the Create Skelegons button, and then drag from the base of the hand toward the little finger to create the first Skelegon. Click again at the base of the little finger, again at the middle knuckle, and again at the little finger's tip. Press Enter to exit Skelegon creation mode.
3. Click the Create Skelegons button again and create a chain of Skelegons for the remaining fingers and the thumb.
4. Select the first Skelegon in the Top viewport and click the Edit Skelegons button. Drag the cross at the Skelegon's base upward in the Back viewport to align the Skelegons with the hand object. Repeat this step for the other Skelegons.
5. Click the Rotate Skelegons button, select the Skelegons that don't follow the curvature of the hand in the Back viewport, and then drag on the center handle to rotate them into position. Repeat for all fingers and the thumb.

   The Skelegons should now be aligned with the hand object, but they still need to be connected into a single hierarchy.
6. Click the Skelegon Tree button, drag each separate chain, and drop it when a light blue line appears underneath the first Skelegon named Bone01. The Skelegons should be structured as shown in Figure 8.16. Then close the Skelegon Tree dialog box.
7. Select the File, Save Object As menu command and save the file as Subpatch hand with Skelegons.lwo.
8. Open the Layout interface, select the File, Load, Load Object menu command and load the Subpatch hand with Skelegons.lwo file.
9. With the hand selected, choose the More, Convert Skelegons Into Bones menu command from the Add section in the Setup tab.

   A small dialog box appears stating that 20 bones were created. After enabling the bones, you can use them to deform the hand object, as shown in Figure 8.17.
10. Select the File, Save, Save Scene As menu command and save the file as Subpatch hand with bones.lws.

LESSON 4

MORPH OBJECTS

What You'll Do

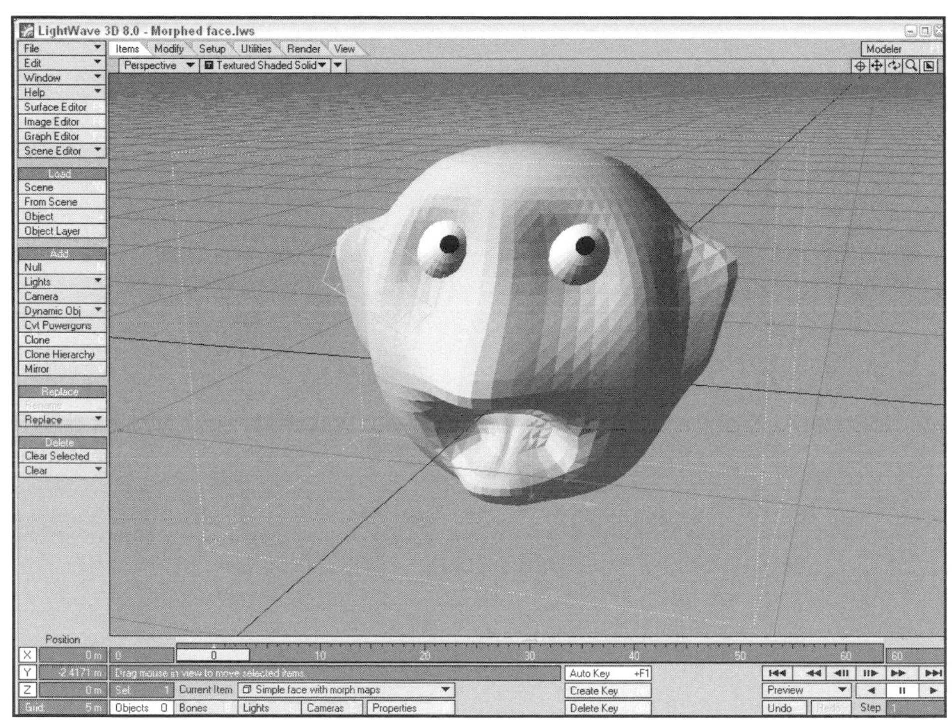

In this lesson, you'll learn how to morph between different objects, create endomorphs in the Modeler, and mix together several morph targets using the Morph Mixer dialog box.

A morphing object is an object that slowly changes from one state to another state. The first state is the source object and each other morph state is known as a **morph target**. Source morph objects and their targets must have an equal number of points and the same point order.

Morphing to a Target

If a scene includes two objects with the same number of points of the same point order, you can specify one of these objects as a morph target for the other. Select the object that you want to be the source object and open the Properties dialog box by clicking the Properties button at the bottom of the interface. In the Deform panel of the Object Properties dialog box, click the Morph Target drop-down list and select the other object as the morph target. After you specify a target, you can change the Morph Amount value to control how much the source object changes to look like the target object. This value can also be animated. Figure 8.18 shows two spheres. The one on the left is the source object that is about halfway through morphing to the target sphere, which is the one on the right.

Creating Endomorphs in the Modeler

Morph targets provide a great way to precisely control how objects are animated, but if you need to load a separate object for each morph target, you'll soon be swimming in objects. The Modeler has a solution: **endomorphs**. With the endomorph commands, you can create morph vertex maps in the Modeler. To create an endomorph, click the New Endomorph button in the Morph section of the Map menu tab in the Modeler. This opens a simple dialog box, shown in Figure 8.19, where you can name the morph map. The named morph map appears in the lower-right corner of the Modeler interface. With the new morph map selected, all point changes are recorded within the vertex map and you can recall them by selecting the morph map. If you need to move the morph map point positions to the base object, use the Apply Morph button.

Accessing the Morph Mixer

When you load an object containing morph maps into the Layout interface, only the base object is visible. You can open the morph maps using the **Morph Mixer**. To access the Morph Mixer, select the base object, open the Properties dialog box, and then select the Morph Mixer option from the Add Displacement drop-down list in the Deform panel. This adds the Morph Mixer to the list of displacements. Select the Morph Mixer from the list and then select the Properties option from the Edit drop-down list, or double-click the Morph Mixer

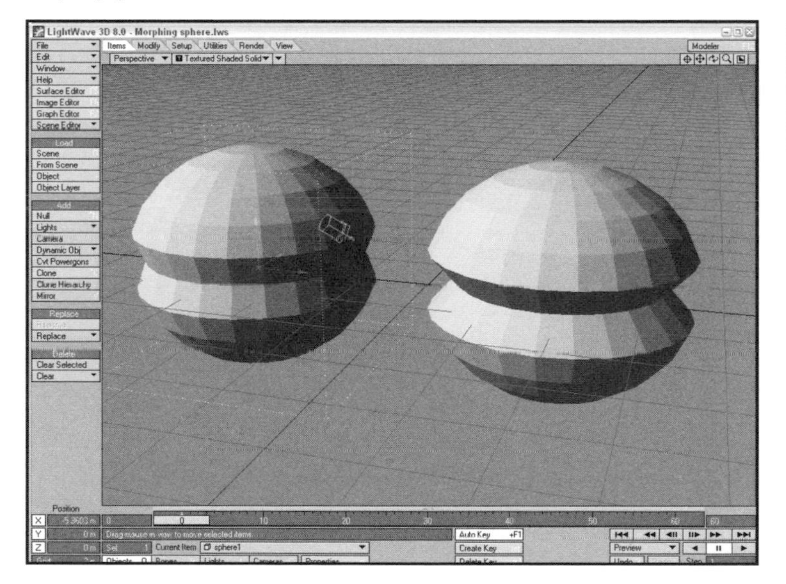

FIGURE 8.18
Morphing sphere

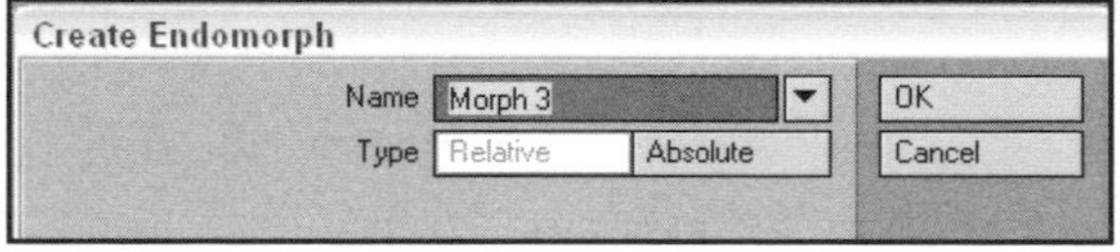

FIGURE 8.19
Create Endomorph dialog box

name in the list. The Morph Mixer dialog box is shown in Figure 8.20.

Using the Morph Mixer

The Morph Mixer shows all the morph maps that are part of the selected object. By dragging the slider associated with each morph map, you can morph the base object toward its morph target. You can also use the Morph Mixer to combine several different morph targets. To create a keyframe for the morph value, click the K icon button to the right of the sliders. Use the arrow icons to move between different keyframes, and the E icon to open the Graph Editor.

FIGURE 8.20
Morph Mixer dialog box

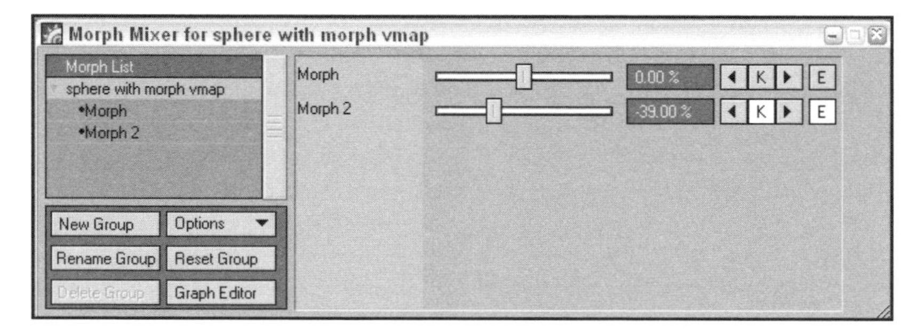

Create and mix endomorphs

1. Open the Modeler interface, click the File, Load Object menu command, and open the Simple face.lwo file.
2. Click the Map tab, click the New Endomorph button, and name the new morph map **Wiggle ears**.
3. In Points mode, hold down the Shift key and select the outer ear points on both ears and move them forward in the Top viewport by dragging them with the Move tool.
4. Repeat steps 2 and 3 to create new morph maps called Twitch nose, Eyes left, Eyes right, and Eyes up.

   The face object now includes five different morph maps.
5. Select the File, Save Object As menu command and save the file as Simple face with morph maps.lwo.
6. Open the Layout interface, select the File, Load, Load Object menu command, and open the Simple face with morph maps lwo file.
7. With the face selected, click the Properties button at the bottom of the interface to open the Object Properties dialog box. Select the Deform tab and then select the Morph Mixer option from the Add Displacement drop-down list.
8. Double-click on the Morph Mixer name to open the Morph Mixer dialog box.

   All five morph maps appear in the Morph Mixer dialog box.
9. Drag the sliders for the eye morph maps in the Morph Mixer and notice the changes in the viewport, as shown in Figure 8.21.
10. Select the File, Save, Save Scene As menu command and save the scene as Morphed face.lws.

FIGURE 8.21
Morphed face

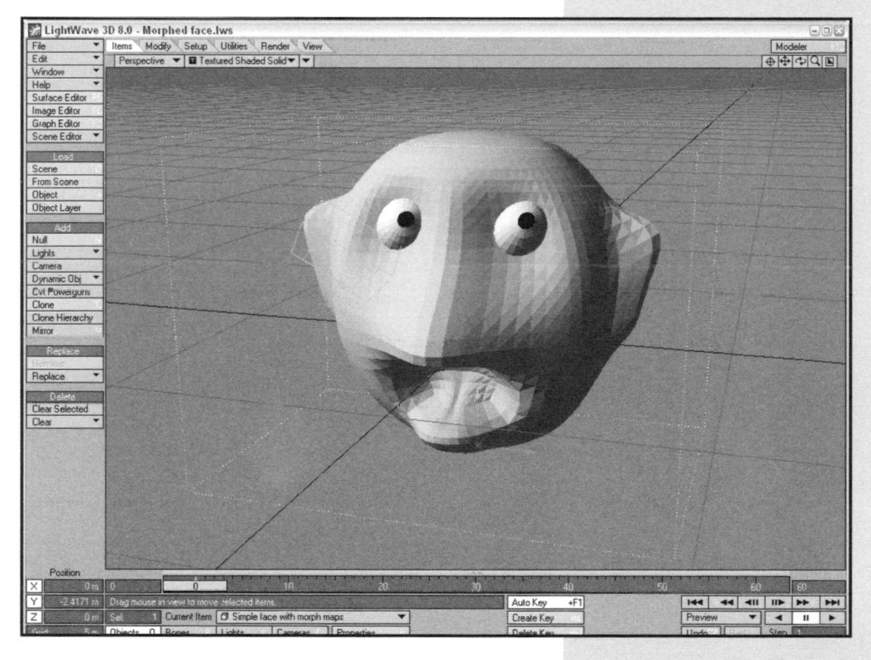

LESSON 5

DEFORM OBJECTS

What You'll Do

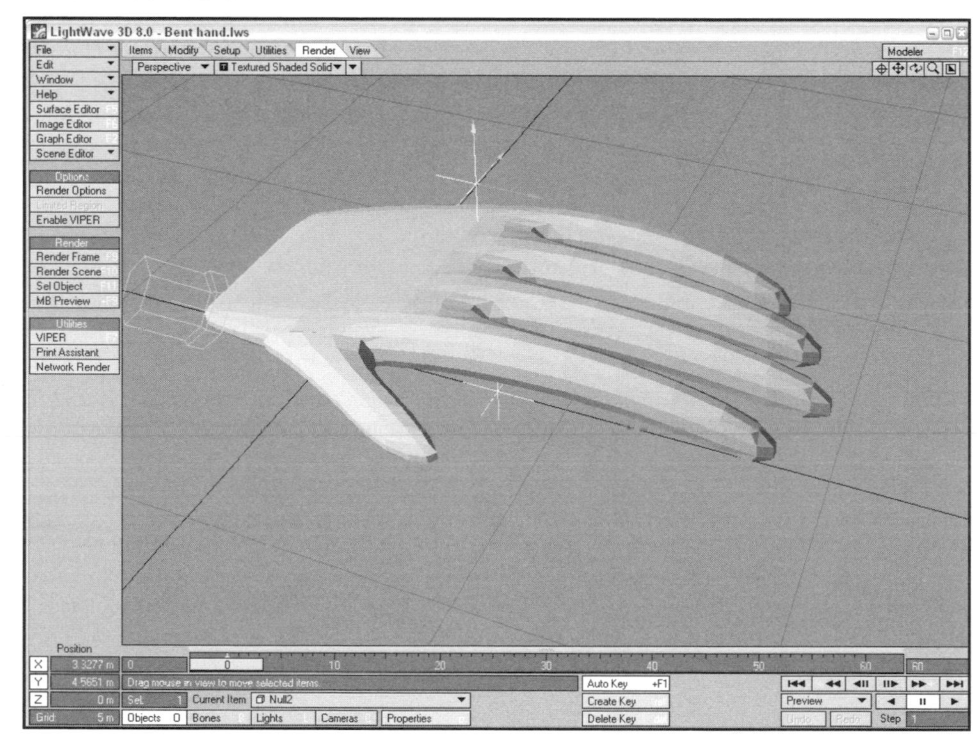

In this lesson, you'll learn how to access deform displacement plug-ins and control them using null objects.

The Modeler provides an unlimited number of ways to deform objects, but after you load objects into the Layout interface, the deformation options are limited. But by using the Object Properties dialog box, you can enable several deformation tools.

Adding a Displacement Texture

Displacement maps are useful for adding texture to an object. Displacement maps work in a similar manner, except they actually change the geometry of the object, which results in better shadows and highlighting. For the displacement map to be effective, the object needs to be sufficiently dense to represent the displacement. To apply a displacement map, select an object, open the Object Properties dialog box, and select the Deform tab. Click the Texture icon (the small icon button with a T on it) and select a texture in the Texture Editor. In Figure 8.22, the Turbulence Procedural Texture was applied as a displacement map to a flat box object.

Using the Deform Displacement Plug-Ins

If you click the Add Displacement button in the Deform panel of the Object Properties dialog box, you can select from a long list of displacement plug-ins, including several deform displacement plug-ins. To use any of these **deform displacement plug-ins**, you need to add two null objects to the scene using the Null button in the Items tab. These null objects are used to define the deformation axis for the various deform plug-ins. Moving the null objects after the deform plug-in is applied changes the amount of deformation. After you select a deform displacement plug-in, you can open a dialog box of its settings by double-clicking on its name. Figure 8.23 shows the Properties dialog box for the Shear plug-in. In the Properties dialog box, you can select one null object as an Effect Base and another as an Effect Handle. You can also specify a falloff curve for the deformation to follow.

FIGURE 8.22
Displacement map

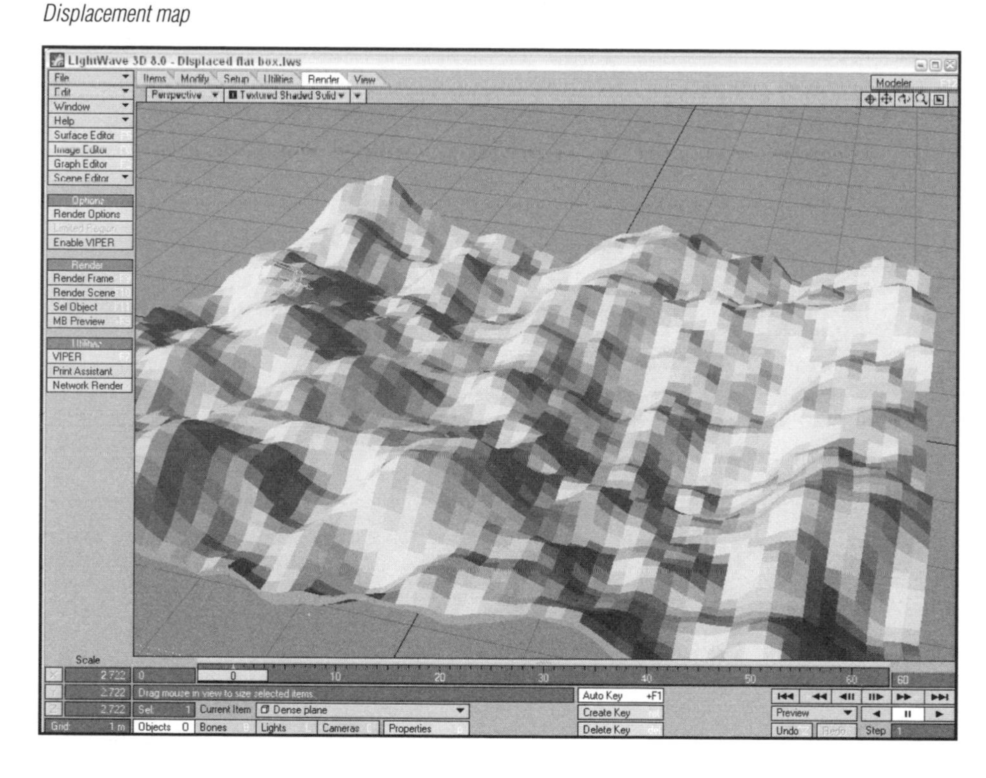

FIGURE 8.23
Shear Properties dialog box

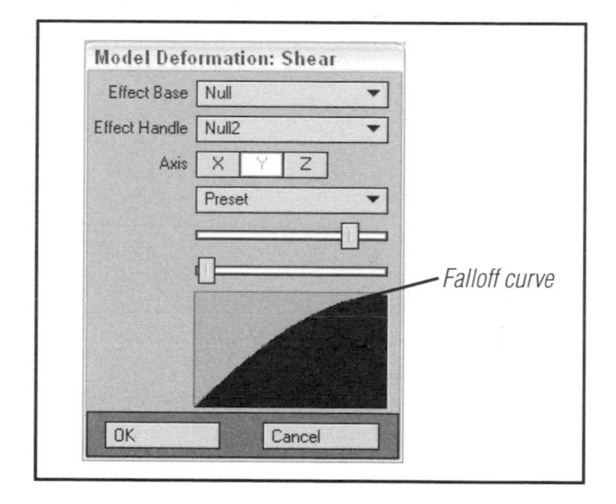

Bending Objects

You can use the Bend deform displacement plug-in to bend objects about the Effect Base null object. Figure 8.24 shows a chair object that was bent over the Z-axis by dragging the top null object.

Shearing an Object

The Shear deform displacement plug-in is like the Bend deform plug-in, except it maintains a straight line between the top and bottom of the sheared object. Figure 8.25 shows a chair object that was sheared by dragging the top null object.

FIGURE 8.24
Bended chair

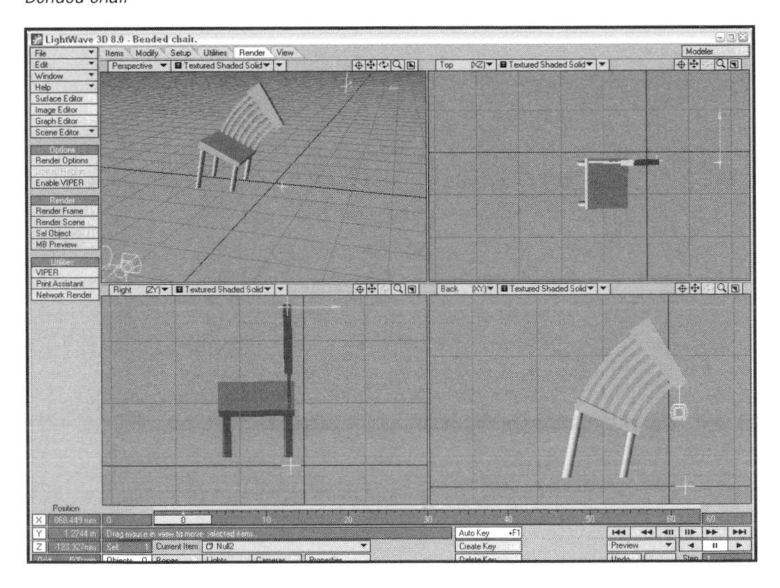

FIGURE 8.25
Sheared chair

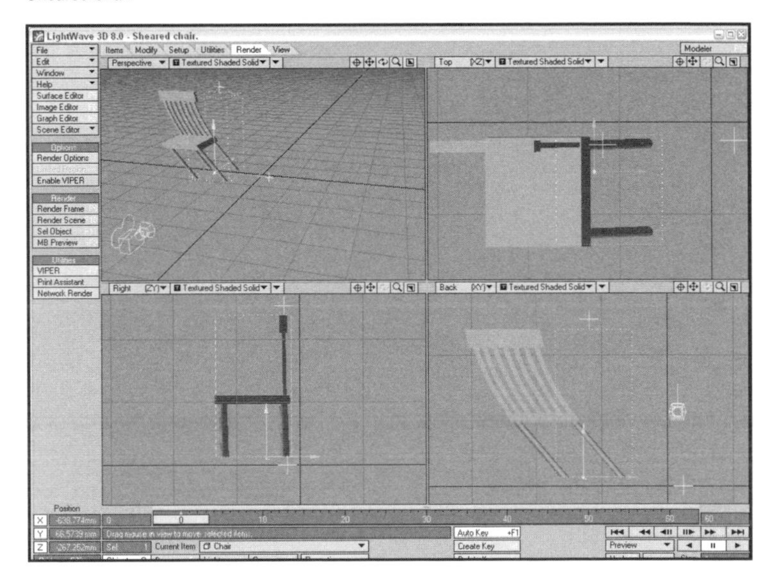

Twisting an Object

You can use the Twist deform displacement plug-in to twist an object about an axis. The twisting action is accomplished by rotating the Effect Handle null object. Figure 8.26 shows a chair object that was twisted by rotating the top null object.

Other Deform Displacement Plug-Ins

In addition to the deform displacement plug-ins covered previously, LightWave also includes Pole, Taper, and Vortex plug-ins. The Pole deform plug-in pushes the center of the object outward as the null object is scaled. The Taper plug-in decreases the scale on one end of an object as the null object is scaled. The Vortex plug-in forms a spiral vortex as the null object is rotated. You can specify that multiple plug-ins are enabled at the same time in the Object Properties dialog box. Figure 8.27 shows a tapered chair.

FIGURE 8.26
Twisted chair

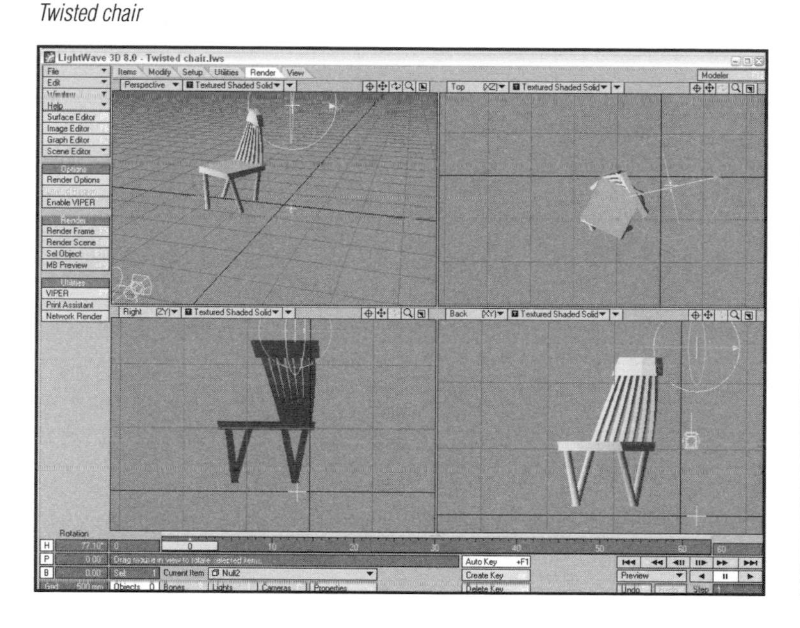

FIGURE 8.27
Tapered chair

Add a displacement map

1. Click the File, Load, Load Object menu command and open the Dense plane.lwo file in the Layout interface.
2. With the box object selected, open the Object Properties dialog box. Select the Deform menu tab and click the Texture icon (the small button with a T on it) to open the Texture Editor.
3. In the Texture Editor, select the Procedural Texture option as the Layer Type and choose the Ripples2 option from the Procedural Type drop-down list. Click on the Automatic Type drop-down list. Click on the Automatic Sizing button. Then click on the Use Texture button to close the Texture Editor. Finally, close the Object Properties dialog box.

   The procedural texture is used to deform the box object, as shown in Figure 8.28.
4. Select the File, Save, Save Scene As menu command and save the file as Hills and valleys.lws.

FIGURE 8.28
Displaced box object

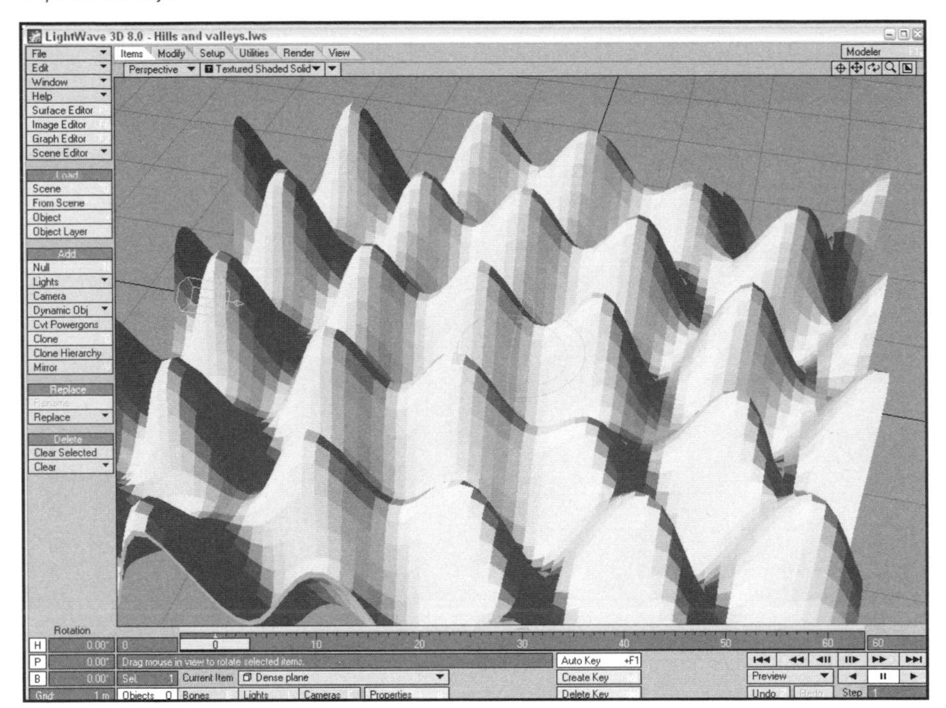

FIGURE 8.29
Displaced hand

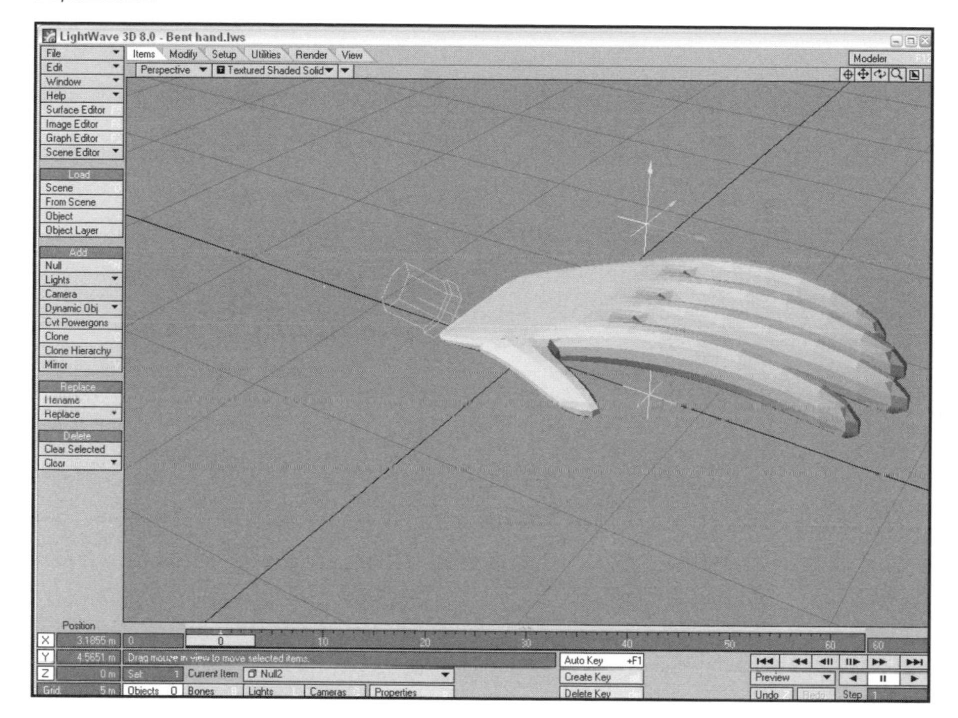

Use a deform displacement plug-in

1. Click the File, Load, Load Object menu command in the Layout interface and open the Subpatch hand.lwo file.
2. Click the Items tab, select the Null button, and name the new null object Null1. Repeat this step to create a second null object named Null2 and move it above the first null object.
3. Select the hand object and open the Object Properties dialog box. Click the Deform menu tab and select the Deform: Bend option from the Add Displacement drop-down list.
4. Double-click the Deform: Bend option in the Displacement list to open its Properties dialog box. Select Null1 as the Effect Base and Null2 as the Effect Handle. Then select the Y-axis and click OK.
5. Back in the viewport, select and drag the top null point to the right.

   As the Effect Handle Null object moves, the hand bends about the Effect Base null object, as shown in Figure 8.29.
6. Select the File, Save, Save Scene As menu command and save the file as Bent hand.lws.

LESSON 6

ADD FUR AND HAIR

What You'll Do

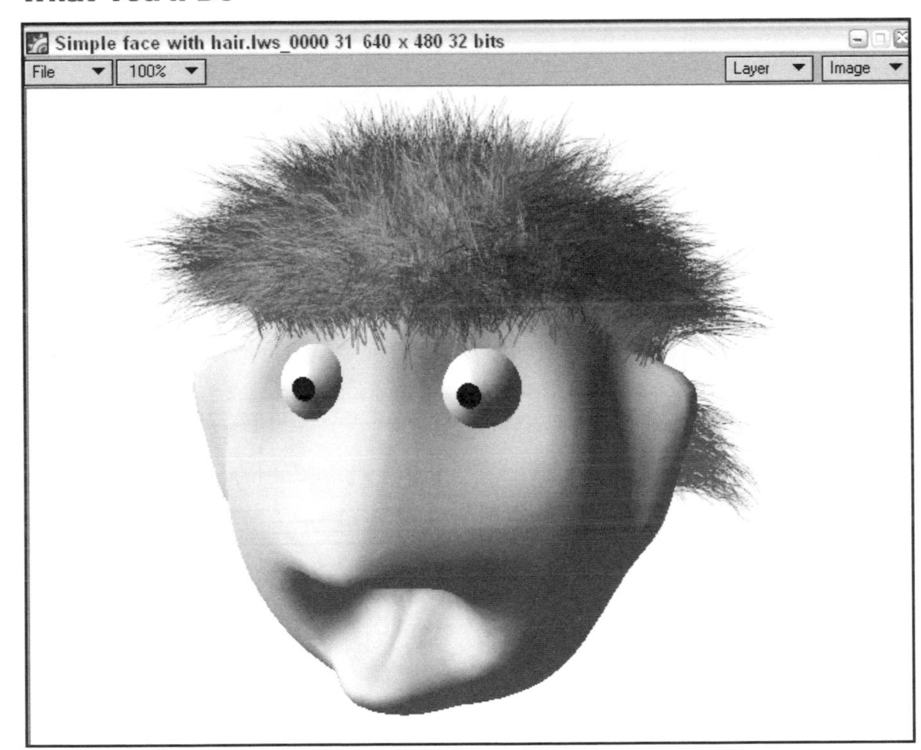

In this lesson, you'll learn how to add fur and hair effects to objects and surfaces.

One aspect of creating characters is so specific that it really needs a separate plug-in to effectively produce it. This aspect is fur and hair. If you imagine trying to place and manage each individual strand of hair as an object, you can begin to appreciate what these plug-ins can do for you. The fur and hair plug-in in LightWave is called **Sasquatch Lite** and you can access it using the Displacement plug-ins in the Object Properties dialog box.

Adding Fur to an Entire Object

To add fur to an entire object, you simply need to select the object, open the Object Properties dialog box, and select the SasLite option from the Add Displacement drop-down list in the Deform panel. Double-clicking the SasLite option opens the Sasquatch Lite dialog box, shown in Figure 8.30. The Sasquatch Lite dialog box includes a wide assortment of properties for controlling the look and feel of the fur and hair, including Color, Glossiness, Coarseness, Frizz, and Density. The default setting at the top of the Sasquatch Lite dialog box is Apply Fur to All Surfaces. With this option selected, click OK to close the Sasquatch Lite properties dialog box.

Enabling a Pixel Filter

After you specify fur for the selected object, the fur won't actually be visible until the object is rendered, Before you can render the object, you need to enable a Pixel Filter for the Sasquatch Lite plug-in. A Pixel Filter is a way to add effects to the object during the rendering phase instead of doing so at the geometry level. To add a Pixel Filter for the Sasquatch Lite plug-in, open the Processing panel of the Effects dialog box, shown in Figure 8.31, by selecting the Window, Image Processing menu command. In the Add Pixel Filter section, select the SasLite option. Double-clicking on the SasLite option opens another Sasquatch Lite dialog box, shown in Figure 8.32, where you can set the antialiasing level and enable shadows.

FIGURE 8.30
Sasquatch Lite dialog box

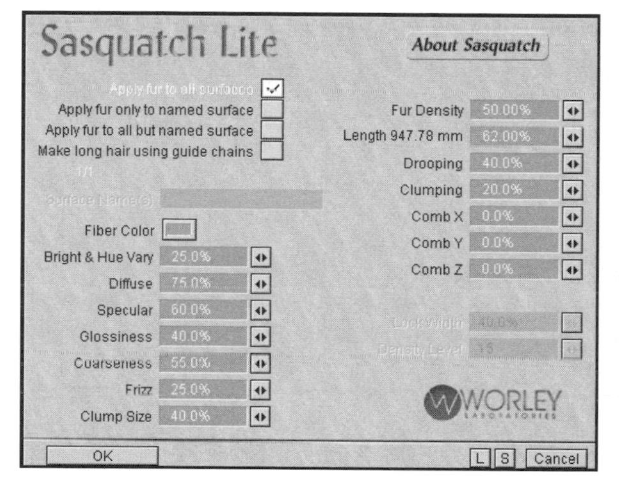

FIGURE 8.31
Image Processing panel of the Effects dialog box

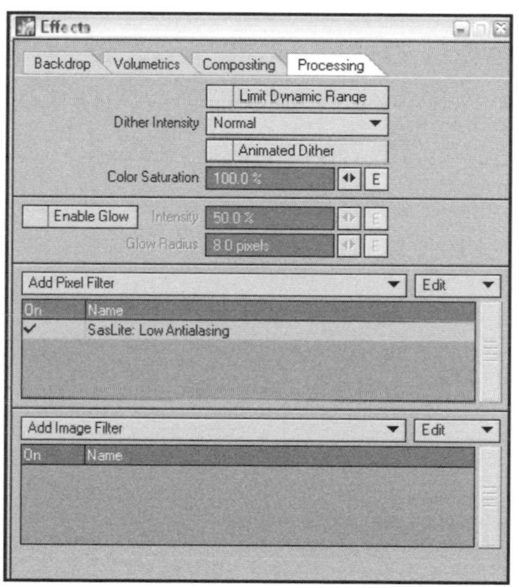

FIGURE 8.32
Image Processing options for the Sasquatch Lite plug-in

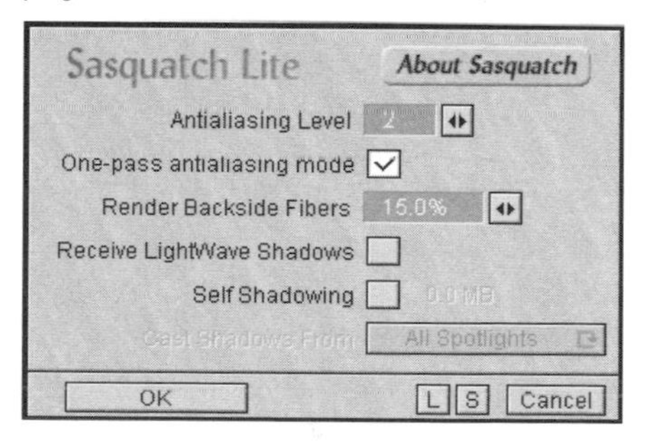

Rendering Fur

After you apply fur to an object's surfaces and enable the pixel filter, you can render the furry object using the Render Frame button in the Render tab. The Renderer has to render the view from a camera in the scene. More on rendering is covered in Chapter 12, but Figure 8.33 shows a sphere rendered with fur.

CAUTION

Adding fur or hair to an object can greatly increase the amount of time it takes the render the scene.

FIGURE 8.33
Sphere object rendered with fur

Adding Fur to a Specific Surface

If you don't want fur to cover the entire object, you can apply the fur to specific surfaces only. In the Sasquatch Lite dialog box, select the Apply Fur Only to Named Surfaces option and type the name of the surface in the Surface Name. To enter multiple surface names, separate each name with a comma. Figure 8.34 shows fur applied to the stripes surface of this ball object.

FIGURE 8.34
Fur applied to a specific surface

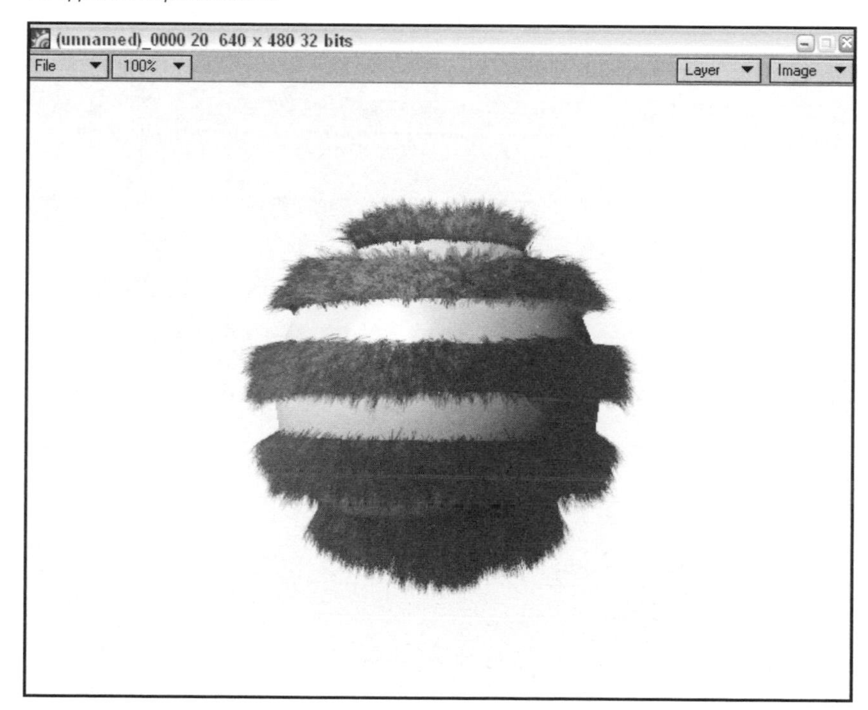

Add hair to a surface

1. Click the File, Load, Load Object menu command and open the Simple face with scalp.lwo file.
2. Select the head object and open the Object Properties dialog box. Click the Deform menu tab and select the SasLite option from the Add Displacement drop-down list.
3. Double-click the SasLite option in the Displacement list to open the Sasquatch Lite Properties dialog box. Select the Apply Fur Only to Named Surface option and type **scalp** in the Named Surface(s) field. Set the Length value to **80%** and then click OK.
4. Click the Window, Image Processing menu command to open the Processing panel of the Effects dialog box. Select the SasLite option from the Add Pixel Filter drop-down list. Then close the Effects dialog box.
5. Click the Render menu tab and then click the Render Frame button.

   The head object is rendered, with fur located only along the scalp surface, as shown in Figure 8.35.
6. Select the File, Save, Save Scene As menu command and save the file as Simple face with hair.lws.

FIGURE 8.35
Simple face with hair

CHAPTER SUMMARY

This chapter explained how to transform objects like you can do in the Modeler interface. It also discussed how to control geometry objects such as characters using an underlying hierarchy of bones and Skelegons. Several commands to morph and deform objects were covered, in addition to the plug-in that enables you to add fur and hair to objects.

What You Have Learned

- How to translate, rotate, and scale objects within the Layout interface.
- How to create a system of bones and use them to control how a geometry object moves.
- How to add Skelegons to an object in the Modeler and convert these Skelegons to bones in the Layout interface.
- How to use the Endomorphs feature to create morph targets.
- How to bend, twist, and shear objects using the deform displacement plug-ins.
- How to add hair and fur using the Sasquatch Lite plug-in.

Key Terms from This Chapter

- **Numeric Adjustment Controls.** A set of text fields that allow you to transform the selected object by entering transform values.
- **bones.** Simple nonrendered objects that control the attached geometry.
- **Inverse Kinematics (IK).** Controls that enable child objects to control the motion of their parent objects.
- **Skelegons.** Objects that can be placed within the Modeler and converted to bones within the Layout interface.
- **morph target.** A state of an object that defines a position during a single frame of an animation.
- **Endomorph.** A single morph target that you can save during the editing phase in the Modeler and access from within the Layout interface.
- **Morph Mixer.** An interface in which you can access all the endomorphs that are added to an object.
- **displacement map.** A 2D bitmap image that controls the displacement of geometry objects.
- **deform displacement plug-ins.** A series of plug-ins you can use to deform geometric objects.
- **Sasquatch Lite.** A specialized plug-in that enables you to add fur and hair effects to objects.

CHAPTER 9

ANIMATING OBJECTS

1. Use the animation controls.
2. Set keys.
3. Work with motion paths.
4. Use animation modifiers.

CHAPTER 9
ANIMATING OBJECTS

It's relatively easy to animate objects in 3D with LightWave because the program stores information on the exact position, orientation, and scale of all objects in the scene at all times. Therefore, LightWave can quickly perform the simple calculation needed to interpolate between different two different states. The different states that an object passes through are called **keyframes**, or keys for short.

You can set keys for several different channels, including the X, Y, and Z axes for Position, Rotation, and Scale. This means that you can specify that a specific animation key only affects the scaling in the X axis and leaves all other channels untouched.

The controls for setting and manipulating keys are located at the bottom on the interface. These controls are the **Time Line**, the **Dope Track**, the Keyframe options, and the Preview buttons. Using these controls, you can not only create keys, but you can also visualize the subsequent animation sequences in the viewports.

In addition to manually setting keys for each channel, you can also enable the **Auto Key** mode, which causes keys to be created automatically for every object that is manipulated in the viewports.

As you animate objects, a **motion path** is created that shows the exact path that the object follows during its animation sequence. You can edit and move these motion paths just as you would edit a curve. You can also save and load motion paths onto other objects, which gives you the ability to reuse animations between objects.

As an alternative to manually keyframing all the object motions, you can use the modifiers in the Motion Options dialog box to automate certain types of motions. Use the variety of modifiers in the Motion Options dialog box to produce motions such as making an object follow a curve, and creating object vibrations, oscillation, and cyclical motion.

Tools You'll Use

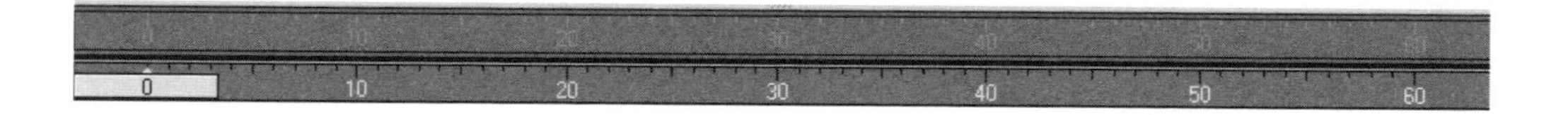

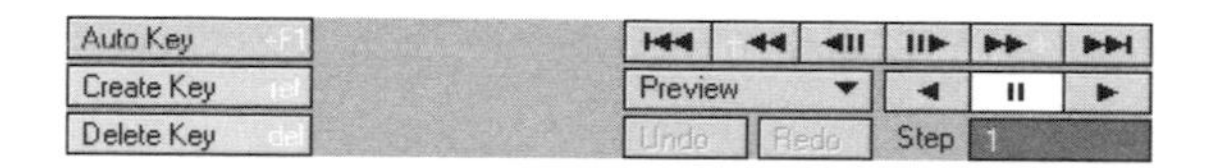

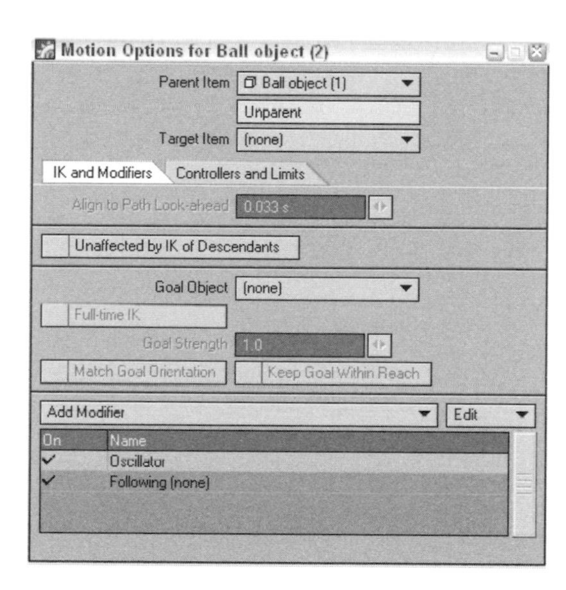

LESSON 1

USE THE ANIMATION CONTROLS

What You'll Do

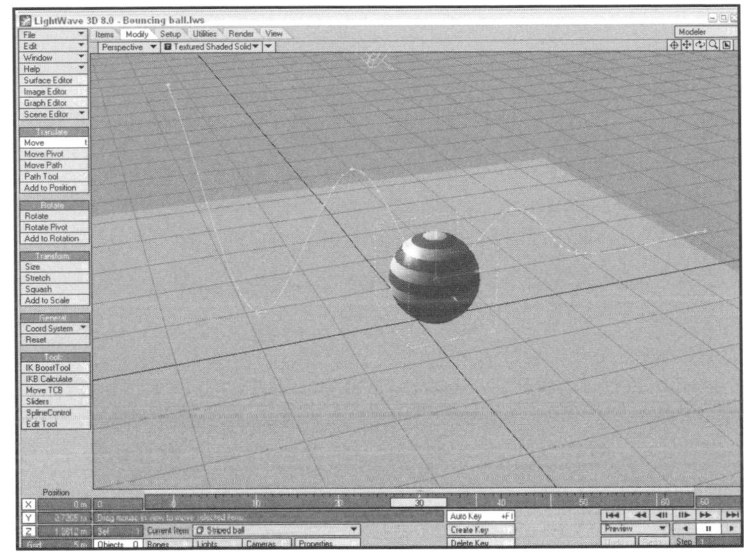

In this lesson, you'll learn how to use the various animation controls.

Several controls for viewing, creating, and altering animation sequences are located at the bottom of the Layout interface. Learning to use these controls is the key to animating objects.

Using the Time Line

The Time Line, shown in Figure 9.1, located directly underneath the viewports, includes markers for all the available frames. By dragging the Frame Slider to the left or right, you can change the current frame number, which is displayed on the Frame Slider. Use the fields to the left and right of the Time Line to set the range of the current frames.

Learning the Animation Preview Controls

Animation Preview controls are located below the Time Line, in the lower-right corner of the interface, as shown in Figure 9.2. Using these controls, you can play the current animation either forward or backward, and move between the different frames and animation keys.

FIGURE 9.1
Time Line control

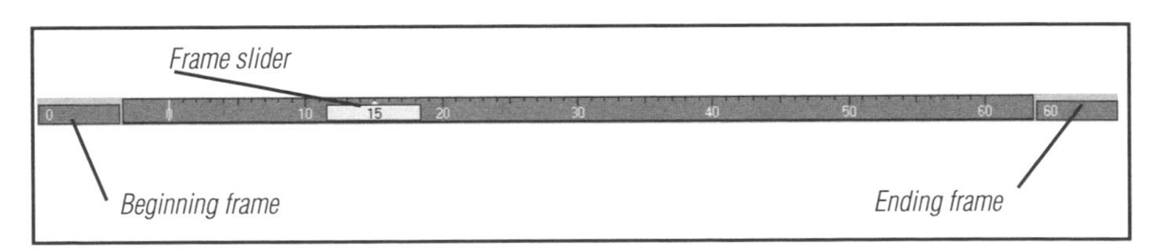

TIP

You an also see an animation by dragging the Frame Slider back and forth on the Time Line.

Accessing the Dope Track

If you look closely above the Time Line, you can see a thick line. Clicking on the center of this thick line moves the Dope Track above the Time Line, as shown in Figure 9.3. Use the Dope Track to work with animation keys. Clicking again on the thick line hides the Dope Track.

Learning the Keyframe Options

Three buttons are also located below the Time Line, as shown in Figure 9.4. Use these buttons to set the Keyframe mode. Using these buttons, you can automatically create keys, manually create keys, or delete keys. The keyboard shortcuts for these buttons are Shift+F1 for Auto Key, Enter/Return for Create Key, and Delete for Delete Key.

FIGURE 9.2
Animation Preview controls

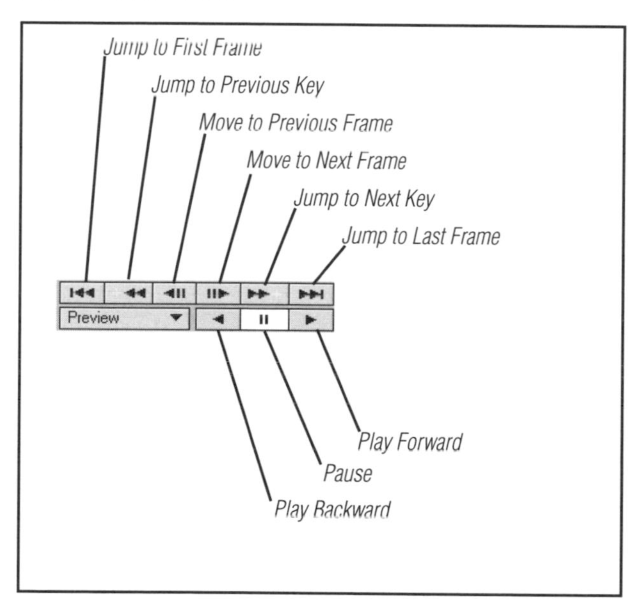

FIGURE 9.3
Dope Track control

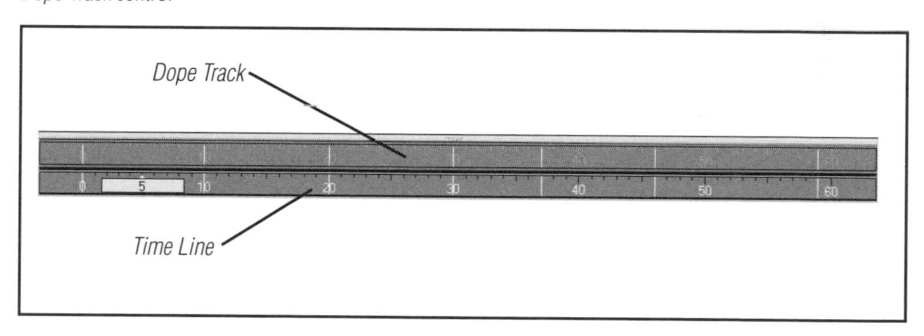

FIGURE 9.4
Keyframe option buttons

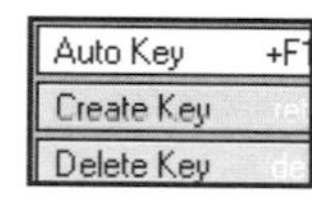

Setting Animation Options

Several animation options are located in the General Options panel of the Preferences dialog box, shown in Figure 9.5. To open this dialog box, use the Edit, General Options menu command. You can set the Auto Key Create option to Off, Modified Channels, or All Channels. For the Frame Slider Label, you can specify that either the Frame Number or Time is displayed. You can also set the Frames Per Second option, which determines how rapidly the animations are played.

FIGURE 9.5

General Options panel of the Preferences dialog box

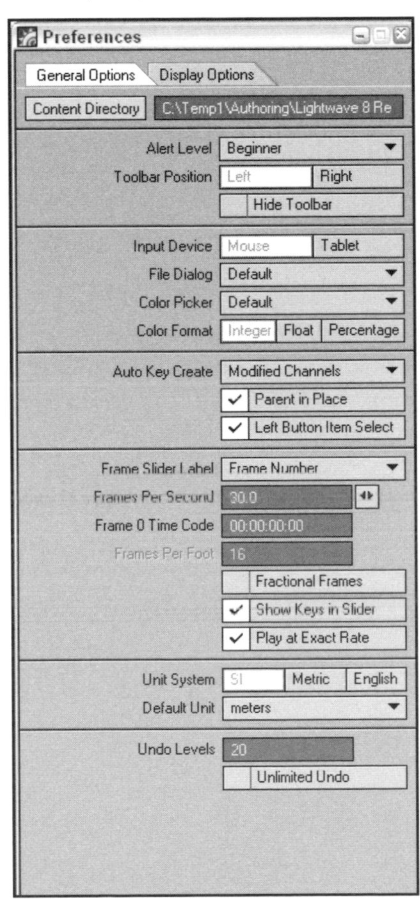

FIGURE 9.6
Animated bouncing ball

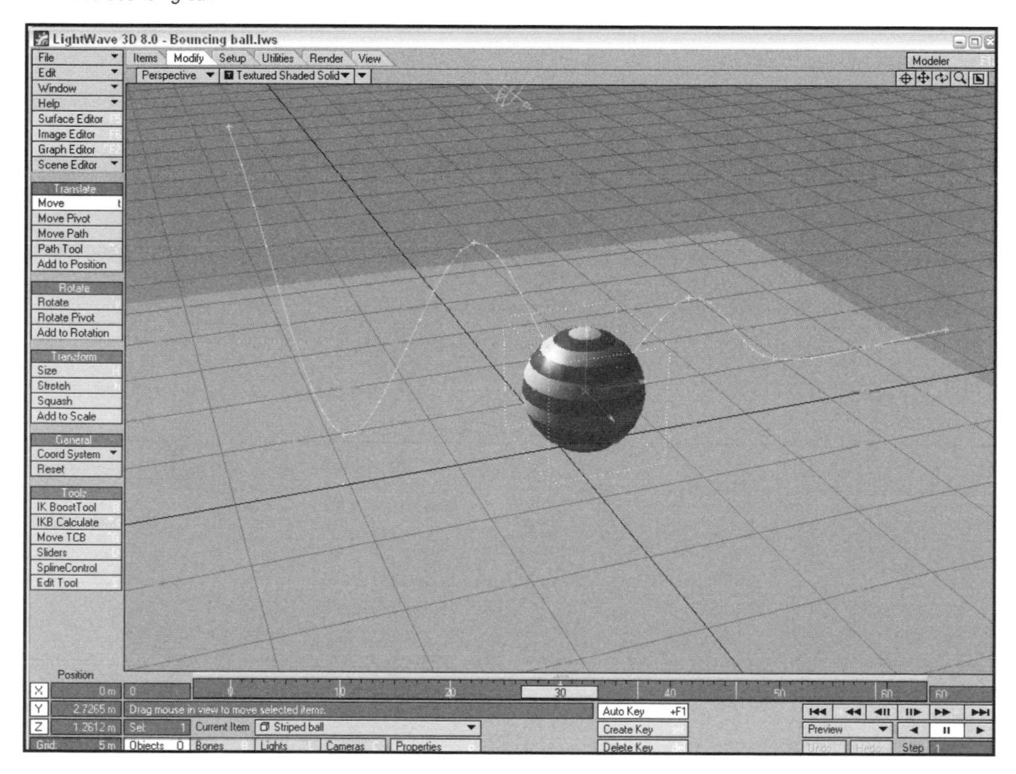

Move objects

1. Click the File, Load, Load Scene menu command and open the Bouncing ball.lws file.

   This file includes a simple ball object that is animated so that it bounces across the scene.

2. Click the Play Forward button.

   The animation sequence starts and the ball bounces across the scene.

3. Click the Pause button, and then click the Jump to First Frame button.

4. Select the ball object and drag the Frame Slider to frame 25. Click the Jump to Next Key button.

   Dragging the Frame Slider animates the ball and clicking the Jump to Next Key button moves the Frame Slider forward to frame 30, where the ball's next key is located, as shown in Figure 9.6.

LESSON 2

SET KEYS

What You'll Do

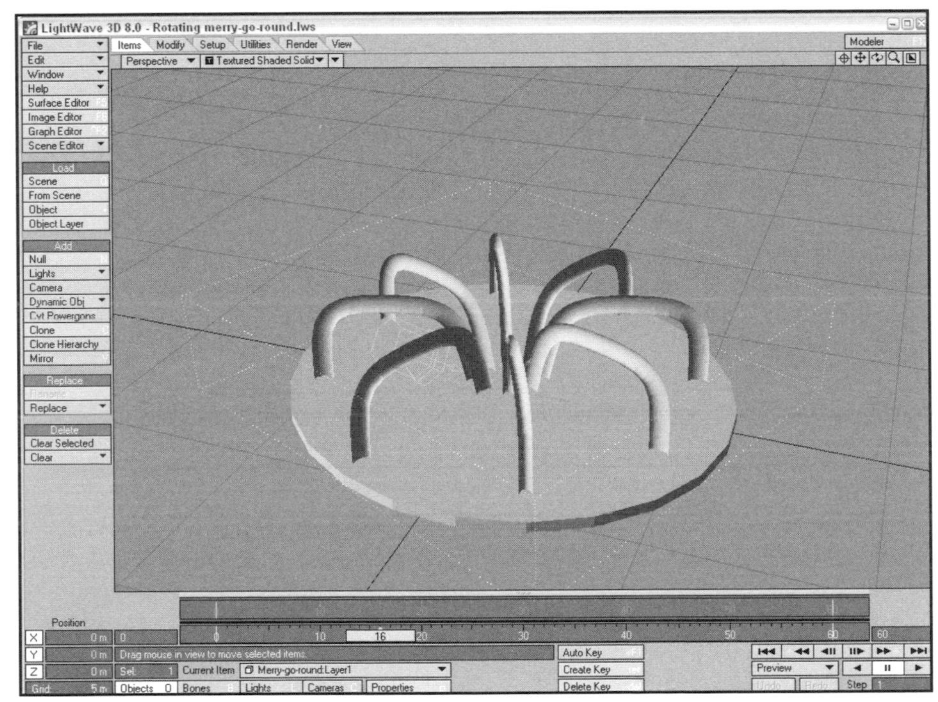

In this lesson, you'll learn how to manually set keys and how to use the Auto Key feature.

Keyframes (or keys for short) define the state of an object during an animation sequence. LightWave is aware of an object's position, orientation, and scaling values, so these values can be recorded into a keyframe for the beginning and ending state of an object. Next, the value of the states between the start and the end keyframe are interpolated to create a smooth animation.

Creating Keys

You can set a key for the selected object at the current frame by clicking the Create Key button at the bottom of the Layout interface (or by pressing Enter) to open the Create Motion Key dialog box, shown in Figure 9.7. The Create Key At field is automatically set to the current frame, but you can enter a different frame value. You also have the option of setting the key for the Selection Items, Current Item Only, Current Item and Descendants, and All Items. Using the Position, Rotation, and Scale buttons, you can limit the key to only specific information. After you create a key, it appears as a thin line on the Time Line and the Dope Track.

TIP

You can also set animation keys for lights and cameras.

Deleting Keys

To open the Delete Motion Key dialog box, click the Delete Key button at the bottom of the interface or press Delete. The Delete Motion Key dialog box is identical to the Create Motion Key dialog box, except that it removes keys.

Enabling Auto Key Mode

If you enable the Auto Key button, every objects movement results in the creation of a key for the current frame. Be careful when the Auto Key button is enabled or you might end up with keys that you don't want.

Moving All Keys

Dragging the Frame Slider from side to side quickly moves through the various frames, but if you hold down the Alt key while dragging the Frame Slider, all the keys on the Time Line are moved along with the Frame Slider. This is a convenient way to reposition a set of keys within the available time range.

Cutting, Copying, and Pasting Keys

With the Dope Track open, you can select multiple keys by dragging over them or select all keys by right-clicking and then selecting the Select All Keys option from the pop-up menu. This menu also includes options to Cut, Copy, and Paste the selected keys.

FIGURE 9.7
Create Motion Key dialog box

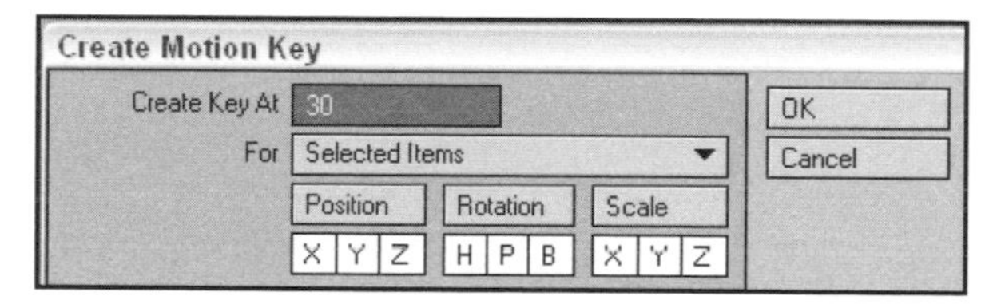

Create keys

1. Click the File, Load, Load Scene menu command and open the Merry-go-round.lws file.
2. Drag the Frame Slider to frame 1 and click the Create Key button. In the Create Motion Key dialog box, click OK.

   A single key is added to the Time Line.
3. Drag the Frame Slider to frame 60. Click the Modify tab and then click the Rotate button. Drag in the Top viewport to rotate the merry-go-round object about three revolutions.
4. Click the Create Key button again and then click OK to accept the key.
5. Click the Play Forward button to see the resulting animation.

   Keys are now positioned at frames 1 and 60, as shown in Figure 9.8.
6. Select the File, Save, Save Scene As menu command and save the file as Rotating merry-go-round.lws.

Use Auto Key mode

1. Click the File, Load, Load Scene menu command and open the Car and block.lws file
2. Drag the Frame Slider to frame 1 and click the Auto Key button.

   The Auto Key button is highlighted white to show that it is enabled.

FIGURE 9.8

Rotating merry-go-round

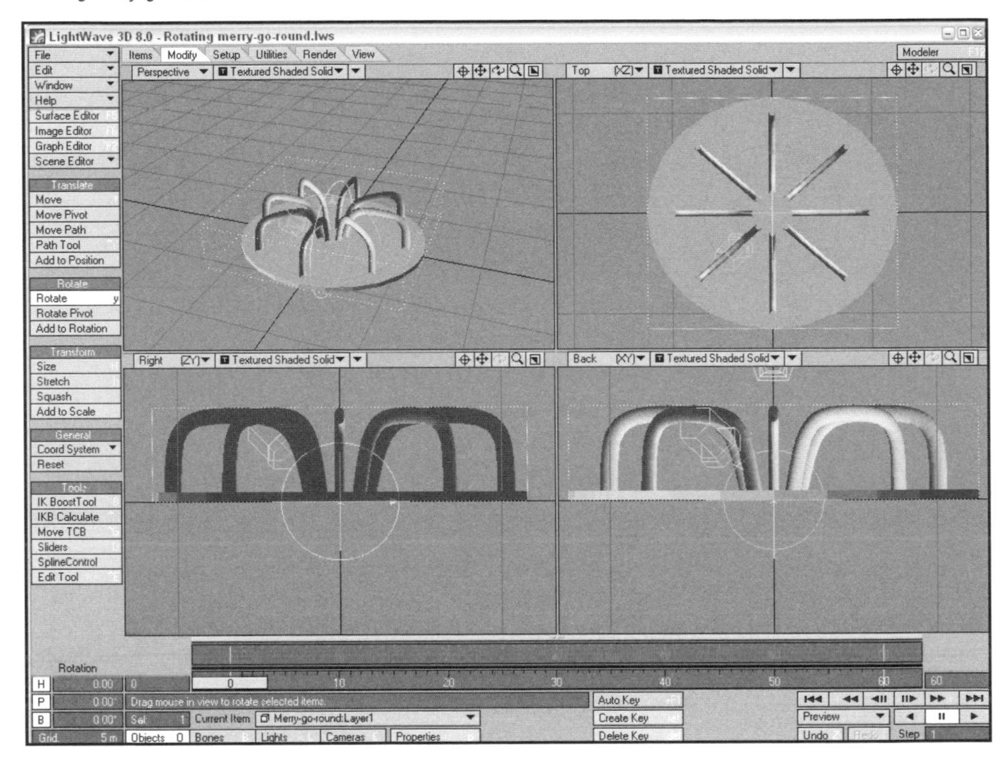

FIGURE 9.9
Pyramid object

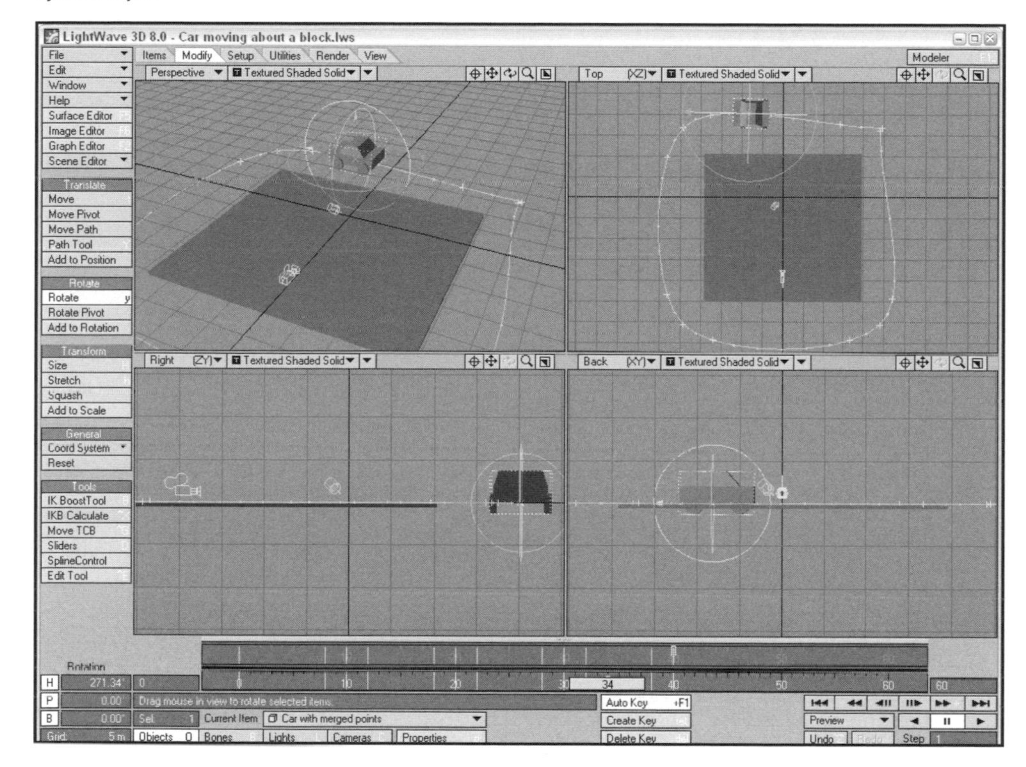

3. Drag the Frame Slider to frame 10 and move the car object to the next corner in the Top viewport. Drag the Frame Slider to frame 20 and move the car to the next corner in the Top viewport. Continue until the car is back where it started at frame 40.

   If you drag the Frame Slider, you'll see the car move around the block, but it maintains the same orientation throughout the sequence.

4. Drag the Frame Slider to frame 8 and slightly rotate the car clockwise in the Top viewport. Drag the Frame Slider to frame 12 and rotate the car clockwise in the Top viewport until it is pointing the correct direction. Repeat this step for each corner until you're back at frame 40.

5. Click the center of the line above the Time Line to open the Dope Track. Select the very first key at frame 0, right-click on the Dope Track, and then select the Copy option from the pop-up menu. Drag the Frame Slider to frame 60 and select the Paste option.

   By copying the beginning key to the end key, you can create an animation sequence that loops smoothly.

6. Click the Play Forward button to see the resulting animation.

   The car moves about the block, as shown in Figure 9.9.

7. Select the File, Save, Save Scene As menu command and save the file as Car moving about a block.lws.

LESSON 3

WORK WITH MOTION PATHS

What You'll Do

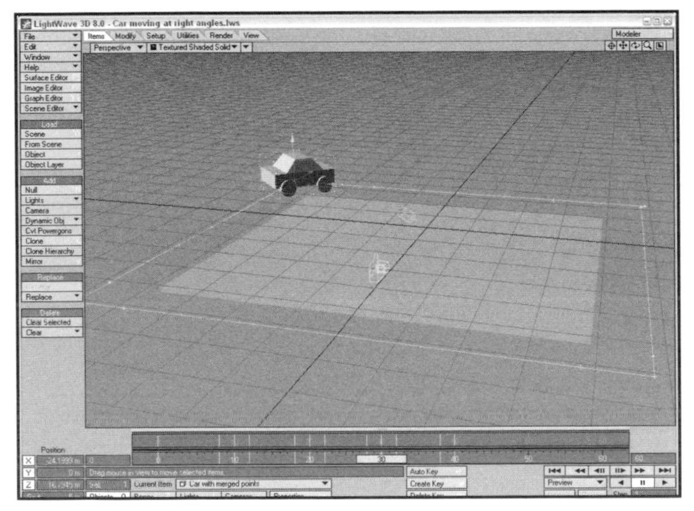

In this lesson, you'll learn how to view, edit, and save motion paths.

Whenever you create a motion key, a motion path is also created and shown for the selected object. This motion path includes a dot for each frame and a cross marker for each key. Figure 9.10 shows a motion path for a bouncing ball.

FIGURE 9.10
Motion path

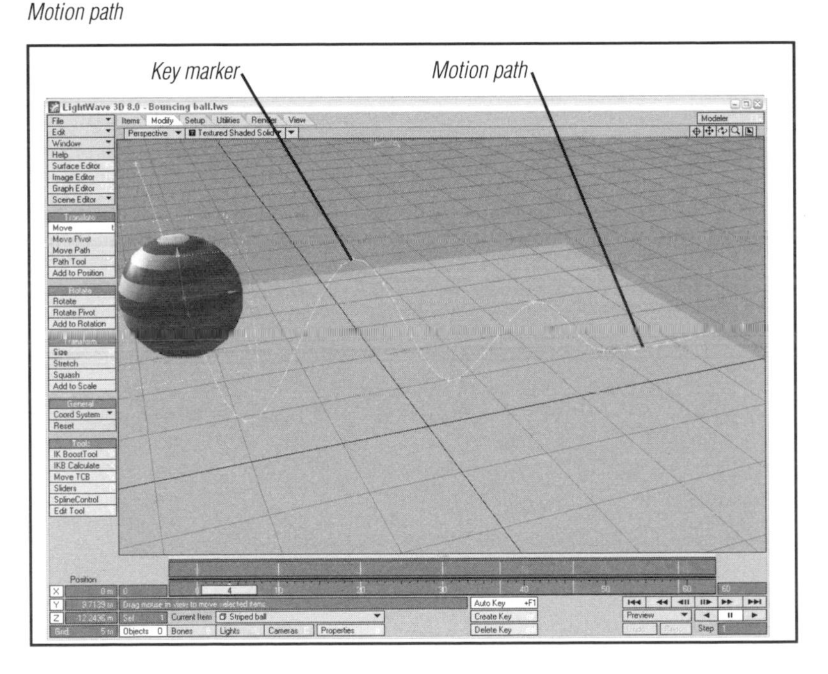

Viewing Motion Paths

The Display Options panel of the Preferences dialog box includes a Show Motion Paths option. Using this option, you can make motions paths visible or invisible.

Moving Motion Paths

Selecting the Move Path button in the Modify tab lets you drag the motion path to a new location along with its object.

Editing Motion Paths

Motion paths are really just simple curves, so you can edit them in the Layout interface using the Path tool in the Translate section of the Modify tab. With the Path tool active, you can select and drag the key markers to a new location, and thus alter the curve. Figure 9.11 shows a motion path that was edited using the Path tool.

Changing Tension, Continuity, and Bias

Another way to alter motion paths is to adjust how smoothly or abruptly the curve moves into and out of a point at the current frame using the Move TCB tool in the Tools section of the Modify tab. TCB stands for **Tension**, **Continuity**, and **Bias**, and each value can range between –1 and 1. The

FIGURE 9.11
Edited motion path

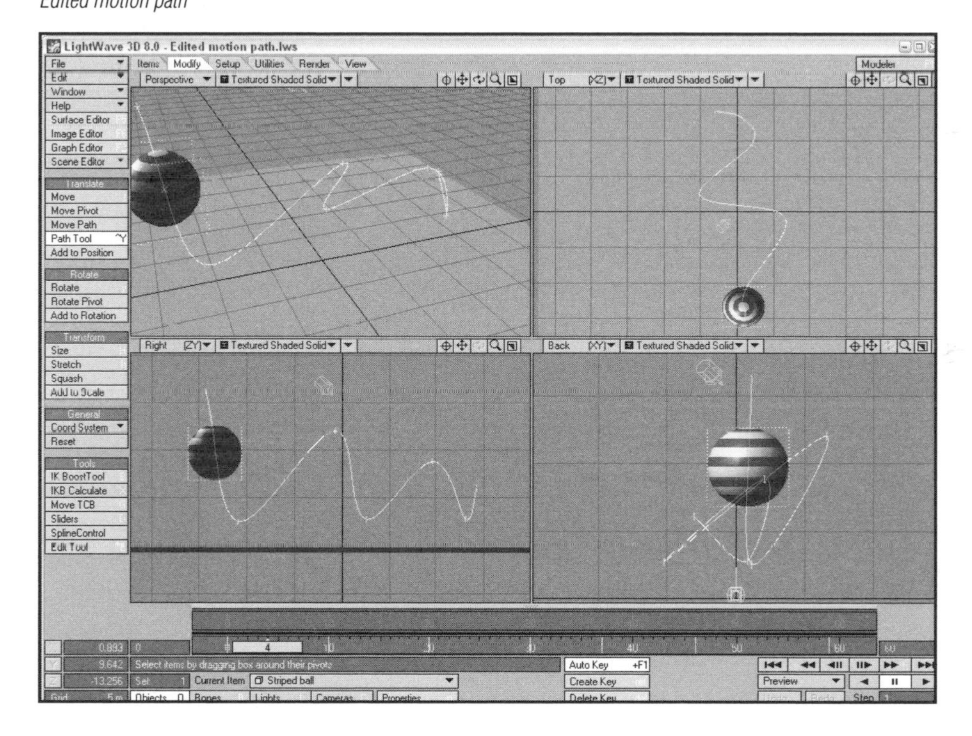

Tension value defines how sharp the point is, with a value of 1.0 being a sharp point and –1.0 a smooth transition. The Continuity value defines the abruptness of the curve at the selected frame point. A Continuity value of 1.0 causes a gradual change into and out of a point, and a value of –1.0 causes an abrupt change. The Bias pushes the points adjacent to the selected frame point toward or away from the current point. You can change the Tension value by dragging in the viewport with the Move TCB tool enabled. To change the Continuity value, hold down the Ctrl key while dragging in the viewports. To change the Bias value, drag in the viewports with the right mouse button.

Figure 9.12 shows three points that were edited using the TCB Move tool. The first point has a Tension value of 10.0, the second point has a Tension value of –1.0 and a Continuity value of 1.0, and the third point has a Bias setting of 1.0.

Saving and Loading Motion Paths

You can save the motion path for the selected object as a file with a MOT extension using the File, Save, Save Motion File menu command. You can load saved motion paths and apply them to other objects in the scene. Figure 9.13 shows the bouncing ball motion path applied to a chess piece.

FIGURE 9.12
TCB edited points

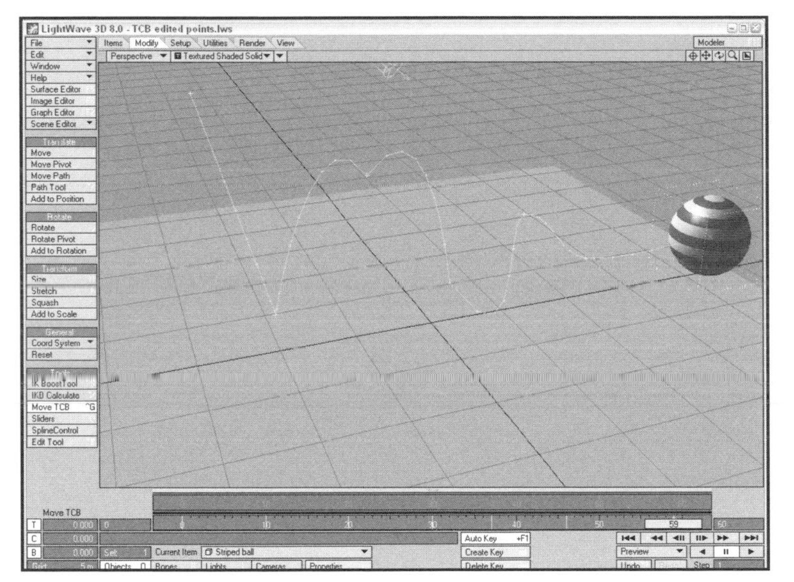

FIGURE 9.13
Loaded motion path

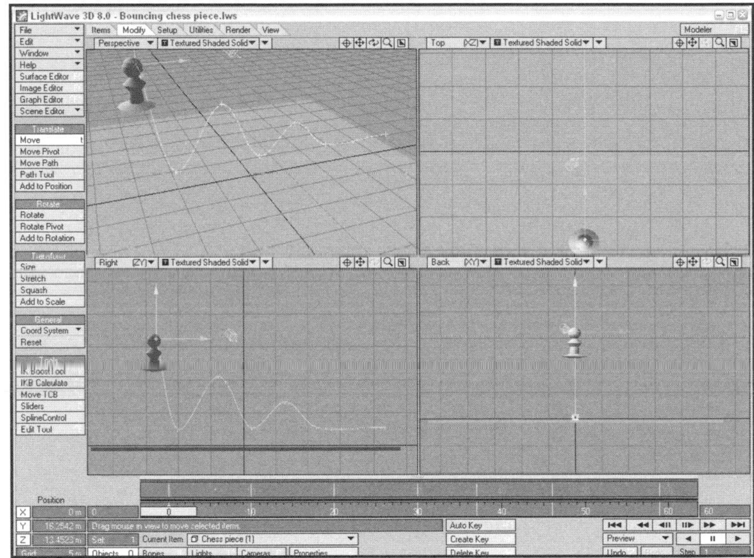

FIGURE 9.14

Car moving about a TCB altered motion path

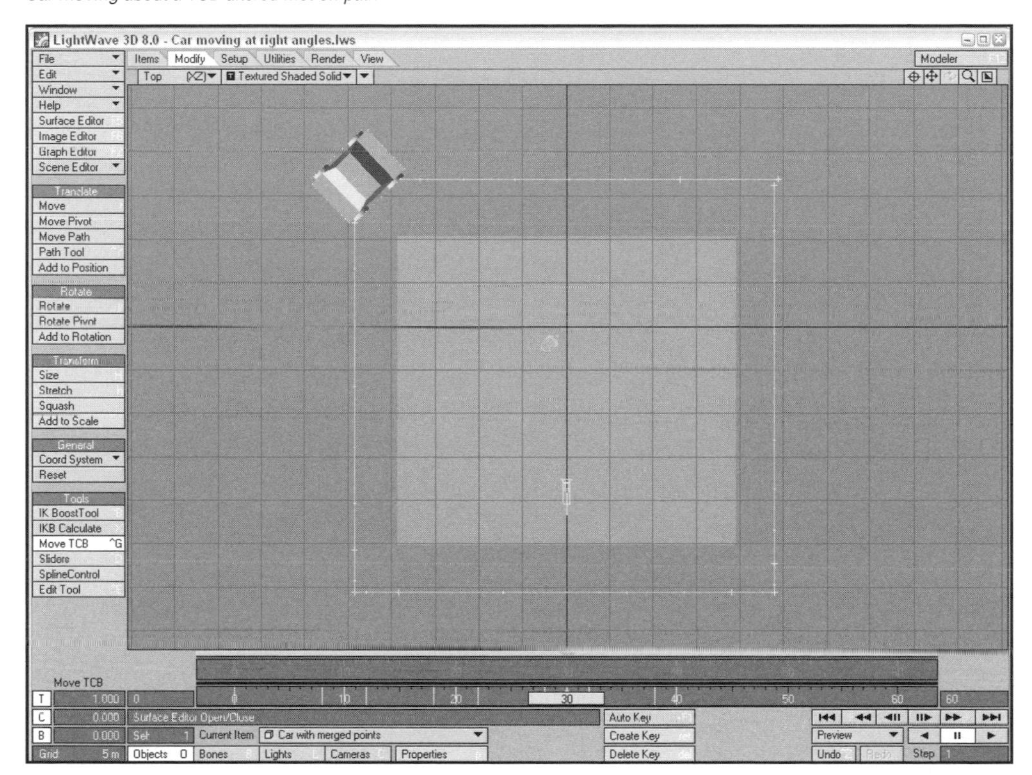

Create a sharp motion path point

1. Click the File, Load, Load Scene menu command and open the Car moving about a block.lws file.

   With the car selected, the motion path is visible.

2. Drag the Frame Slider to frame 10 and click the Move TCB button in the Tools section of the Modify tab. Drag to the right in the Top viewport until the Tension value in the lower-left corner of the interface is set to 1.0.

   The motion path at frame 10 is changed to a sharp right angle.

3. Repeat step 2 for frames 20 and 30.

4. Click the Play Forward button to see the resulting animation.

   The car moves about the block, as shown in Figure 9.14.

5. Select the File, Save, Save Scene As menu command and save the file as Car moving at right angles.lws.

Reuse motion paths

1. With the Car moving at right angles.lws file still open, select the car object and click the File, Save, Save Motion File menu command.
2. In the Save Motion File dialog box, name the file Square motion path.mot and click the Save button.
3. Select the car object and then click the Clear Selected button from the Delete section in the Items tab to delete the car object.
4. Select the File, Load, Load Object menu command and load the Spikey ball.lwo file.
5. Move the spikey ball object to the upper-right corner of the block object in the Top viewport.
6. With the spikey ball object selected, click the File, Load, Load Motion File menu command and load the Square motion path.mot file, and then click the Open button.

   The loaded motion file is applied to the selected object, as shown in Figure 9.15.
7. Click the Play Forward button to see the resulting animation.
8. Select the File, Save, Save Scene As menu command and save the file as Spikey ball moving in a square.lws.

FIGURE 9.15

Spikey ball reusing the car's motion path

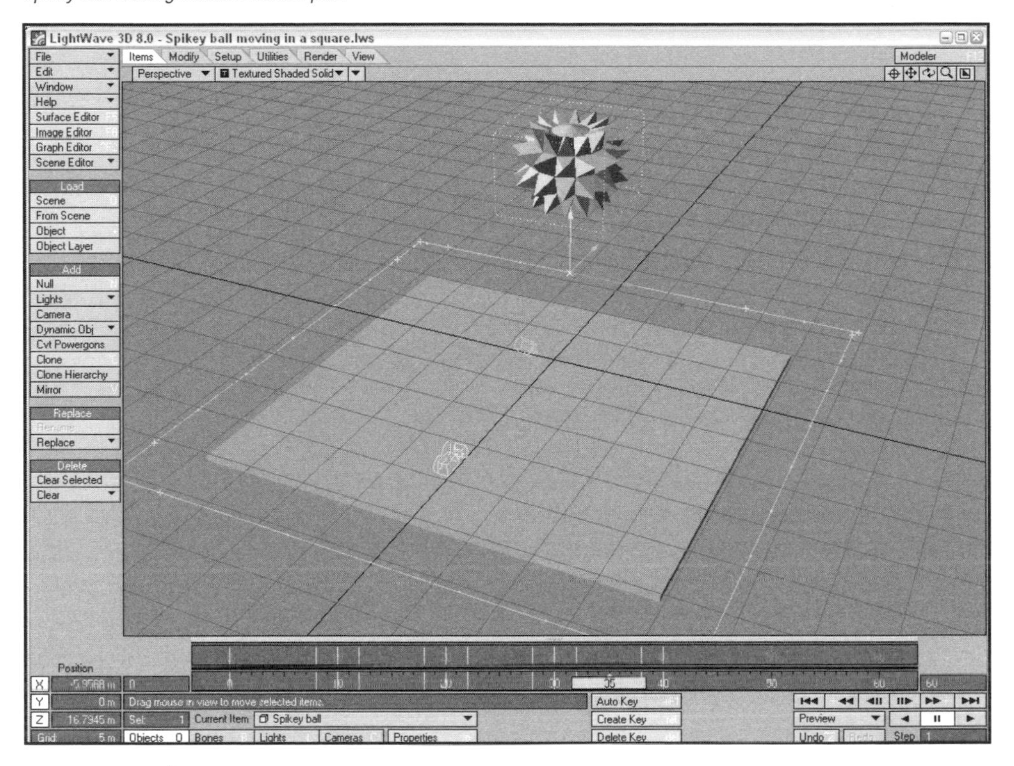

LESSON 4

USE ANIMATION MODIFIERS

What You'll Do

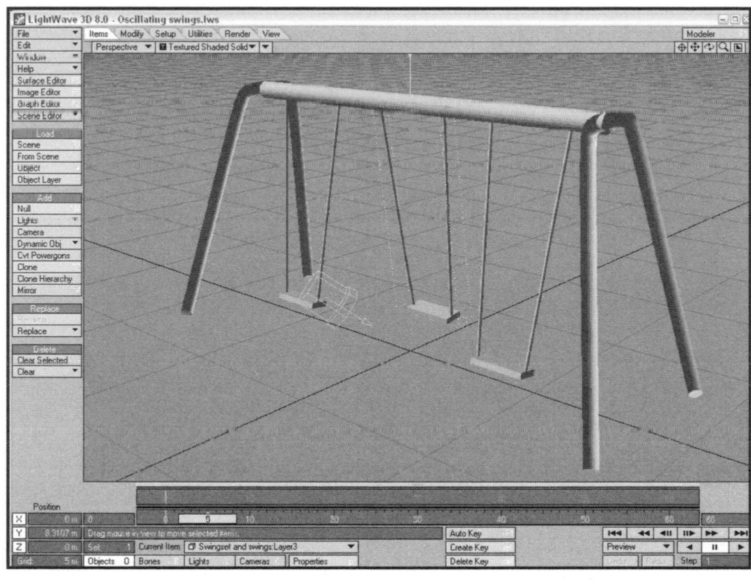

In this lesson, you'll learn how to automate the creation of certain motions using modifiers.

The Motion Options dialog box, shown in Figure 9.16, includes animation modifiers you can apply to the selected objects. You can open this dialog box from the Motions section in the Setup tab. Use these modifiers to automate an object's motion in many different ways, including having one object follow another. Modifiers can streamline the animation process by actually creating the keys for you.

FIGURE 9.16
Motion Options dialog box

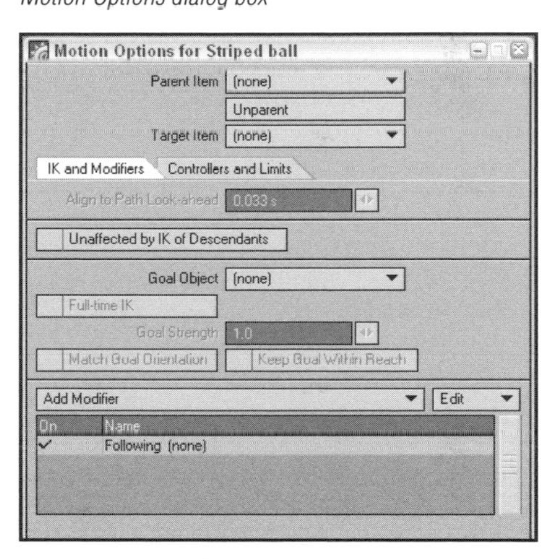

Parenting and Targeting Objects

When an object is parented to another object, it moves along with its **parented object** when the parented object is moved, but the child object can move independently of its parent. To create a parent-child link between the selected object and its parent, select the Parent Item from the drop-down list of objects in the Motions Options dialog box. You can use the Unparent button to break any parent links. When you target an object to another object, its orientation is locked to the **targeted object**. This means that when the targeted object moves, the selected object rotates to stay pointed at the moving target. To select a target for the selected object, select the targeted object from the Target Item drop-down list in the Motion Options dialog box.

Applying Modifiers

To apply modifiers to the selected object, open the Motion Options dialog box by clicking the Motion Options button in the Motions section of the Setup tab (or by pressing m). Clicking the Add Modifier button at the bottom of the IK and Modifiers tab opens a list of available modifiers. When you select a modifier, it is added to the list of modifiers. To disable a listed modifier, click the check mark to the left of the modifier name. When you select a modifier and then click the Edit button, you view its properties, and copy, paste, or remove it.

TIP

You can also access the Properties dialog box for the selected modifier by double-clicking the modifier name.

FIGURE 9.17
Curve Constraint dialog box

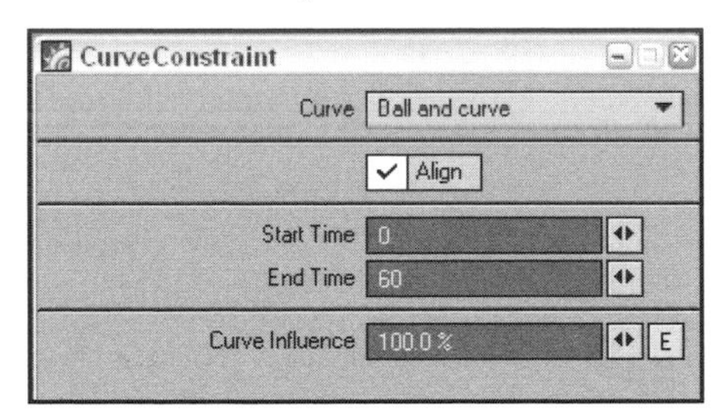

Animating an Object Following a Curve

You can select the Curve Constraint modifier from the Add Modifier list in the Motion Options dialog box. Using the Curve Constraint modifier causes the selected object to travel along the path defined by a curve. This curve can be part of the selected object or another curve loaded into the scene. The Curve Constraint dialog box, shown in Figure 9.17, includes a drop-down list where you can select the curve to use. Using the Align option causes the object to rotate along with the curve. You can also specify the Start and End Times, and use the Curve Influence value to scale the object's motion.

Using the Follower Modifier

Using the Follower modifier, also found in the Add Modifier list in the Motion Options dialog box, causes the selected object to follow along with the targeted item. Using the Follower dialog box, shown in Figure 9.18, you can also specify a Time Delay, or a Path Delay, which is the distance behind the path that the object follows. You can also specify a multiplication factor or an offset value for each channel.

Making Objects Vibrate

You can add small random vibrations to an object using the Jolt modifier, found in the Add Modifier list. In the Jolt dialog box, shown in Figure 9.19, you can set Jolt Keys for when the vibrations begin. You can use the preset Light, Medium, or Heavy settings, or customize the Duration, Position, and Rotation values. In the Events panel, you can set the vibrations to occur when a watched item in the scene meets certain criteria, such as a Position, Rotation, or Scale value that is greater than or less than a certain value.

FIGURE 9.18
Follower dialog box

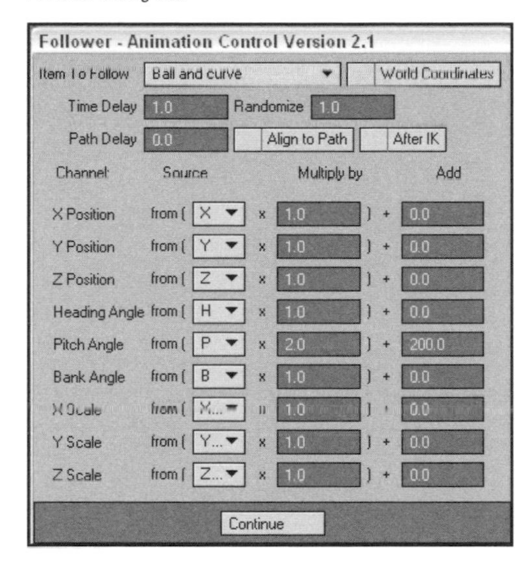

FIGURE 9.19
Jolt dialog box

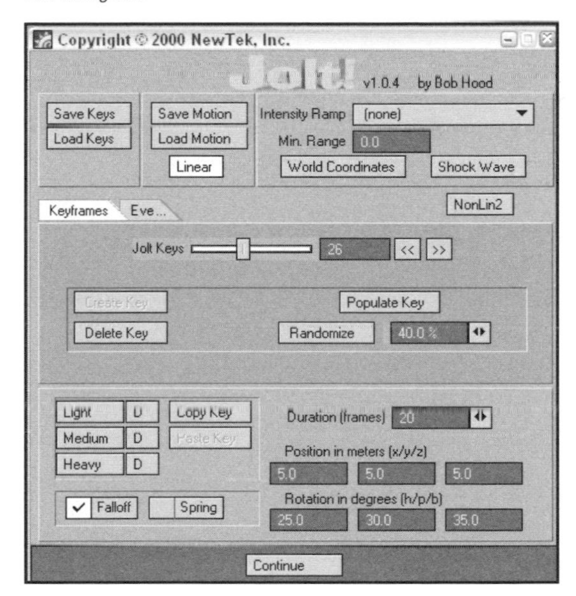

Adding Cyclical Motion

You can use the Oscillator modifier, found in the Add Modifier list, to add sine wave-like motion to a particular channel. This is useful for producing cyclical motion such as waves on the sea, a rocking chair moving back and forth, or the motion of a swing. The Oscillator dialog box, shown in Figure 9.20, shows the wave in a graph and you adjust its Time, Size, Offset, Phase, and Damping here.

Using Dynamic Parenting

When an object is parented to another object, it moves along with the parent. This is convenient for objects such as shoes and watches, but not for objects that the character needs to occasionally set down, like a weapon or a tool. To handle the objects, you can use the Dynamic Parents modifier, found in the Add Modifier list. This modifier opens a dialog box, shown in Figure 9.21. Clicking the Parent button opens another dialog box where you can select a parent object and then specify whether to keep the object's initial position, rotation, and scale. This creates a parent-child link for the selected object at the given frame, but you can break this relationship at a different frame using the Unparent button. The Dynamic Parents dialog box keeps a list of when the selected object is parented and when it is not.

FIGURE 9.20

Oscillator dialog box

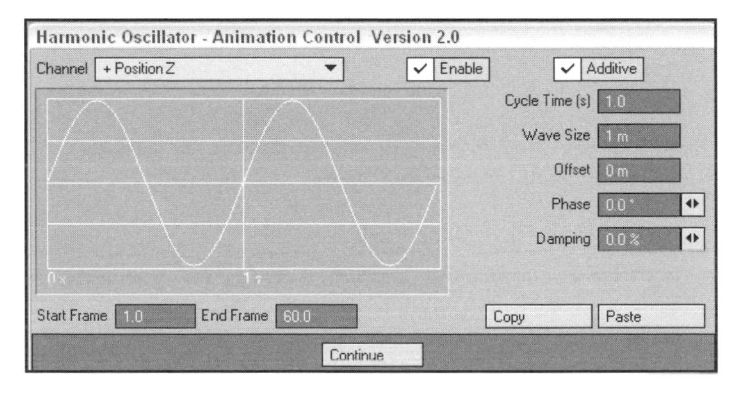

FIGURE 9.21

Dynamic Parents dialog box

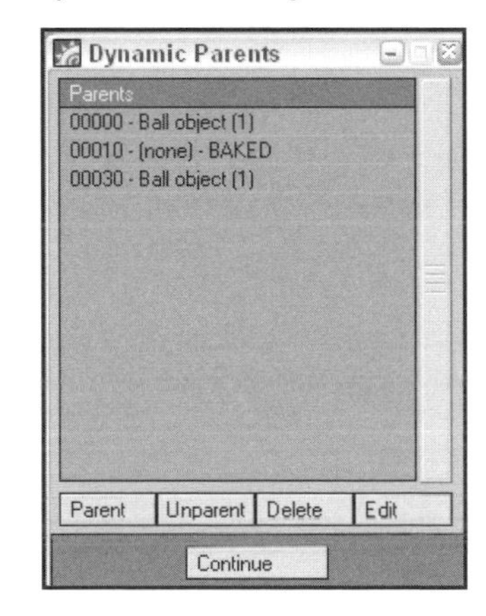

FIGURE 9.22

Parented swings

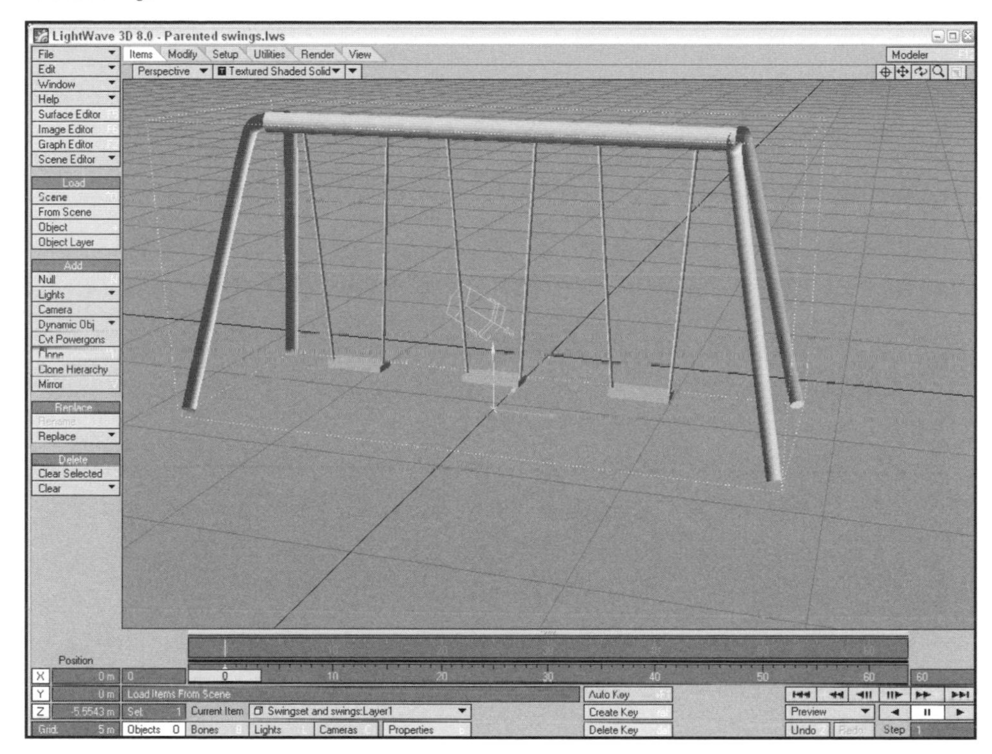

Parent objects

1. Select the File, Load, Load Object menu command and load the Swingset and swings.lwo files.

   This file includes a swingset and each of the three swings as separate layers. Each layer is loaded as a separate object.

2. Select the first swing object and click the Motion Options button in the Motions section of the Setup tab to open the Motion Options dialog box.

3. In the Motion Options dialog box, select the Layer 1 object as the Parent Item. Repeat this step for the remaining swing objects.

4. Select the swingset object and move it about the scene.

   All the children swing objects move with its parent object, as shown in Figure 9.22.

5. Select the File, Save, Save Scene As menu command and save the file as Parented swings.lws.

Use animation modifiers

1. Within an empty scene, select the File, Load, Load Object menu command and load the Ball.lwo and S Curve.lwo files.

2. Select the ball object and click the Motion Options button in the Motions section of the Setup tab to open the Motion Options dialog box. Then close the Motion Options dialog box.

3. Click the Add Modifier button and select the Curve Constraint option. Double-click on the Curve Constraint option, select the S curve from the Curve drop-down list, and then enable the Align option.
4. With the ball object still selected, click the Clone button in the Add section of the Items tab and create a single new ball object.
5. Select the cloned ball object and open the Motion Options dialog box by clicking on the Motion Options button in the Motions section of the Setup tab. Click the Add Modifier button and select the Follower modifier.
6. In the Modifier list, click the check mark to the left of the Curve Constraint modifier to disable it and double-click on the Follower modifier. Double-click the Following option, select Ball Object 1 as the Item to Follow, set the Path Delay value to 2, and enable the Align to Path option. Click the Continue button to close the Follower dialog box.
7. With the cloned ball selected, click the Clone button in the Add section of the Items tab again and create eight more clones.

   Each cloned object will have the same modifiers applied.
8. With the Motion Options dialog still open, press the Down arrow key to cycle through the parent objects until the Ball Object (2) appears in the title bar of the Motion Options dialog box. Double-click on the Following modifier and set the Path Delay value to **4** in the Follower dialog box that opens.

FIGURE 9.23
Using animation modifiers

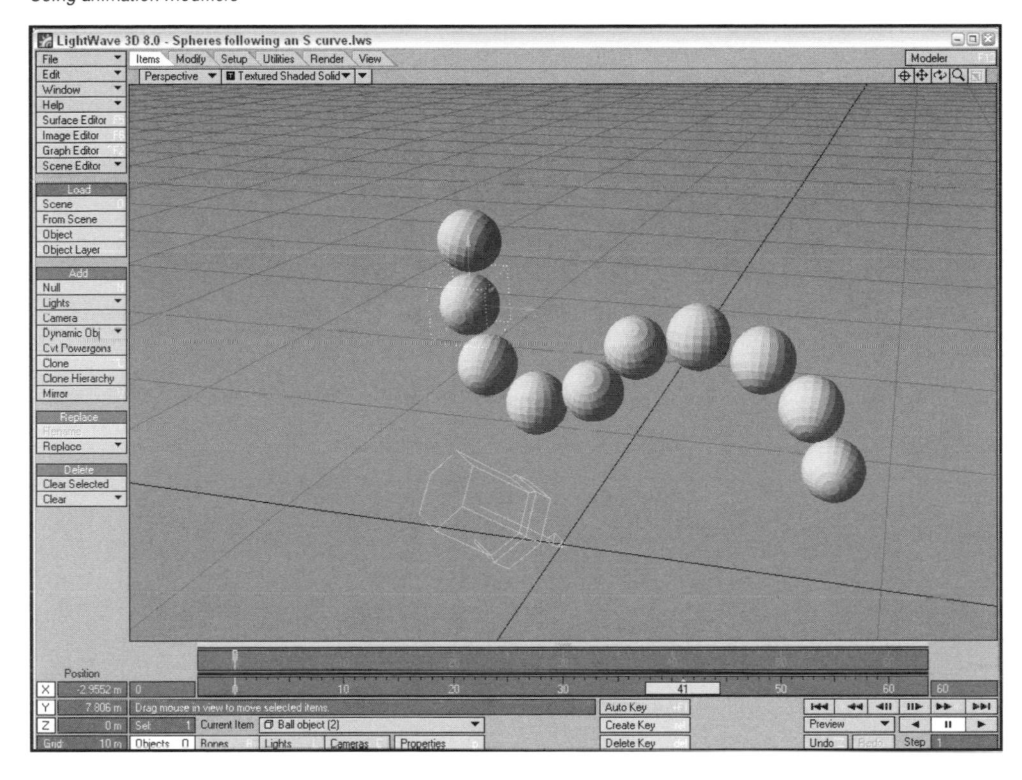

9. Repeat step 6 for the remaining clones, incrementing the Path Delay value by 2 each time.
10. Click the Play Forward button to see the resulting animation.

    The first ball object follows the target S curve, and all other ball objects follow in turn, separated by a designated distance, as shown in Figure 9.23.
11. Select the File, Save, Save Scene As menu command and save the file as Spheres following an S curve.lws.

Create oscillation motion

1. Select the File, Load, Load Scene menu command and load the Parented swings. lws files.

   Because the swings are parented to the swingset, they move along with the swingset, but they can also be animated independent of their parent.
2. Select the first swing object and notice where its pivot point is located. Click the Modify tab, select the Move Pivot button, and then move the pivot point to the top of the swingset bar directly in the middle of the swing in the Back viewport. Repeat this for the other two swings.
3. Click the Motion Options button in the Motions section of the Setup tab to open the Motion Options dialog box.

4. Click the Add Modifier button and select the Oscillator option. Double-click on the Oscillator option to open the Oscillator dialog box. Select the Pitch Angle from the Channel drop-down list, and then select the Enable option. Set the Wave Size value to **10 m**, the Damping value to **50%**, and then click the Continue button.
5. In the Motion Options dialog box, select the Oscillator name and click the Copy option from the Edit drop-down list.
6. Select the second swing object and then click the Paste option from the Edit drop-down list in the Motion Options dialog box. Repeat this step for the final swing object.
7. Double-click on the Oscillate modifier in the Motion Options dialog box and set the Phase values to **60** and **210** for the second and third swing objects.

   Changing the Phase values on the other swing objects causes the swings to swing in different directions at the start. The Damping value causes the motion to die out over time, as shown in Figure 9.24.
8. Select the File, Save, Save Scene As menu command and save the file as Oscillating swings.lws.

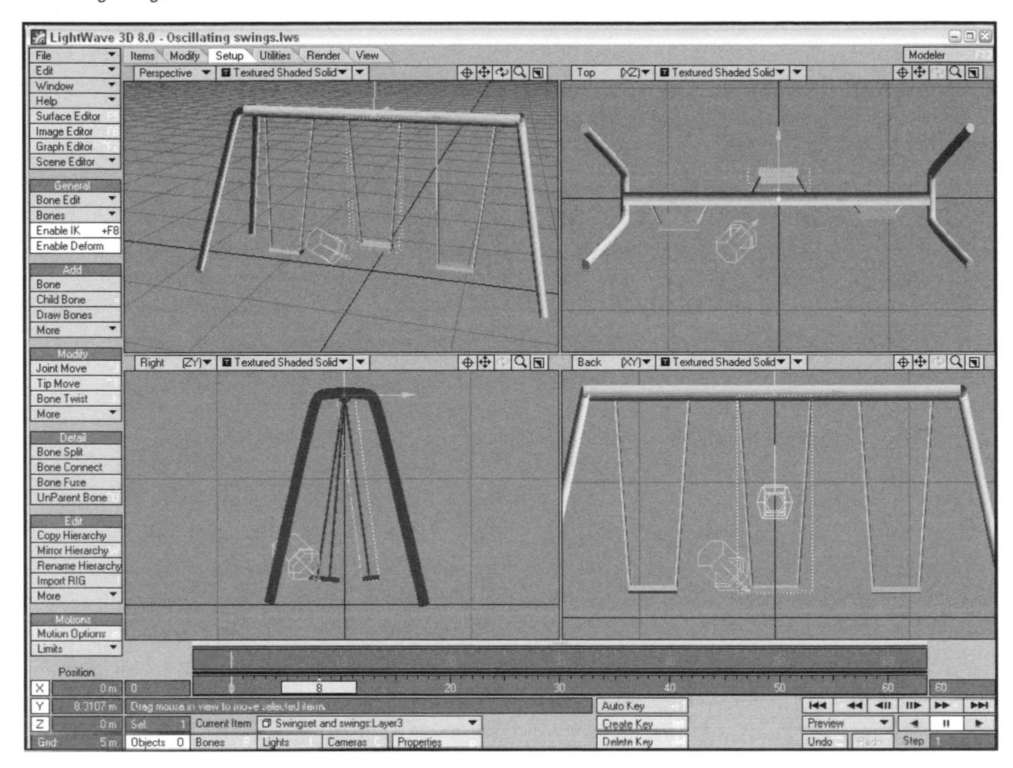

FIGURE 9.24
Oscillating swings

CHAPTER SUMMARY

This chapter explained the basics of animation in LightWave. You can animate objects by setting position, rotation, and scale keys for the scene objects. You can use the Auto Key mode to create keys automatically. You can also animate objects that move along a path by editing the object's motion path. Finally, you can use animation modifiers to automate objects in certain ways, including simple vibrations and wave motions.

What You Have Learned

- How to use the Time Line, the Animation Preview, and the Dope Track controls.
- How to create keyframes using the Create Key and the Auto Key commands.
- How to move, delete, cut, copy, and paste keys.
- How to work with motion paths to view, edit, save, and load them.
- How to parent and target objects to move together.
- How to use animation modifiers to automate the motion of objects.

Key Terms from This Chapter

- **Time Line.** A control at the bottom of the Layout interface that displays all the available frames.
- **Animation Preview controls.** A set of controls in the lower-right corner of the Layout interface that lets you play back the current animation and move between frames and keys.
- **frame.** A single animation state. All frames together make the complete animation.
- **keyframe.** The recorded state of an object that marks a beginning or ending motion of an object.
- **Dope Track.** An interface control that displays and lets you work with all the keys for the current scene.
- **Auto Key.** A toggle mode that automatically creates new keys every time you move an object.
- **motion path.** A curve that shows the path that an object takes during an animation.
- **Tension, Continuity, and Bias.** A set of controls for defining an object's motion path, enabling you to create sharp points and rounded areas.
- **Animation modifier.** A plug-in's module that includes a dialog box for defining certain types of object motions.
- **parented object.** An object that is hierarchically linked to another object, causing the linked object to move with its parent.
- **targeted object.** An object that is linked to another object, causing the linked object to rotate so that it maintains its orientation to the targeted object.

CHAPTER 10

WORKING WITH THE GRAPH EDITOR

1. View animation curves.

2. View different curves.

3. Edit keys.

4. Edit curves.

CHAPTER 10
WORKING WITH THE GRAPH EDITOR

Moving and editing keyframes using the Time Line is fine for linear type motion, but what do you do when you need to create a curved motion path? Well, you could add multiple keys to simulate the curve, or edit the motion path, but LightWave provides an easier method and a powerful dialog box you can use to accomplish this and many more tasks. This dialog box is the **Graph Editor** and it represents all motions as graphs that you can easily manipulate to create the exact motion you want.

You can open the Graph Editor by clicking the Graph Editor button in the toolbar, pressing Ctrl+F2, or clicking one of the Envelope icon buttons located throughout both the Modeler and Layout interfaces.

Within the Graph Editor, you can select the precise **channel** to work on and use the Graph Editor commands and modes to select, move, stretch, and zoom on specific keys. You can also add new keys to the existing channel, and change the shape of the curve using the various curve shape types.

Tools You'll Use

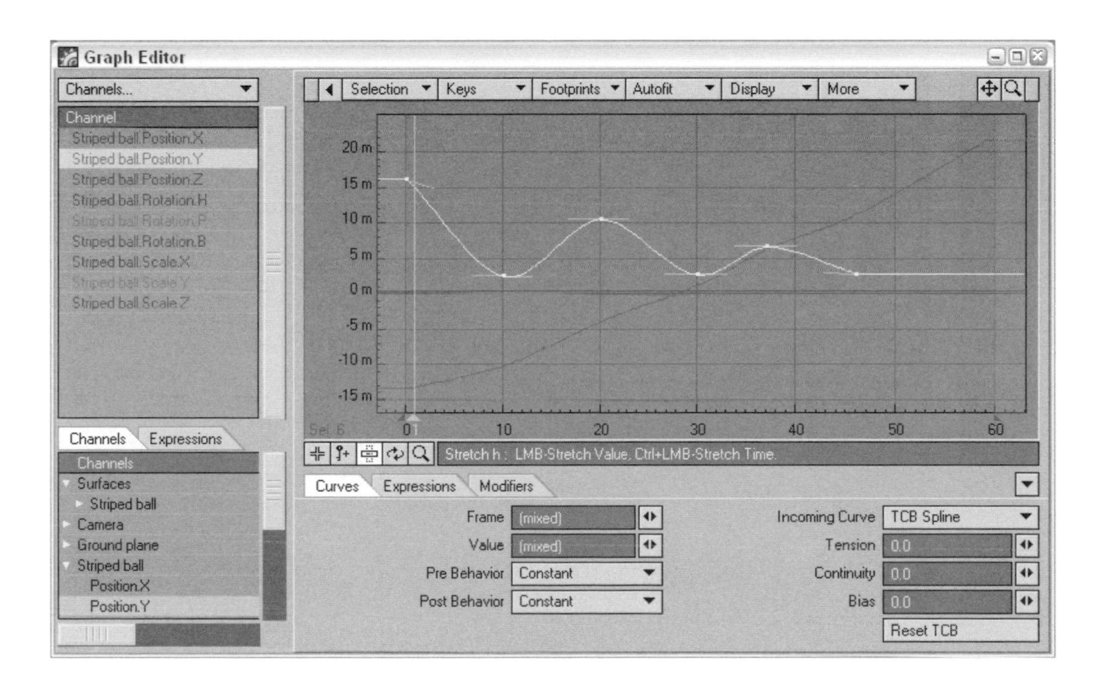

LESSON 1

VIEW ANIMATION CURVES

What You'll Do

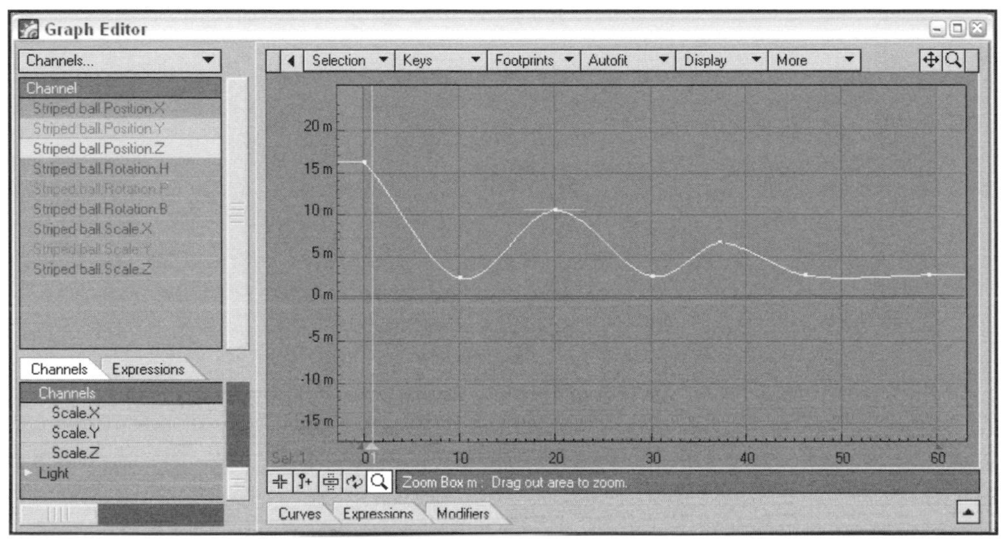

In this lesson, you'll learn how to view various channels in the Graph Editor.

The Graph Editor is divided into several panes. The pane on the left is called the **Channel Bin** and it lists all the available channels for the selected object. The list below the channels lists all the scene items and their respective channels. The right pane shows the actual animation curves and below them, three panels of controls. Several pop-up menus are located along the top of the dialog box.

Selecting a Channel

When you open the Graph Editor, all channels for the selected object are shown in the Channel Bin on the left. To select the channel for any object in the scene, use the list below the Channel Bin. When you select a channel in the left pane, the right pane displays the corresponding animation curve in a bright color that matches the channel's color. To select several channels at a time, use the Shift and Ctrl keys. Figure 10.1 shows the Graph Editor when several channels are selected. The Selection pop-up menu at the top of the dialog box also includes several commands for selecting channels including Clear Unselected Channels, Clear Channel Bin, Remove Channel from Bin, Invert Channel Selection, Select All Curves in Bin, and Reset Bin Selection.

Increasing the Graph Area

To hide the channel selection list and thus increase the space allotted for the channel graph, click the left arrow next to the pop-up menu buttons at the top of the interface. To restore the channel selection list, click the button again. You can also collapse the panels at the bottom of the Graph Editor using the Collapse button that's under the bottom-right corner of the graph pane. Figure 10.2 shows the Graph Editor with the top collapse button clicked. You can also select these collapse commands from the Display pop-up menu. If the graph pane gets large enough, the Options, Undo, and Cancel buttons appear to the right of the pop-up menu buttons.

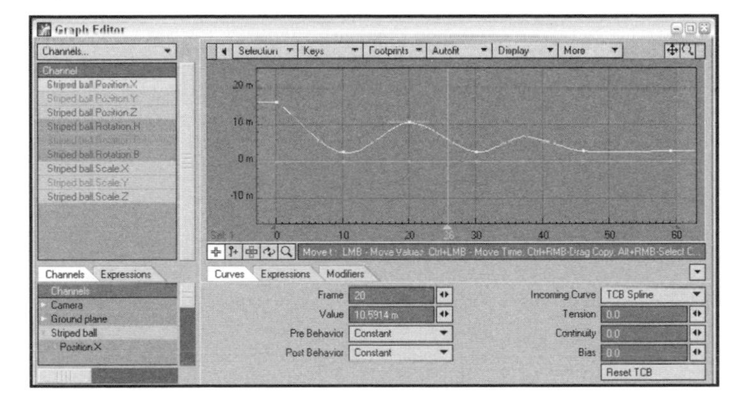

FIGURE 10.1
Graph Editor with several selected channels

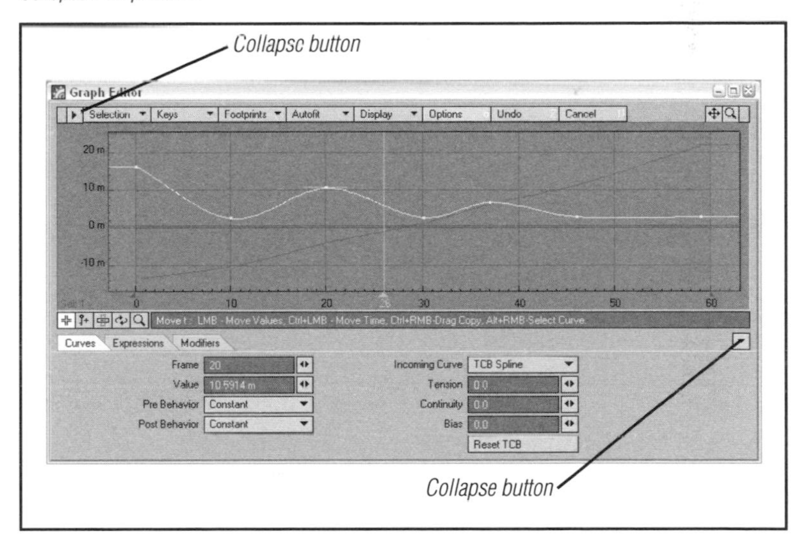

FIGURE 10.2
Collapsed Graph Editor

TIP

You can increase the size of the Graph Editor dialog box even more by dragging on its edges or corners.

Changing the Frame and Frame Range

Within the graph pane, a thin vertical gray line marks the current frame. If you click the small triangle at the base of this line, you can drag it left and right just as you do with the Frame Slider. Changing the current frame in the Graph Editor also changes it in the viewports and in the main Time Line, and vice versa. You can also change the frame range by dragging on the small icons above the beginning and end frames. Figure 10.3 shows the current frame line in the Graph Editor, and the beginning and ending range changing icons. If you want to change these values by entering a number, use the Go to Frame and the Numeric Limits commands in the Display pop-up menu. When you click one of these commands, a simple dialog box opens where you can enter the frame and range values.

FIGURE 10.3

Graph Editor current frame line

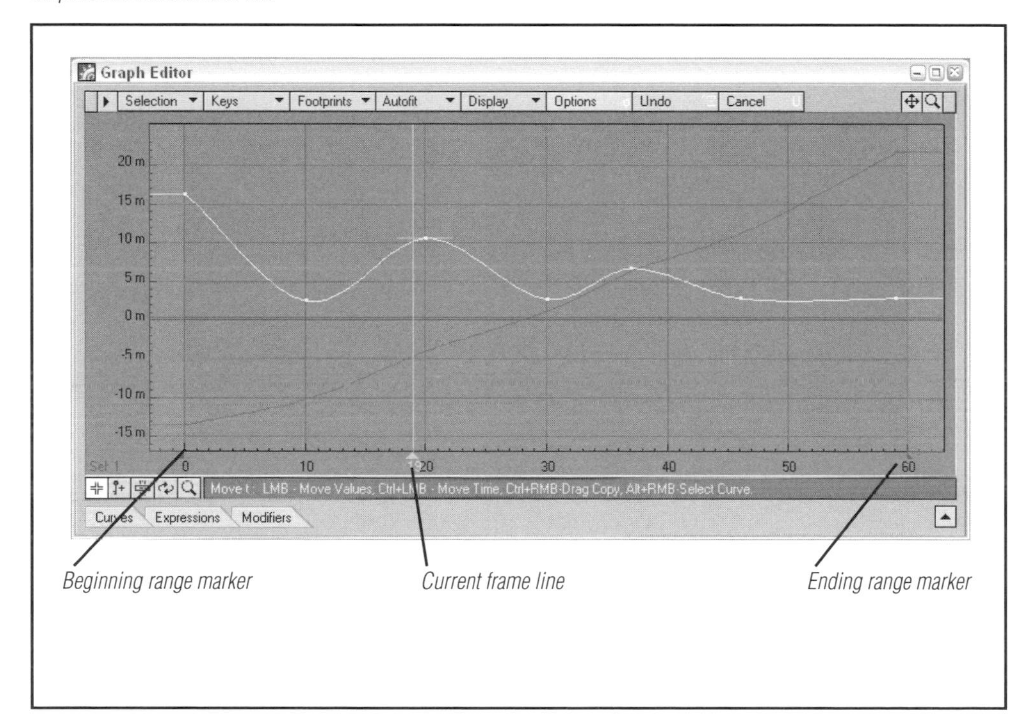

TIP

The dark area in the graph pane represents the active range.

Zooming and Panning the Graph Pane

Notice the two icon buttons in the upper-right corner of the graph pane. They look just like the icon buttons used in the viewports. Using these buttons, you can Zoom and Pan the graph pane. With the Zoom tool, you can scale the graph values and time. Figure 10.4 shows a graph that was zoomed in both time and value.

TIP

The Display, Center Graph pop-up menu option centers the graph about the mouse cursor. The keyboard shortcut for this command is g, so positioning the mouse cursor and then pressing g centers the graph about the mouse cursor.

FIGURE 10.4
Zoomed graph

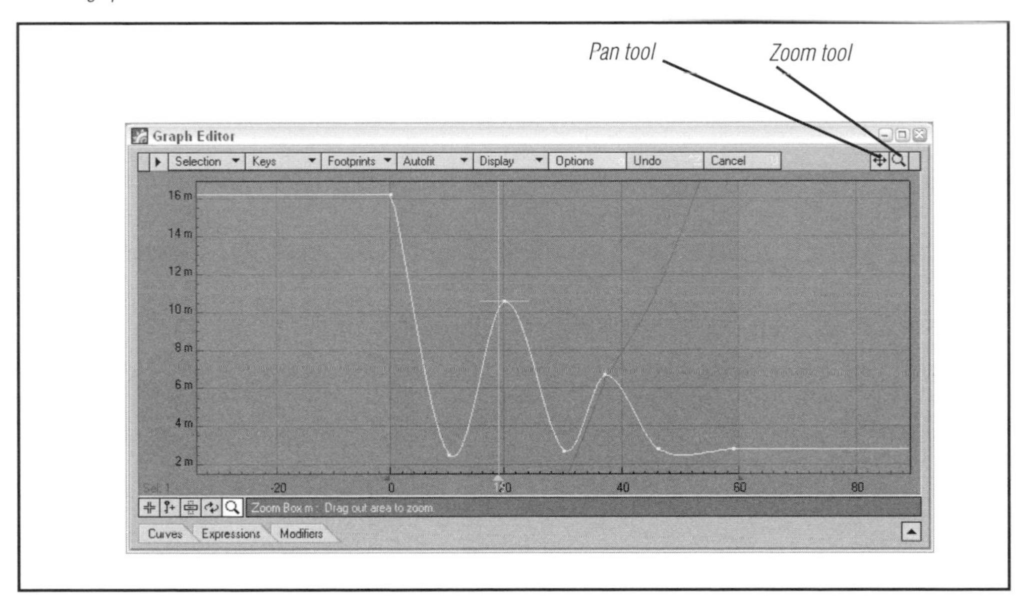

Autofitting a Graph

Using the options found in the Autofit pop-up menu, you can automatically fit the selected channel within the graph pane. Using the Fit Values by Type option scales the value axis to vertically maximize the selected channel, as shown in Figure 10.5.

Setting Graph Editor Options

Selecting the Options button (or selecting the Graph Editor Options menu from the More button if the width of the Graph Editor isn't wide enough to show the Options button) opens a dialog box of options, as shown in Figure 10.6. Use these options to customize how the Graph Editor works with keys. This dialog box also includes many different display options, which are also available in the Display pop-up menu.

FIGURE 10.5
Autofit values graph

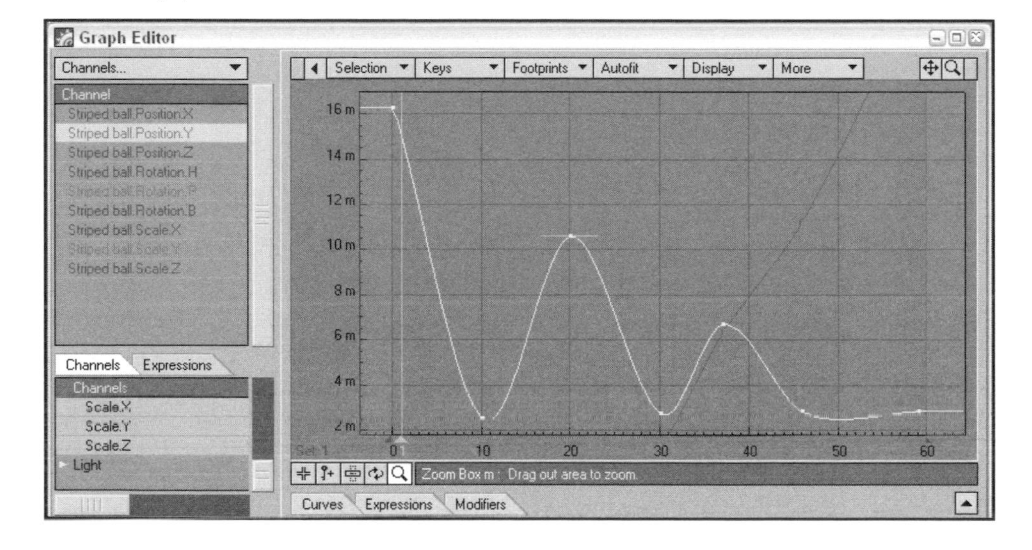

FIGURE 10.6
Graph Editor Options dialog box

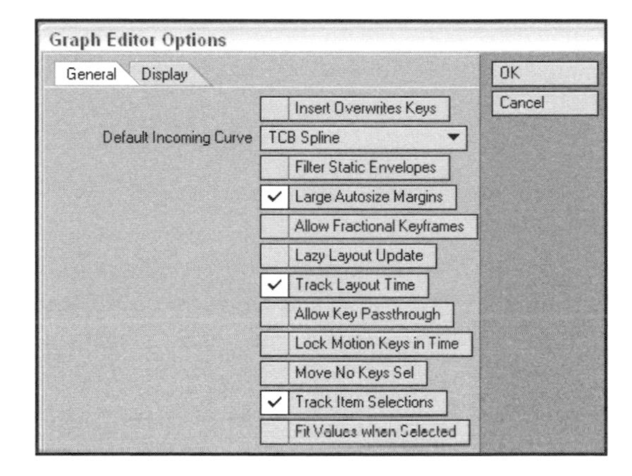

FIGURE 10.7
Selected channels in the Graph Editor

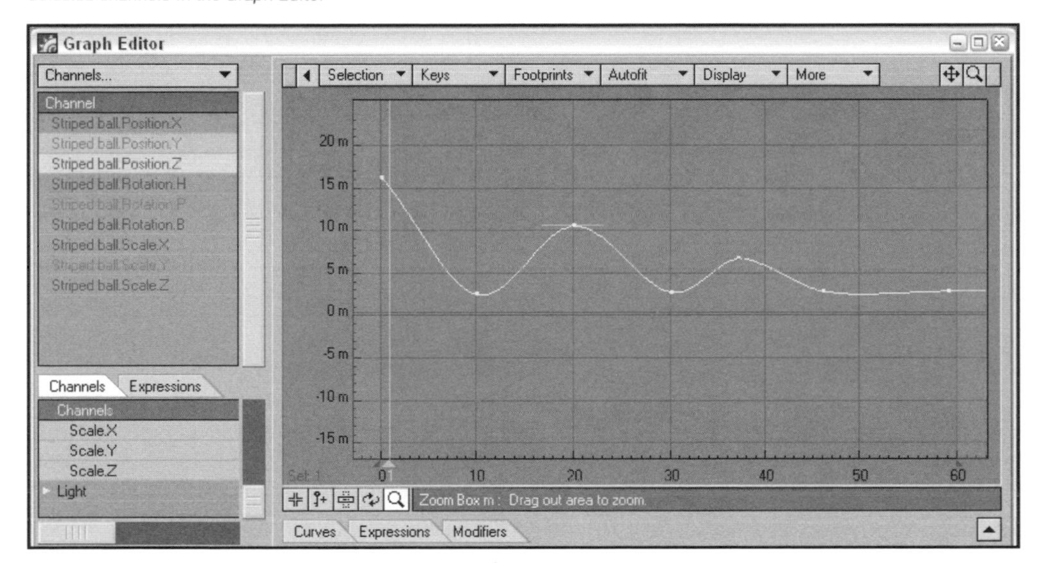

Move objects

1. Click the File, Load, Load Scene menu command and open the Bouncing ball.lws file.
2. Select the ball object, and then click the Graph Editor button in the toolbar.

   The Graph Editor opens and displays the available channels for the ball object.
3. In the Channel List of the Graph Editor, hold down the Ctrl key and select the Striped ball.position.Y and the Striped ball.position.Z channels. Then click the Striped ball.position.X channel to deselect it.
4. Click the lower Collapse button icon to increase the graph area.
5. Select the Autofit, Autofit menu command to size the channel graphs within the graph area.

   The graph for this channel is displayed in the graph pane, as shown in Figure 10.7.
6. Choose the File, Save, Save Scene As menu command. Then select and open the Autofit graph.lws file.

LESSON 2

VIEW DIFFERENT CURVES

What You'll Do

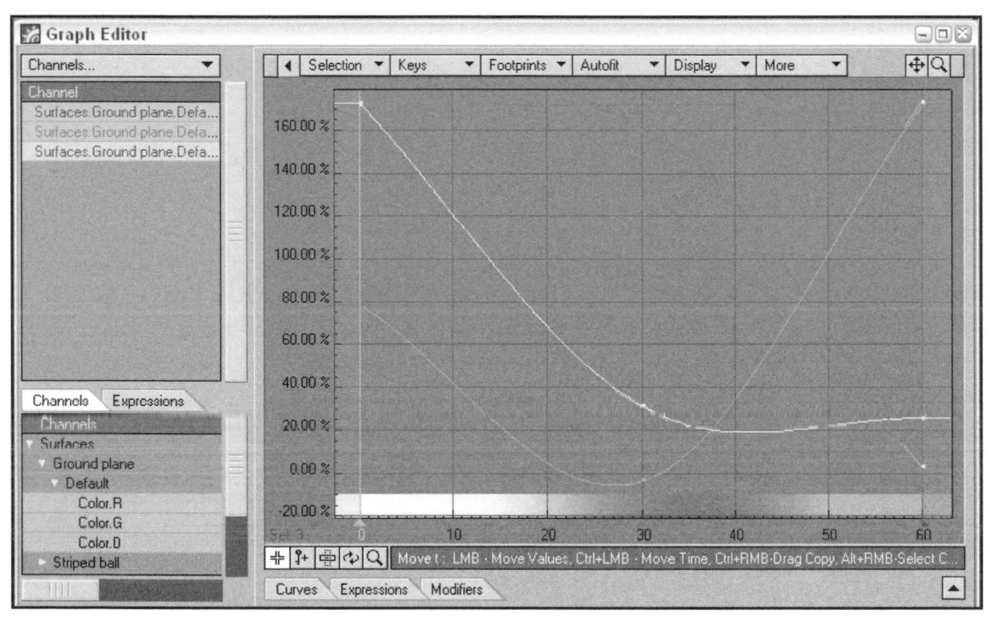

In this lesson, you'll learn how to work with channels and view color value curves.

When you first open the Graph Editor, the position, rotation, and scale channels for the selected object are shown in the Channel Bin, but there are also many other parameter curves that you can edit using the Graph Editor.

Adding Channels to the Channel Bin

The Scene list is located directly below the Channel Bin. This pane includes a hierarchical list of all the items included in the current scene, including all available objects, cameras, and lights. It also includes a Surface listing that holds all the scene surfaces. If you locate a channel with the Scene list that you want to see in the Graph Editor, simply double-click on the channel or an item and all its channels will replace the current channels in the Channel Bin. You can also add a channel to the current set of channels in the Channel Bin by holding down the Shift key while you drag the channel from the Scene list and then drop it in the Channel Bin. After you add a channel to the Channel Bin, you can select it to display its graph in the graph pane. Figure 10.8 shows the Scene list with several expanded hierarchies.

> **TIP**
>
> You can drag the edge between the Channel Bin and Scene list to change the sizes of each.

Removing and Reordering Channels in the Channel Bin

The Channel Bin can hold many different channels, but it is only a staging area for the channel graphs that you want to see. If you delete a channel from the Channel Bin using the menu commands Selection, Remove Channel from Bin, or the Selection, Clear Channel Bin, it has no effect on the scene. You can also reorder the channels listed in the Channel Bin by dragging and dropping them above or below other channels.

Viewing Color Values in the Graph Editor

Each surface within the Scene list has R, G, and B parameter values that you can edit in the Graph Editor. When any of these color channels are displayed in the Graph Editor, a color bar appears below the graph, as shown in Figure 10.9. This color bar shows the change in the color for the entire frame range.

FIGURE 10.8
Scene list

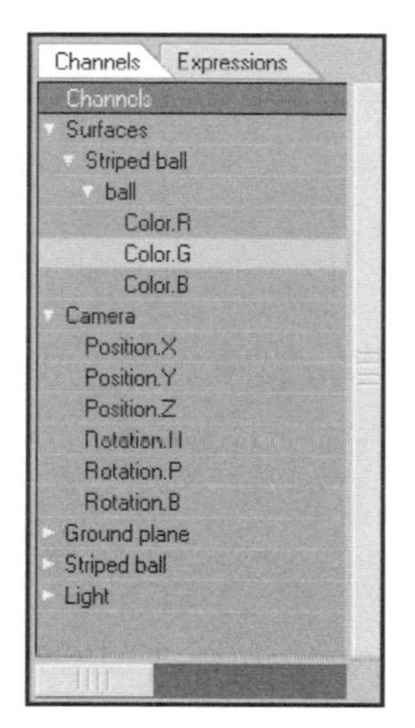

FIGURE 10.9
Color values graph

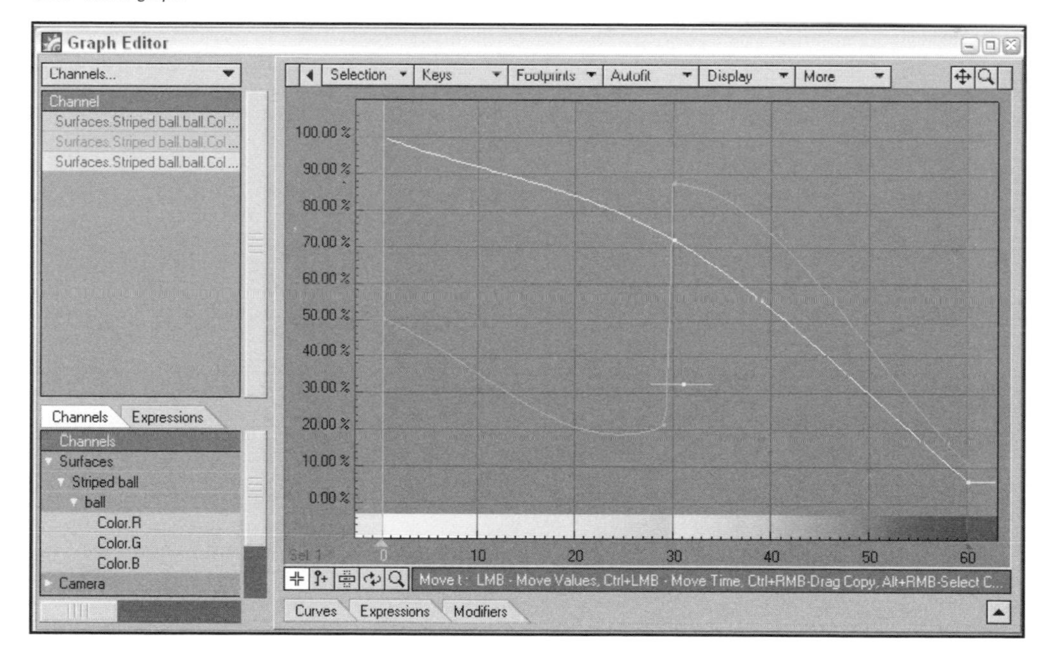

> **TIP**
>
> If you right-click on a color graph key, you can open the Color Picker, where you can select a specific color from a palette.

Editing Envelopes

Many dialog boxes such as the Surface Editor, the Texture Editor, and the Light Properties dialog boxes offer direct access to the Graph Editor via their **Envelope editing** icon, shown in Figure 10.10. These icons are labeled with Es and clicking an Envelope icon opens the Graph Editor with the selected parameter's channel selected in the Channel Bin.

FIGURE 10.10
Envelope editing icon

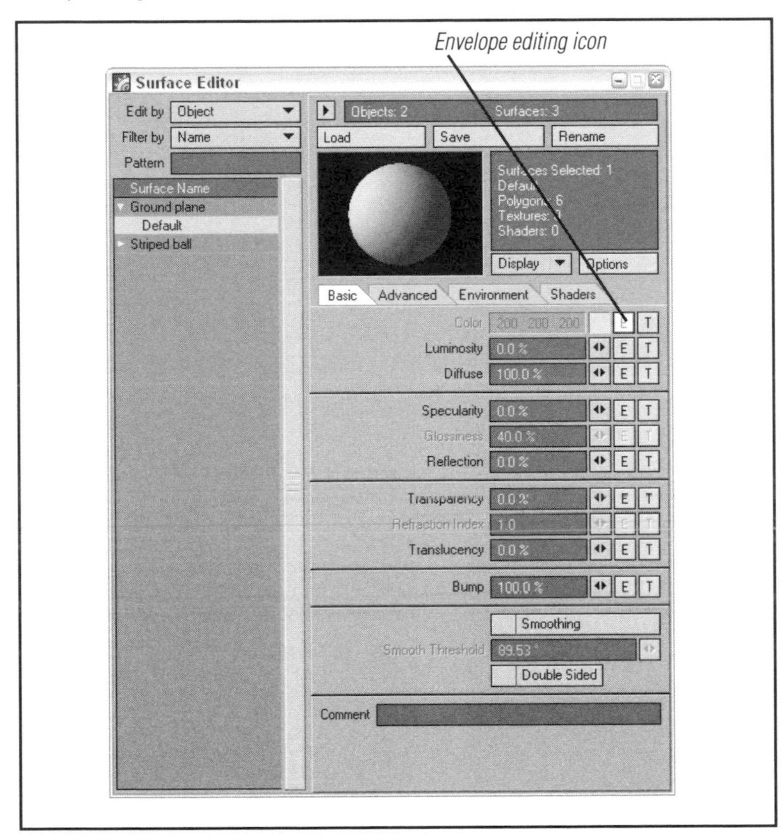

FIGURE 10.11

Graph Editor accessed from the Surface Editor

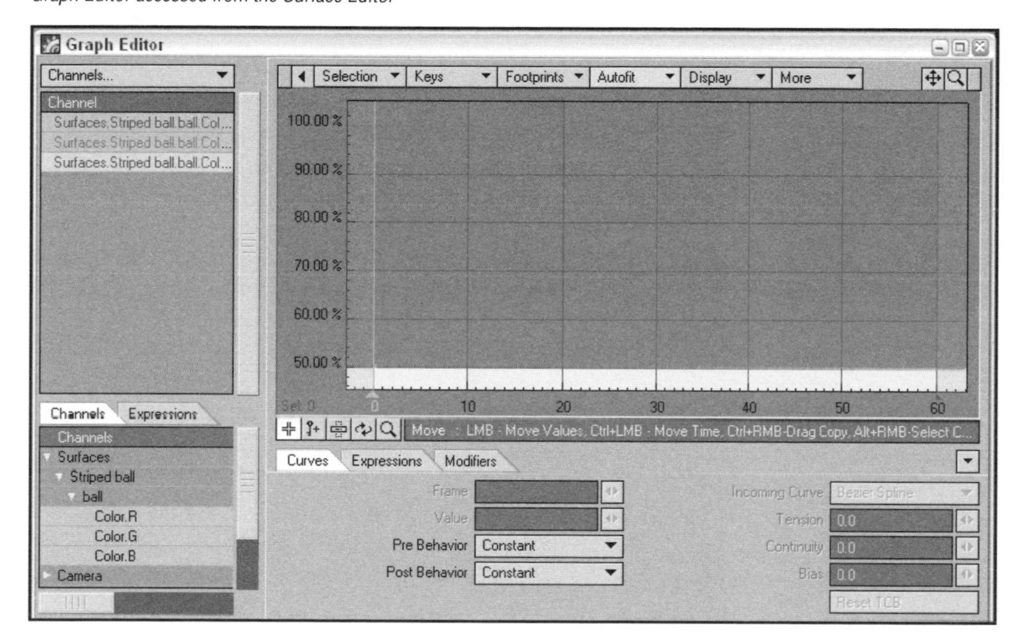

View a color graph

1. Click the File, Load, Load Scene menu command and open the Color values graph.lws file.
2. Select the ball object, and click the Surface Editor button in the toolbar to open the Surface Editor. Then click on the Envelope button to the right of the Color property.

   Clicking on the Envelope button automatically opens the Graph Editor with the Color.R, Color.G, and Color.B channels selected in the Scene list, as shown in Figure 10.11.

LESSON 3

EDIT KEYS

What You'll Do

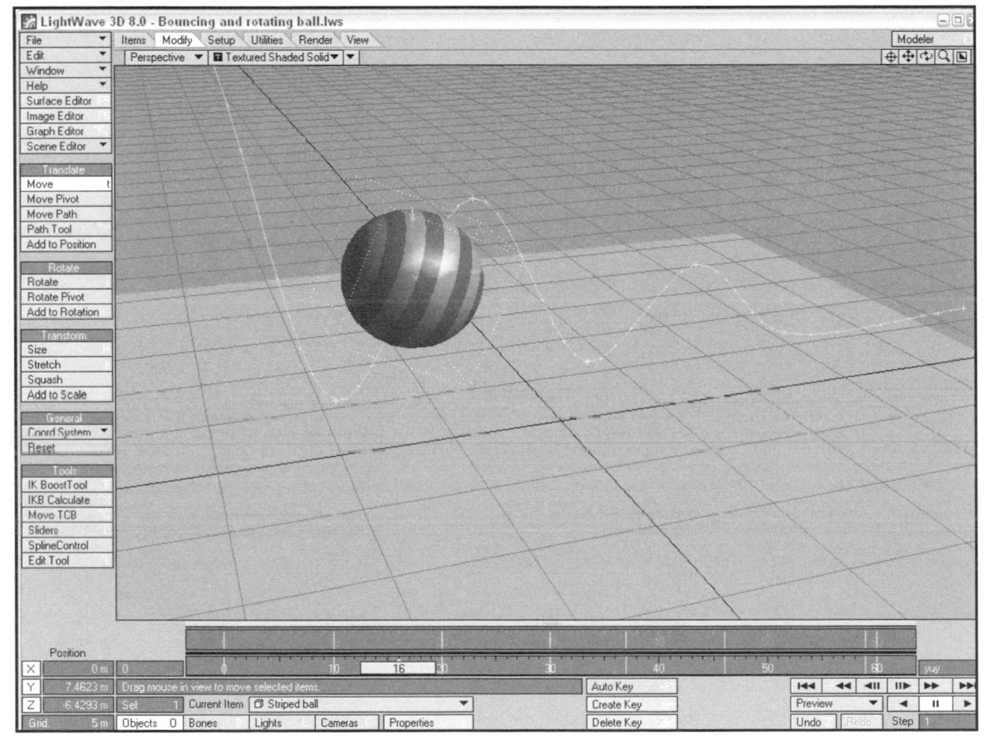

In this lesson, you'll learn how to add new keys and edit existing keys.

The curvature of the curves in the Graph Editor are determined by keys. These keys are displayed as points on the curve. Using the Graph Editor, you can add new keys, select and move keys, and perform functions such as scaling a range of keys. Keys that you add in the Graph Editor also show up on the Time Line and Dope Track. When editing keys, there are several different modes that you an access. To select a mode, use the buttons at the lower-left corner of the graph, as listed in Figure 10.12.

> **TIP**
>
> Pressing the Spacebar cycles through these different modes.

Selecting Keys

You can select keys for the selected channel curves by simply clicking on them in the graph pane. If you select a single key, you can use the left and right arrow keys to the select the adjacent keys. To select multiple keys, drag over them with the right mouse button. You can also select multiple keys by holding down the Shift key and clicking them. The selected keys are highlighted in yellow, as shown in Figure 10.13.

TIP

If you hold the mouse over the top of a curve's key, a pop-up info box displays the key's channel, value, and frame.

Moving Keys

With the Move Key mode enabled, you can click on any key in the active curve and drag up and down to change its value, or hold down the Ctrl key and drag left or right to change its frame.

Adding and Deleting Keys

With a channel graph visible in the Graph Editor, you can add new keys using the Add Key mode. When this mode is active, wherever you click within the graph pane creates a new key for all the selected channels. After clicking to place a key, you can drag it up or down to change its value, or drag while holding down the Ctrl key to change its frame. To delete a key in Add Key mode, press Ctrl and then click the key.

FIGURE 10.12
Key editing modes

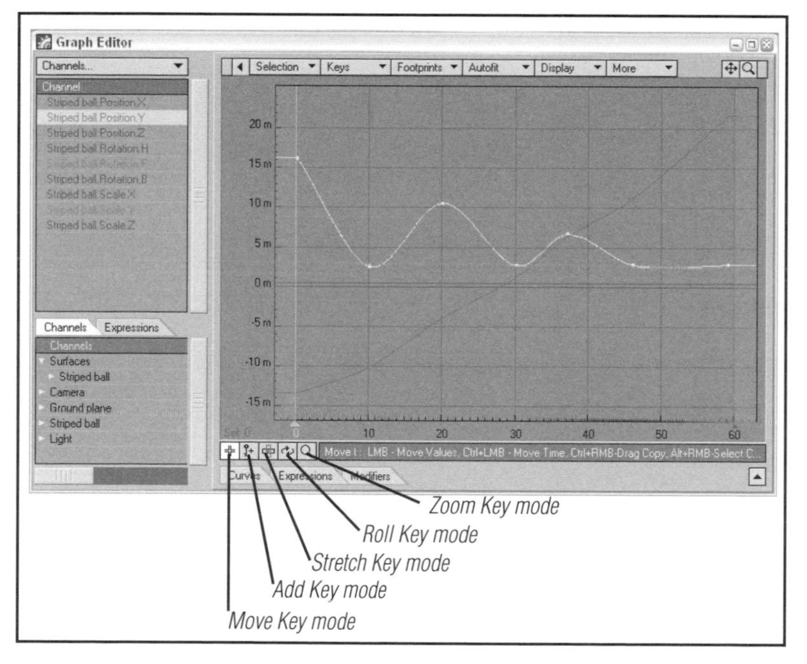

FIGURE 10.13
Selected keys

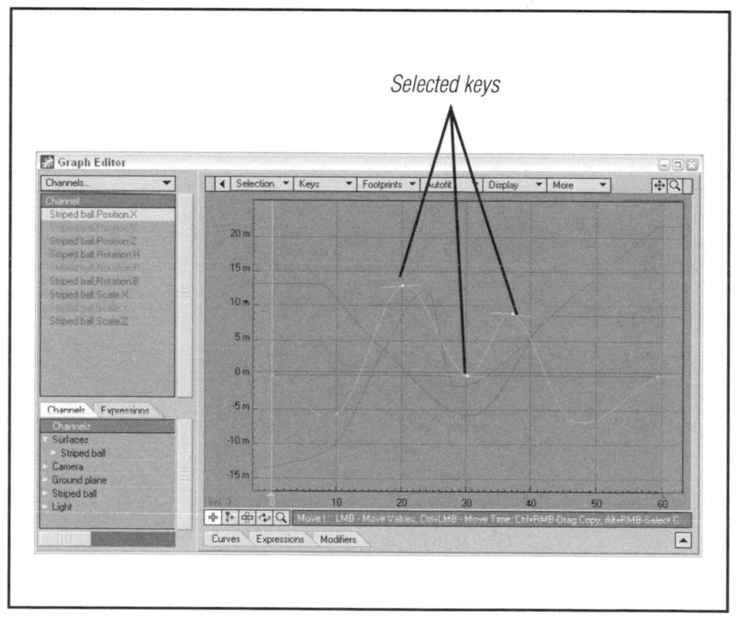

> **TIP**
>
> You can delete selected keys in any mode by pressing Delete.

Scaling Keys

With the Stretch Key mode enabled, you can scale keys toward or away from a point where you initially click in the graph pane. Holding down the Ctrl key while dragging scales keys horizontally along the frame axis.

Rolling Keys

In Roll Key mode, you can select a roll range by dragging with the right mouse button in the graph pane. This roll range is colored darker than the rest of the graph pane, as shown in Figure 10.14. After you define a roll range, dragging left and right with the left mouse causes all keys within the roll range to slide in the direction of the mouse. When a key reaches the end of the roll range, it reappears on the opposite side.

Zooming Keys

Clicking the Zoom Key mode button changes the mouse cursor to a small magnifying glass, which you can use to drag over the area that you want to magnify, as shown in Figure 10.15. Releasing the mouse zooms in on the selected area. To zoom back out, right-click the graph pane.

FIGURE 10.14
Roll Keys mode

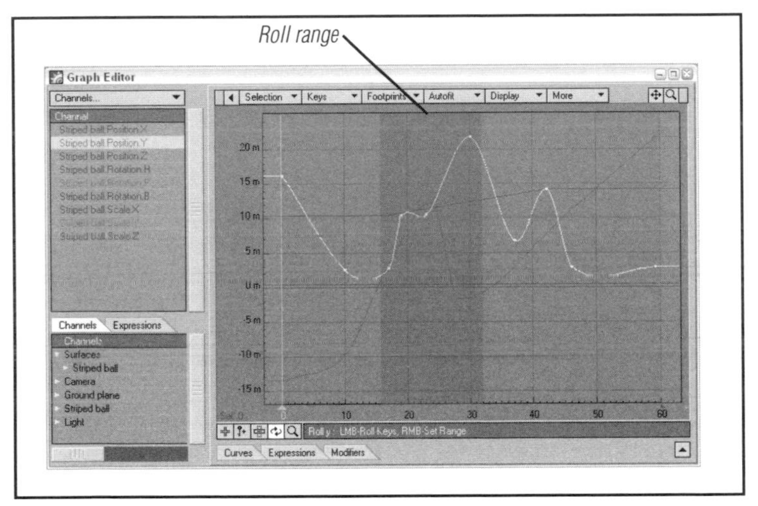

FIGURE 10.15
Zoom Keys mode

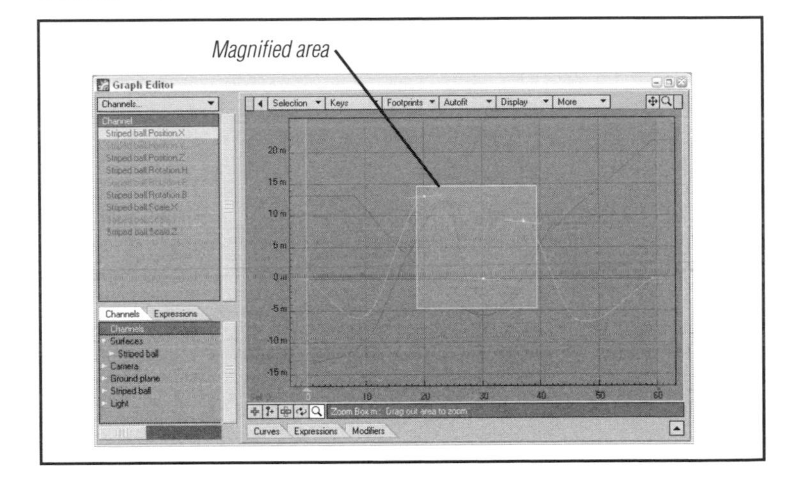

Copying Keys

To copy keys between the same curve or to another curve, select the key to copy, right-click it, and then select the Copy Key Value command from the pop-up menu. Next, select another key on the same curve or on another curve, right-click it, and then select the Paste Key Value option from the pop-up menu. You can also copy keys interactively: Hold down the Ctrl key, right-click on the key to copy it, and then drag it to the position on the curve where you want to paste it. The frame number is displayed, and a small arrow points at the location where the key will be pasted, as shown in Figure 10.16.

FIGURE 10.16
Copying keys

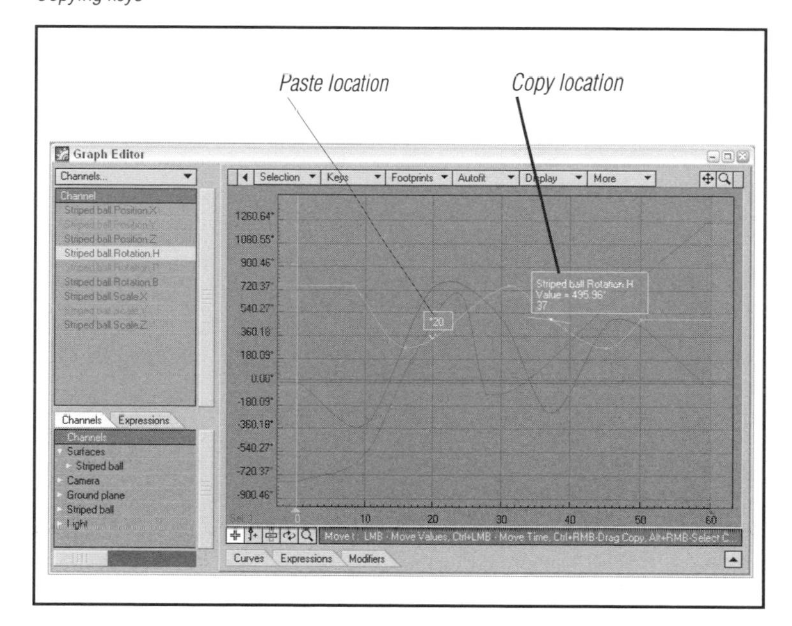

Edit graph keys

1. Click the File, Load, Load Scene menu command and open the Bouncing ball.lws file.
2. Select the ball object, and click the Graph Editor button in the toolbar.
3. In the Channel Bin, select and double-click on the Striped ball.Rotation.P channel.
4. In the lower-left corner of the graph pane, select the Add Key mode, and then click the highlighted line in the graph pane at frame 0 and frame 60.

   Two new keys are added to the channel graph curve.
5. In the lower-left corner of the graph pane, select the Move Key mode and move the key at frame 60 upward to a value of around 1200 degrees.
6. Drag the Frame Slider in the Graph Editor.

   Notice how the striped ball now rotates as it bounces along in the scene, as shown in Figure 10.17.
7. Choose the File, Save, Save Scene As menu command and save the file as Bouncing and rotating ball.lws file.

FIGURE 10.17
Bouncing and rotating ball

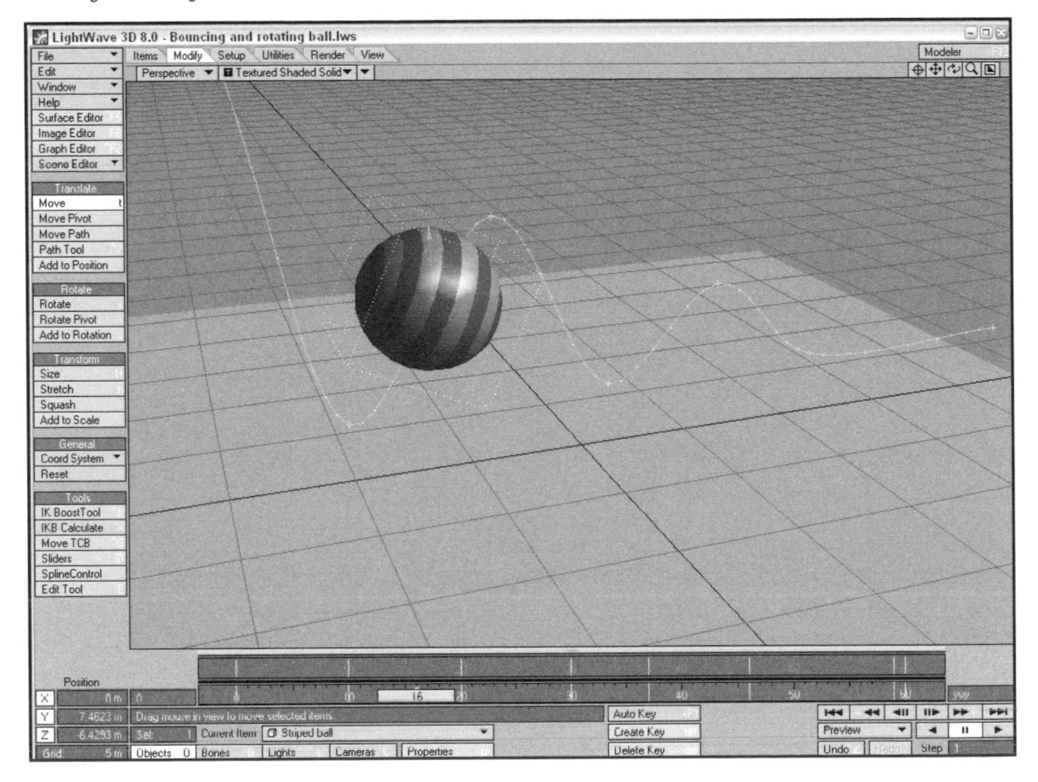

LESSON 4

EDIT CURVES

What You'll Do

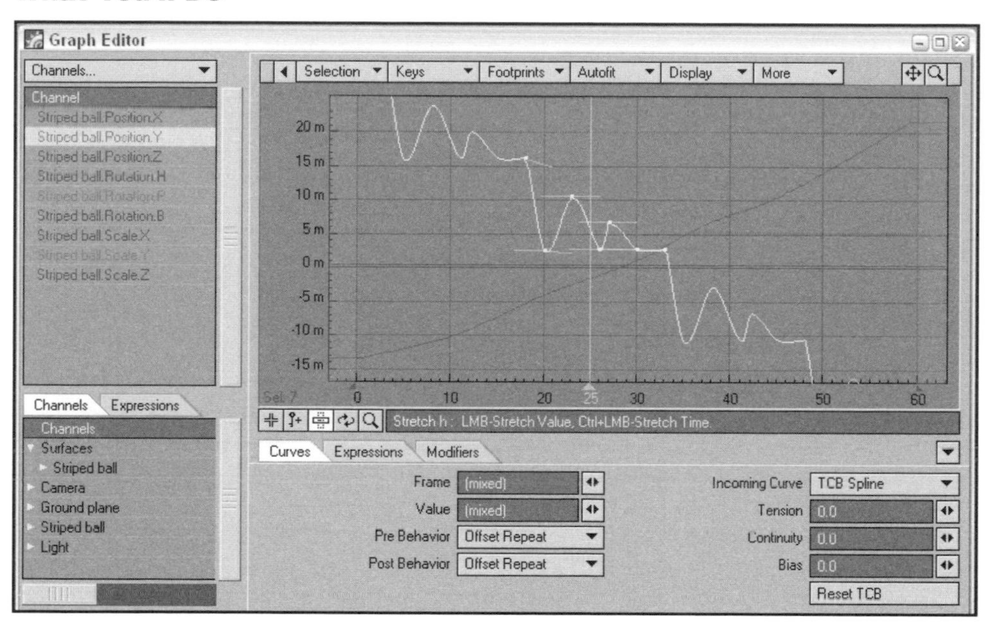

In this lesson, you'll learn how to change and edit the curve shape.

You can change animation curves by moving the keys along the curve, but you can also alter the curves by changing the curve type. You can select a curve type from the Incoming Curve drop-down list in the Curves panel below the graph pane. The available curve types include TCB Spline, Hermite Spline, Bezier Spline, Linear, and Stepped.

Making Curves Loop

In the Curves panel, the **Pre and Post Behavior** options specify how the curve acts before the first and last keys are encountered. The options include Reset, Constant, Repeat, Oscillate, Offset Repeat, and Linear. Using the Constant option maintains the value of the first or last key. If you select the Repeat option, the keys are repeated for the entire range. To continually play the keys forward and backward, use the Oscillate option. Using the Offset Repeat option repeats the keys, but starts from the location where it ends. Use the Linear option to continue the curve in the same direction as the first or last key.

Figure 10.18 shows several Pre and Post Behavior options. The top curve has a Pre Behavior of Constant and the Post Behavior of Linear. The bottom curve has a Pre Behavior of Repeat and a Post Behavior of Offset Repeat.

Using TCB and Hermite Splines

The **TCB Spline** type controls the shape of the curve based on the Tension, Continuity, and Bias values. These values are described in Chapter 9 with the motion paths discussion. Selecting the **Hermite Spline** type adds a single tangent handle to the left of the key. By dragging this handle, you can change the shape of the curve coming into the curve, as shown in Figure 10.19.

FIGURE 10.18
Pre and Post Behavior options

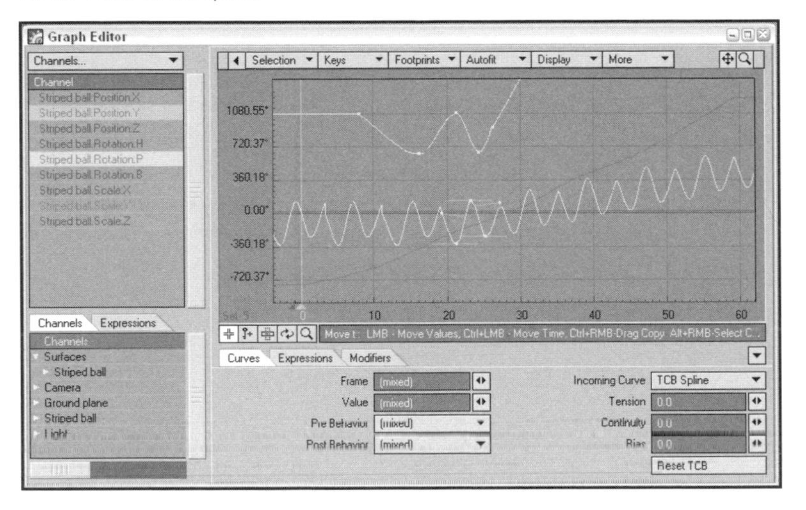

FIGURE 10.19
Hermite spline

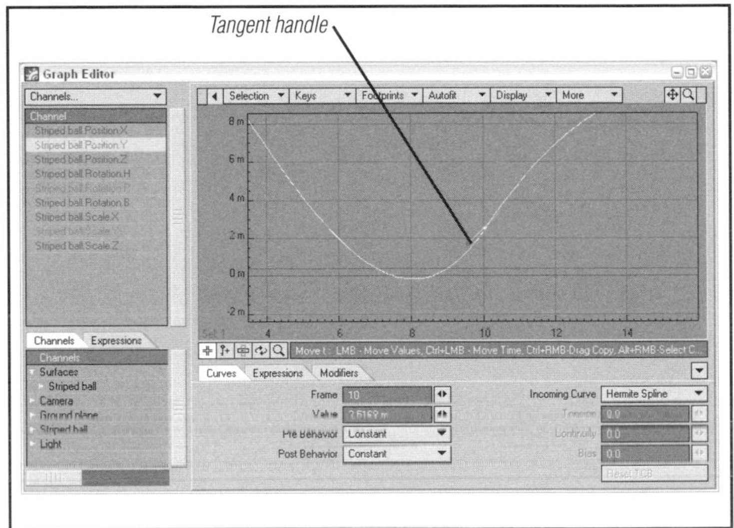

Using Bezier Splines

Selecting the Bezier Spline type adds two tangent handles to the either side of the key, as shown in Figure 10.20. Dragging either of these handles changes the shape of the curve by moving both handles to maintain a straight line between the two handles. If you drag on one of the handles while holding down the Alt key, you can move each handle independently, and thus cause a break in the smoothness of the curve around the key.

FIGURE 10.20
Bezier spline

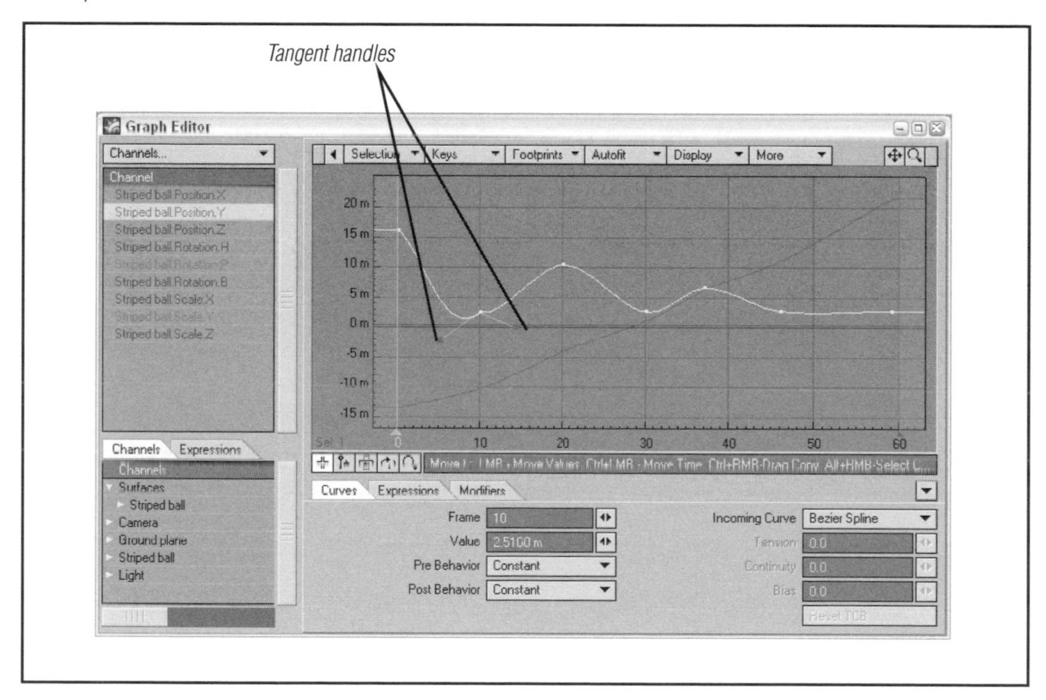

Creating Straight and Stepped Lines

Selecting the Linear type changes all curve segments to straight lines, as shown in Figure 10.21. Using the Stepped type maintains the key value until the next key is reached and then abruptly jumps to the new value, as shown in Figure 10.22.

FIGURE 10.21

Linear option

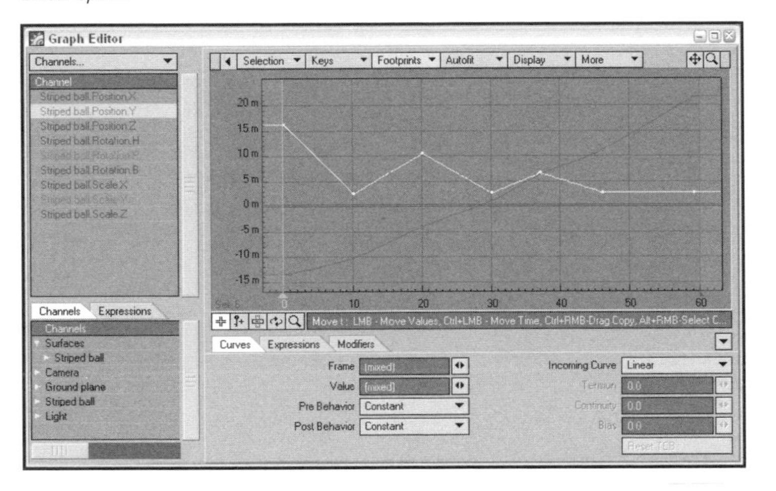

FIGURE 10.22

Stepped option

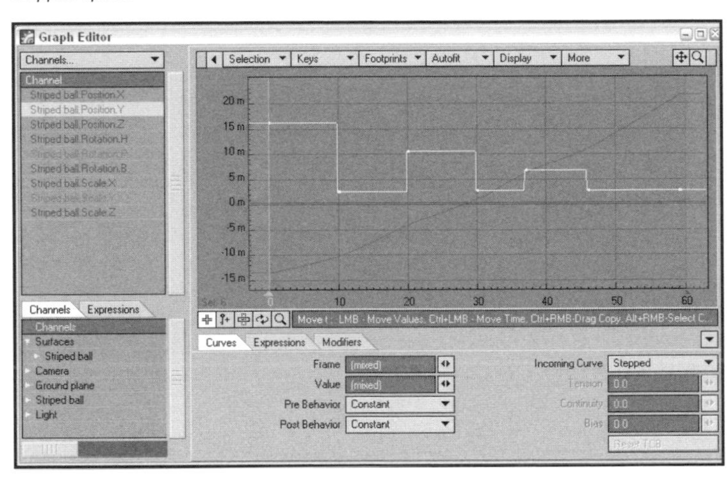

FIGURE 10.23
Bouncing down steps

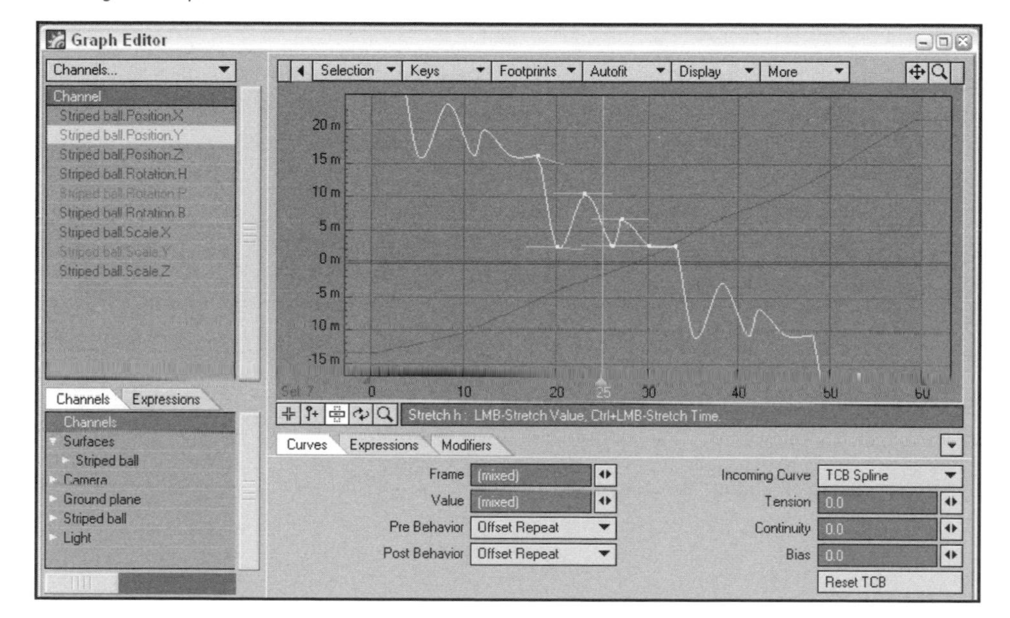

Create looping

1. Click the File, Load, Load Scene menu command and open the Bouncing ball.lws file.
2. Select the ball object, and click the Graph Editor button in the toolbar.
3. In the Channel Bin, select and double-click on the Striped ball.Position.Y channel.
4. In the graph pane, right-click and drag over all the available keys to select them all.
5. In the lower-left corner of the graph pane, select the Stretch Keys mode. Then hold down the Ctrl key and drag to the left until all the keys are scaled to a 15-frame range in the center of the graph pane.
6. In the Curves panel, set the Pre and Post Behavior options to Offset Repeat.

   The graph should now resemble the one shown in Figure 10.23, with the ball animated as if it was bouncing down a series of steps.
7. Choose the File, Save, Save Scene As menu command and save the file as Bouncing down steps.lws.

Change curve shape

1. Click the File, Load, Load Scene menu command and open the Bouncing ball.lws file.
2. Select the ball object, and click the Graph Editor button in the toolbar.
3. In the Channel Bin, select and double-click on the Striped ball.Position.Y channel.
4. In the graph pane, right-click and drag over all the available keys to select them all.
6. In the Curves panel, select the Stepped option from the Incoming Curve drop-down list.

   The ball's motion changes to abrupt steps, as shown in Figure 10.24.
7. Choose the File, Save, Save Scene As menu command and save the file as Bouncing steps.lws.

FIGURE 10.24
Bouncing steps

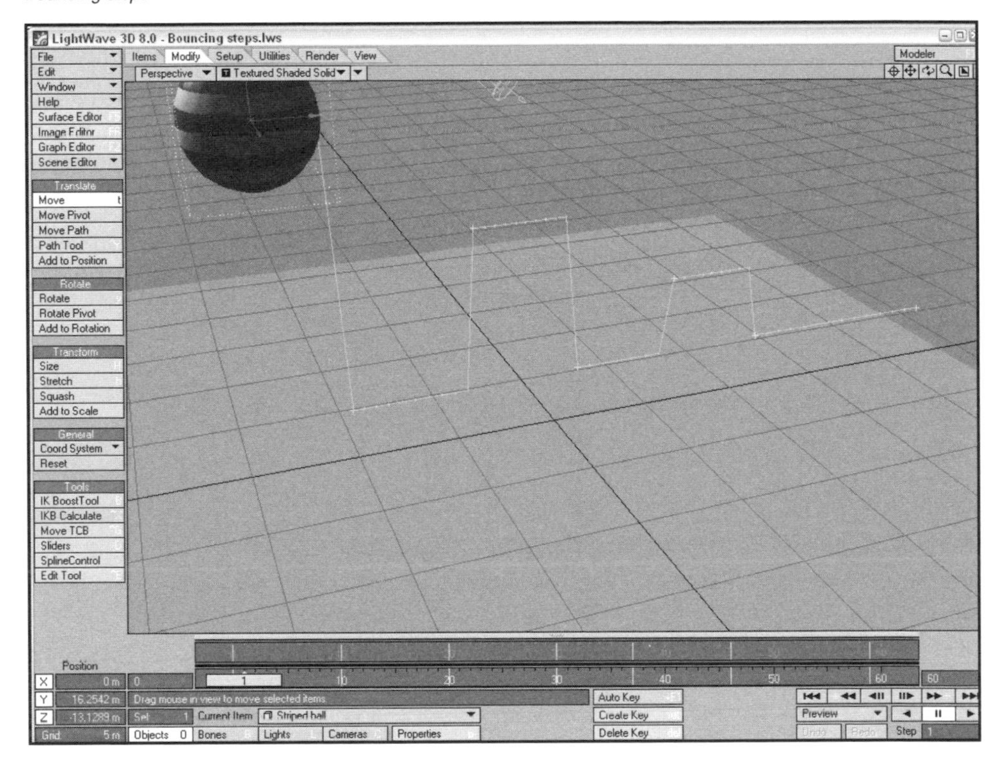

CHAPTER SUMMARY

This chapter explained how to view and edit keys by using the Graph Editor. You can use the Graph Editor to view all animated curves over the total number of frames. You can also use the Graph Editor to edit individual keys and animation curves. In addition, you can edit surface parameters using the Graph Editor by clicking on one of the Envelope editing buttons in the Surface Editor.

What You Have Learned

- How to use the Graph Editor interface and controls.
- How to select and display different channel graphs in the Scene list.
- How to open surface parameters in the Graph Editor by using the Envelope editing icon buttons.
- How you can use the various key editing modes to move, add, stretch, roll, and zoom keys.
- How to copy and paste keys between different graphs.
- How to use Pre and Post Behavior options to make an animation graph loop.

Key Terms from This Chapter

- **Graph Editor.** An interface that displays all animations as graphs and keys as curve points.
- **channel.** The graph curve for a particular object attribute.
- **Channel Bin.** A pane to the left of the Graph Editor where all current channels are listed.
- **Envelope editing icon.** Small icon buttons marked with an E and located in the Surface Editor. They automatically open the Graph Editor.
- **Pre and Post Behaviors.** Used to define the shape of the channel's graph before or after the existing selection of keys, including options for making the curve loop indefinitely.
- **TCB spline.** A curve type that defines the curve based on the Tension, Continuity, and Bias values.
- **Hermite spline.** A curve type that lets you edit the smoothness around the curve point by dragging a control handle.

CHAPTER 11

ENABLING DYNAMICS

1. Create hard-body objects.
2. Create soft-body objects.
3. Create a cloth object.
4. Create a particle emitter.

CHAPTER 11

ENABLING DYNAMICS

Dynamics is the study of motion. In LightWave, you can use dynamics to provide a lot of automated motion, but first, you need to set up the parameters of the objects involved. To assign dynamic objects to objects, use the Dynamics panel in the Object Properties dialog box. The options include hard-body objects, soft-body objects, cloth objects, emitters, wind, collision, and gravity.

Hard-body objects are objects that are rigid and inflexible. **Soft-body objects** are flexible and are easily deformed when colliding with other objects. **Cloth objects** typically conform to objects that they collide with, and **particle emitters** are used to emit **particles** that are grouped together to create certain effects.

Each dynamic object type has several different panels of properties and settings that you can use to control how the object acts during the simulation. After you assign the properties, you can click the Calculate button in the Object Properties dialog box to automatically create the animation keys.

Tools You'll Use

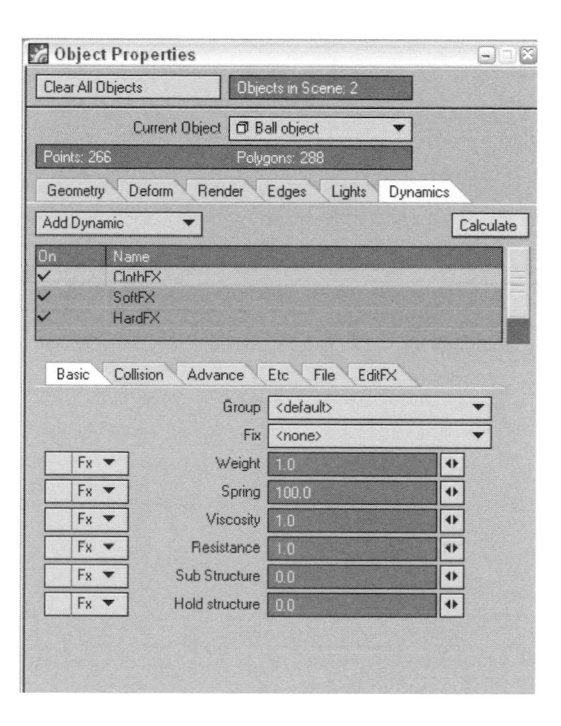

LESSON 1

CREATE HARD-BODY OBJECTS

What You'll Do

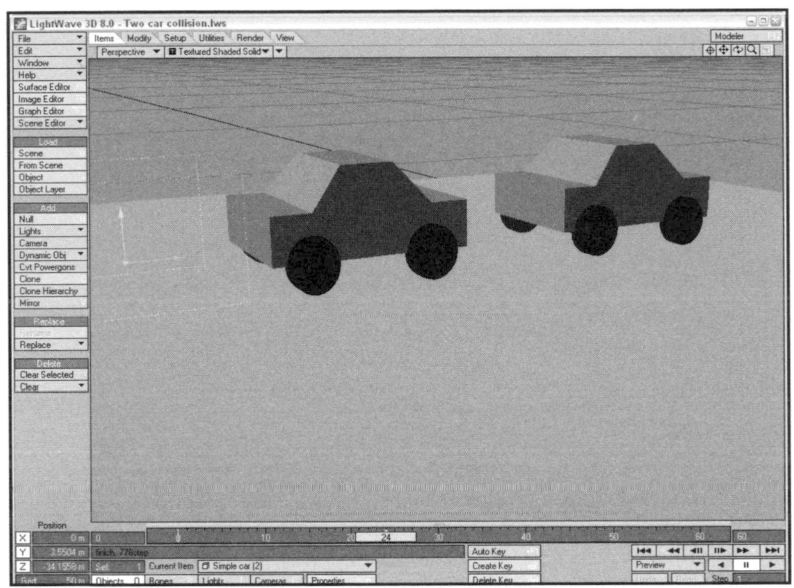

In this lesson, you'll learn how to create dynamic hard-body objects.

A hard-body object has a hard surface that won't give way to other objects such as a bowling ball, a rock, or a chair. To make the selected object a hard-body object, select the Hard option from the Add Dynamic drop-down list in the Dynamics panel of the Object Properties dialog box. When you select the HardFX option that is added to the Dynamics list, the dialog box expands to include several panels of settings, as shown in Figure 11.1.

FIGURE 11.1

Dynamics panel of the Object Properties dialog box

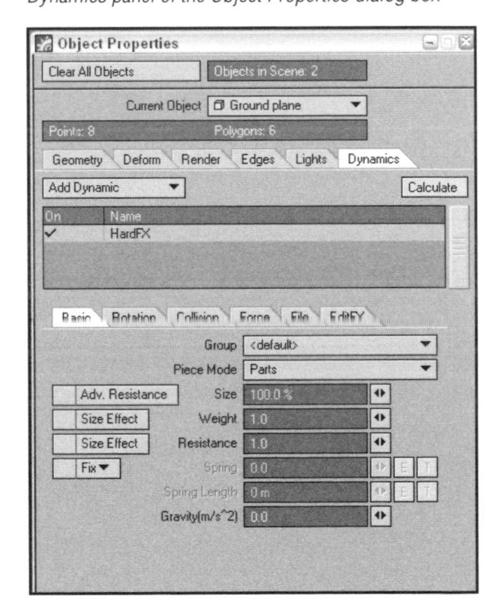

TIP

To disable a dynamic effect for any object, select the check mark to the left of the Dynamic name.

Setting Dynamic Properties

The first panel of settings that appear in the Object Properties dialog box when the HardFX option is selected is the Basic panel. Within the Basic panel, you can set the object's Size, Weight, Resistance to air, and Spring values. The Size and Weight values determine the object's density and how much power the object has when it collides with other objects. You can use the Resistance value to make the object resist gravity forces, and the Spring value to define how much rebound the object has as it strikes other objects.

Setting Object Gravity

For hard-body objects, you can specify a value in the Gravity field in the Basic panel. The typical value of gravity on Earth is $-9.81\ m/s^2$, but you can set it to whatever value you desire. Setting this value to a negative, non-zero value accelerates the object in the negative Y-axis direction. If you set the Gravity value to 0, the object becomes immovable.

CAUTION

In order for collision detection to work, all colliding objects must have a non-zero gravity value. This value can be small like 0.01, but it must not be 0.

Enabling Rotation

Use the Rotation panel for HardFX objects, shown in Figure 11.2, to define how the hard-body object rotates when subjected to dynamic forces. You can set the Impact Effect to Roll, Force, None, or Stop, and the Wind Effect to None, Accelerate, Roll, or Spin. You can also set the Minimum and Maximum Torque values to limit the rotation of an object.

Enabling Collisions

Use the Collision panel for HardFX objects, shown in Figure 11.3, to enable collisions between different dynamic objects. You can

FIGURE 11.2
Rotation panel for HardFX

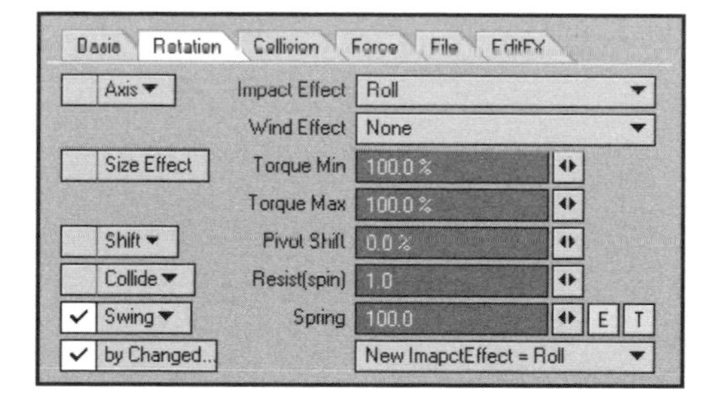

FIGURE 11.3
Collision panel for HardFX

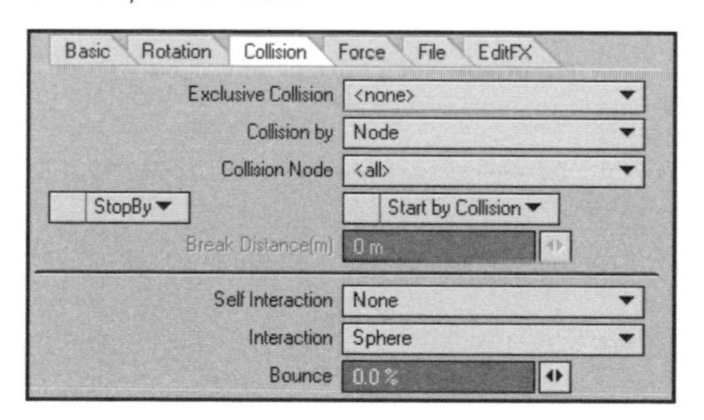

use the Exclusive Collision drop-down list to select a single object to collide with and cause all other collisions to be ignored. The Collision By option defines the shape of the object used to determine a collision. The options include Node (object's vertices), Box (a bounding box), or Sphere (a bounding sphere). Use the Self Interaction option to specify how the interactions are determined for the same object (useful for cloth, but not for hard objects). Use the Interaction option to specify the interaction shape for other objects. The Bounce value defines how much the object rebounds after a collision.

NOTE

For a collision to take place between two objects, you need to enable collision options for both objects.

Adding Forces

Use the Force panel for HardFX objects, shown in Figure 11.4,to add forces to the objects. Use the Force Mode drop-down list to specify when the designated force begins. The options include Start, Break, Rotation Control, and Event. Selecting the Start option adds the force when you click the Calculate button. If you select the Break option, the force is added as the object starts to break into parts. The Rotation control lets you apply a rotation value to the object. When you select the Event option, the force is added when a collision takes place. You can also set the Initial Axis about which the force is applied, and its Velocity and Rotation values about the specified axis.

Saving Motion Files

Use the File panel for HardFX objects, shown in Figure 11.5, to save a motion file for the simulated dynamics. Motion files have BDD file extensions and you can reload them and apply them to other objects using the Copy and Paste buttons.

Breaking into Pieces

A single hard-body object can consist of several different pieces, depending on how it was built in the Modeler. In the Basic panel of the Object Properties dialog box for the HardFX option, you can specify a Piece Mode. The options are 1Piece, which makes the entire object act as a single piece; Parts, which computes each object separately; and two options to convert a single piece to parts when a collision or an event takes place.

FIGURE 11.4
Force panel for HardFX

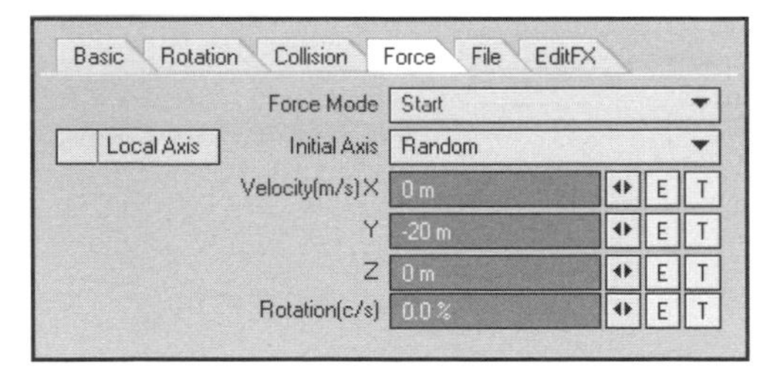

FIGURE 11.5
File panel for HardFX

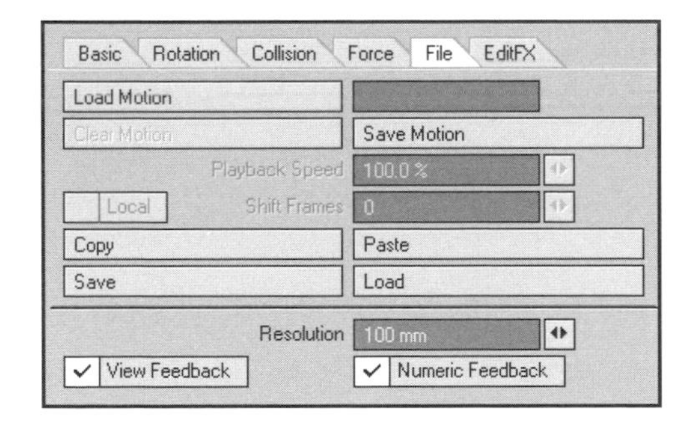

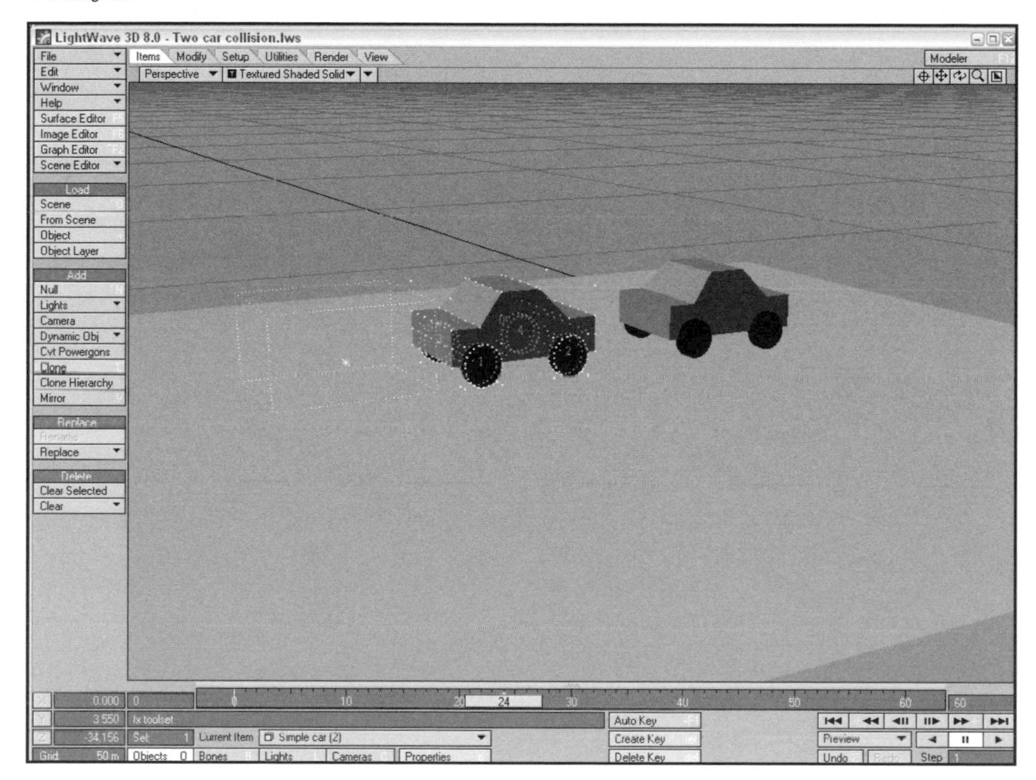

FIGURE 11.6
Colliding cars

Simulate hard-body dynamics

1. Click the File, Load, Load Scene menu command and open the Two cars.lws file.
2. Select one of the car objects, and then open its Object Properties dialog box. Click the Dynamics tab and select the Hard option from the Add Dynamic drop-down list. Click the HardFX option to access its properties.
3. In the Basic panel, select the 1piece option in the Piece Mode drop-down list, set the Weight value to 20, and the Gravity value to –0.01. In the Collision panel, set the Interaction method to Box. In the Force panel, set the Velocity for the Z-axis to 20. Repeat steps 2 and 3 for the other car, but make the Velocity value –20. Also, set the Piece Mode for one of the cars to 1 Piece>Parts (collision).
4. After setting all the properties, click the Calculate button in the Object Properties dialog box.

   The cars are animated moving toward each other and colliding, as shown in Figure 11.6.
5. Select the File, Save, Save Scene As menu command and save the file as Two car collision.lws.

Break into pieces

1. Click the File, Load, Load Scene menu command and open the Eggs.lws file.
2. Select the top set of eggs, and then open its Object Properties dialog box. Click the Dynamics tab and select the Hard option from the Add Dynamic drop-down list. Click the HardFX option to access its properties.

3. In the Basic panel, select the Parts option in the Piece Mode drop-down list, set the Weight value to 20, and the Gravity value to -15. In the Collision panel, set the Interaction method to Box. Repeat steps 2 and 3 for the other set of eggs, but make the Velocity value 0.01.
4. Select the Dozen eggs (1) object from the Current Object list at the top of the Object Properties dialog box. Then repeat steps 2 and 3 for the other set of eggs, but make the Velocity value 0.01.
5. After setting all the properties, click the Calculate button In the Object Properties dialog box.

   The top set of eggs are animated descending toward the second set and when they collide, all the eggs are scattered into pieces, as shown in Figure 11.7.
6. Select the File, Save, Save Scene As menu command and save the file as Egg collision into pieces.lws.

FIGURE 11.7
Eggs breaking into pieces

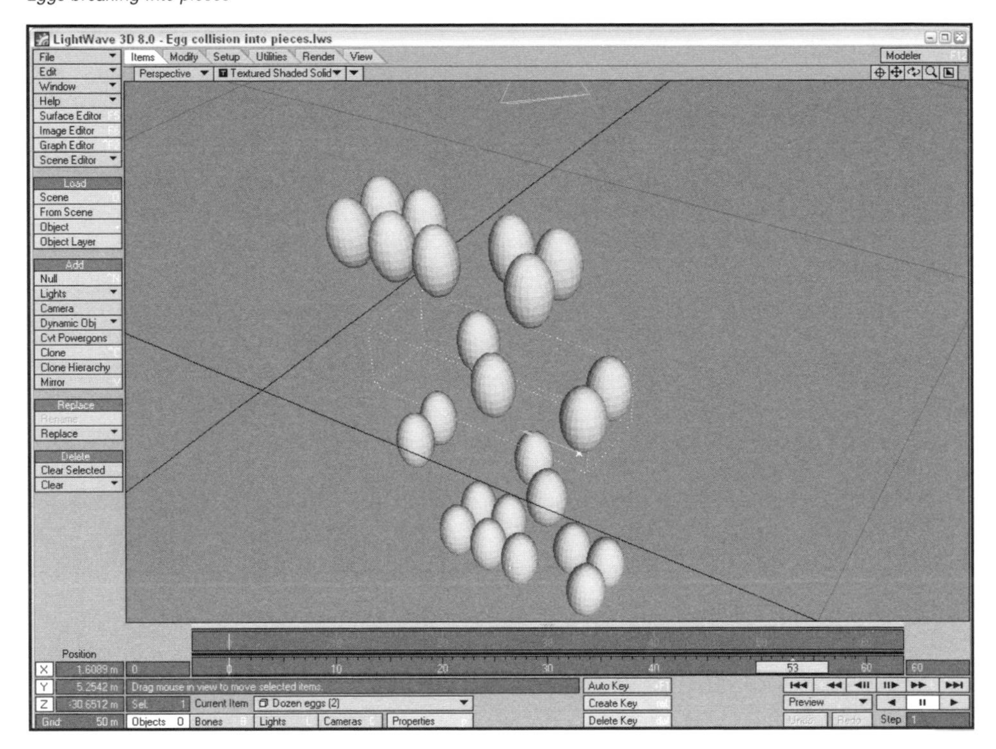

LESSON 2

CREATE SOFT-BODY OBJECTS

What You'll Do

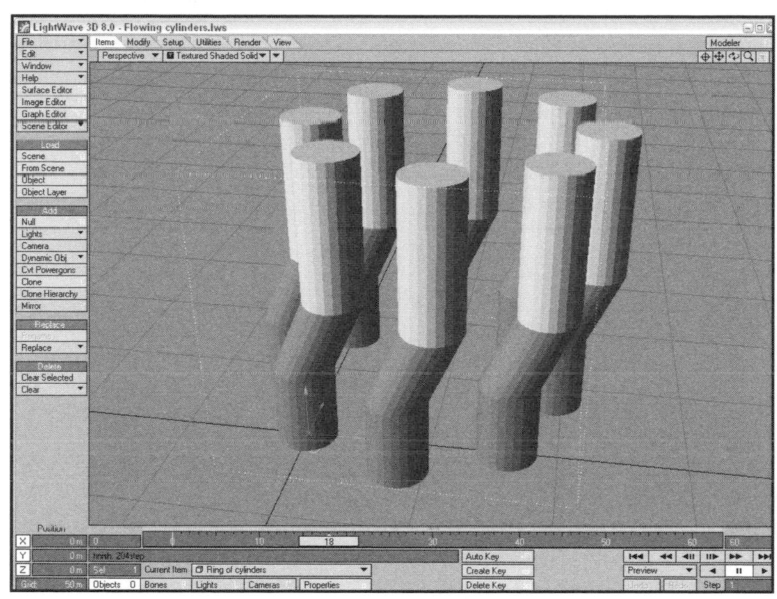

In this lesson, you'll learn how to create dynamic soft-body objects.

Soft-body objects are objects that are the opposite of hard-body objects. Soft-body objects easily give way to other objects such as a pillow or a beach ball. To make the selected object a soft-body object, select the Soft option from the Add Dynamic drop-down list in the Dynamics panel of the Object Properties dialog box. When you select the SoftFX option that is added to the Dynamics list, the Object Properties dialog box expands to include several panels of settings, as shown in Figure 11.8.

FIGURE 11.8
SoftFX properties

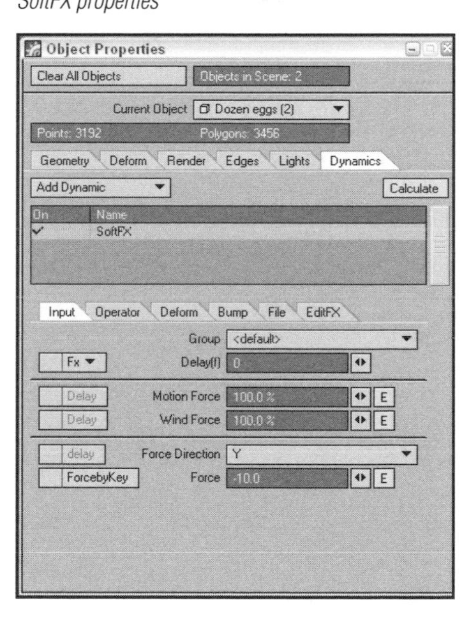

Grouping Objects

The Group field in the Input panel includes a new group option that you can use to create and name a new group of objects. All objects that you place within the designated group are isolated from all outside forces.

Specifying Soft-Body Forces

Soft-body objects can be affected by three forces: a motion force, a wind force, and a directional force. For each of these forces, you can enable a delay before the force is introduced.

Adding a Soft-Body Jiggle

In the Operator panel, shown in Figure 11.9, you can select up to two different oscillating surface motions. These secondary motions are typically used to add a jiggle effect to the soft-body object. Use the Mode list to specify how the motion is damped over time, and the Operator Map to specify the surface that receives the jiggle effect. Use the Effect Size, Wave Cycle, and Wave Size values to set the characteristics of the secondary motion shown in a graph to the left.

Enabling Collisions

In the Deform panel, shown in Figure 11.10, you can select which surfaces are used to detect collisions. The Collision Size value determines the amount of impact the collision has on the soft-body object.

Defining Stretching

In the Bump panel, shown in Figure 11.11, you can select which surfaces are deformed with a bump when collisions occur. The Compress Bump value is the amount the surface bows outward when being compressed. The Negative Bump value is the amount that the surface indents when impacted by another object. You can also control the wave propagated upon impact.

FIGURE 11.9
Operator panel for SoftFX

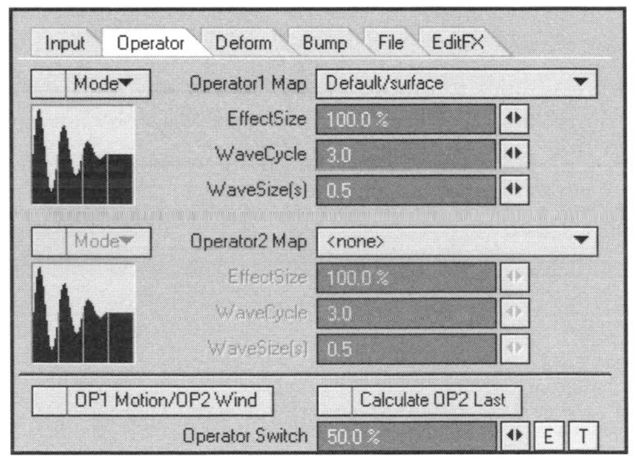

FIGURE 11.10
Deform panel for SoftFX

FIGURE 11.11
Bump panel for SoftFX

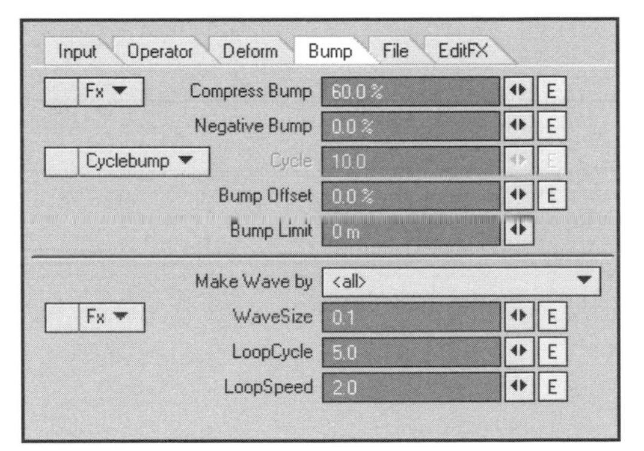

FIGURE 11.12
Soft-body cylinders

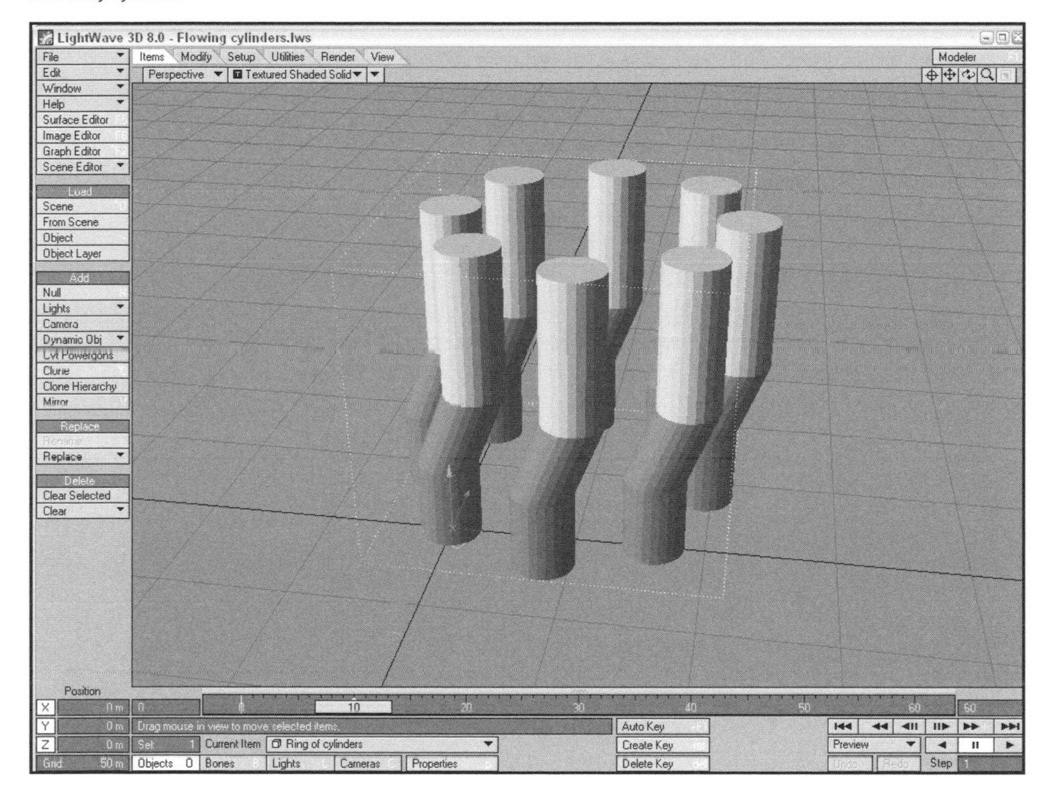

Simulate soft-body dynamics

1. Click the File, Load, Load Scene menu command and open the Ring of cylinders.lws file.
2. Select the cylinder objects, and then open its Object Properties dialog box. Click the Dynamics tab and select the Soft option from the Add Dynamic drop-down list. Click the SoftFX option to access its properties.
3. In the Input panel, select the X-axis Force Direction and set the Force value to 10. Then, in the Operator panel, select the Top half surface for the Operator1 Map setting.
4. After setting all the properties, click the Calculate button in the Object Properties dialog box.

   The top half of the cylinders are animated jiggling relative to their lower half, as shown in Figure 11.12.
5. Select the File, Save, Save Scene As menu command and save the file as Flowing cylinders.lws.

LESSON 3

CREATE A CLOTH OBJECT

What You'll Do

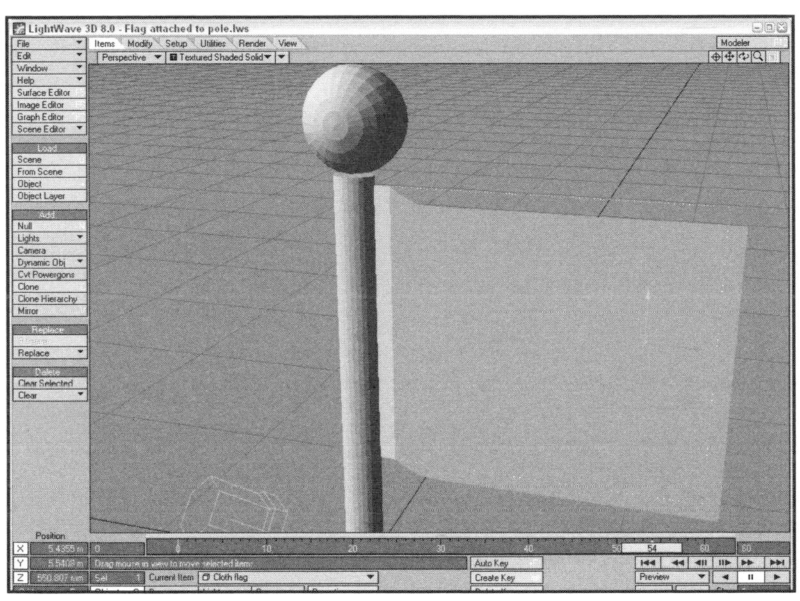

In this lesson, you'll learn how to create dynamic cloth objects.

Cloth objects conform to any surface they collide with, such as a shirt or a flag. They are also easily affected by forces such as wind and gravity. To make the selected object a Cloth object, select the Cloth option from the Add Dynamic drop-down list in the Dynamics panel of the Object Properties dialog box. When you select the ClothFX option that is added to the Dynamics list, the Object Properties dialog box expands to include several panels of settings, as shown in Figure 11.13.

FIGURE 11.13
ClothFX properties

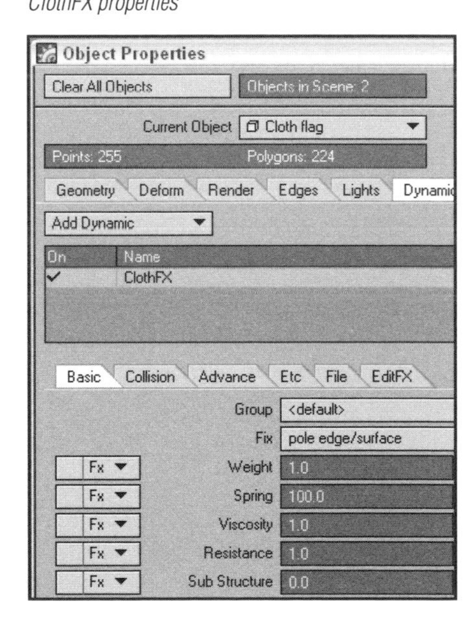

Making an Edge Immovable

From the Basic panel, you specify that a single surface is fixed by selecting it from the Fix drop-down list. This causes the fixed surface to remain unchanged as the dynamics are calculated. Figure 11.14 shows a flag object with a fixed left surface. Notice how the rest of the flag is deforming, but the fixed edge remains intact.

Making the Cloth Stiffer

The property that controls the cloth's stiffness is the Viscosity setting. By increasing this value, you can make the cloth resist some collisions with objects. 2D objects typically work best for simulating cloth, but you can also make a cloth act like a 3D object with some thickness, and thereby increase its stiffness, by increasing the Sub Structure value.

Enabling Collisions

From the Collision panel, shown in Figure 11.15, you can select a single surface to be involved in collisions, an exclusive object for all collisions, and the surfaces that are involved in interactions. Objects colliding with cloth objects can sometimes penetrate the cloth object, so you might want to use the Collision Offset value to define a distance between the cloth and the colliding object that prevents penetration. You can also specify that the cloth object checks for self collisions, and specify whether a surface is double sided.

FIGURE 11.14
Fixed cloth edge

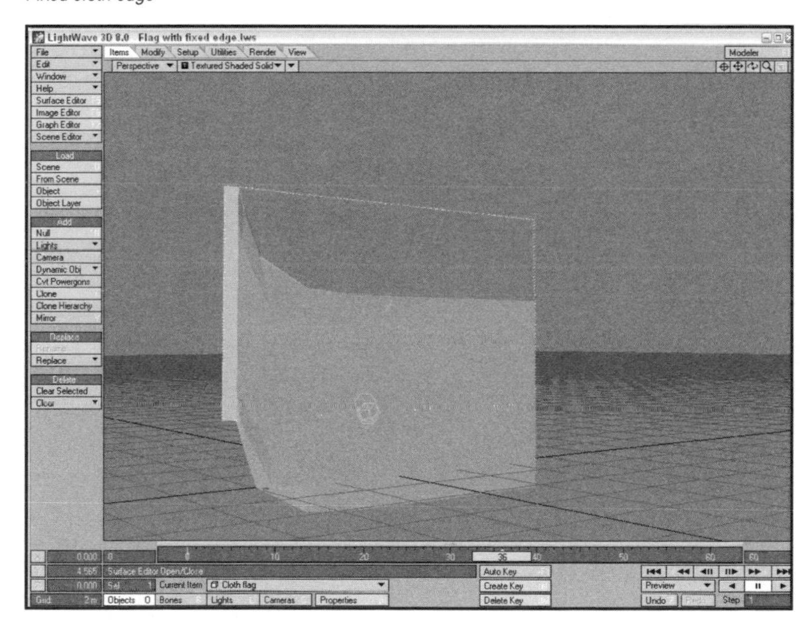

FIGURE 11.15
Collision panel for ClothFX

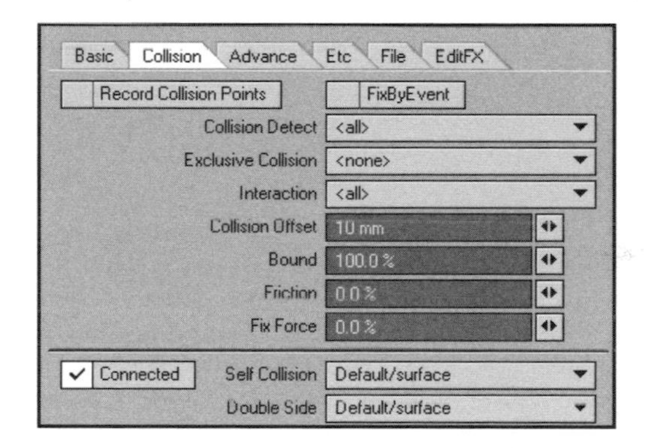

Controlling Stretching

From the Advance panel, shown in Figure 11.16, you can set the Stretch Limit value. A value of 100% allows the cloth object to stretch as it is moved by forces. Lowering this value decreases the amount of stretch for the cloth.

FIGURE 11.16
Advance panel for ClothFX

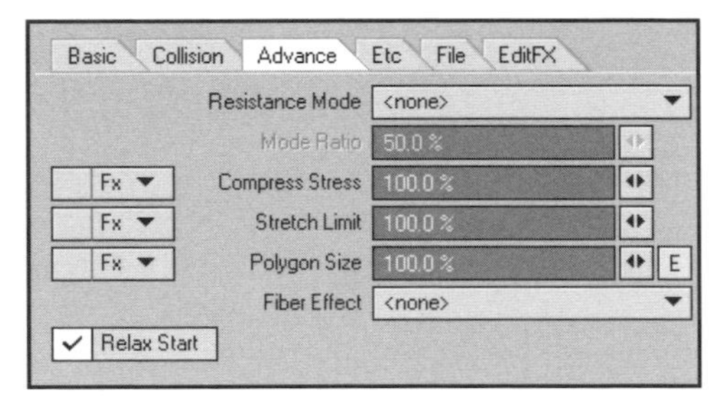

Applying Forces to Cloth

Use the Etc panel, shown in Figure 11.17, to add Gravity forces to the cloth object along any axis. This panel also includes several cloth presets that you can select including Cotton (both thin and thick), Silk, Rubber, and Jelly.

FIGURE 11.17
Etc panel for ClothFX

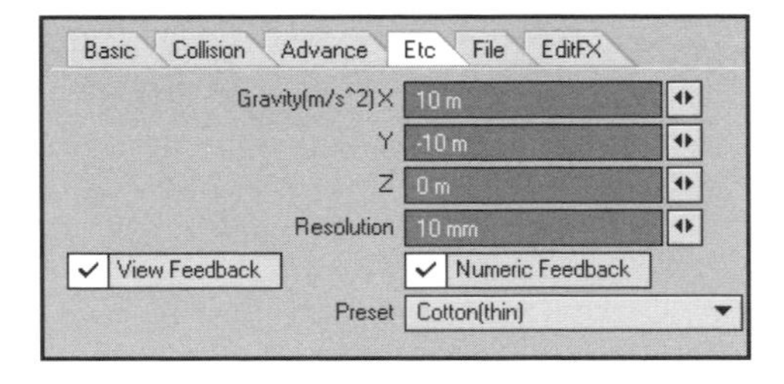

FIGURE 11.18
Flag attached to pole

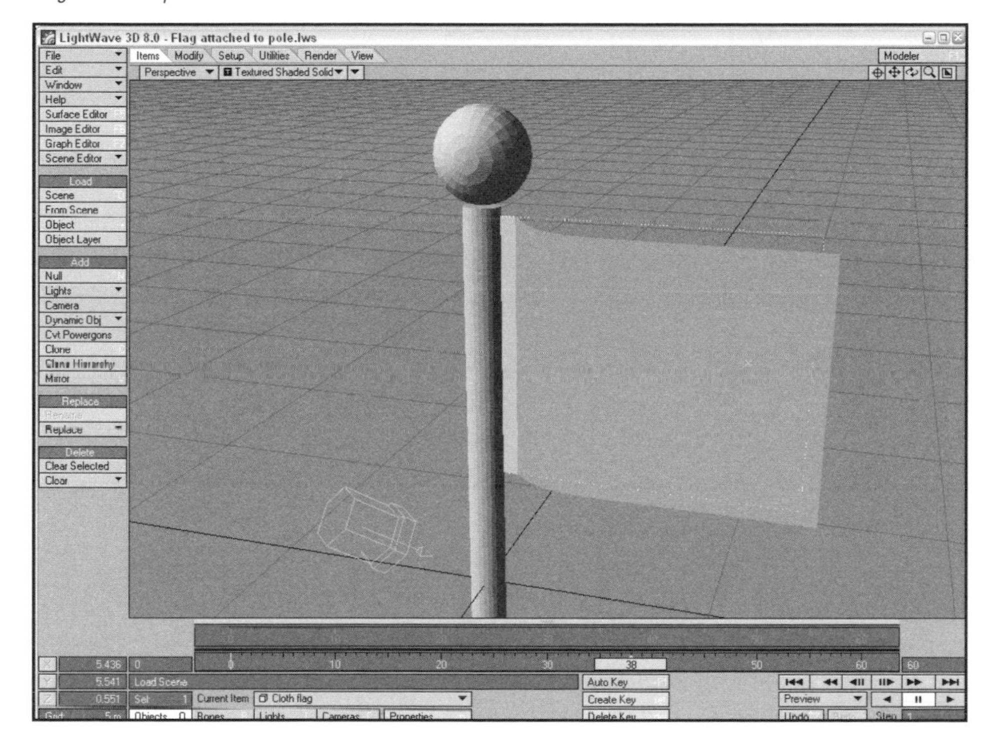

Simulate cloth dynamics

1. Click the File, Load, Load Object menu command and open the Cloth flag.lwo and the Flag pole.lwo files.
2. Select and move the flag object to be aligned with the pole. When it is in place, click the Create Key button at the bottom of the interface. Then click OK in the Create Motion Key dialog box.
3. With the flag object selected, open the Object Properties dialog box. Click the Dynamics tab and select the Cloth option from the Add Dynamic drop-down list. Click the ClothFX option to access its properties.
4. Select the Pole edge surface from the Fix drop-down list in the Basic panel. Set the Hold Structure value to 100.
5. Click the Etc tab and set the Gravity for the X-axis to 10 and the Gravity for the Y-axis to –10.
6. Click the Calculate button to see the dynamic animation.

   The flag stretches slightly under the gravity forces and waves, as shown in Figure 11.18.
7. Select the File, Save, Save Scene As menu command and save the file as Flag on pole.lws.

LESSON 4

CREATE A PARTICLE EMITTER

What You'll Do

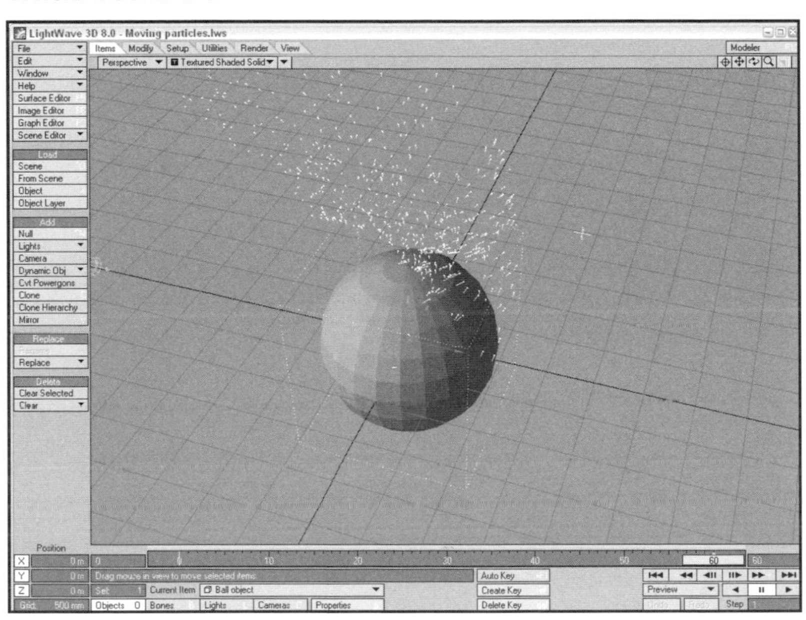

In this lesson, you'll learn how to create particle emitter objects.

Particle emitters are objects that disperse small groups of particles into the scene. You can use these to simulate dust, smoke, or swarms of insects. To make the selected object a Particle Emitter object, select the Emitter option from the Add Dynamic drop-down list in the Dynamics panel of the Object Properties dialog box. When you select the FX Emitter option that is added to the Dynamics list, the Object Properties dialog box expands to include several panels of settings, as shown in Figure 11.19.

FIGURE 11.19
FX Emitter properties

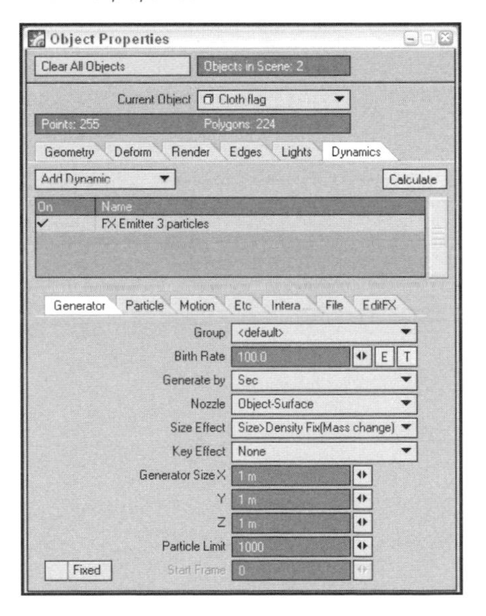

Setting the Number of Particles

The Generator panel includes a **Birth Rate** value, which is the number of particles generated at the designated time specified in the Generate By drop-down list. The options are Frame, Sec, Speed, Collision Event, Wind, and Wind Speed. For example, if you selected a Birth Rate of 10 and a Generate By option of Collision Event, 10 new particles would be created every time a collision occurred.

Using an Object as an Emitter

Using the Nozzle options, standard emitters can emit particles from with an object using the shape of a box, sphere, or cone. However, if you select the Emitter option from the Add Dynamic list for the selected object, you can select the Object Vertices, Object Normal, and Object Surface options from the Nozzle drop-down list. The Generator panel also includes values for setting the Generator's size and a limit to the number of particles it can emit. Figure 11.20 shows the spikey ball used as an emitter, with particles all over its surface.

NOTE

Emitters can also be created by selecting the Dynamic Objects, Particle menu command from the Add section of the Items tab.

FIGURE 11.20
Any object can be an emitter

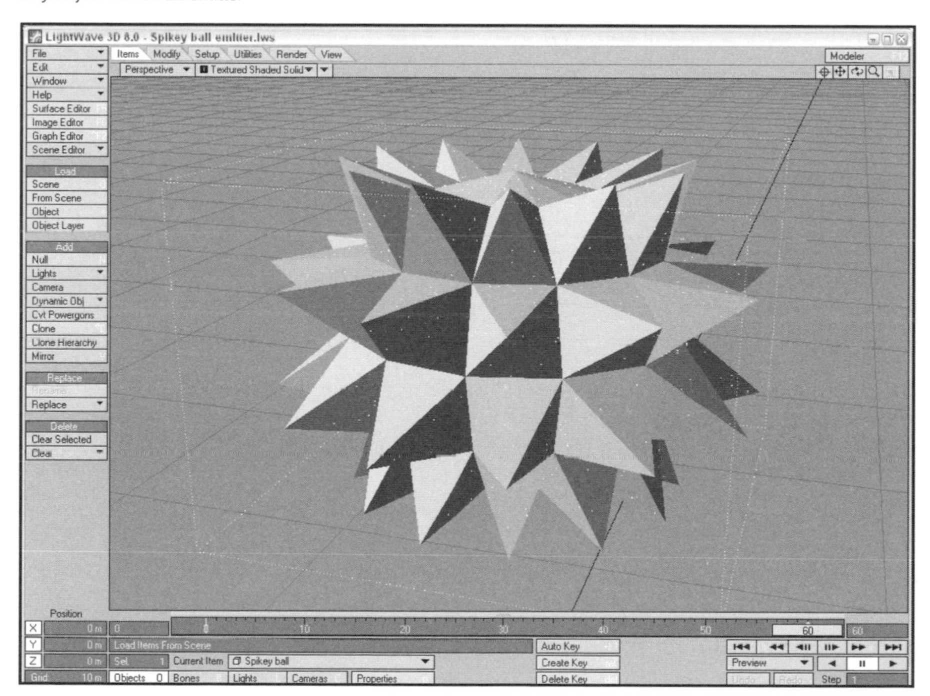

Setting Particle Properties

The Particle panel, shown in Figure 11.21, includes values for setting the particle's Weight, Size, Resistance, and Life Time. Under each of these values is a +/– value that you can use to set the variance of the particles about the designated value.

Setting Particle Motion

The Motion panel, shown in Figure 11.22, includes settings for controlling the direction and speed that the particles move. You can also select a specific object as a target that the particles will move toward within a given threshold. Using the Explosion value causes all particles to move away from the center as if an explosion occurred within the center. You can use the Vibration settings to add some randomness to the particle's motion. Another way to add motion is to enable the Gravity settings in the Etc panel.

FIGURE 11.21
Particle panel for FX Emitter

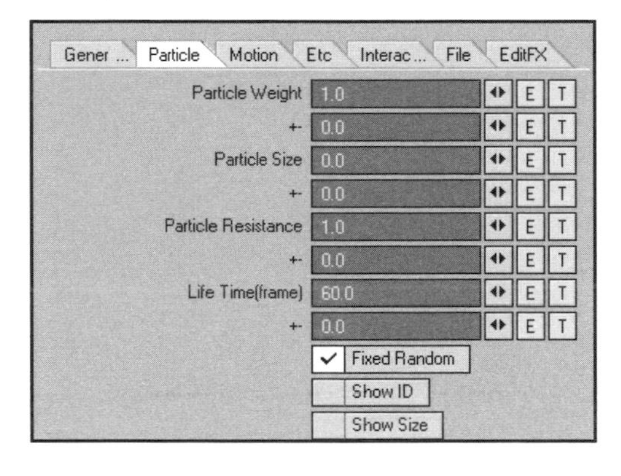

FIGURE 11.22
Motion panel for FX Emitter

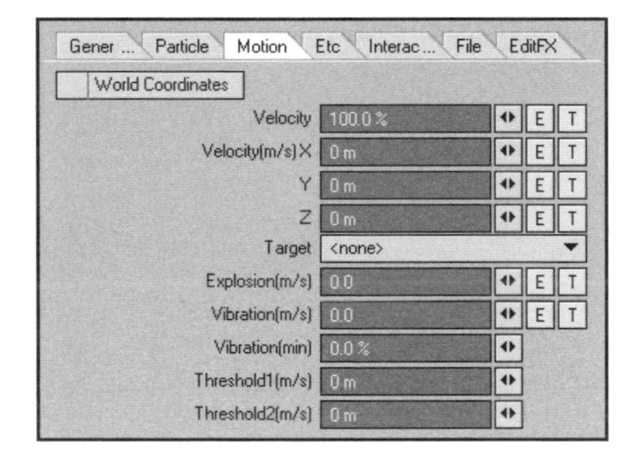

Enabling Particle Interactions

The Interaction panel, shown in Figure 11.23, includes settings for controlling how particles act when they collide with particles from the same emitter and how they react to collisions from another emitter. The options for both of these settings include None, Push, Bounce, Drag, Viscosity, and Crowd. Use the Force setting to specify the strength of the collision impact. In order for interactions to work, you need to enable the Detect Interaction option.

FIGURE 11.23
Interaction panel for FX Emitter

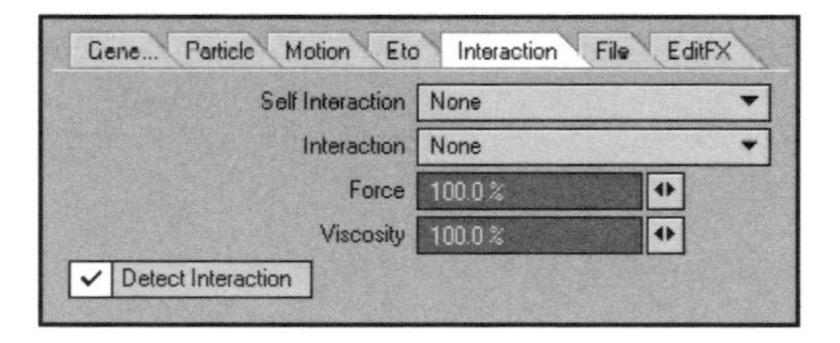

Create a particle emitter

1. Click the File, Load, Load Object menu command and open the Ball object.lwo file.
2. Select the Items tab and click on the Null button in the Add section. Position the Null object above the sphere object and press the Enter key to create an animation key. Then drag the Time Line to the end frame, move the Null object to the right, and create another key.
3. Select the ball object, and then open its Object Properties dialog box. Click the Dynamics tab and select the Emitter option from the Add Dynamic drop-down list. Click the FX Emitter option to access its properties.
4. In the Generator panel, set the Birth Rate to 10, the Generate By option to Frame, and the Nozzle option to Object-Surface.
5. In the Motion panel, set the Velocity value to 300% and the Null object as the Target option.
6. Click the Calculate button to see the dynamic animation.

   The particles are created on the surface of the sphere and immediately move toward the moving Null object, as shown in Figure 11.24.
7. Select the File, Save, Save Scene As menu command and save the file as Moving particles.lws.

FIGURE 11.24
Moving particles

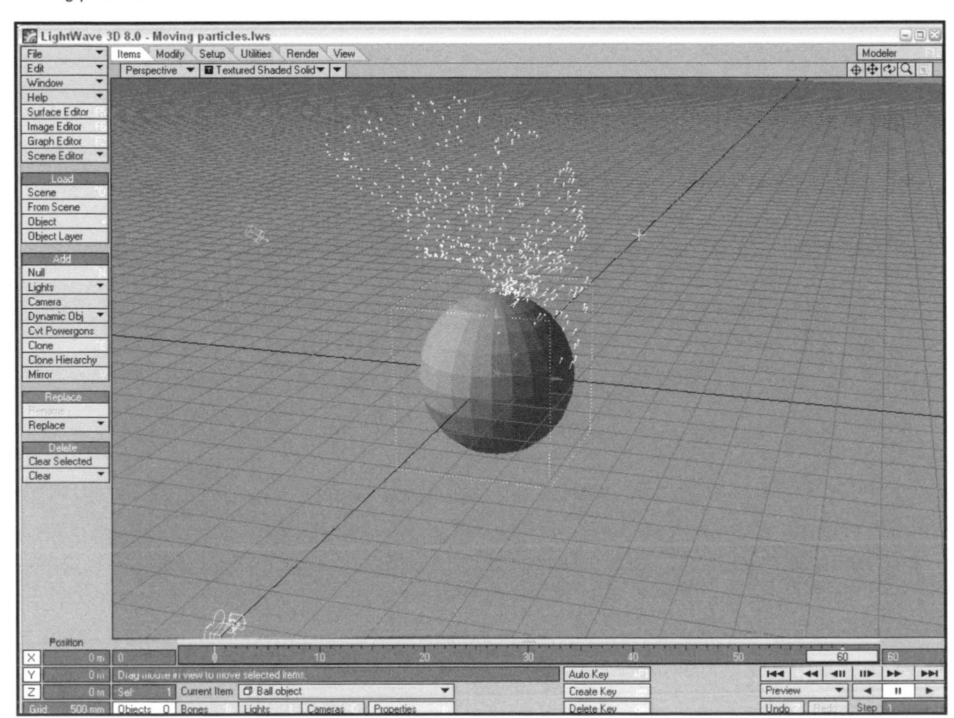

CHAPTER SUMMARY

This chapter explained how to use dynamics to automatically generate animation keys. Dynamics enables objects to be defined as hard-body objects, soft-body objects, cloth objects, and particle emitters. These objects can also interact with forces such as wind and gravity. These dynamic properties are defined in the Object Properties dialog box.

What You Have Learned

- How to create a hard-body object that reacts to gravity, forces, and collisions.
- How objects can break into pieces upon impact.
- How to create a soft-body object with specified jiggle vibrations and stretching.
- How to create a cloth object with an immovable edge.
- How to create a particle emitter using an object as an emitter.
- How to define particle motion and interactions.

Key Terms from This Chapter

- **dynamics.** The study of the motion of objects and how they interact with each other during collisions.
- **hard-body objects.** Objects that are defined as being rigid and inflexible.
- **soft-body objects.** Objects that are defined as being flexible and easily deformed.
- **cloth objects.** Objects that conform to the surface of the object that they collide with.
- **particle emitter.** An object that gradually emits small particle objects into the scene.
- **particles.** A set of small objects that act together as a group to represent smoke, dust, and other effects.
- **Birth Rate value.** The rate at which new particles are created.

CHAPTER 16

RENDERING THE SCENE

1. Add backdrop options.
2. Add fog effects.
3. Work with HyperVoxels.
4. Render scenes.

CHAPTER 12

RENDERING THE SCENE

The final step in the 3D creation process is **rendering**. In this step, you instruct the software to calculate all the light, texture, geometry, and scene settings to produce the final image or animation. You can configure the rendering process to change the final look of the output.

You can add several effects to a scene that aren't visible until you render the scene. These effects include backdrops, fog, and **HyperVoxels**. Backdrops are colors and images that appear behind the rendered scene. Backdrops can be simple solid colors, a gradient that resembles the ground and the sky, or a complex image including clouds that is automatically generated using the **SkyTracer2** plug-in.

Volumetric effects such as fog and HyperVoxels are useful for adding depth and variation to a scene. You can create several different types of fog, including a layered **ground fog** effect. HyperVoxels are volume objects that have a texture applied to them. You can use these volumes to affect the surface or create a sprite. HyperVoxels are useful for creating gaseous effects like fire, smoke, and clouds.

The Render tab includes several different options for rendering, saving, and previewing both images and animations.

Tools You'll Use

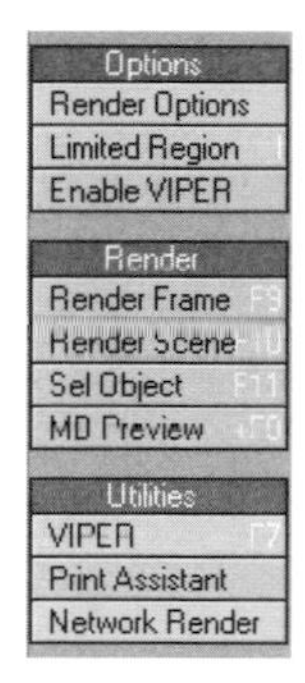

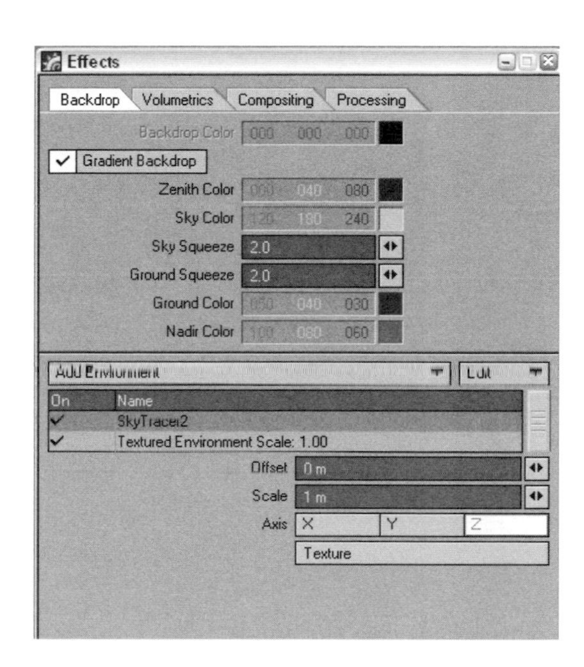

LESSON 1

ADD BACKDROP OPTIONS

What You'll Do

In this lesson, you'll learn how to add backdrop gradients and images to the scene.

The backdrop for the rendered scene can contain objects, a solid color, a gradient, or an image. LightWave also includes several **environment plug-ins** that you can use to create some unique backdrops. All backdrop options are set in the Backdrop panel of the Effects dialog box, shown in Figure 12.1. To access this panel, click the Window, Backdrop Options menu command.

FIGURE 12.1

Backdrop panel of the Effects dialog box

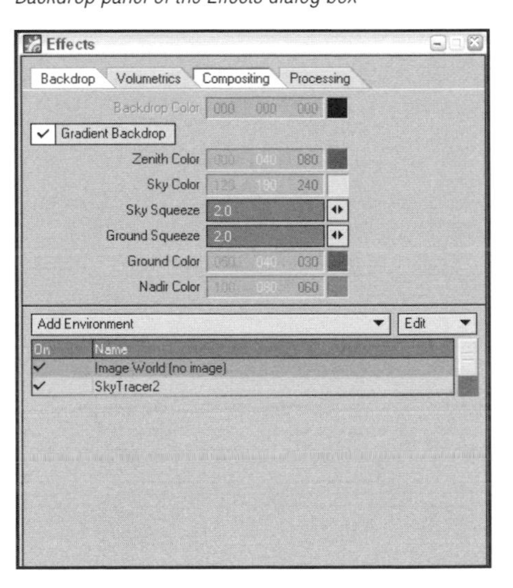

Changing the Background Color

The RGB color values for the backdrop color, along with a color swatch, are located at the top of the Backdrop panel. To change the color values, drag on the RGB values or access a color selector (shown in Figure 12.2) by clicking the color swatch. You can change color values to any value between 0 and 255.

NOTE

The new backdrop color is only visible when the scene is rendered.

Enabling a Gradient Backdrop

If you enable the Gradient Backdrop option in the Backdrop panel, several additional color settings are available. These settings include Zenith, Sky, Ground, and Nadir colors, and Sky and Ground Squeeze values. The Squeeze value determines how quickly the gradient shifts between the sky and zenith colors, and the ground and nadir colors. Figure 12.3 shows a rendered frame with the default gradient backdrop colors.

Using Environment Plug-Ins

Clicking the Add Environment button to choose from several plug-in options. The selected option appears in the Environment list and you can enable and disable it by clicking the check mark to the left of the plug-in name. If you select a listed plug-in, you can open its properties, or copy, paste, or remove it from the Edit drop-down list.

TIP

You can also open the properties for the selected environment plug-in by double-clicking on its name.

FIGURE 12.2
Color selector

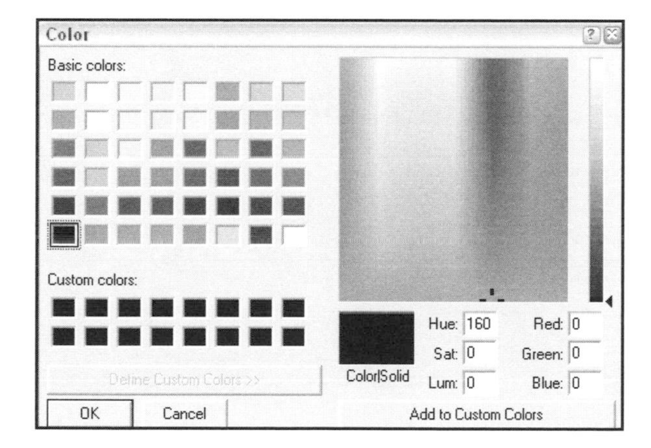

FIGURE 12.3
Gradient backdrop

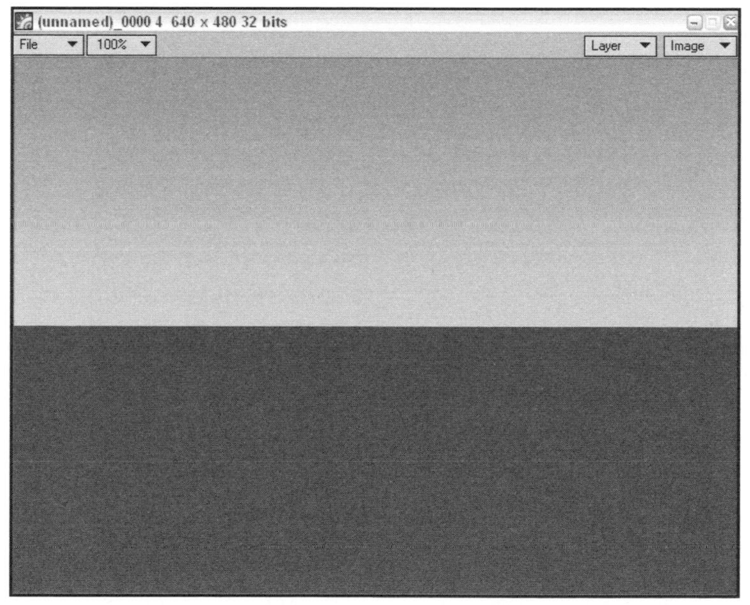

Adding a Textured Backdrop

The Textured Environment plug-in properties includes a Texture button. Clicking this button opens the Texture Editor, where you can specify a texture to use as the backdrop. You can also specify Offset and Scale values to help you position the texture. Figure 12.4 shows a rendered frame that includes a backdrop image.

Using the SkyTracer2 Plug-In

Use the SkyTracer2 environment plug-in to create a backdrop that includes atmospheric effects such as haze, clouds, and sun. The SkyTracer2 properties dialog box, shown in Figure 12.5, includes separate panels for Atmosphere, Clouds, and Suns. Figure 12.6 shows an example of what is possible with the SkyTracer2 plug-in.

FIGURE 12.4
Texture backdrop

FIGURE 12.5
SkyTracer2 properties

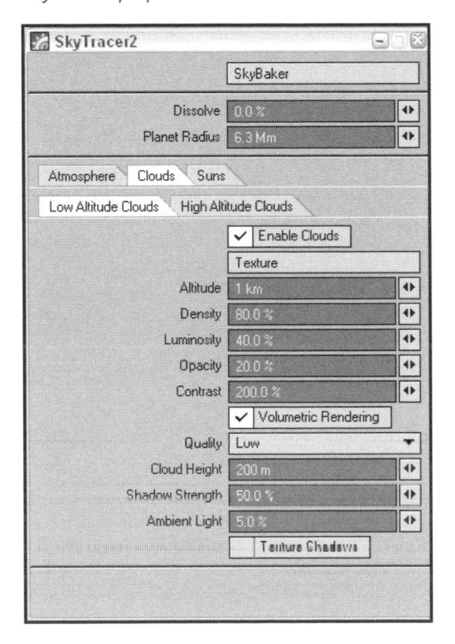

Using the Background Booster

If opening the Effects dialog box just to change the backdrop color or the backdrop gradient colors is a pain, use the Background Booster dialog box, shown in Figure 12.7. To open this dialog box, use the Window, Background Booster menu command. The Background Booster dialog box lists the current backdrop colors. To change all three RGB values at once, use the Boost value.

FIGURE 12.6
SkyTracer2 backdrop

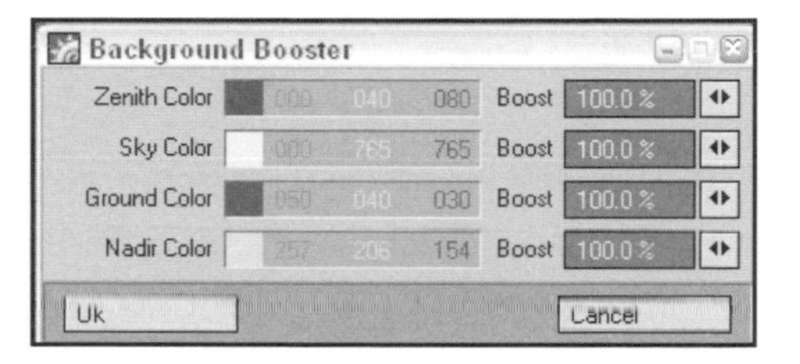

FIGURE 12.7
Background Booster dialog box

Add a SkyTracer2 backdrop

1. Click the File, Load, Load Scene menu command and open the Playground.lws file.
2. Select the Window, Backdrop Options menu command.

   The Effects dialog box opens with the Backdrop panel selected.
3. Click the Add Environment drop-down list and select the SkyTracer2 option.
4. Double-click on the SkyTracer2 option to open its properties dialog box. Select the Clouds tab and enable the Enable Clouds and Volumetric Rendering options.
5. Back in the main interface, click the Render tab and select the Render Frame button.

   The scene is rendered using the active camera including the SkyTracer2 backdrop, as shown in Figure 12.8.
6. Select the File, Save, Save Scene As menu command and save the file as Playground with SkyTracer2 backdrop.lws.

FIGURE 12.8
Playground with SkyTracer2 backdrop

LESSON 2

ADD FOG EFFECTS

What You'll Do

In this lesson, you'll learn how to add fog effects to the scene.

A volumetric effect is a special effect that is added during the rendering process involving a volume of space that changes the look and color of objects in the scene. Fog is a good example of a volumetric effect. Using the Volumetrics panel in the Effects dialog box, shown in Figure 12.9, you can add effects such as fog and other **volumetric plug-ins.** To access the Volumetrics panel, select the Window, Volumetrics and Fog Options menu command.

FIGURE 12.9

Volumetrics panel for the Effects dialog box

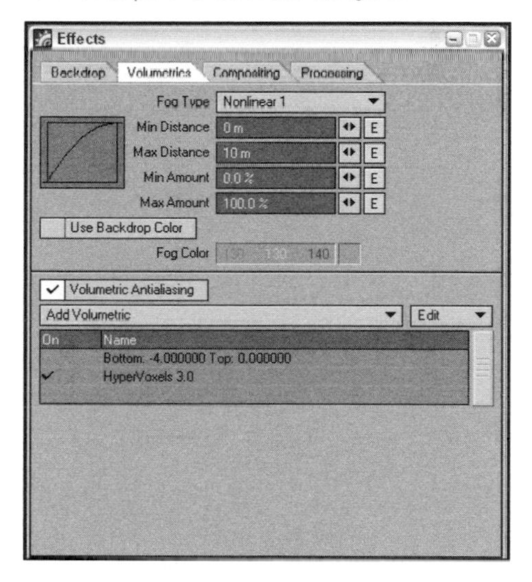

Adding Fog

Using the Volumetrics panel, you can add fog to the scene. From the Fog Type drop-down list, you can select from Off, Linear, and two Nonlinear fog types. You can use the Min and Max Distance values to specify where the fog is located from the camera, and the Min and Max Amount values to set the fog density. Note that the fog doesn't affect the backdrop, only the objects in the scene. In Figure 12.10, notice how the objects farther away from the camera are covered with fog.

Using Volumetric Plug-Ins

You can click the Add Volumetric button to choose from several plug-in options. The selected option appears in the Volumetric list and you can enable and disable it by clicking the check mark to the left of the plug-in name. If you select a listed plug-in, you can view its properties, or copy, paste, or remove the plug-in from the Edit drop-down list.

> **TIP**
>
> You can also open the properties for the selected environment plug-in by double-clicking its name.

FIGURE 12.10
Fog effect

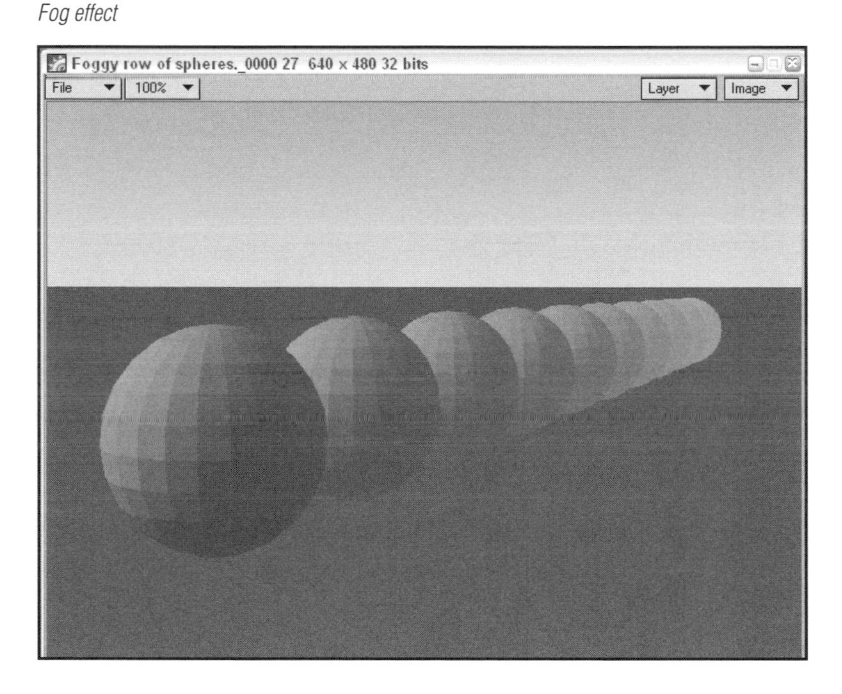

FIGURE 12.11
Ground fog properties

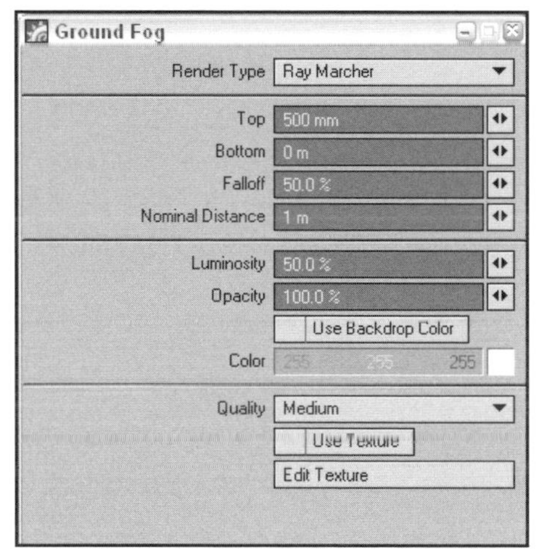

Adding Ground Fog

Use the Ground Fog plug-in to create a layer of fog that covers scene objects. Using the Ground Fog properties dialog box, shown in Figure 12.11, you can select precise location values for the top and bottom of the fog layer, and its Luminosity and Opacity. If the Use Backdrop Color option is disabled, you can select a fog color. For the Render Type option, you can select Fast Fog or Ray Marcher. Fast Fog renders quickly, but the Ray Marcher option is much more accurate. Using the Ray Marcher option, you can also apply textures to the fog. Figure 12.12 shows some ground fog added to the line of sphere objects.

FIGURE 12.12
Ground fog effect

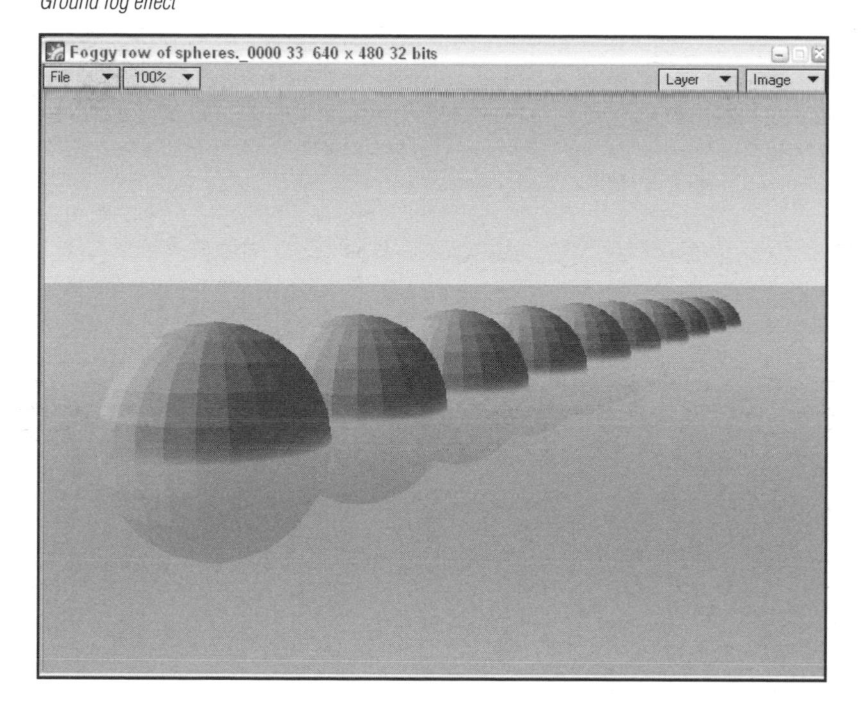

Add ground fog

1. Click the File, Load, Load Scene menu command and open the Playground.lws file.
2. Select the Window, Volumetrics and Fog Options menu command.

   The Effects dialog box opens with the Volumetrics panel selected.
3. Click the Add Volumetric drop-down list and select the Ground Fog option.
4. Double-click on the Ground Fog option to open its properties dialog box. Select Ray Marcher as the Render Type, set the Top value to 1.0, and the Bottom value to–4.0. Make sure the Use Background Color option is disabled and set the fog color to white. Then set the Opacity value to 80%.
5. Back in the main interface, click the Render tab and select the Render Frame button.

   The scene is rendered using the active camera including the ground fog effect, as shown in Figure 12.13.
6. Select the File, Save, Save Scene As menu command and save the file as Playground with ground fog.lws.

FIGURE 12.13
Playground with ground fog

LESSON 3

WORK WITH HYPERVOXELS

What You'll Do

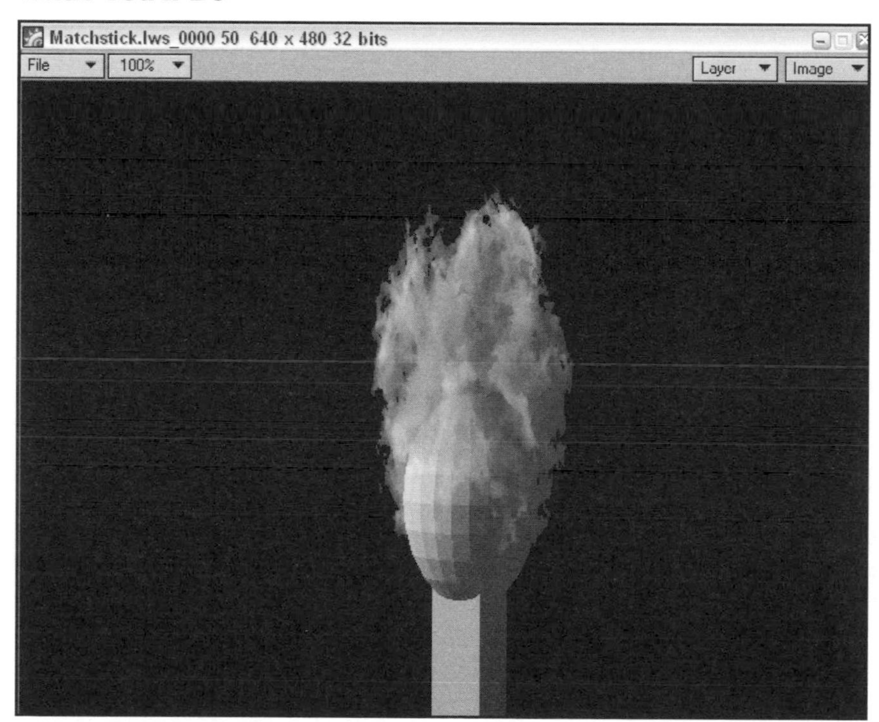

In this lesson, you'll learn how to use HyperVoxels to create effects such as fire, smoke, and clouds.

HyperVoxels provide a way to create gaseous effects such as fire, smoke, clouds, and dust. This is accomplished by rendering a volume that has a particular texture applied to it. You can apply HyperVoxels to the surface of a designated volume, as an actual three-dimensional volume or as a simple two-dimensional sprite. HyperVoxels are available as a volumetric plug-in in the Volumetrics panel of the Effects dialog box. To open this panel, use the Window, Volumetrics and Fog Options menu command.

Selecting a HyperVoxel Type

Double-clicking on the HyperVoxel 3.0 plug-in name in the Volumetrics panel opens its properties dialog box. At the top of this dialog box, you can select an object type. The options include Surface, Volume and Sprite. Selecting the Surface type applies the designated HyperTexture to the surface of the object. Selecting the Volume type renders the entire HyperVoxel as a three-dimensional object, which maintains its texture even if you move the camera to its center. Selecting the Sprite type renders the HyperVoxel as a two-dimensional, flat image. Of these types, the Volume type takes the longest to render and the Sprite type takes the least amount of time. Figure 12.14 shows three HyperVoxel objects, one of each type.

Setting the HyperVoxel Size

In the HyperVoxel 3.0 properties dialog box, shown in Figure 12.15, all the scene objects are listed in a pane to the left. To apply a HyperVoxel to an object, select the object from the list and click the Activate button. You can also apply HyperVoxels to Null objects. After you activate an object, you can set the radius of its volume in the Geometry panel using the Particle Size setting. Use the Size Variation option to specify the maximum size change that each applied HyperVoxel can be. Use the Stretch Direction options to stretch the HyperVoxel along an axis or along with the object's velocity.

FIGURE 12.14
Surface, Sprite, and Volume HyperVoxels

FIGURE 12.15
HyperVoxels properties dialog box

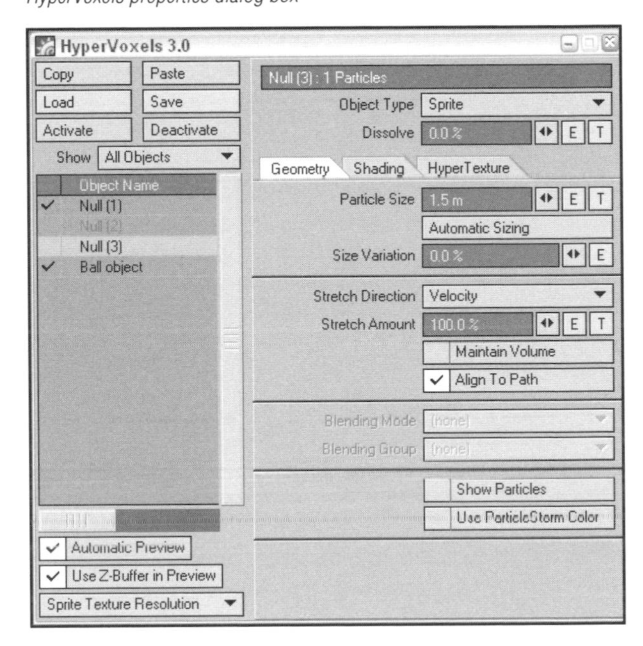

Shading the HyperVoxel

The HyperVoxel Shading panel, shown in Figure 12.16, includes many of the same settings as in the Surface Editor, including Color, Luminosity, and Transparency. The settings in this panel are different for Volume and Sprite types.

Selecting a HyperVoxel Texture

Use the HyperTexture panel, shown in Figure 12.17, to select a texture to apply to the HyperVoxel's volume. The available textures include Smoky (1–3), Turbulence, Dented, FBM, Hetero Terrain, and Hybrid Multi-fractal. A preview of the selected texture is shown in the panel and each texture has several unique settings, such as Frequencies and Contrast. For all textures, you can set a Texture Amplitude value. For Volume and Sprite types, you can select a Texture Effect to further alter the texture's placement.

FIGURE 12.16

Shading panel of the HyperVoxels properties dialog box

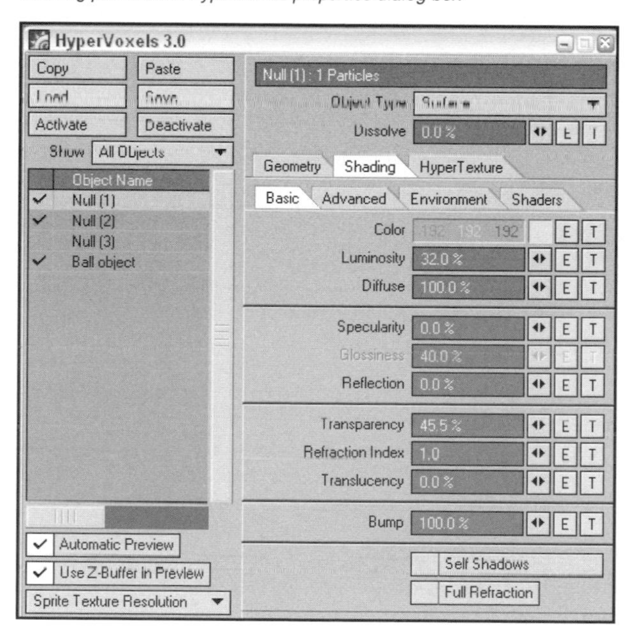

FIGURE 12.17

HyperTexture panel of the HyperVoxels properties dialog box

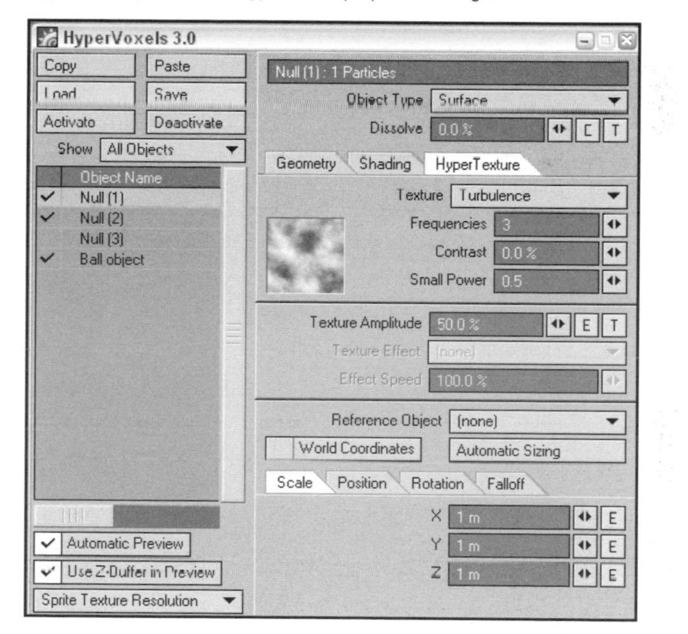

Saving HyperVoxel Settings

Buttons for loading previously saved settings and saving the current settings are located above the object list. You can also copy and paste settings between objects.

Blending HyperVoxels

If two volumes overlap, you can blend their effects using the Blending Mode settings in the Geometry panel. These options are only available for the Surface types. The Blending Mode drop-down list includes three options: Additive, Negative, and Effector.

Figure 12.18 shows three surface HyperVoxels, with the middle one being a blended version of the other two, which includes half of each surface.

FIGURE 12.18
Blended surface HyperVoxels

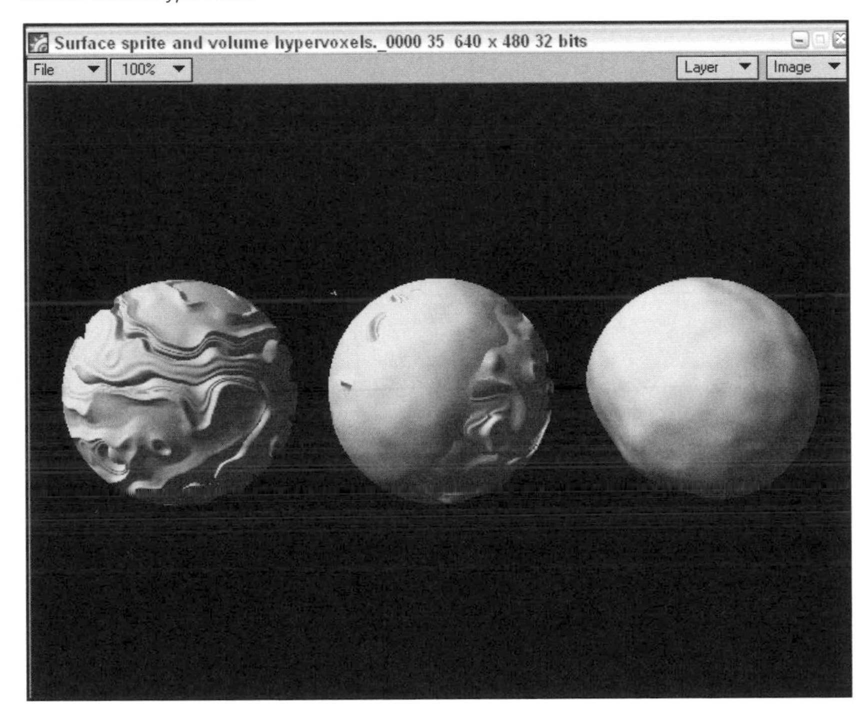

Create a HyperVoxel effect

1. Click the File, Load, Load Scene menu command and open the Matchstick.lws file.
2. Click the Items tab, and then select the Null button from the Add section. Then name the Null object and move it to the top of the matchstick object. Create a key for the Null object to make its new position permanent.
3. Select the Window, Volumetrics and Fog Options menu command. Select the HyperVoxels option from the Add Volumetric drop-down list, and then double-click it to open its properties dialog box.
4. In the HyperVoxels 3.0 dialog box, select the Null object from the object list at the left and click the Activate button. Select the Volume type from the Object Type drop-down list. Set the Particle Size to 5, and the Stretch Direction to the Y-axis with a Stretch Amount of 200%.
5. Click the Shading tab and select the Texture icon for the Color property.

   The Texture Editor opens.
6. In the Texture Editor, select Gradient as the Layer Type. Then click on the Color swatch for the existing marker and change the color to red. Then click halfway down the gradient ramp and change its color to orange. Finally, click at the bottom of the gradient ramp and change its color to yellow to create a gradient that rises from yellow to orange to red. Click the Use Texture button.
7. Back in the HyperVoxels 3.0 dialog box, click the HyperTexture tab and select the Turbulence texture.
8. From the main interface, click the Render tab and select the Render Frame button.

   The scene is rendered using the active camera showing the HyperVoxel, as shown in Figure 12.19.
9. Select the File, Save, Save Scene As menu command and save the file as Matchstick on fire.lws.

FIGURE 12.19
HyperVoxel fire

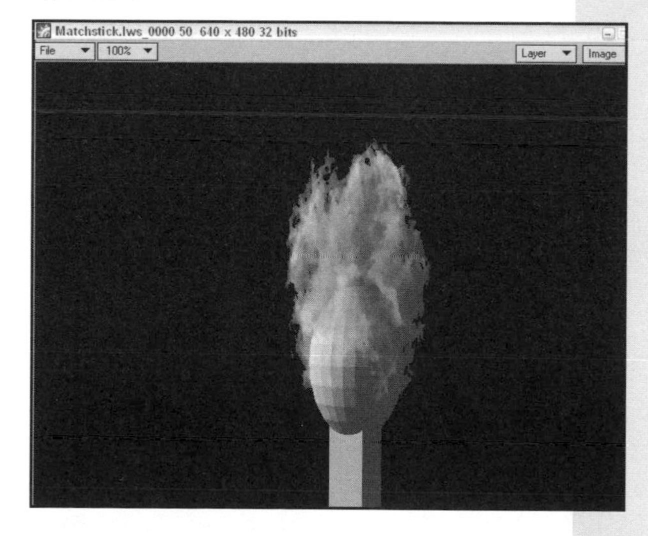

LESSON 4

What You'll Do

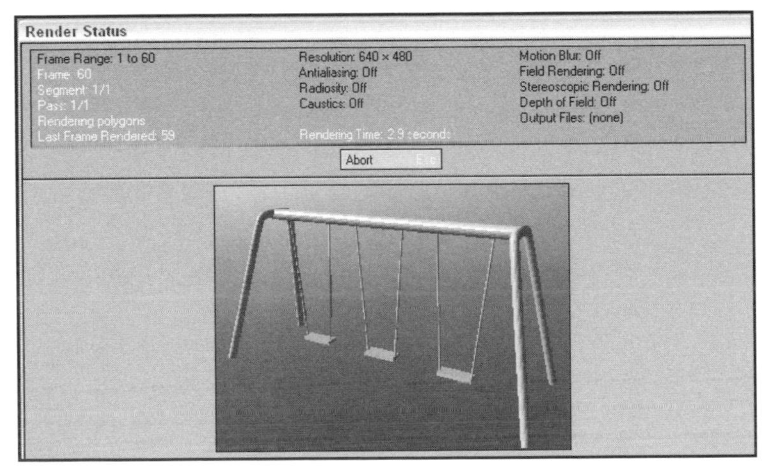

In this lesson, you'll learn how to render images and animations.

The Render tab includes buttons for rendering a single frame or rendering an entire animated sequence. You can also open the Render Options dialog box to change specific settings such as saving the rendered file.

Setting Rendering Options

To set the quality of the final rendered image, use the Render Options dialog box, shown in Figure 12.20. You can open this dialog box by clicking the Render Options button in the Options section of the Render tab. Depending on the options you set and the complexity of the scene, the amount of time it takes to render a scene can vary widely. The Render Options dialog box

FIGURE 12.20
Render Options dialog box

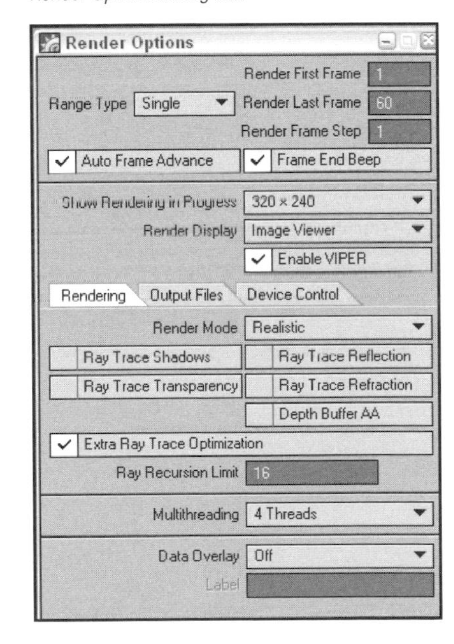

includes a Render Mode drop-down list with Wireframe, Quickshade, and Realistic options. These options provide a way to render the scene quickly. The Output Files panel includes options for saving an animation file, a rendered RGB image, or the scene's Alpha File.

Rendering an Image

To render an image, select the specific frame that you want to render and click the Render Frame button in the Render tab. This opens the Render Status dialog box, shown in Figure 12.21, which lists all the information about the current image and shows the image as the rendering progresses. You can abort the rendering process at any time by pressing Esc. When the image finishes rendering, the final image is displayed in the **Image Viewer**,

FIGURE 12.21
Render Status dialog box

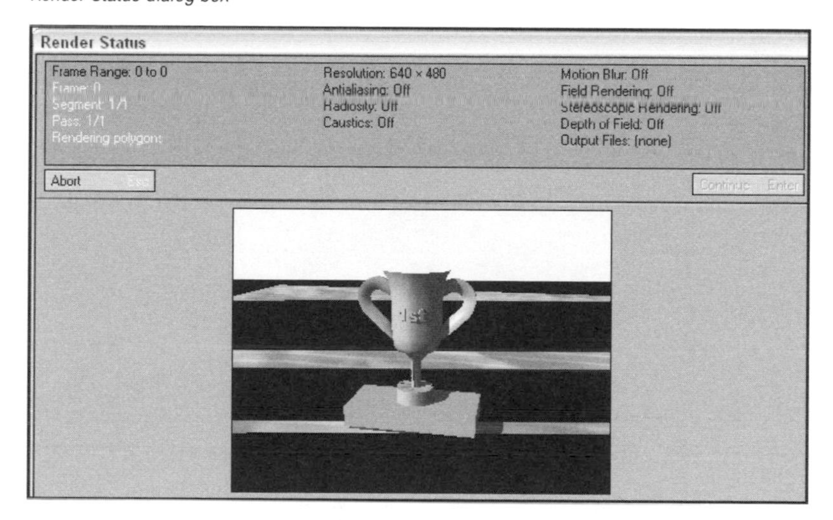

shown in Figure 12.22. Using the Image Viewer, you can save the current image, view the image at different percentages, or view the image's alpha channel.

Rendering a Limited Region

If your scene is complex and takes a long time to render, it can take a long time to check any small changes you make. If you only need to see a small portion of the final scene to check the results, you can render a selected region only using the Limited Region button in the Options section of the Render tab. Clicking this button makes a yellow rectangular square visible in the

FIGURE 12.22
Image Viewer

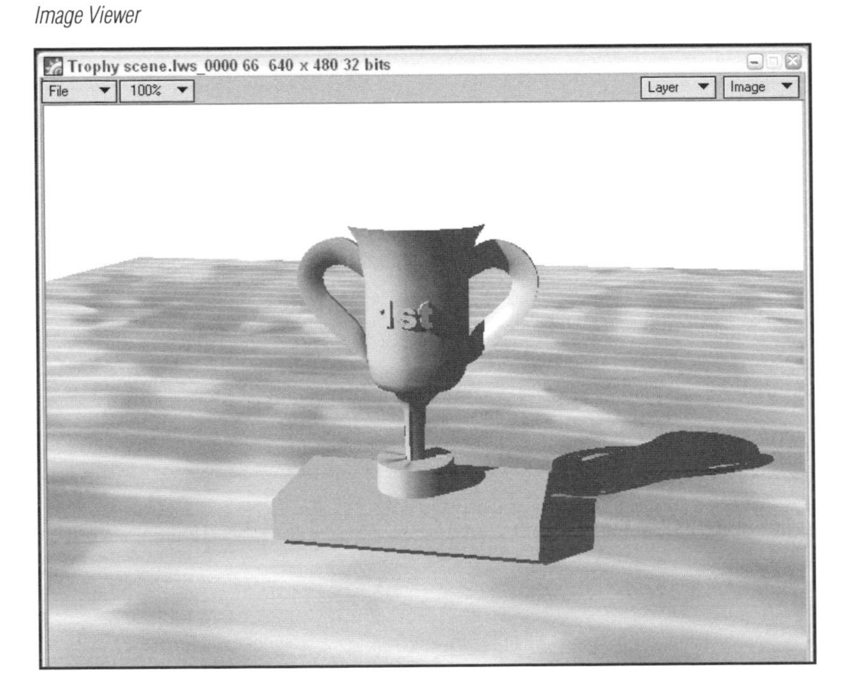

Camera View. By dragging its edges and repositioning it by dragging within the rectangle, you can select the area that you want to render and when you click the Render Frame button, only the selected portion is rendered. Figure 12.23 shows a limited render region selected and Figure 12.24 shows the rendered result.

Rendering an Animation

To render an animation sequence, click the Render Scene button in the Render tab. This opens the Render Status dialog box and proceeds through all the designated frames. If you want to render only a portion of the total frames, select the range to render in the Render Options dialog box. If the Auto Frame Advance option isn't set in the Render Options dialog box, you'll need to press the Continue button in the Render Status dialog box after each frame is rendered.

> **CAUTION**
>
> A warning dialog box appears when the Render Scene button is pressed if the Auto Frame Advance option isn't enabled or if a file save option isn't enabled.

Enabling VIPER

VIPER is an acronym that stands for Versatile Interactive Preview Render. You can open the VIPER interface using the VIPER button in the Utilities section of the Render tab. VIPER uses images that are saved in a buffer from a previous rendering and lets you change scene settings such as object surfaces without requiring a full rerendering. This can speed up the rendering cycle. You can also use the VIPER interface to create and view previews.

FIGURE 12.23
Selected render region

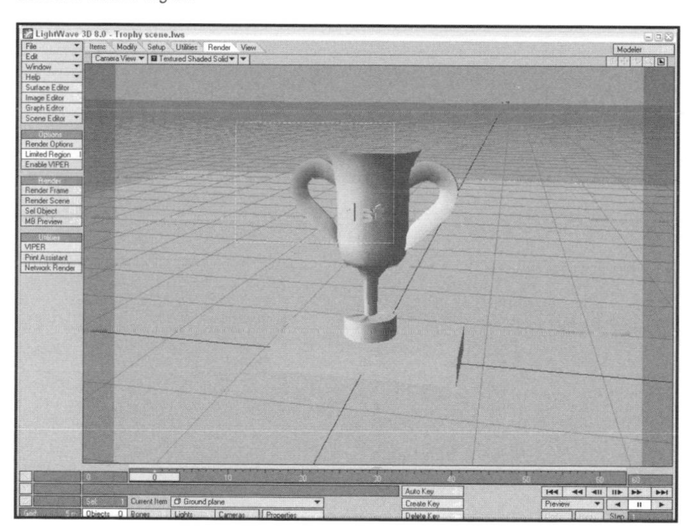

FIGURE 12.24
Rendered region

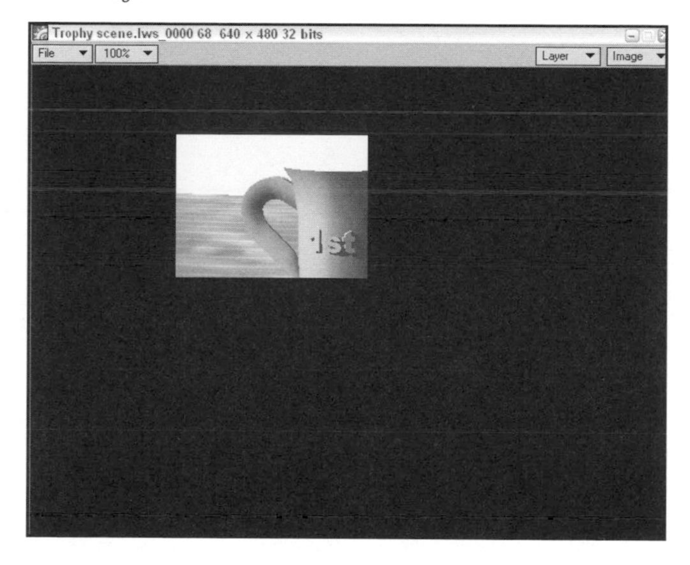

Render an animation

1. Click the File, Load, Load Scene menu command and open the Swingset scene.lws file.
2. Click the Render tab and then click the Render Options button in the Options section.

   The Render Options dialog box opens.
3. Enable the Auto Frame Advance option and set the Render Mode to Realistic.
4. Select the Output Files tab, enable the Save Animation option, and select AVI from the Type drop-down list. Then click on the Animation File button to open a file dialog box. Name the file Swingset animation.avi and click Save. Then close the Render Options dialog box.

   The file name appears in the text field to the right of the Animation File button.
5. Click the Render Scene button in the Render section of the Render tab.

   A warning dialog box appears stating that Auto Frame Advance is on and asking if you want to turn off render display. Click No to continue. Each frame is rendered and displayed in the Render Status dialog box, as shown in Figure 12.25, and the AVI file is saved as specified.

FIGURE 12.25
Rendered animation frame

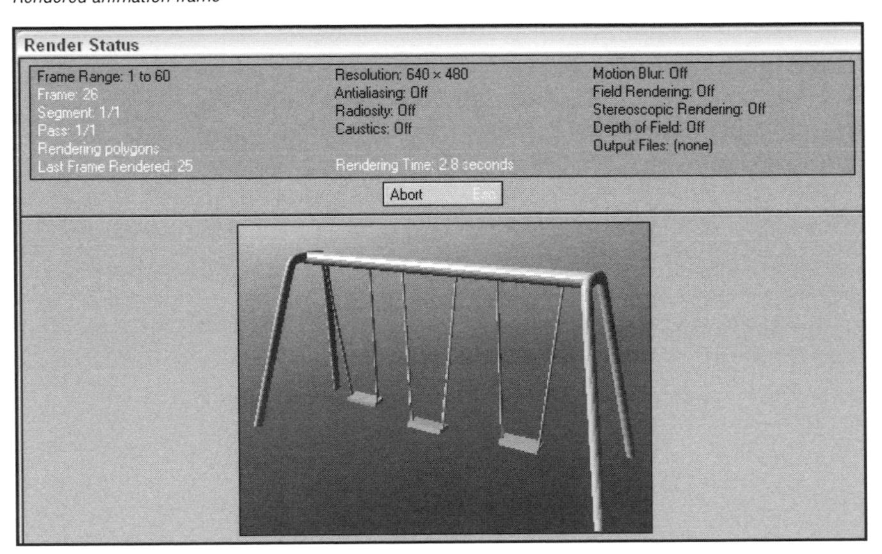

CHAPTER SUMMARY

This chapter covered the details of rendering scenes and animations. It also covered adding backgrounds, effects such as fog and HyperVoxels, and all the render options, including the VIPER interface. You can use HyperVoxels to create gaseous volume effects by adding a surface to a defined volume.

What You Have Learned

- How to change the background to display a solid color, a gradient, or a texture.
- How to use custom environmental plug-ins such as SkyTracer2 to automatically create a background.
- How to add fog to the scene using a volumetric plug-in.
- How to use HyperVoxels to add a surface to a defined volume for creating volume effects such as fire, gas, and explosions.
- How to configure a scene to render using the Render Options dialog box.
- How to render a single image and an animation.

Key Terms from This Chapter

- **environment plug-ins.** Plug-ins that alter the scene background.
- **SkyTracer2.** An environment plug-in that creates a background, including clouds, haze, sun, and ground effects.
- **volumetric plug-ins.** Plug-ins that add volume effects to the scene, such as fog, haze, and fire.
- **ground fog.** A special type of fog that hovers in layers above the ground.
- **HyperVoxel.** A volumetric plug-in that creates gaseous effects such as fire, smoke, clouds, and dust by rendering a volume with a texture applied to it.
- **rendering.** The process of computing the final image or animation by calculating the results of all the lights, objects, and surfaces.
- **Image Viewer.** An interface opening when a scene is being rendered that allows you to save the rendered image.
- **VIPER.** Versatile Interactive Preview Render. An interface that lets you change scene settings such as surfaces and lights and see the results immediately.

CHAPTER 13 USING LSCRIPT

1. View Command History and enter commands.
2. Use LScript.
3. Add plug-ins.

CHAPTER 13

USING LSCRIPT

Behind the scenes, LightWave uses commands to execute all its features. These commands are recorded in the **Command History**. To view the Command History dialog box, click the Command History button in the Commands section from the Utilities tab. If you know a specific interface command, you can enter it in the Command Input dialog box.

You can also use these interface syntax commands with C-based programming constructs to create **LScripts**. LScripts provide a way to extend the features of LightWave. You can load, edit, and save these text-based LScript files. One tool that can help you create LScripts is the LScript Commander dialog box. You can open this dialog box by clicking on the LS Commander button in the LScript section of the Utilities tab. Here you'll see a list of all the available LightWave commands. To execute commands even faster, you can compile LScripts using the LScript Compiler dialog box, available by clicking on the LSCompiler button in the LScript section.

For the ultimate in extendibility, you can add plug-ins to LightWave. These plug-ins are programmed modules that add new functionality to the interface. Using the **Master Plug-Ins** dialog box, available by clicking on the Master Plug-Ins button in the Plug-Ins section, you can access several plug-ins.

Tools You'll Use

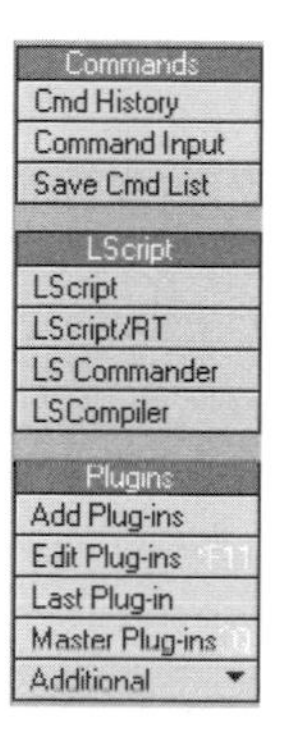

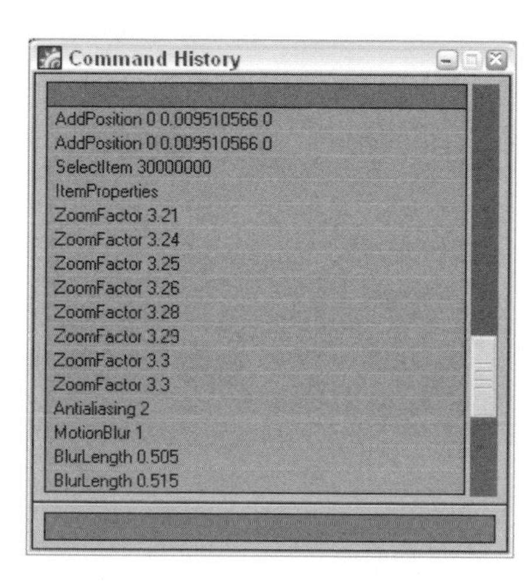

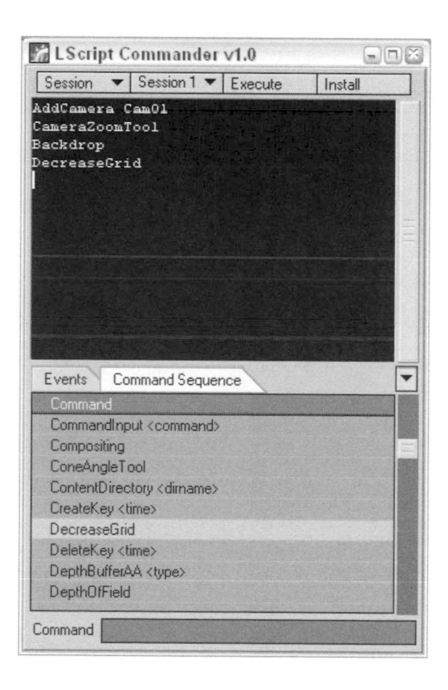

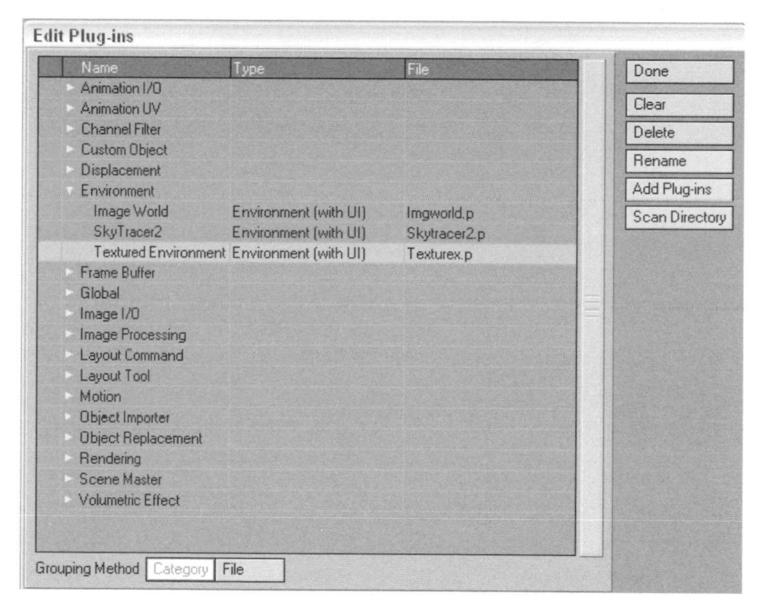

LESSON 1

VIEW COMMAND HISTORY AND ENTER COMMANDS

What You'll Do

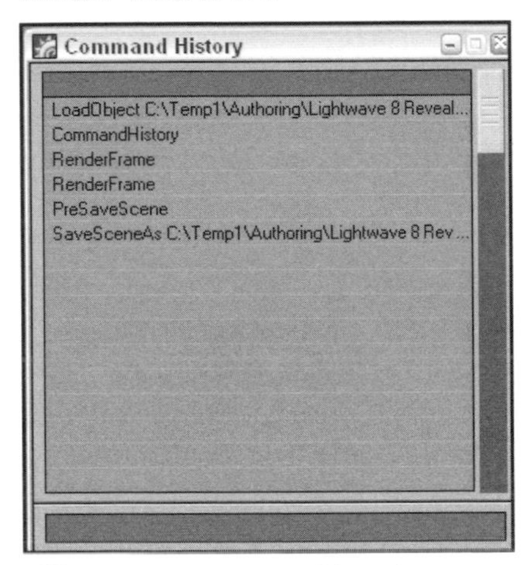

In this lesson, you'll learn how to view the Command History and enter interface commands.

Each command that is issued to LightWave is recorded in the Command History dialog box. This means you can revisit any commands and execute them again as needed.

Viewing Command History

To open the list of Command History, click the Utilities tab and select the Cmd History button in the Commands section. This opens the Command History dialog box, shown in Figure 13.1. If you click on any of the commands in the Command History dialog box, the command is selected and moved to the Input field at the bottom of the dialog box. Pressing the Enter key executes the command that is listed in the Input field. Commands are recorded for the entire active session, but if you close down LightWave and restart it, the Command History is erased.

Entering Commands

You can also enter commands in the Command Input dialog box, which you can open using the Command Input button in the Commands section.

FIGURE 13.1
Command History

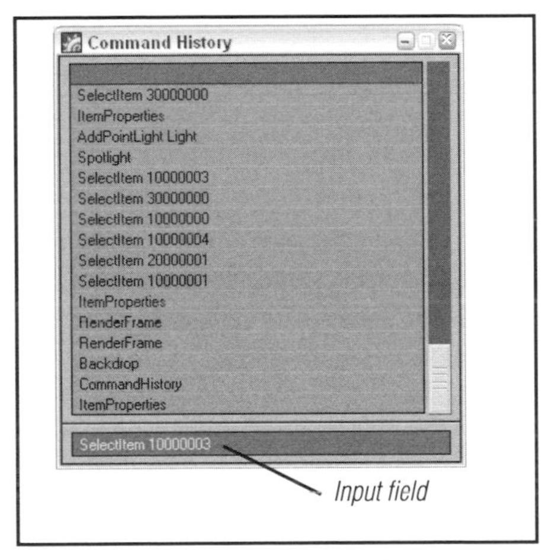

Saving a Command List

If you've performed a series of commands that you want to save to reuse at a later time, you can use the Save Cmd List button to open a file dialog box where you can name and save the commands as a standard text file.

FIGURE 13.2
Command History dialog box

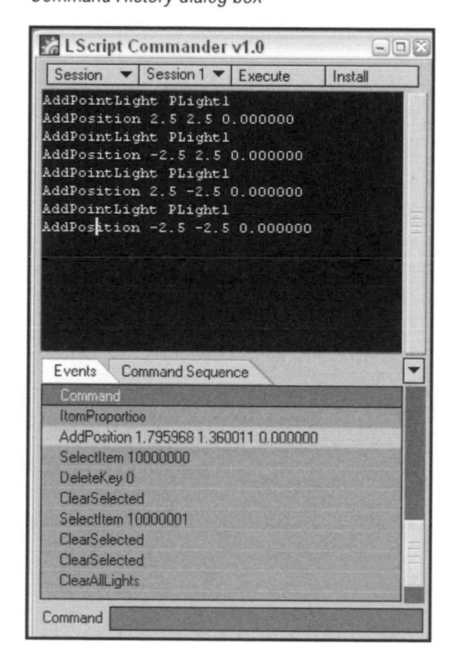

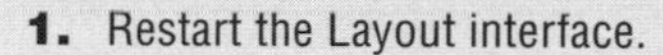

View Command History

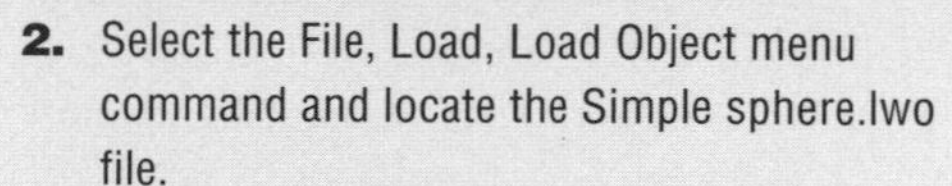

1. Restart the Layout interface.
2. Select the File, Load, Load Object menu command and locate the Simple sphere.lwo file.
3. Click the Utilities tab and then click the Cmd History button from the Command section.

   The Command History dialog box opens, revealing two commands.
4. Click the Render tab and then click the Render Frame button.

   Each of the commands is saved in the Command History dialog box.
5. Click the Utilities tab and then click the Command Input button in the Commands section. Type the command **RenderFrame** and click OK.

   The command is executed and added to the Command History dialog box, as shown in Figure 13.2.
6. Select the File, Save As menu command and save the file as Command loaded sphere.lwo.

USE LSCRIPT

What You'll Do

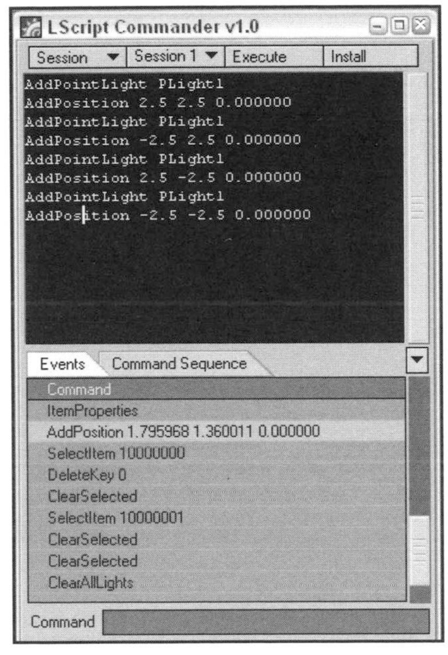

In this lesson, you'll learn how to view LScript commands in the LScript Commander and learn how to compile LScripts.

LScript is a scripting language based on the C programming language. You can use LScript to extend the functionality of LightWave by scripting new functions. These LScripts are text files saved with the LS extension that use specific syntax to execute commands. You can create simple LScripts using the LScript Commander dialog box available by clicking on the LScript Commander button in the LScript section of the Utilities tab, shown in Figure 13.3.

Using the LScript Commander

Use the top pane of the LScript Commander to type LScript syntax or drag commands from the Events and/or Command Sequence panes below. The commands in the Events panel are commands you can execute in the Layout. As in the Command History and the Command Sequence panel, available commands are listed in alphabetical order. Using the Session button at the top of the LScript Commander dialog box, you can open, close, load, and save sessions. Clicking the Execute button runs the current list of commands. Clicking the Install button opens a dialog box where you can name the macro and creates a new button with that name within a new tab named Macros for easy recall.

FIGURE 13.3
LScript Commander dialog box

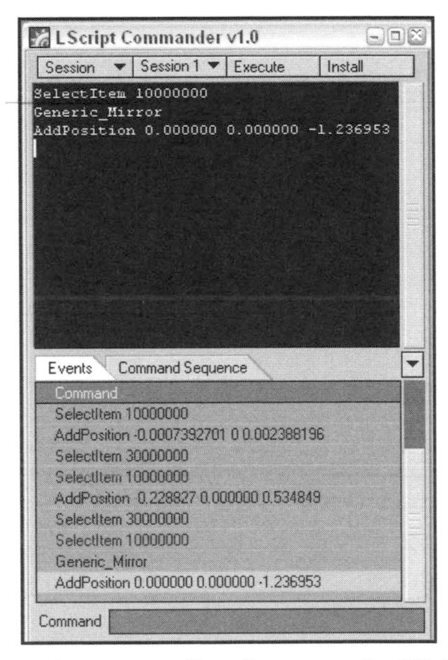

Compiling LScripts

You can run LScripts as LS files using the LScript button in the LScript section, or you can compile and run them as LSC files using the LScript R/T button, also in the LScript section. Compiled LScript files execute more quickly than uncompiled files do. The Target buttons at the top of the **LScript Compiler**, available by clicking on the LScript Complier button in the LScript section, identify the type of script. The options stand for Image Filter, Procedural Texture, Displacement Map, Item Animation, and Object Replacement. To compile an LScript, click the LSCompiler button in the LScript section to open the LScript Compiler dialog box, shown in Figure 13.4. To compile the LScript, load the LS file you want to compile in the Source File field, name the output in the Compiled File field, and click the OK button.

NOTE

You can also save sessions as CS files, which stands for command sequence.

FIGURE 13.4
LScript Compiler dialog box

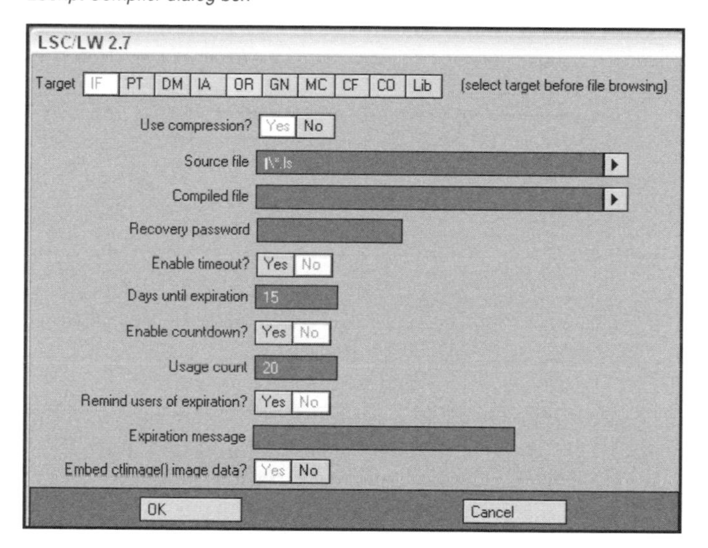

Create and execute an LScript

1. Click the Utilities tab and then click the LS Commander button from the LScript section.

   The LScript Commander dialog box opens.

2. Select the Command Sequence tab at the bottom of the dialog box.
3. Scroll down to the AddPointLight <name> command and drag it to the upper pane. Then replace the <name> text with the light's name, PLight1. Move the yellow insertion cursor to the second line in the upper pane.
4. Click the Execute button at the top of the dialog box.

   A new point light is added to the scene at the origin.

5. Select the new light object and drag it to the right and upward.
6. Click the Events tab in the LScript Commander dialog box and drag the AddPosition command to the top panel. Edit the coordinates to be 2.5, 2.5, and 0.0.
7. Drag over the two commands in the top pane of the LScript Commander and press Ctrl+C to copy the text. Position the cursor below the two commands and then press Ctrl+V three times to copy the commands.
8. Edit the coordinates on the lower set of commands to be –2.5, 2.5, 0.0; 2.5, –2.5, 0.0; and –2.5, –2.5, 0.0.
9. Click the Execute button at the top of the dialog box.

   Four new point lights are created surrounding a center point and the LScript Commander looks like Figure 13.5.

10. Click the Session button at the top of the dialog box and select the Save Session menu command. In the file dialog box that opens, name the file 4 lights.cs and click Save.
11. Click the Install button at the top of the dialog box. In the Name Script dialog box, type the name **4 lights**.

    The command sequence is added as a button to the Macros tab, as shown in Figure 13.6.

12. Select the File, Save, Save Scene As menu command and save the file as 4 lights.lws.

FIGURE 13.5
Edited command sequence

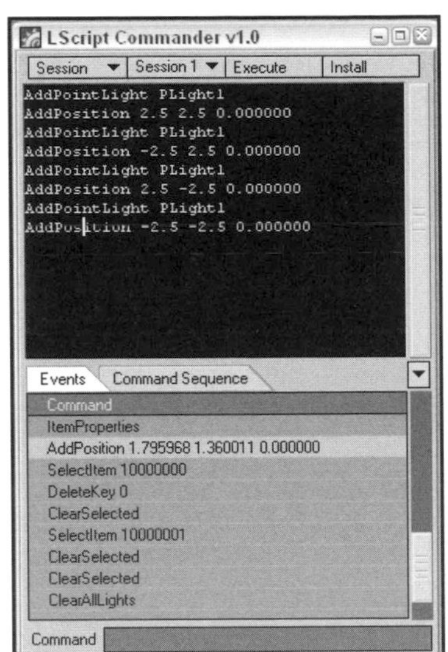

FIGURE 13.6
Installed command sequence

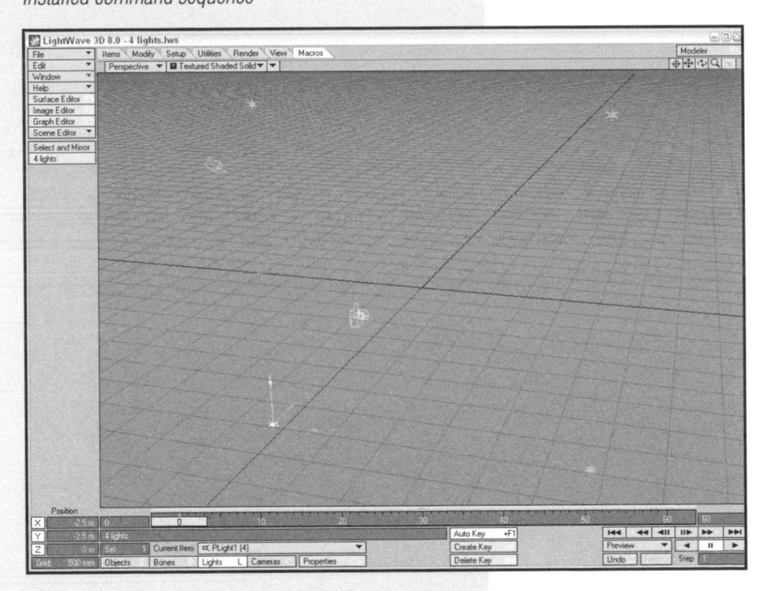

LESSON 3

ADD PLUG-INS

What You'll Do

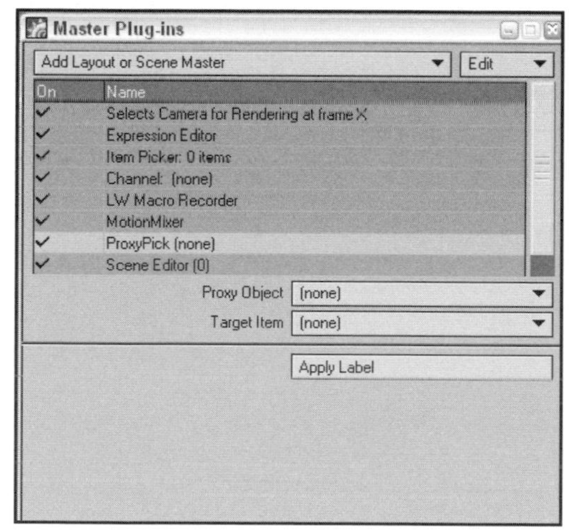

In this lesson, you'll learn how to add plug-ins to LightWave.

Plug-ins are new programmed modules you can use to add new features to LightWave. These features can be fairly simple or complex.

FIGURE 13.7
Edit Plug-Ins dialog box

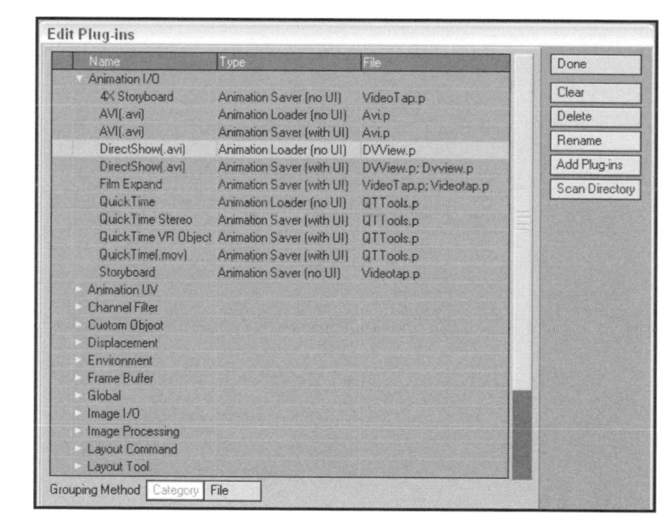

Adding and Editing Plug-Ins

Clicking the Add Plug-Ins button in the Add Plug-Ins section of the Utilities tab opens a file dialog box where you can locate and load plug-ins into LightWave. Once loaded, the available plug-ins appear in the Edit Plug-Ins dialog box, shown in Figure 13.7. Using this dialog box, you can clear, delete, or rename plug-ins. You can use the Scan Directory button for help in locating any plug-ins on your local hard drive.

CAUTION

Many of the core LightWave features are implemented as plug-ins and should not be deleted.

Accessing Master Plug-Ins

Clicking the Master Plug-Ins button, available in the Plug-Ins section, opens a dialog box, shown in Figure 13.8, where you can access several plug-ins by clicking the Add Layout or Scene Master button. When loaded, these plug-ins appear in the list below. If you click the Edit button, you can open a dialog box of properties for the selected plug-in. Some of these plug-ins are accessible through the interface and others are only accessible through this dialog box.

FIGURE 13.8
Master Plug-In dialog box

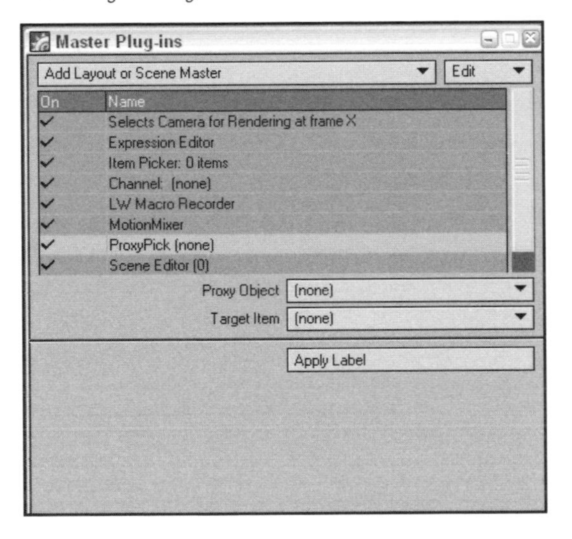

FIGURE 13.9
Located plug-ins

Add Plug-ins
528 Plug-ins found in 241 files.
OK

Scan for plug-ins

1. Click the Utilities tab and then click the Edit Plug-Ins button to open the Edit Plug-Ins dialog box.
2. Click the Scan Directory button, browse to the folder you want to scan, and then click OK.

   After scanning the directory, a simple dialog box returns list the number of plug-ins found, as shown in Figure 13.9.

Access master plug-ins

1. Click the Utilities tab and then click the Master Plug-Ins button to open the Master Plug-Ins dialog box.
2. Click the Add Layout or Scene Master button and select the Expression Editor from the drop-down list.
3. Select the Expression Editor from the list, click the Edit button, and then select the Properties option.

   The Expression Editor opens, as shown in Figure 13.10.

FIGURE 13.10
Expression Editor plug-in

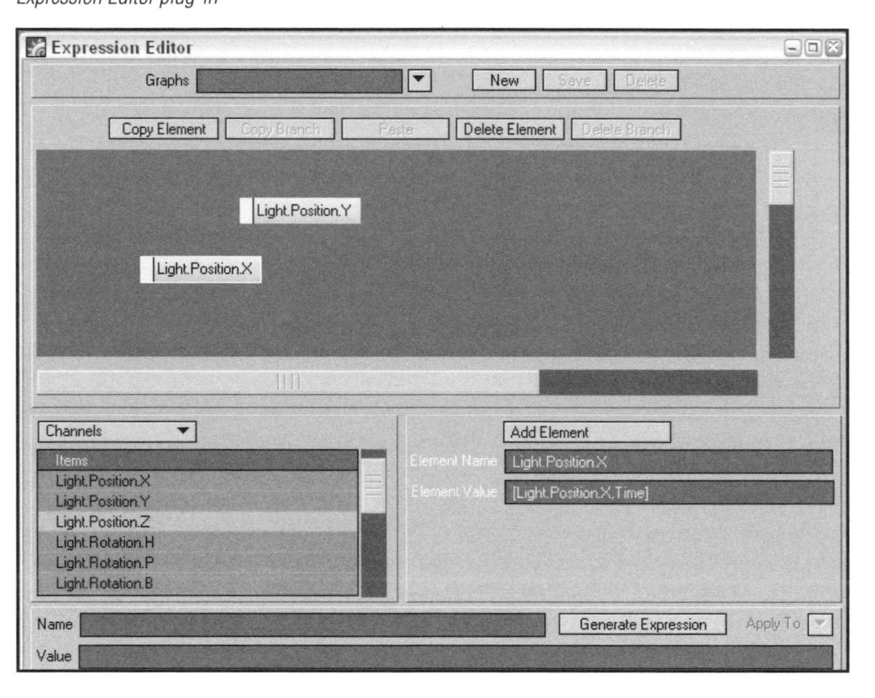

CHAPTER SUMMARY

This chapter explained how several utility commands are available for accessing and executing text-based commands. All executed commands are stored in the Command History, where you can save them as macros to be re-executed. You can use plug-ins and text-based scripts written using a scripting language known as LScript to enhance LightWave features.

What You Have Learned

- How to view the Command History dialog box to see a list of executed commands.
- How to use LScript to create macros and to enhance LightWave features.
- How to load and install plug-ins to add new features to LightWave.

Key Terms from This Chapter

- **Command History.** An interface that keeps a list of all the executed commands.
- **LScript.** A text-based scripting language that can add auto macros and additional functionality to LightWave.
- **LScript Compiler.** An interface that converts macros and text-based LScripts to machine language for quicker execution.
- **master plug-ins.** Additional coded features that you can add to the existing interface.

C

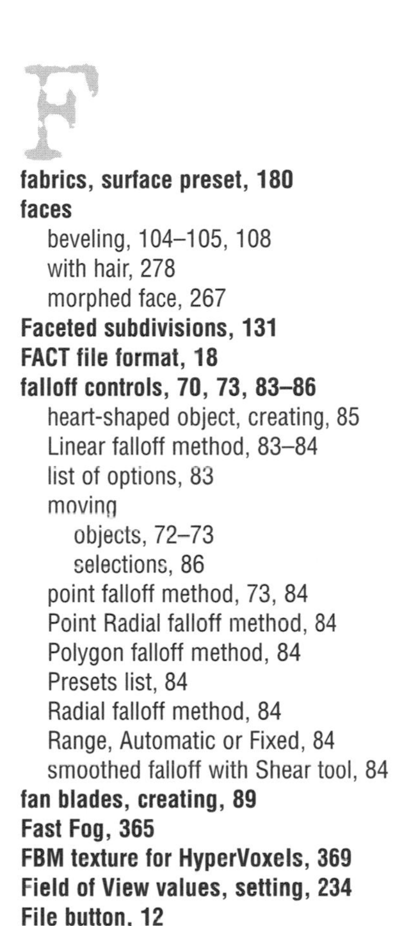

Q–R

U

V

INDEX